Communications
in Computer and Information Science 721

Commenced Publication in 2007
Founding and Former Series Editors:
Alfredo Cuzzocrea, Orhun Kara, Dominik Ślęzak, and Xiaokang Yang

Editorial Board

More information about this series at http://www.springer.com/series/7899

Mayank Singh · P.K. Gupta
Vipin Tyagi · Arun Sharma
Tuncer Ören · William Grosky (Eds.)

Advances in Computing and Data Sciences

First International Conference, ICACDS 2016
Ghaziabad, India, November 11–12, 2016
Revised Selected Papers

 Springer

Editors
Mayank Singh
Krishna Engineering College
Ghaziabad, Uttar Pradesh
India

P.K. Gupta
Jaypee University of Information
  Technology
Waknaghat, Himachal Pradesh
India

Vipin Tyagi
Department of Computer Science
  and Engineering
Jaypee University of Engineering
  and Technology
Guna, Raghogarh, Madhya Pradesh
India

Arun Sharma
Indira Gandhi Delhi Technical University
New Delhi
India

Tuncer Ören
School of Electrical Engineering
  and Computer Science
University of Ottawa
Ottawa, ON
Canada

William Grosky
Department of Computer and Information
  Science
University of Michigan-Dearborn
Dearborn, MI
USA

ISSN 1865-0929   ISSN 1865-0937 (electronic)
Communications in Computer and Information Science
ISBN 978-981-10-5426-6   ISBN 978-981-10-5427-3 (eBook)
DOI 10.1007/978-981-10-5427-3

Library of Congress Control Number: 2017945739

Printed on acid-free paper

This Springer imprint is published by Springer Nature
The registered company is Springer Nature Singapore Pte Ltd.
The registered company address is: 152 Beach Road, #21-01/04 Gateway East, Singapore 189721, Singapore

Preface

In the past few years, the computer science field has gone through several fundamental changes to make computing useful in all aspects of life. State-of-the-art techniques and computing paradigms based on research domains like big data, cloud computing, Internet of Things, and machine learning are working as key technologies to bring comfort and changes in one's life. This volume contains 64 papers presented at the International Conference on Advances in Computing and Data Sciences (ICACDS 2016) held during November 11–12, 2016, and hosted by The Department of Computer Science and Engineering, Krishna Engineering College, Ghaziabad (UP), India in association with Special Interest group on Cyber Forensics of Computer Society of India.

ICACDS 2016 was an attempt to bring together researchers working in these domains to share their knowledge and their work in front of others from around the world. The conference was organized specifically to help the researchers, academics, scientists and industry to derive benefits from the advances of next-generation computing technologies. Invited speakers presented the latest developments and technical solutions in the areas of advanced computing, communications, informatics, Internet of Things (IoT), and data sciences and big data.

The Program Committee of ICACDS 2016 is extremely grateful to the authors whose tremendous response to the call for papers resulted in over 500 papers being submitted in five tracks in Advanced Computing, Data Sciences, Internet of Things, Communications, and Informatics. All submitted papers went through a peer-review process and finally 64 papers were accepted for publication in Springer's CCIS series. We are highly thankful to our potential reviewers for their efforts extended in finalizing the high-quality papers.

The conference featured many distinguished personalities including Prof. Alexendar Horse Norta, Tallinn University of Technology, Tallinn, Estonia; Prof. Ramesh Bansal, University of Pretoria, South Africa; Prof. D.P. Mohaparta, NIT, Durgapur, India; Prof. S.K. Mishra, Majmaah University, Saudi Arabia; Prof. Arun Sharma, Indira Gandhi Delhi Technical University for Women, India; Mr. Anup Girdhar, CEO and Founder, Sedulity Solutions & Technology, India, among many others. We are very grateful for the participation of these speakers in making this conference a memorable event.

The Organizing Committee of ICACDS 2016 is indebted to Dr. Manoj Goel, CAO-KIET Group, Dr. Narendra Kumar, Director, and Prof. S.B. Bajpayee, Dean of Academic Affairs, for their confidence that they invested in us for organizing this international conference. We also wish to thank all faculty members and staff of KEC Ghaziabad for their support in organizing the conference and for making it a grand success.

We would also like to thank the authors of all submitted papers for their hard work, their adherence to the deadlines, and their patience with the review process. Our sincere thanks to CSI, CSI SIG on Cyber-forensics, and DRDO for sponsoring the event.

May 2017

Mayank Singh
P.K. Gupta
Vipin Tyagi
Arun Sharma
Tuncer Ören
William I. Grosky

Organization

Steering Committee

Patron

Narendra Kumar   Krishna Engineering College, Ghaziabad, India

Honorary Chair

Shailendra Mishra   Majmaah University, Kingdom of Saudi Arabia

General Chair

Mayank Singh   Krishna Engineering College, Ghaziabad, India

Program Chair

Arun Sharma   Indira Gandhi Delhi Technical University for Women, Delhi, India

Convener

Pradeep Kumar Gupta   Jaypee University of Information Technology, Solan, India

Co-convener

Vipin Tyagi   Jaypee University of Engineering and Technology, Guna, India

Advisory Board Chair

Tuncer Ören   University of Ottawa, Canada

Technical Program Committee Chair

William I. Grosky   University of Michigan – Dearborn, USA

Organizing Chair

Purnendu S. Pandey   THDC Institute of Hydropower, Engineering and Technology, Tehri, India

Dileep Kumar Yadav   Krishna Engineering College, Ghaziabad, India

Vishwajeet Pattanaik   Krishna Engineering College, Ghaziabad, India

Organizing Secretary

Vipin Dewal	Krishna Engineering College, Ghaziabad, India
Krista Chaudhary	Krishna Engineering College, Ghaziabad, India
Karuna Lochab	Krishna Engineering College, Ghaziabad, India
Pratishtha Singh Raghuvanshi	Krishna Engineering College, Ghaziabad, India

Finance Chair

S.B. Bajpayee	Krishna Engineering College, Ghaziabad, India

Organizing Committee

Registration

Deepali	Krishna Engineering College, India
Parikshit Joshi	Krishna Engineering College, India
Ruchi Goel	Krishna Engineering College, India
Shweta Goel	Krishna Engineering College, India

Publication

Mayank Singh	Krishna Engineering College, India
Vishwajeet Pattanaik	Krishna Engineering College, India
Vipin Dewal	Krishna Engineering College, India
Krista Chaudhary	Krishna Engineering College, India

Cultural

Astha Gupta	Krishna Engineering College, India
Sandhya Awasthi	Krishna Engineering College, India
Surbhi A. Sharma	Krishna Engineering College, India
Vishu Tyagi	Krishna Engineering College, India

Transportation

Birendra Kumar	Krishna Engineering College, India
Mohit Jain	Krishna Engineering College, India
Sandeep Saxena	Krishna Engineering College, India
Vimal Kr. Dwivedi	Krishna Engineering College, India

Hospitality

Karuna Lochab	Krishna Engineering College, India
Pramod K. Sethy	Krishna Engineering College, India
Prerna	Krishna Engineering College, India
Rahul Deva	Krishna Engineering College, India

Stage Management

Krista Chaudhary	Krishna Engineering College, India
Pratishtha Singh Raghuvanshi	Krishna Engineering College, India

Technical Session

Mayank Singh	Krishna Engineering College, India
Vishwajeet Pattanaik	Krishna Engineering College, India
Krista Chaudhary	Krishna Engineering College, India
Karuna Lochab	Krishna Engineering College, India

Finance

Vipin Dewal	Krishna Engineering College, India
Suyash Garg	Krishna Engineering College, India

Food

Gaurav Singh	Krishna Engineering College, India
Jai Singh	Krishna Engineering College, India
Lokesh Jain	Krishna Engineering College, India
Rishu Gupta	Krishna Engineering College, India

Advertising

Vishwajeet Pattanaik	Krishna Engineering College, India
Vikas Mishra	Krishna Engineering College, India

Press and Media

Birendra Kumar	Krishna Engineering College, India
Surbhi A. Sharma	Krishna Engineering College, India
Vipin Dewal	Krishna Engineering College, India

Editorial

Kavita Saxena	Computer Society of India, India
Mayank Singh	Krishna Engineering College, India
Vishwajeet Pattanaik	Krishna Engineering College, India
Vipin Dewal	Krishna Engineering College, India
Lokesh Jain	Krishna Engineering College, India
Krista Chaudhary	Krishna Engineering College, India
Karuna Lochab	Krishna Engineering College, India
Shweta Suran	Krishna Engineering College, India
Rishu Gupta	Krishna Engineering College, India

Advisory Board

A.K. Moudgil	Krishna Engineering College, India
A.K. Nayak	Computer Society of India, India
A.N. Mishra	Krishna Engineering College, India
Anoop Narain Singh	Krishna Engineering College, India
Anirban Basu	Computer Society of India, India
Barbara Masucci	Università di Salerno, Italy
Bharat Bhargava	Purdue University, USA
Christos Bouras	University of Patras, Greece
Deepak Garg	Thapar University, India
Emilio Insfran	Universitat Politecnica de Valencia
Julie Dugdale	Grenoble Informatics Laboratory, France
Klaus Havelund	NASA's Jet Propulsion Laboratory, USA
Maninder Singh	Thapar University, India
Mario Cataldi	Université Paris 8, France
Mohammed Atiquzzaman	University of Oklahoma, USA
Pavel Zezula	Masaryk University, Czech Republic
Piyush Goyal	Computer Society of India, India
R.K. Sharma	Thapar University, India
Rajesh Bhatia	PEC University of Technology, India
Ralf Wimmer	University of Freiburg, Germany
S. Saraswat	Krishna Engineering College, India
Sanjay Mohapatra	Computer Society of India, India
Sanjeev Kumar	Krishna Engineering College, India
Saurabh Aggarwal	Computer Society of India, India
Sulabh Bansal	Krishna Engineering College, India

Technical Sponsoring Institutions

Computer Society of India, Ghaziabad Chapter
Special Interest Group – Cyber Forensics, Computer Society of India

Financial Sponsoring Institutions

DRDO, Ministry of Defence, Government of India

Technical Program Committee

Aaradhana Deshmukh, Denmark	Abhilasha Varshney, India
Abbas Karimi, Iran	Abhinav Vishnu, USA
Abdel Badeeh Salem, Egypt	Abhishek Dixit, India
Abdelhalim Zekry, Egypt	Abhishek Sharma, India
Abdul Jalil M. Khalaf, Iraq	Adarsh Kumar, India
Abhhishek Verma, India	Aditi Gangopadhyay, India

Ahmad Rezaee Jordehi, Iran
Ahmed J. Jameel, Bahrain
Ajay Gupta, India
Ajay Raturi, India
Ajay Sahu, India
Ajeet Kumar, India
Akanksha Bhardwaj, India
Akansha Mehrotra, India
Akhil Balaji, India
Akhilendra Pratap Singh, India
Alex Mason, UK
Alexandra Cristea, UK
Alexandre Carlos Brandão Ramos, Brazil
Alfian Abdul Halin, Malaysia
Alka Singhal, India
Alla Talal Yassin, Iraq
Al-Sakib Khan Pathan, Malaysia
Amandeep Kaur, India
Ambika Nagaraj, India
Amin Al-Habaibeh, UK
Amir Khan, India
Amir Zeid, Kuwait
Amit K. Awasthi, India
Amit Kumar, China
Amit Prakash Singh, India
Amit Sehgal, India
Amit Sharma, India
Amit Upadhaya, India
Amitava Nag, India
Amol D. Potgantwar, India
Amr Ahmed, Brayford Pool
Amrita A. Manjrekar, India
Anburajan M., India
Anil Bist, India
Anil K. Ahlawat, India
Anil Kumar Tripathi, India
Anil Kumar, India
Anita, India
Anju Sharma, India
Ankit Chaudhary, USA
Ankur Saxena, India
Anshuman Prakash, India
Antonina Dattolo, Italy
António Abelha, Portugal
António Silva, Portugal
Anubhav Sharma, India

Anuranjan Mishra, India
Aparajita Ojha, India
Aravind Mekala, Durgapur
Aris Skander, Algeria
Arnab Chakraborty, India
Arun Agarwal, India
Arun Chandrasekaran, India
Arun Kumar Tripathi, India
Arun Solanki, India
Arun Yadav, India
Arup Kumar Chattopadhyay, India
Ashiv Shah, India
Ashok Nanda, India
Asoke Nath, India
Atif Azad, Germany
Atul Sajjanhar, Australia
Avdhesh Kumar, India
Avinash Sharma, India
Ayesha Choudhary, India
Aylin Ahadi, Sweden
B.K. Sharma, India
B.T. Ahmed, Spain
B.K. Tripathy, India
Babu Sena Paul, South Africa
Balu Chettiyar, India
Balwant Rajput, India
Banit Negi, India
Bassim Sayed Mohammed, Iraq
Battula Tirumala Krishna, India
Bestoun S. Ahmed, Switzerland
Bhalaji Natarajan, India
Bharat Bhargava, USA
Bhavnesh Kumar, India
Bhupesh Gour, India
Bimal Ray, India
Birendra Kumar, India
B.N. Pandey, India
Bouhorma Mohammed, Morocco
Brian Manuel González Contreras,
  Mexico
Brijesh Kumar, India
Brijesh Mishra, India
Brijmohan Singh, India
Carlos Becker Westphall, Brazil
Cevdet Gologlu, Turkey
Chanchal Kumar, India

Chandan Kumar Sonkar, India
Chandrabhan Sharma, West Indies
Chandramohan Dhasarathan, India
Charlette Donalds, West Indies
Chembe Christopherm, Zambia
Cheng Luo, USA
Chengcheng Li, USA
Cheng-Chi Lee, Taiwan
Chidananda Mohapatra, India
Ching-Min Lee, Taiwan
Chirag Modi, India
Chockalingam Aravind Vaithlingam,
   Malaysia
Christophe Claramunt, France
Coruzzi P., Italy
Cuong Pham-Quoc, Vietnam
D. Ganeshkumar, India
D.S. Suresh, India
D.K. Chauhan, India
D. Gunaseelan, Oman
D.K. Lobiyal, India
Damodar Reddy Edla, India
Deep Singh, India
Deepak Chaudhary, India
Deepak Garg, India
Deepak Gupta, India
Deepanwita Das, India
Deepika Koundal, India
Deepti Mehrotra, India
Deeshant Rajput, India
Deo Vidyarthi, India
Devesh Srivastava, India
Devpriya Soni, India
Dhairay Ahuja, India
Dhiraj Pandey, India
Dhruv Kaushik, India
Dileep Kumar Yadav, India
Dilip Mali, Ethiopia
Dimitrios A. Karras, Greece
Dindayal Mahto, India
Dinesh Bhatia, India
Divya Jain, India
Donald Adjeroh, USA
Donghyun Kim, USA
Dorian Gorgan, Romania
Ekta Garg, India

Eloi Pereira, USA
Emilio Insfran, Spain
Encik Mohd Helmy Wahab, Malaysia
Eric Wong, USA
Erik Markert, Deutschland
Farqad Farhan, Iraq
Fateh Krim, Algeria
Fazirulhisyam Hashi, Malaysia
Felix J. Garcia Clemente, Spain
Feng Li, USA
Fethi Farhani, Tunisia
Filipe Portela, Portugal
Gautam Tiwari, USA
Gayatri Sakya, India
George Kliros, Greece
Ghanshyam Raghuwanshi, India
Gholamreza Akbarizadeh, Iran
Gholamreza Rouhi, Canada
Goutam Datta, India
Gunaseelan Devaraj, Saudi Arabia
Gunjan Gupta, South Africa
Guoyi Peng, Japan
Gurpreet Singh, India
Gyanendra Saroha, India
H.J. Kamaruzaman Jusoff, Malaysia
Haider Abbas, Iraq
Hamid Magrez, Morocco
Hamir Wasia, India
Hardwari Lal Mandoria, India
Hari Mohan Pandey, India
Harikesh Singh, India
Hariom Sharan Sinha, India
Harpreet Singh, Canada
Harsh Kumar Verma, India
Hasmukh Morarji, Australia
Hassan Aldheleai, India
Haytham El Miligi, Canada
Hazem Ali, Iraq
Hema N., India
Hemant Gupta, India
Himani Mittal, India
Himanshu Monga, India
Hing Keung Lau, Hong Kong,
   SAR China
Hongji Yang, UK
Houbing Song, USA

Huang-Chen Lee, Taiwan
Ian Wells, UK
Ibrar Shah, UK
I-Cheng Chang, Taiwan
Iman Yousefi, Iran
Imran Bashir Bhatti, Germany
Indrasen Singh, India
Ips Sethi, India
J.K. Sahoo, India
J. Maiti, India
Jai Gopal Pandey, India
Jay Singh, Korea
Jayanth J., India
Jayanthi J., India
Jia-Ching Wang, Taiwan
Jianping Zeng, China
Jiayin Wang, China
Jinhai Cai, Australia
Jolly Parikh, India
José Mario De Martino, Brazil
Joy Long-Zong Chen, Taiwan
Joydip Dhar, India
Juan José Martínez Castillo, Venezuela
Juana Canul-Reich, Mexico
Jugal Kishor, India
Jugnesh Kumar, India
Jun Kong, USA
Jun-Dong Cho, Korea
Jyoti Prakash Singh, India
Jyoti Singh, India
Jyoti Singhai, India
K.K. Bharadwaj, India
Kalid Muleta, Ethiopia
Kalikinkar Mandal, Canada
Kamal Saluja, India
Kamaljit I. Lakhtaria, India
Kamlesh Dutta, India
Kapil Kumar, India
Karan Singh, India
Karanbir Singh, India
Kavita Saxena, India
Keith Leonard Mannock, London, UK
Khalid Alemerien, USA
Kiran Pokkuluri, India
Kirat Pal Surya, India
Kirti Jain, India

Komal Kumar Bhatia, India
Krishan Kumar, India
Kshitiz Saxena, India
Kunal Gupta, India
Kunwar Singh, India
Lalit Kumar Awasthi, India
Latha Banda, India
Lavanya Sharma, India
Lefteris Gortzis, Greece
Lei Wu, Texas, USA
Leszek Borzemski, Poland
Linda Mathew, India
Liping Shao, China
Liu Hui, Germany
Lopamudra Mohanti, India
M. Azzouzi, Algeria
M.N. Zaw, Myanmar
M. Sabarimalai Manikandan, India
M. Ubaidullah Bokhari, India
M.K. Singh, India
Madan Singh, Rome, Italy
Madhuparna Biswas, India
Magdiel Ablan, Colombia
Mahdi Jampour, Iran
Mahdi Mahmoodi Vaneghi, Iran
Mahesh Chandra, India
Mahesh Jangid, India
Mahesh Kumar Aghwariya, India
Manas Kamal Bhuyan, India
Mandeep Guleria, India
Mandeep Kaur, India
Maninder Singh Nehra, India
Manish Kumar, India
Manisha Yadav, India
Manju Nanda, India
Manjunath R., India
Manmeet Singh, India
Manoj Pandey, India
Manpreet Kaur Khurana, India
Manpreet Singh, India
Manuel Filipe Santos, Portugal
Manvendra Singh, India
Maode Ma, Singapore
Marut Kumar, India
Maulika Patel, India
Maya Dimitrova, Bulgaria

Mayank Tiwari, India
Md. Farhad Hossain, Bangladesh
Md. Khubeb Siddiqui, Australia
Meenakshi Rana, India
Michael Coyle, USA
Michel Owayjan, Lebanon
Miguel Bordallo Lopez, Finland
Ming-Ching Chang, USA
Mitsunori Makino, Tokyo
Mohamed Ben Halima, Tunisia
Mohammad Alaei, Iran
Mohammad Hashim, Germany
Mohammad Najmuddoja, India
Mohammad Obaidat, USA
Mohammad Shahid, India
Mohammd Pourmahmood Aghababa,
  Iran
Mohd Herwan Sulaiman, Malaysia
Mohd Nazri, Malaysia
Mohd. Ashraf Saifi, India
Mohit Gambhir, USA
Mohit Kumar Singh, India
Mokhtar Beldjehem, Canada
Monika Johri, India
Morteza Saberi Kamarposhti, Iran
Mostafa Fouda, Japan
Moulay Akhloufi, Canada
Mritunjay Rai, India
Muhammad Usman Akram, Pakistan
Mukesh Chandra Negi, India
Munesh C. Trivedi, India
Musheer Ahmad, India
Mushtaq Ahmed, India
N.C. Karmakar, Australia
Nalin Sarda, Australia
Nancy Girdhar, India
Nandita Magon, India
Narayan Gowraj, India
Narottam Chand Kaushal, India
Navaid Rizvi, India
Naveen Aggarwal, India
Navneet Agrawal, India
Nawaz Mohamudally, Mauritius
Neera Batra, India
Neeraj Gupta, India
Neeraj Kumar, India

Neeta Awasthy, India
Neeta Nain, India
Neeta Sharma, India
Neha Gupta, USA
Nenad Stankovic, Japan
Nika Raatikainen, Finland
Nikhil Sinha, India
Niranjan Lal Verma, India
Nirmalya Kar, India
Nisar Ahmad Koka, Saudi Arabia
Nisha Chaurasia, India
Nishant Bhardwaj, India
Nishant Gupta, India
Nisheeth Joshi, India
Nitesh Chauhan, India
Nitin Sharma, India
Om Pradyumana Gupta, India
Omar S. Essa, KSA
Ombretta Gaggi, Italy
P. Karthigeyan Rahul, India
P. Kiran Sree, India
P. Laxmi, India
P. Mythili, India
P. Srinivasa Varma, India
P. Vasant, Malaysia
Padam Singh Saini, India
Padmini Vishwanathan, India
Pankaj Garg, India
Paola Lovanna, Italy
Paolo Crippa, Italy
Parayitam Laxminarayana, India
Paritosh Pandey, India
Parteek Bhatia, India
Partha Pakray, India
Parul Garg, India
Paul O'Leary, Austria
Paulo Neves, Portugal
Paulus Sheetekela, Namibia
Pinku Kumar, India
Piyush Dua, India
Plamen Angelov, UK
Pooja Ganesh, India
Pooja Gupta, India
Pooja Tripathi, India
Poonam Priyadarshini, India
Poonam Tanwar, India

Poornesh Tripathi, India
Prabhat. K. Mahanti, Canada
Pradeep Kumar Vashistha, India
Pradeep Singh, India
Praful Ranjan, India
Pragya Baluni, India
Pramod Shety, India
Prathamesh Churi, India
Pratibha Singh, India
Pratibha Tokas, India
Pratiksha Singh Gaur, India
Pratishtha Singh, India
Praveen Kumar, India
Praveen Saini, India
Preeti Sharma, India
Preety Joshi, India
Pritee Khanna, India
Pritom Rajkhowa, India
Priya Ranjan, India
Priyanshu Saxena, India
Priyanshu Srivastava, India
Pronami Borah, India
Puneet Azad, India
Pushpendra Singh, India
P.V.L. Narayana Rao, Ethiopia
Quazi Md. Alfred, India
Quoc-Tuan Vien, UK
R. Balamurali, India
R.C. Tripathi, India
Rafael Valle, USA
Raghav Mehra, India
Ragini B., India
Ragini Karwayun, India
Rahul Dubey, India
Rahul Johari, India
Rahul Rajput, India
Rahul Singhal, India
Raj Kamal, India
Rajeev Kumar, India
Rajeev Shrivastava, India
Rajendra Prasad Payasi, India
Rajendra Sahu, India
Rajesh Duvvuru, India
Rajesh Kumar, India
Rajesh Mishra, India
Rajesh Prasad, Nigeria

Rajesh Singh, India
Rajeshwar Kumar, India
Rajibul Islam, Malaysia
Raju Kumar Singh, India
Raju Pal, India
Rakesh Shriwastava, India
Ralf Wimmer, Germany
Ram Krishan Mishra, Dubai
Ram Saran, India
Rama Murthy Garimella, India
Rama Shankar Yadav, India
Ramachandran Aarthi, India
Ramesh Rayadu, New Zealand
Ranjeet Kumar, India
Ranvijay Singh, India
Rashidali, Saudi Arabia
Ravi Jain, India
Ravi Shankar Singhal, India
Remus Brad, Romania
Renu Mishra, India
Riaz Ahmed Shaikh, Saudi Arabia
Rinkoo Bhatia, India
Rishav Singh, India
Rishu Gupta, India
R.K. Mohanty, India
R.N.V.J. Mohan, India
Rohit Thanki, India
Rohit Yadav, India
Rohtash Dhiman, India
Rongrong Ji, China
Roshan Lal Chhokar, India
Roy Abi Zeid Daou, Lebanon
Rozmie, Malaysia
Rubina Parveen, India
Ruchin Gupta, India
Rudra Pratap Ojha, India
Ruifan Li, China
S.M. Dilip Kumar, India
S. Abdul Khader Jilani, KSA
S. Hariharan, India
S. K. Pandey, India
S. Leng, China
S. Mini, India
S.P. Syed Ibrahim, India
S.G. Sanjeevi, India
S. Senthilkumar, Malaysia

S.V.A.V. Prasad, India
Saber Mohamed Abd-Allah, Egypt
Sabri Abdelouahed, Morocco
Sachin Agarwal, India
Saeed Olyaee, Iran
Sahadeo Padhye, India
Saikishopr Elangovan, Australia
Saket Chaoudhary, India
Salah Bournnane, France
Samir Kumar Bandyopadhyay, India
Sandeep Lohani, USA
Sandeep Saxena, India
Sandeep Sharma, India
Sanjay Agarwal, Taiwan
Sanjay Rawat, India
Sanjay Singh, India
Sanjeev Sharma, India
Sanjoy Das, USA
Sara Moein, Malaysia
Sarhan M. Musa, USA
Saroj Biswas, India
Sarvesh Kumar Sharma, India
Satish Chand, India
Satnam Mahley, India
Saurabh Agarwal, India
Seema Shah, India
Setiawan Hadi, Indonesia
Shahanawaj Ahamad, Saudi Arabia
Shailendra Singh, India
Shaishav Agarwal, India
Shalini Batra, India
Shalini Bhartiya, India
Shamimul Qamar, Saudi Arabia
Shanu Sharma, India
Sharad Saxena, India
Shashikala Tapaswi, India
Shaveta Bhatia, India
Shilpi Gupta, India
Shiv Nath Verma, New Zealand
Shruti Ray, India
Shuai Wang, New Jersey
Siddeeq Ameen, Iraq
Sivkumar Mishra, India
Skander, Algeria
Sohan Kumar Yadav, India
Sonia Lamba, India

Sonu Yadav, India
Sooraj Tr, India
Sotiris Kotsiantis, Greece
Soubhik Chakraborty, India
Sourav Mukhopadhyay, India
Spyridon Mouroutsos, Greece
Sreesh Gaur, India
Srinivas Chakravarthy, USA
Sritrusta Sukaridhoto, Indonesia
Stjepan Bogdan, Croatia
Subhasish Mazumdar, USA
Subith Babu, India
Sudarshan Deshmukh, India
Suddhasil De, India
Sudhir Sharma, Oman
Sugam Sharma, USA
Sumit Chaudhary, India
Sundeep Raj, India
Sunil Kumar Bharti, India
Sunil Kumar Pandey, India
Sunil Kumar, India
Sunita Yadav, India
Suresh Penamati, India
Surya S.R., India
Sushant Chougule, India
Tamer Nassef, Egypt
Tamoghna Ojha, India
Tanupriya Choudhury, Amity University,
    India
Tapas Kumar, India
Tapas Sinha, India
Tarok Pramanik, India
Tarun Kumar, India
Tole Sutikno, Indonesia
Tomasz Rak, Poland
Tripty Singh, India
Trupil Gordhanbhai Limbasiya, India
Ugrasen Suman, India
Utharn Buranasaksee, Thailand
Uttam Kumar Roy, India
Varma Srinivasa, India
Vasanth Iyer, USA
Vegi Srinivas, India
Vibhash Yadav, India
Victor R. Lazar, India
Vijay Tripathi, India

Contents

Communications

Informatics

Internet of Things

Data Sciences

Advanced Computing

A Survey on Location Recommendation Systems

Meera Narvekar[1], Snehal Nayak[1(✉)], and Jagdish Bakal[2]

[1] D.J. Sanghvi College of Engineering, Mumbai, India
narvekar.meera@gmail.com, nayaksnehal01@gmail.com
[2] Shivajirao S. Jondhale College of Engineering, Dombivli, India
bakaljw@gmail.com

Abstract. Location based service is an integral part of day to day life. Many location recommendation algorithms are proposed in the past. This paper investigates various approaches currently available for implementing location recommendation systems.

Keywords: Collaborative filtering recommendation · Location recommendation and hybrid approach

1 Introduction

Location based service provides information and entertainment service to the user on the move. They are convenient to use with mobile devices and can make use of the global positioning system to ease navigation. Some of the most popular systems that use location-based services are friend finder, shopping alerts, best restaurant and location-based mobile marketing and advertising.

The user can add location dimensions to the location-based social networking services. For example Foursquare, UBER, cool cab and GeoLife. It gives the information about new locations to visitors. When a user visits the place, the users can leave comments about a restaurant, shop etc. in a location-based social networking site. People can find such recommendations useful. Location of user context gives knowledge about an individual's interests and behavior. This allows us to better understand users in a social structure and the user mobility and activities in the physical world [1]. People visiting gyms might like physical exercises and users who have dinner in the same restaurant may share a similar taste [1]. Sometimes individuals who do not have overlaps of physical locations can still be linked, according to categories of their visited locations that are of a similar interest, such as beaches or museums [1]. Such kind of information is useful for targeted marketing. It also is useful for customization and personalization of value added services provided by the service provider to users [2]. This paper contains an analysis of various techniques that can be used to recommend the location.

© Springer Nature Singapore Pte Ltd. 2017
M. Singh et al. (Eds.): ICACDS 2016, CCIS 721, pp. 3–12, 2017.
DOI: 10.1007/978-981-10-5427-3_1

2 Literature Review

Zhou and Wang [3] used both the temporal influence and geographical influence. Temporal pattern is represented by the temporal curve. It extracts a temporal pattern from category information of check-in data. They consider the category to be a coffee shop. The temporal curve represents the user check in behavior for a particular time in a day. The similarity between two users is calculated by the distance between two temporal curves. If two users have a similar temporal curve that means they might share a common interest and have co-related check-in behavior. Coupling method is used to find the difference between two temporal curves. To determine the temporal influence collaborative filtering method is used. The geographical influence measures the probability of checking into a location based on the distance of that location to user's home location. Spatial probability function filters out those locations that are not relevant to the user. Precision and recall are used to measure the performance of the system. It compares the performance with the probability category based location recommendation and periodic mobility model. The advantage of the system is that it recommends the location to the user at a given time of the day by using the category information. This system however has not considered the social tie between users to build the category information.

Jia-Dong et al. [4] describe a personalized location recommendation system which returns the top k locations with highest visiting probability. It used kernel density estimation and fast Gaussian transform technique. Advantages of the Kernel Density Estimation is that it is applicable to arbitrary distribution and requires few samples to give good density estimation. Fast Gaussian Transform is used for pattern recognition [4]. It predicts the probability of the user to visit new location when the user gives home location and a set of the check-in locations. Here a comparative study of the Non-negative Matrix Factorization, Multicenter Gaussian model and power law distribution is done based on the precision and recall. Precision is the ratio of the number of the discovered location to the number of k recommended location. The recall is the ratio of the number of the discovered locations to the number of the positive locations. Discovered location is the number of the visited location by the user in training dataset. The positive location is the number of the visited locations by the user in testing dataset. The dataset containing information of the check-in details of the user is taken from the Foursquare and Gowalla. The advantage is that it models the personalized geographical influence on user's check-in behavior in order to accurately predict the probability of the user visiting a new location. This technique gives the good output in the cold start of the system with the minimum amount of the data. The limitation of the system is that it does not provide any information about the location. It is mostly probabilistic model that depends on probability.

Lin et al. [5] designed an integration framework of three algorithms, which are (i) User based collaborative filtering, (ii) Collaborative filtering based on social influence and (iii) Naive Bayesian classifier. They calculated the distance between the user's current location and the recommended location and compared it with the distance limit parameter of the recommended location. The distance limit parameter of the recommended location can be set by the user. User preference is calculated by user-based collaborative filtering. This algorithm, considers users current location, distance limit factor and user residence. It checks that the recommended location distance is less than the distance limit parameter. It then recommends the top 'n' locations to the user. They divided cold start problem into new users and new location. The new user does not have any previous history so Navies Bayesian cannot be used here. It requires at least two previous records of each dataset. For the new location, there are no check-in records of the user. For the cold start, it gives the average accuracy. The accuracy and the precision is calculated and compared. The accuracy of the user based collaborative filtering based on social influence and the naïve Bayesian classifier is better than all other methods. The limitations of this system is that the cold start problem and spare data reduce the accuracy.

Veningston and Shanmugalakshmi [6] gives location aware review in order to understand user experience and in future to suggest a location according to their interest when they are visiting new places. The input parameters are user location, time the query is issued, the maximum distance the user will travel and a query string. It maintains a user profile. User specific parameter is determined by the probability of the user issuing a query and searching the information on the topic. The user profile contains the terms present in user search history. The system applies Bayes theorem. It uses Kullback-Leibler Divergence between two contextual models to measure the similarity between two contexts is information gain. The Doctor recommendation system authors proposed is built to choose the physician who best suits their need. It is privacy aware recommendation system. User modeling contains standardized electronic patient health records. Document modeling is done on the description of the education resource. The advantages are the similarity matching is done for selection of the resource based on rules given by experts to present personalized resources to users. The limitation of this system is that the use of spare data reduces the accuracy of the recommendation technique.

Bagci and Karagoz [7] designed a random walk based context aware activity recommendation algorithm for the location-based social network. It is an activity based algorithm in which they consider the social, personal and spatial context of the user. The authors propose a graph model to represent the location-based social network [7]. They proposed the algorithm with friend based and expert based recommendation algorithm. It builds the subgraph and gives the input to activity recommendation system and measures its efficiency by calculating the precision and recall. It compares with other techniques like popularity based recommendation, friend-based recommendation, and expert based recommendation. From the comparison of this technique; the random walk based context aware activity recommendation gives better precision, recall and f measure. In [7], algorithm populates a subgraph according to the current context of the user and performs a random walk on this graph to rank the activities. For each location coordinate in the Foursquare dataset, they queried; it is checked whether such a location exists in the Foursquare database. If such a location exists then its category is utilized as activity information. Next; an updated dataset that contains activity information in addition to user and location information is obtained.

Jiang et al. [8] considered the area of interest as standard deviation ellipse which consists of point sets. In Content-Based Recommendations, users will prefer a location near where he or she used to be. The system assumed that the locations recommended to the user will always fall within standard deviation ellipse. Whereas; Collaborative Filtering Recommendation involves evaluating the similarity between users. For evaluating similarity, they proposed two approaches viz. (i) Standard Deviation Ellipse: Locations recommended by user's higher similar value have higher priority than those having lower similar value. (ii) Cosine Distance: While constructing utility matrix; limited data is considered and cosine distance is calculated based on it. However, recommendations made by this system may not reliably every time; as recommendations are made considering the large geographical area. The limitation of the system is that it lacks finer location granularity in the recommendation.

Gupta and Singh [9] describes the restaurant recommendation system. In this, the system retrieves the past history of the user by Foursquare account or Facebook. It maintains the user profile and restaurant database. In [9] system first locates the user using Google geolocation API, it then searches the nearby restaurant and then recommends the restaurant to the user. This whole process is done online. When the user checks in at a particular restaurant it is then added in the restaurant database. User profile and interest are stored. According to the user profile and interest, the restaurant is recommended to the user. This process is done offline so there is no wastage of power and bandwidth. It needs to integrate 'Facebook places' to get user's past visits data. Most recent information on recommended restaurants should be searched online to look for offers and discounts. Locating the user's friends in vicinity for recommendation is also incorporated.

Jin et al. [10] combines the feature of the foursquare and yelp. Location recommendation is done using collaborative filtering. The system uses binary rating for each location. If the user checks into a location, it is marked as 1 or else as 0. The user similarity with the other user is calculated using cosine similarity. In this privacy recommendation engine, data is shared among the specific group of people. It consists of the server side privacy recommendation engine (S-PRE) and client-side privacy recommendation engine (C-PRE). S-PRE can be helpful in the cold start problem for a new user because it contains the record of the anonymous user. In this C-PRE client can make the change to whom their data can be visible. The main goal of this privacy is to allow the user to selectively and securely share their location with the other user and/or service providers. It performs encryption for private sharing between the parties. The advantages of this system is that the accuracy of the recommendation system is good. Collaborative filtering algorithm performs well even with less data. In this system authors aim to give the recommendation system; the data which the user wants to share with others.

Wen-ying and Guo-ming [11] used collaborative filtering algorithm for the recommendation. They used a Rule-based recommendation for the cold start problem. Collaborative filtering recommendation cannot solve the cold start problem. User preference is divided into two-factor subjective factor and objective factor. Subjective factor is the personal preference and habits of the user. Objective factor is the current time, current location and current weather. Location based recommendation system need to use the recommendation algorithm which has the ability to handle multiple discrete attributes. User profile information, context information, restaurant information, restaurant characteristic and usage log record is maintained. The advantages of this system is that they used mix collaborative filtering recommendation to get good results and it can store enough data.

Hongbo et al. [12] used user-based collaborative filtering. In this similarity of the user and check-in activities are recorded. They make a cluster of check-in records based on the position then it calculates the gravity center of the member position to represent the position of the cluster and then selects top N similar user and the user records for the user-based collaborative approach. It is used to predict rating of the unvisited places for making a set of recommendation place. This system constructs semantic hierarchical category graph framework. It consists of three layers, in the bottom layer there is cluster semantics and in the top layer, they assign the most general categories to the categories in the middle layer. It uses inverse document frequency where a cluster is a document and the user who check-in is known as the term. The advantages of this system is that it used the semantic to determine the cluster. Performance is measured using precision and recall.

Authors in [13] proposed a mobile navigation system that combines active RFID indoor localization and hybrid filtering recommendation mechanisms. The localization system is responsible for the real-time localization of the user. It identifies the user's current position. The recommendation system will analyze the questionnaire and score table of the user as well as the navigation records and will then recommend the travel route. In [13] the proposed hybrid filtering algorithm which is a combination of the content-based filtering and collaborative algorithm. The advantage of the hybrid filtering approach, Content-based filtering overcomes the issues of the false failure and Collaborative filtering approach avoids the problem of newly added data. Authors in [14] proposed tourism recommendation system for smartphone devices, it considered group activity and individual profile. A recommendation system is a hybrid approach that combines collaborating filtering with the content-based recommendation. Personalization is obtained by collecting information of the user profile, location and time. Socialization allows people to share their experience in the social networking sites. It used group tag cloud and individual user tag cloud to measure group similarity. The advantage of the system is it has used a hybrid approach. The limitation of this system is that it used group similarity rather than the individual similarity.

Noh et al. [15] consider user spatial information. In this location of the user is traced and according to their location news article is recommended. It uses the topical representation to represent the user preference. When the user read an article from the smart device then for each article there is a GPS tag used for recording the location of the user. Each location has its own location stamp. In this, all words are located in the geographical space. For calculating the similarity score function is used. The geographical pattern of the topic is ruled by the Gaussian distribution. In [15] only the news article recommendation is considered according to the location of the user the article may be recommended to the user. The limitation of this system is that it does not consider the pattern in which user is viewing the news article.

Yawutthi and Natwichai [16] proposed a top k tree index to improve the efficiency of the top k location-based recommendation queries. The tree is developed by the R-tree method. The authors in this used aR-tree method to build the tree one difference between the R-tree and aR-tree is that aR tree store more information than the R-tree. The search method that access only the most likely answer and prunes non-relevant answer from the tree traversal. It uses the bottom-up approach to travel across the tree. To group together the k similar object and to create the higher level of the index entity use k nearest neighbor (KNN) object. The similarity is calculated by the closeness of the object in the multi-dimensional space. The improvement in the aR tree is made by each node is identified using the key composed of the user, location and activity identifier. The score value is stored in the leaf node. Each non-leaf node store the maximum score of the child nodes in its subtree. The limitation of this system is that if the value of the k is increased the search time is increased.

In [17] authors used weighted Voronoi diagram. It gathers the dwell time at certain position from GPS, interest data from social networking sites and analyze the data to construct affinity diagram and affinity matrix. Affinity diagram is constructed using the information collected from the user, location and friendship and then analyzing the data and getting the location similarity. Dwell time is turned into the weight because weight is inversely proportional to the distance. When recommending individual friends, the affinity matrices and interest similarity are used to evaluate the acceptable degree. If the acceptable degree is larger than the threshold then it recommends the persons. To calculate the similarity pattern matching and longest common subsequence is used. In this case the threshold is 75% and acceptable degree is 0.5.

In [18] authors consider the location of the user and service. Location information including the IP address of the user host, autonomous system and ID of the country. Location similarity is calculated based on IP address posed by network (ASN) similarity. User-based collaborative filtering adopts Pearson correlation coefficient to compute the similarity between two users. In [19] recommendation system, random walk based method is used. The similarity of the user is calculated on the basis of the visiting popular venues, attending venue by category, the following a friend, staying close to home and like-mindedness parameters. The performance of this system is calculated on the Foursquare and Gowalla dataset, also precision and recall are calculated. The weight between the user, the location visited and the relationship between the user and place is calculated. To calculate the venue by category, content-based filtering approach is used. To calculate the similarity; collaborative filtering approach is used.

Rahimi and Wang [20] made two assumptions regarding temporal pattern of the user according to the daily activities and check-in data. The probability of the user visiting the location nearby to their home location is more. The daily activity of the user according to the time is taken. The frequency of user visits at the location is mapped to the time difference. Probability density function is used to evaluate the probability of the check-in to the category based on the time of the day. The Probability category recommendation system, recommends the location category the user will visit at a given time of the day. The performance is measured using precision and recall. Authors in [21] proposed a method to recommend a friend based on the location visited by the user. The pattern of the user is recorded. It used the random walk process on the graph. It gives an output 'N'; which is the number of the geo friends.

Waga et al. [22] has described context-aware recommendation system based on the four aspect content, time, location and social network. For trust management, it consists of the trusted services verified by administrator. Collaborative filtering is used with the information about user profile and context. User profile contains behavioral data location and previous usage data. It used scoring function to recommend the top K item. The score function is decided by the location, time, user history and rating of the user. In the query, it checks if any of the keywords associated to the service in question has been searched in nearby locations. The advantage of the system is that it consider the trust management in it and the score function is determine using different factor.

Jamil et al. [23] recommend the name of the friend in Twitter if other user does not have their Twitter id or email id. It uses user based collaborating filtering to recommend a name of a friend of the Twitter user. It is mostly based on the location near to their home location. In this algorithm, the similarity between the user A and user B is calculated. If it is less than the specified threshold it is selected. It also compares user B friend with user A friend and recommends user A the name of the friend. The similarity is calculated by Euclidean similarity score. To measure the performance precision and recall is calculated. The limitation of this system is that the precision was good till 50 km after that the precision value decreases. Zheng and Xie [24] show the correlation between the locations. Stay point is the place where the user stays for the longer time. Location history is given by the sequence of the stay point visited during arrival and departure time. The stay point of all users is a cluster according to the maximum visited stay points by maximum number of the users. Here the density-based clustering algorithm is used and sequence of the user movement is recorded.

Zegarra et al. [25] proposed the structure of the recommendation system for a cellular networking. Cell broadcast message is sent to the user who is in a specific geographical region. The system recommends the user with the number of the services such as sports, entertainment, local news, international news, and health. Cosine similarity is used to measure the similarity. The product is recommended based on the user profile and the item similar to those that are used by the client. It sends an SMS to all the user in a particular range for example the restaurant is being open newly then it sends the information about that restaurant [25]. To subscribe to particular service offered by the mobile subscriber. The advantages of the system are depending on the interest of the user the subscription is given to the user on their particular interest. Gupta and Lee [26] calculate the similarity measure depending on the overlapping area between the active users and the candidate user. The drawback is that it groups together the users visiting the same region. The user in the same region has different access behavior. Grid division cosine similarity (GDCS) form a cluster of the user's location history and capture similarity among users in the group. The area is divided into a grid. It maintains location access vector for each user. It maps each user location to the grid cell. It uses Pearson correlation coefficient to measure the similarity between the user and its neighbor.

3 Comparison of the Recommendation Systems

We now compare three best techniques used for recommendation systems.

1. Collaborative Filtering: It can solve cold start problem and is scalable with respect to number of users. Grouping of users with similar interests is easy. This technique however is not suitable for personalized data. Accuracy degrades with increase in data.

2. Content-Based Filtering: It contains the description of the item determined via user preference. It has a low algorithmic complexity. However it cannot handle the cold start problem.
3. Hybrid Filtering: It handles cold start problem very well. It is also scalable with respect to user preferences and location data. However the algorithm exhibit more time complexity as compared to Content-Based Filtering.

4   Conclusion

Thus, a brief survey of the existing location recommendation systems. We find that the current location and user preferences contribute considerably for improving accuracy of recommendations to the user. With deep impact of social networks and psychological need to stay connected; location recommendation systems are bound to have a profound influence in our day to day lives. In most of the systems, only the one data source is considered including past history of users. Data sources of user social structure need to be considered because they are related to each other. A hybrid approach is necessary to handle the data complexity associated with mobility and user preferences. The user specific parameters like user income, user mood and age must also be considered while recommending the location. The update of the user location history must be made fast. Most of the systems have not considered the security and privacy of the system. Location based service must contain the privacy terms so that they do not share their personal information with anyone. When transmitting user's personal information some encryption mechanism should be used to provide security of the data. Trust management must be included in the recommendation systems.

References

1. Bao, J., Zheng, Y., Mokbelm, M.F.: Location-based and preference-aware recommendation using sparse geo-social networking data. In: Proceedings of the ACM SIGSPATIAL GIS (2012)
2. Narvekar, M., RaviKumar, R., Mantha, S.S.: Algorithm for personalization of mobile value added services. In: International Conference CUBE, Pune, September 2012, ACM International Conference Proceedings (2012). ISBN 978-1-4503-1185-4
3. Zhou, D., Wang, X.: Probabilistic category-based location recommendation utilizing temporal influence and geographical influence. In: International Conference on Data Science and Advanced Analytics (DSAA), pp. 115–121, November 2014
4. Jia-Dong, Z., Chi-Yin, C., Li, Y.: iGeoRec: a personalized and efficient geographical location recommendation framework. IEEE Trans. Serv. Comput. 8(5), 701–714 (2015)
5. Lin, K., Wang, J., Zhang, Z., Chen, Y., Xu, Z.: Adaptive location recommendation algorithm based on location-based social networks. In: 10th International Conference on Computer Science & Education (ICCSE), pp. 137–142 (2015)
6. Veningston, K., Shanmugalakshmi, R.: Personalized location aware recommendation system. In: International Conference on Advanced Computing and Communication Systems (ICACCS 2015), 05–07 January, Coimbatore, India, pp. 1–6 (2015)

7. Bagci, H., Karagoz, P.: Random walk based context-aware activity recommendation for location-based social networks. In: IEEE International Conference on Data Science and Advanced Analytics (DSAA), pp. 1–9 (2015)
8. Jiang, D., Guo, X., Gao, Y., Liu, J., Li, H., Cheng, J.: Locations recommendation based on check-in data from location-based social network. In: 22nd International Conference on Geoinformatics (GeoInformatics), pp. 1–4 (2014)
9. Gupta, A., Singh, K.: Location-based personalized restaurant recommendation system for mobile environments. In: International Conference on Advances in Computing, Communications and Informatics (ICACCI), pp. 507–511 (2013)
10. Jin, H., Saldamli, G., Chow, R., Knijnenburg, B.P.: Recommendations-based location privacy control. In: IEEE International Conference on Pervasive Computing and Communications Workshops (PERCOM Workshops), pp. 401–404 (2013)
11. Wen-ying, Z., Guo-ming, Q.: A new framework of a personalized location-based restaurant recommendation system in mobile application. In: International Conference on Management Science and Engineering (ICMSE), pp. 166–172 (2013)
12. Hongbo, C., Zhiming, C., Arefin, M.S., Morimoto, Y.: Place recommendation from check-in spots on location-based online social networks. In: 3rd International Conference on Networking and Computing (ICNC), pp. 143–148 (2012)
13. Wang, C.-S., Chen, C.-L., Hsu, W.-C., Wei, Y.-C.: A location-aware mobile navigation system integrating recommendation mechanism. In: 4th International Conference on Awareness Science and Technology (iCAST), pp. 122–127 (2012)
14. Rey-López, M., Barragáns-Martínez, A.B., Peleteiro, A., Mikic-Fonte, F.A., Burguillo, J.C.: moreTourism: mobile recommendations for tourism. In: IEEE International Conference on Consumer Electronics (ICCE), pp. 347–348 (2011)
15. Noh, Y., Oh, Y.-H., Park, S.-B.: A location-based personalized news recommendation. In: International Conference on Big Data and Smart Computing (BIGCOMP), pp. 99–104 (2014)
16. Yawutthi, S., Natwichai, J.: An efficient indexing for top-k query answering in location-based recommendation system. In: International Conference on Information Science and Applications (ICISA), pp. 1–4 (2014)
17. Chu, C.-H., Wu, W.-C., Wang, C.-C., Chen, T.-S., Chen, J.-J.: Friend recommendation for location-based mobile social networks. In: 7th International Conference on Innovative Mobile and Internet Services in Ubiquitous Computing (IMIS), pp. 365–370 (2013)
18. Tang, M., Jiang, Y., Liu, J., Liu, X.: Location-aware collaborative filtering for QoS-based service recommendation. In: IEEE 19th International Conference on Web Services (ICWS), pp. 202–209 (2012)
19. Noulas, A., Scellato, S., Lathia, N., Mascolo, C.: A random walk around the city: new venue recommendation in location-based social networks. In: International Conference on Social Computing (SocialCom) Privacy, Security, Risk and Trust (PASSAT), pp. 144–153 (2012)
20. Rahimi, S.M., Wang, X.: Location recommendation based on periodicity of human activities and location categories. In: Pei, J., Tseng, V.S., Cao, L., Motoda, H., Xu, G. (eds.) PAKDD 2013. LNCS, vol. 7819, pp. 377–389. Springer, Heidelberg (2013). doi:10.1007/978-3-642-37456-2_32
21. Yu, X., Pan, A., Tang, L.-A., Li, Z., Han, J.: Geo-friends recommendation in GPS-based cyber-physical social network. In: International Conference on Advances in Social Networks Analysis and Mining (ASONAM), pp. 361–368 (2011)
22. Waga, K., Tabarcea, A., Franti, P.: Context aware recommendation of location-based data. In: 15th International Conference on System Theory, Control, and Computing (ICSTCC), pp. 1–6 (2011)

23. Jamil, N., Alhadi, A.C., Noah, S.A.: A collaborative names recommendation in the Twitter environment based on location. In: International Conference on Semantic Technology and Information Retrieval (STAIR), pp. 119–124 (2011)
24. Zheng, Y., Xie, X.: Learning location correlation from GPS trajectories. In: 11th International Conference on Mobile Data Management (MDM), pp. 27–32 (2010)
25. Zegarra, D., Sousa, J., Faria, B., Alfaia, E.: Recommendation system based on location and presence information of users in a mobile network. In: 5th International Conference on Digital Telecommunications (ICDT) (2010)
26. Gupta, G., Lee, W.-C.: Collaborative spatial object recommendation in location based services. In: 39th International Conference on Parallel Processing Workshops (ICPPW), pp. 24–33 (2010)

A Comparative Study and Performance Analysis of Classification Techniques: Support Vector Machine, Neural Networks and Decision Trees

Kumarshankar Raychaudhuri[(⊠)], Manoj Kumar, and Sanjana Bhanu

Department of Computer Science, Ambedkar Institute of Advanced
Communication Technologies and Research (AIACT&R), GGSIPU,
Delhi 110031, India
ksrc19@gmail.com, sanjanabhanu@gmail.com,
manojgaur@yahoo.com

Abstract. A support vector machine (SVM) is a classification technique in the field of data mining, used for the classification of both linear as well as non-linear data. It learns the decision surface from two different classes of input samples and then performs analysis of new input samples. A neural network is able to learn without the explicit description of the problem or the need of a programmer. Another type of classification technique is the decision tree. In this paper, we are doing a comparative study of the above mentioned classification techniques by analyzing their performance on data sets. We will be comparing the inputs and the observed outputs.

Keywords: Support Vector Machine (SVM) · Artificial Neural Network (ANN) · Decision Trees (DT) · Classification · Hyperplane

1 Introduction

Classification is a data analysis technique, used to categorize data into different classes or to predict future trends in the data. Different classification techniques have been proposed by researchers in the areas of machine learning, pattern recognition, and statistics. Classification is carried out in two phases. During first phase, a classifier is developed by training with a pre-determined set of data inputs, using a classification algorithm. This is referred to as the "training phase" or "learning phase". This type of learning called supervised learning as well. In the second phase, the classifier model, is used for classification. In this phase, another set of data, called the test data set is used. The test data set is prepared by arbitrarily selecting inputs from the general data set, that are not included in the training data set.

Support Vector Machine is an efficient classification technique. As proposed by Vapnik [1]. SVM's is one of the best "off-the shelf" supervised learning algorithm. A special property of SVM is that it can maximize the relative geometric margin, which decreases the future test errors during classification. The SVM maps the input vectors

M. Singh et al. (Eds.): ICACDS 2016, CCIS 721, pp. 13–21, 2017.
DOI: 10.1007/978-981-10-5427-3_2

to a high dimensional feature space by constructing a Decision Boundary, also called "Optimal hyperplane" [2]. Two more hyperplanes are constructed parallelly on either sides of the maximal hyperplane, which ultimately classifies the input data into two different classes. The objective is to find the optimal hyperplane and the solution of the hyperplane is a combination of few input points also known as "Support Vectors."

A neural network is an interconnected network of parallel, distributed information processing elements. The idea to develop artificial neural networks (ANNs) comes from the desire to develop artificial structures capable of doing sophisticated, and fast computations similar to the neurons present in the human brain [3]. It has been observed that SVM classifies with quite a higher accuracy than that of ANN, regardless of the input data set and the algorithm used to train the neural network [3].

Decision tree is another technique for classification. It is basically a binary tree, where the test on an attribute is denoted by an internal node, the outcome of the test denoted by the branch, and the class label is held by leaf node. One of the reason for the popularity of DT classifier is that it can be build without any knowledge about the domain or parameter setting [6].

The paper is divided into VI sections. Section 2 represents details of SVM. Section 3 deals with the Neural Networks. Decision Tree is represented in Sect. 4 and the comparative study of SVM, ANNs, and Decision Tree is described in Sects. 5 and 6 presents Analysis and Conclusion.

2 Support Vector Machines

The classification process in a SVM is done by forming a single or a set of hyperplanes in a high-dimensional feature space. The hyperplanes are defined as the set of points whose dot product with a vector in that space results in a constant. When linearly separable training data is used, two hyper planes are selected in a manner such that none of the points lie in between them, thus leading to the separation of the data. Then, the bounded area is called as the "margin" [1]. Hence, a margin can be defined as the width of the decision boundary, having no training points within. It can vary with the position and orientation of the separating hyperplane. There can be more than one hyperplanes between any two classes of input points in the feature space and the set of all such decision boundaries is known as the "Feasible Region." As the margin keeps on increasing, the feasible region reduces and there reaches an instance, when all the regions will coincide and the margin can no longer be incremented, else, the feasible region will become zero. At this point, all those points, which touch the decision boundary are called the "Support vectors" and they are instrumental in controlling and influencing the decision boundary.

Maximizing the margin is a good idea, because a larger margin ensures that the future test samples are less likely to cross the hyperplane, leading to less errors. By Vapnik [1], it is proved below that there is a bound existing on the expected loss of future test samples also known as Risk, which is presented by the following equation:

Here, in Eq. (1) $R(\omega)$ is the risk in the decision boundary, ($R_{train}(\omega)$ is the error associated with the training data and h is the V.C dimension)

$$R(\omega) \leq R_{train}(\omega) + [f(h)/N]^{1/2} \qquad (1)$$

This equation makes a prediction that in future, whatever risk that may occur from the decision boundary is bounded by the following two factors, as stated below:

i. The training error, $R_{train}(\omega)$
ii. Function f(h), where h is the V.C dimension, and f(h) is given by:

$$F(h) = h + h\log(2N) - h\log(h) - c \qquad (2)$$

The above stated Eq. (2) gives a guarantee that the future test error of unknown samples (that have never been seen), will be less than the training error and a monotonically increasing function

$$[f(h)/N]^{1/2}$$

In order to reduce the test error, the margin needs to be maximized. For this, following two adjustments needs to be done:

i. The training error (R_{train}) should be kept low (say 0).
ii. The V.C dimension, h should be minimized.

Figure 1 represents the smallest sphere (a circle in 2-dimensional space, as shown), with a diameter D that covers all the training points and ρ is taken to be the margin between the two sides of the hyperplane.

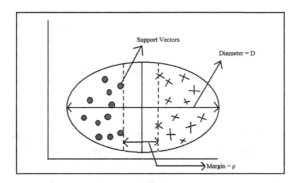

Fig. 1. Relative margin

$$\text{Relative Margin} = \rho/D$$

(The relative margin does not depend on the scale of points).

The main objective is to somehow maximize the relative margin. VC-Dimension (VC-D) is given by-

$$h \leq \left(min\left(d, \frac{D^2}{\rho 2} \right) + 1 \right) \tag{3}$$

Here, in Eq. 3, d refers to the dimensionality of the set of points while D^2/ρ^2 indicates the relative margin. Eq. 3 shows a relation between the VC-D and h. It shows that h is the minimum of d and the relative margin term. What people used to refer to as the "curse of Dimensionality", the fact that when the value of d goes up, the test error also keeps going up and there is no way to control it, a scenario referred to as "over-fitting", the VC-D provides a way to break this curse, where the VC-D would be bounded by the (D^2/ρ^2), and hence it would be independent of the term d (d would not be needed anymore to find the value of h). This forms one of the most important principles of "Maximum Margin Classification" [1].

Now, in order to maximize the relative margin:

Figure 2 shows the hyper plane with its boundaries, where g(x) = 0 is the equation of the hyper plane.

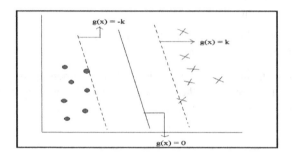

Fig. 2. Hyper plane with decision boundaries

The decision boundary is represented by the equation:

$$W^T X + b = 0 \tag{4}$$

Here, in the above Eq. (4), W^T refers to the coefficient of the hyper plane, X refers to the training sample used, b refers to the bias constant, while d gives the value of the class notion.

In order to maximize k, following conditions needs to be satisfied:

$$W^T X_i + b \geq k, \quad for\ d_i = 1 \tag{5}$$

$$W^T X_i + b \leq -k, \quad for\ d_i = -1 \tag{6}$$

In the above Eqs. (5) and (6), d_i is the label of the samples, where it is +1 for one class of samples and −1 for another class.

3 Artificial Neural Networks

The primary aim for developing neural network is to simulate the working of a human brain, inside a computer system. ANN consists of neurons, which forms a network of interconnected cells.

A graphical representation of a neuron is given in the figure below:

Figure 3 describes the structure of a single neuron in the ANN, indicating the weights, which are outputs from the previous layer but act as input to this particular layer; a weighted sum is calculated and a non-linear activation function is applied to the net input [4].

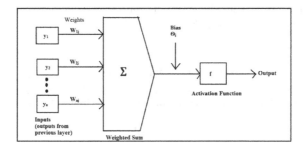

Fig. 3. A single neuron structure

Given a unit j in a output layer, the net input I_j is given by:

$$I_j = \sum_i W_{ij}O_i + \Theta_j \tag{7}$$

In Eq. (10), W_{ij} is the weight of the connection from unit i in the previous layer to unit j; O_i is the output of unit i from the previous layer, and Θ_j is the bias of the unit. The value of O_j is found using the logistic function as shown below:

$$O_j = \left[1 / \left(1 + e^{-I_j} \right) \right] \tag{8}$$

In Eq. (11), I_j is the net input to the unit j. This function is also referred to as the "squashing function" because it maps a large input domain onto a smaller range of 0 to 1 [4]. Therefore, $O_j(1 - O_j)$, used in the previous equation is the derivative of logistic function.

Learning in ANNs can be broadly classified into three types: (i) Supervised Learning (ii) Unsupervised Learning and (iii) Reinforced Learning.

In Supervised Learning, the network computes a response to each of the input value, referred to as the "Output vector". The output vector is then compared with the target vector. If the computed response differs from the target response significantly, then the weights of the network are adjusted according to the learning rule [5].

For a unit j in the output layer, the error E_j is calculated by:

$$E_j = O_j(1 - O_j)(T_j - O_j) \tag{9}$$

Here, in Eq. (12), O_j is the actual output of unit j, and T_j is the known target value of the training tuple.

The weights and the biases are updated to reflect the propagated errors. Weights are updated according to the following equation:

$$\Delta W_{ij} = (l)E_j O_i$$

Here, l is the learning rate, a constant whose value ranges between 0.0 and 1.0 [4]. Now, the adjusted weights are shown by the following equation:

Here, in Eq. (13), (s) indicates the current weights and (s+1) indicates the adjusted weights.

$$W_{ij}(s + 1) = W_{ij}(s) + \Delta W_{ij}(s) \tag{10}$$

After updating the weights, biases are updated according to the following equation:

$$\Delta\Theta_j = (l)E_j \tag{11}$$

$$\Theta_j = \Theta_j + \Delta\Theta_j \tag{12}$$

Here, $\Delta\Theta_j$ is the change in the bias.

As shown above, the weights and biases are updated after the presentation of each tuple. This is referred to as "case updating" [4].

4 Decision Trees

Decision trees provide a simple yet powerful technique for classification of data. It is a flowchart-type structure where the test on an attribute is denoted by an internal node, the outcome of the test denoted by the branch, and the class label is held by leaf node. The error rate and accuracy rate in case of a decision tree are given by the following formulas:

$$\text{Error Rate} = \frac{\text{Total no. of misclassified points}}{\text{Total no. of data points}}$$

$$\text{Accuracy Rate} = (\text{Error Rate} - 1)$$

Information Gain

Information gain is defined as the measure with which an attribute is chosen to perform the testing process at each node. ID3 uses information to select the attributes [4].

To calculate the information gain, it is essential first to calculate the entropy. Entropy, in general, is given by Eq. 13, as shown below:

$$\text{Entropy}(T) = \sum_{i=1}^{n} -\pi \log 2(\pi) \tag{13}$$

Over Fitting Avoidance

In machine learning, "over fitting" is a general problem, especially in case of decision trees. Decision trees are trained to stop when all the data is well classified. In other words each branch is extended enough to classify data in that branch. To overcome the problem over-fitting, following two approaches are:

i. Stop growing the tree before its perfection point.
ii. Post-prune some of the branches of a fully grown tree.

5 Comparison of the Techniques Based on Training, Testing and Validation

The dataset description is as follows:

No. of features: 16
No. of instances: 435 samples
Training data size: 335 samples
Test data size: 50 samples
Validation data size: 50 samples

In this problem, we work with one of the UCI datasets on US congressional voting. The aim is to predict whether a US congressman (equivalent to a Member of Parliament in India) is Democrat or Republican based their voting pattern on various issues. The dataset provided has been split into 3 disjoint subsets: training data, validation data and data set. The simulation tool used for the purpose of carrying out the research work is MATLAB.

Comparison of efficiency measures between SVM and Neural Networks has been shown in Table 1 below, where C is a variable that controls the training error.

Table 1. Comparison of efficiency measures between SVM and neural networks

Cost	C = 1	C = 1000
SVM train	88.95%	94.92%
SVM test	82%	88%
SVM validate	82%	90%
ANN train	92.02%	62.31%
ANN test	82%	61%
ANN validate	89%	66%

Table 2 describes the efficiency of decision trees in training, testing, and validation when net error and information gain are used as best attributes for the growth of the decision trees. Information gain can be referred to as the measure with which an attribute is chosen to perform the testing process at each node. Training error and Testing errors are the two types of errors that can be made during the training and testing of the data sets. However, as the tree grows in size, the training error decreases. The testing error decreases in the beginning upto a certain point, with the increase in size of the tree, after which the training algorithm starts to cater to the noise in the data, which reduces its accuracy on the training data.

Table 2. Efficiency of decision tree with best attributes

Type	Fully grown (net error)	Fully grown (information gain)
Training	100%	100%
Test	90%	96%
Validation	86%	96%

Table 3 gives efficiency of decision trees in training, testing, and validation when the tree is pruned with net error and information gain to avoid over fitting [7]. To control the size of the tree, pruning is done, where the training data set is partitioned into the growing set and the pruning set. The growing set is used to build the tree, while the pruning set is used to find the approximate testing errors in the sub-trees, and the sub-tree having the minimum error is eventually selected as the decision tree.

Table 3. Efficiency of decision tree pruned to avoid over fitting

Type	Pruned (net error)	Pruned (information gain)
Training	88.95%	96.72%
Test	78%	98%
Validation	90%	96%

6   Analysis and Conclusion

In this paper, while comparing the classification techniques, it was observed that there has been variation in the results. It has been found that the accuracy differs in case of SVM and neural Networks (Table 1), when working on the same set of data. From Table 1, it is evident that when C = 1000, the results are in favor of Neural Networks, while the results change when C = 1 i.e. in the latter case, SVM is able to classify the data with more accuracy as compared to Neural Networks.

In case of decision trees, a general trend is that a fully grown tree with net error criteria has a lower accuracy as compared to a fully grown tree with information gain criteria, as evident from Table 2. However, when tree is pruned using net error criteria, the accuracy is far less than the pruned tree with information gain criteria which is clearly shown in Table 3.

The above generated results depend on methods used to choose best attribute and criteria used to grow the tree.

Thus, it can be concluded that the classification techniques employed for the purpose of the research work, clearly depends on many factors. These factors play a major role for selecting one among many, as a result of which, it becomes difficult to state a technique better than the rest, in general. However, when a specific situation is given under certain circumstances, then it might be possible to prove one of the techniques to be superior than the others, which might fit the situation more perfectly than the rest.

References

1. Vapnik, V.N.: An overview of statistical learning theory. IEEE Trans. Neural Netw. **10**, 988–999 (1999)
2. Durgesh, K.S., Lekha, B.: Data classification using support vector machine. J. Theoret. Appl. Inf. Technol. **12**, 1–7 (2010)
3. Byvatov, E., Fechner, U., Sadowski, J., Schneider, G.: Comaprison of support vector mahine and artificial neural network systems for drug/nondrug classification. J. Chem. Inf. Comput. Sci. **43**(6), 1882–1889 (2003)
4. Han, J., Kamber, M.: Data Mining: Concepts and Techniques. Morgan Kauffman Publishers, San Francisco (2007)
5. Nordbotten, S.: Data Mining with Neural Networks. Bergen, Norway (2006)
6. Kotsantis, S.B.: Decision Trees: a recent overview. Artif. Intell. Rev. **39**(4), 261–283 (2013). Springer
7. de Melo, G., Weikum, G.: Constructing and utilizing word nets using Statistical methods. Lang. Resour. Eval. **46**, 287–311 (2012). Springer

A Novel Technique for Segmenting Platelets by k-Means Clustering

Kaushiki Roy[1(✉)], Ratnadeep Dey[1], Debotosh Bhattacharjee[1],
Mita Nasipuri[1], and Pramit Ghosh[2]

[1] Department of Computer Science and Engineering, Jadavpur University,
Kolkata 700032, India
kaushiki.cse@gmail.com, ratnadipdey@gmail.com,
debotoshb@hotmail.com, mitanasipuri@gmail.com
[2] Department of Computer Science and Engineering,
RCC Institute of Information Technology, Kolkata 700015, India
pramitghosh2002@yahoo.co.in

Abstract. Platelet is a major component of various blood cells present in blood that helps in clotting of blood. Platelet count often becomes a crucial diagnostic parameter to identify several diseases like dengue, yellow fever, etc. The traditional process of counting platelets by examining blood slides under a conventional optical microscope is subjected to human errors due to manual inspection. In addition, the overhead on pathologist increases manifold when huge numbers of blood samples are to be tested. In this work, we have developed an Android-based mobile app, which takes as input the microscopic image of blood smear and gives as output the total platelet count present in the image. This system reduces the dependency on expert pathologists and avoids manual errors. A comparative study between platelet counts obtained from expert lab technicians and the one given by our developed app have shown it to be robust and efficient for automated platelet counting.

Keywords: Platelet count · Color-based segmentation · K-means clustering · Android app · L*a*b color space · Telemedicine compatible · Dengue detection

1 Introduction

The blood cells present in our body can be broadly classified into three different types namely red blood cells (RBC), white blood cells (WBC), and platelets. Each one of them [1] is associated with specific functions and should be present in a specific proportion for the proper functioning of the body. RBC, WBC, and platelet count are important diagnostic measures [2] to identify several diseases. The conventional process of counting platelets by keeping blood slides under the optical microscope is time consuming and prone to manual errors. To eliminate these problems and reduce dependency on expert technicians, automated systems for RBC, WBC, and platelet count is urgently needed. A large number of research works has already been done to develop automated systems for counting RBCs and WBCs.

© Springer Nature Singapore Pte Ltd. 2017
M. Singh et al. (Eds.): ICACDS 2016, CCIS 721, pp. 22–29, 2017.
DOI: 10.1007/978-981-10-5427-3_3

Savkare et al. [3] had used k-means clustering with two clusters to segment blood cells from the background. Further Sobel edge detection and watershed transformation were used to separate the overlapping cells. *Sharif et al.* [4] have segmented RBCs from other blood cells using masking and watershed algorithm. *Kareem et al.* [5] have proposed a technique for counting the number of RBCs present in thin blood film using annular ring ratio transform with concentric circular structuring element. *Deb et al.* [6] have proposed a technique for anemia detection through classification of RBCs present in blood smear using image processing techniques like ring ratio transform with concentric circular structuring element, aspect ratio, and Fourier descriptors. *Karunakar et al.* [7] have developed an application in Android mobile for counting the number of RBCs present in a blood smear. *Duan et al.* [8] have proposed a WBC segmentation technique based on color information in HSI color space. The basic segmentation algorithm included color space conversion, histogram based thresholding for segmenting the cytoplasm and WBC nucleus, morphological operations like region growing, region merging, etc. *Nasir et al.* [9] have used k-means clustering for segmentation of WBCs in acute leukemia images.

All the works mentioned above focused on segmenting RBCs and WBCs and hence eliminated platelets along with other artifacts. However, platelet count is a vital measure for diagnosis and treatment of various diseases like malaria, yellow fever, dengue, etc.

We [10] have earlier proposed an algorithm for segmenting platelets. In that work, we had firstly acquired microscopic images of peripheral blood smear. These RGB images were then converted to L*a*b color space followed by the extraction of chromaticity layers "a*" and "b*". The chromaticity layer "b*" was subtracted from "a*" layer making the appearance of platelets and WBCs prominent and the RBCs got faded. Image binarization was applied next to eliminate the RBC pixels completely leaving behind WBC and platelet pixels. Morphological operations were then applied to eliminate WBCs and extracting only platelets. We [11] have also developed a smart-phone based app for the same. This algorithm however had one drawback. It gave good results for well-illuminated images but erroneous results when the images were not well illuminated. To improve the results, in this work we have proposed a new platelet segmentation technique using k-means clustering. The details of this work have been presented in the next sections. We have also developed a smart-phone based app for the same.

2   Methodology

This section describes, in detail, the algorithm for platelet segmentation. We have developed this app for Android since Android phones are readily available to masses owing to their cost-effectiveness. The entire code has been written in Android, and Android Development software kit (SDK) has been used to develop the application.

Platelets are of variable size and shape. Therefore, platelets cannot be segmented by size or shape. However, Leishman stain give platelets and WBCs a bluish appearance and RBCs a reddish appearance. Therefore, platelets can be segmented by color-based segmentation. In this work, platelets have been segmented using color-based segmentation with clustering based approach.

2.1 Image Acquisition

We have collected Leishman stained blood slides of 100 different patients from the nearby laboratory. In our laboratory, the microscopic images of these slides were captured using an optical microscope (Olympus CX21I). These stained slides were placed under the 100x objective of the microscope. This high magnification was required since platelets are very tiny objects and not visible at lesser magnification. In our database, the captured microscopic images of Leishman stained blood slides of 100 different patients were stored. These images were then transferred from the desktop to the Android phone and could be stored either in the internal memory or in a secure digital card (SD card) of a smart phone. Figure 1a, b, c shows some of the microscopic images of blood smear present in our database. Our database is not freely and publicly available.

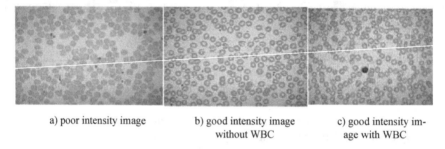

      a) poor intensity image   b) good intensity image   c) good intensity im-
                                 without WBC   age with WBC

Fig. 1. Microscopic image of blood cell captured at 100x objective (Color figure online)

2.2 Platelet Counting App

As already mentioned Android Software Development Kit (SDK) [12] has been used to develop this App. This App consists of four main elements namely text-field [13], text-view [14], button [15] and image-view [16]. In the textfield, the path of the image to be analyzed is provided. The button named "Want to know Platelet Count? Clk" is pressed next. After the button is pressed, the image, whose path is mentioned in the text-field, is fetched, further segmentation takes place on it, and the final image consisting only of platelets is displayed in the image-view along with its count. The detail of this segmentation process is described in the next section. The block diagram of the segmentation process is shown in Fig. 2, and the final App output has been shown in Fig. 4.

Image Preprocessing. The input RGB image was filtered using an average filter of window size 5 × 5 [10] to eliminate unwanted objects and hence filter the input image. The window size was limited to 5 × 5 since higher window size would cause severe smoothening, which would further lead to loss of minute details.

RGB to L*a*b Conversion. The processed RGB image was converted to L*a*b color space. Images captured in the digital microscope are usually in RGB color space whose visual segmentation [10] is difficult. Therefore, for better segmentation, these images were converted to L*a*b color space. Also, L*a*b color space [10] is a device

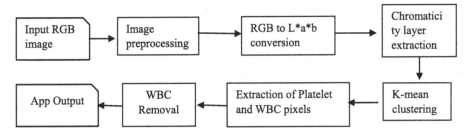

Fig. 2. Block diagram of image segmentation

independent color space, unlike RGB. The "L*" layer represents lightness. The opponent colors red and green is represented in the "a*" axis. The "b*" axis represents opponent colors blue and yellow.

Chromaticity Layer Extraction. As mentioned earlier, the L* layer in L*a*b color space represents only brightness and the actual color information is contained in the chromaticity layers a* and b*. Thus, we extracted the two chromaticity layers and applied k-means clustering on them.

K-means Clustering. K-mean clustering is an unsupervised [17] learning technique that partitions n observation into k-different clusters and each observation is placed into that particular group which has the nearest mean. In our work, we have fed data in "a*" and "b*" sub-bands as features to the k-mean cluster. The number of clusters was set to 2, one for the background and another for the blood cells. The main challenge here was to establish the initial cluster centers randomly. To meet the challenge, two intensities were used, a very low intensity for the background pixels and higher intensities for blood cell pixels. The input RGB images were first converted to L*a*b color space, and k-means clustering has been applied to them. The detail of the process has been stated above. Figure 3 represents the clusters obtained from input image Fig. 1a.

Correct Cluster Identification. For each of the input RGB images, we get two clusters each containing blood cell pixels and background pixels as shown in Fig. 3. The next

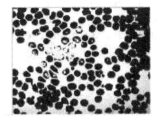
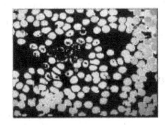

(a) Cluster 1 of image 1a containing background pixels

(b) Cluster 2 of image 1a containing blood cell pixels

Fig. 3. Clusters obtained from input images shown in Fig. 1a (Color figure online)

challenge of our work was to identify the cluster containing the blood cell pixels, which could be used for further segmentation. To achieve this, the cluster center information was utilized. The number of iterations used in k-means clustering algorithm was fixed as seven. The cluster center values obtained for the two clusters after the successful run of the clustering algorithm is a vector of the form $<x1, y1>$ and $<x2, y2>$. Here $x1$ and $x2$ represent the mean of "a*" values of each pixels for cluster 1 and 2 respectively and $y1$ and $y2$ represent the mean of "b*" values of each pixels for both clusters. As stated above "a*" layer of L*a*b color space represents the red and green color information for each pixels. The cluster containing the blood cell pixels have much more reddish component than the cluster containing the background pixels as evident from Fig. 3. This implies that the "a*" layer values for each pixels belonging to the desired cluster will be much more than the other cluster having the background pixels which further implies that the mean of "a*" layer value of the desired cluster will be much more than the other cluster. This information was used for correct cluster identification. We extracted the first components of the vectors represented above namely $x1$ and $x2$ and checked which amongst them had a greater value.

If, $x1 > x2$ then cluster 1 else cluster 2 was identified as the desired cluster. Figure 3b represents the desired cluster obtained successfully using the method described here.

Extraction of WBC and Platelet Pixels. The main aim of this block is to extract platelets and WBCs and eliminate RBCs. As evident from Fig. 3, platelet and WBC pixels have higher bluish component. On the contrary, RBC pixels have higher reddish component. Input images obtained from the previous step were analyzed, and pixels with higher bluish component than the reddish components were all extracted. These pixels belonged to the platelets and WBCs.

WBC Removal. The images obtained from the previous step consist of WBCs and platelets. The main aim of this block was to eliminate WBCs and extract platelets. WBCs have much larger area than platelets. Since platelets are tiny objects, a small threshold (approximately 15) was set and all objects having more pixels than the set threshold were removed, thus retaining only those objects having number of pixels lesser than the set threshold. This process successfully segmented platelets from the other blood cells namely RBCs and WBCs.

Platelet Count. The next goal of our work was to count the number of platelets, which was done using 8-connectivity approach [18]. Figure 4a, b, c shows the output images obtained corresponding to the input image represented in Fig. 1a, b, and c respectively.

3   Result and Discussion

As mentioned earlier, our developed App takes the microscopic images of blood smear as input and produces the segmented image consisting of platelet along with its count as output. Figure 1a, b, c are input images and Fig. 4a, b, c are the corresponding output images. Figure 4 shows the screenshot of our mobile app containing final image and

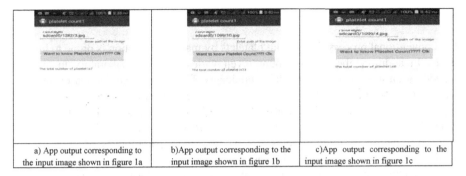

a) App output corresponding to the input image shown in figure 1a	b)App output corresponding to the input image shown in figure 1b	c)App output corresponding to the input image shown in figure 1c

Fig. 4. Output given by the Platelet-Counting App after segmentation

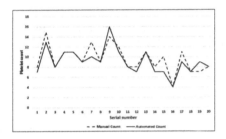

Fig. 5. Graph representing the manual and automated platelet count

corresponding platelet count. Output images are shown in Fig. 4a, b, c. Small black dots are platelets. Above those images the platelet count of that image is shown.

We have tested the App output on the microscopic images of 100 different blood smears and compared the platelet count given by our App and the manual count obtained from expert pathologists and got an appropriate result in most cases. The overall accuracy of this system is 90.625%. Equation 1 is used to calculate the accuracy percentage. Figure 5 shows a comparison graph between manual and automated platelet count for 20 different blood samples. The x-axis represents 20 different blood samples, and the y-axis represents the platelet count of the corresponding sample. The dashed line in Fig. 5 accounts for the manual platelet count whereas the continuous line represents the automated platelet count for each sample. As evident from the graph, the two lines are very close to each other implying that the count given by our app is approximately same as manual or conventional counting in most of the cases.

$$\text{Error}(\%) = \frac{\sum\limits_{i=1}^{n}(m_i - a_i)}{\sum\limits_{i-1}^{n} a_i} \times 100\% \tag{1}$$

4 Conclusion

The conventional process of counting platelets by manual inspection is prone to human errors. In addition, the platelet count given varies from one laboratory to another depending on the expertise of the lab technicians. This dependency on lab-technicians for counting platelets could be eliminated by our developed app. We have tested our app on poor as well as good intensity images and got appropriate results in most of the cases. Thus, this app is not dependent on the intensity of the images. Also, it would be useful for people residing in outskirts where expert pathologists are not readily available. In future, this app could be helpful for detecting diseases like Dengue where platelet count is a vital parameter for treatment and monitoring the health status of patients. This would also avoid the rush to the laboratories, which arise when there is a huge outbreak of endemic diseases like dengue where technicians have to check a huge number of the blood sample and thus helps to reduce human errors.

Acknowledgement. Authors are thankful to Department of Bio-Technology, Govt. of India (Letter No. - Letter No -BT/PR8456/MED/29/739/2013) for their support.

References

1. What does blood do? http://wpww.ncbi.nlm.nih.gov/pubmedhealth/PMH0072576/?report= printable. Accessed 10 July 2016
2. All you need to know about taking a CBC or Complete Blood Count test. http://www.thehealthsite.com/diseases-conditions/complete-blood-count-cbc-test-what-you-need-to-know. Accessed 10 July 2016
3. Savkare, S.S., Narote, S.P.: Blood cell segmentation from microscopic blood images. In: IEEE International Conference on Information Processing (ICIP), pp. 502–505 (2015)
4. Sharif, J.M., Miswan, M.F., Ngadi, M.A., Salam, M.S.H., bin Abdul Jamil, M.M.: Red blood cell segmentation using masking and watershed algorithm: a preliminary study. In: International Conference on Biomedical Engineering (ICoBE), pp. 258–262 (2012)
5. Kareem, S., Morling, R.C.S., Kale, I.: A novel method to count the red blood cells in thin blood films. In: IEEE International Symposium of Circuits and Systems (ISCAS), pp. 1021–1024 (2011)
6. Deb, N., Chakraborty, S.: A noble technique for detecting anemia through classification of red blood cells in blood smear. In: IEEE International Conference on Recent Advances and Innovations in Engineering (ICRAIE), pp. 1–9 (2014)
7. Karunakar, Y., Kuwadekar, A.: An unparagoned application for red blood cell counting using marker controlled watershed algorithm for Android mobile. In: Fifth International Conference on Next Generation Mobile Applications, Services and Technologies, pp. 100–104 (2011)
8. Duan, J., Yu, L.: A WBC segmentation methord based on HSI color space. In: IEEE International Conference on Broadband Network and Multimedia Technology (IC- BNMT), pp. 629–632 (2011)
9. Dey, R., Roy, K., Bhattacharjee, D., Nasipuri, M., Ghosh, P.: An automated system for segmenting platelets from microscopic images of blood cells. In: IEEE International Symposium on Advanced Computing and Communication (ISACC), pp. 230–237 (2015)

10. Dey, R., Roy, K., Bhattacharjee, D., Nasipuri, M., Ghosh, P.: A smart phone based app for automated segmentation and counting of platelets. In: IEEE International Conference on Recent Advances in Information Technology (RAIT), pp. 434–438 (2016)
11. Nasir, A.S.A., Mashor, M.Y., Rosline, H.: Unsupervised colour segmentation of white blood cell for acute leukaemia images. In: IEEE International Conference on Imaging Systems and Techniques, pp. 142–145 (2011)
12. Android Studio Overview. https://developer.android.com/studio/intro/index.html. Accessed 28 June 2016
13. Text Fields. https://developer.android.com/guide/topics/ui/controls/text.html. Accessed 28 June 2016
14. TextView. https://developer.android.com/reference/android/widget/TextView.html. Accessed 28 June 2016
15. Button. https://developer.android.com/reference/android/widget/Button.html. Accessed 28 June 2016
16. ImageView. https://developer.android.com/reference/android/widget/ImageView.html. Accessed 28 June 2016
17. Tan, P.-N., Steinbach, M., Kumar, V.: Cluster analysis: basic concepts and algorithms. In: Introduction to Data Mining. Pearson Education India (2006). Chap. 8
18. Gonzalez, R.C., Woods, R.E.: Digital image fundamentals. In: Digital Image Processing. Pearson Education International (2006). Chap. 2

Additive Noise Removal by Combining Non Local Means Filtering and a Local Fuzzy Filter – A Fusion Approach

Raju G., Farha Fatina Wahid$^{(\boxtimes)}$, and Sugandhi K.

Department of Information Technology, Kannur University,
Kannur, Kerala, India
kurupgraju@gmail.com, sugandhikgs@gmail.com,
farhawahid@yahoo.co.in

Abstract. Additive noise is one among the prominent types of noises which degrades the quality of images. A very large number of algorithms, in spatial, frequency and wavelet domain have been proposed to enhance images corrupted with additive noise. All the methods suggested have their own advantages as well as disadvantages. With the availability of parallel processing capability, in low end workstations and systems, fusion of two or more de-noising methods has become a topic of interest. In this paper, we have implemented one of the recent contributions to mean filter - a fuzzy filter. Also, as a complementary filter, the basic Non Local Means filter is implemented. Experiments were carried out by fusing the results obtained through the two filters. The results obtained establish the merit of the fusion approach.

Keywords: Additive noise · Image de-noising · Image fusion · NLM · Fuzzy filter

1 Introduction

Though image de-noising is a pre-processing step in any image processing application, it is impracticable to attain 100% de-noising results. Noise estimation and design of suitable filters are the basic steps of image de-noising. Additive noise is a commonly known noise model which includes salt and pepper, Gaussian and uniform noise. Among these noises, Gaussian noise is the prominent one. Local filters have evolved in the field of image de-noising few decades back. These filters showed their significance in computational as well as application environments. The process of convolution is the basic thought behind any local filter [1]. Local filters vary from mean filters [1, 2] to the recently developed fuzzy filter [3]. Local filters have their own advantages and disadvantages. As an alternate approach to the local neighborhood concept, the non-local neighborhood concept was introduced by Buades et al. [2]. This concept got wide acceptance and several image de-noising problems got solutions using this concept. Non local neighborhood filters ranges from the basic Non-Local Means filtering (NLM) [2] to the recently developed Non-Local Fuzzy Means (NLFM) filtering [4].

© Springer Nature Singapore Pte Ltd. 2017
M. Singh et al. (Eds.): ICACDS 2016, CCIS 721, pp. 30–39, 2017.
DOI: 10.1007/978-981-10-5427-3_4

The recent trend in image de-noising is the fusion concept. Fusing relevant information from input images results in an image that contains much better details than the individual input images [5]. Registered images are mainly used so as to overcome alignment problem that might occur during fusion. Fusion techniques are broadly categorized into three – namely pixel level fusion [6, 7], feature level fusion [8] and data/decision level fusion [9]. Among these techniques, pixel level fusion is simple as it's directly applied on image pixels in spatial domain.

In this paper, a novel natural gray image de-noising method using pixel level fusion technique is proposed. A local fuzzy filter and the classical Non-Local Means filter are selected for applying pixel level fusion. The individual results obtained from the above filters are fused so as to obtain a finer resultant de-noised image. The idea behind this thought is that, these two concepts namely the local and the non-local filtering approaches have shown their own significance as image de-noising algorithms and works in a different manner.

The paper is organized as follows: Sect. 2 gives an overview of the fuzzy filter followed by the NLM filtering in Sect. 3. Section 4 explores the proposed fusion approach. Results and discussions are given in Sect. 5. Finally, conclusion is given in Sect. 6.

2 A Fuzzy Filter for Additive Noise Removal

In this section, we present a fuzzy filter [3], a recent addition to the family of mean filters. The filter was proposed as an alternate to existing local filters and reported better performance in denoising color images. It is a two-step fuzzy based filtering technique used for restoring images corrupted with additive noise. In the first step, a membership function is used to compute membership values of all pixels with respect to the central pixel in a selected pixel neighborhood. The membership values are appropriately modified and used as weights for the pixels in the neighborhood. The weighted average of these pixels gives the filtered pixel at the center point of pixel neighborhood. In the second step, the results obtained in the first step are improved by reducing the noise in the color component differences without destroying the fine details of the image. In this work, we deal with gray images rather than color images, hence only the first step in the filter is considered.

Given a noisy image I of size m × n, corrupted with additive noise, for filtering a pixel $I(i,j)$, where i,j denotes the spatial coordinates of the pixel, a neighborhood of size $(2k+1)$ centered at (i,j) is selected. Here, k indicates half the window size. Initially, the absolute difference of each pixel in the neighborhood with respect to the central pixel is calculated as

$$diff_{i,j,r,s} = \left| diff_{i,j} - diff_{r,s} \right| \tag{1}$$

where $r,s \in \{-k,\ldots,0,\ldots+k\}$.

Once the absolute difference is found, the next step is to find mean and variance of the difference. Let $L\_mean\_diff_{i,j}$ and $L\_std\_diff_{i,j}$ denote the local mean and standard deviation of the differences respectively. Then, the membership values for each difference value can be calculated as

$$\mu_{diff(i,j,r,s)} = e^{\frac{-\left(diff_{i,j,r,s} - L\_mean\_diff_{i,j}\right)^2}{2 * L\_std\_diff_{i,j}^2}} \tag{2}$$

The fuzzy membership values thus obtained is multiplied with a scaling parameter α so as to give higher weights for those pixel positions whose membership degree is high for the difference values.

The weights are given as

$$w_{i+r,j+s} = \left\lfloor \alpha * \mu_{diff(i,j,r,s)} + 0.5 \right\rfloor \tag{3}$$

The final filtered pixel is calculated as the weighted average of all pixels in the neighborhood.

$$I'_{(i,j)} = \frac{\sum_{r=-k}^{+k} \sum_{s=-k}^{+k} w_{i+r,j+s} * I_{i+r,j+s}}{\sum_{r=-k}^{+k} \sum_{s=-k}^{+k} w_{i+r,j+s}} \tag{4}$$

In this work, the difference computation step for each pixel within its neighborhood is kept intact as in the existing fuzzy filter. These neighborhood differences are combined together and its global mean and standard deviation are used for membership computation rather than considering local mean and standard deviation. i.e., if G_mean_diff and G_std_diff denotes the mean and standard deviation of entire difference values, Eq. 2 is replaced as

$$\mu_{diff(i,j,r,s)} = e^{\frac{-\left(diff_{i,j,r,s} - G\_mean\_diff\right)^2}{2 * G\_std\_diff^2}} \tag{5}$$

We have carried out experiments with global mean and standard deviation as well as local mean and standard deviation and found that global mean and standard deviation always results in better performance.

3 Non Local Means Filter

The Non Local Means (NLM) filtering [2] was proposed by Buades et al. in 2005. Here, in order to restore a noisy pixel, either the entire image pixels or pixels within a search window centered about the noisy pixel are selected. From the search window, neighborhood patches are extracted. The similarity between neighborhood patches plays a key role in NLM filtering. Basically, it uses weighted average of all pixels in the search window surrounding a pixel to modify it. The weights are calculated based on the similarity between the neighborhood patches. The contribution of all pixels in the search window to modify the current pixel is directly proportional to their respective weights. Hence, high weights indicate more contribution and vice versa.

Given an image I corrupted with additive white Gaussian noise, the de-noised image I' is given as

$$I'(i) = \sum_{j \in I} w(i,j).I(j) \qquad (6)$$

where $w(i,j)$ is the weight assigned to the jth pixel for modifying the value of the ith pixel. The weight can be calculated as

$$w(i,j) = \frac{1}{z(i)} e^{\frac{-\|I(N_i) - I(N_J)\|_{2,a}^2}{h^2}} \qquad (7)$$

where $z(i) = \sum_j e^{\frac{-\|I(N_i)-I(N_J)\|_{2,a}^2}{h^2}}$.

Here, N_i and N_j are neighborhood of pixels i and j respectively, h is the filtering parameter and $\|.\|_{2,a}^2$ denotes squared Euclidean norm with a Gaussian kernel standard deviation, $a > 0$. The weights are always in the range $0 \leq w(i,j) \leq 1$ and must satisfy the condition $\sum_j w(i,j) = 1$ [10]. A special case that occurs in weight calculation is when $i == j$. In such situation, in order to overcome the overweighting of the noisy pixel to itself, the weight value is replaced by the maximum weights among the remaining pixels [11].

4 The Fusion Approach

In the previous sections, a local and a Non-local filtering technique are discussed. Each filter has its own merits and demerits. Both the methods use weighted average of pixels to modify a noisy pixel. In this work, for restoring an image corrupted with additive noise, a simple and efficient pixel level fusion technique is adopted. As an initial step, de-noised images are obtained using fuzzy filter and NLM filter. Then the weighted average of pixels from both the images is found, there by obtaining a new fused image containing properties from both the input de-noised images.

4.1 Fusion Using Weighted Average

Let FZ be the de-noised image obtained using fuzzy filter and NL be the de-noised image using NLM filter. Then, the de-noised image F_Wt_Avg is mathematically represented as

$$F\_Wt\_Avg(i) = \beta.NL(i) + (1 - \beta).FZ(i) \qquad (8)$$

where β denotes the weight and satisfies the condition $0 < \beta < 1$ and i denotes image pixel position. By varying β, it is possible to improve the quality of the fused image.

5   Experimental Results and Discussions

Experiments are carried out with different natural gray images. The images under consideration are corrupted with additive white Gaussian noise with four different noise densities (σ) 5, 10, 15 and 20 respectively. In case of fuzzy filter, the parameter k is

Table 1. List of images

Image ID	Image name
1	Cameraman
2	House
3	Lake
4	Lena
5	Living room
6	Mandril
7	Peppers
8	Pirate
9	Walk bridge
10	Barbara

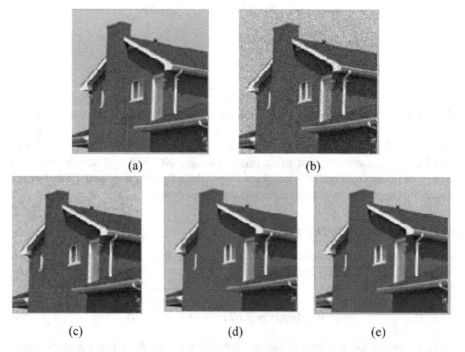

Fig. 1. (a) Original house image (b) Image corrupted with noise standard deviation 10 (c) De-noised image using fuzzy filter (d) De-noised image using NLM filter (e) De-noised image using weighted average fusion.

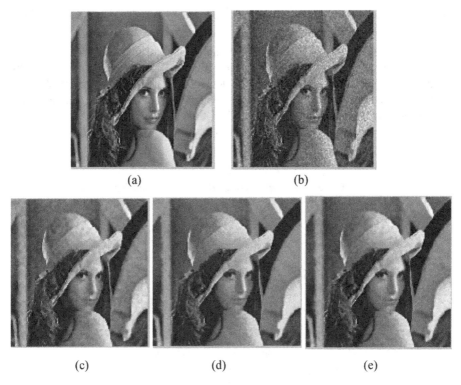

Fig. 2. (a) Original Lena image (b) Image corrupted with noise standard deviation 15 (c) De-noised image using fuzzy filter (d) De-noised image using NLM filter (e) De-noised image using weighted average fusion.

fixed to 1 and the scaling parameter α is fixed to 10. For the implementation of NLM filter, a search window of size 21 and patch size of 7 is selected. The parameter h is found to depend on noise standard deviation and its value is fixed using trial and error scheme [10]. For applying fusion using weighted average, the optimal β value is selected based on trial and error scheme, independently for each noise density.

In order to evaluate the performance of the fusion technique over classical NLM and fuzzy filter, two different performance evaluation measures, namely Peak Signal to Noise Ratio [12] and Structural Similarity Measure [13] are considered.

The similarities between the structures of two images are found using the structural similarity index (SSIM). SSIM can be measured using Eq. 9 [13].

$$SSIM = \frac{\left(2\mu_x\mu_y + c_1\right)\left(2\sigma_{xy} + c_2\right)}{\left(\mu_x^2\mu_y^2 + c_1\right)\left(\sigma_x^2\sigma_y^2 + c_2\right)} \tag{9}$$

where, x and y are two windows of identical size. Here, μ_x and μ_y are the average of x and y, σ_x^2 and σ_y^2 are the variance of x and y and σ_{xy} is the co-variance. $c_1 = (k_1 L)^2$, $c_2 = (k_2 L)^2$, $k_1 \ll 1$, $k_2 \ll 1$ and L is the dynamic range of pixel values.

Table 1 gives the set of natural images. Figure 1 gives the de-noised results obtained for house image for noise standard deviation 10 using fuzzy filter, NLM filter and the proposed fusion approach. The results obtained using these three techniques for Lena image corrupted with noise standard deviation 15 is given in Fig. 2.

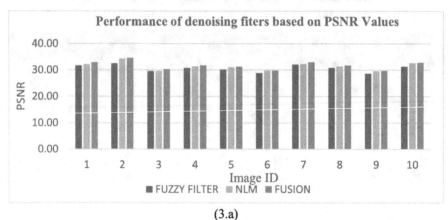

(3.a)

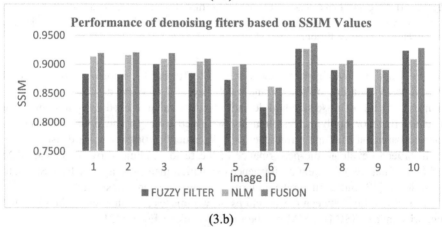

(3.b)

Fig. 3. Comparison of fuzzy filter, NLM filter and fusion approach ($\beta = 0.7$) for $\sigma = 10$ based on performance evaluation parameter (a) PSNR value (b) SSIM value

Figure 3 shows the graphical representation of the comparisons between the performances of fuzzy filter, NLM filter and the proposed fusion approach using performance evaluation parameters PSNR and SSIM for noise standard deviation 10. The comparisons of the de-noising filters for noise standard deviation 15 and 20 are given in Fig. 4 and Fig. 5 respectively.

Based on an overall analysis, it is evident that the de-noising results obtained using fusion of a local neighborhood filter – fuzzy filter and a non-local neighborhood filter- NLM filter using weighted average gave better performance than the individual de-noised results for images corrupted with additive white Gaussian noise at all noise densities for natural gray images based on quantitative as well as qualitative analysis.

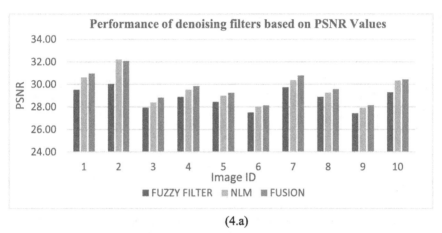

(4.a)

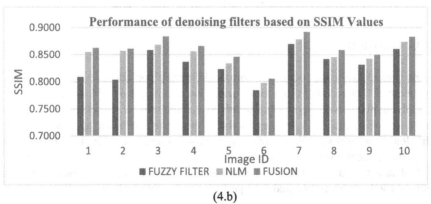

(4.b)

Fig. 4. Comparison of fuzzy filter, NLM filter and fusion approach ($\beta = 0.6$) for $\sigma = 15$ based on performance evaluation parameter (a) PSNR value (b) SSIM value.

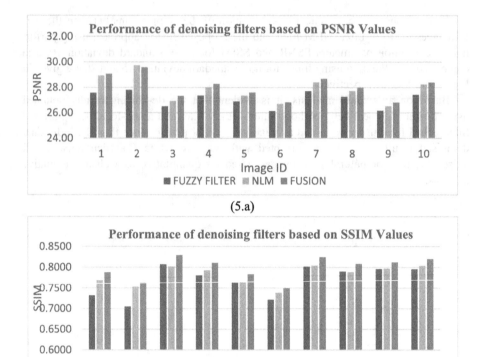

(5.a)

(5.b)

Fig. 5. Comparison of fuzzy filter, NLM filter and fusion approach ($\beta = 0.6$) for $\sigma = 20$ based on performance evaluation parameter (a) PSNR value (b) SSIM value

6 Conclusion

In this paper, fusion of local and non-local filtering for additive noise removal is implemented. The results from a local fuzzy filter and Non-Local Means filter are used for applying pixel level fusion using weighted average scheme. Experiments carried out with a set of natural gray images establish the merit of fusion approach over the individual approaches at all noise densities. Fusion outperforms the individual results of the above mentioned de-noising filters.

A detailed study of different fusion rules or various combinations of filtering methods can be explored to find best performing filtering technique.

Acknowledgement. The authors would like to acknowledge the University Grants Commission for the financial support extended under the Major Project Scheme.

References

1. Gonzalez, R., Woods, R.: Digital Image Processing, 3rd edn. Pearson Education Inc., Upper Saddle River (2009)
2. Buades, A., Coll, B., Morel, J.: A review of image denoising algorithms, with a new one. Multiscale Model. Simul. **4**, 490–530 (2005)
3. Nair, M., Raju, G.: Additive noise removal using a novel fuzzy-based filter. Comput. Electr. Eng. **37**, 644–655 (2011)
4. Lan, R., Zhou, Y., Tang, Y., Chen, C.: Image denoising using non-local fuzzy means. In: 2015 IEEE China Summit and International Conference on Signal and Information Processing (ChinaSIP) (2015)
5. James, A., Dasarathy, B.: Medical image fusion: a survey of the state of the art. Inf. Fusion **19**, 4–19 (2014)
6. Li, M., Dong, Y., Li, J.: Overview of pixel level image fusion algorithm. AMM **519–520**, 590–593 (2014)
7. Anita, S., Moses, C.: Survey on pixel level image fusion techniques. In: 2013 IEEE International Conference ON Emerging Trends in Computing, Communication and Nanotechnology (ICECCN) (2013)
8. Ganasala, P., Kumar, V.: Multimodality medical image fusion based on new features in NSST domain. Biomed. Eng. Lett. **4**, 414–424 (2014)
9. Gu, L.: Research on multi-sensor data level fusion based on artificial neuron. Chin. J. Mech. Eng. **39**, 89 (2003)
10. Buades, A., Coll, B., Morel, J.: A non-local algorithm for image denoising. In: 2005 IEEE Computer Society Conference on Computer Vision and Pattern Recognition (CVPR 2015) (2015)
11. Raju, G., Wahid, F., Shareekhath, K.: Modified non-local means filtering. In: 2015 IEEE International Conference on Signal Processing, Informatics, Communication and Energy Systems (SPICES) (2015)
12. Hore, A., Ziou, D.: Image quality metrics: PSNR vs. SSIM. In: 2010 20th International Conference on Pattern Recognition (2010)
13. Wang, Z., Bovik, A., Sheikh, H., Simoncelli, E.: Image quality assessment: from error visibility to structural similarity. IEEE Trans. Image Process. **13**, 600–612 (2004)

An Incremental Verification Paradigm for Embedded Systems

Hara Gopal Mani Pakala[✉]

Matrusri Engineering College, Saidabad, Hyderabad 500059, Telangana, India
gopalmaniph@yahoo.com

Abstract. Embedded Systems complexity is enhancing many folds in most of the product domains. Changing requirements and uncertainty during early stages of development are of greatest concern for the developing community, as they enhance system development complexities. Verification encompasses all aspects of system development process. This paper proposes an incremental paradigm that incorporates early integration and reduces uncertainty during initial phases of development under changing conditions of requirements. The method can be represented by a cascaded V-model. The verification methodology implementation issues are presented.

Keywords: Embedded systems · Changing requirements · Uncertainty in development · Verification method · Early integration · Division of design-verification-cycle · Cascaded V-model · Implementation of verification method

1 Introduction

Complex embedded systems (CES) have mission critical requirements like real-time and high-confidence performance; accommodate frequent changes in requirements, environment, and technology; large embedded software running on different embedded computing platforms; etc. Examples are robots, modern cars, airplanes, radars, sonar's, missiles, etc., [1–8]. At present ES are being researched in all aspects and in all phases of development. From requirements uncertainty [1, 2], to system design [3], to Verification and Validation [6–8] to the requirement of new approaches/theories [9], all are being focused by the embedded community. Verification and validation (V and V) activities are associated with all stage of the product lifecycle and account for a substantial share of project budgets, both time and money. Strictly, V and V Stringent market and economic considerations are forcing all concerned into reducing V and V process deficiencies [10] and introducing design methodologies with dedicated resources for important phases of development [5, 11]. All these efforts are directed towards reducing overall cost or to meet market deadlines or to improve performance. This paper focus is design/implementation verification of CES-product under development.

© Springer Nature Singapore Pte Ltd. 2017
M. Singh et al. (Eds.): ICACDS 2016, CCIS 721, pp. 40–49, 2017.
DOI: 10.1007/978-981-10-5427-3_5

2   Related Work

The verification and validation methodologies reported so far can be categorized into (a) language dependent [3, 6], (b) specific tool (development framework) [4–6], and also commercially available tools [8]. But these tools are not available in all application areas, very expensive (if available), not qualified and also are not easily accessible. Most tools do not cater to incomplete requirements. Such solutions are not easily accessible to the embedded community. As such general method for 'ES verification and validation' is required which is useful to the development community. A frame work for re-verification of component-based software systems [5] after modifications of components is presented. The tool supported frame work uses high-level algebraic representations to identify and execute.

In [6] an approach to improve the formal verification process on system-level model is presented using SystemC. The V and V for a safety critical embedded system, part of a larger system-of-systems, are presented in [7]. The V and V approach reported is iterative and uses random and non-real time testing apart from the static and dynamic tests. The process phases are carried out in parallel and the results of the different phases are considered to ensure that an error free embedded system is given for the field testing.

This paper proposes a general incremental approach to Verification, derived from the V and V space. It is based on the idea of division of design-implementation-verification cycle into multiple design-evaluation cycles and the number is under the control of designer.

3   Verification and Validation Aspects in Embedded Systems

A Complex Embedded System (CES) consists of various subsystems as shown in Fig. 1, and also software. These subsystems (including embedded software) should be developed for implementing on the target architecture. Verification starts with an implementation (product-prototype) and confirms that the implementation meets its specifications. The system specifications are transformed into an implementation by the design-development process. Thus the task of verification is to assess if the implemented design performs according to the anticipated functionality and fulfills the design constraints on throughput, precision, etc. Normally the Verification approach is to test the embedded system with the test cases till all the faults are presumed to be detected and all the tests generated for the system pass. This means, for example, apart from the 'Final System Integration', a minimum of four integration tests must be executed, as shown in Fig. 1. The V-model normally hides several important design steps associated with the development of Embedded System.

If there is no change in requirements, specifications can be easily finalized. The simplified development and evaluation process of Embedded System is as shown in Fig. 2. The testing architecture requires a reference system, test-suites and a comparator. However the method implicitly places condition that the output responses of the System under Test to be observable by the tester. Another point is regarding availability of "reference system". Test techniques employed are functional/black-box

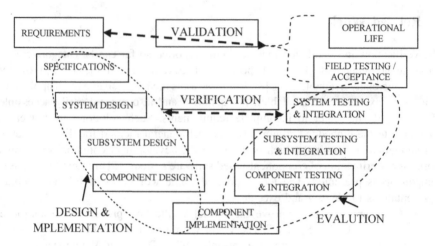

Fig. 1. V-Model system development life cycle

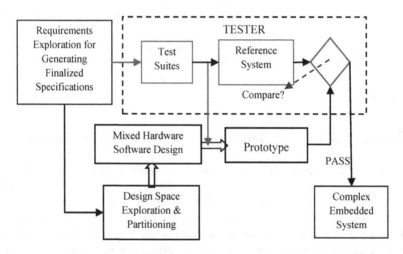

Fig. 2. Embedded system development (simplified)

and structural/white-box testing. Due to System complexity, structure testing is difficult. It is to be noted that after completion of "design-implementation-cycle" only the verification activities can be started. It can be seen that subsystems integration testing and resulting verification effort required is an expensive process without any assurance on the outcome of product development activity.

The scope of the functional test cases at each test level is extended in relation to the prior test level. Moreover, the functionality of every integrated component that interacts with the rest needs to be tested. Most test objectives at these different test levels can be achieved by the application of functional testing. The challenge of software-hardware integration is their differing natures and observability of interaction among components.

If observability of component/subsystem interaction is necessary then dynamic test architecture like 'run time monitoring' may have to be combined with testing [12]. The changing requirements and the necessity to modify specifications will alter the development process shown in Fig. 2 drastically.

4 Verification and Validation Trade-Off Space

The formal V and V (FVV) process tradeoff space shown in Fig. 3, developed for software development [13] can also be applied for Embedded Systems. The specification/validation axis associates several aspects of formal specification like work, value, etc. The System axis deals with the adaptability of the complex system implementation to a specific FVV technique. The verification axis links the specification and implementation axis. The verification axis represents the work, value and other overheads of verification. The FVV trade-off space can be applied for both coverage and cost between FVV techniques. Qualitatively three formal techniques compared are [13] - Theorem Proving (TP), Model Checking (MC) and Execution based Model Checking (EMC). EMC is a mixture of Runtime Verification (RV) and Automatic Test Generation (ATG). Based on automation of level of ATG tool, the EMC technique automation can be partial or total. With ATG it is possible that the EMC's verification coverage cannot be 100% and also low cost. Summary of the comparison results are:

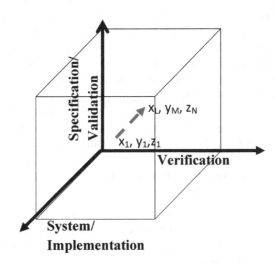

Fig. 3. FVV trade off space - effect of incremental design evaluation cycle

- TP and MC can provide good verification. However several behavioural requirements of interest cannot be addressed by them.
- EMC has better coverage and cost in specification and system dimensions. But in the "verification dimension" the EMC has lower coverage and cost compared to other two techniques.

The trade-off space indicates that no ideal FVV technique is available. However it also hints at the possibility of a novel "incremental verification scheme" for the CES. As such it is possible to improve coverage on the verification axis, by combining runtime verification with proper selection of test- sequence generator technique [13]. Next section describes necessary structure for implementing the new incremental verification methodology.

5 An Incremental Verification Paradigm

The normal development cycle is denoted as "design-implementation verification-cycle (DVC)" or simply DVC is shown in Fig. 2 and normally called as V-model. For iteration this normal single development cycle DVC is to be divided into a reasonable "set of k design-evaluation-cycles (DEC)" where 'k' is verification step size which is selected by the developer, based on the modification required. The verification coverage is expected to increase step-wise with each 'verification step-k', as shown using dotted arrow (may not be linear as shown) in Fig. 3 from a point (x_1, y_1, z_1) to some other point (x_L, y_M, z_N) as 'k' increases. This implies iteration of integration and verification for each executed DEC cycle. For example requirement got modified from previous DEC. Then the test sequence should be generated for each DEC, based on updated set of requirements.

An important point on Test sequence generation is highlighted here. The V-model (Fig. 1) left hand side represents step-wise progression of partial-specification C_1 into a realization C_n; where C_1 to C_n are called *contracts*. The right side of V-model represents corresponding test sets. It is clear that C_j and TS_j are related. If C_{j+1} are the progression of C_j then corresponding test sets TS_j and TS_{j+1} are related in terms of refinement calculus [14]. It is possible to generate and use updated test sequence using the relation between TS_j and TS_{j+1} [14]. It is to be noted that the verification coverage/costs are also dependent on Test sequence Generator [13]. The jth test sequence $(TS)_j$ should be generated for $(DEC)_j$, starting from j^{th} partial set of requirements and after each update to $(j + 1)^{th}$ of requirements a new $(TS)_{(j + 1)}$ should be generated.

The requirements for building the incremental verification paradigm highlights the following set of important activities.

(1) Limited set of real life requirements – partial specifications are generated and used for system design. However for ES (Product)-prototype architecture some of the candidates are – rapid prototyping, modular, and other flexible architectures.
(2) Product-Prototype Implementation.
(3) Verify – Determine the Product-prototype is meeting the initial set of real-life requirements. This also implies addition of integration testing at appropriate level in this step. This requires development of
    (a) Test sequence generating System based on system requirements.
    (b) Independent Instrumentation support and criterion for evaluation.

(4) Updating requirements – improving/modifying specifications based on performance and user/other requirements of the application. This step implies the following:

   (a) Complete requirements (validated also)/specifications are available and the developer is addressing them in some logical way one by one. This is quite rare.

   (b) The developer is implementing a base line system with clear specifications. There are anticipated changes. These changes are under validation, using simulation, etc., and will be rolled-down after validation. These are future requirements.

   (c) User is involved and can spell clear requirements/inform adequacy of implementation by observing the performance for certain test cases.

In all these cases the proposed verification paradigm becomes applicable and provides adaptive methodology.

(5) Augment prototype –This implies addition of resources (hardware and software) for the prototype. Example if the target architecture is modular bus based computing-boards, then adding additional computing/other board.

(6) Verify – Determine the augmented-product-prototype is meeting the updated requirements. The Test generating method and criterion should be selected for reusing already generated test-sequences, if possible.

(7) Repetition of steps supports update/evaluation and for checking performance requirements of application (i.e., validation). For iteration the normal single development cycle is to be divided into a reasonable "set of k design-evaluation-cycles (DEC)".

The division of DVC and iteration of DEC procedure automatically incorporates integration and evaluation in each step, viz., for each step-k the V-model of Fig. 1 is executed completely. Step 3; clearly indicates the requirement for an independent "Dynamic Real-time Evaluation System" as a support system for the development. All these aspects form foundations for the novel Systems Level framework for adaptive methodology for evaluation (FAME) described in the next section.

The incremental verification method consists of k-sets of Design Evaluation Cycles that can be represented as a cascaded V – model as shown in Fig. 4. The cascaded V-model is superimposed on another normal V – model shown in dotted lines in the figure. The requirements exploration and its link in generation of partial specifications and updating specifications are given. Each DEC (from partial specifications to prototype evaluation) is depicted as a V-model. The V-model steps are same as that shown in Fig. 1. The cascaded V-model is different from multiple V-models and nested V-model [15]. Between the 1st V-model and the kth V-model, the iteration, verification and up-gradation with increasing-k are shown with 'dashed arrow'. Each of the Design-Evaluation-Cycles is marked appropriately. After the kth V-model (Design-Evaluation-Cycle-k) the final system evaluation takes place. Each Design Evaluation Cycle while providing a prototype reduces product uncertainty/remaining-risk incrementally.

The details of kth-V-model; from k^{th}-partial specifications to prototype ($Proto_k$) design/evaluation are similar to the V-model shown in Fig. 1. The kth-V represents

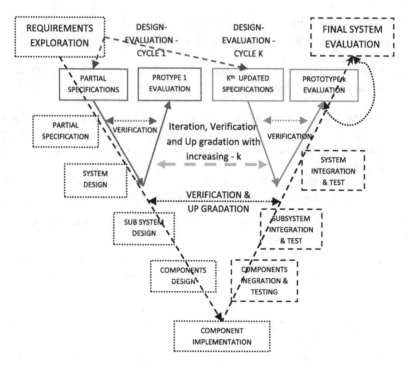

Fig. 4. Cascaded V model

"partial specifications to prototype evaluation" indicating the adaptive creation of $Proto_k$ and its verification with the support of a specially designed dynamic real time evaluation system [16]. The $Proto_{k-1}$ is tested with corresponding test sequence TS $_{(k-1)}$ and verified. Once verified the uncertainty or risk, in the $Proto_{k-1}$ is taken to be zero. The iterative implementation of $Proto_k$ and its verification provides a structured way of removing ambiguity in the interpretation of requirements. During improvements and or for up-gradation, the DEC's are performed until 'finalization of specifications and final-product' verification.

6   The Role of FAME in the Embedded System Development Process

The role of the proposed verification method in the Embedded System development is clearly implementation of the "Evaluation Process" shown in dotted lines in Fig. 1, under changing specifications. A simplified development process including the FAME method is shown in Fig. 5. The Evaluation paradigm, FAME, is shown as two-boxes within dotted lines. Ideally, the (product) development process can be divided into five major steps, for dealing with changing requirements:

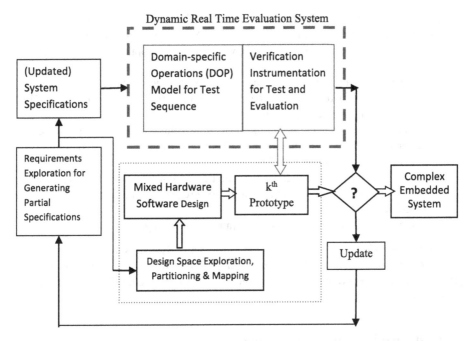

Fig. 5. Role of incremental verification paradigm in embedded system development

A. An iterative exploration of requirements for translating to partial specifications. Here it is assumed that the specifications do not change during the design-evaluation cycle.

B. Translate partial-specifications into implementation of a prototype (Target system architecture is modular/flexible with updatable resources) using any standard procedure.

C. Verify the prototype under development with the help of "Dynamic Real time Evaluation System (DRES)".

D. Update/improve the specifications and repeat the steps (B and C) till finalization of specifications and prototype development.

E. Develop engineered product from prototype (if required).

F. The core of FAME methodology is clearly the development of "Dynamic Real-time Evaluation System (DRES)" for implementing the "Evaluation Process" shown in Fig. 1. The 'C-point' given above indicates that the components of "Dynamic Real time Evaluation System (DRES)" and the prototype design/implementation tasks have to be concurrently carried out. It is to be noted that both systems are application and implementation dependent. Especially the prototype architecture is required to be modular. However other types can be used if it is decided to use different architectures for engineered product, after evaluation. Also the components of DRES will be very useful for discussions with customer/user and in the validation process.

G. The proposed methodology addresses the following embedded system issues, and provides systematic procedure for verification. Note that the method assumes usage of some standard design methodology for the development of *prototype of embedded system* per se.

   (1) Uncertainties in early design stages and resulting Risk in the development of ES. A probabilistic metric based on "remaining risk" for the DVC and DEC can be defined for comparison [17].
   (2) Accommodate changes in requirements and technology dependent choices.
   (3) User feedback is taken based on the results of evaluation for update of specifications at the end of each DEC.
   (4) Early and Step-wise design implementation and verification. The step size 'k' can be varied based on User/Developer expertise level and linked to changes in specifications.
   (5) Spreads system-level multiple integration and testing costs.

An example Complex Embedded Signal Processing System is taken for illustrating the methodology and for the development of Dynamic Real time Evaluation System [16, 17]. The methodology shows reduction of initial development risk for the example considered.

7 Conclusions and Future Work

Present work proposed an *incremental verification paradigm* based on the idea of division of single "design and verification cycle" into "k-multiple steps of design and evaluation cycles". The methodology is illustrated by defining a cascaded V-model. A framework is presented that adapts the "formal incremental verification scheme" for the development of complex embedded systems. The method requires development of (a) Test sequence generating System and (b) dedicated Real time Instrumentation support and criterion for evaluation.

References

1. Jeannet, B., Gaucher, F.: Debugging embedded systems requirements with stimulus: an automotive case-study. In: Proceedings of the 8th European Congress on Embedded Real Time Software and Systems (ERTS 2016), Toulouse, France, January 2016
2. Chang, C.-H., et al.: SysML-based requirement management to improve software development. Int. J. Softw. Eng. Knowl. Eng. **26**(03), 491–511 (2016)
3. Saeedloei, N., Gupta, G.: A methodology for modeling and verification of cyber-physical systems based on logic programming. ACM SIGBED Rev. **13**(2), 34–42 (2016)
4. Johnson, K., Calinescu, R., Kikuchi, S.: An incremental verification framework for component-based software systems. In: CBSE 2013, 17–21 June 2013, Vancouver, BC, Canada (2013)
5. Wagner, F.R., Nascimento, F.A.M., Oliveira, M.F.S.: Model-driven engineering of complex embedded systems: concepts and tools. ftp://143.54.11.3/pub/simoo/papers/cbsec12.pdf. Accessed 20 Oct 2016

6. Elshuber, M., Kandl, S., Puschner, P.: Improving system-level verification of systemC models with SPIN. In: Choppy, C., Sun, J. (eds.) 1st French Singaporean Workshop on Formal Methods and Applications (FSFMA 2013), vol. 31. Schloss Dagstuhl–Leibniz-ZentrumfuerInformatik (2013)
7. Nanda, M., Jayanthi, J.: An effective verification and validation strategy for safety-critical embedded systems. Int. J. Softw. Eng. Appl. (IJSEA) 4(2), 123–142 (2013)
8. Tatar, M., Mauss, J.: Systematic test and validation of complex embedded systems. In: ERTS-2014, Toulouse, pp. 05–07 (2014)
9. Liggesmeyer, P., Trapp, M.: Trends in embedded software engineering. IEEE Softw. 26(3), 19–25 (2009)
10. The Economic Impacts of Inadequate Infrastructure for Software Testing. Technical report, National Institute of Standards and Technology, May 2002
11. Hoppe, M., Engel, A.: Improving VVT process in SysTest project: evaluating results of pilot projects in six industries. In: 2005 Fifteenth Annual International Symposium on Systems Engineering: Bridging Industry, Government, and Academia, 10–15 July 2005, NY, USA (2005)
12. Watterson, C., Heffernan, D.: A runtime verification monitoring approach for embedded industrial controllers. In: IEEE International Symposium on Industrial Electronics, ISIE 2008, pp. 2016–2021. IEEE (2008)
13. Drusinsky, D., Michael, J.B., Shing, M.-T.: A visual trade-off space for formal verification and validation techniques. IEEE Syst. J. 2(4), 513–519 (2008)
14. Aichernig, B.K.: The commuting V-diagram: on the relation of refinement and testing. UNU/IIST Report No. 254 (2002)
15. Broekman, B., Notenboom, E.: Testing Embedded Software. Addison-Weseley, Boston (2003)
16. Pakala, H.G.M., et al.: Development of instrument for test and evaluation of a signal processing system. J. Instrum. Soc. India 42(1), 40–43 (2012)
17. Pakala, H.G.M., et al.: An adaptive design verification methodology for embedded systems. Int. J. Ad hoc Sens. Ubiquit. Comput. (IJASUC) 2(3), 35–55 (2011)

Artificial Intelligence Based Recommender Systems: A Survey

Goldie Gabrani[1], Sangeeta Sabharwal[2],
and Viomesh Kumar Singh[2(✉)]

[1] BML Mujal University, Gurgaon, India
goldie.gabrani@bml.edu.in
[2] Netaji Subhas Institute of Technology, Delhi, India
ssab63@gmail.com, singh.viomesh@gmail.com

Abstract. In recent years, Artificial Intelligence (AI) techniques like (a) fuzzy sets, (b) Artificial Neural Networks (ANNs), (c) Artificial Immune Systems (AIS) (d) Swarm Intelligence (SI), and (e) Evolutionary Computing (EC) are used to improve recommendation accuracy as well as mitigate the current challenges like Scalability, Sparsity, Cold-start etc. Aim of the survey is to incorporate the recommender system in light of the AI techniques. Various AI techniques are presented and recommender system's challenges are also presented. Moreover, we have tried to study the ability of AI techniques to deal with the above mentioned challenges while designing recommender systems. Furthermore, pros and cons of AI techniques are discussed in detail.

Keywords: Recommender system · Collaborative filtering · Hybrid recommender system · Sparsity · Scalability · Cold-start problem

1 Introduction

With the recent advancements in the field of Internet Technology, information overload has turned into an immense issue. Recommender system (RS) enables online users to cope with the information overload and supports in various decision-making processes by providing most important and relevant information that are likely to interest customers and assists them in making better decisions [1].

"Recommender Systems are software tools that predict and suggest items that is worth recommending as user might like them or may want to buy them" [1]. The recommendation take into account in many different kind of decision-making processes, for example which city/places to visit, what items to buy, what movie to watch to, or what books, news/articles to read etc. RS recommend an item that is worth recommending. RSs plays an indispensable role in various websites such as Netflix, Amazon.com, YouTube etc. because they provide suggestions of more relevant items to their users. Thereby, companies may see a hike in their sales and come up with more diverse items in the market.

In this paper, the author focuses on the applications of AI techniques to develop RS that can resolve current challenges. The rest of the paper is organized in the following manner, Sect. 2 discusses the traditional RS techniques. In Sect. 3, we present current

M. Singh et al. (Eds.): ICACDS 2016, CCIS 721, pp. 50–59, 2017.
DOI: 10.1007/978-981-10-5427-3_6

challenges in detail. In Sect. 4, we highlight different AI techniques along with their basic attributes and properties. Some recently developed AI based RS are presented in Sect. 5. Finally Sect. 6 concludes the survey.

2 Traditional Recommender System Techniques

Recommending techniques are broadly classified as: Personalized and Non-Personalized (Fig. 1). In case of Non-Personalized Recommendations, users get recommendation about the most popular items. Non personalized RSs simply rely on the concept of popularity. But the complexity of Personalized RSs offer, the most reasonable items or products taking into account the client's profile [1]. It also requires techniques to predict the most suitable item for an individual user based on his preferences. However, in this case different users will receive different suggestions. This is in contrast to the Non-Personalized RS where each user gets the same recommendations. Personalized RS techniques are classified into three main categories (i) Content based, (ii) Collaborative filtering and (iii) Hybrid.

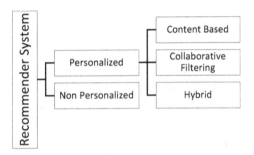

Fig. 1. Techniques for recommender system

2.1 Content Based Recommender System

This system figures out how to suggest items that are similar to the ones that user liked in the past. The correlation among items is computed based on the properties and attributes of compared items [1, 2]. For instance, if a client has provided positive rating to some superhero movies, then Content Based (CB) RS can learn to suggest other movies belong to superhero genre (Fig. 2).

2.2 Collaborative Recommender System/Collaborative Filtering (CF)

This approach recommends items that other users with similar tastes liked in the past [1]. The correlation between two users is computed based on the correlation in the rating provided by those users. It can be accomplished by establishing relation between the users or between items therefore, CF is further divided into two categories (i) user-based and (ii) item-based filtering.

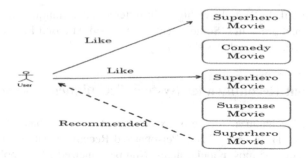

Fig. 2. Content based recommender system

User-Based Collaborative Filtering

User-based approach finds a set of highly correlated users based on theirs taste and behavior. It compute correlation between users based on rating given to the items [3]. As shown in Table 1, User 1 is related to User 3 because the rating given by User 3 is quite similar to that of User 1. That's why item 3 is recommended to the User 1.

Table 1. User-based collaborative filtering

	Item 1	Item 2	Item 3	Item 4
User 1	Like	Unlike	?	Unlike
User 2	Unlike	Unlike	Like	Like
User 3	Like	Like	Like	Unlike

Item-Based Collaborative Filtering

Item-based approach finds a set of highly corelated items instead of set of users with similar taste [3]. As shown in Table 2, Item 1 and Item 3 are highly corelated as they got quite similar ratings. So whoever likes Item 1 may also interested in Item 3. That's why Item 3 is recommended to the User 1.

Table 2. Item-Based Collaborative Filtering

	Item 1	Item 2	Item 3	Item 4
User 1	Like	Unlike	?	Unlike
User 2	Unlike	Unlike	Unlike	Like
User 3	Like	Like	Like	Unlike
User 4	Like	Unlike	Like	Like

2.3   Hybrid Recommender System

These Recommender Systems are based on the combination of the aforementioned recommendation approaches to obtain synergy [1, 4]. CF methods suffer from new items problems, those are not rated by any of user. Since content-based RS predict item based on their properties and attributes so they can resolve new items issue with ease. So in such cases, Hybrid RS are used to avoid drawback of individual RS. To build Hybrid RSs, CB and CF can be combine in various way:

- Implement collaborative and content-based methods individually and joining their results.
- Utilize content-based properties into a collaborative filtering.
- Utilize collaborative filtering attributes into a content-based RS.
- Generate a unified RS that incorporates both approaches.

3 Challenges in Recommender Systems

Scalability: There are millions of users and items, this volume creates numerous problems because of inadequate computational resources. Fundamental issue for RSs is, determination of a way to embed recommendation techniques in real time environment [5]. Furthermore, how to manage with huge monstrous and dynamic information due interactions among users and items (reviews, interests, ratings, implicit feedback etc.).

Cold Start Problem: System can't provide accurate recommendation for new user or new item, this problem is known as cold-start problem. In case of new user, system won't be able to determine similar neighbors as it doesn't have much information about new user. In case of new item, no rating is available [6].

Sparsity: Several times, user doesn't bother to provide rating to items so user-item matrix becomes large and sparse. Sparsity is a very basic issue to most of RS because of the way that clients regularly rate just a little extent of the accessible items.

Limited Coverage: Similarity among users can be measured by comparing their ratings for the same items; so if clients have evaluated common items in similar way than only they can be neighbors. This assumption doesn't work, in the case of where users doesn't provide rating or rate very few common items, may still have similar preferences. This results limited coverage as recommendation is based on items rated by neighbors.

Diversity: Client may locate appropriate items if there is diversity among recommended items. In many cases, there is no value in having same kind of products in recommended list, such as news/articles recommendation.

Over-Specialization: System recommend items according to user profiles. It doesn't recommend unexpected items which aren't mentioned in user's profile. So user doesn't get any new kind of recommendations which might be interesting. This issue is known as over-specialization Problem.

4 Artificial Intelligence (AI) Techniques

Artificial Intelligence (AI) techniques such as: (a) fuzzy sets, (b) Artificial Neural Networks (ANNs), (c) Artificial Immune Systems (AIS) (d) Swarm Intelligence (SI), and (e) Evolutionary Computing (EC) have abilities of learning, reasoning, planning, knowledge creation, natural language processing, perception, prediction, also to move and manipulate data [7]. Due to these propensities, AI techniques are employed in RS to make efficient recommendations and to overcome challenges.

Fuzzy Logic is a multi-value logic which is widely used for data analysis, pattern recognition and decision making processes. Fuzzy logic are capable to quantify uncertainty. Due to these characteristics, fuzzy logic is employed in RS to provide accurate recommendations.

The ANNs are apt to learn, memorize, and model the non-linear dependencies. ANNs are capable to perform classification problems. It can be used to estimate or approximate the relationships among the input data. ANNs apply error back propagation method to train data. Among the different sorts of ANNs it is most prominent methodology Feed-forward ANN. For the multilayered ANN, Back Propagation method is used for training purpose. Except these two method, Self-organizing map (SOM) is widely used for clustering purpose because of its competitive unsupervised learning ability.

Artificial Immune System (AIS) is yet another computationally intelligent adaptive technique inspired by structure and function of the immune system. AIS is quite feasible for ever changing Web environment. AISs are have been applied for classification, scheduling, data clustering, Web mining, pattern recognition and security.

Swarm intelligence is biological organisms technique which is non-linear, decentralized behavior and very efficient to determine optimal solution. Because of the attributes, SI can be used in RS to find out nearest neighbor and clustering purpose. Particle Swarm Optimization (PSO), Bat algorithm, Ant Colony Optimization (ACO) are widely used SI algorithms.

Evolutionary computing (EC) is based on Darwinian principal of biological evolution (survival of the fittest). EC provides efficient solution for optimization problems and approximation problems in dynamic environment. EC have several variants namely Genetic Programming (GP), Genetic Algorithms (GA), Evolutionary Programming (EP), and Evolutionary Strategies (ES). These algorithms are used in RS mainly because of robustness to dynamic changes; wherever encountered.

5 Recent Recommender Systems Based on the AI Techniques

Zhang et al. [8] proposed a hybrid RS based on Fuzzy Set Technique to deal with data sparsity and uncertainty. The approach combines Fuzzy Set Techniques with User-based and Item-based Collaborative Filtering Techniques for Telecom products and services. This approach was useful to overcome the sparsity issue and cold start problem with less scalability.

Serrano-Guerrero et al. [9] developed fuzzy linguistic RS which enables users to communicate and collaborate with others who are interested in the same field by using Google Wave capabilities that enables association between multi-disciplinary researchers. For dealing with cold start problem, with this approach new users need to select two-tuple linguistic value to define their profiles. They determine the similarity by comparing the vector representation of new user's preferences with the other vectors. This approach doesn't resolve the issue of scalability and sparsity.

Li and Kao proposed [10] Trust-Based Recommender System for Peer Production Services (TREPPS) depend upon the trust factor of social network. Proposed approach utilizes fuzzy inference system to find out trust worthy service provider and determine best service provide by applying Multi Criteria Decision Making (MCDM) on fuzzy environment. This approach minimizes the information overload and determine optimal recommendations for the peer services.

Krstic and Bjelica [11] developed Context-Aware RS for TV program recommendation by applying Feed-forward Neural Network. This approach analyzes user's TV viewing habits to overcome cold start problem.

Ansari et al. [12] proposed a framework to find out clusters of web session based on fuzzy neural clustering network (FNCN). The proposed approach utilizes Fuzzy C-Means (FCM) clustering technique and the Modified Self-Organizing Map (MSOM). FCM incorporates the idea of partial membership & empowers the development of overlapping clusters to create Fuzzy C-Partitions of web client sessions. To find out most reasonable cluster centers, they applied unsupervised learning neural network model MSOM which consists of an input layer and an output layer. User session object is presented at input layer, whereas each neuron (associated with weight vector) competes amongst themselves at output layer and neuron with minimum dissimilarity weight becomes cluster center. Proposed method's computational timing is considerably higher because neural network suffers from poor convergence rate.

Chou et al. [13] proposed personalized RS based on Back Propagation Neural Networks (BPNN). BPNN training model is used to classify the users into clusters based on their navigation behavior. Unsupervised Web Mining approach is applied to further analyze the user navigation behaviors by extracting the navigation pattern. In addition, for the clients and items with the less events, proposed RS was not able offer the exact suggestions.

Devi et al. [14] developed a collaborative RS based on Probabilistic Neural Networks (PNNs) to handle sparsity and cold start problems. PNNs are applied on user-item rating matrix to determine trust among users. This trust among user is used to predict value of non-rated items to remove sparsity. The presented approach is effective to find trusted clusters by applying self-organizing map (SOM) technique and cluster center is determined by using trust values among users in those clusters. PNN is fast and single pass technique due to which, Proposed RS is very effective in real world environment.

Wan and Niu [15] proposed Mixed Concept Mapping (MCM) and Immune Algorithm (IA) based RS for e-learning recommendation. Initially, MCM is applied on learners and learning objectives models to understand their attributes. Thereafter, IA is applied to provide personalized recommendation. This RS is highly adaptive due to IA. To optimize the IA author also design and applied monomer vaccine and block vaccine.

Acilar and Arslan [16] proposed Collaborative RS based on Artificial Immune Network (AINet). To overcome the sparsity problem, AINet's hyper-mutation mechanism is applied to produce implicit ratings. The saprsity is reduced at iteration. Whereas, to resolve the scalability problem they utilized two different suppression methods (clonal and network) which provides efficient neighborhoods. Afterward by utilizing k-means algorithm, authors clustered the reduced dataset.

Chen et al. [17] presented an AIS Collaborative Filtering System for movie recommendation. In the training stage, authors defined every record of client rating information as antigen and the similarity is refereed as the affinity in AIS. The antigens invade the immune system and number of immune networks were created by replicating the antigens as the antibodies. After completion of training stage, AIS generates a wide range of classification principles by implementing evolution process. Authors applied AINet to CF for computing the affinity and users' rating prediction based on associated antibodies. By considering past factors into account, Author also modified the Pearson correlation coefficient for similarity estimation. This system is not effective for data scalability and cold start kind of memory-based problems.

Bedi and Sharma [18] developed Trust based Ant Recommender System (TARS) that uses the ACO for locating similar neighbors. TARS produces recommendation along with explanation of recommendations. He also focused on strengthening the level of connectedness for all users by developing trust graph each edge represents trust intensity between users. Dynamic behavior of ACO to establish trust between the clients results in more precise suggestions.

Hsu et al. [19] implemented Artificial Bee Colony (ABC) algorithm on Facebook to analyze individual style. The approach recommends personalized auxiliary items based on difficulty level of auxiliary items.

Kim and Ahn [20] applied genetic algorithm (GA) to find out the relevant clusters for the customers and thereafter authors utilize K-means algorithm to analyze cluster optimized by GA. That's why this method is named as GA K-means RS. This RS using GA K-means clustering improves segmentation performance to offer accurate suggestions in comparison to other typical clustering algorithms.

Al-Shamri and Bharadwaj [21] proposed a RS based on Hybrid Fuzzy-Genetic Approach. For minimizing the sparsity of user-item matrix and system complexity, authors first enable the hybrid filtering by applying a concise user model. Based on user rating, weights are assigned to user preferences. Then the Fuzzy Distance Function is used to calculate similarity among user preferences. A user model is built using Hybrid feature that helps to reduce sparsity problem whereas information integration smaller than the entire set, improves scalability.

Alahmadi and Zeng [22] proposed a Twitter based RS using GA and Probabilistic Sentiment Analysis to resolve cold start problem. To retrieve friends' opinions, authors applied probabilistic sentiment analysis in form of multi-point scale of ratings from tweets. GA is applied on extracted trust relation among user friends to obtain optimized trust parameters. Finally, the system predicts rating for active user by applying Support Vector Regression algorithm (SVR). This methodology is extremely appropriate to take care of cold start problem utilizing understood social trust for dynamic clients of Online Social Networks.

We summarize characteristics of AI techniques, their strengths and weaknesses. Based on the aforementioned study of various AI techniques based RS, we also concludes the AI techniques utility for development of RS and their performances regarding RS challenges in Table 3.

Table 3. AI techniques: characteristics and utility in RS

AI techniques	Characteristics	Pros.	Cons.	Application in RS	Performance for current challenges
Fuzzy logic	• Handle ambiguity/undecidability • Robust • Stable • Model • Pattern recognition • Data analysis	• Suits for "One-To-One" mapping • Acceptable reasoning • Handle uncertainty	• Difficult to model • Multiple rules • Continuous • Effort • To resolve • Ambiguities	• Effective for handling • Ambiguity & uncertainties • Handle fuzzy • Similarities • Ability to deal with incomplete data	• Suitable for cold start, & uncertainty problems • Not effective to resolve scalability issue
Artificial Neural Networks (ANNs)	• Suits for approximation & classification • Learning ability • Self-organization • Real time operation • Distributed	• Unsupervised learning ability • Capable to classification problems	• Limited explanation • Inefficient to learn new data	• Effectively determines similar users • Suitable to approximate relationships among the input data	• Effective to handle cold start problems • Not effective to resolve sparsity and scalability
Artificial Immune Systems (AIS)	• Adaptive • Clustering, • Pattern recognition • Classification • Optimization	• Feasible for dynamic web environment • Efficient for preference matching	• Profile adaptation is tricky • Computation complexity is high	• Well suited for web personalization • Useful to overcome ambiguity	• Effective to solve sparsity and cold start problems
Swarm Intelligence (SI)	• Non-linear, • Decentralized • Self-organized • Optimization • Scalable	• Personalized sequencing • Web mining • Understand collective behavior	• Not suitable when accuracy required • In effective to model contextual information	• Suitable to determine nearest neighbor • Effective for clustering in dynamic environment	• Effective to resolve scalability issue • Resolve sparsity and cold start problem
Evolutionary Computing (EC)	• Optimization • Parallel Processing • Robust • Dynamic	• Query Optimization • Efficient in dynamic environment	• Sometimes not suitable for well-defined problems • Computation cost is high	• Effective to determine best neighborhood. • Optimize online tasks	• Not well suited to solve scalability • Descent performance in case of sparsity.

6 Conclusion

In this study, a cutting edge of Recommender Systems is introduced in light of the AI procedures, for example, the Fuzzy Sets, ANNs, AIS, SI and EC. However, the major focus has been put on the design challenges being encountered by various Recommender Systems and key features of each of aforementioned AI techniques. Likewise the top-level curve has been drawn by cluster of difficulties being met by each of the introduced approaches. It is watched that each of the AI methods is equipped for managing one or more difficulties. In general, AI based Recommender Systems are highly methodical. However, these AI techniques are required to explore further in order to achieve complete coherency to resolve the challenges of RS and to provide optimal solution in efficient way.

References

1. Ricci, F., Rokach, L., Shapira, B.: Introduction to Recommender Systems Handbook. Springer, Heidelberg (2011)
2. Mooney, R.J., Roy, L.: Content-based book recommending using learning for text categorization. In: Proceedings of the Fifth ACM Conference on Digital Libraries, pp. 195–204. ACM (2000)
3. Schafer, J.B., Frankowski, D., Herlocker, J., Sen, S.: Collaborative filtering recommender systems. In: Brusilovsky, P., Kobsa, A., Nejdl, W. (eds.) The Adaptive Web. LNCS, vol. 4321, pp. 291–324. Springer, Heidelberg (2007). doi:10.1007/978-3-540-72079-9_9
4. Burke, R.: Hybrid recommender systems: survey and experiments. User Model. User-Adap. Interact. 12(4), 331–370 (2002)
5. Sarwar, B.M., Karypis, G., Konstan, J., Riedl, J.: Recommender systems for large-scale e-commerce: scalable neighborhood formation using clustering. In: Proceedings of the Fifth International Conference on Computer and Information Technology, vol. 1 (2002)
6. Schein, A.I., Popescul, A., Ungar, L.H., Pennock, D.M.: Methods and metrics for cold-start recommendations. In: Proceedings of the 25th Annual International ACM SIGIR Conference on Research and Development in Information Retrieval, pp. 253–260. ACM (2002)
7. Engelbrecht, A.P.: Computational Intelligence: An Introduction. Wiley, Hoboken (2007)
8. Zhang, Z., Lin, H., Liu, K., Dianshuang, W., Zhang, G., Jie, L.: A hybrid fuzzy-based personalized recommender system for telecom products/services. Inf. Sci. 235, 117–129 (2013)
9. Serrano-Guerrero, J., Herrera-Viedma, E., Olivas, J.A., Cerezo, A., Romero, F.P.: A Google wave-based fuzzy recommender system to disseminate information in University Digital Libraries 2.0. Inf. Sci. 181(9), 1503–1516 (2011)
10. Li, Y.M., Kao, C.P.: TREPPS: a trust-based recommender system for peer production services. Expert Syst. Appl. 36(2), 3263–3277 (2009)
11. Krstic, M., Bjelica, M.: Context-aware personalized program guide based on neural network. IEEE Trans. Consum. Electron. 58(4), 1301–1306 (2012)
12. Ansari, Z.A., Sattar, S.A., Babu, A.V.: A fuzzy neural network based framework to discover user access patterns from web log data. Adv. Data Anal. Classif. 1–28 (2015)
13. Chou, P.H., Li, P.H., Chen, K.K., Wu, M.J.: Integrating web mining and neural network for personalized e-commerce automatic service. Expert Syst. Appl. 37(4), 2898–2910 (2010)

14. Devi, M.K.K., Samy, R.T., Kumar, S.V., Venkatesh, P.: Probabilistic neural network approach to alleviate sparsity and cold start problems in collaborative recommender systems. In: IEEE International Conference on Computational Intelligence and Computing Research (ICCIC), pp. 1–4 (2010)
15. Wan, S., Niu, Z.: A learner oriented learning recommendation approach based on mixed concept mapping and immune algorithm. Knowl.-Based Syst. **103**, 28–40 (2016)
16. Acilar, M., Arslan, A.: A collaborative filtering method based on artificial immune network. Expert Syst. Appl. **36**(4), 8324–8332 (2009)
17. Chen, M.H., Teng, C.H., Chang, P.C.: Applying artificial immune systems to collaborative filtering for movie recommendation. Adv. Eng. Inform. **29**(4), 830–839 (2015)
18. Bedi, P., Sharma, R.: Trust based recommender system using ant colony for trust computation. Expert Syst. Appl. **39**(1), 1183–1190 (2012)
19. Hsu, C.C., Chen, H.C., Huang, K.K., Huang, Y.M.: A personalized auxiliary material recommendation system based on learning style on Facebook applying an artificial bee colony algorithm. Comput. Math Appl. **64**(5), 1506–1513 (2012)
20. Kim, K.J., Ahn, H.: A recommender system using GA K-means clustering in an online shopping market. Expert Syst. Appl. **34**(2), 1200–1209 (2008)
21. Al-Shamri, M.Y.H., Bharadwaj, K.K.: Fuzzy-genetic approach to recommender systems based on a novel hybrid user model. Expert Syst. Appl. **35**(3), 1386–1399 (2008)
22. Alahmadi, D.H., Zeng, X.-J.: Twitter-based recommender system to address cold-start: a genetic algorithm based trust modelling and probabilistic sentiment analysis. In: 27th International Conference on Tools with Artificial Intelligence (ICTAI). IEEE (2015)

Assembling Swarm with Limited Visibility in Presence of Line Obstacles

Pratibha Tokas$^{(\boxtimes)}$, Aravind Mekala, and Deepanwita Das

National Institute of Technology, Durgapur, Burdwan 713209, West Bengal, India
pratibhatokas89@gmail.com

Abstract. In this paper, we have proposed a distributed algorithm for assembling of swarm of autonomous mobile robots on the left boundary of a rectangular region in presence of opaque horizontal line obstacles. The robots are having limited visibility capabilities and they are randomly scattered inside the region together with the obstacles. The robots do not have any message exchange among themselves. In the proposed algorithm, the robots follow the CORDA model for computation. In addition to that, synchronous/semi-synchronous timing model and full compass model are also followed. Our algorithm guarantees successful assembling of all the robots on the left boundary of the given region in a collision free manner.

Keywords: Swarm robots · Assembling · Passive communication · Limited visibility · Distributed algorithm

1 Introduction

Swarm of mobile robots work collectively to accomplish various complex tasks that are impossible to be completed by individual robots [10]. They perform the task by maintaining the internal coordination among the members of the swarm. The act or coordination is inspired by the natural behavior of insects like, movement of ants while searching and fetching of food [7], flocking of birds [9], schools of fishes etc.

Assembling of swarm robots along a particular boundary of a region may be considered as a preliminary step towards solving a complex problem like the problem of area partitioning. Area partitioning is an important problem and has several applications like scanning or coverage of a free space [1,6], terrain mapping, car body painting etc.

Das et al. [2] proposed a distributed algorithm for assembling of swarm robots along left boundary of a rectangular region in presence of horizontal line obstacles with negligible height without any collision. No other work except this has been reported on assembling using CORDA. However, in this work, the visibility range is assumed to be unlimited. Here, the view of any robot may get restricted due to the presence of robot or obstacle(s) in its line of sight. The inter-robot spaces among unassembled robots is at least δ and among the assembled robots are not fixed.

© Springer Nature Singapore Pte Ltd. 2017
M. Singh et al. (Eds.): ICACDS 2016, CCIS 721, pp. 60–69, 2017.
DOI: 10.1007/978-981-10-5427-3_7

This paper presents a distributed algorithm for assembling randomly scattered swarm of robots along left boundary of a given rectangular region in presence of several horizontal line obstacles. The robots are assumed to have limited visibility where the visibility can also be restricted by presence of robot and obstacle within the visibility range. Total number of obstacles and position of robots as well as obstacles are unknown to the robots. This algorithm guaranteed a collision free assembling of robots along left boundary of the rectangular region. Basically this is an extension of the work done by Das et al. [2].

We have used the basic $CORDA$ model [8] for computation in our proposed algorithm. In this model, robots go through multiple computational cycles until they finish their task. Each cycle consists of 3 phases namely *Observe*, *Compute* and *Move*. Robots follow *Full compass* and *Synchronous/Semi-Synchronous* timing model. It is assumed that initially any two objects (robots and obstacles) are separated by a minimum distance δ. The robots are assumed to be oblivious i.e. they can retain only $O(1)$ amount of information pertaining to the current computational cycle and there is no direct communication among them.

The organization of the paper is as follows. In Sect. 2, the problem definition, models and characteristics of the robots are discussed; Sect. 3.1 presents the algorithm $ASSEMBLE$, Sect. 3.2 gives the correctness proofs and Sect. 3.3 gives the Simulations and Result. Section 4 is conclusion of the paper along with the future scope of work.

2   Problem Definition, Assumptions and Models

Robots and line obstacles are randomly distributed over a rectangular region. All the robots are autonomous, anonymous, mobile, have same computational power. Robots have limited visibility where they can view within a radius of V. Robots are unaware of the position of other robots and obstacles. Our task is to assemble all the robots along left boundary of the given rectangular region in a collision free manner. The characteristics of the robots and the models assumed in the paper are listed below: (a) Robots are *identical and homogeneous* with respect to their computational power. (b) Robots are *autonomous* that is, there is no governing authority. (c) Each robot executes the same algorithm in distributed manner, independent of each other. (d) *Full-compass* [3,4]: Each robot has its own local coordinate system in which it is placed at the origin. And all the robots agree on orientation and direction of axes. (e) There is no direct communication among the robots. But each robot observes the position of every other robot with respect to its local coordinate system. (f) Robots have *limited* visibility. Each robot can view only within a radius of V. And its view can be restricted by presence of robot and/or obstacle(s). (g) The robots follow $CORDA$ model [5]. In $CORDA$ model, each robot goes through a sequence of *computational cycle*, each consisting of three phases namely, *Look*, *Compute* and *Move*. In *Look* phase, each robot observes the environment and gets the position of all other robots with respect to its local coordinate system. In *Compute* phase, based on the observations made in look phase, robots compute the destination. And in *Move* phase, robots move towards the destination. (h) Robots are assumed to be oblivious or memoryless. That is, robots can only remember the observations made during the *Look* phase of the current computational cycle. (i) Robots are assumed to be mobile and their movement is rigid, that is, robot reaches the computed destination in an uninterrupted way. (j) The robots can be in, *active* state or *sleep* state. In the *active* state, the robots execute the computational cycles continuously. In the *sleep* state, robot remain idle. However, a robot can be in *sleep* state for a bounded amount of time and then becomes *active*. (k) *Fully Synchronous/Semi-Synchronous Model* [3,4]: Our algorithm works in both fully synchronous and semi synchronous timing models. In Fully synchronous model, all robots follow common clock and execute the three phases of CORDA model synchronously. Semi-Synchronous model, is quite similar to fully synchronous model, but with a slight difference that all robots need not be active in each computational cycle. But all the active robots work synchronously that is, following a common clock.

3   Assembling Algorithm

The first part of this section describes the proposed algorithm. The second part presents the correctness proofs and the third part shows the simulation and results.

3.1   Algorithm *ASSEMBLE*

The objective of the problem is to assemble all the randomly scattered robots on the left boundary of a known rectangular area under limited visibility of the robots. The environment consists of robots and horizontal line obstacles (with negligible heights) of variable lengths. The length of the obstacle can at most be, say l, which is assumed to be less than L, the length of the rectangular area. It is also assumed that the minimum horizontal and vertical distance between any two objects (robot or obstacle) is δ. The robots are having limited visibility that is, can view only up to a range of V which is also called the visibility radius of the robot. However, robots' view may also get restricted due to the presence of obstacle(s).

Look
STEP 1: According to the local co-ordinate system, a robot R first observes the position of all other robots. Let the co-ordinates be (a_1, b_1), (a_2, b_2), ..., (a_{N-1}, b_{N-1}), whereas, its own co-ordinate would be $(0,0)$. It is to be noted that some of these (a_i, b_i) values might be negative also.

Compute
STEP 1: Robot R checks the status of the boundary flag FLG. If $FLG = 1$, that means R is already on the boundary of the target region and the algorithm terminates. If $FLG = 0$ then R will execute the following steps to assemble on the left boundary of the region.

STEP 2: Robot R checks the list of visible neighbors within its visibility range V. There may be two possible cases:

Case I: No obstacle nor any robot is visible along the $-ve$ X -axis of R.
R calculates a point $D(x, y)$ on the $-ve$ X-axis at V distance away from it, as shown in Fig. 1. R will skip all the remaining compute steps and directly goes to the *Move* step.

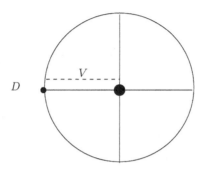

Fig. 1. Computing destination point D on $-ve$ X-axis

Case II: Any robot or any obstacle is visible at a point $Q(-\alpha, 0)$ (where $-\alpha \leq$ 0 on the x-negative axis of R) then robot R checks whether it is lying on the right boundary or not. If yes, then it will move through a small distance, say ϵ, towards left along X-axis.

If robot R is not located on the upper boundary, then R will execute Step 3 else Step 4.

STEP 3: This step will be executed if the robot is not located on the upper boundary of the region. There may be two possible cases:

Case I: R does not find any robot or obstacle along $+ve$ Y -axis within V.
Robot R computes a point $P(0, \gamma)$ where, $\gamma = V$ on the $+ve$ Y-axis as shown in Fig. 2. Next, R finds midpoint $D(x, y)$ between P and Q, where $D(x, y) = (\frac{-\alpha}{2}, \frac{\beta}{2})$. Next, R will skip the remaining steps and goes to the *Move* step.

Case II: R finds a robot or an obstacle along $+ve$ Y -axis within V.
R may identify a robot or an obstacle or both that is vertically closest to R. Let the co-ordinate of that vertically closest neighbour be (α, β). This can be obtained by sorting all the visible elements above the X-axis, according to their Y-coordinate and identifying the one having smallest positive non-zero value.

Then R identifies a point $P(0, \beta)$ on $+ve$ Y-axis which is the intersection of the $+ve$ Y-axis and the horizontal line passing through (α, β). Robot R then finds the midpoint $D(x, y)$ between P and Q as shown Fig. 3, where $D(x, y) = (\frac{-\alpha}{2}, \frac{\beta}{2})$.

After D, R will skip all the remaining compute steps and directly goes to the *Move* step.

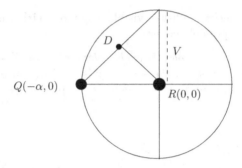

Fig. 2. Computing destination point D, when there is no robot or obstacle found above the X-axis as per Case 1

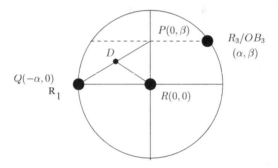

Fig. 3. Computing destination point D, when R finds a robot on the upper side of X-axis

STEP 4: This step will be executed if the robot is located on the upper boundary of the region. Here R checks the list of visible neighbours within its visibility range V. There may be three possible cases:

Case I: R does not find any robot or obstacle below the X-axis within V.
Robot R computes a point $P(0, \frac{-\gamma}{2})$ (where $\gamma = V$) along $-ve$ Y-axis. R then computes the midpoint $D(x, y)$ between points P and Q as shown in Fig. 4(a), where, $D(x, y) = (\frac{-\alpha}{2}, \frac{-\gamma}{4})$.

After computing D, robot R will skip all the remaining compute steps and directly goes to the *Move* step.

Case II: R finds a Robot R_2 as its nearest neighbour within V below the X-axis.
Robot R computes a horizontal line passing through robot R_2, which intersects the $-ve$ Y-axis at $T(0, -\beta)$. Let the line be AB.

Then robot R computes another horizontal line CE at a distance $(\frac{-\beta}{2})$ from AB, which intersects the $-ve$ Y-axis at point $P(0, \frac{-\beta}{2})$. Next robot R computes the midpoint $D(x, y)$ between P and Q as shown in Fig. 4(b), where, $D(x, y) = (\frac{-\alpha}{2}, \frac{-\beta}{4})$.

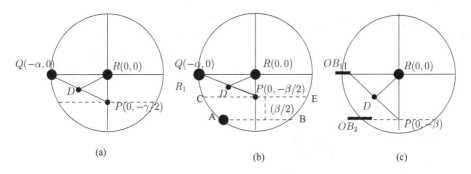

(a)   (b)   (c)

Fig. 4. Computing destination points D in case I, case II and case III respectively

After computing destination point D, R will skip all the remaining compute steps and directly goes to the *Move* step.

Case III: R finds an obstacle OB as a nearest neighbour within V below the X-axis.
R computes a horizontal line passing through OB which intersects the $-ve$ Y-axis at point P i.e., $P(0, -\beta)$. Next, R draws line between P and Q, and finds the midpoint D as shown in Fig. 4(c), where, $D(x, y) = (\frac{-\alpha}{2}, \frac{-\beta}{2})$.

After computing the destination point D, R will skip all the remaining compute steps and directly goes to the *Move* step.

Move

Robot R will move to the point D as computed in the *Compute* phase.

3.2   Correctness Proof

Observation 1: Algorithm ASSEMBLE successfully assembles all the robots in finite time along the left boundary of a given rectangular region in the presence of horizontal line obstacles, under synchronous/semi-synchronous timing model.

Proof: Initially all the robots and obstacles are scattered randomly in a rectangular region. As the algorithm uses the synchronous/semi-synchronous timing model, no robot will be in the *Sleep* state infinitely. Each robot executes the ASSEMBLE algorithm with $O(1)$ time complexity, as the algorithm does not contain any loop, recursion or call to any other non-constant time function. Hence, each robot can reach the target boundary with in a finite amount of time using the ASSEMBLE algorithm.

Observation 2: Algorithm ASSEMBLE provides a collision free path to assemble all the robots along the left boundary of the rectangular region.

Proof: Throughout the algorithm, the movement of the robots are collision free. *Case I:* Let's assume there are two robots R and R_2 on the same vertical axis, and robot R is on the upper boundary. R views another robot R_1 along $-ve$ X-axis and robot R_2 along $-ve$ Y-axis. R_2 also observes R along $+ve$ Y-axis

---

Algorithm 1. ASSEMBLE

State *Look*

R takes a snapshot of the positions of all the visible robots, obstacles (end points) and boundaries of the region, according to the local coordinate system of R, where R occupies the origin $(0,0)$.

State *Compute* (returns destination point D(X,Y))

if *(R is on left boundary)* **then**
 | $X = 0$; $Y = 0$; and the algorithm terminates
else
 | **if** *(R does not find any other robot or obstacle to left of X-axis within its visibility)* **then**
 | | $X = -V$; $Y = 0$;
 | **else**
 | | **if** *(R finds itself on the right boundary)* **then**
 | | | $X = -\epsilon$; $Y = 0$;
 | | **else**
 | | | **if** *(R is not on upper boundary of the region)* **then**
 | | | | Case I: R does not find any obstacle along $+ve$ Y-axis within its visibility.
 | | | | $X = \frac{-\alpha}{2}$; $Y = \frac{\gamma}{2}$,(where $(\gamma = V)$;
 | | | | Case II: R finds an obstacle at $P(\alpha,\beta)$ along $+ve$ Y-axis within its visibility.
 | | | | $X = \frac{-\alpha}{2}$; $Y = \frac{\beta}{2}$;
 | | | **else**
 | | | | Case I: R does not find any obstacle or robot below X-axis within its visibility
 | | | | $X = \frac{-\alpha}{2}$; $Y = \frac{-\gamma}{4}$, (where $(\gamma = V)$;
 | | | | Case II: R finds a robot as its nearest neighbour at $P(\alpha,\beta)$ below X-axis within its visibility
 | | | | $X = \frac{-\alpha}{2}$; $Y = \frac{-\beta}{4}$;
 | | | | Case III: R finds an obstacle as its nearest neighbour at $P(\alpha,\beta)$ below x-axis within its visibility
 | | | | $X = \frac{-\alpha}{2}$; $Y = \frac{-\beta}{2}$;

State *Move*
Move to (X,Y);

---

and an obstacle OB_1 along the $-ve$ X-axis. Then R computes the destination D (using case II in step 4 of ASSEMBLE algorithm) and R_2 computes its destination D_2 (using case II in step2) as shown in Fig. 5. In this case, when one robot R_2 is moving upward and robot R moving downward along the same vertical line, then R_2 computes the midpoint of the line joining obstacle OB_1 and robot R. Whereas R computes a point at the half distance of its visibility range along $-ve$ Y-axis. The destinations D and D_2 are computed in such a way that they do not overlap each other. So during the movement of robot R and R_2, there will be no chance of collision.

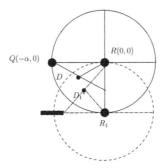

Fig. 5. Computing destination points D and D_1 of robots R and R_1 respectively, when encountered each other along Y-axis

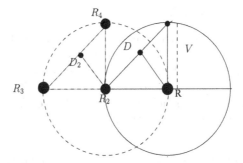

Fig. 6. Computing destination points of R and R_2, D and D_2 respectively

Case II: Let's assume there is a robot R that does not lie on the upper boundary. If R observes a robot R_2 along $-ve$ X-axis and it does not find any robot along $+ve$ Y-axis, R_2 observes R_3 along $-ve$ X-axis and R_4 along $+ve$ Y-axis, then R will compute the destination D (using Case I in step 3 of ASSEMBLE algorithm) and R_2 will calculate destination D_2 (using Case II in step 3 of ASSEMBLE algorithm). The destinations D and D_2 are computed in such a way that they do not overlap each other. So during the movement of robot R and R_2, there will be no chance of collision as shown in Fig. 6.

Case III: Let's assume there is a robot R which does not lie on the upper boundary. If R does not find any robot or obstacle along $-ve$ X-axis and there exists another robot R_2 along $+ve$ Y-axis of R then both R and R_2 calculate destinations D and D_2 respectively (using Case I of step 2 of ASSEMBLE algorithm). In such a way that they do not overlap each other. So during the movement of robot R and R_2, there will be no chance of collision as shown in Fig. 7. So, the algorithm provides a collision free assembling of all the robots on the left boundary of the given rectangular region in both *fully-synchronous* and *semi-synchronous* timing model. In *semi-synchronous* model, robot's active cycles may be interleaved by sleep cycles. But when the robot becomes active, they will compute the destination and move towards the destination at the same time.

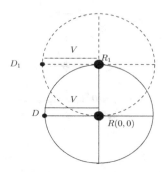

Fig. 7. Computing destination points of R and R_2, D and D_2 respectively

3.3   Simulations and Result

The algorithm has been simulated using the C. The result has been plotted in a graph using gnuplot software. We have taken seven robots and recorded the movement of the robots in each cycle. Table 1 shows the positions of obstacles and Table 2 shows the position of robots in each cycle. The simulation result shows that all the robots able reach the left boundary of the rectangular region within finite number of cycles and without collision.

Table 1. Positions of obstacles (left end point)

Obstacle	1	2	3	4	5
Left end point	$(-1, 0.5)$	$(1, 1.5)$	$(-1, 2)$	$(2, 3)$	$(-3, 4)$

Table 2. Positions of robots in each cycle

Robot	Cycle 1	Cycle 2	Cycle 3	Cycle 4	Cycle 5	Cycle 6	Cycle 7	Cycle 8	Cycle 9
R1	$(1, 0.5)$	$(0, 0.5)$	$(-0.5, 1)$	$(-1.5, 1)$	$(-2.5, 1)$	$(-3.5, 1)$	$(-4.5, 1)$	$(-5, 1)$	$(-5, 1)$
R2	$(-3, 1.5)$	$(-4, 1.5)$	$(-5, 1.5)$	$(-5, 1.5)$	$(-5, 1.5)$	$(-5, 1.5)$	$(-5, 1.5)$	$(-5, 1.5)$	$(-5, 1.5)$
R3	$(2, 2)$	$(1.5, 2.5)$	$(0.5, 2.5)$	$(0, 3)$	$(-1, 3)$	$(-2, 3)$	$(-3, 3)$	$(-4, 3)$	$(-5, 3)$
R4	$(1, 2)$	$(0, 2)$	$(-0.5, 2.5)$	$(-1.5, 2.5)$	$(-2.5, 2.5)$	$(-3.5, 2.5)$	$(-4.5, 2.5)$	$(-5, 2.5)$	$(-5, 2.5)$
R5	$(-2, 4)$	$(-2.5, 4.5)$	$(-3.5, 4.5)$	$(-4.5, 4.5)$	$(-5, 4.5)$	$(-5, 4.5)$	$(-5, 4.5)$	$(-5, 4.5)$	$(-5, 4.5)$
R6	$(-2, 5)$	$(-2.5, 4.75)$	$(-3.5, 4.75)$	$(-4.5, 4.75)$	$(-5, 4.75)$	$(-5, 4.75)$	$(-5, 4.75)$	$(-5, 4.75)$	$(-5, 4.75)$
R7	$(-3, 5)$	$(-4, 5)$	$(-5, 5)$	$(-5, 5)$	$(-5, 5)$	$(-5, 5)$	$(-5, 5)$	$(-5, 5)$	$(-5, 5)$

4   Conclusion and Future Work

The proposed algorithm with *full-compass* and *synchronous/ semi-synchronous* timing model. There is passive communication among the robots in the sense that they observe positions of other robots. The algorithm guarantees successful assembling of all the robots on the left boundary within finite time in a collision free manner. The proposed algorithm can be extended for different shapes and types of obstacle (static or mobile, convex or concave). We can also extend the algorithm to work in *asynchronous* timing model.

References

1. Das, D., Mukhopadhyaya, S.: An algorithm for painting an area by swarm of mobile robots. Int. J. Inf. Process. **7**(3), 1–15 (2013)
2. Das, D., Mukhopadhyaya, S., Nandi, D.: Multi-robot assembling along a boundary of a given region in presence of opaque line obstacles. In: Deiva Sundari, P., Dash, S.S., Das, S., Panigrahi, B.K. (eds.) Proceedings of 2nd International Conference on Intelligent Computing and Applications. AISC, vol. 467, pp. 21–29. Springer, Singapore (2017). doi:10.1007/978-981-10-1645-5_3
3. Efrima, A., Peleg, D.: Distributed algorithms for partitioning a swarm of autonomous mobile robots. Technical report MCS06-08, The Weizmann Institute of Science (2006)
4. Pagli, L., Principe, G., Viglietra, G.: Getting close without touching: near-gathering for autonomous mobile robots. Int. J. Distrib. Comput. **28**(5), 333–349 (2015). Springer
5. Flochinni, P., Prencipe, G., Santoro, N., Widmayer, P.: Distributed coordination of a set of autonomous mobile robots. In: Proceedings of the IEEE Intelligent Vehicles Symposium, pp. 480–485 (2000)
6. Das, D., Mukhopadhyaya, S.: Painting an area by swarm of mobile robots with limited visibility. In: Venugopal, K.R., Patnaik, L.M. (eds.) ICIP 2012. CCIS, vol. 292, pp. 446–455. Springer, Heidelberg (2012). doi:10.1007/978-3-642-31686-9_52
7. Hoff III, N.R., Sagoff, A., Wood, R.J., Nagpal, R.: Two foraging algorithms for robot swarms using only local communication. In: IEEE International Conference on Robotics and Bioinformatics, pp. 123–130 (2010)
8. Prencipe, G.: Corda: distributed coordination of a set of autonomous mobile robots. In: Proceedings of 4th European Research Seminar on Advances in Distributed Systems, pp. 185–190 (2001)
9. Ballerini, M., Cabibbo, N., Candelier, R., Cavagna, A., Cisbani, E., Giardina, I., Lecomte, V., Orlandi, A., Parisi, G., Procaccini, A., Viale, M., Zdravkovic, V.: Interaction ruling animal collective behavior depends on topological rather than metric distance: evidence from a field study. Proc. Natl. Acad. Sci. USA **105**(4), 1232–1237 (2007)
10. Murphy, R.R., Kravitz, J., Stover, S.L., Shoureshi, R.: Mobile robots in mine rescue and recovery. Robot. Autom. Mag. **16**(2), 91–103 (2009). IEEE

Clustering Proficient Students Using Data Mining Approach

M.V. Ashok[1] and A. Apoorva[2(✉)]

[1] Department of Computer Science, Teachers Academy, Bangalore, India
ashokmv@ymail.com
[2] Department of MCA, GIMS, Bangalore, India
a.apoorva89@gmail.com

Abstract. Every educational institution strives to be the best in terms of quality. Quality is measured using many parameters. One such parameter of measuring quality is proficient students. Hence the objective of this study is to Cluster proficient students of an educational institution using data mining approach. Clustering is based on knowledge, skill and ability concept known as KSA. A model and an algorithm are proposed to accomplish the task of Clustering. A student data set consisting of 1,434 students from an institution located in Bangalore are collected for the study and were subjected to preprocessing. To evaluate the performance of the proposed algorithm, it is compared with other Clustering algorithm on the basis of precision and recall. The results obtained are tabulated. The performance of the proposed algorithm was better in comparison with other algorithms.

Keywords: Educational data mining · Clustering · Proficient student · KSA

1 Introduction

In an educational institution student fraternity is combination of excellent, good, average, and weak students. The study is based on Knowledge, Skills and Attitudes popularly known as KSA's concept. It is a list of special qualifications and personal attributes that a student should possess to get placed. A primary purpose of KSAs is to measure those qualities that will differentiate candidate from the others. KSAs are defined as the factors that identify better person basically qualified for a position from a group of candidates. Attributes considered for skills are Coding, preparing business plans, communication etc. and Responding, Judgment, Competence etc. are the attributes considered for attitude. Students having good score of KSA will have better chance of placement. It is assumed that the students with effective score (KSA score) more than 50% are proficient students. Identifying such students is the primary objective of this study.

2 Problem Statement

Normally hundreds of students will be there in institutions. It is a tedious task and time consuming to predict placement chance for all students and it is not necessary also to predict placement chance for those students who are considered weak academically.

© Springer Nature Singapore Pte Ltd. 2017
M. Singh et al. (Eds.): ICACDS 2016, CCIS 721, pp. 70–80, 2017.
DOI: 10.1007/978-981-10-5427-3_8

Hence there is a need for Clustering the proficient students who scores well in KSA, whose placement chance can be predicted.

3 Related Works

Performance appraisal system is basically a formal interaction between an employee and the supervisor or management conducted periodically to identify the areas of strength and weakness of the employee. The objective is to be consistent about the strengths and work on the weak areas to improve performance of the individual and thus achieve optimum process quality [8]. (Chein and Chen [9], Pal and Pal [10], Khan [11], Baradwaj and Pal [12], Bray [13], Yadav et al. [14]. K-means is one of the best and accurate Clustering algorithms. This has been applied to various problems. K-means approach belongs to one kind of multivariate statistical analysis that cut samples apart into K primitive Clusters. This approach or method is especially suitable when the number of observations is more or the data file is enormous. K-means method is widely used in segmenting markets. (Kim et al. [1], Shin and Sohn [2], Jang et al. [3], Hruschka and Natter [4], Bottou and Bengio [5], Fabere [6], Bydovska and Popelinsky [7], Jamesmanoharan et al. [15].

4 Proposed Methodology

4.1 Explanation for the Proposed Model

The algorithm of the projected model, along with its computational processes for determining the proficient student, is outlined below:

Step 1: Data collection
The goal is to find the proficient students in the college under consideration viz., XX for the year 2016. In this college there were 1,434 students. These students hailed from various courses that were operative in the college. The courses are MBA, MCA, BCA, B.Com, and BBA.
Step 2: Data preprocessing
Preprocessing was done using chi-square test for the goodness of fit to remove the attributes such as address, contact number, gender which doesn't contribute to the result.
Step 3: Clustering technique
This step Clusters proficient students among all the students of the institution using Proposed Clustering algorithm.
Step 4: Evaluate the result
The obtained result is compared in terms of precision, accuracy, variance with other algorithms such as K-means, K-Medoids, X-Means, K-Means fast (Fig. 1).

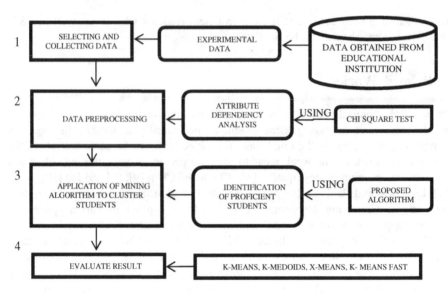

Fig. 1. Flowchart of the proposed model

4.2 Data Description

Reg-no – Register number of the student. It can take any integer values; Branch – represents the name of the Branch. It can take only text values ranging from A–Z; Percent – It is a weighted average in terms of percentage. Percentage = Assignments + tests + presentations + seminars (20% + 40% + 20% + 20% = 100). It can take only the numeric values from 0 to 100; Skills – It shows the overall Skills of the student. It can take only the numeric values from 0 to 10; Effective_score -it shows the overall performance of the student (Effective_score = percent + skills * 10) in this I used this formula to calculate Effective-score. It can take only the numeric values from 0 to 200 (Table 1).

Table 1. Data description

Variables	Description	Possible values
Reg-no	Register number of the student's	{Int}
Branch	Branch (MCA, MBA, BSC ....etc.) of the student	{Text}
Percent	Percentage = Assignments + tests + presentations + seminars (20% + 40% + 20% + 20% = 100)	{65, 71, 82, ..., 100}
Skills	Knowledge, skill and ability	{1, 2, 3, 4, 5, ..., 10}
Effective_score	Effective_score = percent + skills * 10, it shows the overall performance of the student	{50, 99, 154, ..., 200}

4.3 Proposed Algorithm

The main algorithm in turn is divided into 3 sub- algorithms represented as step 1, step 2 and step 3 as shown below (Fig. 2):

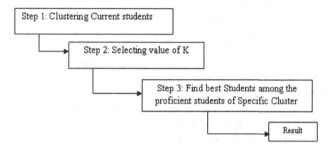

Fig. 2. Steps of the main proposed algorithm

5 Experimental Evaluation

The above table is an extract of the current students i.e., 2015 batch along with the attributes that are considered for the study. Here attribute skill value is taken from 0 to 10. The effective score is calculated using
effective score = percent + skills * 10

Example:
In row 1: 23 + 10 (3) => 53
By using the above formula, maximum value of effective score is

$$= 100 + 10\,(10) => 100 + 100 => 200$$

Minimum value of effective score is = 0 + 10(0) => 0 + 0 => 0
Hence the effective score value ranges from 0–200.
Similarly the other values in the Table 2 are calculated.

Table 2. Extract of current student details

Reg_No	Branch	Percent	Skills (0–10)	Effective_Score
1	MCA	23	3	53
2	MCA	32	4	72
3	MCA	80	3	110
4	MCA	21	2	41
5	MCA	79	5	129
6	MCA	76	7	146
7	MCA	26	8	106
8	MCA	50	5	100
9	MCA	54	5	104
10	MCA	85	8	165

5.1   Proposed Algorithm

Steps of the proposed algorithm are explained below:

Step 1: Clustering Current students

Input: Current Student List, K
Output: K number of Clusters of Students

1. Read all current Student Data and Store in List Student List
2. Read the number of Clusters and store in k
3. Initialize a List of size k with random values and Store as centroids List
4. Perform Post Evaluation Loop
    [Begin Loop]
5. Initialize a List of size k with 0 and store it as centroid Count
6. Initialize a List of size k with 0 and store it as centroidS
7. For every student in Student List
    [Begin Loop]
8. Initialize a List of size k with values of centroid List and store as old Centroid List
9. Initialize centroid Index as -1
10. For every centroid and centroid List
    [Begin Loop]
11. Find index of centroid having least distance from student and store it at centroid Index
    [End Loop at Step 9]
12. set student.centroid as centroid a centroid List[centroid Index].centroid
13. add student.score at centroidS[centroid Index]
14. increment value at centroid Count[centroid Index]
    [End Loop at Step 7]
15. For every centroid Index in indexes of centroid List
    [Start Loop]
16. Calculate centroid[centroid Index] = centroidS[centroid Index] / centroid Count[centroid Index]
    [End Loop at Step 15]
17. If centroid List = old Centroid List or centroid Count has value 0
    [End Loop at Step 4]
18. Write Clusters

For Clustering the current student data, Table 2 is used as the input.

Main objective of this algorithm is to Cluster the given data into 'k' Clusters.

In our algorithm value of k is determined and den used to make clusters on the basis of effective score.

According to the proposed algorithm, initially k-values among the effective_ score will be selected as initial centroids in random. Other values in the attribute will be compared with the initial centroids. One which is nearest to the first centroid will form a group. Same happens with the other centroid also forming the other groups. The same process is repeated to ensure better accuracy of Clustering.

In the input Table 2, values 53 and 110 is considered as the initial centroids when k = 2, the values 53, 72, 41 etc. are nearest to 53. Hence this forms a first group with centroids 55.33. Other values viz., 129, 100, 104 etc. forms the second group with centroids 122.85 as shown in Table 3.

Note: Every Cluster is identified by its centroid values.

Table 3. Centroids for different values of K

Sl. No.	K	No. of clusters	Centroids
1	2	2	55.33 and 122.85
2	3	3	55.33, 105.0 and 146.66
3	4	4	55.33, 105.0, 129 and 155.5
4	5	5	55.33, 103.33, 105.0, 129.0 and 155.5
5	6	6	55.33, 100.0, 105.0, 110.0, 129.0 and 155.5
6	7	7	41.0, 62.5,100.0, 105.0, 110.0, 129.0 and 155.5

If centroid values = effective score; No. of Clusters = value of k.

In the above table centroid values 41, 110, 129, 100 are same as effective score. Hence it is concluded that the maximum possible Clusters are 7. If the process is continued centroid values of most of the students will be same as their respective effective scores. Hence the process is stopped.

Hence at the end of the module 'Clustering current students' the number of Clusters formed is 7.

Step 2: Selecting value of K

Selecting the value of 'k' in other words number of Clusters to be selected among the total Clusters formed is the next objective of our study.

According to the step 2 of proposed algorithm a method is devised where in variance centroid distance explained as a function of the number of Clusters: One should choose a number of Clusters so that adding another Cluster doesn't give much better modeling of the data. This is explained as follows

Centroid Distance = Highest Centroid − Lowest Centroid
Variance Centroid Distance = (Centroid Distance * Centroid Distance)/value of K

The above table depicts the calculation of centroid distance and variance centroid distance using the method described above.

In the table lowest and highest centroid values are obtained from the Tables 3.

For the value k = 2
Centroid Distance = 67.52
Variance Centroid Distance
=67.52 * 67.52/2
=2279.73

Similarly other variance centroid distance values are calculated (Fig. 3).

ADVERTISING SCHEDULING USING EDUCATIONAL DATA MINING

Clustering Students and Finding Centroid Distances
Centroid Distance for k = 2 is 2279.7324263038545
Centroid Distance for k = 3 is 2780.5925925925912
Centroid Distance for k = 4 is 2508.3402777777774

Selected k : 3

INPUT VALUE

Fig. 3. Screenshot of selected Cluster with k = 3

Form the observation of Table 4 it is found that variance centroid distance increases starting from k = 2 to k = 3, and then suddenly drops from k = 4 to k = 7, the value of k at which variance centroid distance suddenly decreases is selected as the value of k. This is represented using the graph (Fig. 4).

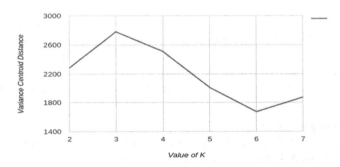

Fig. 4. Variance centroid distance against Clusters number

Table 4. Variance centroid distances

Value of K	Lowest centroid	Highest centroid	Centroid distance	Variance centroid distance
2	55.33	122.85	67.52	2279.73
3	55.33	146.66	91.33	2780.59
4	55.33	155.5	100.17	2508.34
5	55.33	155.5	100.17	2006.67
6	55.33	155.5	100.17	1672.22
7	41.0	155.5	114.5	1872.89

More precisely, if a graph is plotted with variance centroid distance against the number of Clusters, much information is added by the first Clusters (explain a lot of variance), but at some point the marginal gain will drop, giving divergence in the graph. At this point number of Clusters is chosen.

From the observation of the graph it is inferred that when the value of k = 3 the angle drops indicating the value of k that need to be selected which is the objective of module 'Selecting the value of K'.

Similarly Clustering was done with few other algorithms, and Precision and recall of all algorithms are provided in the tables shown below and represented graphically.

By the data available in Table 5 it can be observed that the precision and recall values are comparatively better for proposed algorithm (Fig. 5).

Table 5. Comparative analysis of algorithms

Algorithm	TA	FA	TB	FB	Precision	Recall
k-means	429316	34478	495081	68586	0.92	0.86
k-medoids	437508	50440	480293	59220	0.89	0.88
k-means fast	397940	61802	397940	169779	0.86	0.81
X-Means	386752	69788	480457	90464	0.84	0.81
Proposed algorithm	443506	24428	502455	53772	0.94	0.89

*TA- True class A, TB- True class, FA- False class A, FB- False class B

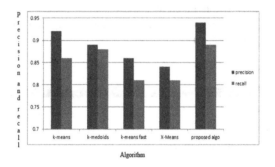

Fig. 5. Bar graph representing the comparison of precision and recall of different algorithms

Step 3: Find best Students among the proficient students of Specific Cluster

        Input : Centroid Value
        Output : Student List
1. Read Centroid Value as centRal
2. Read All Student List
3. For Each student in All Student List
        [Begin Loop]
4. If student is in Cluster of Centroid as centRal
5. add Student to student Write Post
        [End If]
        [End loop at Step 3]
6. Write students Write List

Since the value of k = 3 is selected, the data table for k = 3 is taken as input (Table 6).

Table 6. List of selected students

reg_no	1	2	3	4	5	6	7	8	9	10
Centroids of Cluster	55.33	55.33	105.0	55.33	146.66	146.66	105.0	105.0	105.0	146.66
Selection	Not selected	Not selected	Selected	Not selected	Selected	Selected	Selected	Selected	Selected	Selected

The above table indicates selected list of students who are the best among proficient students.

Criterion of Selection:
Those Clusters whose centroid values greater than or equal to 100 are selected as best Clusters who has more proficient. Since the maximum value of effective score is calculated as 200, students whose effective score more than 100 is considered, reason being, student should atleast have good marks or have good attitude or should have both. Hence the value of 100 is taken as criterion.

Hence at the end of the this module only 2 lusters are selected with centroids 105.0 and 146.66 as the output (Fig. 6).

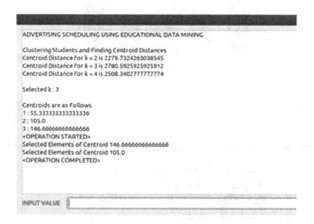

Fig. 6. Screenshot displaying selected cluster with k = 3

The above screenshot depicts the selected Clusters with k = 3 and also those Clusters whose centroid values are greater than or equal to 100 who are best among the rest. This completes the process of Clustering.

6 Results

From the deduction the Cluster 3 is found to be the best Cluster having the number of proficient students

7 Conclusion and Future Enhancement

The main objective was to identify the proficient students by Clustering using proposed algorithm. It was found that Cluster 3 having proficient students emerged among the students of the institution. The proposed methodology has an accuracy of 89%. Thus the solution for the above problem was found successfully. This work can be extended to predict placement chance of the proficient students selected.

References

1. Kim, S.Y., Jung, T.S., Suh, E.H., Hwang, H.S.: Student segmentation and strategy development based on student lifetime value: a case study. Expert Syst. Appl. **31**(1), 101–107 (2006)
2. Shin, H.W., Sohn, S.Y.: Product differentiation and market segmentation as alternative marketing strategies. Expert Syst. Appl. **27**(1), 27–33 (2004)
3. Jang, S.C., Morrison, A.M.T., O'Leary, J.T.: Benefit segmentation of Japanese pleasure travelers to the USA and Canada: selecting target markets based on the profitability and the risk of individual market segment. Tour. Manag. **23**(4), 367–378 (2002)
4. Hruschka, H., Natter, M.: Comparing performance of feed forward neural nets and k-means of cluster-based market segmentation. Eur. J. Oper. Res. **114**(3), 346–353 (1999)
5. Bottou, L., Bengio, Y.: Convergence Properties of the K-Means Algorithms. In: Advances in Neural Information Processing Systems 7 (1995)
6. Fabere, V.: Clustering and the continuous k-means algorithm. Los Alamos Sci. (1994)
7. Bydovska, H., Popelinsky, L.: Predicting student performance in higher education. In: 2013 24th International Workshop on Database and Expert Systems Applications (DEXA), pp. 141–145. IEEE (2013)
8. Archer-North and Associates: Performance Appraisal (2006). http://www.performance-appraisal.com. Accessed Dec 2012
9. Chein, C., Chen, L.: Data mining to improve personnel selection and enhance human capital: a case study in high technology industry. Expert Syst. Appl. (2006, in Press)
10. Pal, K., Pal, S.: Analysis and mining of educational data for predicting the performance of students. (IJECCE) Int. J. Electron. Commun. Comput. Eng. **4**(5), 1560–1565 (2013). ISSN: 2278-4209
11. Khan, Z.N.: Scholastic achievement of higher secondary students in science stream. J. Soc. Sci. **1**(2), 84–87 (2005)
12. Bharadwaj, B.K., Pal, S.: Mining educational data to analyze students' performance. Int. J. Adv. Comput. Sci. Appl. (IJACSA) **2**(6), 63–69 (2011)
13. Bray, M.: The Shadow Education System: Private Tutoring and Its Implications for Planners, 2nd edn. UNESCO, Paris (2007)

14. Yadav, S.K., Bharadwaj, B.K., Pal, S.: Data mining applications: a comparative study for predicting student's performance. (IJITCE) **1**(12), 13–19 (2011)
15. Jamesmanoharan, J., Hari Ganesh, S., Felciah, M., Shafreenbanu, A.K.: Discovering students' academic performance based on GPA using k-means clustering algorithm. In: 2014 World Congress on Computing and Communication Technologies (WCCCT), pp. 200–202. IEEE (2014)

Designing of a Gender Based Classifier
for Western Music

Anam Tasleem[1,2], Satbir Singh[1,2], Balwinder Singh[1,2(✉)],
and Hitesh Pahuja[1,2]

[1] Centre for Development of Advance Computing, Mohali, Punjab, India
anam.tasleem92@gmail.com, {balwinder,hitesh}@cdac.in
[2] A Scientific Society of Ministry of Electronics and Information Technology,
New Delhi, India

Abstract. A musical piece constitutes of vocals and background music which
is repetitive in nature. Their separation is an essential job in many applications,
like music information retrieval (MIR), gender recognition and lyrical recognition. In this paper, we propose a classifier which cleaves the music/song on the
basis of gender of the singer without having to listen to it. The basic idea is the
music/vocal using REPET algorithm and using the vocals extracted for
parameter extraction. The parameters used here are pitch, ZCR and MFCC.
Based on these values, a classifier was designed using fuzzy inference system
(FIS). A dataset of 43 songs was prepared to check the validity of the system.
These songs were experimented upon and showed the accuracy of 82.6% by
using the classifier designed.

Keywords: MIR · Gender identification · REPET · Pitch · ZCR · MFCC ·
Fuzzy inference system

1 Introduction

Singing voice is an important feature of western songs. It is that part of the song that
captures the attention of the listeners the most. In the past, systems have been developed for identifying the gender of the speaker of speech signal but singing is different
than speaking. Singing is the continuous form of speech. Thus, the methods used for
speech analysis and speaker identification are quite different from the one required for
singing voice analysis. The identification of the gender of the singer is an important
part of music information retrieval (MIR) system. Many a times, a person is interested
in listening to a song of a particular gender. So, to cater to this requirement, there is a
need to develop a method which gives the option to the user for availing such facility.
The proposed system can classify a song based on its gender for superior listening
experience. This system can be used to classify the songs based on their gender after its
identification. The chore of singer identification is very complex because of the mixing
of the voice and instruments which constitute a song. Another issue which needs to be
handled is the background noise and silence removal. In this paper, we propose a
system which helps in singer's gender identification and keeping the issues mentioned
above in check. A simple algorithm chosen for extracting the vocal counterpart from

© Springer Nature Singapore Pte Ltd. 2017
M. Singh et al. (Eds.): ICACDS 2016, CCIS 721, pp. 81–90, 2017.
DOI: 10.1007/978-981-10-5427-3_9

the complete song is Repeating Pattern Extraction Technique (REPET) [1]. The notion behind this algorithm is identifying the repeating patterns occurring periodically in the audio of the song and then separating the "background" (instruments and acoustical music) which is repeating from the "foreground" (singing vocals) which is non-repeating. After the retrieval of vocals from the song, there is a need to find out its gender. For this purpose, some features of singing voice are extracted. Various acoustic vectors or features which are used in this system are pitch, ZCR, MFCC and short time energy (STE) as they can collectively provide robust gender identification. After setting their thresholds to a particular value, the vectors extracted from the vocals are then classified using the fuzzy inference system (FIS). The rest of the paper is organized as follows: Sect. 2 consists of related work. Section 3 has basic concepts and practical representation of REPET along with the specifics of parameters selected. Section 4 has the details of the database, classifier and results.

2 Related Work

In the past, extensive work has been done on speech processing. Various ways have been introduced through which we can identify the gender of a speaker. But, not much has been researched on gender identification of a singer per se. In some studies, separation of background music and foreground singing voice has been performed. Rafi and Pardo contended that repetition is the basic concept in music [1]. In music analysis, a song constitutes of repeating and non-repeating parts. They put forward a novel method, REPET, to identify the repeating segments occurring at periodic intervals and by comparing them to a model of repeating segment, the repeating patterns could be extracted through time frequency masking. REPET could be efficiently applied for music/voice separation and being resilient to real-world audios could be easily extended to whole songs. But, there has been no method put forward to directly perform gender identification without any intermediary steps. Jena et al. worked on the idea of a relative inspection on speech signals to concoct a gender classifier. The analysis comprises of a contrast of dissimilar pitch values of male and female speech samples [2]. This significant contrast is executed using MATLAB programming by ascertaining pitch through the method of autocorrelation. Autocorrelation algorithm is the measure of similarity of a signal with itself after a time lag. In the end, it was indicated that there was enough dissimilarity among the value of pitch of male and female samples to be used in the working of gender classifier by setting a threshold value [3, 5]. Another method was studied upon by Ghosal et al. for classifying the audio speech signals into male speech and female speech through various time-domain acoustic parameters like zero crossing rate (ZCR), short time energy (STE) and spectral flux [8]. Random Sample and Consensus (RANSAC), a re-sampling method that gives solutions by using the least observations and Neural-Net, consisting of interconnecting patterns, learning process and the activation function, were used as standard classifier. RANSAC was found to have much better accuracy compared to Neural-Net [7, 9]. Archana et al. proposed to identify gender by extracting features like Mel Frequency Cepstral Coefficient (MFCC), energy entropy and frame energy estimation, gender classification was done. Artificial Neural Network (ANN) and Support Vector Machines

(SVM) were used for classification of the gender [4]. The features extracted were put to use in classification of the gender of the speaker. As the main difference was in the value of pitch, the median value for male was 186.8644 and that of female was 380.1724 for the word 'hello'. From the chosen classifiers, SVM was found better than ANN. If one wants to hear only male singer's track/female singer's track out of an unsorted database of western song tracks, the only way is to first listen to the songs. To arrange the songs in a list on the basis of duration, day modified etc. has been done. But arranging the songs on the basis of the gender of the singer has not been performed yet. This feature could enhance the productivity of media players and other gender utilizing systems in the field of music.

3 Proposed System

This project is based on the build out of a classifier which would arrange the music by the gender of the artist. An audio-visual signal consists of numerous acoustics such as different languages, noise, compressed speech, speech over background score. So, a gender identification system must be potent enough to process a variety of speech signals and exude good performance. This was done by making use of the REPET [1] algorithm. The computation of the MFCC value included a series of steps which were to be followed in order. The ZCR value is the measure of times the sign of the signal changes during the course of audio. Pitch is the elemental frequency of the source of excitation. The algorithm used for the purpose of finding out pitch of a particular vocal sample was the fast autocorrelation algorithm. The threshold values were set for differentiating between the genders and by taking the average of these values through a classifier, the final output is given. This classifier was based on the fuzzy inference system.

3.1 REPET

This is an algorithm based on the fact that a song consists of a repeating background (music) and a non-repeating foreground (vocals/singing voice). The separation of the repeating background from the non-repeating foreground was performed in this method. The original output obtained was the repeating background. So, to get the non-repeating foreground as output, subtraction was performed. This technique can be divided in to an array of steps:

– Identification of repeating pattern - A given sample of a mixture signal is subject to the STFT (Short Time Fourier Transform) after windowing. Then a magnitude spectrogram is prepared and then forwarded for autocorrelation. The repeating period is evaluated and used for time segmenting the spectrogram.
– Reproduction of repeating segment - Through time-frequency masking, the part of the song which is recurring periodically is identified.
– Extraction of repeating portion - A repeating spectrogram model is prepared. After obtaining time- frequency masks, they are applied to STFT of the mixture signal (whole song). The resulting short time Fourier transform is inverted in to time

domain to give the output. This output is the repeating part which is subtracted from the mixture signal to obtain the non-repeating part of the song (vocals).

3.2   Representation of REPET

From the database of 43 songs, we select a song to showcase the proper working of REPET in the form of various steps. In the following figures, X- axis represents sample signal and Y- axis represents intensity of signal (Figs. 1, 2 and 3).

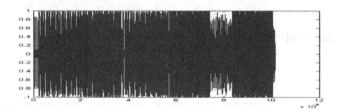

Fig. 1. Original song (Blank space by Taylor swift)

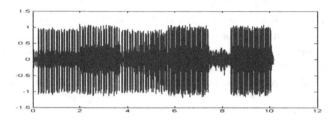

Fig. 2. Instrumental signal

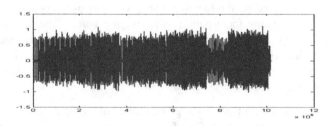

Fig. 3. Vocal extract

3.3   Parametric Extraction

The parameters selected for extraction are MFCC (Mel Frequency Cepstrum Coefficient), ZCR (Zero Crossing Rate) and pitch. These parameters are:

(i) MFCC – These coefficients constitute the Mel scale. Mel scale is a type of a scale which is linear at low values of frequency (<1000 Hz) and logarithmic at high values of frequency (>1000 Hz). In a normal cepstrum, frequency bands are linearly arranged whereas in Mel scale frequency bands are spaced equally [6]. The equation to convert the frequency to Mel scale is given below.

$$m(F) = 1125 \ln(1 + F/700) \tag{1}$$

In Eq. (1), F is the frequency value to be converted to Mel scale. For finding out the value of MFCCs, there are well defined steps which need to be followed (Fig. 4).

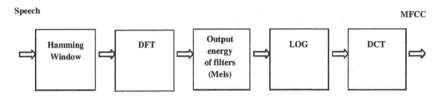

Fig. 4. Steps to find MFCCs

1. Hamming window - Windowing is done to avoid sudden jumps at the end of the frame and it efficiently reduces the side lobes.
2. DFT - Discrete Fourier Transform is performed to convert the signal from time domain to frequency domain.
3. Output energy (in Mels) - This is done to map the powers of the spectrum in Mels.
4. Log - This is inspired by the phenomenon of human hearing. Humans hear loudness on a logarithmic scale.
5. DCT- Discrete Cosine Transform of Mel log powers is performed next. As the filter banks might overlap. The energy of the filter banks is correlated to each other. To de-correlate these energies, DCT is used.
6. The amplitude of the resulting spectrum will give the MFCCs.

ZCR - The ZCR value is taken as the next parameter which is the rate of change of sign along the path of a signal. Zero crossing in particular is a point at which no voltage is present. The figure below shows the zero crossing where X- axis depicts voltage and Y- axis depicts time (Fig. 5):

Fig. 5. Zero crossing point

If the sign of the output of the product of present value and past value has not changed, then there has been no zero crossing. If the sign of the product of present and past value has led to change of sign, then zero crossing has occurred.

$$zcr = \frac{1}{P-1}\sum_{p=1}^{P-1} I\{s_p s_{p-1} < 0\} \tag{2}$$

The above Eq. (2) is used to find the value of ZCR. Here, S is the signal of length P and I (a) is the indicator function whose value is 1 if argument 'a' is true else 0.

(ii) Pitch - It can be defined as an auditory perception using which the listener decides its place on the musical scale (low or high). Pitch is the elemental frequency of the origin of excitation [2]. The algorithm used for the purpose of finding out pitch of a particular vocal sample is the fast autocorrelation algorithm. Autocorrelation algorithm is the measure of similarity of a signal with itself after a time lag or at different points in time. This can be done by performing short time autocorrelation for a signal. The value of this short time autocorrelation can be found by following equation:

$$s_n(T) = \sum_{n=-\infty}^{\infty} \frac{[y(n)z(p-n)]}{[y(n+T)z(p-n-T)]} \tag{3}$$

In the Eq. (3) above, $s_n(T)$ = Short time autocorrelation, y = Speech signal, z = Window, and T = Sample time at which autocorrelation was evaluated.

3.4   Fuzzy Classification

The gender classifier is based on fuzzy logic. This utilizes the FIS (Fuzzy Inference Systems). It is a type system which makes use of fuzzy sets to give outputs. The mapping between input and output becomes a base through which decisions are made and various patterns are defined. The first step towards designing a fuzzy inference system is the formation of a set of rules. These rules strictly follow the ranges set for each parameter. A few of the rules are shown below:

If (pitch minimum) and (ZCR is minimum) and (MFCC is minimum) then gender is male,
If (pitch minimum) and (ZCR is minimum) and (MFCC is medium) then gender is male,
If (pitch minimum), and (ZCR minimum) and (MFCC maximum), then gender is male,
If (pitch minimum) and (ZCR is medium) and (MFCC minimum), then gender is male,
If (pitch minimum) and (ZCR maximum) and (MFCC minimum), then gender is male,
If (pitch minimum) and (ZCR is medium) and (MFCC medium), then gender is male,

If (pitch is minimum) and (ZCR medium) and (MFCC maximum), then no conclusion...

The command 'gensurf' is used to generate a plot of the output surface of a FIS. This uses the first output and first two inputs. The third window that is used to show results is the plot of degree of membership and GCS (Gender Classifier System). It is used to graphically depict the ranges (female, male and no conclusion) in which the output might lie. This will ensure the result as per the range in which it falls. The window is displayed as shown below in Fig. 6. The last step of FIS is defuzzification. This step is implemented only if a crisp output is required. It constitutes the conversion of fuzzy output to crisp output. The method used here for defuzzification is centroid method. This method returns the center of the area under the curve as shown in Fig. 7.

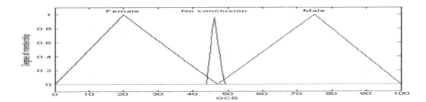

Fig. 6. Plot of degree of membership and GCS

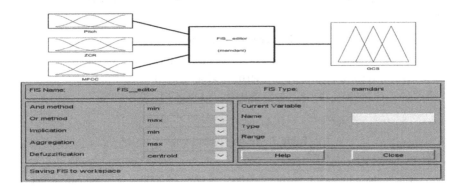

Fig. 7. FIS editor

4 Database and Results

The table below is used to showcase the song database. In addition to the songs, the extracted values of parameters from the mixture of a song are also shown (Tables 1, 2, 3 and 4).

Table 1. Training phase songs

S. No.	Name of the song	ZCR	Pitch	MFCC (STD)
1.	Strange desire-The black keys	0.02	67.56	3.4561
2.	George Harrison-While my guitar gently	0.01	49.60	2.4919
3.	Misery by Maroon 5	0.06	58.74	3.6646
4.	Save room by John Legend	0.05	56.93	2.9732
5.	Thinking out loud by Ed Sheeren	0.05	99.12	6.6305
6.	Recovery by James Arthur	0.05	100.56	4.3980
7.	You're beautiful by James blunt	0.06	72.88	2.6038
8.	Here without you by 3 Doors down	0.04	72.62	4.7248
9.	No freedom by Dido	0.03	149.06	3.0664
10.	Sand in my shoes by Dido-	0.04	140.24	3.6062
11.	Get down by James Arthur	0.05	61.65	4.1780
12.	Impossible by James Arthur	0.07	66.29	4.8876
13.	Suicide by James Arthur	0.05	197.76	5.8536
14.	Story of my life by Boyce avenue	0.03	72.69	4.1970
15.	Summertime sadness by Lana del ray	0.06	20.470	7.2776
16.	Born to die by Lana del ray	0.06	18.28	4.7665
17.	Pretty girl rock by Keri hilson	0.05	84.65	3.9743
18.	Energy by Keri hilson	0.08	3.43	2.4776
19.	Suicide by James Arthur	0.05	197.76	5.8536
20.	Like I would by Zayn Malik	0.06	108.58	4.9780

Table 2. Range of given parameters

S. No	Gender of the speaker	ZCR	Pitch	MFCC (Std. deviation)
1.	Female	>0.05	>130	≥ 4.1
2.	Male	≤ 0.05	≤ 130	<4.1

Table 3. Testing phase songs

S. No.	Name of the song	ZCR	Pitch	MFCC (STD)	Gender
1.	Blank space by Taylor swift	0.06	117.3	4.2008	No conclusion
2.	Chasing pavements by Adele	0.07	169.72	3.8994	Female
3.	How deep by Calvin Harris	0.05	127.09	5.0387	Male
4.	Life for rent by Dido	0.04	151.42	3.8597	Female
5.	Burn by Ellie Goulding	0.05	120.58	4.0443	Female
6.	Shake it out by Florence	0.06	206.65	4.2817	Female
7.	Unconditional by Katy Perry	0.05	131.38	4.5959	Female
8.	Chandelier by Sia	0.05	156.16	5.0467	Female
9.	White flag by Dido	0.04	229.28	5.8656	Female
10.	Cry by Rihanna	0.05	104.14	3.6801	Female

(continued)

Table 3. (*continued*)

S. No.	Name of the song	ZCR	Pitch	MFCC (STD)	Gender
11.	I got you by Leona Lewis	0.05	112.45	3.4914	No conclusion
12.	Impossible by Shontelle	0.1	119.18	6.8893	Female
13.	Young and beautiful by Lana	0.0368	104.43	3.1073	Out of memory
14.	Bleeding love by Leona Lewis	0.05	123.92	4.1697	Female
15.	Angel and the fool Broken bells	0.03	64.87	1.4553	Male
16.	In the room by Dmb	0.13	75.36	4.2416	No conclusion
17.	Tuesday by Drake	0.03	89.93	1.6691	Male
18.	Did you by George Ezra	0.07	66.02	3.988	Male
19.	Happy by Pharrel Williams	0.009	56.89	3.8036	Male
20.	Impossible by James Arthur	0.04	87.01	4.6510	Male

Table 4. Accuracy of results

S.No.	Feature of the song	Total songs to be tested	True outcomes	False outcomes	Accuracy %
1	ZCR	23	16	7	69.5
2	Pitch	23	17	6	73.9
3	MFCC	23	17	6	73.9
4	GCS	23	19	4	82.6

5 Conclusion

This field of identifying the gender of singing voice signal along with application of fuzzy logic/neural network has not been explored in the past. MIR is the process of identification of various features of a song. Identifying the gender of the singer is an important part of MIR. To find out a way for adding a feature other than the usual ones like name of the artist, duration, type of audio etc. is the basal motive of this research. Gender of a singer could be the added feature. There are various fields which require the need to know the gender of the singer like in the case of arranging the songs sung by various artists, for a singing competition, according to the gender and could be highly useful in karaoke gaming. Moreover, knowing the gender of the artist, while listening to a song in the media player, can act as an added feature. This feature could be a part of a bigger project in future.

References

1. Rafii, Z., Pardo, B.: Repeating pattern extraction technique (REPET): a simple method for music/voice separation. IEEE Trans. Audio Speech Lang. Process. **21**(1), 73–84 (2013)
2. Jena, B.L., Panigrahi, B.P.: Gender classification by pitch analysis. Int. J. Adv. Comput. Theory Eng. **1**(1), 2319–2526 (2012)

3. Chen, O.T.-C., Gu, J.J., Lu, P.-T., Ke, J.-Y.: Emotion-inspired age and gender recognition systems. In: IEEE 55th International Midwest Symposium on Circuits and Systems, pp. 662–665, August 2012

4. Archana, G.S., Malleswari, M.: Gender identification and performance analysis of speech signals. In: Global Conference on Communication Technologies (GCCT), pp. 483–489. IEEE, April 2015

5. Gupta, S., Mehra, A.: Gender specific emotion recognition through speech signals. In: International Conference on Signal Processing and Integrated Networks (SPIN), pp. 727–733. IEEE, February 2104

6. Patel, K., Prasad, R.K.: Speech recognition and verification using MFCC & VQ. Int. J. Comput. Sci. Inf. Technol. 5(5(2)), 1139–1143 (2014)

7. Daqrouq, K., Hilal, T.A., Sherif, M., El-Hajjar, S., Al-Qawasmi, A.: Speaker identification system using wavelet transform and neural network. In: International Conference on Advances in Computational Tools for Engineering Applications, ACTEA 2009, pp. 559–564. IEEE, July 2009

8. Ghosal, A., Dutta, S.: Automatic male-female voice discrimination. In: International Conference on Issues and Challenges in Intelligent Computing Techniques (ICICT), pp. 731–735. IEEE, February 2014

9. Yucesoy, E., Nabiyev, V.V.: Gender identification of a speaker from voice source. In: Signal Processing and Communications Applications Conference (SIU) pp. 1–4. IEEE, April 2013

Detecting Malwares Using Dynamic Call Graphs and Opcode Patterns

K.P. Deepta[(✉)] and A. Salim

College of Engineering Trivandrum, Thiruvananthapuram, Kerala, India
deeptakp6@gmail.com, salim.mangad@gmail.com

Abstract. Classification and detection of malware includes detecting instances and variants of the existing known malwares. Traditional signature based approaches fails when byte level content of the malware undergoes modification. Different static, dynamic and hybrid approaches exist and are classified based on the form in which the executable is analyzed. Static approaches include signature based methods that uses byte or opcode sequences, printable string information, control flow graphs based on code and so on. Dynamic approaches analyze the runtime behavior of the malwares and constructs features. Hybrid methods provide an effective combination of static and dynamic approaches. This work compares the classification accuracy of static approach that employs opcode sequence analysis and dynamic approach that uses the call graph generated from the function calls made by the program and an integrated approach that combines both these approaches. Integrated approach shows an improvement of 2.89% than static and 0.82% than dynamic approach.

Keywords: Dynamic analysis · Integrated approach · Malware · Static analysis

1 Introduction

Malware or malicious software is any software which has the potential to damage the information stored in a computer. There are different categories of malware including viruses, worms, spyware and so on. There has been a profound increase in the number of malicious samples due to the deployment of morphing techniques, which prevents the anti-malware software from detecting them. Researchers and anti-malware vendors face the challenge of how to detect previously unseen malware (also called zero-day attack).

Malware detection involves identification of both instances and variants of the existing malware. For this, it is essential to observe and study the organization of the malicious code and its behavior. This gives an understanding about the nature of infection caused by the code and thus identifies similar ones.

1.1 Basics of Malware Analysis

Malware analysis can be considered as an art of dissecting the malware to find out the way it works, methods to identify it and how to trash and wipe it out. Malware analysis is critical area as it is a threat to security of computer systems.

© Springer Nature Singapore Pte Ltd. 2017
M. Singh et al. (Eds.): ICACDS 2016, CCIS 721, pp. 91–101, 2017.
DOI: 10.1007/978-981-10-5427-3_10

1.1.1 Static Analysis

Static analysis consists of examining the executable file without viewing the actual instructions. It can be applied on different representations of a program like binary code, source code etc. It can be used to find memory corruption issues and prove the correctness of models if the source code is available.

Some of the techniques used for static malware analysis are file fingerprinting, extracting hard coded strings, file format inspection, disassembling of machine code etc.

Islam et al. presented an automatic malware classification method based on function length frequency and Printable String Information [1]. Their results demonstrated that a combined approach of string and function length features into a single test provides a superior result than they were used individually. Even though these features are easier to collect, the use of static features alone, fails when obfuscation and packing is performed.

Santos et al. proposed a malware detection system that uses semi-supervised learning to detect malicious programs [2]. This method is useful when a limited amount of labeled data exists for benign and malware classes. N-gram distribution is used to represent the executables. The main contribution of this paper is the reduction in the number of required labeled instances while maintaining a good precision of above 90%. However, due to the use of static nature of features, the system will be unable to counter packed malware.

Ye et al. proposed a detection system based on static analysis to generate signatures for clustering malwares [3]. Two features have been considered here, namely Instruction Frequency and Function-based sequences. A Hybrid hierarchical clustering algorithm which combines the advantages of hierarchical clustering and k-medoids algorithm was used to cluster the malwares.

Cesare et al. has proposed a static method of malware detection [4]. Initially the system unpacks the executables and disassembles the code. Malware signature is generated based on the set of control flow graphs (from high level source code) the malware contains. Feature vector is a decomposition of the set of graphs into either fixed size k-subgraphs, or q-gram strings. Similarity with the known malwares is computed using string distance matching methods like edit distance. This method is more efficient than signature based methods as the control flow overcomes the limitations of byte level and instruction level classification but cannot properly handle packing and obfuscation issues. The major drawback of the approach is that it considers the static control flow of the program and this can be easily bypassed by the code obfuscation techniques.

The key advantage of static malware analysis is that it permits a comprehensive analysis of a given binary i.e., it can cover all possible execution paths of a malware sample. Additionally, as the source code is not actually executed, static analysis is generally safer than the dynamic analysis. But the drawback is that static analysis is usually conducted manually and thus consumes time and requires expertise.

1.1.2   Dynamic Analysis

Executing a given malware sample within a controlled environment and monitoring its actions to analyze the malicious behavior is called dynamic malware analysis. Zhao et al. proposed a vector space model where API sequences were translated into features [5].

Another approach is a graph based model where API calls and OS resources are represented as graph nodes and edges representing reference between them [6]. The Graph Edit Distance algorithm was used to find the match between different graphs.

Anderson et al. proposed a malware detection algorithm that analyzes the graphs constructed from dynamically collected instruction traces of that executables [7]. The nodes of the graph represent instructions and the transition probabilities are estimated by the data in the trace. Using the concept of graph kernels, similarity matrices between instances in training set were constructed. Gaussian kernel and spectral kernel were the two measures used to construct kernel matrix.

Borojerdi and Abadi proposed MalHunter, which is a method for generating behavioral signature [8]. Sequence-based clustering algorithm is based on the Basic Sequential Algorithmic Scheme (BSAS). The steps involved in generating the signature were identifying semantic behaviors, clustering the behavior sequences, generalizing these sequences and generating multiple behavioral signatures.

As the analysis and detection is during runtime and malware unpacks itself, dynamic malware analysis avoids the restrictions of static analysis like unpacking and obfuscation issues. The main drawback is the issue of dormant code. Also if the analysis environment is not properly managed, the system itself may get damaged. Furthermore, malware samples may change their behavior or stop the execution when they detect that execution is taking place in a controlled analysis environment.

Observing the runtime-behavior of an application is currently the most promising approach. It is mostly conducted utilizing sandboxing. A sandbox refers to a controlled runtime environment which is partitioned from the rest of the system in order to isolate the malicious process. This partitioning is typically achieved using virtualization mechanisms on a certain level.

1.1.3   Integrated Approach

Integrated approaches are the combination of static and dynamic malware analysis techniques. Sharma proposed a combination of dynamic representation of program calling structures, with a static analysis applied to a region of that structure with observed performance problem [9]. Suspicious behavior showing portions are taken as signatures and searched for similar patterns. This was a theoretical work and does not contain any experimental results for evaluating the actual performance.

Nguyen et al. proposed a method to identify real target of an indirect jump [10]. This work was aimed at reducing the false target identification that could happen when processing such jumps and during CFG construction. The framework consists of two phases: Static and Dynamic. In the static phase, the program was divided into regions and sub-CFGs were generated. During the dynamic analysis Intermediate labeled transition system is generated and test cases are executed and then the CFG is updated, followed by first step and this continues.

2 Proposed Architecture

Figure 1 shows the proposed architecture of the malware detection system. It consists of a static, dynamic and integrated approach for fast and accurate detection of malware.

2.1 Static Feature Extraction

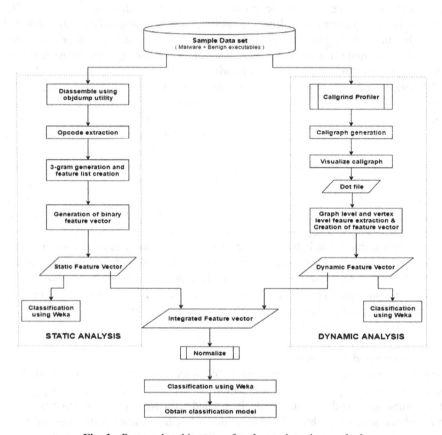

Fig. 1. Proposed architecture of malware detection method

2.1.1 Disassemble the Executable

A disassembler is a computer program that translates machine language into assembly language. Objdump command in Linux is used to disassemble the codes.

2.1.2   Feature Vector Formation

The disassembled code contains the opcode sequence of the program. Opcodes from the disassemble input has been separated using a python program and 3-gram patterns were generated using the Linux utility text2ngram.

Initially all the opcodes from the disassembled code were extracted and frequency of every possible 3-gram sequence were computed. The 3-grams with frequency above a threshold were filtered from both malware and benign samples. To get a feature vector that represent malware family more precisely, we extracted all frequent 3-grams and filtered out that are common in both classes. Various length feature vectors (size 10, 20, 50, 80 and 100) were considered. The feature vector consists of strings of 1 s and 0 s depending on the presence of 3-gram patterns. This was done for each pattern and feature vectors corresponding to each sample was generated. Algorithm 1 describes the steps in Static feature extraction.

```
Algorithm 1 static feature extraction
      S : Sample set containing malware and benign files
      B : Binary  feature vector
      begin
      for each sᵢ in S do
            Extract all the opcodes in sᵢ;
            Generate all 3-grams from opcodes;
            Add each unique 3-gram to a csv file f_csv;
      for each 3-gram in f_csv do
            counter :=0;
            for each sᵢ in S do
                  Increment counter if 3-gram is present
                  in sᵢ and store 3-gram and its counter
                  in file f_c;
      Sort f_csv based on frequency of 3-grams;
      Remove 3-gram having frequency < Threshold
      Store the new list in file f_c;
      i=0;
      for each sᵢ in S do
            i = i+1;
            for each 3-gram in f_c do
                  k = 0;
                  if 3-gram present in sᵢ then
                        b_ik :=1;
                  else
                        b_ik :=0;
                  k = k+1;
                  //Each bi is a feature vector
            Tabulate the binary feature vectors of all sᵢ
            in S and Input this to classifiers;
      end.
```

2.2   Dynamic Feature Extraction

The core idea is to make malware detection system more resilient to byte- and instruction-level modifications and obfuscations. A call graph derived from the binary code provides a reasonable approximation of the program's run time behavior. So we translate the problem of finding similar graphs into that of extraction of different features of the graph and analyze the similarities in them.

The executable files were analyzed using *Callgrind*, a profiling tool that records the call history among functions in a program's run as a call-graph. By default, the collected data consists of the number of instructions executed, their relationship to source lines, the caller/callee relationship between functions and the numbers of such calls.

We used Callgrind to analyze the executables. This is a profiling tool which records the call history of functions in a program during execution as a call-graph. The output generated by Callgrind was visualized using KCachegrind. Figure 2 shows a section of a sample call graph. The nodes of the graph contain the function name, its memory location, number of instructions and cost and the edges represent time consumed. The graph needs to be exported to Dot format for further analysis. The following features were extracted from graph corresponding to each of the sample. We ranked the features based on the information gain and Table 1 shows the features in descending order of ranks.

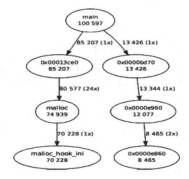

Fig. 2. A section of a sample call graph

2.3   Classifier Model

Dataset consisted of 787 malicious and 425 benign samples. Malware samples were collected from malware repositories Virusshare [13] and AVCaesar [14] and benign samples were obtained from Windows system directory. BayesNet and RandomForest classifiers were chosen to implement the classification model. BayesNet has the capability to find interdependencies between different attributes. Unlike decision tree, in Random forest the best parameter at each node in the tree is selected from a randomly chosen set of features. This helps Random Forest to perform well and makes it less vulnerable to noise in the data. An open source machine learning tool, Weka was used to implement the models [12].

Table 1. Ranking of features extracted from graph

Rank	Feature	Description
1	Network diameter	Longest graph distance between any 2 nodes. ie. How far apart are the two most distant nodes?
2	Average path length	Average number of steps along the shortest paths for all possible pairs of nodes
3	Average weighted degree	Ratio of sum of the in- and out-degree of all nodes to the number of vertices
4	Average degree	Ratio of sum of the in-degree of all nodes to the number of vertices
5	Modularity	Measures the density of links inside communities as compared to links between communities
6	Graph density	How close network is to complete? Ratio of number of edges to the possible number of edges
7	Strongly connected components	A directed graph is strongly connected if there is a path between all pair of nodes. A strongly connected component of a directed graph is a maximal strongly connected subgraph
8	Edge count	Number of edges
9	Node count	Number of nodes
10	Average clustering coefficient	Indicates how nodes are embedded in their neighbourhood
11	Weakly connected components	

3   Experimental Results and Discussion

Performance of the classification models were evaluated using measures like True Positive Rate (TP Rate), False Positive Rate (FP Rate), Precision, Recall, F-Measure (Harmonic mean of precision and recall), ROC Area (ROC curve is the curve created by plotting TPR against FPR at various threshold settings) and Accuracy.

3.1   Static Approach

Tables 2 and 3 show the classification results obtained using RandomForest and BayesNet classifiers respectively. Experiments have been repeated with varying number of static features from 10 to 100. Classification results of static analysis using RF classifier indicate that the features do not show much variation in accuracy between lengths 20 and 50. 95.87% is the best accuracy observed from RF classifier when feature length was 20.

Table 2. Weighted average of classification results with RandomForest classifier

Feature vector length	TP rate	FP rate	Precision	Recall	F-Measure	ROC area	Accuracy (%)
10	0.941	0.092	0.942	0.941	0.941	0.952	94.14
20	0.959	0.06	0.959	0.959	0.959	0.973	95.87
30	0.959	0.06	0.959	0.959	0.959	0.983	95.87
40	0.957	0.063	0.957	0.957	0.957	0.983	95.71
50	0.957	0.062	0.957	0.957	0.957	0.985	95.71
80	0.95	0.075	0.951	0.95	0.95	0.964	95.05
100	0.945	0.086	0.945	0.945	0.944	0.956	94.47

Table 3. Weighted average of classification results with BayesNet classifier

Feature vector length	TP rate	FP rate	Precision	Recall	F-Measure	ROC area	Accuracy (%)
10	0.87	0.145	0.871	0.87	0.87	0.916	86.96
20	0.823	0.183	0.83	0.823	0.825	0.889	82.26
30	0.771	0.227	0.787	0.771	0.775	0.869	77.06
40	0.744	0.237	0.771	0.744	0.75	0.854	74.42
50	0.732	0.24	0.766	0.732	0.738	0.849	73.18
80	0.721	0.253	0.755	0.721	0.727	0.833	72.11
100	0.716	0.258	0.75	0.716	0.723	0.826	71.62

3.2 Dynamic Approach

We conducted experiments with complete set of dynamic features and Tables 4 shows the classification results obtained using RF classifier with dynamic approach. Dynamic feature analysis shows an improvement of 1.65% over static feature analysis with RF classifier.

Table 4. Weighted average of classification results with RFclassifier

Classifier	TP rate	FP rate	Precision	Recall	F-Measure	ROC area	Accuracy (%)
Random Forest	0.975	0.042	0.976	0.975	0.975	0.97	97.52
Bayes Net	0.979	0.038	0.98	0.979	0.979	0.962	97.93

3.3 Integrated Approach

We conducted experiments by taking complete set of dynamic features and varying number of static feature lengths. Tables 5 and 6 shows the classification results obtained using RF and BayesNet classifiers using integrated approach. Figure 3 depicts the variation in ROC curves obtained from RF classifier with change in static feature vector length. Classification results obtained after integrating the features obtained from

Table 5. Weighted average of classification results with RFclassifier

Feature vector length	TP rate	FP rate	Precision	Recall	F-Measure	ROC area	Accuracy (%)
10	0.979	0.034	0.979	0.979	0.978	0.993	97.85
20	0.982	0.027	0.982	0.982	0.982	0.983	98.18
30	0.985	0.026	0.985	0.985	0.985	0.993	98.51
40	0.985	0.024	0.985	0.985	0.985	0.995	98.51
50	*0.988*	*0.019*	*0.988*	*0.988*	*0.988*	*0.997*	*98.76*
80	0.987	0.019	0.987	0.987	0.987	0.998	98.68
100	0.985	0.9024	0.985	0.985	0.985	0.998	98.51

Table 6. Weighted average of classification results with BayesNetclassifier

Feature vector length	TP rate	FP rate	Precision	Recall	F-Measure	ROC area	Accuracy (%)
10	0.978	0.034	0.978	0.978	0.978	0.992	97.77
20	0.971	0.042	0.971	0.971	0.971	0.988	97.11
30	0.975	0.036	0.975	0.975	0.975	0.991	97.52
40	*0.979*	*0.04*	*0.979*	*0.979*	*0.978*	*0.993*	*97.85*
50	0.967	0.041	0.967	0.967	0.967	0.985	96.70
80	0. 912	0.075	0.918	0.912	0.913	0.975	91.17
100	0. 869	0.101	0.886	0.869	0.871	0.969	86.88

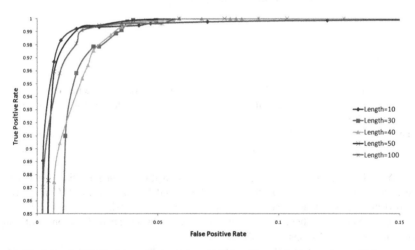

Fig. 3. Variation in ROC curves obtained from RF classifier with change in static feature vector length (Integrated approach)

static and dynamic analysis shows an improvement of 2.89% than static and 0.82% than dynamic approach.

On analyzing the classification results, we observed that the accuracy shows a declining trend on increasing the static feature vector length beyond 50. On an average both classifiers gives best accuracy rates for vector length between 30 and 50. The average time taken to build the model was 0.07 s. This is faster than the Control flow based malware variant detection [4] which took 0.7 s and Hybrid concentration based feature extraction approach for malware detection [11] which took 0.99 s on an average.

4 Conclusion

Dynamic malware analysis is done by watching and logging the behavior of the malware while running on the host. As most of the malwares pack themselves or morph their code during execution, static analysis alone is not efficient in malware detection. So here we have proposed a method that extracts features by analyzing the dynamic behavior of the malware and also static properties of the binaries and identifying whether the new sample possess similar features. The experimental results show that the method is more efficient than the static and dynamic analysis methods alone and also will be able to identify the polymorphic variants of the malware. The detection accuracy of integrated approach is comparatively better than several existing approaches. Integrated approach shows an improvement of 2.89% than static and 0.82% than dynamic approach. A practical extension to this work is to improve the static analysis part by incorporating the concept of function length analysis and also to consider files other than executables while constructing the model.

References

1. Islam, R., Tian, R., Batten, L., Versteeg, S.: Classification of malware based on string and function feature selection. In: IEEE Second Cybercrime and Trustworthy Computing Workshop (2010)
2. Santos, I., Nieves, J., Bringas, P.G.: Semi-supervised learning for unknown malware detection. In: 9th International Conference on Practical Applications of Agents and Multi-agent Systems (PAAMS) (2011)
3. Ye, Y., Li, Y., Chen, Y., Jiang, Q.: Automatic malware categorization using cluster ensemble. In: Proceedings of the 16th ACM SIGKDD International Conference on Knowledge Discovery and Data Mining, KDD 2010, pp. 95–104. ACM, New York (2010)
4. Cesare, S., Xiang, Y., Zhou, W.: Control flow-based Malware variant detection. IEEE Trans. Dependable Secure Comput. **11**, 307–317 (2014)
5. Zhao, Z., Wang, J., Bai, J.: Malware detection method based on the control flow construct feature of software. IET J. Inf. Secur. **8**, 18–24 (2014)
6. Elhadi, A.A.E., Maarof, M.A., Osman, A.H.: Malware detection based on hybrid signature behavior application programming interface call graph. Am. J. Appl. Sci. **9**, 283 (2012)

7. Anderson, B.H., Quist, D.A., Neil, J.C.: Graph-based Malware Detection Using Dynamic Analysis. Los Alamos National Laboratory Associate Directorate for Theory, Simulation, and Computation (ADTSC) LA-UR 12-20429

8. Borojerdi, H.R., Abadi, M.: MalHunter: automatic generation of multiple behavioral signatures for polymorphic Malware detection. In: 3rd International Conference on Computer and Knowledge Engineering (ICCKE 2013), 31 October–1 November 2013. Ferdowsi University of Mashhad (2013)

9. Sharma, V.: A theoretical implementation of blended program analysis for virus sign extraction. In: IEEE International Carnahan Conference on Security Technology (ICCST), October 2011

10. Nguyen, M.H., Nguyen, T.B., Quan, T.T., Ogawa, M.: A hybrid approach for control flow graph construction from binary code. In: IEEE Software Engineering Conference (APSEC) (2013)

11. Zhang, P., Tan, Y.: Hybrid concentration based feature extraction approach for malware detection. In: 2015 IEEE 28th Canadian Conference on Electrical and Computer Engineering (2015)

12. http://www.nilc.icmc.usp.br/elc-ebralc2012/minicursos/WekaManual-3-6-8.pdf

13. https://virusshare.com

14. https://avcaesar.malware.lu

Development of Secured Trust SLA Model from SLA Life Cycle Phases

Manjula Shanbhog[1(✉)], Krista Chaudhary[2], Mayank Singh[2], and Shailendra Mishra[3]

[1] School of Science, Noida International University, Greater Noida, India
manjulashanbhog@gmail.com
[2] CSED, Krishna Engineering College, Ghaziabad, India
krista2330@gmail.com, mayanksingh2005@gmail.com
[3] CSED, BTKIT, Dwarahat, India
Skmishra1@gmail.com

Abstract. This is the era of Cloud Computing which shares on-demand computing resources and disposes off efficiently. It has a wide range of benefits for business and consumers. In spite of several benefits, there embeds numerous challenges such as data integrity, authenticity, data security, data locking, access control, data confidentiality, auditability, trust on cloud service provider, well management of service level agreement (SLA). Trust – is a key differentiator in defining the success or failure of many business companies. Service Level Agreement builds trust between cloud providers and cloud consumers. This research proposes a secured trust SLA model that builds trust on cloud service provider and helps in providing data security, confidentiality and integrity for cloud user.

Keywords: Message digest · Service level agreement · Confidentiality · Cloud service provider · Activation

1 Introduction

Cloud computing is a flourishing service oriented paradigm where the user don't require to buy the computing resources for his use, instead he can hire the virtual resources dynamically form the cloud service provider, and scale down or scale up the resources according to his requirement through internet and pay as per the usage. The required resources to the user are made available by the service provider primarily in the form of 'plat form as a service' infrastructure as a service, software as a service.

When consumers have migrated their core business functions onto their entrusted cloud. Cloud consumers do not have control over the underlying computing resources. It is vital for consumers to obtain guarantees from providers on service delivery (Subramanyam and Hari 2014). Typically, these are provided through Service Level Agreements (SLAs) negotiated between the providers and consumers. The very first issue is the definition of SLA specifications in such a way that has an appropriate level of granularity, namely the tradeoffs between expressiveness and complicatedness, so that they can cover most of the consumer expectations and is relatively simple to be

© Springer Nature Singapore Pte Ltd. 2017
M. Singh et al. (Eds.): ICACDS 2016, CCIS 721, pp. 102–111, 2017.
DOI: 10.1007/978-981-10-5427-3_11

weighted, verified, evaluated, and enforced by the resource allocation mechanism on the cloud (Subramanyam and Hari 2014). Through Service level agreement the service provider adhere to the commitments, and ensures suitable service support and service deliverance to their customer.

2 Research Objectives

The Two main objectives of this research are

Objective 1: To identify the security issues in the cloud computing technology.
Objective 2: To provide the solutions for the security issues identified above.

3 Research Methology

Objective 1: The security issues in the cloud computing technology are identified from the literature review.

This section presents the methodology used during the design phase to solve the objective 2.

The solution for the complex research problem is obtained from the knowledge about the problem domain (Rubach 2010). In every domain with a high level of uncertainty and, consequently in the domain of research, it is necessary to confront the requirements and the resulting conceptual design with state-of-the-art solutions drawn from the available literature. The solution is obtained through iterative phases. During the initial phase the problem is analyzed in detail. Divide and Conquor rule is used to reduce the complexity, i.e. the complex problem is divided into smaller problem, and each problem is studied in detail. During the second phase, extensive literature is explored, analysed and reviewed which helped in getting ideas, plans or traces of hints for solving the problem. In the third phase, the solutions are proposed and designed. In the next phase, extensive feasibility analysis is made for the conceptual design obtained from the previous phase, as a result the design may have altered or a new design may have developed. The above phases are repeated until the design obtained is convinced and feasible.

4 Literature Review

Cloud computing comes with numerous possibilities and challenges simultaneously. Of the challenges, security is considered to be a critical barrier for cloud computing in its path to success (Khorshed et al. 2012). Mainly, confidentiality, integrity, authentication, & Trust are the primarily concerned areas (Kant and Sharma 2013; Hussain and Ashraf 2014; Talib 2015). Confidentiality means to prevent the disclosure of private and important information. Since all the information is stored on geographically dispersed locations, confidentiality becomes a big issue. Confidentiality defined as ensuring that user data which resides in the cloud cannot be accessed by unauthorized party. This can be achieved through proper encryption techniques taking into consideration the type of encryption: symmetric or asymmetric encryption algorithms, also key length and key management in case of the symmetric cipher (Talib 2015; Hussain and Ashraf 2014). In Cloud security, authentication is the most important factor. Authentication is generally referred to as a mechanism that establishes the validity of the claimed identity of the individual (Ziyad and Rehman 2014; Panse and Haritha 2014). One important security problem is guaranteeing the integrity of remotely stored data. Data integrity in simple terms can be understood as the maintenance of intactness of any data during transactions like transfer, retrieval or storage (Rao et al. 2014). In terms of customers' personal or business data security, the strategic policies of the cloud providers are of highest significance (Joint et al. 2009) as the technical security solely is not adequate to address the problem. Trust is another problem which raises security concerns to use cloud service (Ryan and Falvey 2012). Trust establishment might become the key to establish a successful cloud computing environment. The provision of trust model is essential in cloud computing as this is a common interest area for all stakeholders for any given cloud computing scenario. Trust in cloud might be dependent on a number of factors among which some are human factors, processes and policies (Abbadi et al. 2011). Trust in cloud is not a technical security issue, but it is the most influential soft factor that is driven by security issues inherent in cloud computing to a great extent (Ahmed and Hossain 2014).

The security issues in the cloud computing technology are identified and they are Confidentiality, Authenticity, Integrity and Trust.

Service Level Agreement: Service level agreement is a legal contract between service provider and client, which documents the key services provided by the service provider, specification of the service attribute, if the performance degrades and falls down the agreed level, penalties and the corrective measures to be undertaken.

5   Development of Model

5.1   SLA Lifecycle

Ron and Aliko (2001) defines the life cycle of SLA cycle using three phases. Firstly, the creation phase, in which the customers find service provider who matches their service requirements. Secondly, the operation phase, in which a customer has read-only access to the SLA. Thirdly, the removal phase, in which SLA is terminated and all associated configuration information is removed from the service systems.

Using this model as a base, we propose the improvisation in the SLA life cycle by adding more phases to get into more details. The mapping between the base model and the proposed model is given in Table 1.

This section discusses the phases of the Proposed SLA life cycle (Fig. 1).

Discover Service Provider: One of the most fascinating aspects of the cloud is the cost effectiveness and easy entry and exit freedom. The organizations are now looking for cloud because they want to transfer and manage their IT resources to cloud, which helps their business to achieve the objectives efficiently. As their exist many types of cloud, each providing different types of services to the user. Organizations have to choose service provider according to their needs and demands. Discovering Service

Table 1. Mapping of base and proposed SLA phases

Base model phases	Proposed model phases
Creation phase	Discover service provider, initial specification
Operation phase	Activation
	Measure the performance
	Compare the performance with initial specification
	To manage the existing service or modify
Removal phase	Apply penalty
	Continue servicing with the service provider
	Terminate

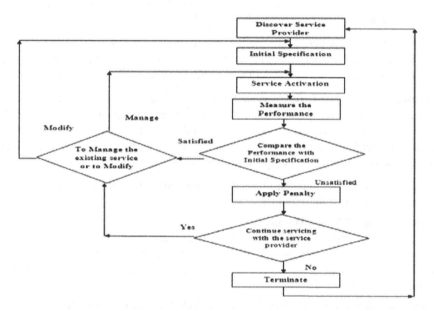

Fig. 1. Proposed SLA life cycle

Provider from the existing many is a very tedious task because different service provider have different pricing technique, performance parameters and service level agreement.

Initial Specification: Specification is a task that serves as a communication abet and disagreement preventing tool. It specifies services provided by the service provider which serves the needs of the customer. It specifies metrics for measuring the services so that cost for the service can be calculated, expectations from the service can be measured and conflicts can be prevented between service provider and service consumer. Initial specification defines the services, behavioral expectations, performance measurement in an unambiguous way.

Service Activation: The negotiated services are now implemented; consumer uses the services provided by the service provider according the business need of the customer.

Measure the Performance: Third party may be involved in measuring the service performances. The level of services agreed by the customer and service provider are monitored and measured. The level of service objective boundary has to be clearly mentioned so that any unfulfillment of any service can be easily identified.

Compare the Performance with Initial Specification: The measured services are compared to the agreed initial specification, if the customer is satisfied for the services received; he pay as he uses, and provider receives the cost for provision of the services so that there exist no conflicts between them.

To Manage the Existing Service or Modify: When the customer is satisfied with the services, he maintains and continues the relationship according to his need. The customer may wish to obtain the defined services or he may require to modify the existing services and accordingly SLA may be redefined.

Apply Penalty: If the performance of the service is not according to the agreed level specified in the Initial specification and the cloud consumer may be dissatisfied with services of the cloud service provider then the penalty is applied to the service provider.

Continue Servicing with the Service Provider: Cloud consumer has to decide to continue the services from the same provider, if he wants to continue, he may wants to get the predefined services or may wish to modify the services, accordingly cloud service provider helps to provide the service. On the other hand cloud consumer may want to discontinue with service provider, so requests to terminate the services.

Terminate: During termination all related configuration information is deleted from the service systems of the provider.

Proposed Secured Trust Model
The proposed Secured Trust SLA model consists of the phases of the SLA life cycle and also provides confidentiality, authenticity and integrity solution, the proposed model also contains the SLA and Service performance monitoring system to maintain the quality of service (Fig. 2).

Cloud Providers: are those who possess cloud infrastructure and provides cloud services such as IAAS, PAAS, SAAS to the cloud consumer.

Cloud Consumer: are those who uses the services provided by the cloud providers according to their business needs.

End User: are those who uses the services provided by the cloud consumers.

Phase I - Discover Service Provide: Information Centre: There can be many cloud service providers and cloud consumers will not have any information about the existence of cloud service providers unless the service providers advertise about themselves. Advertising about their cloud services can be done in a common place called "Information Centre" by registering themselves. At present there is no such common Information centre which records the details of the cloud services provided by the service provider. The information Centre has to generate an identification code for each cloud provider who gets registered, and has to collect the Contact details, Service template pool and calculates and generates the Reputation of Service Provider by taking input from the Cloud Consumer.

Contact Details: Contact details should have the information and method to contact the Service Provider.

Service Template Pool: It is a set of service templates which contain different predefined services, where the cloud consumer can choose a Service Template or can customize the service according to his business requirement.

Reputation of Service Provider: Reputation of Service Provider has to contain a numerical digit provided by the consumer for the quality of the services, attitude of the services and cost of the services provided by the provider. The cloud consumer will choose a particular provider from the list in the Information centre. Now the Cloud Service Provider has to provide contact details about their consumer so that the Information Centre collects the feedback credibility points about the service providers and calculates and display the Ranking or Reputation of the Service Provider.

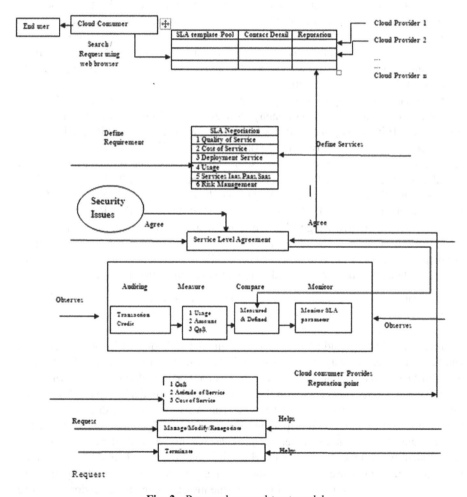

Fig. 2. Proposed secured trust model

Phase II - Initial Specification: SLA Negotiation: In this phase, the Cloud Consumer defines his business requirements and provider defines his services in front of the third party called Cloud Brokers, which maintains the unbiasedness. The Cloud Consumer can choose the service template from the template pool or can ask to customize the services according to the consumer's requirement.

Service Level Agreement: Finally an agreement is made between Cloud Consumer and Cloud Service Provider stating the services provided and not provided in a clear, simple, and precise language. Both the parties need to sign on the SLA negotiated documents. The metrics for each service is defined. The services are broadly categorized into Quality of service which may include reliability, availability, integrity etc., cost of service, deployment of service such as private, public, hybrid, Usage of each negotiated service, service types such as IAAS, PAAS and SAAS, risk measurements such as security, privacy, backup, recovery etc.

Security Issues: Confidentiality: One of the security issues concerned with the user data is confidentiality. To protect a user's data in the cloud, encryption is considered as influential tool that can be used efficiently. User can confidently utilize cloud services by knowing that their confidential data is protected by encryption. Confidentiality of data in the cloud can be achieved by cryptography. The main role of encryption is to secure data from attackers (Soofi et al. 2014).

Public key cryptography is an important means of ensuring confidentiality. It is also known as asymmetric key cryptography. It uses two different keys public key and a private key. Private Key needs to be kept secret with the CSP while public key is announced or shared publicly in the Information Centre. The advantage of public-key cryptography is increased security because private keys never need to be transmitted or revealed to anyone. One of the secured asymmetric algorithms is RSA. In this method; from one key, the data is encrypted while from the other the data is decrypted. This is one of the advantages of RSA. According to Soofi et al. (2014) RSA is the most popularly used asymmetric algorithm. The confidentiality of the data can be maintained by the above algorithm. Cloud service Providers or cloud user can take the help of certification Authority (CA) to distribute the public key without getting forged. CA is a federal or state organization that binds a public key to an entity and issues a certificate.

Authentication: Authentication is generally referred to as a mechanism that establishes the validity of the claimed identity of the individual (Ziyad and Rehman 2014). Verification of eligible users' credentials and protecting such credentials are part of main security issues in the cloud (Ahmed and Hossain 2014). Violation in these areas could lead to undetected security breach (Kumar 2012). The proposed Secured Trust model uses third party to authenticate the client. In this method, the cloud user who wishes to use the cloud services registers with the Authentication provider's Server (AS), which grants a user identity and a symmetric key. The AS maintains the database with the provided identities and the corresponding symmetric key. The cloud user who wishes to communicate with the cloud service provider has to get verified by using the registered identity with the AS. The AS verifies the cloud user, sends two messages. First message to the cloud user, which contains a message encrypted with the permanent symmetric key known only to the cloud user, the message contains a session key to be used between Cloud server, and a voucher for cloud server encrypted with symmetric key known between the AS and Cloud server and the time stamp. Second message to the cloud server which contains the session key to be used between the cloud users encrypted with symmetric key known only between the cloud server and the authentication server. The cloud user receives the encrypted message, decrypts the message with the symmetric key, extracts encrypted voucher and the session key to be used between cloud server and itself. The cloud user now uses the session key and encrypts the encrypted voucher and the time stamp received from the AS and sends to the cloud server, The cloud server receives two messages one from AS and other from cloud user. The cloud server first decrypts the message received from the AS with the symmetric key and extracts the session key, now decrypts the message received from the cloud user with the session key. The AS authenticates both the cloud user and the server with the symmetric keys. The introduction of third party authentication and identity management has the objective to strengthen the robustness of security in the concerned area which the cloud service provider itself is not capable of to deploy or offer.

Integrity: Data integrity refers to maintaining and assuring the accuracy and consistency of data over its entire life-cycle and is a critical aspect to the design, implementation and usage of any system which stores, processes, transmits or retrieves data (Data Integrity 2010). The data integrity provides the validity of the data, assuring the consistency or regularity of the data (Rawat et al. 2013). One important security problem is guaranteeing the integrity of remotely stored data (George and Sabitha 2013). In this proposed model the integrity of the data can be provided by the message digest method. To preserve the integrity of a encrypted message, the encrypted message is passed through an algorithm called a hash function. The hash function creates a compressed image of the encrypted message that can be used as a finger print. The message digest is created at the sender site. It is sent with the encrypted message to the receiver. To check the integrity of a encrypted message, the receiver creates the hash function again and compares the new message digest with the one received. If both are the same, the receiver is sure that the original encrypted message has not been changed.

Firewall: Firewall is a protection build around network so as to check ingress and egress of data packets across the firewall. It is a specially programmed machine. It is programmed to filter packets that flow through it (Gupta 2011). Firewall have been employed on large public networks for many years and are a great starting place in the development of a security strategy and cloud computing can be regarded as a public network (Ameen and Nourildean 2014). In our proposed secured trust SLA model, the cloud service provider implements the firewall. The unauthorized access from the extranet is filtered and from the intranet it filters the packet going to unauthorized user in the extranet.

Phase III - Activation: Cloud provider activates the negotiated services to the consumer, the consumer uses the services and both the parties observe the services.

Phase IV - Measure the Performance: The service transaction are credited and accounted. All the three parties cloud consumer, cloud brokers and cloud providers will have knowledge about service credentials. The measurement involves the usage of the service and accordingly amount for usage is calculated and quality of the service is measured according to the defined metrics.

Phase V - Compare the Performance with Initial Specification: The measured services are compared with the defined or negotiated SLA metrics.

Monitors: All the three parties monitors and evaluates the SLA parameters to check the under performances or default performances which may lead to unfulfillment of the defined service. According to the observation by the cloud consumer on quality of service, attitude of service and cost of service he provides points to the information centre to calculate the reputation of the service provider.

Phase VI - Manage/Modify SLA: If the cloud consumer is satisfied with the services received by the provider, he may request to manage the existing services or may request to renegotiate to modify defined services, and service provider helps the consumer to get the desired service.

Phase VII - Apply Penalty: If the performance of the services is not up to the defined standard then service provider may need to pay the penalty.

Phase VIII - Continue Servicing with the Service Provider: Cloud consumer has to decide to continue the services from the same provider, if he wants to continue, he may wants to get the predefined services or may wish to modify the services, accordingly cloud service provider helps to provide the service. On the other hand cloud consumer may want to discontinue with service provider, so requests to terminate the services.

Phase IX - Terminate: Finally the consumer may request to end the provision of services and all the configuration and data of the consumer are deleted from the providers environment.

6 Conclusion

The research proposes security and Trust model which provides the solution to the main security issues. The confidentiality of the cloud users data can be maintained by the Public Key Cryptography RSA, the authenticity of the cloud user and cloud providers can be obtained from the authenticating third part, the integrity of the data can be obtained by using message digest and filtration of the unauthorized user can be done by using firewall at the cloud service providers network. The trust on the Service provider is built because of informed & maintained transparency through SLA.

References

Abadi, H.R., Hafshejani, S.N., Zadeh, F.K.: Considering factors that affect users' online purchase intentions with using structural equation modeling. Interdisc. J. Contemp. Res. Bus. 3(8), 463–471 (2011)

Ahmed, M., Hossain, M.A.: Cloud computing and security issues in the cloud. Int. J. Netw. Secur. Appl. (IJNSA) 6(1), 25–36 (2014)

Ameen, S.Y., Nourildean, S.W.: Firewall and VPN investigation on cloud computing performance. Int. J. Comput. Sci. Eng. Surv. (IJCSES) **5**(2), 15–25 (2014)

Data Integrity, November 2010. https://en.wikipedia.org

George, R.S., Sabitha, S.: Survey on data integrity in cloud computing. Int. J. Adv. Res. Comput. Eng. Technol. (IJARCET) **2**(1), 123–125 (2013)

Gupta, P.C.: Data Communications and Computer Networks. PHI, New Delhi (2011)

Hussain, I., Ashraf, I.: Security issues in cloud computing - a review. Int. J. Adv. Netw. Appl. **6**(2), 2240–2243 (2014)

Joint, A., Baker, E., Eccles, E.: Hey, you, get off of that cloud? Comput. Law Secur. Rev. **25**, 270–274 (2009)

Kant, C., Sharma, Y.: Enhanced security architecture for cloud data security. Int. J. Adv. Res. Comput. Sci. Softw. Eng. **3**(5), 570–575 (2013)

Khorshed, T., Ali, A., Wasimi, S.: A survey on gaps, threat remediation challenges and some thoughts for proactive attack detection in cloud computing. Future Gener. Comput. Syst. **28**, 833–851 (2012)

Kumar, A.: World of cloud computing & security. Int. J. Cloud Comput. Serv. Sci. **1**(2), 53–58 (2012)

Panse, D., Haritha, P.: Multi-factor authentication in cloud computing for data storage security. Int. J. Adv. Res. Comput. Sci. Softw. Eng. **4**(8), 629–634 (2014)

Rao, S., Gujrathi, S., Sanghvi, M., Shah, S.: Analysis on data integrity in cloud environment. IOSR J. Comput. Eng. (IOSR-JCE), **16**(5) (2014). E-Issn: 2278-0661, P-Issn: 2278-8727

Rawat, S., Chowdhary, R., Bansal, D.A.: Data integrity of Cloud Data Storages (CDSs) in cloud. Int. J. Adv. Res. Comput. Sci. Softw. Eng. **3**(3), 585–592 (2013)

Ron, S., Aliko, P.: Service level agreements. Internet NG. Internet NG project (1999–2001) (2001). http://ing.ctit.utwente.nl/WU2/

Rubach, P.: Optimal resource allocation in federated metacomputing environments. Ph.D. thesis. Warsaw University of Technology, Electronics and Information Technology, Warsaw (2010)

Ryan, P., Falvey, S.: Trust in the clouds. Comput. Law Secur. Rev. **28**, 513–521 (2012)

Soofi, A.A., Khan, M., Fazal-E-Amin: Encryption techniques for cloud data confidentiality. Int. J. Grid Distrib. Comput. **7**(4), 11–20 (2014)

Subramanyam, K.J., Hari, K.K.: The Proceedings of the International Conference on Information Engineering, Management and Security (2014)

Talib, A.: Ensuring security, confidentiality and fine-grained data access control of cloud data storage implementation environment. J. Inf. Secur. **6**, 118–130 (2015)

Ziyad, S., Rehman, S.: Critical review of authentication mechanisms in cloud computing. IJCSI Int. J. Comput. Sci. Issues **11**(3), 145–149 (2014)

Dimensionality Reduction by Distance Covariance and Eigen Value Decomposition

S. Nithya$^{(\boxtimes)}$ and A. Salim

College of Engineering Trivandrum, Thiruvananthapuram, Kerala, India
haripriya.nithya@gmail.com, salim.mangad@gmail.com

Abstract. Dimensionality reduction is the transformation of high-dimensional data into a meaningful representation of reduced dimension. In this paper, we investigate how much dimensionality reduction can be achieved with distance covariance and eigen value decomposition. The proposed method starts with data normalization, calculation of euclidean distances matrices of each attributes, and a recentralization followed by eigen value decomposition on the distance covariance matrix. We repeated experiment with a different normalization technique. Applied these reduction techniques on few public data sets, and results were compared with that of conventional Principal Component Analysis. The distance covariance matrix for dimension reduction yields better performance than that of PCA on the basis of the classification efficiency parameters.

Keywords: Dimensionality reduction · Distance covariance

1 Introduction

The advent of information technology and advances in data collection during the past few decades have led to an information overload or infobesity in most field of scientific research and development. Researchers working in diverse domains face larger and larger observations on a daily basis [1]. Such datasets, in contrast with smaller ones, face new and bigger challenges in data analysis because such an uncontrollable flood of data overwhelms us. The term *curse of dimensionality* or *Hughes effect* is used to refer various phenomena that arise when analyzing and organizing data in high-dimensional spaces [2]. Data processing with high dimensions incur higher computational overhead and complexity.

Dimensionality reduction is of great need in such a situation because it increase efficiency, reduce measurement cost, storage and computation cost and it leads to ease of interpretation and modelling. It is useful in visualizing data and discovering a compact representation. Reducing the number of dimensions helps to separate the important features from the less important ones and provides additional understanding of the nature of data. Ideally, the reduced representation of data should have a

© Springer Nature Singapore Pte Ltd. 2017
M. Singh et al. (Eds.): ICACDS 2016, CCIS 721, pp. 112–122, 2017.
DOI: 10.1007/978-981-10-5427-3_12

dimensionality that corresponds to the intrinsic dimensionality of the data. The intrinsic dimensionality of data is the minimum number of parameters needed to account for the observed properties of the same [3].

2 Related Work

Dimensionality reduction techniques can be broadly classified into linear and non-linear dimensionality reduction techniques. These methods of dimension reduction produce a low dimensional mapping of original high dimensional data that preserves some feature of interest in the data.

Pearson in 1901 introduced the Principal Component Analysis (PCA), also known as *Karhunen-Love transform*, for dimension reduction [4]. PCA derive new variables that are linear combinations of original variables and which are uncorrelated. Covariance between all the dimensions are computed and first few eigen vectors of the covariance matrix is calculated. These eigen vectors represent the prominent features of the input data. It is useful in reducing dimensionality and finding new, informative, uncorrelated features. However, this is a method of linear dimensionality reduction technique and may not be adequate for non-linear data analysis. In addition, it may not be good at data clustering. Also, PCA is based on the assumption that most of the information is contained in those directions where input data variance is maximum. This becomes a disadvantage of PCA because of the fact that the directions maximizing variance do not always maximize information.

Multi-Dimensional Scaling (MDS) is one of the several multivariate techniques which achieves a lower dimensional representation of data, while trying to preserve the distances between data points [5]. The input data for MDS is in the form of distance matrix representing the distances between pairs of objects. Given n, items in a p-dimensional space and an $n * p$ matrix of proximity measures among the items. Multidimensional scaling (MDS) produces a k-dimensional, $k \leq p$, representation of the items such that the distances among the points in the new space maintains the proximities in the data. There are various MDS methods, differing in the types of metrics used. But, MDS is difficult in representing small distances corresponding to local structure.

Tenenbaum et al. introduced a non-linear dimension reduction method called Isomap or Isometric Feature Mapping [6]. Isomap combines the major algorithmic features of PCA and MDS such as computational efficiency and global optimality. It builds on classical MDS but seeks to preserve the intrinsic geometry of the data by considering geodesic manifold distances between all pairs of data points, instead of Euclidean distances. Geodesic distances represent the shortest path distance between the objects. Algorithm first constructs a neighbourhood graph by determining neighboring data points, either by choosing all points in a fixed radius or by finding the K nearest neighbors. Later the shortest path between two nodes is computed using Floyd's algorithm or Dijkstra's algorithm. Then, lower dimensional embedding is constructed using Classical MDS. Isomap is considered as a Global approach, which maintains the closeness and nearness properties of objects.

An improved version of Isomap called S-Isomap or Supervised Isomap [7] is another nonlinear dimensionality reduction technique. When Isomap is applied to real-world data, it shows limitations, such as being sensitive to noise. S-Isomap utilizes the class information to do the non-linear dimensionality reduction. In this method, the neighbourhood graph of input data is constructed according to a certain kind of dissimilarity between data points, which is designed to integrate class information. This makes S-Isomap a robust technique.

Fisher developed LDA or Linear Discriminant Analysis [8]. Objective of LDA is to project data in such a way that separation between classes is maximized and the class discriminatory information is preserved. LDA and PCA look for linear combinations of variables, which best explains the data. LDA explicitly attempts to model the differences between the classes of data.

Distance covariance, introduced by Szekely et al. in 2005 is an elegant contribution to the statistical theory, which measures the degree of any kind of relationship between two vectors of arbitrary dimensions p and q [9, 10]. Distance covariance was introduced to address deficiency of Pearson correlation, where there are chances of zero value for dependent variables. It is a class of multivariate dependence coefficients applicable to random vectors of arbitrary and not necessarily equal dimension. They are analogues to product-moment covariance, which is a measure of linear correlation between two variables [11, 12]. Correlation equal to zero (uncorrelatedness) does not imply independence while a zero distance correlation imply independence.

3 Proposed Method

PCA and MDS are two of the widely used feature extraction techniques for dimensionality reduction. The first one make use of the data covariance and the latter method rely on distance between data points. PCA retain features with largest variance. The idea of *distance covariance* combines the distance as well as dependence between data points. We propose a novel method for dimension reduction, by making use of distance covariance as a measure. Also we propose a second method by altering the pre-processing step of PCA and repeated testing, then compared the performance.

3.1 Dimension Reduction with Distance Covariance (DRD)

Proposed idea of applying distance covariance for dimension reduction is depicted in Algorithm 1. Initially, input raw data is mean centered by subtracting column mean

```
Algorithm 1: DRD
    Data: Input data with number of instances
          n and dimension p
    Result: Data of dimension k, where k<<p
    begin
    Read input data in the form of an n*p matrix, M
          // n: no.of instances, p: no.of attributes
    Subtract column mean from each element to get M'
    For i = 1 to Column_Max
     For j = 1 to i
                    //Column_Max is the number
                    of dimensions p of M'
       Dᵢⱼ = Dⱼᵢ = Distance_Covariance(Xᵢ, Yⱼ)
                //distance covariance of the
                    pairwise attributes of M'
      end for
    end for
    Eigen(D) //Compute eigen vectors of the
                    distance covariance matrix D
    Sort the eigen vectors in the decreasing order
    of eigen values
    Select the top k eigen vectors, that correspond
    to the largest k eigen values and let that matrix
    be W
    Compute reduced dimension data set O = Wᵀ * M'ᵀ
    end.
```

from each element and distance covariance matrix is computed. Distance covariance matrix is obtained by performing series of matrix operations, which starts with calculation of euclidean distance matrix of each set of attributes. Then, it is re-centered using row mean, column mean and grand mean. Eigen values and vectors are computed on resultant distance covariance matrix and vectors are sorted in the descending order based on eigen values. The top k principal components are vectors corresponding to top k eigen values, where k is far less than actual dimension of the data. See Algorithm1 for details.

The method of finding Distance_Covariance is explained in Algorithm 2.

```
Algorithm 2: Distance_Covariance
      Data: A pair of attribute values (X,Y) of
            all observations, {Xi ; i = 1,2 ..n},
            {Yi ; i = 1,2 ..n}
      Result: Distance covariance value of the two
             input attributes
    begin
    Calculate euclidean distance matrices of
    attributes    (X,Y), where,
    For i = 1 to n
       For j = 1 to n
          aij = (Xi - Xj)1/2
          bij = (Yi - Yj)1/2
          //a and b are the n*n euclidean
             distance matrices of X and Y respectively
       end for
    end for
    For i = 1 to n
       Find the ith row mean of matrix a to Ri
       For j = 1 to n
         Raij = Rj
         //Ra is the n*n matrix of row mean of matrix a
       end for
    end for
    For i = 1 to n
       Find the ith column mean of matrix a to Ci
       For j = 1 n
           Caji = Ci //Ca is the n*n matrix of
                    column mean of matrix a
       end for
    end for

    For i = 1 to n
      For j = 1 to n
        Sa = Sa + aij
      end for
    end for
    a.. = (1/n2) Sa
       //a.. is n*n matrix of mean of all elements
          of the distance matrix a

    For i = 1 to n
       Find the ith row mean of matrix b to Ri
       For j = 1 to n
         Rbij = Rj
         //Rb is the n*n matrix of row mean of matrix b
       end for
    end for
```

```
For i = 1 to n
   Find the iᵗʰ column mean of matrix b to Cᵢ
   For j = 1 n
      Cbⱼᵢ = Cᵢ //Cb is the n*n matrix of
                   column mean of matrix b
   end for
end for

For i = 1 to n
   For j = 1 to n
      Sb = Sb + bᵢⱼ
   end for
end for
b.. = (1/n²) Sb
   //b.. is n*n matrix of mean of all elements
      of the distance matrix b
Define the re-centered matrices, A and B
   Aᵢⱼ = a - Ra - Ca + a.. and   Bᵢⱼ = b - Rb - Cb + b..
Compute squared distance covariance,
```

$$\hat{v}(X,Y) = \frac{1}{n^2} \sum_{i,j=1}^{n} Aij * Bij$$

```
Return DCov(X,Y) = v²(X,Y)
end.
```

3.2 Dimension Reduction by Double Centering the Data (DRR)

We propose a new dimension reduction method by double centering the data. This is achieved by a new pre-processing step to the conventional PCA approach. Rather than just normalizing data along the column by subtracting the column mean from each attribute, in DRR, data is centered by the row mean, column mean and grand mean. Data is re-centered here. Covariance matrix computation and eigen value decomposition steps are same as that of PCA. Dimension reduction by double centering the data (DRR) is depicted in Algorithm 3.

3.3 Datasets for Validation

To validate the proposed algorithm, we used data sets collected from UCI machine learning repository [13]. The data sets collected are an Ionosphere data set and Ozone depletion data set.

Ionosphere data set consists of 351 instances of radar collected data which includes 35 attributes in total. All attributes are numeric, except the class attribute. The 35ᵗʰ attribute is the class attribute, which is either *Good* or *Bad*. *Good* indicates instances that has some type of structure in the ionosphere where as *Bad* are those signals that pass through the ionosphere.

```
Algorithm 3: DRR
    Data: Input data with number of instances
          n and dimension p
    Result: Data of dimension k, where k<<p
  begin
    Read input data in the form of an n*p matrix, M
         // n: no.of instances, p: no.of attributes
    Subtract column mean from each element to get M'
    For i = 1 to n
        Find the iᵗʰ row mean of matrix M to Rᵢ
        For j = 1 to n
            Rmᵢⱼ = Rᵢ
            // Rm is the n*n matrix of row mean
               of matrix M
        end for
    end for
    For i = 1 to n
        Find the iᵗʰ column mean of matrix M to Cᵢ
        For j = 1 to n
            Cmᵢⱼ = Cᵢ
            // Cm is the n*n matrix of row mean
               of matrix M
        end for
    end for
    For i = 1 to n
        For j = 1 to n
            Sm = Sm + Mᵢⱼ
        end for
    end for
    m.. = (1/n²)Sₘ  // m.. is n*n matrix of mean of
                    all elements of distance matrix M
    Define re-centered matrix, M'
    M'ᵢⱼ = M - Rm - Cm + m..
    D = Covariance_Matrix(M')
       //Compute covariance matrix of M'
    Compute eigen vectors of D
    Sort the eigen vectors in the decreasing order
    of eigen values
    Select the top k eigen vectors, that correspond
    to the largest k eigen values and let that matrix
    be W
    Compute reduced dimension data set O = Wᵀ * M'ᵀ
  end.
```

A total of 73 attributes and 1050 observations are there in the Ozone level detection data set. Attributes consists of a class attribute to differentiate between an *ozone day* and *normal day*. Attributes mainly details about variation in temperature as well as solar radiation.

4 Results and Discussions

The data sets were processed with PCA, DRD and DRR methods and the results were tested for classifier performance using the open source machine learning tool, Weka. The performance measures includes classification Accuracy, Precision and Recall. The Percentage of correctly classified instances by a classifier, is called as accuracy [14]. The fraction of retrieved instances that are relevant are termed to be precision and fraction of relevant instances that are retrieved is called recall.

The procedure for dimension reduction is all about reducing the number of attributes and hence to alleviate the issue of processing overhead, without much disgrace of performance. Thus we tested and verified the performance in terms of Accuracy, Precision and Recall when the total attributes of the data are reduced to lesser number of principal components. Dissection of the test results in this manner is to check whether the reduction in dimension would degrade the performance of transformed data set. Following are the tabular representations of classification efficiency of top components after dimension reduction on two data sets and their comparisons and explanations.

Table 1 details the performance of Ozone depletion data set after dimension reduction tested under the J.48 classification method. When top 70 components, after dimension reduction are used to test under the J.48 classifier, accuracy is greater than 98% for all three methods. The top 50 components, after dimension reduction, provides about 97% accuracy on an average (considering all the three methods of DR). When we reduce the dimension from 73 to 10, accuracy is maximum for DRD data and is equal to 97.33%. If the dimension is further reduced to 5, by taking only top 5 components, accuracy is 95.14% for DRD data and 95.62% for DRR. An important observation to be considered here is that, when the components are reduced to less than 15% of the original, there is no drastic drop in accuracy of DRD scheme. This indicates that for ozone deletion data, the reduced dimension of just 15% of original is giving sufficiently good results. Usefulness of any dimension reduction method lies in providing maximum accuracy when the total components are reduced to minimum.

Table 1. Comparison of J.48 classifier performance of top components of Ozone_Depletion

	Method	Top 70 components	Top 50 components	Top 30 components	Top 20 components	Top 10 components	Top 5 components
Accuracy	PCA	98.86%	97.71%	97.62%	96.10%	95.62%	95.14%
	DRD	98.29%	97.43%	97.52%	97.62%	97.33%	95.14%
	DRR	98.47%	98.48%	98.47%	95.90%	96.10%	95.62%
Precision	PCA	0.988	0.976	0.975	0.959	0.952	0.905
	DRD	0.982	0.973	0.975	0.976	0.973	0.905
	DRR	0.984	0.984	0.986	0.953	0.959	0.952
Recall	PCA	0.989	0.977	0.976	0.961	0.956	0.951
	DRD	0.983	0.974	0.975	0.976	0.973	0.951
	DRR	0.985	0.985	0.986	0.959	0.961	0.956

Similar is the case of precision. When top 70 components are kept and calculated the precision, it is greater than 0.98 for all three methods. If dimension is reduced to 10, DRD data is classified under J.48 with precision of 0.973 which is greater than that of PCA and DRR. On reducing dimension to five, PCA and DRD data provides precision of 0.905 and DRR data gives precision of 0.952. It is clear that that there is no much tarnish of performance in terms of precision as well for DRD and DRR.

Table 1 also shows how recall value changes with reduction in dimension. DRD keeps recall value greater than 0.97 even if we reduce the dimension to 10% of the original. If it is reduced to just five by picking up top five components, recall is 0.951 for DRD which is same as that of PCA. At the same time DRR is having recall of 0.956, which is the maximum with five components.

Table 2 tabulates the performance of proposed dimension reduction methods on Ionosphere data set, which contains 35 attributes in total and tested under J.48 classifier. Performance efficiencies are tested for top 33, 30, 20, 15 and top 10 components respectively.

Table 2. Comparison of J.48 classifier performance of top components of Ionosphere Dataset

	Method	Top 33 components	Top 30 components	Top 20 components	Top 15 components	Top 10 components
Accuracy	PCA	99.15%	97.72%	96.86%	97.44%	93.16%
	DRD	98.01%	98.01%	97.44%	97.43%	98.58%
	DRR	98.01%	98.29%	97.44	97.15	95.72
Precision	PCA	0.991	0.975	0.969	0.974	0.932
	DRD	0.98	0.98	0.974	0.974	0.986
	DRR	0.98	0.983	0.974	0.972	0.958
Recall	PCA	0.991	0.974	0.969	0.974	0.932
	DRD	0.98	0.98	0.974	0.974	0.986
	DRR	0.98	0.983	0.974	0.972	0.957

When the total 35 attributes are reduced to 30 top components, accuracy provided by the DRD and DRR are 98.01% and 98.29% respectively, which is higher than PCA. If we intend to keep only top 15 components, all the three methods on an average gives accuracy of 97.3%. When only the top 10 components are picked, DRD method of dimensionality reduction yields maximum accuracy of 98.5% for J.48 classifier. Visible change in performance can be observed when we reduce the components from 30 to 10. As the dimension reduces to much lesser number accuracy obtained with DRD and DRR are much better than that of PCA.

If the dimension is reduced from 35 to 20 by picking up top twenty components, precision obtained under J.48 for DRD and DRR are the same and is equal to 0.974. PCA data is classified with the precision of 0.969 in this case. Now, when we reduce dimension to just 10, maximum precision is obtained for the DRD data and is equal to 0.986, while for DRR it is 0.958. Performance in terms of precision value is always greater than 0.97 for DRD and DRR even if we reduce dimensions to lesser number. It is not the case of PCA because, after reducing dimension to 10 precision obtained is 0.932, which is minimum among the three.

Change in recall value is almost similar here. If all the components of the transformed data are kept, PCA data gives a recall value of 0.991 for J.48. Recall is 0.98 for DRD and DRR at the same time. As the dimension goes down to less than 15, recall is maximum for DRD data and is greater than 0.97. When the dimension is reduced to ten, recall obtained with DRD is 0.986 and it is 0.97 for DRR. PCA holds the minimum value of recall in this case.

5 Conclusion

Distance covariance is a simple procedure involving matrices and Euclidean distances between sample data points. The proposed methods for dimensionality reduction, DRD and DRR, were tested using two different data sets on J.48 classification model. The results obtained in terms of classification accuracy, precision and recall are promising in all the test cases, even after testing with variety of classifiers which are not tabulated in this paper. Also, the classifier efficiency of DRD and DRR are better than that of PCA. Thus, it is a valuable, practical, and natural tool in data analysis and inference along with the consideration of intrinsic geometry of the system.

References

1. Cunningham, J.P., Ghahramani, Z.: Linear dimensionality reduction: survey, insights, and generalizations. J. Mach. Learn. Res. **16**, 2859–2900 (2015)
2. Houle, M.E., Kriegel, H.-P., Kröger, P., Schubert, E., Zimek, A.: Can shared-neighbor distances defeat the curse of dimensionality? In: Gertz, M., Ludäscher, B. (eds.) SSDBM 2010. LNCS, vol. 6187, pp. 482–500. Springer, Heidelberg (2010). doi:10.1007/978-3-642-13818-8_34. ISBN 978-3-642-13817-1
3. Tsai, F.S., Chan, K.L.: Dimensionality reduction techniques for data exploration. IEEE (2007). 1-4244-0983-7/0
4. Pearson, K.: On lines and planes of closest fit to systems of points in space. Philos. Mag. Ser. B **2**(11), 559–572 (1901)
5. Cox, T., Cox, M.: Multidimensional Scaling, 2nd edn. Chapman & Hall, New York (2001)
6. Tenenbaum, J., de Silva, V., Langford, J.: Global geometric framework for nonlinear dimensionality reduction. Science **290**, 2319–2323 (2000)
7. Geng, X., Zhan, D.-C., Zhou, Z.-H.: Supervised nonlinear dimensionality reduction for visualization and classification. IEEE Trans. Syst. Man Cybern.-Part B Cybern. **35**(6), 1098–1107 (2005)
8. Fisher, R.A.: The use of multiple measurements in taxonomic problems. Ann. Eugen. **7**(2), 179–188 (1936)
9. Szekely, G.J., Rizzo, M.L.: Brownian distance covariance. Ann. Appl. Stat. **3**(4), 1236–1265
10. Cowleyand, B., Vinci, G.: Summary and discussion of: brownian distance covariance. Stat. J. Club 36–825
11. Szekely, G.J., Rizzo, M.: On the uniqueness of distance covariance. Stat. Probab. Lett. **82**(12), 2278–2282 (2012)

12. Lyons, R.: Distance covariance in metric spaces. Ann. Probab. **41**(5), 3284–3305 (2013)
13. Ics.uci.edu: Donald Bren School of Information and Computer Sciences @ University of California, Irvine (2015). http://www.ics.uci.edu
14. Srivastava, S.: Weka: a tool for data preprocessing, classification, ensemble, clustering and association rule mining. Int. J. Comput. Appl. **88**(10), (2014). (0975-8887)

Exploration of GBP2MP Network Performance for Next Generation Using Artificial Neural Network (ANN)

Sanjeev Verma[✉] and Anita Thakur

Amity School of Engineering & Technology, Amity University, Noida, India
Verma.sanjeev1992@gmail.com, athakur@amity.edu

Abstract. New era of world needed fast communication network for that optical fiber communication is promising solution. Optical networks are used in closed systems to open systems for various application like video on demand, voice over internet, video conference and real time broadcast. So fast performance criteria prediction of optical fiber network is time and cost saving solution. The aim of this paper is to determine the performance characteristic of Gigabit point to multipoint (GBP2MP) optical fiber network using artificial neural network. In artificial neural model (ANN), the input is frequency and fiber length in kilometres. Performance of optical network checked in term of minimum bit error rate (BER) parameters and results are discussed the performance of optical fiber network (OFN) when varying the length of fiber and frequency respectively.

Keywords: Optical passive network · Bit error rate · Artificial neural network

1 Introduction

Optical fiber communication is the process of spreading data from one place to other place through an optical fiber in the form of light. Fiber optical communication network are used for various application such as Live T.V broadcast, video on demand, voice over internet, video conference, local area network etc. Nowadays, Fiber has many advantages such as Data Security Immunity to electromagnetic interference (EMI), eliminating spark hazards, ease of installation, high Bandwidth over long distances but there are some disadvantages of optical fiber such as price, fragility, affected by chemicals and it requires special skills to install the network. Recently, optical networks have been evolving from closed systems to open systems, in which the optical layer is designed to allow transmitter/receiver add and drop without affecting the current structure. In Optical fiber networks, a GPON system is a bi-directional gigabit point-to-multipoint network architecture deploying optical access lines between a carrier's central office and customer sites [1]. There are several other techniques that provide fiber to the home, building, office, urban area, rural area etc. but GPON is considered as the strongest for widespread deployments. Because GPON is based on time division multiplexing (TDM) technique where downstream wavelength is used for digital and one downstream is used for analog video services [2]. The GBP2MP is a

© Springer Nature Singapore Pte Ltd. 2017
M. Singh et al. (Eds.): ICACDS 2016, CCIS 721, pp. 123–131, 2017.
DOI: 10.1007/978-981-10-5427-3_13

gigabit point to multipoint execution and its main purpose is to use a power splitter and an encryption to secure data. Gigabit Passive Optical Network (GPON) is defined by ITU-T recommendation series G.984.1 through G.984.4. G.984 standard series define general characteristics of GPON (G.984.1) as well as physical layer specification (G.984.2), transmission layer specification (G.984.3) and ONU (Optical Network Unit) management and control specification (G.984.4). GPON can transport not only Ethernet, but ATM and TDM (including PSTN, ISDN, E1 and E3) traffic by using GPON encapsulating method (GEM) [3].

Large data handling is difficult in optical fiber network such as a variation in kilometres, frequency, Min. BER, Eye Height, threshold, dispersion and their effects on communication. It needed a system which can easily handle the large amount of data and predict the performance of the system in less time and cost effective. For this Artificial Neural Network is optimal solution. In this study ANN model is used for the exploration of the performance of GBP2MP network. Artificial Neural Network is the manmade network that mimic the human brain and hence it's called the "Artificial". ANN model can handle non-linear relationship of input output data [4]. The best quality of ANN is that it is Non-parametric model which does not require higher background of statistic as required by the statistical model. Generally, ANN system is used with the Back propagation (BP) learning algorithm for predicting problems and solving numerous problems [5, 6]. The main disadvantage of back propagation (BP) is its slow convergence but it provides the convergence guarantee. In earlier research, main focus putted on wavelength, differential phase-shift-keying (DPSK) systems, Dense Wavelength Multiplexing [7, 8]. In this study simulation set up of GBP2MP is done in software "OPTISYSTEM". Which is a simulation system for designing, testing and intensification of optical link and optical signal noise ratio (OSNR), chromatic dispersion (CD) and polarization mode dispersion (PMD). Artificial Neural Network is used to predict the performance analysis of optical fiber communication network at varying the length and frequency of fiber.

This paper is organized as follows. Section 2, discussed the simulation setup of proposed network, Sect. 3 cover briefly working and architecture of artificial neural network model. Section 4 shows simulation result and performance graph. Short concluding remark is given in Sect. 5.

2 Simulation Setup

An efficient optical fiber communication network is proposed in this study which is trained using artificial neural network (ANN). In Sympathetic perception GBP2MP is generally a passive optical network (PON). The simulation set up of the network is made by using the software "OPTISYSTEM". In Fig. 1, shows the simulation set up that the transmitter section consists of PRB sequence, NRZ pulse Generator, CW laser and Mach-Zehnder modulator which is further surveyed by the Fiber Bragg's Grating (FBG). At receiver section used a Bessel optical filter, PIN photo detector, low pass Bessel filter and eye diagram analyzer to get the desired original signal and measured various parameters.

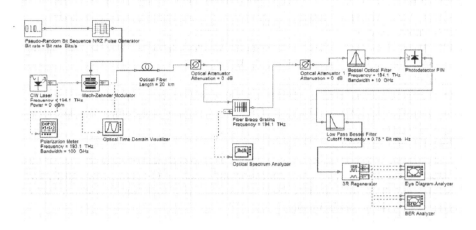

Fig. 1. Gigabit passive optical network (GBPON) simulation setup

2.1 Transmitter Section

In transmitter section, they consist of following components:

1. NRZ pulse generator
   Non Return to Zero(NRZ) modulator is binary code in line code system where one is represented by positive voltage and zero are represented by Negative voltage. Generally, we prefer NRZ over RZ because it RZ has low energy as compared to NRZ.
2. Mach-Zehnder Modulator
   The main purpose of using Mach-Zehnder Modulator is to control the amplitude of an optical wave in optical fiber networks. Generally, Mach-Zehnder Modulator is used in transmitter section of optical fiber networks, which divide the given inputs into two waveguide infero-meter armaments.
3. Continuous Wave (CW) Laser
   CW laser is a device which is generally used to emit an electromagnetic wave in continuous way from the device in which fields are spatially and temporarily intelligible in CW laser.
4. Optical Attenuator (OA)
   The main purpose of using optical attenuator is used to control or reduce the optical power signal in optical fiber networks in free space system and sometimes it is also known as optic fiber attenuator device.

2.2 Receiver Section

In receiver section, it is mainly designed to receive efficient signal having Min. BER, they consist of following components:

1. Bessel Filter
   Bessel filter(BF) is used to provide group delay and shaping factor to the received signal in the receiving section. Generally, it is comparable to Gaussian filter.
2. PIN Photo-detector
   PIN Photo-detector is used to pass more wavelength in receiver section having efficient optical fiber signal which is in light form.
3. Optical Regenerator
   Optical generator is used to identify optical signal which is in light form, convert them into desired electrical signal. Optical regenerator sometimes also knows as optical repeater.
4. Eye diagram Analyzer
   Eye diagram analyser is a test tool, which is used to calculate or measure the various parameter in optical fiber communication link such as Q-Factor, Min. BER, Eye height, threshold. It is mainly used when there is a high speed communication system exits in an environment.

3   Artificial Neural Model for GBP2MP Network

Neural Network model have ability to work with flexible functional form and universal functional approximator for prediction [9]. In this proposed study three-layer neural model is used for performance monitoring of GBP2MP Network. Figure 2 shows the neural network architecture for GBP2MP network. Input to the model is length of fiber and frequency and output is the minimum bit error rate of GBP2MP network. Middle layer is hidden layer where number of neuron are varied to get best performance result. Sigmoid Activation is used in proposed neural model. For learning of network supervised error back propagation (BP) algorithm is used. Back propagation is the most efficient learning algorithm, in which at the end of each iteration output error is propagated back to input adjusting the weight and biases. To overcome the slow

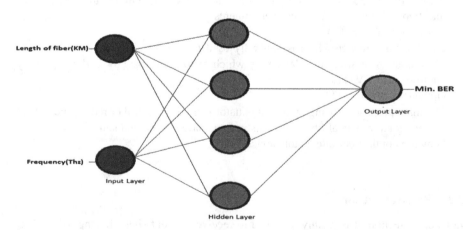

Fig. 2. Shows the neural network architecture for GBP2MP network

convergence rate of the back propagation algorithm, two parameters, learning rate and momentum can be adjusted. For training we implemented the Levenberg-Marquardt algorithm because of its rapid convergence.

3.1 Levenberg-Marquardt Algorithm

Levenberg-Marquardt (LM) algorithm is used to detects the local minimum of many local multivariate functions. Which is expressed as a sum of square of several non-linear and some of real valued functions. Levenberg-Marquardt (LM) become a standard algorithm for some problems of non-linear least squares, which is extensively used in the various applications for large Data-Fitting application. Generally, it is thought that LM is a combination of both Gauss-Newton method and Steepest descent method. Algorithm behaves as a steepest descent method when a current solution is far from a local minimum, converge is slow but guaranteed. Similarly, algorithm behaves as a Gauss-Newton method when a current solution is close to a local minimum and convergence is fast as compared to steepest descent method. LM is considered much faster algorithm than a Gradient descent (GD) algorithm but it is costlier than GD algorithm.

LM algorithm training method can be demonstrated in the following steps:

(1) User provide the initial guess for the parameter vector μ.
(2) After each iteration, parameter vector changes to $\mu + \beta$.
(3) To determine β, Eq. 1 is used

$$f\left(P_{i}, \mu + \beta\right) \approx f\left(P_{i}, \mu + Ji\ \beta\right)$$
$$J_{i} = \frac{\partial f\left(Pi,\ \mu\right)}{\partial \mu} \tag{1}$$

P_i = Input factor

(4) First order approximation of Eq. 1 is given as

$$\left(J^{T}J\right) \beta = J^{T}[Y - f(\mu)] \tag{2}$$

J = Jacobian matrix, α is the Levenberg's damping factor, τ is the weight vector that is to be find. The τ predicted how much change should be made in a network weight accomplished an improved solution.

Y and f are vectors with i^{th} component f (P_i, μ) and P_i.

(5) Lavenberg replaced with a damped version

$$\left(J^{T}J + \tau I\right) \beta = J^{T}[Y - f(\mu)] \tag{3}$$

Where I = Identity matrix

4 Results and Discussion

The transmitter section, which is designed with help of few components such as Pseudo-Random Bit sequence generator which have a bit rate of 2e+010 having order of 8, which is further connected to Non return to zero (NRZ) Generator having a sample rate of 7.4e+011, then Mach-Zehnder Modulator with excitation ratio of 30 db connected to optical fiber and CW Laser. The continuous wave laser having a frequency 194.1 THz produces a noise threshold of −100 db. The polarization meter which is connected to CW laser have frequency of 194.1 THz and bandwidth 100 GHz. The optical fiber having a length of L = 20 km with transmitted wavelength of 1550 nm, shows an attenuation 0.3 db/km, group delay of 0.3 ps/km.

The fiber Bragg's Grating functioned at a frequency of 194.1 THz by means of effective index 1.45 for restored communication. The Bessel optical filter operated at a frequency of 194.1 THz of bandwidth of 10 GHz is used in receiver section with almost zero insertion loss with PIN photo detector of 1 A/W responsivity responsible for obtain anticipated signals. In this paper simulation set up of GBP2MP is evaluated in "OPTISYSTEM" software. Their simulation result is in Table 1 which shows the comparison results of performance matrix of GBP2MP network with varying the frequency and length of fiber.

Table 1. Comparison of performance matrix of GBP2MP network

Length (km)	Frequency (THz)	Min. BER	Frequency (THz)	Min. BER	Frequency (THz)	Min. BER	Frequency (THz)	Min. BER
20	193.1	1.60951e−020	194.1	3.98552e−021	195.1	2.5594e−020	196.1	8.21438e−021
25	193.1	3.18314e−019	194.1	1.58061e−019	195.1	6.55621e−020	196.1	8.32498e−020
30	193.1	5.60283e−018	194.1	2.43522e−018	195.1	1.12774e−019	196.1	1.73403e−018
35	193.1	1.44445e−016	194.1	1.08397e−016	195.1	4.20143e−017	196.1	1.70366e−017
40	193.1	2.74574e−015	194.1	1.25124e−015	195.1	2.044213e−015	196.1	3.51015e−016
45	193.1	2.72545e−013	194.1	1.34926e−014	195.1	3.93182e−015	196.1	7.03234e−016
50	193.1	2.21226e−012	194.1	3.5223e−013	195.1	3.3667e−013	196.1	7.99708e−014

Figure 3 shows Eye diagram analyzer with varying the length of optical fiber (20 km to 50 km). For 50 km Min. BER is the order of 10^{-12}, q-factor of order of 8 a.u and an eye height of 33 a.u.

In neural model nftool fitting tool of MATLAB is used for GBP2MP network. In fitting nftool the input layer, hidden layer and the activation function is assigned according to architecture of GBP2MP network. Length and frequency of fibre network is the input of network and output of network is Bit error rate. By changing the number of neuron in hidden layer we trained the network. Figure 4 shows the neural network training (nntraintool) which shows the proposed neural network architecture of GBP2MP network.

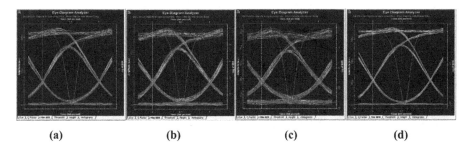

| | | | |
| (a) | (b) | (c) | (d) |

Fig. 3. Eye diagram analyzer for (a) 20 km (b) 30 km (c) 40 km (d) 50 km

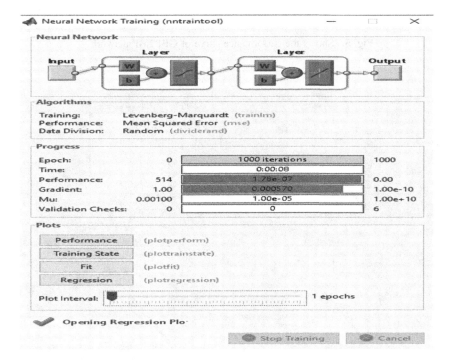

Fig. 4. Shows the neural network training of GBP2MP network

Best model is selected according to minimum mean square error. Minimum MSE is 2.091e−007 at 1000 epoch are achieved. Figure 5 shows the performance of GBP2MP network in term of mean square error with respect to number of iteration. The best fitting of model is predicted by regression graph which shows the targeted output is equal to actual output that is generated by neural network. Figure 6 shows the regression graph of proposed neural network model of GBP2MP network.

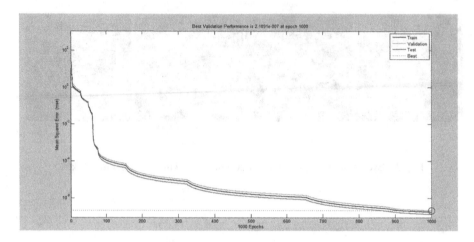

Fig. 5. Shows the performance curve of GBP2MP network

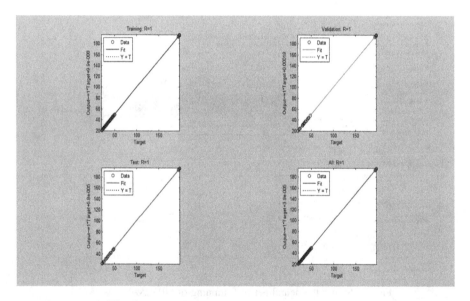

Fig. 6. Regression graph of proposed neural network

5 Conclusion

In this paper, GBP2MP network simulation is created in "OPTISYSTEM" software and their performance of network is explored by artificial neural networks with varying length and frequency of fiber. In simulation design, Kilometres are vary from 20 km to 50 km, similarly frequency varies as 193.1 THz, 194.1 THz, 195.1 THz and 196.1 THz. Here, kilometres and frequency is carry as input and Min. BER as output in

ANN model. Best performance is getting with 2.1091e−007 at epoch 1000, training regression is nearly equal to one. The qualitative analysis of signal is done by Eye Diagram Analyser by varying the length and frequency of fiber. Study shows that ANN model have capability to predicts the behaviour and performance of optical fiber network in fast and cost saving manner. It also opens the path for making better network with upcoming technique and design.

Acknowledgements. We would like to thanks Department of Electronics and Communication, Amity School of Engineering & Technology-Amity University Uttar Pradesh, for providing us resources and facilities for implementation this research.

References

1. Kim, H., et al.: An Electronics Dispersion Compensator (EDC) with an analog Eye Opening Monitor (EOM) for 125-Gb/s Gigabit Passive Optical Network (GPON) upstream links. IEEE Trans. Microw. Theory Tech. **55**, 2942–2950 (2007)
2. Llorente, R., Morant, M., Beltran, M., Pellicer, E.: Fully converged optical, millimetre-wave wireless and cable provision in OFDM-PON FTTH networks. In: 15th IEEE International Conference on Transparent Optical Networks (ICTON), pp. 1–4 (2013)
3. Gerstel, O., Cassata, R., Paraschis, L., Wakim, W.: Operational solutions for an Open DWDM layer. In: Presented at the Optical Fiber Communications (OFC) and the National Fiber Optic Engineers Conference (NFOEC) 09 March 2009
4. Güney, K., Erler, M., Sagiroglu, S.: Artificial neural networks for the resonant resistance calculation of electrically thin and thick rectangular microstrip antennas. Electromagnetics **20** (5), 387–400 (2000)
5. Thakur, A., Bhanot, S., Mishra, S.N.: Early diagnosis of ischemia stroke using neural network. In: Proceedings of the International Conference on Man-Machine Systems (ICoMMS), Malaysia (2009)
6. Patnaik, A., Anagnostou, D.E., Mishra, R.K., Christodoulou, C., Lyke, J.C.: Applications of neural networks in wireless communications. IEEE Antennas Propag. Mag. **46**, 130–137 (2004)
7. Davey, R.P., et al.: DWDM reach extension of a GPON to 135 km. J. Lightwave Technol. **24**, 29–31 (2006)
8. Jarajreh, M.A., Ghassemlooy, Z., Ng, W.P.: Improving the chromatic dispersion tolerance in long-haul fibre links using the coherent optical orthogonal frequency division multiplexing. IET Microw. Antennas Propag. **4**(5), 651–658 (2010)
9. Haykin, S.: Neural Networks. A Comprehensive Foundation, 2nd edn. Prentice Hall, Upper Saddle River (1999)

Hybrid Segmentation Technique Using Wavelet Packet and Watershed Transform for Medical Images

K. RajMohan[(✉)], G. Thirugnanam, and P. Mangaiyarkarasi

Department of Electronics and Instrumentation Engineering,
Annamalai University, Chidambaram, Tamil Nadu, India
ggtt_me@yahoo.com

Abstract. Image segmentation is necessary but significant element in less intensity image investigation, pattern recognition, and in robotic systems. It is one of the most complex and demanding tasks in image processing. Image segmentation is the process of separating an image into various regions such that each region is identical. This paper proposes a new medical image segmentation method that integrates multi-resolution wavelet packet decomposition with the watershed transform for MRI image. The wavelet packet transform (WPT) is applied to the input image, creating detail and approximation coefficients. If watershed technique alone is used for segmentation, then over cluster is present. To overcome this, the proposed technique which combines wavelet packet and watershed algorithm is developed. First, the wavelet packet transform is applied to produce multi-resolution images, followed by applying watershed for segmentation to the approximation sub-bands. Finally, Inverse WPT is implemented to obtain the segmented image. Due to wavelet packet decomposition, the quantity of the disturbance can be decreased and leads to a tough segmentation. This proposed work concludes that wavelet packet and watershed transform facilitate to get the elevated precision even in strident images.

Keywords: Magnetic resonance imaging · Wavelet packet transform · Watershed algorithm · Image segmentation

1 Introduction

Image segmentation is the division of an image into significant areas relies on uniformity [1]. The objective of this is to make things easier the depiction of an image into something that is further significant and easier to evaluate. It is applied to establish substance and borders in pictures. Attributes can be taken from images like buildings, roads, water bodies and vegetation etc. Though the performance of conventional segmentation techniques are restricted by shadow problems and noise leads to over-segmentation in few places, less segmentation in others, resulting in inferior precision. To prevail over these complications, inspecting the images at multi-resolution is being measured [2].

© Springer Nature Singapore Pte Ltd. 2017
M. Singh et al. (Eds.): ICACDS 2016, CCIS 721, pp. 132–139, 2017.
DOI: 10.1007/978-981-10-5427-3_14

A foremost crisis in watershed algorithm is stern above-segmentation due to the immense and variety of commotion inside the image. Two limitations in registering this technique and they are susceptivity to tough clamor and calculation necessities to combine these areas. This trouble is surmount once segmentation technique is incorporated in a multi-decree attitude [3].

2 Wavelet Packet Transform (WPT)

Two levels WPT analysis tree as shown in Fig. 1. The approximate image is steady when decomposition level increases [8]. On the other hand, embedding strength is decreased. So in this work, the input image is analyzed to two levels. In this technique,

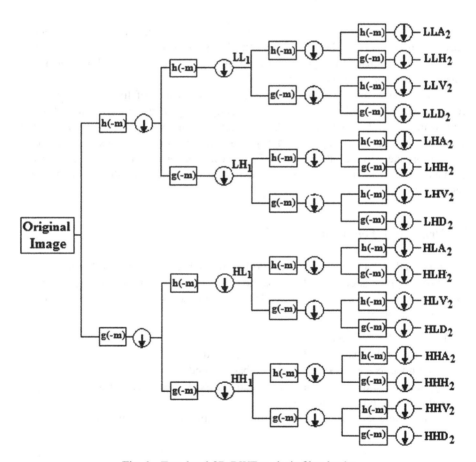

Fig. 1. Two level 2D DWT analysis filter banks

input image is analyzed to approximate image and 3 detail images. In WPT, the detailed coefficients like LH, HL and HH can be decomposed further as shown in Fig. 1. This furnishes an random pyramidal structure equivalent to WP bases.

This leads to narrower frequency bands at higher frequencies and assures the capture of the image significant points. For a input of 2N, it generates a 2j sets of sub-band co-efficient. Every set is down-sampled, band-pass filtered with added resolve in instance. Similarly, the same procedure can be extended to two dimensional analyses. It produces sixteen sub-bands from LLA_2 to HHD_2 as depicted in Fig. 1. This coefficient produces further decree in strength and to be perceived. Therefore, in this work WPT is projected to execute. To do this, the Haar wavelet is applied in this method, because it requires low calculation difficulty [7].

3 Watershed Algorithm

The watershed transform realizes the catchment basins and ridge lines in such a grayscale image. In stipulations of the setback related to image segmentation the key perception is to change the preliminary image into a different one whose catchment basins are the objects to identify [6].

In the image investigation, noise exclusion, exclusive of filtering the edge, is complicated. Classically, noise is specifying by sharp details in an image. Fourier transform generally restrain the sharp details constituent which is enviable, but decreases the edge unevenness. So applying Fourier transform for noise elimination is not appropriate. On the other hand, WPT allocates better in both spatial and spectral domains. Hence in this work, hybrid wavelet packet and watershed is applied for segmentation [4].

4 Proposed Technique

The proposed technique is Marker Controlled watershed segmentation. In this section, watershed segmentation is used to separate emotive items in an image. The watershed exists as catchment basins in an image [5]. The proposed Marker-controlled watershed segmentation process is (Fig. 2):

1. To assess the function of segmentation.
2. To evaluate the markers belongs to foreground.
3. To enumerate the markers belongs to background.
4. To modify the minima at the foreground and background marker locations so that segmentation utility is modified.
5. To determine the watershed transform of the modified segmentation.

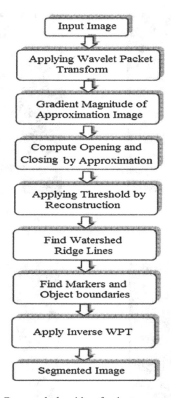

Fig. 2. Proposed algorithm for image segmentation

5   Result and Discussion

In this work, MRI brain input image of size 512×512 is considered. Primarily the input image is analyzed to two levels using WPT for the development of multi-resolution sub-bands. The input image and wavelet packet sub-bands are shown in Figs. 3 and 4 Gradient magnitude segmentation function is used in the approximation sub-band and the boundaries of the objects are shown in Fig. 5. Using watershed transform directly on the image outcome in over segmentation. Hence to avoid these further preliminaries such as marker calculations are given below.

To mark the foreground techniques called opening and closing by reconstruction are shown in Figs. 6, 7, 8, 9 and 10. The regional maxima are superimposed on input image for comparison is shown in Figs. 11 and 12. To compute background markers, the thresholding operation is performed to generate binary image as shown in Fig. 13. Now the surroundings is insipid by calculating the regions using watershed transform on the binary image. The resultant image has watershed ridge lines as shown in Fig. 14. Now the forefront and back ground markers are overlying on the input image to obtain the segmented output image as shown in Fig. 15. The segmented output image is converted to true color image for visualization purpose to identify the segmented thing as shown in Fig. 16 (Table 1).

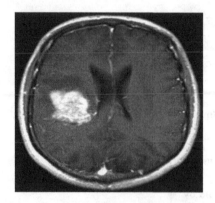

Fig. 3. Input image

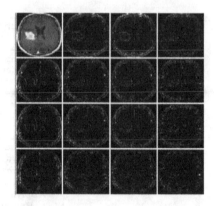

Fig. 4. Two level WPT coeffcients

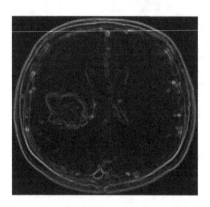

Fig. 5. Gradient magnitude

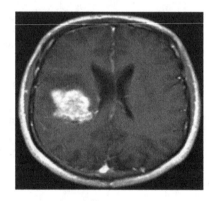

Fig. 6. Opening by approximation

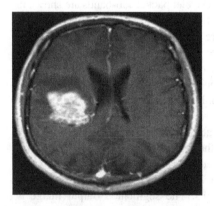

Fig. 7. Opening by reconstruction

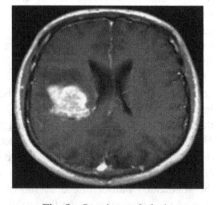

Fig. 8. Opening and closing

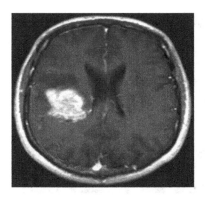

Fig. 9. Opening and closing by reconstruction

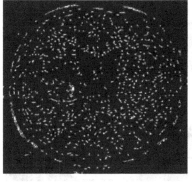

Fig. 10. Regional maxima of opening and closing by reconstruction

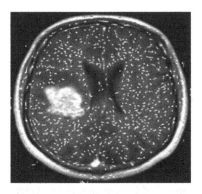

Fig. 11. Regional maxima on input image

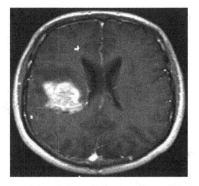

Fig. 12. Modified regional maxima on input image

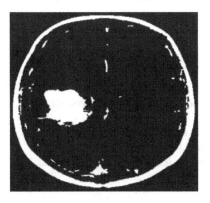

Fig. 13. Threshold opening-closing

Fig. 14. Watershed ridge lines

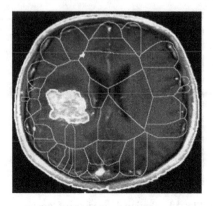

Fig. 15. Segmented output image

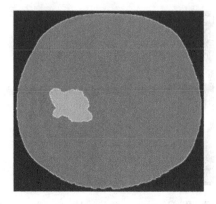

Fig. 16. Coloured watershed output

Table 1. Evaluation indices of hybrid wavelet transform and hybrid wavelet packet transform

Images	Wavelet and watershed transform	Wavelet packet and watershed transform
Completeness (%)	92.9856	96.4765
Correctness (%)	93.6882	97.7403
Quality (%)	93.9034	97.2341

6 Conclusion

In this work, an advance for image segmentation is described by merging the wavelet packet and watershed transforms. Watershed is extremely susceptible to blare and results in excess segmentation. To resolve this setback, the proposed transforms are synthesized for escalating the result precision. The simulation results reveal that this proposed technique can able to segment the object in accurate manner. The proposed Wavelet packet based scheme performs better for segmentation when compared to wavelet transform based segmentation.

References

1. Pal, N.R., Pal, S.K.: A review on image segmentation techniques. Patt. Recognit. **26**(9), 1277–1294 (1993)
2. Kim, H.J., Kim, E.Y., Kim, J.W., Park, S.H.: MRF model based image segmentation using hierarchical distributed, genetic algorithm. IEE Electron. Lett. **34**(25), 1394–1395 (1998)
3. Kim, J.B., Kim, H.J.: Multi-resolution based watersheds for efficient image segmentation. Patt. Recogn. Lett. **24**, 473–488 (2003)

4. Beucher, S., Meyer, F.: The morphological approach to segmentation: the watershed transformation. In: Mathematical Morphology in Image Processing. Marcel Dekker, New York (1993)
5. Haris, K., Efstratiadis, S.N., Maglaveras, N., Katsaggelos, A.K.: Hybrid image segmentation using watersheds and fast region merging. IEEE Trans. Image Process. **7**(12), 1684–1699 (1998)
6. Gies, V., Bernard, T.: Statistical solution to watershed over-segmentation. In: International Conference on Image Processing, pp. 1863–1866 (2004)
7. Ma, W.Y., Manjunath, B.S.: Edge flow: a technique for boundary detection and image segmentation. IEEE Trans. Image Process. **9**(8), 1375–1388 (2000)
8. Mallat, G.: A theory for multiresolution signal decomposition: the wavelet representation. IEEE Trans. Pattern Anal. Mach. Intell. **11**(7), 674–693 (1989)

Image Modelling: A Feature Detection Approach for Steganalysis

Anuj Rani[1(✉)], Manoj Kumar[2(✉)], and Payel Goel[1]

[1] Department of Computer Science, GLBITM, Greater Noida, India
Anuanuj1989@gmail.com, payalsmile86@gmail.com
[2] Departmet of Computer Science,
JIMS Engineering Management Technical Campus, Greater Noida, India
wss.manojkumar@gmail.com

Abstract. The most popular challenges in steganalysis is to identify the char-acterstics, to discover the stego-images. In this, we derive a steganalysis measure using Gaussian distribution, for image modeling. By using Gaussian distribution model the distribution of DCT coefficients and quantify a ratio of two Fourier coefficients of the distribution of DCT coefficients [9]. This derive steganalysis measure is evaluated against three steganographic methods i.e. first one is LSB (Least Significant Bit), the second one is SSIS (Spread Spectrum Image Steganography), and the last one is Steg-Hide tool, which is based on graph theoretic approach. Classification of image features dataset is done by using different classification techniques such as SVM.

Keywords: Steganography · Steganalysis · Gaussian-distribution · Stego-image · Cover-image · Laplace-distribution

1 Introduction

Steganography is the science that deals with covert communication [1]. This is done by hiding the message into some other media such as images, audio, video, text files, etc. The word steganography is taken from Greek language that splits into two words, i.e., 'steganos' and 'graphie' which means 'hidden' and 'writing' respectively. Thus, steganography means 'hidden writing.' The main aim of steganography is to keep off casting intuition from the transmission of the message.

Steganalysis is the complicated sequential process of finding the existence of hidden text or information which is not known while forensics refers to searching known hidden information in carrier-object. It is typical to find the existence of the hidden message as there are many steganographic techniques and tools that can be used for hiding the information. Even knowledge of the technique or tool used for hiding the information can be of no use in finding the actual message because some cryptography techniques might be used to encrypt the message.

Steganography and steganalysis these are two terms which are mainly used with information hiding process. Steganography deals with hiding the text whereas steganalysis is a method of detecting the hidden information. Steganalysis methods are broadly divided into two categories-specific and Universal which is also known as

© Springer Nature Singapore Pte Ltd. 2017
M. Singh et al. (Eds.): ICACDS 2016, CCIS 721, pp. 140–148, 2017.
DOI: 10.1007/978-981-10-5427-3_15

Blind Steganalysis. In steganalysis technique, the embedding technique is known and according to embedding technique steganalysis technique will be applied. But in universal or blind steganalysis, it works with any embedding technique not designed for specific embedding technique. The general framework for Blind Steganalysis is shown below in Fig. 1. In universal steganalysis, a classifier is used to detect the stego-images based on some features calculated from images using the different-different steganographic technique. When any steganographic technique is applied on cover-image some features of its gets violated.

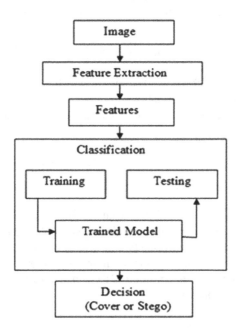

Fig. 1. General framework of Blind Steganalysis

There are various steganography techniques available for embedding the information in images. Steganography techniques can be categorized into: substitution method, transform domain methods, spread spectrum technique, statistical method, cover generation techniques and last one is distortion. In images, steganography can be done in different ways i.e. first one is image domain or spatial domain and the second one is transform domain or frequency domain. In the image domain, information is hidden in the intensity of the pixel directly but in the transform domain, first any transformation technique will be applied, and then information will be embedded in the image. For hiding the data different transform domain like DCT or DWT are used.

The main challenge in steganalysis is to identify the characteristics that are constant for cover images but vary after embedding process. Wavelet decomposition is used on images to capture higher-order statistics [2]. The reason behind, is to detect the difference between cover images and stego images while stego images are generated using different steganographic techniques. Various image quality metrics identified like

Spectral Phase, Cross Correlation, Image Fidelity and much more and these metrics are used to differentiate cover images and stego images [3]. For steganalysis of the JPEG images, the comparison is done between cover images and stego images by calculating the calibrated features from the same set of cover images and stego images [4].

Rather than using the predefined set of features, we derive a measure, which is the ratio of two Fourier coefficients of the distribution of DCT coefficients, modeled DCT coefficients by using Gaussian distribution [9]. In this approach, we are embedding the information in transform domain by choosing the DCT coefficients for hiding purpose. DCT coefficients preserve the first-order statistics in the embedding process.

Gaussian distribution is chosen because it has several advantages over another distribution.

- Gaussian distribution is important in statistics, because of Central Limit Theorem (CLT).
- Gaussian distribution is the only distribution which closed under multiplication, convolution, and linear transformations.
- It comes in machine learning, because of standard deviation and maximum entropy principle.

2 Image Modeling

This is the main challenge to identify the features, which are used to differentiate the cover image and stego image. Our approach is to analyze the frequency component of an image by quantifying the ratio of two Fourier coefficients of the distribution of DCT coefficients [9]. Hiding the information in frequency component reveals the clue whether any information is hidden or not. DCT coefficients are chosen because we are analyzing the frequency component.

2.1 Cover Images

In the frequency domain, let C be the cover image. Then the distribution of the DCT coefficients of C is modeled as a Gaussian,

$$f_c(x) = \frac{1}{\sigma\sqrt{2\pi}} e^{-(x-\mu)^2/2\sigma^2} \tag{1}$$

Where x is, $-\infty < x < +\infty$, Where parameters μ is the location parameter which derives mean and σ is scaling parameter which is used to calculate standard deviation. At $\mu = 0$, Gaussian distribution is symmetric.

Since the fc is non-periodic so it is difficult to find the Fourier coefficients, therefore, we analyse the distribution of $\hat{C} = C \bmod m$ for some $m \in R+$.

$$f_c^{\sim}(x) = fc(x) * \sum\nolimits_{k=-\infty}^{\infty} \delta(x - km) \tag{2}$$

$$= \sum\nolimits_{k=-\infty}^{\infty} fc(x - km) \tag{3}$$

Where * is the convolution operator, δ is Dirac's delta function. $f\hat{c}(x) = fc^{\sim}(x)$, x $\in [0, m]$.

Since $fc^{\sim}(x)$ is periodic, therefore its Fourier coefficients are,

$$c_k = \frac{1}{m} F_c(\omega)|_{\omega=\omega_0} \tag{4}$$

$Fc(\omega)$ is the Fourier transform of $fc(x)$, $\omega_0 = \frac{2\pi k}{m}$
Fourier transform of $f_c(x)$ at $\mu = 0$ is

$$F_c(\omega) = \frac{1}{2} \exp - (\frac{\sigma^2 \omega^2}{2}) \tag{5}$$

From Eq. (4) the Fourier coefficients is,

$$c_k = \frac{1}{m} \left(\frac{1}{2} \exp - \left(\frac{\sigma^2 \omega^2}{2}\right)\right) \omega_0 = \frac{2\pi k}{m} \tag{6}$$

$$c_k = \frac{1}{m} \left(\frac{1}{2} \exp - \left(\frac{2(\sigma\pi k)^2}{m^2}\right)\right) \tag{7}$$

Fourier coefficients are depending upon the value of modulo m and standard deviation σ.

2.2 Stego Images

Stego-images are quantified by Fourier coefficient using additive model like cover-images. Additive model for stego-images is S = C + M, where S is the stego-image, C is the cover-image and M is the message to be hidden. The distribution for stego-image and the message is represented by fs(x) and fM(x) respectively. The Fourier coefficients for fS(x) are,

$$c_k = \frac{1}{m} F_s(\omega)|_{\omega=\omega_0} \tag{8}$$

Where $Fs(\omega)$ is the Fourier transform of fs(x). Convolution of the distribution of two normal variables is calculated as shown in Eq. (9).

$$f_s(x) = f_c(x) * f_M(x) \tag{9}$$

Then the Fourier transform of a convolution is the product of the transforms is:

$$F_S(\omega) = f_c(\omega)\, F_M(\omega), \tag{10}$$

And

$$c_k = \frac{1}{m}\exp - \left(\frac{2(\sigma\pi k)^2}{m^2}\right) F_M\left(\frac{2\pi k}{m}\right) \tag{11}$$

From Eqs. (7) and (11), it is clear that coefficient for stego-images and cover-images dependent upon the same parameter m and σ.

3 Steganalysis Measure

We want a measure that should be constant for cover-image and vary for stego-image because of the embedding process. Let us take m = σ, where $1 \le c < \infty$, then Eq. (7) is looking like this,

$$c_k = \frac{c}{\sigma}\exp\left(-2(\pi kc)^2\right) \tag{12}$$

Now, take the ratio of two coefficients ck and cl for a choice of c as,

$$r_{k,l}(c) = \frac{c_k}{c_l} = \frac{\exp(-2(\pi kc)^2)}{\exp(-2(\pi lc)^2)} \tag{13}$$

For stego-images the ratio r k, l(c) is,

$$r_{k,l}(c) = \frac{c_k}{c_l} = \left(\frac{FM\left(\frac{2\pi k}{m}\right)}{FM\left(\frac{2\pi l}{m}\right)}\right)\left(\frac{\exp(-2(\pi kc)^2)}{\exp(-2(\pi lc)^2)}\right) \tag{14}$$

This relation relies only on the frequency distribution of DCT coefficients.

4 Identifying the Hidden Message

Now our aim is to propose a method using the above relation to identifying transform domain steganography. The relation of r k, l(c) does not makes any bench mark to particular steganographic algorithm. This is worthy, we do not know what embedding method was used to hide the message.

4.1   Ratio Selection

From (14), it is understood that the execution of the detector not only depend upon the distribution of the message, but also the choice of k, l, and c. With just one ratio, we are taking care of two frequencies in the spectrum. Any advanced hiding scheme can easily manipulate detection. Let us take, for different value of c, we have different value of k and l for reducing the error, small value of k should be used.

For different value of c, obtain a vector r. We make constant k and l to some small integers.

$$r = (r\,k, l(c1), r\,k, l(c2), r\,k, l(c3), r\,k, l(c4), \ r\,k, l(c5)) \tag{15}$$

In experiment, r is,

$$r = \left(r_{1,2}(5), \ r_{1,2}(10), \ r_{1,2}(15), \ r_{1,2}(20), \ r_{1,2}(25) \right) \tag{16}$$

In experiment r k, l(c) is difficult but we use its values after applying modulus operator. Our choice of c covers a wide range of frequencies. By detecting these variations, we should be capable to identify stego-images.

4.2   Steganography Techniques

In experiment r k, l(c) is difficult but its used after applying modulus operator. Value of c includes a large number of frequencies.

Least significant bit substitution is more popular approach to hide the information in a cover-image. In LSB method, the least significant bit of some bytes of image is modified according to the message bits [5]. Human eye is not able to find little variations in the original image. Consider first three pixels of an image to be used as:

```
00101101   11010000   10110001
11011000   00101101   11100101
00010111   11010001   10011011
```

In order to hide an image inside the cover image, let the binary value of one pixel of the secret image be 11011001. The resulting pixels of the cover image are as follows:

```
00101101   11010001   10110000
11011001   00101101   11100100
00010110   11010001   10011011
```

On an average, only half of the bits have been changed.

Another data hiding method is Spread Spectrum Image Steganography (SSIS) which uses the digital image as a cover-image. SSIS has a feature to hide and recover error free, digital images. Original image is not required to take out the covered data. Spread Spectrum Image Steganography works by hiding a message as a Gaussian noise in the image [6].

Steghide uses a graph theoretic approach [7]. In this technique of steganography exchanging is more preferable rather than overwriting pixels. Then by using the covered data and secret message construct a graph, in which nodes represent pixels that need to be modified and arcs show the connection between possible partner of an. This is solved by combinatorial problem of calculating a maximum cardinality matching. The useful information is then embedded by matched arcs. Additionally, the edge weights are introduced for minimizing visual changes [8].

5 Experimental Result

In our experiment, the image database contains various images which are different in size and dimensions. The images are collected from different-different sources. For experiment all images are in BMP format. First, calculate the ratio vector for cover images using the derived measure which is ratio, of two Fourier coefficients of the distribution of DCT coefficients modeled as Gaussian [9]. Ratio vector is calculated at the different-different frequency which covers a wide range of frequency in an image. Create the database of features calculated from cover images using derived measure.

The same procedure for stego images and these are generated from the corresponding cover images using three different steganography techniques LSB, SSIS, and Steghide. We use random message size embedded into the cover images. Same ratio vector is calculated for the stego images using the derived measure for stego-images. And database is also created for the stego-images, features are calculated using measure.

The ratio vector is calculated at different-different frequency like r 2,1(5), r 2,1(10), r 2,1(15), r 2,1(20), and r 2,1(25). For the classification of cover images and stego images we have used Support Vector Machine (SVM). Support Vector Machine is a relatively new learning method used for binary classification. Support Vector Machine uses different-different kernel functions like a polynomial kernel, Gaussian Radial Basis Function, Exponential Radial Basis Function and Multilayer-Perceptron. But we use SVM with Gaussian Radial Basis Function (RBF). We use WEKA tool for the classification of images, which is an open source tool for Data Mining. Classifier is trained at different-different percentage like 10%, 20%, 30%, 40%, 50% and last is 60%. The performance of the classifier is measured by the correctly classified images and incorrectly classified images (Table 1).

Table-1. The classification accuracy for Laplace Distribution and Gaussian Distribution at different percentage split

Algorithm	Percentage-split					
	10	20	30	40	50	60
Classification accuracy using Laplace-Distribution (LD)	72	71.21	70.90	70.45	66.66	63.63
Classification accuracy using Gaussian- Distribution (GD)	80	80.3	81.81	81.81	81.81	86.36

On an average Laplace-image modeling giving the 57.4% and Gaussian-image modeling giving the 82.01% classification accuracy, which is better than the Laplace-image modeling. Figure 1 graphically represents a comparison between Laplace-image modelling and Gaussian-image modelling (Fig. 2).

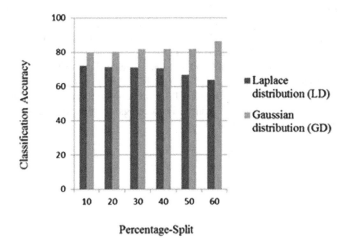

Fig. 2. Classification accuracy at different percentage-split for Laplace Distribution (LD) and Gaussian Distribution (GD).

6   Conclusion

Steganography is an art of science which influences the secure communication between parties through hiding the message in some cover-object. And steganalysis is a process of detect/extract the information from cover-object. We derive a unit which shows a ratio of Fourier coefficients of the distribution of the DCT coefficients by modeling image using Gaussian distribution and also did comparison between Laplace-image modeling and Gaussian-image modeling by classification accuracy. This is another measure for blind steganalysis. Universal or blind steganalysis techniques are the cover wide range of steganalysis because they are not designed for particular steganography algorithm. Our proposed scheme is more effective then Laplace-image modeling.

References

1. Adhiya, K.P., Patil, S.A.: Hiding text in audio using LSB based steganography. Inf. Knowl. Manag. **2**(3), 8–15 (2012)
2. Lyu, S., Farid, H.: Steganalysis using higher-order image statistics. IEEE Trans. Inf. Forensics Secur. **1**(1), 111–119 (2006)
3. Avcibas, I., Menon, N., Sankur, B.: Steganalysis using image quality metrics. IEEE Trans. Image Process. **12**(2), 221–229 (2003)

4. Fridrich, J.: Feature-based steganalysis for JPEG images and its implications for future design of steganographic schemes. In: Fridrich, J. (ed.) IH 2004. LNCS, vol. 3200, pp. 67–81. Springer, Heidelberg (2004). doi:10.1007/978-3-540-30114-1_6
5. Dumitrescu, S., Wu, X., Wang, Z.: Detection of LSB steganography via sample pair analysis. IEEE Trans. Sig. Process. **51**(7), 1999–2007 (2003)
6. Marvel, L., Boncelet Jr., C., Retter, C.: Spread spectrum image steganography. IEEE Trans. Image Process. **8**(8), 1075–1083 (1999)
7. Hetzl, S., Mutzel, P.: A graph–theoretic approach to steganography. In: Dittmann, J., Katzenbeisser, S., Uhl, A. (eds.) CMS 2005. LNCS, vol. 3677, pp. 119–128. Springer, Heidelberg (2005). doi:10.1007/11552055_12
8. Bera, S., Sharma, M.: A review on blind still image steganalysis techniques using features extraction and pattern classification method. IJCSEIT **2**(3), 117–135 (2012)
9. Gonzalez, F.P., Heileman, G.L., Quanch, T.T.: Model-based steganalysis using invariant features. In: Media Forensics and Security. Proceedings of SPIE, vol. 7254, p. 72540B, 4 February 2009. doi:10.1117/12.810507

Implementation of Medical Image Watermarking Technique Using FPGA

S. Sivakannan$^{(\boxtimes)}$, G. Thirugnanam, and P. Mangaiyarkarasi

Department of Electronics and Instrumentation Engineering,
Annamalai University, Chidambaram, India
sivakannan87@gmail.com, ggtt_me@yahoo.com

Abstract. Protection and confidentiality are essential for Medical Image Watermarking because thorough analysis on health pictures is needed for proper diagnosis. In this paper we address this problem and designed a watermarking algorithm for medical images. Protection resolutions are increasingly joined alongside biomedical images. The patient data and patient fingerprint are added to the medical images, without disturbing the essential information in an image. Consequently, watermarking algorithms that involve embedding the patient report and finger print are proposed. In this method we are separating Region of Interest and Region of noninterest pixels from medical image using MATLAB. We have used RONI for adding watermark (patient report and fingerprint) to the medical cover image. In this paper we designed a new method to protect and authenticate medical images. We developed Independent Component Analysis on A Field programmable Gate Array (FPGA) and applied to RONI image that enables the addition of watermark. In this way X ray or scan report are utilized for watermark creation and for patient authentication. The aim of proposed technique is assembly of Independent Component Analysis watermarking to insert two autonomous data's for accuracy and authentication.

Keywords: Image segmentation · Watermarking · Authentication · ICA · FPGA

1 Introduction

Telemedicine removes inconvenience arising from different geographic locations and provides health services at far-away places. In the recent years, use of digital equipment's in health care sector has increased considerably [6]. Modern technology allows doctors to diagnose their patients using digital parameters. In numerous medical applications, distinct protection and secrecy is needed for patient records, reason being thorough analysis on health pictures is needed for proper diagnosis. Tampering images will lead to surface unwanted consequences as an aftermath of defeat of crucial information [9, 11].

Watermarking is utilized to deal alongside the above problems. Instituted on the method utilized for embedding data onto an image, watermarking methods are categorized into two types. They are spatial and frequency. In spatial area watermarking

© Springer Nature Singapore Pte Ltd. 2017
M. Singh et al. (Eds.): ICACDS 2016, CCIS 721, pp. 149–157, 2017.
DOI: 10.1007/978-981-10-5427-3_16

methods, data is implanted undeviatingly onto the cover image. In frequency area methods, data is inserted in the transformed host image [3, 6].

Medical images grasp pivotal property and are extremely critical and vital portion of health information. Region of interest (ROI) contains important information in the medical images. These type of regions are helpful diagnosing the patients problems by the doctor. Small amount of changes in ROI could lead to unwanted treatment for patient by the doctor. Across watermarking ROI, the medical images are safeguard by indicating to be upheld and the watermarks can stay in some portion of the picture is Region of Non Interest (RONI) [7]. So the request in medical images for watermarking can done through two step procedure including:

   i. Determining ROI from the health images
  ii. Watermarking request on RONI

This paper proposes medical image segmentation and a new algorithm on water-marking established on Independent Component Analysis of the medical picture (CT Scan, MRI scan etc.), which enables the digital images authentication. In this paper new algorithm derived with biometric watermarks established on fingerprint mark and template of patient data are embedded invisibly in a medical images. Once the extraction of watermark is done, instead original watermarks, just one more example needed of biometric traits to present patient authentication. Our paper includes ICA rotting of the cover picture into four frank constituents and selecting two, with the highest power ones for inserting watermark [3]. Early constituent (cover image approximation) varied alongside fingerprint picture, but in the subsequent constituent (cover image details) patient data template is inserted by quantization of pixels [6].

2 Preliminary

In this section, we give an introduction to the image segmentation method and the properties of average watermarking algorithm in ICA area. Next a little data concerning biometric verification methods, exceptionally established on fingerprint that will be utilized for watermarks assembly, are provided.

2.1 Region of Interest (ROI) Segmentation

Segmentation is the early pace to be considered in medical image, to avoid distortion in ROI [8]. Medical image segmentation is utilized for extracting the feature, measure-ment of image and for image display [8, 9]. The aim of image segmentation is to tear whole image into sub spans (gray and white). In supplement, this helps in categorizing pixels of image into anatomical spans (such as ligament, bones and muscles) [8, 9].

2.2 ICA for Watermarking

The constituents are statistically independent in Independent Component Analysis [7]. We can use this method for Blind Source Separation. The additional ICA is applied to watermarking by many researchers who endeavored to apply with its blind separation method, frequently emphasizing the similarity amid critical periods of these procedures [3]. The watermarking extraction period can be believed as a de blending procedure of ICA, whereas the original picture and the watermark are statistically autonomous origins that ought to be taken out from the watermarked image. MRICA (Multi resolution Independent Component Analysis) is an example to request ICA in watermarking that decomposes each image into statistical autonomous constituents to use for watermark insertion [3]. Exactly, the watermarking procedure starts alongside splitting cover image size N × M into blocks size k × k to attain k^2 observation picture of size N/k × M/k. The value of k have to set initially for number of observation image are desired. Then ICA algorithm de blends observation images to attain k^2 autonomous Images that craft ICA centers. This procedure needs reshaping of all observation pictures to the vectors x_1, for $l = 1;...; k^2$, sized $1 × NM/k^2$, that come to be lines of matrix X sized $k^2 × NM = k^2$. The ICA algorithm finds $k^2 × k^2$ de blending matrix B and $k^2 × NM = k^2$ matrix Y, such that Y = BX. Finally, lines of Y are statistically autonomous and afterward resizing to N/k × M/k are seized as ICA centers (autonomous constituent). As it is the constituent alongside the high power denoted as IC_H is the most robust, the watermark W of the size N/k × M/k is embedded in it [6].

According to the rule

$$IC_W^H = IC_H + \alpha W \qquad (1)$$

Where α = embedding strength and IC_W^H = watermarked constituent.

Then to reinstate watermarked image constituent IC_W^H and $k^2 - 1$ early detail constituents as well as blending matrix B^{-1} are used. For watermark extraction, we have to do the ICA reverse process.

3 Proposed Method

Segmentation procedure in the original image, embedding the watermark onto cover picture and extraction of the counseled watermarking technique gave uniqueness of this method compare to MRICA that was explained in Sect. 2.2. For authentication, two watermarks extracted from the watermarked image.

Our work focuses on embedding watermark in RONI span of medical image by maintaining ROI. This way helps in isolating ROI span i.e. not to distort the critical span of medical image that will be denoted by physician for the diagnosis. The arrangement diagram for this way is shown in Fig. 1.

In an Initial phase of system separating the ROI from the Original medical picture provides RONI span for embedding watermark. This pace isolates ROI from embedding process. In this period multiple watermarks are embedded into the RONI span of health image. Embedding several watermarks safeguard elevated protection of medical image as it carries elevated payload and it will be complex to break the system. After the completion of embedding procedure the separated ROI is joined alongside the produced watermarked image. The resultant watermarked medical image is next

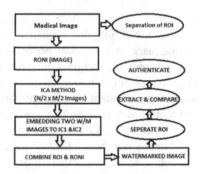

Fig. 1. Medical image watermarking approach

dispatched to the receiver. In watermark extraction period, initial pace is to distinct the ROI from the watermarked medical image. The stayed watermark extraction procedure is precise reverse of embedding procedure, whereas the embedded watermark will be removed from the watermarked medical image. The watermark authentication is attained by contrasting the extracted watermark alongside the original watermark. This procedure helps in recognizing if each tampering or manipulation to the watermarked medical image.

3.1   Seperation of ROI

Distortion may occur in ROI, if we use traditional watermarking techniques onto the medical image. Then diagnosis information could be lost. So RONI taken for embedding the watermark onto a cover image. The ROI can be taken out from the cover picture. Excluding ROI, the watermark images are inserted to cover image. Figure 1 shows selection of ROI in Matlab from the medical image for proper diagnosis by the physician. Figure 2 shows one of the option for ROI selection in Matlab. Thus, ROI and RONI of images are to be separated before inserting the watermark to a cover picture.

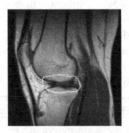

Fig. 2. Selecting ROI

3.2   Embedding

In this work we have used Multi Resolution Independent component Analysis (MRICA) to insert two different watermark images. In this original image is divided into four observation images (i.e. N × M is converted to N/2 × M/2 images). To make ICA bases (ICA1 to ICA4) like standard MRICA the observation images are transformed by de blending matrix. Then we can use two ICA bases for watermarking onto the medical image. To achieve highest robustness we have to insert watermark image in highest energy observation image. The first watermark image(fingerprint) size is changed to N/2 × M/2 and then inserted to IC1(highest energy observation image) (Fig. 3).

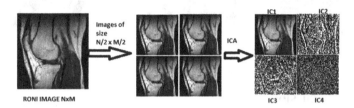

Fig. 3. Splitting Image into N/2 x M/2 Images and ICA applied image

This embedding procedure is consistent alongside MRICA way, as watermark is varied alongside IC1 from the Eq. (1) little embedding strength α to attain watermarked component IC1' shown in Fig. 4. Though, seizing into report protection of watermark content, that is biometric trait of the patient.

Fig. 4. Adding IC1 with fingerprint

The uniqueness of this way is that additionally IC2 component is utilized for insertion of the subsequent watermark W2 shown in Fig. 5.

Fig. 5. Adding IC2 with patient report

3.3   Extraction

First the modified components along with high energy IC1" is selected to remove fingerprint picture using ICA to these elements and resized cover picture. The result is we will get two source images, i.e. resized medical image and fingerprint picture W1'. To remove both watermarks, watermarked picture is decomposed into $k^2 = 4$ observation images which are extracted by ICA (Fig. 6).

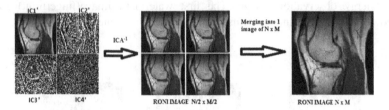

Fig. 6. Inverse ICA process

4   Result Discussion

In this work segmentation portion is implemented in Matlab and ICA design and watermarking algorithm is implemented employing FPGA Altera stratix. We used 512×512 pixel size image cover picture (medical image) and 64×64 pixel finger print and Patient data template as watermark for testing. Perceptual transparency and Robustness are the performance evaluation metrics taken here. Measure of quality of processed image is done using PSNR & SNR. Greater the PSNR, greater the image quality.

4.1   Validation of Functionality

To analyze the accuracy of the proposed ICA watermarking design, the proposed design is delineated alongside Verilog HDL, as algorithm by matlab programming language has additionally been industrialized, that has the alike data precision in the data path (Fig. 7) .

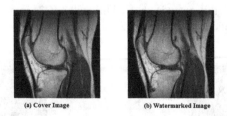

(a) Cover Image   (b) Watermarked Image

Fig. 7. Cover image and watermarked image

The cover image is early utilized as the input for Verilog HDL testbench simulation. The aftermath of watermarking algorithm created using testbench simulation is imported to a txt doc. Next cover image is processed by Watermarking with matlab. The modified coefficients are made into another text document. Final analysis is done by comparing both the results. The Watermarking output coefficients got from test bench simulation are given for an Inverse ICA procedure program of matlab, that displays the recovery image. PSNR for picture size M × N is given by:

$$PSNR(db) = 10 \log_{10} \frac{(Max_I)^2}{\frac{1}{M*N} \sum_{j=i}^{M} [f(i,j) - f'(i,j)]^2} \tag{2}$$

Where, f (i, j) = pixel values cover image. f '(i, j) = pixel values of watermarked image. Max_I = maximum pixel worth of picture. Using correlation factor robustness is measured. The correlation factor is used to measure the similarity and difference between inserted data(watermark image) and removed data(watermark image). Its value is usually 0 to 1. Ideally it ought to be 1. Robustness is given by (Fig. 8):

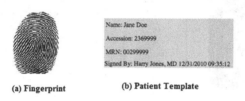

(a) Fingerprint   (b) Patient Template

Fig. 8. Recovered watermark

$$\rho = \frac{\sum_{i=1}^{N} w_i w_i'}{\sqrt{\sum_{i=1}^{N} w_i} \sqrt{\sum_{i=1}^{N} w_i'}} \tag{3}$$

Where, N = number of pixel in watermark, w_i = original watermark, w_i' = removed watermark. Here, we are getting PSNR 42.55 dB and $\rho = 1$, for weighting factor F PSNR and ρ for 'standard database of health corresponding examination picture shown in Table 1.

4.2   Benefits

Cloud computing has wide benefits and applications in various fields including Information technology, Academics, Medicine etc., It provides flexibility, Security, cost wise services with powerful computing technology and effective performance. In this domain, Cloud Computing has been able to deliver rapid data sharing and storage

Table 1. Result for medical image

Watermarked Images	Recovered Watermark	Weighting factor (F),PSNR(db), Correlation(ρ), SNR
	Name: Jane Doe Accession: 2369999 MRN: 0029999 Signed By: Harry Jones, MD 12/31/2010 09:35:12	F=0.02 PSNR=42.55 ρ=1 SNR=41.25
	Name: Jane Doe Accession: 2369999 MRN: 0029999 Signed By: Harry Jones, MD 12/31/2010 09:35:12	F=0.06 PSNR=48.34 ρ=1 SNR=46.12
	Name: Jane Doe Accession: 2369999 MRN: 0029999 Signed By: Harry Jones, MD 12/31/2010 09:35:12	F=0.06 PSNR=47.56 ρ=1 SNR=45.91

with security being the prime concern. Cloud computing in the field of biomedical Image Watermarking has been exploited in such a way that the external resources has been reduced by utilizing Watermarking Technology, where the Patient's Template and Fingerprint can be fully watermarked on the Cover Image itself.

4.3 Limitations

The Digital Watermarking Technology used here is limited to Biomedical Applications as the ROI (Region of Interest) and RONI (Region of Non Interest) has been identified as the prime source of acquiring and embedding the data related to the Patient's Medical Condition. It enables the system to utilize the RONI for Watermarking the Patient's Template and Fingerprint which is considered to be less effective in other applications apart from Biomedical.

5 Conclusion

Healthcare industry nowadays requires more sophisticated services like sending medical pictures from one place to other. Through cloud, enhancement in data and contact technologies made it probable to grasp such requests. In this paper we proposed a Digital Watermarking Technology that effectively utilizes the Services of Cloud Computing in delivering an Authentic Scheme for obtaining the patient's Data by reducing the use of Hardware Resources. It makes use of the patient's Template and Fingerprint which are to be watermarked on the Independent Component in the cover Image thereby enabling the Secure Transfer of Information.

References

1. Al-Otum, H.: Semi-fragile watermarking for grayscale image authentication and tamper detection based on an adjusted expanded-bit multiscale quantization-based technique. J. Vis. Commun. Image Represent. **25**(5), 1064–1081 (2014)
2. Bounkong, S., Toch, B., Saad, D., Lowe, D.: ICA for watermarking digital images. J. Mach. Learn. Res. **4**, 1471–1498 (2003)
3. Hajisami, A., Hosseini, S.: Application of ICA in watermarking. In: Gupta, M.D., (ed) Watermarking, vol. 1. InTech (2012)
4. Rao, N., Thrimurthy, P., Babu, B.: A novel scheme for digital rights management of images using biometrics. Int. J. Comput. Sci. Netw. Security **9**(3), 157–167 (2009)
5. Giakoumaki, A., Pavlopoulos, S., Koutsouris, D.: Multiple image watermarking applied to health information management. IEEE Trans. Inf. Technol. Biomed. **10**(4), 722–732 (2006)
6. Wójtowicz, W., Ogiela, M.R.: Digital images authentication scheme based on bimodal biometric watermarking in an independent domain. J. Vis. Commun. Image Represent. **38**, 1–10 (2016)
7. Badakhshannoory, H., Saeedi, P.: A model-based validationscheme for organ segmentation in CT scan volumes. IEEE Trans. Biomed. Inf. **58**(9), 2681–2693 (2011)
8. Forouzan, A.H., Zoroofi, R.A., Hori, M., Sato, Y.: Liver segmentation by intensity analysis and anatomical information in multislice CT images. Intensity Anal. Anat. Inf. Multi-slice CT Images **4**, 287–297 (2009). In: Proceedings of Liver Segment
9. Memon, N.A., Gilani, S.A.M., Qayoom, S.: Multiple watermarking of medical images for content authentication and recovery. IEEE (2009)
10. Shoshan, Y., Fish, A., Li, X., Jullien, G.A., Yadid-Pecht, O.: VLSI watermark implementations and applications. Int. J. Inf. Technol. Knowl. **2**(4), 379–386 (2008)
11. Grzeszczak, A., Mandal, M.K., Panchanathan, S.: VLSI implementation of discrete wavelet transform. IEEE Trans. Very Large Scale Integr. Syst. **4**(4), 421–433 (1996)
12. Sharma, S., Tim, U.S., Gadia, S., Wong, J.: Growing Cloud Density& as-a-Service Modality and OTH-CLOUD Class (2015)

IoV: The Future of Automobiles

Preethi Pattabiraman[1], R. Dhaya[2(✉)], B. Sasidhar[1], and R. Kanthavel[3]

[1] Department of CSE, Velammal Engineering College,
Anna University, Chennai, India
preetiauguststar@gmail.com
[2] Department of CSE, Rajalakshmi Engineering College,
Anna University, Chennai, India
Dhayave12005@gmail.com
[3] Department of ECE, Rajalakshmi Institute of Technology,
Anna University, Chennai, India

Abstract. Internet of Things is an extension of WSN (Wireless Sensor Networks) in which every WSN is connected via the Internet such that in the end every "thing" is connected to the Internet, which will eventually ensure that the world becomes a "connected village". Any "thing" in IoT should be able to sense, compute and communicate. Of those "things", automobiles are an integral part. That's why this field can be aptly called "Internet of Vehicles". To integrate all these vehicles together and to ensure QoS and QoE for the end users is now a challenging need that is put forth the telecom providers and car manufacturers. This paper surveys on different applications that can be created with vehicles of day-to-day usage.

Keywords: Internet of things · Internet of Vehicles · Vehicles · Automobiles

1 Introduction

Internet of things is a buzzword that is expected to rule the markets at least till 2035 (Until every "thing" is connected!). IoT an old idea, its architecture is old (architecture of IoT is flexible; it can be changed accordingly based on the application that is to be designed), and the devices that are the "things" are day to day devices that are nothing sophisticated or complicated. IoT is a "smart" move towards the concept of remote access that brings together everything together [1]. About $4.5 trillion is invested in IoT and about $14.4 billion is expected by 2022 (Courtesy: http://www.cisco.com/web/about/ac79/docs/innov/IoE_Economy.pdf) by the business, which can give just an insight on how important this is to the market.

The next important thing in the market is automobiles. According to recent statistics, about 1.2 billion vehicles are on the road, with an estimation that at least 2 billion vehicles are expected to be on road by 2035. (Courtesy: http://www.greencarreports.com/news/1093560_1-2-billion-vehicles-on-worlds-roads-now-2-billion-by-2035-report). Figures 1 and 2 depict the current status in India and in the world. Thus there is a big market when it comes to IoT and vehicles put together.

North Korean telecom provider SK Telecom has already implemented IoT and thus, IoT is not longer a dream that cannot be made true. Gone are the days when

© Springer Nature Singapore Pte Ltd. 2017
M. Singh et al. (Eds.): ICACDS 2016, CCIS 721, pp. 158–164, 2017.
DOI: 10.1007/978-981-10-5427-3_17

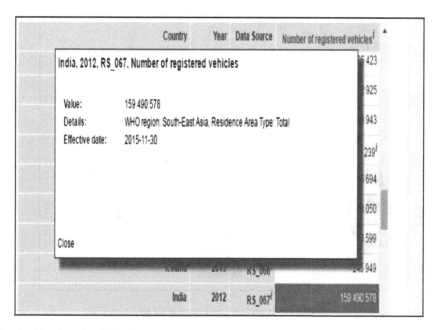

Fig. 1. Number of vehicles in India (Courtesy: WHO http://apps.who.int/gho/data/node.main. A995)

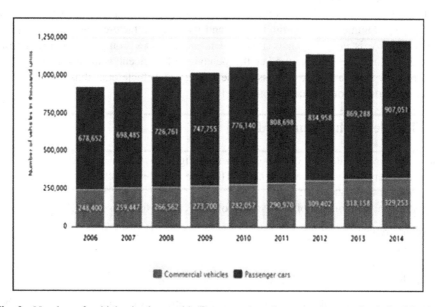

Fig. 2. Number of vehicles in the world (Courtesy: http://www.statista.com/statistics/281134/ number-of-vehicles-in-use-worldwide/

Fig. 3. High level architecture of IoV

people have to ensure that all is fine in their homes or at work. With IoT everything connected together, one can reap the benefits of remote connectivity with the help of Internet and Cloud server [10].

Bringing together IoT and vehicles, a fusion aptly named Internet Of Vehicles (IoV), creates numerous opportunities for end users, manufacturers and telecom providers [2]. IoV is in itself a new area, which encompasses from even buying a new vehicle, routing the vehicle, predict the behavior of adjacent vehicle on the roads, repairing the vehicle during any issues, servicing the vehicle etc., thus ensuring the customers worry about virtually nothing [4].

2 Flexible Architecture of IOT

The high level architecture of IoT is shown in Fig. 3, which is flexible, so it can be adapted to any application as per need. Thus the high level architecture that can be proposed for IoV can be as:

The main components of architecture of IoV can be listed as

1. Smart vehicle
2. Cloud service
3. Traffic carrier
4. Application

Of course, a natural question of whether a vehicle can be made "smart" can be answered by the Fig. 4. A high level picture of a smart car has about 25+ sensors which can help the driver to understand the current status of the vehicle [3]. Cloud services can be private, public or enterprise. Cloud services are the backend, they process the data that are uploaded from the sensors by the traffic carriers; this processing is coupled with decision making based on the data uploaded. Traffic carriers are telecom providers that can pass data in 3G/LTE/WiMAX [5]. This network forms the crux of the system. Depending on the speed and agility of the networking, is the performance of IoV [9]. The application is the actual front end; which is the end point from the user's end [6]. This should be seamless so that there is less latency in data transmission and reception, since this traffic is pure real time.

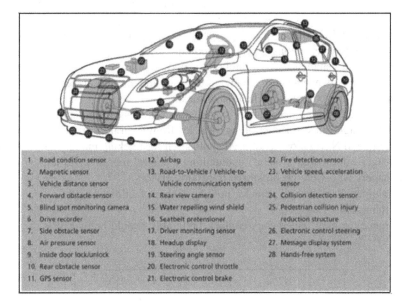

Fig. 4. Sensors in current vehicles

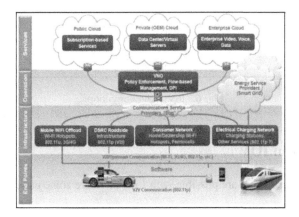

Fig. 5. IoV technologies

3 Various Applications with IOV

IoV and its flexible architecture provides with enormous openings for applications. The Fig. 5 shows the IoV Technologies. All this applications help in all ways to make the lifetime of the customers better [7]. The IoV technology loop gives an idea on how to begin and how to process. It depicts the flow of operations in the IoV [8]. Figure 6 shows the flow of control and its various components.

1. IoV is actually Mobility as a Service. It forms the topmost element in IoV software architecture. Thus this service can be classified as
   a. Vehicle and Driver service: Taxi services, lend vehicle and driver services
   b. Vehicle service: renting a car, car pooling
   c. Enterprise vehicle services: public transport.
2. Tire pressure management system: monitoring and monitoring of tire pressure; maintaining tire pressure can help save fuel.
3. Anti theft: already in place (alarm systems); can extend to immobilizers.
4. Remote Diagnostics: for controlling vehicles from central location.
5. Tracking and Navigation: most used application for tracking unregistered vehicles.
6. Passenger information systems: maintaining a central repository of all.
7. Passengers who were on board the transport services.
8. Infotainment services: all vehicles now have these facilities to get.
9. Entertainment.
10. Emergency calling: emergency contact; preferably should be over IP.

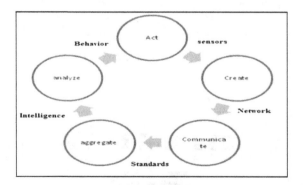

Fig. 6. IoV technology loop

4 Use Cases in IOV

Given the applications that are possible with IoV, there are some use cases that should be scrutinized.

S. No	Management	Functions	Examples
1	Mobility	Allow driver to reach destination safely	Traffic information, parking
2	Vehicle	Reduce OPEX and increase	Servicing, condition checking
3	Entertainment	Enjoyment of drivers and customers	Smartphone, WiFi, music, Social Media
4	Safety	Warn driver of external hazards	Collision, emergency functions, ir
5	Assistance	Partial or full automatic driving	Autopilot in traffic or highway
6	Well-being	Comfort, ability and fitness	Fatigue deduction, medical assistance

Thus an IoV design should satisfy the above use cases to ensure the completeness of the process. There are again two perspectives of IoV:

- Market: how to support and promote the applications.
- Government: how to ensure that these applications are available for all registered users.
- It requires all the stakeholders to come together to make this possible.

5 Conclusion

With the advent of IoT, people have started to think smart, and have invested huge amount of money. Market is such that any smart application defines their success, since it makes them stand out among their peers. IoT makes life easier; and IoV makes driving easier. A lot of applications are already available; they are in stand alone systems (they are single applications). When they are combined, it can create a full force of data with which manufacturers can improve their design, market can invest more and government can bring more security to the transport environment. But the main challenges include:

- Security of the data in cloud.
- Authentication of registered users.
- Authorization of drivers with registered users.
- Interoperability among telecom providers.
- Customers will now want to share vehicles, less will buy.
- High pressure on manufacturers to constantly change their designs an ensure that they are upgradable.
- Have now to invest more on cloud servers to handle these EBs of data But the market is supportive for the grant entrance of IoV.

References

1. Bonomi, F.: The Smart and Connected Vehicle and The Internet of Things. Cisco, San Jose (2013)
2. Singh, S., Aujla, G.S.: A closer look through routing protocols invehicular ad hoc networks VANETs. IOSR J. Eng. IOSRJEN 4(2), 58–64 (2016)
3. Mitra, S., Mondal, A.: Secure inter-vehicle communication: a need for evolution of VANET towards the internet of vehicles. In: Mahmood, Z. (ed.) Connectivity Frameworks for Smart Devices. CCN, pp. 63–96. Springer, Cham (2016). doi:10.1007/978-3-319-33124-9_4
4. Chatrapathi, C., Rajkumar, M.N., Venkatesakumar, V.: VANET based integrated framework for smart accident management system. In: 2015 International Conference on Soft-Computing and Network Security ICSNS-2015 (2015)
5. Shekar, M.: M2 M/IoT Applications in automotive and intelligent transportation systems (2012)
6. http://dupress.com/articles/internet-of-things-iot-in-automotive-industry
7. Dhaya, R., Pattabiraman, P., Shahrukh, S., Chandrasoodan, M.S., Kanthavel, R.: Smart grid: the future of power transmission. In: Proceedings of ARC 2016 8th International Conference on Applied Research in Engineering and Management Sciences (2016)
8. http://topelectronicpro.blogspot.in/2016/05/iotvehiclesimulationsystem.html
9. https://www.element14.com/community/groups/internetofthings/blog/2014/04/29/vehiclesimulationsystemproject
10. http://www.simafore.com/blog/bid/207243/7-applications-of-IoT-connected-vehicles

Measuring Branch Coverage for the SOA Based Application Using Concolic Testing

A. Dutta, S. Godboley$^{(\boxtimes)}$, and D.P. Mohapatra

Department of Computer Science and Engineering,
National Institute of Technology Rourkela, Rourkela, India
arpitad10j@gmail.com, sanghu1790@gmail.com,
durga@nitrkl.ac.in

Abstract. This work describes the working of white-box testing for the Service-Oriented Architecture (SOA) based Application. Now, a days it is very essential to perform code coverage testing to understand the quality of software. This paper deals with the measurement of branch coverage percentage for the BPEL architecture that orchestrates all the services, which are distributed geographically. Here, we are testing the code coverage of BPEL architecture, which actually shows the invocations of services when it is required. This work integrates the existing open source tools, to automate the computation of branch coverage for SOA based application. This paper shows a novel technique for generation of test cases and computing branch coverage through our proposed tool.

Keywords: SOA · Hit ratio · Black-box testing

1 Introduction

Service-Oriented Architecture (SOA) is an application of cloud computing. It is a systematic arrangements of loosely coupled services, that organized to provide a communication between services and business processes. These services are orchestrated by BPEL architecture. A service is an individual unit component of programming that is proposed to perform a specific task. Service consists of *interfaces*, *agreement*, and *execution*. Interface deals with the function of service supplier, which fulfilling all demands which were demanded by service customer. Agreement deals with the contract between service supplier and the service purchaser. Implementation of service shows the actual service code. Development Of software is always on top of SOA and are programmed prominent yet to be testing. Therefore, SOA based application must to be tested.

SOA has the important following characteristics: SOA services consists of interfaces in XML document, which are platform independent. Web Service Description Language (WSDL) is a standard that used to depict the SOA services. SOA services communicate with messages formally characterized by means of XSD (also called XML schema) [6]. Supplier and customers communicate among themselves using SOA services. This interactions are in heterogeneous environment. There is no actual information about the service supplier. But, the messages between services can be seen

© Springer Nature Singapore Pte Ltd. 2017
M. Singh et al. (Eds.): ICACDS 2016, CCIS 721, pp. 165–172, 2017.
DOI: 10.1007/978-981-10-5427-3_18

as key business records handled in an enterprise. Application can look for services in the registering and invoking it. Universal Description Definition and Integration (UDDI) is the standard for SOA service registry.

Software testing is the important phase in Software Development Life Cycle to detect and correct the bugs present in the software. Software testing is of two types: Black-box and White-box testing [11–17]. In this paper, we focus on white-box testing. Since, services are orchestrated by BPEL architecture so, there is the possibility of selection and invocation of services by the users. This invocations must have some clauses and decision. The communication of services with BPEL architecture must have source code with the SOA application developers. Since, invocation of correct and expected services are required, so, it is very essential to perform the testing for especially the source code of this communications. Here, we understood that there must be clauses or decisions, therefore white-box testing is much suitable for testing this source code. Hence, we measure branch coverage metric for the Java code generated for SOA based Application.

In this paper, we propose an approach to generate test cases for SOA based application using concolic testing to measure branch coverage. We integrate some open source tools to develop a single final tool to produce the desired output. These open source tools are: OPENESB, CODE CONVERTER, JAXB, JCUTE. Our main contribution is to propose this novel technique and to perform experiments of some case studies.

The rest of the article is organized as follows: Sect. 2 deals with basic definitions. Section 3 describes our proposed approach. Section 4 shows experimental study. Section 5 shows the comparison with related work. Section 6 concludes the proposed approach and suggesting some possible future work.

2 Basic Concepts

In this section, we discuss some important basic definitions.

Service-Oriented Architecture (SOA): It is an architecture for building business application as systematic arrangements of loosely coupled black-box components organized to results some characterized level of services by communication together with business process [1].

Web Service Definition Language (WSDL): It standardizes messages formats and communications protocols in the web community. WSDL addresses an XML documents for describing network services as a set of communication terminal points that are able to exchanging messages. WSDL service definitions provide documentation for distributed systems. WSDL service definitely used for automating the details provided in application communications.

Business Process Execution Language (BPEL): It is a language providing the means to implement service compositors, because BPEL is backed by many software vendors, it is often chosen by enterprises.

Concolic Testing: It is a systematic testing that simultaneously executing concrete and symbolic executions.

Branch Coverage: Branch Coverage is calculated by γ and $\gamma^{executed}$ functions. Computing these two functions for every activity type in BPEL to calculate the number of all branches and other number of branches executed in tests. Since, the process element is the basic activity in every BPEL processes, so how we use the β function for the process element to provide the Branch Coverage definition in BPEL as executed:

$$Branch\ Coverage = \frac{\gamma^{executed}(process)}{\gamma(process)} \tag{1}$$

3 Proposed Approach: TOMBSO

In this section, we discuss our proposed approach in detail.

3.1 Description Through Schematic Representation

Figure 1 shows the schematic representation of Tool to measure Branch Coverage for SOA Application (TOMBSO). TOMBSO is the integration of open source tools. The flow starts with the designing SOA application using OPENESB. Then, Code Converter

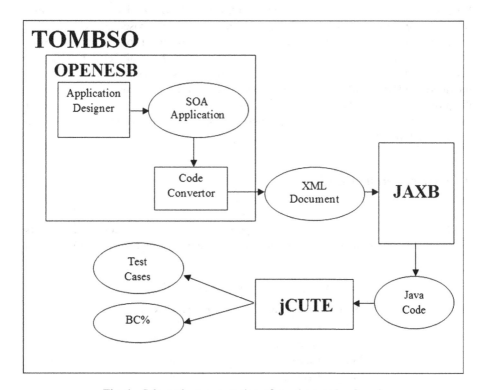

Fig. 1. Schematic representation of our proposed approach

generates XML document for the designed SOA application. Java Architecture XML Binding (JAXB) generates Java code for the provided XML document, please note that here JAXB produces the Java code, which requires some manual modification so that it can proceed to the jCUTE tool. Then, jCUTE tool accepts this Java code to generate test cases automatically. Based in these recorded test cases, jCUTE computes Branch Coverage percentage.

3.2   Algorithmic Representation

Algorithm-1-TOMBSO

Input: SOA Application
Output: Test Cases, BC%
1. Design a SOA Application for the goal of case study using OPENESB.
2. Generate the XML document from the designed SOA Application using code converter.
3. Execute JAXB using XML document to produce an executable Java code.
4. Generate test cases for the executable Java code using jCUTE.
5. Using the test cases, jCUTE computes Branch Coverage percentage.

Description: Algorithm 1 deals with the function of TOMBSO. Line 1 of Algorithm 1 shows the development of service oriented architecture (SOA) based application using OPENESB. Line 2 deals with the generation of XML document for the designed SOA application using Code Converter. This Code Converter is the small developed module inside the OPENESB. Line 3 presents the generation of executable Java code for provided XML document through JAXB. Now, Line 4 discusses the important step of the process. Hence, JCUTE uses this generated executable Java code to generate test cases automatically. Line 5 uses these generated test cases to measure Branch Coverage percentage through JCUTE.

4   Experimental Results

In this section we discuss the detail experimental information for five case studies.

Table 1 shows the characteristics of experimental case studies. Column 2 presents the Name of case studies taken. Column 3 shows the total number of SOA services

Table 1. Characteristics of applications

Sl. no.	Case study	Services	Classes
1	Calculator	5	4
2	Quadratic	4	3
3	Cramer's	7	3
4	Geometry	5	4
5	Producer consumer	4	3

developed. Column 4 shows the total number of Classes exist for the communication between BPEL architecture and SOA services. BPEL architecture manages these invocations.

Table 2 deals with the coverage summary of case studies through jCUTE. Column 3 presets the total number of test cases generated through jCUTE. Column 4 deals with total number of functions invoked. Column 5 shows total number of branches covered through jCUTE. Column 6 presents total number of explored paths. Column 7 shows the total execution time to execute the Java code through jCUTE which is generated form JAXB. Column 8 deals with final coverage metric i.e. Branch Coverage percentage. On an average of five Case Studies we measured 90.6% as Branch Coverage.

Table 2. Experimental results

Sl. no.	Case study	Test cases	Functions invoked	Branches covered	Paths explored	Execution time (ms)	BC%
1	Calculator	11	1	22	12	4346	100%
2	Quadratic	10	2	18	8	4117	87%
3	Cramer's	17	2	33	18	5124	74%
4	Geometry	3	1	17	5	3877	100%
5	Producer consumer	7	2	15	11	3924	92%

5   Comparison with Related Work

In this section we discuss some related work.

Karimi et al. [1] proposed a technique to identify with the full service that they offer for enterprise Integration. They have concluded their approach as the use of service oriented architecture instead of object oriented orchestrated and component-based architecture has proven to be efficient and better. Karimi et al. [1] have not proposed any technique for SOA based technique unlike Karimi et al. [1]. We also showing the efficiency and betterment of SOA and as compared to object-oriented and component based testing, but in testing scenario.

A white paper by oracle [2] consulting proposed and provided a detailed information into why and how SOA enablement will documents the cost rate and risk rate of Application upgrades. Their white paper [2] support to understand the lifetime value of investing SOA technology. In our proposed approach, we are performing testing of SOA based applications. In our work we also computed the cost rate but in term of testing execution time.

Kumar et al. [3] discusses various testing perspective challenges of service oriented architecture testing. They have reviewed some testing approach and presented. They have identified the limitations and improved the testability of service oriented architecture based services. In our proposed approach we are also performed testing of SOA based application. But, the concern of our proposed work is with the code coverage of invocations of services which are orchestrated with BPEL architecture.

Kumar et al. [4] proposed a new testing model that helps to get the automatic test cases of services oriented architecture based application. At last, they have generated the test suite execution results and computed the coverage as XML schema elements present in the WSDL. In our proposed approach, we also compute the code coverage for SOA based application. They have measured contract coverage metric with their proposed technique.

Lubke et al. [5] proposed some useful metrics, such as activity coverage, branch coverage, link coverage, handles coverage. These BPEL test coverage metrics are calculated through Instrumentation technique. In our proposed work, we also computing branch coverage testing. But, our test cases generation process is more efficient and better than Lubke et al. because we are using more exhaustive and thorough testing i.e. concolic testing.

Godboley et al. [7–10] presented an automated approach to generate test data that helps to achieve an increase in MC/DC coverage of a program under test. Transformation techniques are used for transforming program. This transformed program is inserted into the CREST TOOL to generate test suite and increase the MC/DC coverage.

In Table 3, we compare our proposed approach with other existing work in terms of technique used and tools developed. Some papers exist with no information of their tools used such as Karimi et al. [1], White paper by oracle [2], Kumar et al. [3], and Lubke et al. [5]. Table 4 shows the brief description of related work comparing with our proposed work. Table 5 deals with the characteristics considered or not. We can observe from the Table 5 that all the authors mentioned in the table used SOA as their input application, except Godboley et al. [7–10]. Also, we can observe that except Karimi et al. [1], and White paper by oracle [2], all have performed testing process.

Table 3. Technique used and tools developed for related work

Sl. no.	Authors	Technique used	Tools developed
1	Karimi et al. [1]	SOA system integration	–
2	White paper by oracle [2]	SOA-enablement methodologies	–
3	Kumar et al. [3]	Service perspectives of SOA apps	–
4	Kumar et al. [4]	SOA based Services	UDDI, Soap UI tool
5	Lubke et al. [5]	Coverage criteria	–
6	Godboley et al. [7–10]	White - box testing criterion	PCT, EXNCT, JPCT
7	Proposed approach	Branch coverage %	TOMBSO

Table 4. Brief descriptive comparison of related work

Sl. no.	Authors	Description
1	Karimi et al. [1]	They have developed a three-step process for integrating services organizations
2	White paper by oracle [2]	They have provided a detailed information into why and how SOA enablement will documents the cost rate and Risk rate of Application upgrades
3	Kumar et al. [3]	They have reviewed some testing approach and identified the limitations and improved the testability of SOA based services
4	Kumar et al. [4]	They have generated the test suite execution results and computed the coverage as XML schema elements present in the WSDL
5	Lubke et al. [5]	They have defined test metrics to generate an extension to the BPEL Unit testing framework, testers are able to assess whether their white box tests cover all important areas of a BPEL process
6	Godboley et al. [7–10]	They have presented an automated approach to generate test data that helps to achieve an increase in MC/DC coverage of a program under test and also proposed transformation techniques
7	Proposed approach	They have proposed a novel technique to calculate the branch coverage for the SOA based application using concolic testing

Table 5. Characteristic comparison with related work

Sl. no	Authors	Whether SOA used	Whether apply testing
1	Karimi et al. [1]	✓	X
2	White paper by oracle [2]	✓	X
3	Kumar et al. [3]	✓	✓
4	Kumar et al. [4]	✓	✓
5	Lubke et al. [5]	✓	✓
6	Godboley et al. [7–10]	X	✓
7	Proposed approach	✓	✓

6 Conclusion and Future Work

In this work, we proposed a novel technique to calculate the branch coverage for the SOA based application using concolic testing. We computed 90.6% as Branch Coverage for the average of five case studies.

In future work, we will extend our proposed work to compute some more coverage metrics.

References

1. Karimi, O., Nasser, M.: Enterprise integration using service oriented architecture. Adv. Comput.: Int. J. (ACIJ) 2(5), 41–47 (2011)

2. An Oracle White Paper, Application Upgrades and Service Oriented Architecture, Oracle (2008)
3. Kumar, A., Manindra, S.: An empirical study on testing of SOA based services. I.J. Inf. Technol. Comput. Sci. **1**, 54–66 (2015)
4. Kumar, A.: A novel testing model for SOA based services. I.J. Mod. Educ. Comput. Sci. **1**, 31–37 (2015)
5. Lubke, D., Singer, L., Salnikow, A.: Calculating BPEL test coverage through instrumentation. In: ICSE Workshop on Automation of Software Test AST 2009, pp. 115–122. IEEE (2009)
6. Shamsoddin-Motlagh, E.: Automatic test case generation for orchestration languages at service oriented architecture. Int. J. Comput. Appl. **80**(7), 35–44 (2013)
7. Godboley, S., Mohapatra, D.P.: Time analysis of evaluating coverage percentage for C program using advanced program code transformer. In: 7th CSI International Conference on Software Engineering, pp. 91–97, November 2013
8. Godboley, S., Prashanth, G.S., Mahapatro, D.P., Majhi, B.: Increase in modified condition/decision coverage using program code transformer. In: IEEE 3rd International Advance Computing Conference (IACC), pp. 1400–1407, February 2013
9. Godboley, S., Prashanth, G.S., Mahapatro, D.P, Majhi, B.: Enhanced modified condition/decision coverage using exclusive-nor code transformer. In: 2013 International Multi-conference on Automation, Computing, Communication, Control and Compressed Sensing (iMac4s), pp. 524–531, March 2013
10. Godboley, S., Mohapatra, D.P., Das, A., Mall, R.: An improved distributed concolic testing. Softw.: Pract. Exper. (2016). doi:10.1002/spe.2405
11. King, J.C.: Symbolic execution and program testing. Commun. ACM **19**(7), 385–394 (1976)
12. Godefroid, P., Klarlund, N., Sen, K.: DART: directed automated random testing. In: Proceedings PLDI, pp. 75–84, New York, USA (2005)
13. Das, A.: Automatic generation of MC/DC test data. Master thesis, Computer Science & Engineering, Indian Institute of Technology, Kharagpur, India (2012)
14. Bokil, P., Darke, P., Shrotri, U., Venkatesh, R.: Automatic test data generation for C programs. In: 3rd IEEE International Conference on Secure Software Integration and Reliability Improvement (2009)
15. Godboley, S., Dutta, A., Mohapatra, D.P., Mall, R.: J^3 model: a novel framework for improved modified condition/decision coverage analysis. Comput. Stand. Interfaces **50**, 1–17 (2016). Elsevier
16. Godboley, S., Dutta, A., Mohapatra, D.P., Das, A., Mall, R.: Making a concolic tester achieve increased MC/DC. Innov. Syst. Softw. Eng. **12**, 1–14 (2016). Springer
17. Godboley, S., Dutta, A., Mohapatra, D.P.: Java-HCT: an approach to increase MC/DC using Hybrid Concolic Testing for Java programs. In: Proceedings of the Federated Conference on Computer Science and Information Systems (36th IEEE Software Engineering Workshop), Annals of Computer Science and Information Systems, vol. 8, pp. 1709–1713. Gdansk University of Technology, Gdansk (2016)

Mutation Analysis of Stateflow to Improve the Modelling Analysis

Prachi Goyal[1](✉), Manju Nanda[2], and J. Jayanthi[2]

[1] Manipal Institute of Technology, Manipal, Karnataka, India
goyalprachi001@gmail.com
[2] Aerospace Electronics Division, CSIR-NAL, Bangalore, India
{manjun,jayanthi}@nal.res.in

Abstract. Formal methods possess great analyzing capability that has led to an increasing use by engineers in the development and verification-validation life-cycle of hardware and software critical systems. Mutation Analysis has been very effective in model design and safety analysis. In this paper primary idea is to integrate the mutation analysis of stateflow to the Integrated Mutation Analysis Tool. This enhanced property of the IMAT tool after integration will be able to analyze the functionalities of stateflow models of the highly critical systems. The effectiveness of the Stateflow mutation analysis can be validated using the case-study of Autopilot Mode Transition Logic.

Keywords: Formal methods · Mutation analysis · Stateflow integration · Safety critical systems

1 Introduction

In today's scenario, systems are increasingly dependent on software components. The complexity of systems with embedded software has increased and is increasing rapidly. The use of formal methods is motivated by performing appropriate analysis in the engineering discipline that can contribute to the correctness and robustness of the highly critical computer based systems. Formal methods are being used as a complementary technique for the reduction of errors in computer-based systems [1]. Model based designing and development approach is being extensively used in industries for implementing a safe and reliable system. Simulink tool is used for modelling and analysis of the control applications [11].

The primary idea of this proposed work is to improve the modelling analysis by adding new feature to the in-house developed mutation tool. The stateflow mutation is added as a new feature. Control algorithm in the aerospace domain use Simulink model for design and analysis. These control algorithms are developed using Stateflow parameters. Stateflow is a graphical design and development tool for control and supervisory logic used along with SIMULINK. Stateflow provides clear and concise descriptions of various complex model behavior using finite state machine theory, flow diagrams notations and state transitions diagram all in the same stateflow diagrams [9]. As high critical systems uses the stateflow so it is necessary to perform the fault analysis of these systems. For fault analysis of the model, mutation tool is used.

© Springer Nature Singapore Pte Ltd. 2017
M. Singh et al. (Eds.): ICACDS 2016, CCIS 721, pp. 173–182, 2017.
DOI: 10.1007/978-981-10-5427-3_19

By integration of stateflow to IMAT tool it will be easy to do the fault based analysis. This integration is being implemented by the GUI building in MATLAB R2013a. Integration of the stateflow to mutation tool helps in enhanced fault analysis of the critical model design.

This paper is divided into seven sections as follows: First section gives the introduction about the proposed work. It tells about the overview of the workflow which is required to be followed. Second Section tells about the related which is done in this field and tells that how the proposed approach will help in improving the analysis of the more complex models. Third section tells about the IMAT tool i.e. mutation tool and how it helps in doing the faulty analysis of the system. Fourth section tells about the workflow of the integration of the stateflow to the IMAT tool. This section is one the important aspect of our proposed work. Fifth section tells about the proven case study Autopilot Mode Transition Logic (MTL) is taken for the mutation analysis. Sixth section concludes the proposed work and tells the advantages of this work in the avionics industry.

2   Related Work

Various work has been done regarding the implementation of the mutation analysis on the safety critical systems. Singh [1] has found that the use of a formal methods eliminates ambiguity of the models and reduces the chance of errors being introduced during software development. Cachia [13] stated Mutation Testing is a technique which determines if a test suite thoroughly tests a codebase.

Okun [12] analyzed that to detect a fault in a program, a test case must cause the fault to affect the outputs, not just intermediate variables. Nayak [3] has done the mutation analysis for the Simulink models with the IMAT tool in which test cases are generated based on the models and the validity of the models is checked. Many highly critical systems uses the stateflow for defining their functionality because control laws are defined with the help of stateflow. It is necessary to validate the stateflow model with the help of faulty analysis. This paper discusses the new feature added to the mutation tool developed in-house. The newly added feature enhances the tool capability for analyzing critical system models such as control aircraft models.

3   IMAT- In-House Powerful Mutation Tool

Mutation analysis in model-based and software testing is observed as the most effective way to validate the software under inspection [2]. Integrated Mutation Analysis Tool (IMAT) is used for the fault analysis of the Simulink models. For the fault analysis the imported model should be correct and compatible. Mutation testing is a fault-based testing method that estimates the effectiveness of test cases of the Simulink models [2, 4]. While importing the test model to IMAT Tool, SLDV (Simulink Design Verifier) verifies the functionality and correctness of the imported model. Simulink Design Verifier uses the model-checker formal methods to identify intricate design errors in the models without large number of simulation runs [10]. After the verification of the imported model, the mutation tool generates the mutants of the model. Mutants are generally known as bugs. Bugs are the semantic/functional changes in the Simulink models [3]. Approach may fall under model based testing techniques where the GUI model is tested for its ability to kill wrong test cases [5]. Mutation testing is a fault based testing. The IMAT tool developed by CSIR-NAL generates test cases for the imported Simulink models. Each test case is compared with imported model and the mutation analysis is done in the form of "mutation adequacy score" [8]. IMAT is able to generate mutants for logical, mathematical, gain, constant, relational, sign, sum, min-max, trigonometric [3] functions.

Mutation generation for Simulink stateflow is not there in the current version of the IMAT Tool. This feature is essential as most of the avionics system software have complex logic. The best way to depict and implement the logic is by means of stateflow. Hence there is a requirement to integrate and mutate stateflow in the IMAT tool.

4   Approach for Integration of Stateflow to IMAT

Generating mutants for the stateflow models is quite complicated. Every component of the stateflow model should be correct and considered during programming of the generation of mutants. The transition of the states are of great importance. Every transition should be taken care of while generating mutants such that the functionality of the model is not affected. For the generation of mutants of stateflow, the stateflow is parsed and the mutants for the stateflow logic are created. These mutants are created using MATLAB code. This MATLAB mutant generation code is integrated with the IMAT mutation blocks. To execute the Stateflow mutants in IMAT Tool and push-button in the MATLAB GUI Building (Graphical User Interface) is created. The press of the pushbutton in the IMAT Tool will generate the mutants, generate test cases and test-report. The Fig. 1 shows the flowchart for the implementation of this new feature into the IMAT Tool.

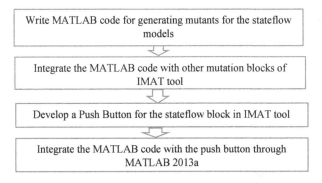

Fig. 1. Workflow of integration of stateflow to IMAT tool

After the MATLAB code, it should be integrated with the other mutation blocks such as relational, sum, logic etc. for the integration of the stateflow block with other blocks write the MATLAB code in the IMAT mutation blocks.

4.1 Workflow for Generation of Mutants for Stateflow

Before doing analysis of the model, the system should be loaded in the MATLAB workspace by using the load_system command in MATLAB. The imported Simulink model may be a masked subsystem or a stateflow chart. Initially the Simulink/stateflow models are generated as.mdl files which are being parsed using the Application Program Interface (API) [7]. To load the Simulink/Stateflow model into the memory it should be first connected to its object before accessing the stateflow chart [10]. It is necessary to use the Root object returned by the function sfroot to access the Model object [10]. If the model is locked at the system level it is necessary to unlock it. The MATLAB code for generating mutants is given as:

```
function [c] = Mutant_state (modelname,blockname)
open_system(modelname)
mkdir(modelname);
cd(modelname)
warning off
load_system(modelname);
x=find_system(bdroot,'MaskType','Stateflow');
x=char(x);
[m]=size(x);
c=0;
Mutantcount=0;

for j=1:1:m
    if strcmp(x(j,:), blockname)
        c=c+1;
    end
end
rt=sfroot;
S=rt.find('-isa','Stateflow.State');
save_system(modelname);
close_system(modelname);

for i=1:1:length(S)
    if  c ~= 0
        break;
    else
        Mutantcount = Mutantcount+1;
        load_system(modelname);
        rt=sfroot;
        s=rt.find('-isa','Stateflow.State');
        if (strcmp(get_param(modelname,'Lock'),'on'))
            set_param(modelname,'Lock','off');
        end
        save_system(modelname,[modelname, num2str(Mutantcount)]
,'BreakUserLinks', true);
        load_system([modelname,num2str(Mutantcount)]);
        open_system([modelname,num2str(Mutantcount)]);
```

```
            state=s(i).name;
            path=s(i).path;
            path=char(path);
path=strrep(path,[modelname,num2str(Mutantcount)],modelname);
            s(i).delete;
        disp([modelname,num2str(Mutantcount) ', Deleted the state '
state ' from ' path]);
        close_system(modelname);
        sfsave([modelname,num2str(Mutantcount)],
[modelname,num2str(Mutantcount)])
        close_system([modelname,num2str(Mutantcount)]);
    end
end
end
```

The flowchart for creating mutants of the stateflow models is shown in the flow-chart Fig. 2.

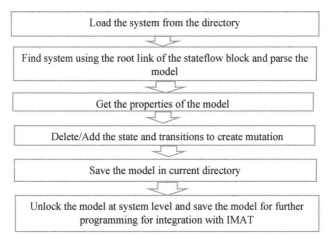

Fig. 2. Workflow for generating mutants

The mutants are generated by deleting one state at a time. If one of the states is deleted from the model then it will turn into a fault model. The parameters of the stateflow models can be parsed using the get function. New parsed parameters can be used to set new system parameters. Mutants can be generated by altering the states of the stateflow models. Mutants are saved automatically in current directory.

5 Case Study: Autopilot Mode Transition Logic (MTL)

An autopilot is a control system used to control the path of a vehicle without constant requirement of manual control by a human operator. Autopilots do not replace a human operator, but assist them in controlling the vehicle, allowing them to focus on broader aspects of operation, such as weather and systems. Autopilots are used in aircraft, boats, spacecraft, missiles, and others.

The MTL is a discrete event system consisting of a state, inputs and outputs. The state of the system is uniquely defined by its state vector, which comprises of state variables. The possible transitions values from a current value of a state variable are specified in the state transition matrix (STM) [6]. The actual transition of a state variable from the current value to a new value is based on condition(s) given in the condition matrix (CM) [6]. If the condition is true, then that element of the state vector is updated to the new value and this value is stored in the corresponding location in a temporary vector of same dimension as the state vector [6]. This is repeated for each of the elements of the state vector. The outputs corresponding to the current state vector are to be read out from the output matrix (OM). These outputs are passed on to the CG. Logical combinations of these outputs are computed to decide the status of the annunciators and the steering bars. [6] The state transition model for MTL an indigenous aircraft is shown as in Fig. 3.

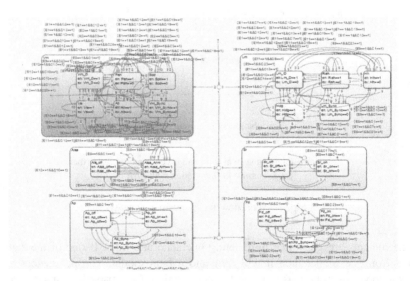

Fig. 3. The state transition model for Mode Transition Logic (MTL) of an indigenous Aircraft

The discrete inputs of the MTL block are: Sync switch on control yoke (SYNC), Total system health (Sheath), Autopilot failure flag (AFF), Weight on wheels (WOW), Stall warning (SW), Elevator trim switch (Err), Actuators monitoring flag (AMF), Manual pitch trim on CW (pilot/copilot) (MPT) [6]. There are 11 outputs of the MTL block: PAH, SPD Hold, VS Hold, Altitude Hold, Altitude Select Arm, RAH, Heading Hold, Heading select, Autopilot engage, Soft Ride, and Flight Director On [6].

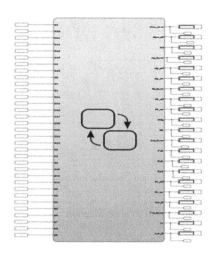

Fig. 4. Stateflow chart of mode transition logic of an indigenous aircraft

The State Transition Matrix consists of six superstates: Vm, Alsa, Lm, AP, Sr, and FD. Each substates have some substates. Vm has 6 substates. Alsa has 2 substates. Lm has 5 substates. AP has 3 substates. Sr has 2 substates. FD has 3 substates [6]. There are twelve events for the MTL: Bap, Bs, Bv, Ba, Bals, B0cap, BH, Bsr, BQDec, ALcap, Bfd, and SYNC. The output matrix consists of the same superstates and substates as of the State Transition Matrix. The outputs of MTL are: Pah, Sh, Vh, Ah, As, Rah, Hh, Hs, Ape, SRon, FDon [6]. The stateflow block of MTL of indigenous Aircrafts given in Fig. 4.

This case-study demonstrates the capability of the IMAT tool to uncover the design flaws in the Simulink model of complex systems. The tool provides the ease of selection of the mutants and generates optimized test cases to verify the design.

6 Results

The above stateflow diagram is used for the mutant generation. The mutants generated are shown in Fig. 5. The autopilot has total six Superstates from which one of the states Vm is deleted to create the fault model to verify the Vm design for its functionality and safety.

The vertical mode (Vm) state is used as an example for generating the mutant of the Mode Transition Logic. This vertical mode state is highly critical state in the Mode Transition Logic. It depends on six state variables functionalities: Disconnect, Pitch Altitude Hold, Speed Hold, Vertical speed, Altitude Hold, SYNC. These states plays an important role in controlling the aircraft for e.g. Pitch Altitude mode maintains the current pitch altitude of the aircraft at the time of engagement and it is a default vertical mode.

The pushbutton of stateflow in IMAT Tool is created as shown in Fig. 6.

The Fig. 6 lists the mutants created for the MTL logic. The mutant for the stateflow is being be used to analyze the stateflow models for its functionality. The tool creates the mutants for the Mode Transition Logic are successfully generated. Similar analysis can be carried out for complex Simulink models. This will help in detecting design flaws earlier in the system life-cycle.

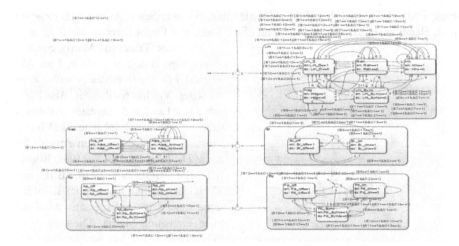

Fig. 5. Mutant generated deleting the state Vm from state diagram

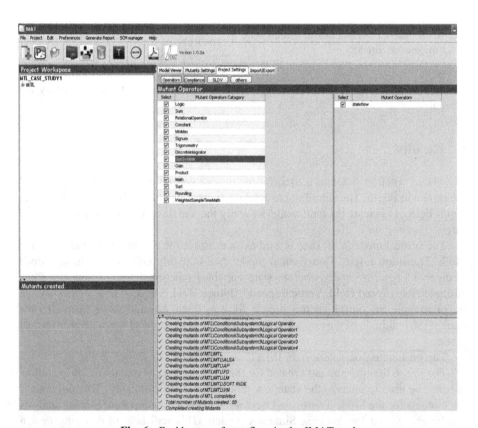

Fig. 6. Pushbutton of stateflow in the IMAT tool

7 Conclusion

In this paper, it is shown that integration of the stateflow will enhance the analyzing capacity of IMAT tool and the mutants of the Autopilot Mode Transition Logic (MTL) are generated which validates the workflow. Like the critical state Vm is altered to create mutant of the model, other states can also be altered to create the mutants of the parent model. The verification of the proposed work can be done by any proven system to verify their critical design and analyze their effectiveness under various conditions. The effectiveness of the system can be analyzed by the mutation score generated by the IMAT tool. IMAT tool integrated with the aspect will give better analysis of the critical systems and can reduce more human and modelling errors, prevent the catastrophic conditions and thus save many human lives. More complex and critical systems can be analyzed by using this approach.

8 Future Work

In this approach, there is a main drawback that for high critical systems it is very tedious task to analyze that which state can be deleted one at a time thus it is more time consuming to analyze the safety critical systems. In this paper mutants are created by deleting only one state at a time as a result it will generate a low mutation score. Currently the work is in progress that more number of mutants can be generated for a particular system and generate the test cases for the stateflow models. After full integration the stateflow models can be analyzed more effectively. Integration of other model checker to IMAT tool will increase the capacity of IMAT Tool for analysis of model-based validation.

Acknowledgement. The authors thank Director, CSIR-National Aerospace Laboratories Bangalore for supporting this work.

References

1. Singh, M.: Formal methods: a complementary support for testing. Int. J. Adv. Res. Comput. Sci. Softw. Eng. **3**(2), 320–322 (2013)
2. Singh, P.K., Sangwan, O.P., Sharma, A.: A study and review on the development of mutation testing tools for java and aspect-j program. Int. J. Mod. Educ. Comput. Sci. **11**, 1–10 (2014)
3. Jayanthi, J., Nanda, M., Nayak, S.: A lightweight integration of mutation analysis with the model checker for system safety verification. In: IEEE International Systems Conference (SysCon) (2013)
4. DeMillo, R.A., Lipton, R.J., Sayward, F.G.: Hints on test data selection: help for the practicing programmer. Computer **11**(4), 34–41 (1978). IEEE
5. Sujata, P.G., Sonali, I.R.: Investigation of mutation testing & its operators for testing case generations. Int. J. Adv. Res. Comput. Sci. Softw. Eng. **3**(10) (2013)

6. Jayanthi, J., Nanda, M., Sreekath, K.P., Lakshmi, P.: Software design description for SARAS SWS/AIC System. National Aerospace Laboratories_ ALD, Vol.-10, Rep No: DR-22
7. Mathworks Inc.: Application Program Interface Guide Version 5 http://www.mathworks.com
8. Jia, Y., Harman, M.: An analysis and survey of the development of mutation testing. IEEE Trans. Softw. Eng. **37**(5), 649–678 (2011)
9. Baier, C., Katoen, J.P.: Principles of Model Checking. MIT Press, Cambridge (2008)
10. The MathWorks, Mathworks MATLAB Simulink. http://www.mathworks.com/products/simulink
11. Mahesh Gowda, N.M., Kiran, Y., Parthasarthy, S.S.: Modelling of Buck DC-DC Converter Using Simulink. Int. J. Innov. Res. Sci. Eng. Technol. **3**(7), 14965–14975 (2014)
12. Okun, V.: Specification mutation for test generation and analysis (Doctoral dissertation. University of Maryland, Baltimore County) (2004)
13. Cachia, M.A.: Investigating ways to make mutation testing feasible in agile environments. Report submitted in University of Malta (2012)

Prioritization of Near-Miss Incidents Using Text Mining and Bayesian Network

Abhishek Verma[✉], Deeshant Rajput, and J. Maiti

Department of Industrial and Systems Engineering,
Indian Institute of Technology Kharagpur, Kharagpur 721302, India
abhishekverma.cs@gmail.com, deeshantrajput@gmail.com,
jhareswar.maiti@gmail.com

Abstract. Near-Miss incidents can be treated as events to signal the weakness of safety management system (SMS) at the workplace. Analyzing near-misses will provide relevant root causes behind such incidents so that effective safety related interventions can be developed beforehand. Despite having a huge potential towards workplace safety improvements, analysis of near-misses is scant in the literature owing to the fact that near-misses are often reported as text narratives. The aim of this study is therefore to explore text-mining for extraction of root causes of near-misses from the narrative text descriptions of such incidents and to measure their relationships probabilistically. Root causes were extracted by word cloud technique and causal model was constructed using a Bayesian network (BN). Finally, using BN's inference mechanism, scenarios were evaluated and root causes were listed in a prioritized order. A case study in a steel plant validated the approach and raised concerns for variety of circumstances such as incidents related to collision, slip-trip-fall, and working at height.

Keywords: Bayesian network · Word cloud · Narrative text · Near-miss incidents · Workplace safety

1 Introduction

Near miss reporting produces the same amount of information as an accident reporting provides, without any serious consequences. It gives the opportunity to move from reaction to prediction of incident. Quantitative estimation of near miss events is very important; otherwise it may escalate to accident in near future with lack of imposed constraints or loss of control on the chain of events. The aim of this study is to investigate and model the root causes of near miss incidents of a steel plant. Data were captured as incident reports contain incidents' information in textual format. The narrative text field provides user to include the details about the incident, such as description about the machine, exact location, surrounding condition, summary about the incidents etc. However, it also increases the complexity of analysis to extract meaningful information. To serve this purpose both the structured and narrative text data were analyzed using text mining and Bayesian network (BN). The approach has been implemented to prioritize the root causes behind near-miss events.

© Springer Nature Singapore Pte Ltd. 2017
M. Singh et al. (Eds.): ICACDS 2016, CCIS 721, pp. 183–191, 2017.
DOI: 10.1007/978-981-10-5427-3_20

The rest of the paper is organized in the following manner. Related literature review is discussed in brief in Sect. 2. In Sect. 3, preparation of data and employed techniques are discussed in short. The results obtained from the model and its practical implications are given in Sect. 4. Finally, conclusions of the study with scope of future research are given in Sect. 5.

2   Literature Review

Research in near-miss management is still in infancy state leaving avenues, scopes and opportunities to structure and develop models around it. Importance of near-miss incident data analysis, for safety improvement in the organization was discussed and inverse proportionality between near-misses and actual accident cases was found [1]. So, learning from near-miss events and prioritization of causal factors behind near-miss incidents are utmost required. Some safety related studies incorporated narrative text to extract and predict incident scenarios [2–4]. Bayesian auto coding methods have been applied to near miss data for minimizing the human effort required to manually code the large descriptive dataset [5]. Bier and Mosleh [6] analyzed the near-miss cases for nuclear plant using probabilistic model and suggested that near-miss events should be given more preference than experts' claim. A study was conducted to evaluate and prioritize the different risk associated with water mains failure using a Bayesian belief network model [7]. BN was also used to prioritize the incidents with help of score collected from expert opinion. Recently, Bayesian network combined with analytic hierarchy process (AHP) has been used to prioritize the factors behind the near-miss events [8]. In that study the prior probability of factors causing near misses was decided by the experts' judgement. It is better to include the information provided by organization's employees about the near-miss incidents, experienced by them. Our study incorporates the information from all the workers instead of relying only on the expert judgement.

3   Methodology

Figure 1 presents the conceptual framework of this study in qualitative and quantitative aspect. The network structure of BN for identifying incident factors corresponds to qualitative aspect, while estimating the probabilities of factors and inference form the networks correspond to the quantitative aspect. The factors (root causes) are identified under coded primary causes by text mining the narrative text. The prior probability is calculated for each factor by measuring their frequency in incidents reports for corresponding coded primary cause. After finding the prior probability of root causes, the conditional probability is calculated for every dependent node in BN to know the cause-consequence relationship among them. Hypothetical evidence then considered about the absence of individual root cause to see the effect on overall BN. Scenarios were generated to draw the conclusion about the top contributing root causes. R language and OpenMarkov software were utilized to build word cloud and Bayesian network respectively. The hardware configuration for the analysis includes: Intel-core(TM) i5-4200 M CPU@ 2.50 GHz, 4 GB RAM and Windows 8 (64 bit).

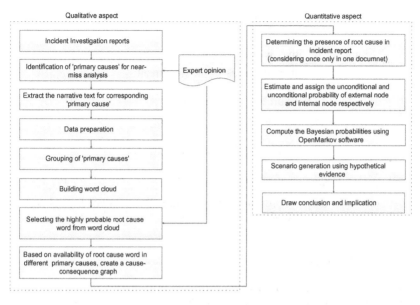

Qualitative aspect   Quantitative aspect

Fig. 1. Conceptual framework for study

3.1 Data Collection and Preparation

For this study, incident investigation data of a steel plant is considered. Data preparation involves resolving various issues related to data like missing values, duplicate data points, spelling errors, non-vocabulary words, incomplete information, etc. Raw file extracted from the safety management system (SMS) database of the plant studied, in MS excel format, originally had 9086 records. After pre-processing, 8877 records were considered for further analysis. After considering 16 primary causes listed in the SMS (out of these 8877 records), 2984 cases were found as near-miss incidents.

3.2 Word Cloud Preparation

Word cloud can extract the information from the text contents and provides overview of the key points. Weighting function is used to calculate the weight of the words using term frequency-inverse document frequency (tf-idf) [9], which magnifies the importance of words occur frequently within a document and rarely across the documents. Brief description of the steps to create the word cloud using R language is given as follows:

1. The brief description of incidents is extracted for individual primary cause.
2. Stop words like "a", "an", "the", "and", "or" were removed.
3. Corpus is created through 'Corpus()' function and structured dataset is created by using 'TermDocumentMatrix()' function.

4. Scoring of words is done by using the 'tf-idf' statistic given as follows:

$$tf(t,d) = \frac{\text{number of times word t appears in a document}}{\text{total number of words in the document}} = \frac{f_d(t)}{\max_{w \in d} f_d(w)} \quad (1)$$

$$idf(t,D) = \ln \frac{\text{total number of documents}}{\text{number of documents with word t in it}} = \ln \frac{|D|}{|\{d \in D : t \in d\}|} \quad (2)$$

$$tfidf(t,d,D) = tf(t,d).idf(t,D) \quad (3)$$

where, $f_d(t) = $ *frequency of word t in report d*, and $D = $ *corpus of documents*.

5. The structured format of words and their corresponding estimated weightages have been found, will be finally put into the 'wordcloud()' function to build word cloud.

3.3   Bayesian Network

Bayesian networks (BNs) use a directed acyclic graph (DAG) to represent conditional probability relationships between a set of variables [10]. As shown in Fig. 2, a BN is composed of set of variables (e.g., X, Y1, Y2 and Z) and a set of directed links between vertices that represent the relationships between these variables. Each variable have mutually exclusive states (e.g., for X, Y1, Y2 and Z, the states are {Pr = present, Ab = absent}). The nodes with arcs directed into are called "child" node and the nodes from which arrows comes from are called "parent" nodes (e.g., Y1 and Y2 are child of X and the parents of Z). Edges show conditional dependencies between these variables such that the value of any variable is a probabilistic function of the values of the variables which are its parents in the DAG. These dependencies on predecessor nodes are quantified through conditional probability tables (CPTs) attached to each node.

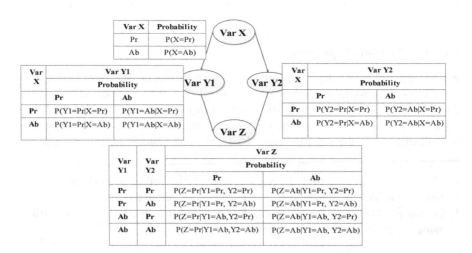

Fig. 2. Sample of Bayesian network (BN)

In Bayesian analysis the relation between parent nodes Y_i ($i = 1, 2, ..., n$) and the evidence or child node Z can be computed as:

$$p(Y_i|Z) = \frac{p(Z|Y_i) \times p(Y_i)}{\sum_{j=1}^{n} p(Z|Y_j) \times p(Y_j)} \tag{4}$$

where, p(Y|Z) represents the posterior probability of occurrence of variable Y with the given condition that Z occurs, p(Y) is the prior probability of Y, and p(Z|Y) denotes the hood distribution of Z given the occurrence of Y.

4 Results and Discussion

4.1 Root Cause Extraction from Word Cloud

Comparison word-cloud allows studying the differences or similarities between two or more primary causes by plotting the word cloud of each primary cause against the other. Figure 3 shows the comparison cloud of "collision and fall related" incidents grouped by the primary causes: dashing/collision, skidding, slip/trip/fall, and working at height. Due to space limitation all clouds are not shown in the paper. Readers are encouraged to contact authors of this study regarding it. Keywords (root causes) were extracted on the basis of presence in number of incident reports (counted only once for individual report).

Fig. 3. Comparison word cloud of collision and fall related incidents

4.2 BN Causal Model from Data

In the Fig. 4, model based on the root causes extracted from the word cloud is constructed. In BN, the conditional probability table (CPT) structure depends upon the conditional independence of nodes. In our study for every node, two states were defined as 'present' and 'absent'. The probability of independent nodes was calculated by its frequency in all the reports of particular primary cause. In this study, Open-Markov software [11] has been employed to perform the model construction and CPT calculation. Four groups were formed on the basis of similarity and to minimize the mathematical calculation by clubbing different primary causes as per experts' opinions. So, three levels of causal factors (group, primary, root level) were considered for building the BN. Finally, the conditional probabilities of all the child nodes are computed assuming all possible combination of probability values of its parents. For making BN, total 57 nodes (36 independent nodes, 21 dependent nodes), 88 links and 1200 conditional probabilities were estimated. After calculating all the prior and conditional probability at every node, the probability of occurrence of near-miss event comes out to be 36.04%. Due to high connectivity and low probability of root cause node, it is important to note that this causes small change in near-miss index, contributed by a particular node.

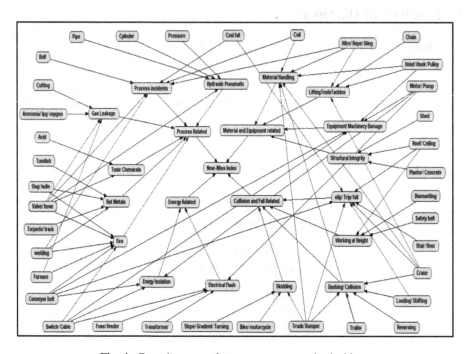

Fig. 4. Bayesian network to measure near-miss incidents

Table 1. Prioritized order of groups after incorporating the hypothetical evidence about their absence

Order	Group	Posterior probability	Near-miss node probability in absence of group cause
1	Collision and fall related	75.19	32.40
2	Process related	18.66	35.24
3	Energy related	6.34	35.91
4	Material and equipment related	32.77	36.00

Table 2. Prioritized order of primary cause after incorporating the hypothetical evidence about their absence

Order	Primary cause	Posterior probability	Near-miss node probability in absence of primary cause
1	Slip/trip/fall	47.11	35.03
2	Working at height	59.78	35.13
3	Process incidents	32.45	35.55
4	Fire	19.77	35.82
5	Dashing collision	15.80	35.83
6	Electrical flash	54.06	35.92
7	Skidding	4.84	35.99
8	Material handling	32.77	36.00
9	Gas leakage	4.56	36.02
10	Energy isolation	14.81	36.03
11	Hot metals	2.97	36.03
12	Hydraulic/pneumatic	2.30	36.03
13	Equipment machinery damage	13.94	36.04
14	Structural integrity	7.18	36.04
15	Lifting tools tackles	1.93	36.04
16	Toxic chemicals	0.97	36.04

Table 3. Prioritized order of root causes obtained from word cloud after incorporating the hypothetical evidence about their absence

Order	Root cause (primary cause)	Probability (%)	Near-miss node probability in absence of root cause
1	Switch/cable	23.16	36.02
2	Stairs/floor condition	15.87	36.02
3	Wire/rope/sling	16.23	36.03
4	Crane	13.74	36.03
5	Valve/hose	10.64	36.03
6	Truck/dumper	8.44	36.03
7	Loading/shifting	7.46	36.03

To prioritize the causal factors at three different levels of network, their effect on near-miss node was estimated by incorporating the hypothetical evidence of absence of different nodes. It will help in indicating the effect of the particular node on overall near-miss node. Prioritized order of particular group, primary cause and root cause level are given in Tables 1, 2 and 3 respectively. In Table 1, all groups are listed in prioritized order of their effect on near-miss node. Similarly in Table 2, primary causes are listed down in prioritized order to show their individual impact on the near-miss node. In Table 3, the root causes extracted from narrative text using text mining are listed and their effect on near-miss node is measured. It will help the safety practitioners to put focused intervention and safety control measures to improve the safety performance at workplaces.

5 Conclusions

The proposed model can extract information at lowest level using word cloud and combines with BN to help in prioritizing the near-miss incidents. The model is capable to provide qualitative and quantitative information of different causes of near-miss. Slip/trip/fall, material handling, electrical flash, dashing/collision and energy isolation are found to be the top five primary causes out of 16 primary causes reported in preliminary investigation report data. At the lowest level, 36 root causes were extracted and their impact on overall network was measured by providing hypothetical evidence. It was found that switch/cable, condition of stair/floor, wire/rope/sling, crane operation, valve/hose dysfunction, and heavy vehicle like truck or dumper and loading or shifting operation and have more propensity of the causing incident. Other root causes can also be prioritized on the basis of their probability and impact on intermediate nodes. It can help to focus the attention of management to improve on particular area. Our future work would focus to analysis organizational hierarchy to find out the location specific causes. Moreover, validation of model can be done by using expert opinions as the gold standard, or using the developed near-miss based system to predict actual accidents and measuring its predictive power.

References

1. Jones, S., Kirchsteiger, C., Bjerke, W.: The importance of near miss reporting to further improve safety performance. J. Loss Prev. Process Ind. **12**(1), 59–67 (1999)
2. Abdat, F., Leclercq, S., Cuny, X., Tissot, C.: Extracting recurrent scenarios from narrative texts using a Bayesian network: application to serious occupational accidents with movement disturbance. Accid. Anal. Prev. **70**, 155–166 (2014)
3. Lincoln, A.E., Sorock, G.S., Courtney, T.K., Wellman, H.M., Smith, G.S., Amoroso, P.J.: Using narrative text and coded data to develop hazard scenarios for occupational injury interventions. Inj. Prev. **10**(4), 249–254 (2004)
4. Sawaragi, T., Ito, K., Horiguchi, Y., Nakanishi, H.: Identifying latent similarities among near-miss incident records using a text-mining method and a scenario-based approach. In: Salvendy, G., Smith, M.J. (eds.) Human Interface 2009. LNCS, vol. 5618, pp. 594–603. Springer, Heidelberg (2009). doi:10.1007/978-3-642-02559-4_65
5. Taylor, J.A., Lacovara, A.V., Smith, G.S., Pandian, R., Lehto, M.: Near-miss narratives from the fire service: a Bayesian analysis. Accid. Anal. Prev. **62**, 119–129 (2014)
6. Bier, V.M., Mosleh, A.: The analysis of accident precursors and near misses: implications for risk assessment and risk management. Reliab. Eng. Syst. Saf. **27**(1), 91–101 (1990)
7. Kabir, G., Tesfamariam, S., Francisque, A., Sadiq, R.: Evaluating risk of water mains failure using a Bayesian belief network model. Eur. J. Oper. Res. **240**(1), 220–234 (2015)
8. Zubair, M., Park, S., Heo, G., Hassan, M.U., Aamir, M.: Study on nuclear accident precursors using AHP and BBN, a case study of Fukushima accident. Int. J. Energy Res. **39**(1), 98–110 (2015)

9. Manning, C.D., Raghavan, P., Schütze, H.: An Introduction to Information Retrieval. Cambridge University Press, New York (2008)
10. Pearl, J.: Probabilistic Reasoning in Intelligent Systems: Networks of Plausible Inference. Morgan Kaufmann Publishers Inc., San Francisco (1988)
11. Arias, M., Díez, F., Palacios, M.: OpenMarkovXML. A format for encoding probabilistic graphical models (2010)

Security Integration in Big Data Life Cycle

Kanika$^{(\boxtimes)}$, Alka Agrawal, and R.A. Khan

Department of Information Technology, BBA University, Lucknow, India
Sharma.kanika247@gmail.com, alka_csjmu@yahoo.co.in,
khanraees@yahoo.com

Abstract. We are living in a modern age, where technology is all around us. On single click user can do anything just like book a ticket, shopping, take an appointment to anyone, see medical reports, etc. Technology is so accessible because smart phones ownership. Large amount of data about users which is generated from various sources such as social networking sites, sensors devices, medical data etc. is called big data. With the increased use of big data, there arise many issues; especially security issues which may badly impact a person's or an organization's privacy. Yazan et al., presented threat and security attack model for big data security lifecycle. In this paper authors presents a critical review of the work and describes some security issues of big data. An approach to secure threat model for big data lifecycle has been proposed as a main contribution of the paper.

Keywords: Big data · Security issues · Security threat model for big data lifecycle

1 Introduction

A huge amount of data about individuals related to their medical, internet activity, social networking, energy usage, communication patterns and social interactions is called big data. From these sources, data is being collected and processed by various survey organizations, national statistical agencies, medical centers, The Web, and companies etc. [1]. Now a day's people are living in a technology era, where people connect with each other, through internet. They are known to each other on facebook, twitter on different social sites but unfortunately they don't know each other as a neighbor. They share photos, messages, exchange their number etc. Big data is very huge and its size is increasing day by day [2]. According to IDC report, it is assumed that till 2020 data will grow from 130 exabytes to 40,000 exabytes, or 40 trillion gigabytes [7]. With this enormous size of data, the privacy and security breaches are expected to increase exponentially [7]. The researcher must be cared out to protect the data provided by the user. According to IBM, 80% of the data generated by various organizations is unstructured [16] (Fig. 1).

© Springer Nature Singapore Pte Ltd. 2017
M. Singh et al. (Eds.): ICACDS 2016, CCIS 721, pp. 192–200, 2017.
DOI: 10.1007/978-981-10-5427-3_21

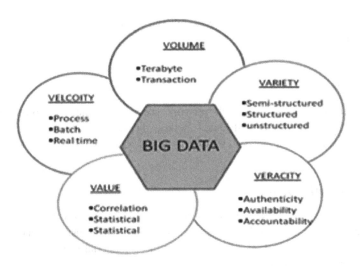

Fig. 1. Big Data Characteristics

Since last two years, users are facing the many issues due to increasing amount of the data. Due to its difficulty and volume, it cannot be handled through existing conventional techniques [1]. There is many privacy issues and breach occurred in 2006. 20 million search queries were released by America Online (AOL). According to this information, couple of reporters of New York Times were able to locate the individuality of user No. 4417749 based on just explore history [10].

To preserve the big data security, Yazan et al. projected a Big Data Lifecycle threat model. This threat model is advancement of the work of Xu et al. [5]. According to Yazan et al., the life span of big data can be further sub divided into four phases such as data collection, data storage, data analytics, and knowledge creation. For all phase, they have explained security attacks and threats. Proposed threat model by the authors has some drawbacks. The researcher critically examines the model and proposed improved threat model.

This paper as organized as Sect. 2 describing security issues of big data, Sect. 3 of this paper briefly describes yazan's security life cycle. In Subsects. 3.2 and 3.3 describes the merits and demerits of life cycle. Section 4 presents some suggestions to improve the cycle, and a pictorial representation of the improved security process has been depicted and explained and Sect. 5 explain the threats and attacks on each phase with solutions.

2 Security Issues of Big Data

Security and privacy plays an prominent role in the respect of big data. The fast data introduce vast open access and big difficulties for big data [3]. During the availability of data, it is compulsory that data security has to be preserved, but it is not possible to securely recover data. Here we have talked over some security points such as network level issues, verification level issues, data level issues, and generic level issues and so on. They are mentioned below.

2.1 Network Level

Network level challenges deal with network security and network protocols, like Inter-nodes communication, distributed nodes, distributed data. Many nodes are existing in clusters and on those nodes, processing or estimation of data is done [7, 13].

2.2 Authentication Level

User authentication level issues tackle with encryption/decryption methods, authentication technique and logging. Various nodes are existing in a cluster. Every node has a other priorities or rights. If malicious nodes get the managerial rights, then it will take away or change the confidential data [4, 7].

2.3 Generic Types

In distributed environment, many technologies used for data computation, as well as some conventional security kit for providing security features. Some conventional security kits were developed over few years ago. So these kits may not be well-matched with the latest distributed structure of big data [4, 7].

2.4 Distributed Data

To minimize parallel processing, a big data set can be planted away in many parts across numerous system. Moreover, redundant copies of data are made to assured the data consistency. In the heterogeneous atmosphere, it is very difficult to discover the particular location, where of a file are kept [8].

3 Security Life Cycle of Big Data

This Big data security lifecycle is projected by Yazan et al. [3], having four phases, i.e. data collection, data storage, data analytics, and knowledge creation. The target of the researchers is to protect data in the diverse atmosphere (Fig. 2).

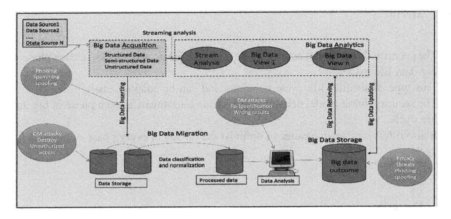

Fig. 2. Big data life cycle threat model

3.1 Phases of the Model

Big data life cycle threat model has following phases:

Data Collection Phase
The first phase of the threat model is data collection phase. In this phase, data comes from different sources and with different formats. The author has described that in order to be secure big data collection phase must be secured and protected. They have emphasized that data should be gathered from reliable sources [1].

Data storage phase
The next phase of this life cycle is data storage phase. In this phase, the data is stored and prepared to be used for the another phase. As data is sensitive, it is essential to take sufficient precautions during data storage for the safety of data in this phase, the author have explained few security measures including, data anonymization data partitioning, and permutation [1].

Data Analytics Phase
Data analytics phase is the third phase and it is used to generate knowledge. Authors have explained data mining methods such as clustering, association rule mining and classification. To protect data, in this phase, data mining process and its output must be secured against data mining based attacks [1].

Knowledge Creation Phase
The last phase of this life cycle is knowledge creation phase. In this phase generated knowledge, is considered as sensitive to crucial data. The authors have emphasized that the organizations should be very careful with data protection. It should not be display in public [1].

3.2 Merits

– The security threat model addresses the security threats and attacks in each phase of big data life cycle.
– This type of security life cycle is unique and can be adapted easily.
– The security threat model delivers depth vision into threats at each phase of big data life cycle.
– It also offers counter-measures to diminist the threats in every phase of big data life cycle.

3.3 Demerits

– The big data lifecycle threat model is unfinished because it does not deliver the source of data evidently. They do not describe the character of data creator. Does it overlook the user who deliver or makes data?
– The researchers have unsuccessfull to explain step by step procedure of the life cycle.
– The life cycle conferred, seems vague and imperfect.
– In the terms of this life cycle, they have not discussed the terms streaming analysis, big data migration, and big data analytics.

4 An Enhanced Security Threat Model

4.1 Data Creation Phase

The most vital phase of enhanced security threat model for big data life cycle is data Creation phase. A data creator is a person who delivers data to the data collector. When a creator gives his information to others, there is always a chance of attacks. A hacker/attacker can exploit his material provided to the data collector. So an originator is too conscious of such type of occurrences on his data. A creator must take into account that the following recommendation to avoid an attack on his data. While providing the data, creator must keep in mind the following recommendations:

• A creator should deliver only appropriate data to the data collector.
• The creator must be definite about the genuineness of the data collector. The creator must not deliver his delicate data until mandatory.
• The creator must retain in his mind that once any evidence dispersed from his side, he loses control over it, regardless of the sensitivity of data (Fig. 3).

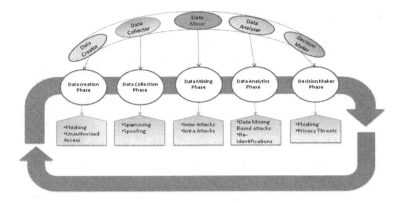

Fig. 3. The new security threat model for big data life cycle

4.2 Data Collection Phase

The another stage of the projected security threat model is data collection phase. Data collection phase is susceptible to several attacks like phishing, spoofing attacks [1].

4.3 Data Mining Phase

The data collector delivers changed data to the data miner. The main alarm of data miner is to save sensitive data from rogue. Data mining stage is vulnerable to numerous attacks like novel networks attacks, content-based attacks [11], distributed/denial of service attacks [9], etc.

4.4 Data Analytics Phase

The fourth segment of this planned security threat model is data analytics phase. In this segment, the data examined the data attained from data mining phase. the analyzer observes huge amounts of data to determine hidden forms, to cite sensitive data [5].

4.5 Decision Maker Phase

The last phase of this planned security threat model is decision maker phase. This segment uses verified and appreciated information attained from the last phase. The exact goal of data mining is to deliver the valuable information to the decision maker so, that decision maker can select a optimal way to attain organization's targets [5].

5 Threats and Attacks of Big Data

Data is in a huge amount that is known as Big Data. An attacker can use data mining methods and procedures to fetch out the confidential data and can misuse it or can release in public. Table 1 list out the threats and their suggested defense for each phase of big data life cycle:

Table 1. Threats and countermeasures for big data life cycle

Phases	Threats and attacks	Description	Suggested defense
Data creation phase	Phishing	Attempt to obtain sensitive information often for malicious reasons [1]	Security awareness program
	Unauthorised access	When a person wants to access a website, services, or another system through else's account or other methods [12]	Access control
Data collection phase	Spamming Spoofing	These attacks are hacking data provider and collector to get access to the data in the collection phase [1]	Security awareness program
Data mining phase	Inter attacks Intra attacks	Malicious attack committed on a network or system by a person with official system right of entry [14, 15]	Antivirus and Internal intrusion detection systems (IDS)
Data analytics phase	Data mining Based attacks	Using data mining methods to extract sensitive knowledge [6]	Divide datasets (vertically and Horizontally) and use access control
	Re-identification	the attack on the confidentiality of data collection [12]	Core attributes encryption
	Wrong result threat	Using incorrect analysis process, which lead to incorrect results [1]	Follow correct analysis procedures and document, audit, and review the process
Decision-making phase	Privacy threats	The release of obtained knowledge [1]	Encrypt the resulting knowledge and adopting access control strategy
	Phishing	Attempt to acquire sensitive information often for malicious reasons [1]	Security awareness program

6 Conclusions

In today's era, data and information are created and processed at very high speed producing large volume of data added to the database from various sources. This large volume of data is known as 'Big Data. To maintain big data in a heterogeneous environment is a difficult task. It is very vast in size that cannot be easily handled through traditional database handling techniques. With the increase in the use and demands of big data, software industries are facing security issues such as authentication level, network level etc. Individual's privacy is still a major problem and providing security has become very sensitive. In this paper authors have presented a security approach to measures the attacks in big data life cycle. In this paper authors explain big data security lifecycle consists five phases including data creation phase, data collection phase, data mining phase, data analytics phase and decision-making phase. The paper explains about threats and their countermeasures for big data while it is moving through different phases of its life cycle.

References

1. Alshboul, Y., et al.: Big data life cycle: threats and security model. Am. Conf. Inf. Syst., 1–7 (2015)
2. Shirudkar, K., et al.: Big data security. Int. J. Adv. Res. Comput. Sci. Softw. Eng., 1100–1109 (2015)
3. Puthal, D., et al.: A dynamic prime number based efficient security mechanism for big sensing data streams. In: IEEE International Conference on Trust, Security and Privacy in Computing and communications (IEEE TrustCom-2015), pp. 1–31 (2015)
4. Savant, V.G., et al.: Approaches to solve big data security issues and comparative study of cryptographic algorithms for data encryption. Int. J. Eng. Res. Gen. Sci. **3**, 425–428 (2015)
5. Xu, L., et al.: Information security in big data: privacy and data mining. IEEE Access **5**, 1149–1176 (2014)
6. Bhaya, W., et al.: A proactive DDoS attack detection approach using data mining cluster analysis. J. Next Gener. Inf. Technol. (JNIT) **5**, 36–47 (2014)
7. Sharma, P., et al.: Securing big data Hadoop: a review of security issues, threats, and solution. Int. J. Comput. Sci. Inf. Technol. (IJCSIT) **5**(2), 2126–2131 (2014)
8. Inukollu, V.N., et al.: Security issues associated with big data in cloud computing. Int. J. Netw. Secur. Appl. (IJNSA), 45–46 (2014)
9. Gantz, J., et al.: The digital universe in 2020: big data, bigger digital shadows, and biggest growth in the Far East. IDC Analyze the Future, pp. 1–16 (2012)
10. Machanavajjhala, A. et al.: Big privacy: protecting confidentiality in big data. XRDS: Crossroads ACM Mag. Stud. **19**, 20–23 (2012)
11. Levent, E., Eilertson, E., Lazarevic, A., Tan, P., Dokas, P., Srivastava, J., Kumar, V.: Detection and summarization of novel network attacks using data mining. Minnesota INtrusion Detection System (MINDS) Technical report (2003)
12. Malin, B.: Compromising privacy with trail re-identification: the REIDIT algorithms. Carnegie Mellon University, Center for Automated Learning and Discovery (2002)

13. Benantar, M., et al.: Method and system for maintaining client server security associations in a distributed computing system. US Patent (2000)
14. https://www.techopedia.com/definition/26217/insider-attack
15. http://resources.infosecinstitute.com/insider-vs-outsider-threats-identify-and-prevent
16. http://www.computerhope.com/jargon/u/unauacce.htm

Trust Based Energy Efficient Clustering Protocol in Wireless Sensor Networks for Military Applications

T.P. Rani[1,2(✉)] and C. Jayakumar[3]

[1] Department of Information and Communication Engineering,
Anna University, Chennai, India
[2] Department of Information Technology,
Sri Sai Ram Engineering College, Chennai, India
`rani.it@sairam.edu.in`
[3] Department of Computer Science and Engineering,
Sri Venkateswara College of Engineering, Chennai, India

Abstract. Wireless sensor network finds its prominence in military applications because the sensing nature of sensors deduces uncertainty. As the sensors may work in harsh environments, minimal or no manual attention can be given to the sensors. Hence they are prone to adversary attacks. With the objective of obtaining security in these environments, trust based energy efficient method TBEM is suggested for clustered wireless sensor networks. By energy efficient and trust based clustering, security and decrease in energy deprivation in Wireless sensor networks can be achieved. The method is compared with existing Low Energy Adaptive Clustering Hierarchy LEACH protocol. The achieved minimal false positives and false negatives are presented for performance analysis.

Keywords: Trust · WSN · Network security

1 Introduction

Wireless sensor networks (WSN) find its prominence in military applications due to its sensing nature [1]. The use of sensors can reduce uncertainty by deducing intrusions. In military, communication requires end to end message security as they are highly confidential. The military applications may work in different environment such as battlefield, urban area or in disaster reliefs. Depending upon the environment, the application requirements may vary. Sensors sensing light, pressure, sound and chemical vapors may be used in perilous circumstances and to detect the change in environment behavior. Ultrasonic Sensors and radars are widely used in intrusion detection for distance estimations. Image processing enhances the intrusion detection through object detection and tracking techniques.

In military applications, security has remained as a major challenge in WSN [2, 3]. Such harsh environments require minimal manual interference. One time sensor nodes

© Springer Nature Singapore Pte Ltd. 2017
M. Singh et al. (Eds.): ICACDS 2016, CCIS 721, pp. 201–209, 2017.
DOI: 10.1007/978-981-10-5427-3_22

are required in these applications as sensors cannot be reused. Except solar sensor nodes, the sensor nodes do not have alternate power source after deployment. Hence the sensor nodes have limited transmission range, processing and storage capabilities. Due to these challenges, the adversaries may target the energy source of WSN and make it paralytic for further communications.

2 Related Works

Clustering [4–6] is a prominent method for communication as several nodes are clustered under cluster heads. The communication to a cluster requires only a communication to the cluster head and the cluster head is responsible for communicating it to the cluster members. The clustering protocols such as Low Energy Adaptive Clustering Hierarchy (LEACH) [7] serve the purpose. A cluster head must not be a malicious node as the communication to a cluster depends on the cluster head. A malicious cluster head may turn a cluster to be infertile for further communications. This paper provides a novel method Trust Based Energy Efficient Method TBEM for cluster head election. It is based on Trust and Energy efficiency of nodes for cluster head election.

Trust [8–11] serves as a major source for security as it is a trait based on past behaviors of a node. It helps in identifying the genuineness of nodes. Trust is of types: Direct and Indirect trust. Direct trust serves as storing traits by observing the behavior of the nodes within the communication range. Indirect trust is based on reputation of the nodes. It is based on recommendations of the nodes from neighboring nodes. In clustering, direct communication serves as a prime source for gathering information of the genuine nodes. Hence TBEM uses only the direct trust to evaluate the trust of cluster members.

3 TBEM

In TBEM, the direct trust is calculated by considering communication trust, energy trust and data trust. The cluster member nodes in WSNs collaborate to arrive at a common solution and perform their tasks. The communication behavior is used to evaluate whether the sensor node is normal or not. A node consumes some amount of energy to transmit data packets. The data packets thus sent may be a false data as false data may be introduced in network through a malicious node. Hence in TBEM, direct trust is computed by considering the factors of communication, energy and data.

3.1 Communication Trust Computation

Calculation of communication trust T_c is based on subjective logic frame work. The T_c calculation is based on the past communications of the nodes in a network. But the nodes may not be responsible for the uncertainty in communication that may arise in network due to noise and communication instability. To tackle uncertainty, subjective logic framework is used [12]. According to this phenomenon the T is a triplet T = {b; d; u} where b, d and u correspond to belief, disbelief and uncertainty respectively and {b, d, u} = [0, 1] b + d + u = 1. T_c is calculated based on successful (s) and unsuccessful (f) communication packets using the formula given in Eq. 1

$$T_c = 2b + \frac{u}{2} \tag{1}$$

Where

$$u = \frac{1}{s+f+1}, \quad b = \frac{s}{s+f+1}$$

3.2 Energy Trust Computation

Energy is a prime factor for calculating trust. A node which spends more energy on communication may be deprived of energy in the near future. Hence the energy level of a node is predicted. It is based on Ray projection method [13]. The energy consumption rates of node n_i for timeslots (1, 2, ... n) is found and tabulated as $(p_{e1}, p_{e2}, p_{e3} \cdots p_{en})$. Change in energy consumption rate is found as $c_{e1}, c_{e2} \cdots c_{en}$ where $c_{ei} = c_{ei} - c_{ei} - 1$. Average of ce ace is found. The differenced ace and $c_{e1}, c_{e2} \cdots c_{en}$ is found and arranged in ascending order $d_1, d_2 \ldots d_n$. The predicted energy consumption rate p_{en+1} is calculated as $p_{en+1} = p_{en} + d_1$ where d_1 is the minimum difference in energy consumption rates. The Energy trust is calculated from the formula given in Eq. 2.

$$T_e = \begin{cases} 1 - p_e, & if\ E_r > 0 \\ 0 & otherwise \end{cases} \tag{2}$$

3.3 Data Trust Computation

Malicious nodes may inject false data and these false data may be transmitted to the entire network. To prevent such data transmissions, identifying the nodes which involve in such false data transmissions is required. The data transmitted in a cluster will be related data as they are generated in the same region and should follow spatial correlation [14]. Such a data exhibits' continuous behavior [14]. If a data deviates from the normal data, it can be identified by using normal distribution [14]. The probability density function for a data set is given in Eq. 3.

$$f(x) = \frac{1}{\sigma\sqrt{2\pi}} e^{\frac{(x-\mu)^2}{2\sigma^2}} \tag{3}$$

where x is the data, μ and σ are the mean and variance of the data respectively.

If the data is closer to mean, its data trust will be higher. Data trust is computed using the formula given in Eq. 4.

$$T_{d=2\left(0.5-\int_{\mu}^{v_d} f(x)dx\right)=2\int_{v_d}^{\infty} f(x)dx} \tag{4}$$

Based on the values of Communication trust, Energy trust and the direct trust is computed from the using the formula given in Eqs. 5 and 6

$$T_{direct} = w_c T_c + w_e T_e + w_d T_d \tag{5}$$

$$w_c, w_e, w_d \in [0, 1] \text{ and } w_c + w_e + w_d = 1 \tag{6}$$

Where w_c, w_e and w_d are the weight values of the trust values for communication, energy and data. The T_{direct} is calculated for all nodes in a cluster. The nodes with $T_{direct} > 0.5$ is considered for cluster head election.

4 Cluster Head Election Based on Trust and Energy Efficiency

The Energy has remained as a main challenging constraint in WSN. In TBEM, the nodes which satisfy the condition of $T_{direct} > 0.5$ are trustworthy nodes. The residual energy level of the nodes is considered further for cluster head election. Among the trustworthy nodes, the node with maximum residual energy is selected as cluster head. For selecting the node with maximum residual energy, max heap algorithm is used. A Max-heap is a widely used data structure for sorting as it reduces the number of comparisons. A Max-heap is used here to arrange the nodes based on their energy level in descending order. Using this technique, the root node will always have the maximum residual energy. The steps for Max-heap are presented in Algorithm 1. Algorithm 2 shows the steps required for clustering in TBEM.

Algorithm 1 : Max-Heap Construction for Residual Energy
Input: List of trust worthy nodes with their residual energy

1. Max-Heap(A,i)
2. initialise h=length[A] // heaplength
3. for i = length[A] to 2
   { Max-Heapform(A,i)}
4. Function Max-Heapform(A,i)
   {// large is the node with maximum residual energy
5. large=i
6. $l = 2 \times i + 1$//left node of heap
7. $r = 2 \times i + 2$/right node of heap
8. if $l \leq$h and A[l]>A[large] then
9. large=l
10. if r$\leq$h and A[r]>A[large] then
11. large=r
12. if large≠i then
13. swap(A [i], A[large])   //A[i] ↔ A[large]
14. Max-Heapform(A,large) }

Algorithm 2: Clustering protocol working method

Steps of clustering protocol in TBEM

1. Nodes in one hop distance propagate their id and their residual energy. Node with highest residual energy announces itself as cluster head.
2. All the other nodes send the Join request message to the cluster head. The cluster head makes a list of all the cluster members. The cluster head maintains a table for Communication, data and energy trust and Residual energy for these cluster members.
3. For each unit of time the trust is calculated for the cluster members. Among the trust worthy nodes, the node with the next high residual energy is elected as the next cluster head.

5 Performance Analysis

The protocol is analyzed against the LEACH clustering protocol for performance analysis. The simulations were performed using NS2 simulator. For analysis 20, 40 … 100 nodes were considered. Malicious nodes such as hello flood nodes and non-cooperative nodes were introduced in the network and the false positive and false negative rates were analyzed.

The average residual energy of the nodes is analyzed and it is found that TBEM is found to be efficient. As the node with highest energy among the trust worthy nodes is elected cluster head, the nodes average residual energy is found to be high when compared to LEACH protocol. Figure 1 presents the detection rate of malicious nodes using TBEM as 100%.

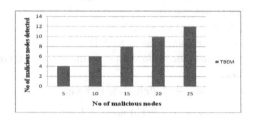

Fig. 1. Malicious node detection in TBEM

As discussed in Sect. 3, based on the past history of the nodes, the malicious nodes can be identified and hence the high detection rate is achieved. Figure 2 depicts the average residual energy of nodes. It is observed that TBEM has higher average residual energy than LEACH. This is due to the phenomenon of electing the high energy node from the list of trustworthy nodes.

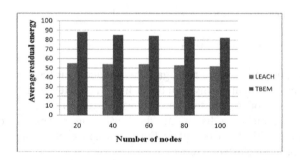

Fig. 2. Average residual energy of nodes

Figure 3 depicts the number of false positives and negatives occurrence in TBEM. It is observed that there are no false negatives in TBEM and the false positives are lesser compared to LEACH. Hence there are no active malicious nodes which can go undetected in TBEM. But there are possibilities of false positives. It is because a node's communication may be affected by noise or other phenomenon. The presence of noise results in packet loss. The packet loss can be calculated by determining the number of packets received successfully. Due to these facts a genuine node may be detected as malicious. But the rate of false positive is minimal.

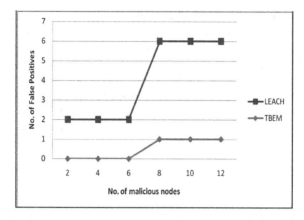

Fig. 3. Number of false positives and negatives

6   Security Analysis

The clustering protocol TBECP is a generic clustering protocol but serves to be secure as the cluster members and the cluster head are trustworthy nodes. To prove that the protocol is secure, it has been analyzed against various types of security attacks. They are Non-cooperative node, false data propagator and Flooding attacks.

6.1   Non-cooperative Node Attack

A node is non cooperative and hence it does not respond to the cluster head messages. It does not involve in any of the communications as the peer nodes. In this case the unsuccessful communication packets will be more and the communication trust calculated for this node will not reach the threshold value and hence the node fails to be trustworthy.

6.2   False Data Propagator

A false data propagator node may transmit false data in the network. As a result the network may have false data packets being transmitted and it may in turn consume energy of the nodes. Using data trust, the nodes are revoked and false data is prevented from roaming in the network.

6.3   Flooding Attacks

Nodes may send hello messages to neighboring nodes to target energy loss of nodes in its vicinity. In long term this malicious activity may produce energy deprived nodes. Using Communication trust, such nodes which often send hello messages to attract neighboring nodes is identified and revoked.

The proposed system is resistant against any type of active attacks. Active attack nodes are malicious or misbehaving nodes. Passive attack nodes remain silent and are difficult to analyze as they behave like a genuine node. Passive or node identity based attacks such as Sybil or Replica attacks may not be identified by the system. In Sybil and replica attacks, a node can impersonalize as another node. In these types of attacks, if the node is active attacker, it will be identified in TBEM. The nodes may not be identified, if the nodes are passive. But it is assumed that nodes may not be passive for a long term as they do not serve the purpose of attack if they remain passive.

7 Conclusion

Clustering protocols are widely used in sensor networks to reduce the communication cost. The proposed TBEM adds trust and energy efficiency for clustering protocol. By adding trust, nodes are evaluated based on its past history. Hence threats based on communication, data and energy can be overcome to improve network lifetime, trustworthy nodes with high energy levels are selected as cluster heads. The proposed system is compared to existing LEACH protocol and it is found to have minimal false positives. In future works the system can be analyzed with clustering mechanisms such as k-means and the system can be enhanced to be resilient against replica or Sybil attacks.

References

1. Durisic, M.P., Tafa, Z., Milutinovic, V.M: A survey of military applications of wireless sensor networks. In: Proceedings of the Mediterranean Conference on Embedded Computing (MECO), pp. 12–20, June 2012
2. Anwar, R.W., Bakhtiari, M., Zainal, A., Abdullah, A.H., Qureshi, K.N.: Security issues and attacks in wireless sensor network. World Appl. Sci. J. **30**(10), 1224–1227 (2014). doi:10.5829/idosi.wasj.2014.30.10.334
3. Xing, K., Sundhar, S., Srinivasan, R., Rivera, M., Li, J., Cheng, X.: Attacks and counter measures in sensor networks: a survey. In: Huang, S.C.-H., MacCallum, D., Du, D.-Z. (eds.) Network Security, pp. 251–272. Springer, Heidelberg (2010). doi:10.1007/978-0-387-73821-5_11
4. Thakkar, A., Kotecha, K.: Cluster head election for energy and delay constraint applications of wireless sensor networks. IEEE Sens. J. **14**(8), 2658–2664 (2014). doi:10.1109/JSEN.2014.2312549
5. Liu, C.-M., Lee, C.-H.: Distributed algorithms for energy-efficient cluster-head election in wireless mobile sensor networks. In: Proceedings of the International Conference on Wireless Networks, ICWN, pp. 405–411 (2005)
6. Mahajan, S., Malhotra, J., Sharma, S.: An energy balanced QoS based cluster head selection strategy for WSN. Egypt. Inform. J. **15**(3), 189–199 (2014). doi:10.1016/j.eij.2014.09.001
7. Tyagi, S., Kumar, N.: A systematic review on clustering and routing techniques based upon LEACH protocol for wireless sensor networks. J. Netw. Comput. Appl. **36**(2), 623–645 (2013). doi:10.1016/j.jnca.2012.12.001

8. Yanli, Yu., Li, Y., Zhou, W., Li, P.: Trust mechanisms in wireless sensor networks attack analysis and countermeasures. J. Netw. Comput. Appl. **35**(1), 867–880 (2011). doi:10.1016/j.jnca.2011.03.005
9. Ishmanov, F., Kim, S.W., Nam, S.Y.: A robust trust establishment scheme for wireless sensor networks. Sensors **15**(3), 7040–7061 (2015). doi:10.3390/s150307040
10. Ahmed, A., Abu Bakar, K., Channa, M.I., et al.: A trust aware routing protocol for energy constrained wireless sensor network. Telecommun. Syst. **61**, 123 (2016). doi:10.1007/s11235-015-0068-8
11. Ahmed, A., Bakar, K.A., Channa, M.I., et al.: A secure routing protocol with trust and energy awareness for wireless sensor network. Mobile Netw. Appl. **21**, 272 (2016). doi:10.1007/s11036-016-0683
12. Gao, W., Zhang, G., Chen, W., Li, Y.: A trust model based on subjective logic. In: Proceedings of the International Conference on Internet Computing for Science and Engineering, pp. 272–276 (2009)
13. Chen, M., Zhou, Y., Tang, L.: Ray projection method and its applications based on Grey Prediction. Chin. J. Stat. Decis. **1**(1), 13–20 (2007)
14. Shao, K., Luo, F., Mei, N., Liu, Z.: Normal distribution based dynamical recommendation trust model. J. Softw. **23**(12), 3130–3148 (2012). doi:10.3724/SP.J.1001.2012.04204

Using Morphological Features to Simplify Complex Sentences in Punjabi Language

Sanjeev Kumar Sharma[(✉)]

Department of Computer Science and Applications,
DAV University, Jalandhar, India
Sanju3916@rediffmail.com

Abstract. In this research paper, a technique for automatic identification and simplification of long and complex sentences in Punjabi language has been proposed. In this research, mainly compound and complex sentences have been simplified. Various morphological features of non-finite verb and type of conjunctions used in complex sentences are used for identification of complex sentences. Sentence structure and conjunction are used for identification of compound sentences. Structure of clauses has been used to mark the start and end position of the dependent and independent clauses present in complex sentences. Syntactic technique has been used for simplification of compound and complex sentences. Author tested this system on compound and complex sentences and obtained an accuracy of 98% in case of compound sentences and 78% for complex sentence.

Keywords: Punjabi sentences · Compound sentences · Complex sentences · Sentence simplification

1 Introduction

In our daily life, whether we read the newspaper, checks email or follow some instruction, we interact with the text and this text is very important to understand. If some text is complex then it is need to simplify it. Sentence simplification is a technique to modify the natural language so that its complexity is reduced and its readability and understandability is improved. The task of sentence simplification is to convert large and complex sentences into simple sentences. While doing the simplification, various constructs and clauses of the large and complex sentence are identified and then two or more than two simple sentences are constructed from these clauses and constructs of the sentence. The goal of sentence simplification is to reduce the syntactic complexity of a large and complex sentence so as to help in the development of various natural language processing and text mining tools. Various syntactic construct considered while simplifying the sentences includes appositions, parenthesized elements, relative clauses, nonfinite verb and conjunctions (coordinate and subordinate). This has applications in different natural language processing resources like text summarization, machine translation [20], grammar checking and in assistive technology [2]. In all these resources sentence simplification is used as pre-processor. As this application reduces the complexity of the sentence hence it is also highly useful for second language

© Springer Nature Singapore Pte Ltd. 2017
M. Singh et al. (Eds.): ICACDS 2016, CCIS 721, pp. 210–218, 2017.
DOI: 10.1007/978-981-10-5427-3_23

learner and lay readers. In the research paper, Sects. 2 explains various existing systems and techniques used for simplification, Sect. 3 explains proposed system for simplification of sentences and in Sect. 4, various results and comparison with existing system is provided.

2 Existing Work

Although much of the wok has been done in manual text simplification [6], very less effort is done to develop automated text simplification system. The first effort was done by Boeing for English language by developing a grammar and style checking system [7]. Further [4, 9, 10] used phrase based statistical machine translation method for simplification of English sentences. Most of the techniques used for text simplification are same as used for paraphrase generation, text summarization, text to text generation and machine translation [9, 11]. Other than English language, sentence simplification has been done for Dutch [3], Brazilian Portuguese [14], French [19], Vietnamese [20], Basque [21], Italian [22], Korean [23], Spanish [26] etc.

2.1 Techniques Used

Various techniques have been use for simplification of large sentences by different researchers. These techniques can be broadly classified into two categories; first the techniques used for simplification of English language and second the techniques used for simplification of other than English language. The approaches used for English language are:

Lexical Approach. In this approach input sentence is scanned for complex words and these complex words, if present, are substituted with simple words. Hence no grammatical simplification is used and only vocabulary simplification is used. This approach has been used for development of PSET (The Use of a Psycholinguistic Database in the Simplification of Text for Aphasic Readers) [4], KURA (Text Simplification for Reading Assistance) [15], HAPPI (Helping Aphasic People Process Online Information) [16], SIMPLEX (Putting It Simply: a Context-aware Approach to Lexical Simplification) [5], LexSiS: Lexical Simplification for Spanish [17] etc. General architecture of this approach is shown in Fig. 1.

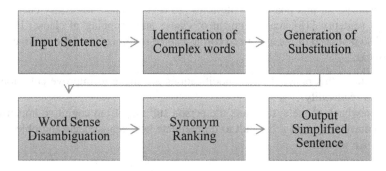

Fig. 1. General architecture of lexical approach

As shown in Fig. 1, initially, the complex words are identified from the input sentence. Then the possible substitutions of these complex words are generated. After this the generated substitutions are refined so that the sense of the input text is not changed. In the last step the refined substitutions are ranked in their order of simplicity. This technique has a drawback that many times the simplified sentence may loss the information. This happens due to word sense disambiguation i.e. the situation when a word has more than one meaning and it is difficult to pick the one that will not change the meaning of the sentence.

Syntactic Approach. In this technique, grammatical complexities of the sentence are identified and then it is rewrite into simple structure. Various types of grammatical complexities that can be resolved by using this technique includes: splitting of compound and complex sentences into their clauses, rewriting of passive voice sentences and resolution of anaphora. Working architecture is shown in Fig. 2.

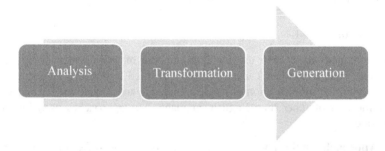

Fig. 2. General architecture of syntactic approach

As shown in Fig. 2, Syntactic simplification takes place in three stages:

Analysis. In this phase, complexity of the sentence is calculated, the input sentence in analyzed for whether it require simplification or not. Language rules and SVM binary classifier can be used for this.

Transformation. In this phase, rewrite rules are used to make necessary changes like splitting a sentence [18], rearrangement of clause and dropping of clause. Rules are preferred so that need of the annotated corpus can be minimized and the accuracy could be improved.

Generation. In this phase, further modifications are made to improve cohesion, relevance and readability.

Few drawback of the system are; the person suffering from cognitive impairments such as aphasia may find it difficult to differentiate between subjects and object when passive voice is used.

This approach has been successfully used for automatic Induction of rules for text simplification [1], simplification of Newspaper text to assist Aphasic reader [18], text simplification for information seeking applications [3], maintaining discourse when performing syntactic simplification [8], splitting of long sentence after explanation generation [12], developing an authoring tool which provides text simplification techniques whilst writing a document [14], acquisition of syntactic simplification rules for French [19], splitting of Vietnamese sentences for Vietnamese English machine translation [20], automatic simplification of Bosque complex sentences using dependency tree [21], sentence simplification to enhance multi-document summaries [13], development of sentence simplification tool for children's stories in Italian [22], simplification of Korean sentences for deaf readers [23], direct manipulation of parse tree [24], removing unnecessary parts of sentences [25] and Spanish sentence simplification [26].

3 Proposed System

In this research, author has used syntactic simplification for converting long Punjabi sentences in to simple sentences. Punjabi long sentences basically fall in two major categories [27, 28]; one is compound sentences and second is complex sentences. Compound sentences are composed of independent clauses only [27, 28] and complex sentences are composed of dependent and independent clauses [27, 28]. Compound sentences are simplified by splitting them in individual independent clauses and then rewriting each independent clause as a separate simple sentence. As the compound sentences are composed of independent clauses joined by coordinate conjunctions therefore these sentences can be split in independent clauses by breaking them from these coordinate conjunctions. On the other hand complex sentences have relatively different structure. These are composed of dependent and independent clauses and position of dependent and independent clauses is different in different types of sentences. In Punjabi language, depending upon the type of dependent clause, complex sentences are basically categorized into four categories [27, 28]; complex sentence having adverb dependent clause, complex sentence having KI dependent clause, complex sentence having relative dependent clause and complex sentence having non-finite dependent clause. Each of these types has different structure. In author's proposed system, all these types of complex sentences are identified by using features of each dependent clause and then different algorithm are used depending upon the type of dependent clause to split the complex sentence in dependent and independent clauses. After splitting, each dependent clause is converted to independent clause by using conversion rules. The complete architecture of the system is shown in Fig. 3.

As shown in Fig. 3, overall system works in two phases. In the first phase, candidate sentences (compound and complex sentences) that need to simplified are identified by using CRF based classification technique. In the second phase, these candidate sentences are simplified as per their type. For simplification, compound and complex sentences are split into clauses. In this research work, three types of clauses that are responsible for complexity of a sentence are handled. These clauses includes; Relative clause, KI clause and Adverb clause. Various possible patterns of these

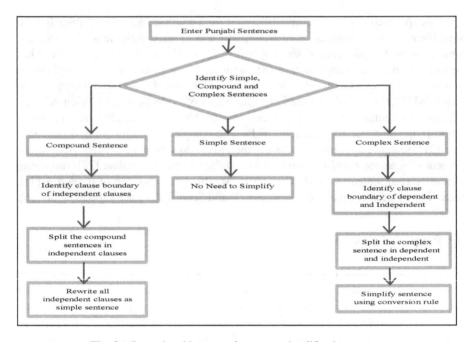

Fig. 3. General architecture of sentence simplification system

dependent clauses with independent clauses and other clauses are examined and then based upon their position in the sentence conversion transformation rules are designed to convert these clauses in simple sentences. Various possible patterns along with example and conversion rules for Relative clause are shown in Table 1, for KI clause are shown in Table 2 and for Adverb clause are shown in Table 3.

Table 1. Various possible patterns and conversion rules for relative clause

Pattern	Example	Conversion rule	Simplified complex sentences
Independent clause + relative clause	ਉਸ ਕੁੜੀ ਨੇ ਸ਼ਹਿਰ ਜਾਣਾ ਹੈ ਜਿਹੜੀ ਕੱਲ੍ਹ ਪਿੰਡ 'ਤੇ ਆਈ ਸੀ ।	Replace the relative clause conjunction with the subject of the independent clause	ਉਸ ਕੁੜੀ ਨੇ ਸ਼ਹਿਰ ਜਾਣਾ ਹੈ । ਕੁੜੀ ਕੱਲ੍ਹ ਪਿੰਡ 'ਤੇ ਆਈ ਸੀ ।
Relative clause + independent clause	ਜਿਹੜਾ ਕਮ ਤੁਹਾਨੂ ਦੱਤਿ ਗਿਆ ਸੀ ਅੱਜ ਓਹ ਪੂਰਾ ਹੋ ਗਿਆ ਹੈ	First apply anaphora resolution and then remove the conjunction form Relative clause	ਕਮ ਤੁਹਾਨੂ ਦੱਤਿ ਗਿਆ ਸੀ ਅੱਜ ਕਮ ਪੂਰਾ ਹੋ ਗਿਆ ਹੈ
Common subject + relative clause + independent clause	ਉਹ ਮੁੰਡਾ ਜਿਹੜਾ ਮੇਰੇ ਨਾਲ ਪੜਦਾ ਸੀ ਅੱਜ ਬਹੁਤ ਸੋਹਣਾ ਗਾਉਦਾ ਹੈ ।	Replace the conjunction of relative clause with common subject. Add common subject to the independent clause	ਉਹ ਮੁੰਡਾ ਮੇਰੇ ਨਾਲ ਪੜਦਾ ਸੀ ਉਹ ਮੁੰਡਾ ਅੱਜ ਬਹੁਤ ਸੋਹਣਾ ਗਾਉਦਾ ਹੈ ।

Table 2. Various possible patterns and conversion rules for KI clause

Pattern	Example	Conversion rule	Simplified complex sentence
Independent clause + KI clause	ਉਹ ਦਸ ਰਿਹਾ ਸੀ ਕਿ ਉਸ ਨੇ ਅੱਜ ਸਕੂਲ ਵਿਚ ਕੀ ਕੀਤਾ	First write KI clause after removing the Ki conjunction and then write the independent clause	ਉਹ ਦਸ ਰਿਹਾ ਸੀ । ਉਸ ਨੇ ਅੱਜ ਸਕੂਲ ਵਿਚ ਕੀ ਕੀਤਾ ?
Independent clause + PAR clause + KI clause	ਤੁਸੀ ਲੋਕਾਂ ਨੂੰ ਵੇਖ ਰਹੇ ਹੋ ਪਰ ਉਨ੍ਹਾਂ ਨੂੰ ਪਤਾ ਨਹੀ ਕਿ ਤੁਸੀ ਉਹਨਾਂ ਨੂੰ ਵੇਖ ਰਹੇ ਹੋ ।	First apply anaphora resolution and then rewrite the PAR Clause and KI Clause after removing PAR and KI keyword Remove duplicate clauses if any	ਤੁਸੀ ਲੋਕਾਂ ਨੂੰ ਵੇਖ ਰਹੇ ਹੋ । ਲੋਕਾਂ ਨੂੰ ਪਤਾ ਨਹੀ ।
Dependent clause + KI clause + Independent clause	ਉਸ ਨੇ ਇਹ ਸੋਚ ਕੇ ਕਿ ਪੇਪਰਾਂ ਵਿੱਚ ਪਾਸ ਤਾਂ ਹੋ ਹੀ ਜਾਣਾ ਹੈ ਪੜ੍ਹਨਾ ਛੱਡ ਦੀਤਾ	Write the KI clause after removing the Ki conjunction Join the dependent clause with independent clause	ਪੇਪਰਾਂ ਵਿੱਚ ਪਾਸ ਤਾਂ ਹੋ ਹੀ ਜਾਣਾ ਹੈ । ਉਸ ਨੇ ਇਹ ਸੋਚ ਕੇ ਪੜ੍ਹਨਾ ਛੱਡ ਦੀਤਾ ।
Independent Clause + KI Clause + TAN clause	ਬਲਕਾਰ ਸਿਂਘ ਇਹ ਜਾਂਦਾ ਸੀ ਕਿ ਜੇ ਉਹ ਮੇਰੀ ਗੱਲ ਮੰਨ ਲੈਂਦਾ ਤਾਂ ਉਹ ਅੱਜ ਜਾਉਂਦਾ ਹੁੰਦਾ	First apply anaphora resolution Write independent clause Write KI clause after removing KI and J-conjunction. Write TAN clause after removing TAN	ਬਲਕਾਰ ਸਿਂਘ ਇਹ ਜਾਂਦਾ ਸੀ । ਉਹ ਬਲਕਾਰ ਸਿਂਘ ਦੀ ਗੱਲ ਮੰਨ ਲੈਂਦਾ । ਉਹ ਅੱਜ ਜਾਉਂਦਾ ਹੁੰਦਾ ।

Table 3. Various possible patterns and conversion rules for adverb clause

Pattern	Example	Conversion Rule	Simplified complex sentence
J-Adverb:- e.g. ਜੋ, ਜਦੋ, ਜਬਿ, ਜਵਿ, ਜਯਿਰ, ਜਦ, ਜਸਿ ਤਰ੍ਹਾਂ etc.	ਜਦੋ ਉਸ ਦੀ ਜਾਗ ਖੁੱਲ੍ਹੀ ਚੋਰੀ ਹੋ ਚੁੱਕੀ ਸੀ।	Remove the J-Adverb from dependent clause and write both the clauses separately	ਉਸ ਦੀ ਜਾਗ ਖੁੱਲ੍ਹੀ ਚੋਰੀ ਹੋ ਚੁੱਕੀ ਸੀ
F-Adverb:- e.g. ਕਿਉਂਕਿ, ਭਾਵੇ, ਸਗੋ, ਜੇ etc.	ਜੇ ਮੁੰਡਾ ਸਕੂਲ ਜਾਏਗਾ ਤਾਂ ਮੁੰਡਾ ਪਾਸ ਹੋ ਜਾਏਗਾ ।	Remove F-Adverb from dependent clause and insert the subject rewrite the sentence as two simple sentences	ਮੁੰਡਾ ਸਕੂਲ ਜਾਏਗਾ ਮੁੰਡਾ ਪਾਸ ਹੋ ਜਾਏਗਾ ।

4 Result and Discussion

It is difficult to measure the simplicity because if we consider a simple sentence to be short in length then it may be possible that understandability of sentence becomes difficult. If a sentence is not understandable then it could not be simpler than its original sentence. Although in some systems like information retrieval, reduce in accuracy can be accepted as the system will still enable the user to find some portion of the document. Author tested his system for 100 compound and 100 complex sentences collected from various Punjabi newspaper websites. For compound sentences 3 sets were created. Two sets having 33 sentences and 3rd set having 34 sentences. For complex sentences, out of 100 sentences, 33 sentences were taken from Relative clause, 33 from Adverb clause and 34 from KI clause. The result obtained for compound sentences are shown in Table 4 and for complex sentences are shown in Table 5.

Table 4. Experimental evaluation for compound sentences

Set number	Total number of sentences in the test data	Correctly simplified	In-correctly simplified	Not simplified
Set 1	33	32	1	0
Set 2	33	33	0	0
Set 3	34	33	1	0
Total	100	98	2	0

Table 5. Experimental evaluation for complex sentences

Type of complex sentence	Sentences in the test data	Correctly simplified	In-correctly simplified	Not simplified
Relative clause	33	21	12	0
Adverb clause	33	28	05	0
Ki clause	34	29	05	0
Total	100	78	22	0

As shown in Table 4, compound sentences show 98% accuracy in simplification of sentences and complex sentences shows 78% accuracy. The low accuracy of complex sentence simplification is due to difficulty in simplification of Relative type clauses.

5 Future Scope

This research can be helpful for researcher working in the field of language processing especially for summarization, machine translation from Punjabi language to other languages, grammar checking of Punjabi language etc. This work can also be used as assistive technology.

References

1. Chandrasekar, R., Srinivas, B.: Automatic induction of rules for text simplification. Knowl.-Based Syst. **10**(3), 183–190 (1997)
2. Devlin, S., Tait, J.: The use of a psycholinguistic database in the simplification of text for aphasic readers. Linguist. Databases, pp. 161–173 (1998)
3. Klebanov, B.B., Knight, K., Marcu, D.: Text simplification for information-seeking applications. In: Meersman, R., Tari, Z. (eds.) OTM 2004. LNCS, vol. 3290, pp. 735–747. Springer, Heidelberg (2004). doi:10.1007/978-3-540-30468-5_47
4. Coster, W., Kauchak, D.: Learning to simplify sentences using Wikipedia. In: Proceedings of the Workshop on Monolingual Text-To-Text Generation. Association for Computational Linguistics, Portland, June 2011, pp. 1–9 (2011)
5. Biran, O., Brody, S., Elhadad, N.: Putting it simply: a context-aware approach to lexical simplification. In: Proceedings of the 49th Annual Meeting of the Association for Computational Linguistics: Human Language Technologies: Short Papers, vol. 2. Association for Computational Linguistics, Stroudsburg, pp. 496–501 (2011)
6. Blum, S., Levenston, E.A.: Universals of lexical simplification. Lang. Learn. **28**(2), 399–415 (1978)
7. Hoard, J.E., Wojcik, R., Holzhauser, K.: An automated grammar and style checker for writers of simplified English. In: O'Brian Holt, P., William, N. (eds.) Computers and Writing, pp. 278–296. Springer, Dordrecht (1992). doi:10.1007/978-94-011-2854-4_19
8. Siddharthan, A.: Syntactic simplification and text cohesion. Res. Lang. Comput. **4**, 77–109 (2006)
9. Zhu, Z., Bernhard, D., Gurevych, I.: A monolingual tree-based translation model for sentence simplification. In: Proceedings of the 23rd International Conference on Computational Linguistics, pp. 1353–1361 (2010)
10. Wubben, S., van den Bosch, A., Krahmer, E.: Sentence simplification by monolingual machine translation. In: Proceedings of the 50th Annual Meeting of the Association for Computational Linguistics. Long Papers, vol. 1, pp. 1015–1024, July 2012. Association for Computational Linguistics, Jeju Island (2012)
11. Woodsend, K., Lapata, M.: Learning to simplify sentences with quasi-synchronous grammar and integer programming. In: Proceedings of the Conference on Empirical Methods in Natural Language Processing, pp. 409–420. Association for Computational Linguistics, Stroudsburg (2011)
12. Kandula, S., Curtis, D., Zeng-Treitler, Q.: A semantic and syntactic text simplification tool for health content. In: AMIA Annual Symposium Proceedings, pp. 366–370. American Medical Informatics Association (2010)
13. Silveira, S., Branco, A.: Combining a double clustering approach with sentence simplification to produce highly informative multi- document summaries. In: 2012 IEEE 13th International Conference on Information Reuse and Integration (IRI), pp. 482–489, August 2012
14. Scarton, C., de Oliveira, M., Candido Jr., A., Gasperin, C., Aluísio, S.M.: Simplifica: a tool for authoring simplified texts in Brazilian Portuguese guided by readability assessments. In: Proceedings of the NAACL HLT 2010 Demonstration Session, pp. 41–44. Association for Computational Linguistics, Stroudsburg (2010)
15. Inui, K., Fujita, A., Takahashi, T., Iida, R., Iwakura, T.: Text simplification for reading assistance: a project note. In: Proceedings of the Second International Workshop on Paraphrasing, pp. 9–16. Association for Computational Linguistics, Sapporo, July 2003

16. Devlin, S., Unthank, G.: Helping aphasic people process online information. In: Proceedings of the 8th International ACM SIGACCESS Conference on Computers and Accessibility, pp. 225–226. ACM, New York (2006)

17. Bott, S., Rello, L., Drndarević, B., Saggion, H.: Can Spanish be simpler? LexSiS: lexical simplification for Spanish. In: Proceedings of COLING 2012. The COLING 2012 Organizing Committee, Mumbai, India, pp. 357–374, December 2012

18. Carroll, J., Minnen, G., Canning, Y., Devlin, S., Tait, J.: Practical simplification of English newspaper text to assist aphasic readers. In: Proceedings of AAAI-1998 Workshop on Integrating Artificial Intelligence and Assistive Technology, pp. 7–10 (1998)

19. Seretan, V.: Acquisition of syntactic simplification rules for French. In: Proceedings of the Eighth International Conference on Language Resources and Evaluation (LREC 2012). European Language Resources Association (ELRA), Istanbul, May 2012

20. Hung, B.T., Minh, N.L., Shimazu, A.: Sentence splitting for Vietnamese-English machine translation. In: 2012 Fourth International Conference on Knowledge and Systems Engineering (KSE), pp. 156–160, August 2012

21. Aranzabe, M.J., de Ilarraza, A.D., Gonzalez-Dios, I.: Transforming complex sentences using dependency trees for automatic text simplification in Basque. Procesamiento del Lenguaje Natural **50**, 61–68 (2012)

22. Barlacchi, G., Tonelli, S.: ERNESTA: a sentence simplification tool for children's stories in Italian. In: Gelbukh, A. (ed.) CICLing 2013. LNCS, vol. 7817, pp. 476–487. Springer, Heidelberg (2013). doi:10.1007/978-3-642-37256-8_39

23. Chung, J.-W., Min, H.-J., Kim, J., Park, J.C.: Enhancing readability of web documents by text augmentation for deaf people. In: Proceedings of the 3rd International Conference on Web Intelligence, Mining and Semantics, pp. 30:1–30:10. ACM, New York (2013)

24. Feblowitz, D., Kauchak, D.: Sentence simplification as tree transduction. In: Proceedings of the Second Workshop on Predicting and Improving Text Readability for Target Reader Populations, pp. 1–10. Association for Computational Linguistics, Sofia, August 2013

25. Klerke, S., Søgaard, A.: Simple, readable sub-sentences. In: 51st Annual Meeting of the Association for Computational Linguistics Proceedings of the Student Research Workshop, pp. 142–149. Association for Computational Linguistics, Sofia, August 2013

26. Štajner, S., Drndarević, B., Saggion, H.: Corpus-based sentence deletion and split decisions for Spanish text simplification. Revista Computación y Sistemas **17**(2), 251–262 (2013)

27. ਡਾ.ਬਲਦੇਵ ਸਿੰਘ ਚੀਮਾ: ਪੰਜਾਬੀ ਵਾਕ ਪ੍ਰਬੰਧ (ਬਣਤਰ ਅਤੇ ਕਾਰਜ), ਪਬਲੀਕੇਸ਼ਨ ਬਿਊਰੋ ਪੰਜਾਬੀ ਯੂਨੀਵਰਸਿਟੀ ਪਟਿਆਲਾ | (2005)

28. ਬੂਟਾ ਸਿੰਘ ਬਰਾੜ: ਪੰਜਾਬੀ ਵਿਆਕਰਨ (ਸਿਧਾਂਤ ਅਤੇ ਵਿਹਾਰ), ਪਬਲੀਕੇਸ਼ਨ ਬਿਊਰੋ ਪੰਜਾਬੀ ਯੂਨੀਵਰਸਿਟੀ ਪਟਿਆਲਾ | (2008)

Communications

A Comparative Study of Internet Protocols in MANET

Shweta Singh[1(✉)] and Arun Kumar Tripathi[2]

[1] Vidya Knowledge Park, Baghpat, India
shweta.vidudi272@gmail.com
[2] KIET Group of Institutions, Ghaziabad, India
mailtoaruntripathi@gmail.com

Abstract. In present era, a growing ease to work in an more sophisticated environment, independent of geographical locations, ease to use resources at distant devices on an anytime-anywhere basis with higher space availability is seen. Taking this into consideration a technology has introduced, namely cloud computing. To emerge with this situation a factor of cloud computing is established that provides an environment with no or minimum infrastructure physically to establish a communication in between the two communicating devices. Besides this, to provide an operating unit of smartness ad-hoc technology along with IPv6 protocol came into existence that is being proven as one of the most encouraging and satisfactory way to use technology and meet today's IT needs and deeds. To attain this infrastructure OPNET IT GURU EDUCATIONAL VERSION 14.5 Modeler is being used.

Keywords: Cloud computing · Ad-hoc network · MANET · Delay · Throughput · PPP · Digital signal · IP routing protocol · IPv4 · IPv6 · RIPng · OSPF · IS-IS · TORA

1 Introduction

Cloud Computing [1] is a technology that is generally utilized through an Internet connection. Cloud Computing is a mechanizing technique that facilitates computing and access to number of applications and information at distant geographical locations. It allows access to all the devices onto network to share and exchange information in-between them, devices involved can be: hubs, repeaters, routers, switches, etc.

To enable the cloud computing mechanism a third party is needed to allow access to shared resources respectively in an on-demand basis. Hence cloud computing is formally known as an on-demand service, i.e. it allows access to all the information and shared resources whenever needed. In collaborating with cloud computing, it has been experienced that there are certain factors to which cloud computing has improved. It enables to work in a pretty faster way while accessing the applications and services, enables a scenario with improved maintainability and manageability factors, facilitates a reliable factor for IT so that they can adjust situations where fluctuating unpredictable business demands can be efficiently fulfilled.

© Springer Nature Singapore Pte Ltd. 2017
M. Singh et al. (Eds.): ICACDS 2016, CCIS 721, pp. 221–231, 2017.
DOI: 10.1007/978-981-10-5427-3_24

One of the main element in cloud computing is 'virtualization' factor, that facilitates number of services to be accessed by number of user as an when needed in a cloud based i.e. virtual environment with a sort of security factor. Work in virtual environment can be accomplished by making use of certain number of either or both of the software and hardware components. Cloud computing is based on Service Oriented Architecture (SOA) [2]. SOA defines the standards that need to be set for accessing every aspect as service globally.

Cloud computing can act as centralized and decentralized in different aspects, such as in an ad hoc network. Ad hoc networking is one of the computing mechanisms that provide a decentralized manner with wireless network. The environment is said as ad hoc because it doesn't actually needs any pre-specified infrastructure to establish communication in between the proposed devices.

Usually, numbers of Access Point (AP) [3] are specified at are responsible to accomplish every communication in between the connected devices. No individual communicating device can act as an AP and cannot determine who all will be communicating at what time span. When an ad hoc network is implemented, it is granted to each of the individual to communication freely in a network. All the workstations are allowed to forward or flood the information (packets) at anywhere and anytime basis, hence is called as 'on the fly' network.

The decision to forward data packets is performed on dynamic basis. The stations in wireless mobile ad hoc network are allowed to forward their individual data to other devices so that communication is achieved dynamically at a much faster basis using minimal configuration requirements. Unless the use of routers, switches, hubs in a traditional way, ad hoc stands off clear in this aspect.

When device(s) in ad hoc network is made to move freely in a network along with roaming capability, it is justified as Mobile Ad Hoc Network (MANET) [4]. MANET is one of the network that is self-configuring and infrastructure-less network on a continuous basis. In MANET, devices are set free to move independently in any direction and it doesn't make any effect on performance factor if we change the links related to other devices.

Furthermore, paper can be sectioned as following. Section 2 defines ad hoc routing protocols [5], Internet Protocol (IP) [6], wireless routing protocol, signaling scheme. Section 3 defines simulation process consisting of proposed scenarios and technology description. Section 4 includes an analysis of proposed scenarios and concluding performance analysis for each of the device in each proposed scenario. Section 5 includes conclusions and results depending on the analysis made in Sect. 4; and references to work with the future perspective to achieve communication in a more efficient manner.

2 Related Work

In MANET, every device is given control to set their own routes to send data packets following with a mobile architecture. Prior to forward any data packet, each of the device(s) in MANET is intended to forward presence-listen acknowledgements to every other individual device. With this process, every individual device establishes an appropriate topological structure of network, and can now use any route to forward or transmit data packet. This process will also let devices to select the most reliable and appropriate route to transmit the data packet.

To communicate in a wireless environment through Internet, some sort of protocol set is also associated to better the performance of devices engaged in network. Indeed, in case of ad hoc or wireless MANET, certain set of routing protocols are used so that the communication is attained in a much higher and in efficient manner. The set of protocols is generally facilitated in an ad hoc network:

Table-Driven (Proactive) Routing [7]. In this routing protocol, a routing table is maintained on continuous basis. Every device will maintain its own destination list and will distribute then to all other devices in a network.

On-Demand (Reactive) Routing [7]. This protocol works on request that is made every-time by devices in a network. Devices send or flood Router Request packets onto the network on on-demand basis.

Hybrid (Both Proactive and Reactive) Routing [7, 21]. This protocol is a combination of both table-driven and on-demand routing protocols, consisting of pros and cons of both the protocols.

Hierarchical Routing Protocols [8]. It is a protocol that fulfils the needs of an effective and efficient routing mechanism. Initially all the devices will follow some aspects of proactive routing, then will individually can choose other way (on-demand) to provide a reliable communication in a network.

To accomplish a reliable end-to-end connection in a communicating network, some sort of end-to-end linking system is required. For this purpose, Point-to-Point (PPP) [9] is being introduced.

PPP is one of the protocols that is usually stacked by in data link layer (layer 2 of OSI model). This layer is responsible to maintain or establish communication in between the connected devices providing them with physical communication link. This protocol provides high standards to be accomplished including encryption during transmission, compression of data packets, and authentication for every data packet that travels in a network. When PPP links are being utilized in a cloud computing and ad hoc network, it is being generalised as T-carrier system, i.e. a carrier system which is responsible to operate using digital signals. The two very famous T-carrier schemes can be as:

Digital Signal 1 (DS1). DS1 [10, 11] is a traditional or a primarily used digital standard in telephonic conversations. It uses a logical bit-pattern to transfer information in form of signal. It is formally known as T1 line or signalling scheme, intended to use 1.544 Mbps of speed consisting of 24 8-bit channels.

Digital Signal 3 (DS3). DS3 [11] is a 3 T-carrier scheme i.e. is known formally as T3 signalling scheme. It is a combination of 28 DS1 or T1 carrier scheme, with speed of 44.736 Mbps. This scheme can be easily accomplished with both wired and wireless communication.

When is dealt with services based on Internet, some address scheme is facilitated to every device that communicates in a network. The protocols required while communication through Internet is referred to as Internet Protocol (IP). IP defines a boundary for each data packet to be communicated in a network. It defines at which network a data packet need to travel and to which destination device it should reach. A data packet is encapsulated with certain blocks containing of information or message to send, source device address and destination device address along with justified path sometimes. The two very famous addressing formats can be as:

Internet Protocol Version-4 (IPv4). IPv4 [12] is a fourth version format to address a data packet. It is a basic or traditional and connectionless protocol that uses a standardised manner of addressing each communicating device or accomplishes efficient internetworking. This protocol doesn't guarantee delivery for each packet or doesn't guarantee of duplicate delivery of packets.

To rectify all these cons, a newer version of IP is launched, which is formally known as Internet Protocol version-6 (IPv6).

Internet Protocol Version-6 (IPv6). IPv6 [12, 13] is the updated version to IPv4 protocol. It is recently launched to provide better aspects to communicate in Internet-based network. Two new factors were launched i.e. unique identification for each communicating device and its location that could be measured geographically.

- It follows packet-switching to travel a packet to a route.
- Includes stateless configuration automatically, announcements from routers, and remembering a network.
- It has much larger address pace than justified in an IPv4 version format for addressing.
- Fragmentation for larger packets to utilize bandwidth efficiently.

In any network, we need to maintain all information that travels in, to maintain all the hops (intermediate devices), routes to travel to easy communication process. For this scenario, certain routing protocols can be implemented for both the efficiency in communication and also for end-to-end reliability. These can be as follows:

Routing Information Protocol Next Generation (RIPng) [6]. This protocol is responsible to maintain a table consisting of source address, number of hops in between any two source and destination devices and destination device address. RIPng is a next generation routing protocol of Routing Information Protocol (RIP). It support IPv6 configuration, supports updates and authentication processes also, and includes a specific format of coding to specify number of hops in between two communicating devices.

Open Shortest Path First (OSPF) [14]. This routing protocol works under a single autonomous segment in any network. This is an interior routing protocol and hence is generally not used by large enterprises. It is a link-state routing protocol. Devices with OSPF functionality, usually collects all information regarding number of hops, routes, etc. from routers available in particular autonomous segment of network and then form their own topological structure and the begins communication.

Intermediate System-Intermediate System (IS-IS) [15]. This protocol is intended to work with an end-to-end basis, i.e. it provides mechanism that can improve end-to-end communication in between to physically connected devices. It follows a router justified using packet-switching scheme and stores this information using certain datagrams. It is also one of the link-state routing protocol. Devices entitled in this mechanism are intended to build up their topological structure by flooding the network information.

3 Simulation

The simulation [16] section defines the operating environment that provides certain factors or parametric factors that can easily affect the performance metrics for each proposed scenario in this section. The simulation environment is implemented using OPNET IT GURU EDUCATIONAL VERSION 14.5 Modeler. The environment is basically consisting of cloud based network and then is bifurcated to number of autonomous network segments. Each of the autonomous segments is then responsible to maintain or manage its level of communication and traffic generation.

Two addressing formats are used namely: IPv4 and IPv6 to two scenarios for each addressing scheme. Each autonomous segment is then constituting an ad hoc computing mechanism using MANET workstations. The detailed description for each autonomous segment can be as justified (Figs. 1 and 2).

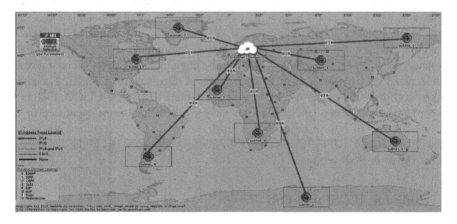

Fig. 1. Internet connection following cloud-based network

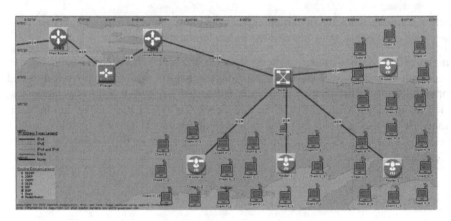

Fig. 2. Simple autonomous ad hoc network

3.1   Ad Hoc with IPv4

This is the first scenario that operates on providing an addressing format of IPv4 version. One more protocol is associated to compare the performance metrics of devices in two addressing formats, i.e. Temporally Ordered Routing Algorithm (TORA) [17].

3.2   Ad Hoc with IPv6

This scenario is implemented to operate on IPv6 address scheme for each of the communicated device. TORA is introduced in this scenario too for better comparison in between the two addressing schemes in familiar with ad hoc networking mechanism.

The working scenario is composed of 324 workstations, 54 routers, 9 switch, 9 firewalls, and an ip_cloud to provide cloud computing to all the autonomous segments in this particular environment. Almost 9 subnets are associated in a cloud computing environment each consisting of its own autonomous segment including the following: Each subnet consists of 4 further sub-autonomous segments each connected with a switch. A switch is made to connect the 4 segments of 4 MANET stations communicating with their own routers as Base Stations (BS). Two CISCO 4000 [18] series routers are also implemented in each subnet or autonomous segment to provide relevant filtering of information along with the firewall. All the stations are implemented with TORA, RIPng, IS-IS, and OSPF routing protocols, out of these some are not facilitated in IPv4 version.

4   Analysing the Simulation

This section performs an analysis of the two proposed scenario in the cloud based ad hoc network. The performance of stations, Internet connection, and firewall are depicted strictly by the justified results in graphs so generated during simulation. A comparison is made to measure performances on the basis of delay and throughput factors while communication.

4.1   Queuing Delay

Queuing delay [19, 20] is an amount of time span that is kept in consideration by a data packet in a queue to reach its destination device before timeout has occurred. Figures 3 and 4 depicts queuing delay occurred in Internet connection and firewall respectively.

Figure 3 depicts performance on Internet connection as queuing delay factor. It can be easily generalised that the IPv6 environment performs much better than IPv4 version of addressing. This can be because IS-IS and OSPF are generally facilitated in IPv6 format, but not in IPv4 format.

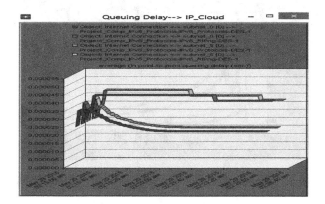

Fig. 3. Internet connection (subnet 0 and subnet 5): queuing delay

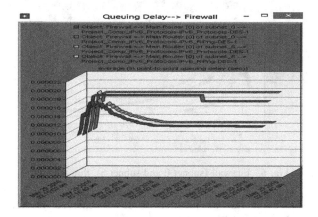

Fig. 4. Firewall (subnet 0 and subnet 5): queuing delay

TORA is most reliable routing protocol to be used in ad hoc networking, as this consist of a functionality that it can propagate data packets ta to the much larger geographical locations; And for this IPv6 performs much faster and is relevant in such a network to be used. And so IPv6 performs better than IPv4 with TORA.

4.2   Throughput

Throughput [3] is defined as the rate at which a data packet is said to be delivered successfully to the destined device respectively. It is said that greater the throughput is, greater the reliability and performance is. Figures 5 and 6 depicts throughput in each of the Internet connection and firewall in an ad hoc network.

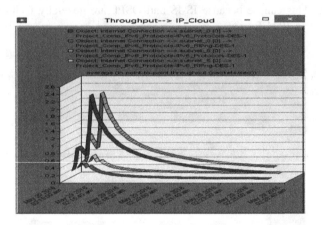

Fig. 5. Internet connection (subnet 0 and subnet 5): throughput

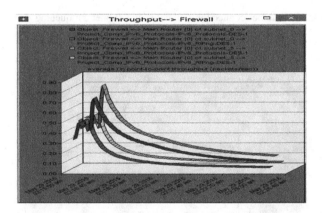

Fig. 6. Firewall (subnet 0 and subnet 5): throughput

Clearly by Fig. 5, it can be justified as IPv6 achieved greater strengths at throughput factor. Because of its availability of larger address space, identification of each individual work station, and better utilization of bandwidth, so IPv6 here too performs in much efficient manner than that of IPv4 formatting type.

Figure 6 represents throughput in firewall that is put in each of the individual autonomous system. From the above graph it can be clearly justified that higher level of throughput is attained when it is dealt with IPv6 encouraging IS-IS, OSPF, TORA in an IPv6 ad hoc network.

The overall comparison in tabular format can be as described below (Table 1):

Table 1. Overall evaluation of internet protocols in MANET

Performance analysis	Internet connection (Subnet 0 and 5)	Firewall (subnet 0 and 5)
IPv4	(1) Queuing Delay in this scenario is increased as numbers of packet are increased (2) As queuing delay is increased as time passes with an increment in numbers of packets, this can conclude to a decrement in throughput factor. Hence performance is decreased	Since IPv4 comes with limited space availability, hence when packet travel all along the network to reach to its destination; point-to-point transmission got affected and so includes up with an increased queuing of data packets to each successfully before time out, and so affects throughput
IPv6	(1) Since IPv6 performs its working in a smarter way, hence it uses a fragmentation methodology for larger packets, and so queuing delay reduces (2) When queuing delay is reduced up to an extent, the performance factor will be increased, i.e. higher rate of successful transmission will be attained	(1) IPv6 comes with extended space availability, hence when data packet travels along the boundaries of network, less time is spent for each data packet for successful transmission (2) Since IPv6 introduces an intelligent aspect of multicasting and acting smartly in any environment, this enhanced the performance factor for all the stations configured for IPv6 environment
Overall evaluation	The overall conclusion for the above proposed scenario and comparison for IPv4 and IPv6 environments. It has been analysed that IPv6 performance much better than IPv4 scenario. This can be accomplished as IPv6 is an extended version of IPv4 protocol, IPv6 includes a process of multicasting and management of bandwidth in a smarter-manner, it ensures or guarantees of successful delivery of every data packet that operates in an IPv6 environment Along with these factors queuing delay has reduced and hence higher rate for throughput has been obtained	

5   Conclusion

The simulation section in this paper composed of a scenario consisting of two different addressing formats, each of which is then intended to operate in a cloud based cum ad hoc networking mechanism. The two addressing formats are being analysed on their performance on factors such as: queuing delay, and throughput. The two factors: queuing delay and throughput truly depends on bandwidth provided, transmitting speed of each work station, methodology used in work stations to provide access mechanism. These two factors are analysed for each working station in the proposed environment consisting of autonomous segments connected via DS3 signalling scheme. It has been analysed from above section that IPv6 performs at much higher rate than IPv4 addressing scheme. There are numbers of factor that encourage this statement that IPv6 is better than IPv4b in very sense. These can be as because of availability of larger space addresses in IPv6, its factor to identify uniquely each operating station in a network, and also, it can provide location management for every possible communication for a particular network. Also, when IPv6 is implemented with routing protocols such as IS-IS and OSPF, performance is increased gradually.

References

1. Sill, A.: Standards underlying cloud networking. IEEE Cloud Comput. **3**(3), 76–80 (2016). ISSN: 2325-609
2. Yu, W.D., Ong, C.H.: A SOA based software engineering design approach in service engineering. In: IEEE International Conference on e-Business Engineering, ICEBE 2009, pp. 409–416, October 2009. ISBN: 978-0-7695-3842-6
3. Singh, S., Ahlawat, A.K., Tripathi, A.K.: Mechanizing wireless LAN (WLAN) using compression techniques. Free J. (IJEAST), 110–116 (2016). ISSN: 2455-2143
4. Prabha, R., Ramaraj, N.: An improved multipath MANET routing using link estimation and swarm intelligence. EURASIP J. Wirel. Commun. Netw. **2015**, 173 (2015). doi:10.1186/s13638-015-0385-3
5. Sanzgiri, K., Dahill, B., Levine, B.N., Shields, C., Belding-Royer, E.M.: A secure routing protocol for ad hoc networks. In: Proceedings of the 10th IEEE International Conference on Network Protocols (ICNP 2002). IEEE (2002). 1092-1648/02
6. https://en.wikipedia.org/w/index.php?title=Routing_Information_Protocol&oldid=718424189
7. Patil, V.P.: Reactive and proactive routing protocol performance evaluation for qualitative and quantitative analysis in mobile ad hoc network. Int. J. Sci. Res. Publ. **2**(9), 1–8 (2012). ISSN: 2250-3153
8. Sen, A., Gupta, M.D., De,D.: Energy efficient layered cluster based hierarchical routing protocol with Dual Sink. In: 5th International Conference on Computers and Devices for Communication (CODEC) (2012). ISBN: 978-1-4673-2619-3
9. Karotiya, N.A., Wyawahare, N.P., Haridas, S.L.: Review paper on point to point communication with the use of power over Ethernet based on VOIP system on asterisk. In: 2nd International Conference on Advances in Electrical, Electronics, Information, Communication and Bio-Informatics (AEEICB), February 2016 (2016). ISBN: 978-1-4673-9746-9
10. Henderson, P.M.: DS1/E1 framing and line codes, 11 November 2002
11. Palme, C., Hummel, F.: Restoration in a partitioned multi-bandwidth cross-connect network. In: Global Telecommunications Conference, 1990, and Exhibition. 'Communications: Connecting the Future', GLOBECOM 1990. IEEE, August 2002. Print ISBN: 0-87942-632-2
12. Cerf, V.G., Kahn, R.E.: A protocol for packet network intercommunication. IEEE Trans. Commun. **22**(5), 637–648 (1974)
13. Mi, W., Zhang, X.: The applicability analysis of IPv6 translation transition mechanisms. IJCNS **8**(4) (2015)
14. Damara, A., Damara, V., Yadav, N., Sexana, A.: A review of IPV6: feature and importance. Int. J. Innov. Res. Comput. Sci. Appl. **1**(1) (2015)

15. ISIS Extensions Supporting IEEE 802.1aq Shortest Path Bridging. IETF, April 2012
16. Law, A.M., Kelton, W.D.: Simulation Modeling and Analysis, 3rd edn. McGrawHill, New York City (2000)
17. Sari, A.: Lightweight robust forwarding scheme for multi-hop wireless networks. IJCNS **8**(3), 19–28 (2015)
18. http://www.cisco.com/c/en/us/products/routers/4000seriesintegratedservicesroutersisr/index.html
19. Tripathi, A.K., Singh, S.: Ensuring reliability in cloud computing and comparison on IPv6 encouraged with protocols. In: Proceedings of International Conference on Science, Technology, Humanities and Business Management, Bangkok, 29–30 July 2016, pp. 9–14 (2016)
20. Bisnik, N., Abouzeid, A.A.: Queuing delay and achievable throughput in random access wireless ad hoc networks. In: 2006 3rd Annual IEEE Communications Society on Sensor and Ad Hoc Communications and Networks, vol. 3, pp. 874–880, September 2006. ISSN: 2155-5486
21. Das, S.R., Perkins, C.E., Royer, E.M.: Performance comparison of two on-demand routing protocols for ad hoc networks. In: Proceedings of INFOCOM 2000, Tel Aviv, Israel, March 2000 (2000)

A Novel Bulk Drain Connected 6T SRAM Cell

Shobhit Kareer[1(✉)], Anchit Kumar[1], Kirti Gupta[1], and Neeta Pandey[2]

[1] Department of Electronics and Communication, Bharati Vidyapeeth's College
of Engineering, New Delhi, India
Shobhitk.95@gmail.com, anchitkumarr@gmail.com,
kirtigupta22@gmail.com
[2] Department of Electronics and Communication, Delhi Technological
University, New Delhi, India
n66pandey@rediffmail.com

Abstract. Static Random Access Memory (SRAM) being the fastest on chip memory is scaled everyday making a challenge to reduce the leakage current and to sustain its consistency. This paper focuses on the six transistor (6T) realization of the SRAM cell. Two existing SRAM architectures are analyzed and their drawbacks in the deep submicron regions are identified. A novel bulk-drain connected architecture of a six transistor (6T) SRAM cell is proposed. The proposed structure exhibits the capability of minimizing the leakage current in deep submicron region and at the same time maintaining the optimum hold and read noise margins. The performance of the proposed circuit is compared with the conventional 6T SRAM cell using a PTM 32 nm CMOS technology parameters. It is found that the proposed cell structure reduces the leakage current by 44% in comparison to conventional SRAM architecture.

Keywords: Static Random Access Memory (SRAM) · Leakage current · Bulk drain

1 Introduction

Historically, CMOS digital circuits exhibit the unique advantage of dissipating negligible static power. Now-a-days, with the rapid scaling down of CMOS technology, the static power is becoming dominant in digital circuits. The static power measured in terms of leakage power increasing as we move deep in the submicron region. Leakage power is an important issue for all the circuits, but it is a critical problem for the static random access memories (SRAMs) because of their extensive used in microprocessor devices such as Alpha 21264 and Strong ARM [1]. A SRAM cell consists of two cross-coupled CMOS inverters whose leakage power majorly contributes to the total SRAM cell power. Hence, leakage current reduction is the main motive of the researchers and forms the basis of the paper.

The paper focuses on the leakage reduction in SRAM cell. The rudimentary six transistor based realization of SRAM cell (6T SRAM cell) has been considered [2]. The two leakage reduction techniques namely sleep transistor and source biasing techniques are analyzed in deep submicron region. These two techniques have been considered as they add the least number of transistors in the 6T cell. Their performance is evaluated

© Springer Nature Singapore Pte Ltd. 2017
M. Singh et al. (Eds.): ICACDS 2016, CCIS 721, pp. 232–242, 2017.
DOI: 10.1007/978-981-10-5427-3_25

in terms of leakage current and stability [3]. The stability is yet another criterion to fulfill the data retaining capability of the memory. It is found that the source-biased 6T SRAM cell reduces the leakage but lacks on the stability issue. Therefore, a new bulk-drain 6T SRAM cell is proposed and is performance is analyzed in deep submicron regime.

The paper first briefly reviews the leakage current in MOSFET working in deep submicron region. Thereafter the basic architecture and operation of the conventional SRAM cell is discussed. The two available techniques for leakage reduction are reviewed. A novel 6T SRAM topology with better performance in deep submicron is presented. Spice simulations using PTM 32 nm CMOS technology parameters are performed and the results are presented in Sect. 4.

2 Leakage Current

In deep submicron regimes, leakage current has become a major contributor to power dissipation of CMOS circuits as threshold voltage, channel length, and gate oxide thickness are scaled down to enhance the performance of the circuits. Therefore, the identification of different leakage components is very important for estimation and reduction of leakage power. This section reviews various factors causing leakage currents in the CMOS transistors. There are three major components that contribute to the leakage currents namely reverse junction current (Irev), subthreshold current (Isub) and gate and tunneling current (Ig) as shown in Fig. 1 [4]. The bulk-drain/source-bulk junctions in a MOSFET forms PN junction, such that minorities charge carrier start flowing from the depletion region or source/drain (heavily doped) to the substrate-well due to band-to-band tunneling effect. This contributes to Irev. The Isub flows when the power supply id less than the threshold voltage. This leakage current is very prominent in the short channel devices due to the strong depletion region, making and exponential relation with the threshold voltage. Lastly, the tunneling current, is due to the tunneling effect occur from gate to the bulk in the active mode and gate to channel during standby mode of the MOSFET.

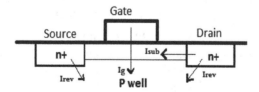

Fig. 1. Leakage currents in MOS.

3 SRAM Architecture

A SRAM cache mainly composed of an array of bit cells, row and column decoders and a sense amplifier [2]. A bit cell stores the information in the cross-coupled inverters, row and column decoders are used to select particular cells for read/write operations. A sense amplifier is sensitive to the output voltage difference of the cell. The SRAM cell is further categorized on the basis of the transistors in the realization. The basic one is the structure employing six transistors and is named as 6T SRAM cell. The paper addresses the leakage and the stability issue in the conventional and the modified 6T SRAM cell.

3.1 Conventional Architecture [2]

A 6T SRAM cell has two CMOS cross-coupled inverters (M2–M4, M3–M5) as shown in Fig. 2. There are two more access transistors (M1, M6) controlled by an external signal wordline (WL) for performing the read and write operation on the cell. The cell has two complementary output lines bitline (BL) and bitline (BLB) for the purpose. The cell works in various states such as write, read and hold depending on the value of the signals at WL, BL and BLB [2]. The combination of the control signals to attain various states is depicted in Table 1.

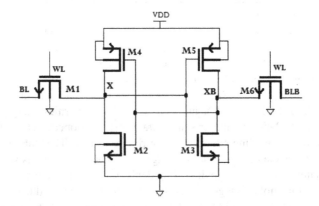

Fig. 2. Conventional 6T cell

Table 1. Operating states of the SRAM cell

State	WL	BL	BLB
WRITE	1	0/1	1/0
READ	1	1	1
HOLD	0	1	1

3.2 Performance Analysis

The performance of the SRAM cell can be evaluated in terms of the leakage current and the stability. A description on the leakage current and stability analysis is covered in the subsection.

3.2.1 Leakage Current Analysis [2]

A SRAM cell works in the read, write and hold states. At the individual cell, the leakage current in the read and hold states predominantly affect the performance. In the read state, the signals WL, BL, and BLB are at high logic levels. For a read '0' operation, the transistors M4 and M3 are OFF and contributes to the read leakage current as shown in Fig. 3. The figure also illustrates the two components of the leakage current named as subthreshold and the gate currents. Out of which the subthreshold leakage current dominates over the other. Similarly during a read '1' operation, the transistor M3 and M6 are OFF resulting in leakage power.

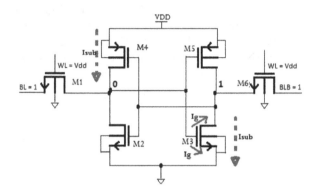

Fig. 3. Read leakage current path

Analogously, in the hold state, the signals WL is at low level while the control signals BL and BLB are maintained at high logic levels. For a holding a low level in the cell, the transistors M1, M2, M3 and M5 are OFF and M2 and M6 are ON. The leakage current flow during this state is shown in Fig. 4. In practical situations, it found that the gate leakage current is negligible in comparison to subthreshold leakage current, so from this point onwards, leakage current due to subthreshold is considered during analysis.

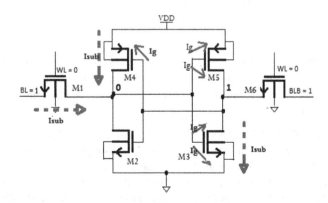

Fig. 4. Hold leakage current path

3.2.2   Stability Analysis [3]

The stability of a SRAM cell measured in terms of the static noise margin (SNM). It measures the confrontation of the cell to any disturbance, such that the value in the cell does not toggle and give redundant data. It forms the basic and a very important issue in SRAM cell. Based on the state of operation either read or hold, Read SNM and Hold SNM are defined for a SRAM cell. Practically, SNM are measured through the Butterfly curve which combines the voltage transfer characteristic (VTC) of the two cross-coupled inverters i.e. X-XB and inverse VTC of XB-X, to demonstrate the bi-stable nature of the cell. The butterfly curve of the 6T SRAM cell to measure the read and the hold SNM are plotted in Fig. 5(a), (b) respectively. SNM is estimated by embedding the largest square inside the lobe of the curve and finding the length of the square which graphically shows the SNM of the circuit. It is very important for a cell maintain to good SNM values since the hold SNM defines the retention capability of the cell while the read SNM is required for marinating proper voltage levels in the difference of the bit lines to be sensed by the sense amplifier.

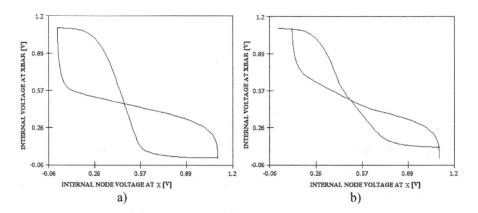

Fig. 5. Butterfly curves of the 6T SRAM cell (a) Hold SNM (b) Read SNM

4   Modified SRAM Architectures

While working in deep submicron regions, leakage current increases exponentially [4]. The techniques which reduce the leakage current as well as maintain good SNM are preferred. Modified 6T SRAM cell structures are available in the literature; out of them the sleep based and source biased structures have been chosen in the work since they add least number of transistors in the basic SRAM cell. A brief discussion on the structure is presented.

Sleep Transistor Based SRAM Cell [5]: This cell structure adds two sleep transistors at the header and the footer in between the two power supplies in the conventional 6T SRAM cell architecture. The complete schematic is shown in Fig. 6. An additional control signal S and S-bar controls the operation of the two architectures. Depending on the value of the S and Sbar signal the cell works in the active and the standby mode. In the active mode, the signal S and S-bar are at low and high logic levels such that both the sleep transistors are ON and the cell work as the regular SRAM cell. Conversely in the standby mode both the sleep transistors are OFF to reduce leakage by providing a high resistance [3, 5].

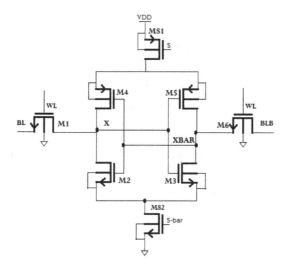

Fig. 6. Schematic of sleep transistor based SRAM cell

Source Biasing Technique Based SRAM Cell [6]: The above cell structure possess a drawback of large size of sleep transistors and more switching power dissipation [3]. Another modification in the SRAM cell architecture is used to source biasing technique as elaborated in Fig. 7. A transistor (MS1) controlled by the WL signal at the footer is added to the basic structure. The reason is that when the cell is active (read or write) MS1 is ON and when the cell is in hold state it is OFF, providing high resistance in the path [6]. The source biasing technique reduces the leakage current drastically but has a serious issue with stability. It poses poor hold SNM as shown through the butterfly curve in Fig. 7b. So, it is not suitable for SRAM cell implementation in deep submicron region.

5   Proposed Architecture

5.1   Bulk-Drain Technique

Unlike in the conventional PMOS, bulk is not connected to the source instead it is connected to the drain terminal, such MOS have almost linear region in the I_{DS}-V_{DS} offering high resistance which aids in reducing the leakage current in the cell even in submicron region [7].

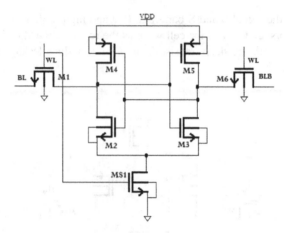

Fig. 7. (a) Schematic of source biasing technique, (b) Hold SNM butterfly curve

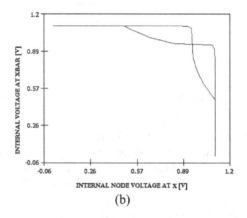

(b)

Fig. 7. (continued)

5.2 Proposed SRAM Cell

In this paper, the incorporation of bulk-drain connected PMOS transistors (Fig. 8) in the 6T SRAM cell is proposed. The complete schematic of the proposed SRAM cell architecture is shown in Fig. 9. The two bulk-drain connected PMOS transistors (M8–M7) are stacked with the PMOS transistors (M5, M6). The working of the proposed architecture is same as that of conventional 6T SRAM cell, that is during read operation the signals value are WL = BL = BLB = 1; during write operation these values are WL = 1 BL = 0 and BLB = 1 or WL = 1 BL = 1 or WL = 1 BL = 1 and BLB = 0 whereas in hold state, the signals maintain WL = 0 and BL = BLB = 1 logic levels.

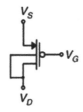

Fig. 8. Connection of bulk drain PMOS [7]

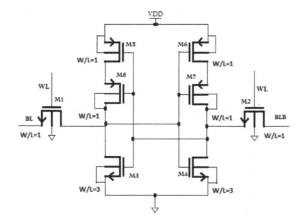

Fig. 9. Schematic diagram of proposed SRAM architecture.

6 Simulation Results

In this section, the functionality of the proposed bulk-drain connected SRAM cell is verified. The leakage and the stability analysis of the proposed cell are performed and is compared with the conventional SRAM cell. The simulations are done using 32 nm PTM CMO technology parameters in SYMICA simulation environment. Simulations are performed at 27 °C and supply is 1.1 V, width of M1, M2, M5, M6, M7, M8 is 32 nm and M3, M4 is 96 nm.

The proposed SRAM cell is simulated and the waveforms at different nodes in the cell are plotted in Fig. 10. It can be observed the SRAM cell operates in the write '1' and write '0' state in the interval 1 ns to 40 ns and 41 ns to 70 ns respectively. Also, it stores the last value in the duration 70 ns to 90 ns. In the interval 100 ns to 110 ns, it reads the stored value. Thus, the proposed architecture conforms to the functionality of the SRAM cell.

The performance of the proposed and the conventional 6T SRAM cell structures is evaluated in terms of the leakage current and the SNM through butterfly curve. The leakage currents during the read and the hold states are listed in Table 2 for supply

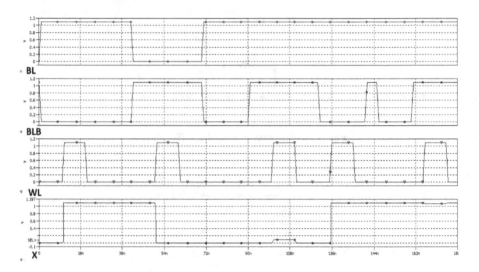

Fig. 10. Simulation waveforms of the proposed SRAM cell

Table 2. Leakage currents measurements

State	Architecture	
	Conventional	Bulk-drain
$V_{DD} = 1.1$ V		
Read leakage	393 nA	327.9 nA
Hold leakage	95.3 nA	53.17 nA
$V_{DD} = 0.4$ V		
Read leakage	1.51 nA	1.30 nA
Hold leakage	2.67 nA	2.41 nA

voltages of 1.1 V and 0.4 V respectively. The results show a maximum reduction of 44% in the hold leakage current values by using the proposed bulk-drain connected SRAM cell. The butterfly curves during the read and hold states obtained from the proposed SRAM cell are shown in Fig. 11. It can be observed that due to the stacking, there is an increase in the Hold SNM, and due to the same there is slight decrease in the Read SNM. Also, it is found that the read SNM increases by increasing the V_{DD} which is confirmed by simulating the proposed cell at different power supply values. The results for the same are noted in Table 3.

The SNM results in Table 3 clearly verifies that the gated technique SRAM cell has a poor hold SNM value (35 mV), having a great disadvantage of stability.

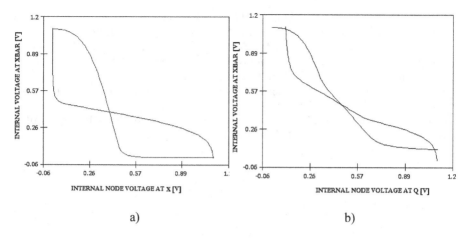

a)   b)

Fig. 11. Butterfly curve of the proposed SRAM cell (a) Hold SNM, (b) Read SNM

Table 3. SNM measurements

State	Architecture		
	Conventional	Bulk-drain	Gated technique
Read SNM	172 mV	122 mV	148 mV
Hold SNM	253 mV	258 mV	35 mV

7 Conclusion

In this paper, new 6T SRAM cell architecture suitable for deep submicron region operation is presented. The architecture introduces two bulk drain connected PMOS transistors in the cross-coupled inverters. This modification reduces the leakage current by providing a high resistance path. Also it is capable of maintaining optimum noise margins which the existing modified SRAM cell architectures fails to maintain. SPICE simulations are done using PTM 32 nm CMOS technology parameters. It is observed that the proposed cell reduces the leakage current by 44% in comparison to conventional SRAM architecture.

References

1. Kim, N.S., Flautner, K., Blaauw, D., Mudge, T.: Circuit and microarchitectural techniques for reducing cache leakage power. IEEE Trans. Very Large Scale Integr. (VLSI) Syst. **12**(2), 167 (2004)
2. Kang, S.M., Leblebici, Y.: CMOS Digital Intrigated Circuit: Analysis and Design, 3rd edn. McGraw-Hill, New York (2003)
3. Singh, J., Mohanty, S.P., Pradhan, D.K.: Robust SRAM Design and Analysis. Springer, Heidelberg, p. 13. ISBN 978-1-4614-0818-5 (eBook)

4. Roy, K., Mukhopadhyay, S., Meimand, H.M.: Leakage current mechanisms and leakage reduction techniques in deep-submicrometer CMOS circuits. Proc. IEEE **91**(2) (2003)
5. Povlov, A., Semenov, O., Sachdev, M.: Sub-quarter micron SRAM cells stability in low voltage operations: a comparative analysis. In: IEEE International Integrated Reliability Workshop Final Report, pp. 168–171, 21–24 October 2002
6. Zang, L.-J., Wu, C., Ma, Y.-Q., Zheng, J.-B., Mao, L.-F.: Leakage power reduction technique of 55 nm SRAM cell. IETET J. (2011)
7. Cannillo, F., Toumazou, C., Lande, T.S.: Bulk-drain connected load for subthreshold MOS current-mode logic. Electron. Lett. **43**(12), 1 (2007)

Blood Pressure Control During Anaesthesia With and Without Transport Delay

Varun Gupta[1(✉)], Abhas Kanungo[1], Piyush Chandra Ojha[1],
and Pankaj Kumar[2]

[1] K.I.E.T, Ghaziabad, India
vargup2@gmail.com, {abhas.kanungo,piyush.ojha}@kiet.edu
[2] S.C.R.I.E.T, Meerut, India
nadarpankaj.miet@gmail.com

Abstract. Regular monitoring of the anaesthetic drug dosage during a surgery is required to avoid the patient's inter operative awareness due to inadequate levels of anaesthesia. The traditional methods of assessing the anaesthetic depth levels such as heart rate, blood pressure, pupil size, sweating, etc are not very accurate as these responses may differ from patient to patient depending on the type of surgery and the anaesthetic drug administered. Sometimes during the process of anesthesia some time delay may occurs and this time delay is very dangerous for our life during anesthesia. In this paper Transport delay that comes in the process of annesthesia have investigated and analysed. Z-Transform have been shown its incapability for fractional time delay processes. So, Modified Z-Transform is preffered for fractional time delay processes. Further effect of this time lag (Transportation delay) on system performance is minimized with PID controller. Relative, absolute stability have been calculated through which blood pressure is effectivly controlled during annesthesia.

Keywords: Depth of anesthesia (DOA) · Heart rate · Time delay · PID controller · Modified Z-Transform

1 Introduction

The main objective of anesthesia is to eliminate pain and awareness so that surgery is successfully done. Earlier alcohol and opium method have been used for anesthesia [1]. Depth of anesthesia includes blood pressure, heart rate and blood oxygenation. Anaesthesia is used in surgery to minimize pain, shock, and discomfort for surgical patients. There are several types of anaesthesia which can be used depending on the needs of the surgeries it may be general, local, regional, and conscious sedation. When anaesthesia works as expected, the patient feels no pain [3, 4]. During Anesthesia study reveals brain-wave patterns that mark loss of consciousness. Study reveals brain patterns produced by a general anaesthesia drug, work could help doctors better to monitor patients. Neuroscientists find that Ritalin could help bring surgical patients out of surgery much more quickly [2]. To provide optimal working environments for surgeons in the operating room as well as ensuring patient's safety, an anesthesiologist's effort is absolutely essential [1].

© Springer Nature Singapore Pte Ltd. 2017
M. Singh et al. (Eds.): ICACDS 2016, CCIS 721, pp. 243–251, 2017.
DOI: 10.1007/978-981-10-5427-3_26

Complete loss of consciousness is a general anaesthesia in the patient. General anaesthesia carries the most surgical risk because of the state of complete unconsciousness [4, 6–10]. Modern anaesthesia objective is to ensure sufficient depth of anaesthesia to prevent awareness and the specialist must be able to monitor DOA. Estimating the patient's anaesthesia depth during the surgery has an important role to prescribe suitable doses of anaesthetic agents; because there is the possibility of sudden awareness if the prescribed dose is not sufficient and the overdose agents can also increase the patient's DOA and result in irretrievable consequences. Therefore, it is necessary to have accurate information about DOA to balance the injected dose of anaesthetic agents [3, 4, 8, 9].

Artificial neural network (ANN) based detection of anaesthetic levels have been proposed by several researchers. The method proposed by Watt et al. [4] uses a three layered feed forward neural network to categorize the spectral signatures associated with EEG recorded at three distinct levels of anaesthesia [5, 8, 10].

As an anaesthesia professional, always need to take complex decisions every day to balance the unique anaesthetic needs of individual patients. It is essential to have the most accurate, relevant patient data possible. BIS monitoring can be especially useful for patients whose status may change unpredictably, such as those with cardiovascular conditions, obesity, trauma, genetic disorders or hypnotic sensitivity [11–13].

All patients underwent general anaesthesia induced with clinically appropriate doses of conventional pharmaceuticals including midazolam (4 ± 1 mg); alfentanil (850 ± 150 mg), fentanyl (135 ± 35 mg) and propofol (170 ± 60 mg). Loss of consciousness (LOC) was clinically assessed by lack of response to verbal and tactile stimuli [12].

2 Control System Model of Blood Pressure

(See Fig. 1).

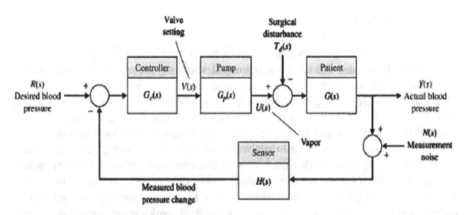

Fig. 1. Figure shows that complete model in which controller, pump, sensors, measurement noise and patient on which experiment is to be performed.

3 Mathematical Modelling of System with Transportation Delay

(See Fig. 2).

Fig. 2. Process with time delay T_d

The time that takes controller for correcting error is known as dead time. When fractional delay comes they are analysed by modified-Z-transform. If input is R(s), output is Y(s), input sampler and output sampler are having sampling time T sec, then

$$\frac{Y(Z)}{R(Z)} = Z\left[G(s)e^{-T_d s}\right]$$

$$Let\ G(s) = \frac{1}{(s+\alpha)}\ and\ T_d = (N+\Delta)T$$

$$So\quad \frac{Y(Z)}{R(Z)} = Z^{-N} Z\left[\frac{1}{(s+\alpha)}e^{-\Delta Ts}\right] \tag{1}$$

Using time shifting property of Laplace transform
$\frac{1}{(s+\alpha)}e^{-\Delta Ts} = e^{-\alpha(t-\Delta T)}u(t-\Delta T)$ and $put\ t = KT$

$$Z[\frac{1}{(s+\alpha)}e^{-\Delta Ts}] = \sum_{k=0}^{\infty} e^{-\alpha(kT-\Delta T)}u(kT-\Delta T)Z^{-k}$$

$$Z[\frac{1}{(s+\alpha)}e^{-\Delta Ts}] = e^{\alpha\Delta T}\sum_{k=0}^{\infty}\left(e^{\alpha T}Z^1\right)^{-k}u(kT-\Delta T)$$

$$Z[\frac{1}{(s+\alpha)}e^{-\Delta Ts}] = e^{\alpha\Delta T}[u(-\Delta T)+\left(e^{\alpha T}Z^1\right)^{-1}u(T-\Delta T)+\left(e^{\alpha T}Z^1\right)^{-2}u(2T-\Delta T)$$

$$+\left(e^{\alpha T}Z^1\right)^{-3}u(3T-\Delta T)+\ldots]\ where\ \Delta = 1-m$$

$$Z[\frac{1}{(s+\alpha)}e^{-\Delta Ts}] = e^{\alpha\Delta T}\left[\frac{\left(e^{\alpha T}Z^1\right)^{-1}}{1-\left(e^{\alpha T}Z^1\right)^{-1}}\right] = \frac{e^{-\alpha mT}}{Z-e^{-\alpha T}} \tag{2}$$

put the value of $Z[\frac{1}{(s+\alpha)}e^{-\Delta Ts}]$ *from* Eq. (2) in Eq. (1)

$$\frac{Y(Z)}{R(Z)} = Z^{-N} Z \left[\frac{1}{(s+\alpha)} e^{-\Delta Ts} \right] = Z^{-N} \frac{e^{-\alpha mT}}{Z - e^{-\alpha T}}$$

Thus for second order system (blood pressure transfer function)- (Table 1, Figs. 3 and 4).

Table 1. Different constants values for the blood pressure control process

N	α	Δ	m	T(in sec)	Stability
1	0.1	0.1	0.9	1	Stable
1	0.1	0.2	0.8	1	Stable
2	0.1	0.3	0.7	2	Stable
2	0.1	0.4	0.6	3	Stable
3	0.1	0.5	0.5	4	Marginal stable
3	0.1	0.6	0.4	10	Marginal stable
4	0.1	0.7	0.3	100	Unstable

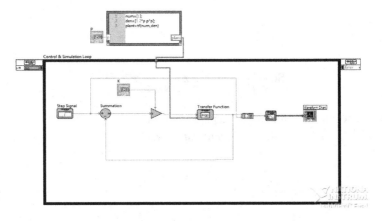

Fig. 3. Proposed VI for proportional controller

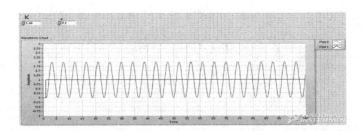

Fig. 4. Sustained oscillation (tuning of proportional controller) using Runge-Kutta-1(Euler) method

$$\frac{Y(Z)}{R(Z)} = Z^{-N} Z \left[\frac{1}{(s+\alpha)^2} e^{-\Delta Ts} \right] \text{ or } \frac{Y(Z)}{R(Z)} = Z^{-N} Z_m \left[\frac{1}{(s+\alpha)^2} \right] \text{at } m = 1 - \Delta$$

$$K_p = 1.99$$

$$p = 0.1$$

$$K_u (ultimate\ gain) = 1.99 \times \frac{1}{2} = 0.995$$

$$P_u = 4.725 \text{ and } \tau_I = \frac{P_u}{1.2} = 3.9375$$

4 Analysis of System Without PID Controller

Without PID controller anaesthesia process is very dangerous for patient. Patients are survived only when transportation delay is minimized. In PID controller PI increase the transient performance and PD increases the steady state performance (accuracy).

5 Analysis of System with PID Controller

(See Fig. 5).

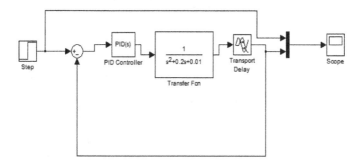

Fig. 5. Step response of the blood pressure control system having transport delay and PID controller

Patient who's blood pressure is to be controlled of blood pressure transfer function $(\frac{1}{(s+p)^2})$ with p = 0.1 and p = 2 have been analysed. PID controller is placed at the error generating stage and it enhances the transient and steady state performance. Analysis of PID controller is done using w^I plane because mapping of w^I is one to one i.e. free from frequency warping. The whole system analysis is done on the basis of transfer function in w^I plane.

$$\frac{Y(Z)}{X(Z)} = \text{Digital PID controller Transfer Function} X \, Z_m \left[\frac{1}{s^2 + 0.2s + 0.01}\right] \text{at m} = 1 - \Delta$$
$$= 0.09$$

Relation between Z and w^I plane, $w^I = \frac{2}{T}\left(\frac{Z-1}{Z+1}\right)$.

Digital Domain Error Coefficient values are calculated using Final value of the Z-transform and these values are as follows- (Fig. 6, Table 2).

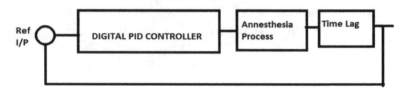

Fig. 6. Digital PID controller with anaesthesia process and transportation delay

Table 2. Different fractional values with calculated digital error coefficients

p	K_P	K_v	K_a	Δ
0.1	1.99	21.45	0.87	0.2
0.4	3.45	23.76	0.81	0.06
100	8.81	34.21	0.31	0.21
1000	9.99	39.21	0.67	0.34
10000	99.21	71.21	0.67	0.54

$$K_P = \lim_{Z \to 1} G_{ho}G(Z) = 119.023$$

$$K_v = \frac{1}{T}\lim_{Z \to 1}(Z - 1)G_{ho}G(Z) = 1.73/T$$

$$K_a = 1/T^2 \lim_{Z \to 1}(Z - 1)^2 G_{ho}G(Z) = 0$$

$$M(Z) = K_P E(Z) + K_v \frac{T(Z+1)}{2(Z-1)} + K_a \frac{(Z-1)}{TZ}$$

6 Results

Various results (step response) have been obtained with PID controller at different frequencies.

Robustness and performance parameters like rise time = 11.7 s, settling time = 34.1 s, % overshoot = 7.43, Phase cross-over frequency w_p = 0.421 rad/sec, w_g = 0.107 rad/sec, Gain Margin (G.M) = 17.8 db, Phase Margin (P.M) = 60° using Runge-Kutta −1 (Euler) method have been calculated. Stable blood pressure control system during annesthesia have been obtained (Figs. 7, 8, 9, 10, 11 and 12).

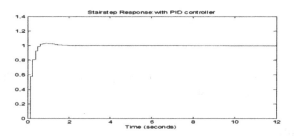

Fig. 7. Stair step response of blood pressure control system with PID controller (ZoH included)

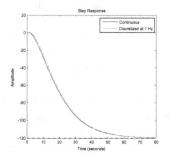

Fig. 8. Step response of blood pressure control system discretized at 1 Hz

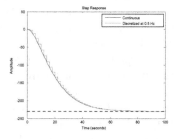

Fig. 9. Step response of blood pressure control system discretized at 0.5 Hz

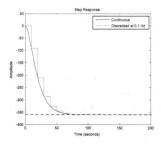

Fig. 10. Step response of blood pressure control system discretized at 0.1 Hz

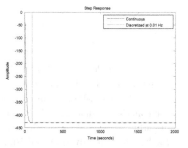

Fig. 11. Step response of blood pressure control system discretized at 0.01 Hz

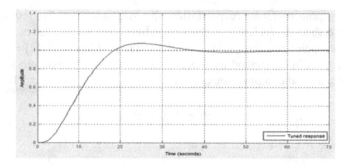

Fig. 12. Step response of the stable, controlled blood pressure control with PID controller that removes (minimizes) transportation delay

7 Conclusion

In this paper blood pressure control system during anaesthesia with and without time delay has been investigated. The delay induced due to any circumstances is analysed by modified-Z-Transform and nullified by the PID controller on the basis of time domain specifications and stable system (after tuning of the PID controller) is obtained. PID controller is used because it is used in 95% industrial processes and it is also suitable for our application. In observation Rise time, overshoot, settling time, closed loop stability and steady state error are obtained. The values of all constants (K_p, K_v, K_a) using Ziegler-Nicholas (Tuning of PID controller) are calculated. In this paper step response for discrete time systems with zero order hold system is also investigated and the truth that comes behind this is as sampling period increases system gets instability. Data processing combined with enhancement in computer and control technology has revolutionized monitoring of patients under anaesthesia.

References

1. Taheri, M., Ahmadi, B., Amirfattahi, R., Mansouri, M.: Assessment of depth of anesthesia using principal component analysis. J. Biomed. Sci. Eng. **2**, 9–15 (2009)
2. http://news.mit.edu/topic/anesthesia
3. Bailey, J., Haddad, W., Im, J., Hayakawa, T., Nagel, P.: Adaptive and neural network adaptive control of doa during surgery. In: Proceedings of the American Control Conference, pp. 3409–3414, Minneapolis, Minnesota, USA, 14–16 June 2006
4. Rabbani, H., Dehnavi, A.M., Ghanatbari, M.: Estimation the depth of anesthesia by the use of artificial neural network. In: Proceedings of the Artificial Neural Networks - Methodological Advances and Biomedical Applications, pp. 283–302 (2011)
5. Mallat, S.G.: A Wavelet Tour of Signal Processing: The Sparse Way. Academic Press, San Diego (2009)
6. Srinivasan, V., Eswaran, C., Sriraam, N.: EEG based automated detection of anesthetic levels using a recurrent artificial neural network. J. Med. Syst. **7**, 267–270 (2005)

7. Moerman, N., Bonke, B., Oosting, J.: Awarness and recall during general anesthesia: facts and feelings. Anesthesiology **79**, 454–464 (1993)
8. Huang, J.W., Lu, Y., Nayak, A.: Depth of anesthesia estimation and control, IEEE Trans. Biomed. Eng. **46**
9. Gibbs, G.A., Gibbs, E.L., Lennox, W.G.: Effect on the electroencephalogram of certain drugs which influence nervous activity. Arch. Int. Med. **60**, 154–166 (1937). (pp. 71-81, 1999)
10. Watt, R.C., Navabi, M.J., Scipione, P.J., Hameroff, S.R., Maslana, E.S.: Neural network estimation of anesthetic level using EEG spectral signatures. Ann. Int. Conf. IEEE Eng. Med. Biol. Soc. **12**(5), 2017–2018 (1990)
11. https://www.uhms.org/images/MEDFAQs/BIS_brochure.pdf
12. Kelly, S.D.: Monitoring Consciousness Using the Bispectrum Index during Anaesthesia, A pocket guide for Clinicians, Aspect medical systems (2007)
13. Furutani, E., Bao, S., Araki, M.: A-TDS: a CADCS package for plants with a pure delay. In: Jamshidi, M., Herget, C.J. (eds.) Recent Advances in Computer-Aided Control Systems Engineering, pp. 247–272 (1992)
14. Astron, K.J., Huggland, T.H.: New tunning methods for PID Controllers. In: Proceedings of the 3rd European Control Conference (1995)
15. Dorf, R.C., Bishop, R.H.: Modern Control Systems, 7th edn. Pearson Prentice Hall, Upper Saddle River (2016)
16. Manitius, A., Olbrot, A.W.: Finite spectrum assignment problem for systems with delays. IEEE Trans. Autom. Contr. **AC-24**(4), 541–553 (1979)
17. Onodera, H., Maetani, S., Aung, T., Kan, S., Sakamoto, T., Shirakami, G., Furutani, E., Araki, M., Imamura, M.: Clinical application of a blood pressure autoregulation system during hypotensive anesthesia. World J. Surg. **23**, 1258–1263 (1999)

Brain-Bot: An Unmanned Ground Vehicle (UGV) Using Raspberry Pi and Brain Computer Interface (BCI) Technology

Vishal Chaurasia$^{(\boxtimes)}$, Vikas Mishra, and Lokesh Jain

Department of Computer Science & Engineering, Krishna Engineering College,
Ghaziabad, India
vchaurasia95@gmail.com,
vikas.mishra@krishnacollege.ac.in,
nsitlokesh.jain@gmail.com

Abstract. Since the last decade, internet has become an essential part of our lives and all the major devices no matter in what field and utility they are used for, connectivity through Internet has become an essential requirement for the users. One of the two major objectives this project was to build an Unmanned Ground Vehicle (UGV) providing with a set of different functionalities such as: GPS tracking, Real-Time Face Detection, Location Tagging, Live Streaming, etc. functionalities such that these functionalities could be used from anywhere in the world irrespective of the distance between the Bot and the controller and this Bot can be controlled through any device so that there is no need of a specialized controller in order to control and access it. The second objective was to introduce a methodology through which people suffering from motor disabilities can interact with physical devices using the Brain Computer Interface (BCI).

Keywords: Raspberry Pi · Brain computer interface (BCI) · Electroence phalography (EEG) · Live stream · Local network/internet · Face detection · Location tracking · Brain-Bot

1 Introduction

Traditionally, near border our security forces need to patrol the area from time to time and due to this there is always a chance of human error but this slight possibility of error can be removed by deploying Brain-Bot in those areas due to its small size it will not be easily detected and because of its live streaming and real-time face detection features [3] one can easily detect and identify the person who is trying to sneak inside.

Apart from all this in the case of any natural/man-made epidemics such as earthquakes, gas leakage, radiation leak Brain-Bot can prove itself useful. In some cases there is sometimes need to collect samples from the affected area the Brain-Bot can be simply deployed in those areas and using its one of the several attachments such as robotic arm, samples can be collected very easily. The previous papers have also discussed similar type of system made using Arduino or any other microcontrollers having the same capabilities but using Raspberry Pi in place of any microcontroller

© Springer Nature Singapore Pte Ltd. 2017
M. Singh et al. (Eds.): ICACDS 2016, CCIS 721, pp. 252–261, 2017.
DOI: 10.1007/978-981-10-5427-3_27

gives much more flexibility to add as many sensors and components as required and in addition to this using Raspberry Pi makes the proposed system accessible from anywhere which can be controlled using a number of devices [2].

In addition to all these functionalities, Brain-Bot can be controlled using the Brainwaves using the Brain Computer Interface (BCI) technology. Though, in the previous papers the use of BCI technology has been made and with the help of eye blink/eye brow movements primarily the object is being moved but this method requires much more effort and time in order to train the mind of the users to adapt and use the proposed device effectively [4, 6]. Hence in order to reduce the time and effort required to control the proposed system a new method is being introduced through which physical device can be controlled (in this case an Unmanned Ground Vehicle). This method can also be applied to help people suffering from motor disabilities and hence making their lives simpler to some extent [4–6].

2 Hardware Requirements

Since one of the main objectives is to build a UGV, the first and foremost thing that will be required in order to build this project is a microcontroller that will communicate with the motors and sensors on receiving the command but the major disadvantage of using a microcontroller is that though it can perfectly communicate with motors or retrieve the readings from any type of sensor whether analog or digital it won't be able to perform complex computations such as face detection, motion tracking, etc. [1]. So in order to overcome this disadvantage Raspberry Pi 2 (Model B in this case) should be used which is a low-cost credit card sized computer and is capable enough to perform all the computations needed and with the help of its 26 GPIO (General Purpose Input/Output) pins motors and sensors can also be connected.

Apart from Raspberry Pi the hardware which will be required are as follows:

1. Motor Drivers (L293d or L298)
2. 2 Axis Pan-Tilt Camera Mount (For Camera Movement)
3. Wi-Fi/GSM Dongle
4. GPS Module
5. LDR based Light Sensor Module
6. Electroencephalography (EEG) Headset
7. Power Bank (For Raspberry Pi) and 12 V Battery Pack (For Motors)

In addition to all the above components, parts such as 4wd robot chassis, wheels, dc motors, servo motors, etc. should be implicitly understood. Now coming to the one of the many design challenges while designing the 4wd (4 wheel drive) chassis one of the most important among them is to design the chassis in such a way that it can easily move on most of the terrains [2] and can easily overcome most of the obstacles having a height of around 3 cm.

Hardware/sensors such as thermal sensors, robotic arm, etc. can also be added the same way as other hardware/sensor will be added which is further discussed under the next heading.

3 System Working and Hardware Assembly

Before going into any further details of how the hardware's were connected to each other one must first understand the logic of how our system will work and for better understanding, it can be further divided into three main parts.

3.1 Control Logic

The basic control logic behind Brain-Bot's working can be understood as a client-server connection where one end of the connection is the Brain-Bot and the other end is the controlling system. One end is the Brain-Bot which will always be fixed and another end can a phone, tablet, laptop, etc. running on different operating systems [1]. From the controlling end, a set of instructions will be sent to Brain-Bot and it will perform a specific operation associated with those instructions once the operation is performed successfully it will send an acknowledgment to the controlling end and if some error has occurred it will send the error code for the same.

3.2 Brainwaves Control Methodology

Now, in order to control the Brain-Bot using brainwaves first of all one needs to understand what an EEG headset and Brain Computer Interface (BCI) technology are and how they work.

Electroencephalography (EEG) Headset
Electroencephalography (EEG) Headset is basically a headset which contains one or more electrodes which are to be placed along the scalp. It uses the method of electro-physiological monitoring through which the electrical activity of the brain is recorded. It measures the voltage fluctuations resulting from the ionic activities from the neurons of the brain [4, 6, 10].

Our brainwaves change according to what we are doing and feeling. Brainwaves are divided into bandwidths to describe their functions. The brainwaves are mainly divided into 6 categories according to their bandwidths:

- INFRA-LOW (< .5 Hz)
  - Infra-Low brainwaves (also known as Slow Cortical Potentials) the slow nature of these brainwaves make them very difficult to detect and measure accurately and hence very little is known about it.
- DELTA WAVES (.5 TO 3 Hz)
  - Delta brainwaves are slow, loud brainwaves (low frequency and deeply penetrating). These are generated in deep mediation and in dreamless sleep. These waves suspend external awareness and are a source to empathy. Healing and regeneration take's place in this state.

- THETA WAVES (3 TO 8 Hz)
  - In theta, our senses are withdrawn from the external world and focused on signals originating from within. It is that state which we only experience fleetingly as we wake up or drift off to sleep.
- ALPHA WAVES (8 TO 12 Hz)
  - These waves are dominant during quietly flowing thoughts, and in some meditative states. It is the resting state of the brain. Alpha waves aid overall mental coordination, calmness, alertness, mind/body integration and learning.
- BETA WAVES (12 TO 38 Hz)
  - Beta is a 'fast' activity, present when we are alert, attentive, engaged in problem-solving, judgment, decision making, and engaged in focused mental activity.
- GAMMA WAVES (38 TO 42 Hz)
  - These are fastest of all the brain waves and are related to a simultaneous processing of information from different brain areas. Gamma is also above the frequency of neuronal firing, so how it is generated remains a mystery. It is speculated that Gamma rhythms modulate perception and consciousness, and that a greater presence of Gamma relates to expanded consciousness and spiritual emergence (Fig. 1).

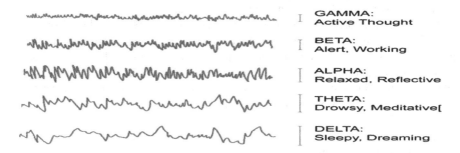

Fig. 1. Brainwaves representation [14]

In this case, the proposed system uses Neurosky MindWave Mobile EEG headset which is single channel and uses dry type electrode [4, 12]. Single channel means that only one electrode is present in the sensor/headset which is placed on the forehead. The MindWave Mobile safely measures and outputs the EEG power spectrums (alpha waves, beta waves, delta waves, theta waves, and gamma waves). It uses TGAM1 (Thinkgear chip) module which removes noise from the raw brainwaves anal it also provides with eSense meters which provide the normalized values of attention, meditation and intentional eye blinks strengths [4].

Brain Computer Interface (BCI) Technology
Brain Computer Interface (BCI) or sometimes called as Mind-Machine Interface (MMI) is nothing but the direct connection between the computer or any other computing device and the EEG headset through a wire or any other wireless methodologies [5] such as Bluetooth, RF Port, etc.

In this method the readings from the EEG headset are sent to the computer which further processes these values such as removal of noise from the raw data and normalizing the raw data and then based on the values of the processed raw data certain predefined actions can be performed [5, 6]. In order to fully understand the concept of BCI refer to the below diagram (Fig. 2).

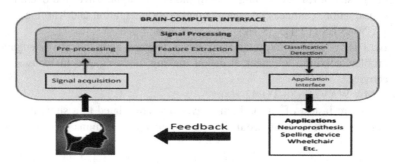

Fig. 2. Brain Computer Interface (BCI)

Now after thoroughly understanding the concept of EEG and BCI the main question is "how to control the Brain-Bot movement using brainwaves?"

As mentioned earlier the MindWave mobile produces eSense values (containing Attention and Mediation strengths) and Eye Blink strength. So, one of the many possible solutions to the above-mentioned problem is to use Eye-Blink to change the direction of motion whenever its strength crosses the threshold value and use the attention values in order to start the motion in the selected direction whenever the attention level crosses a predefined threshold value.

3.3   Hardware Assembly

The next part is assembling all the components together. The Raspberry Pi 2 (in this case) contains a single 40-pin expansion header labeled as 'J8' providing access to 26 GPIO pins [1] (Fig. 3).

Fig. 3. Raspberry Pi J8 header

Since Pi4J will be used as an external library which enables us to control the GPIO pins using Java [9].

In order to understand how the components are to be connected with the pi and the flow of data in the Brain-Bot refer to diagram below (Fig. 4).

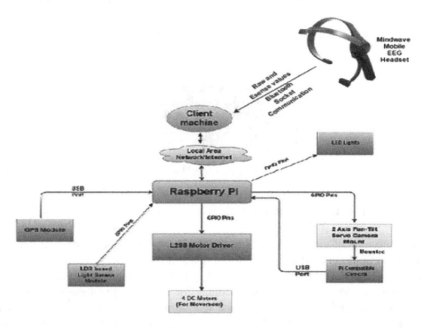

Fig. 4. Flow of data

In the above chart the arrows which are going towards the Pi means that readings such as GPS coordinates and Light Sensitivity values will be read by the Pi and the arrows which are in the opposite direction as of Pi, indicate that Pi will send signals and they will move accordingly. The below diagram of L298 Motor driver module describes how motors are to be connected to it. Here motors A & B are considered as two different pairs of motors i.e.: 'A' indicates one pair & 'B' as another (Fig. 5).

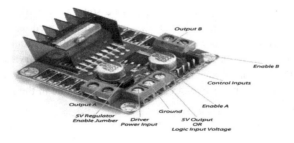

Fig. 5. L298 motor driver

Here control input and enable pins will be connected to Pi's GPIO pins and in the case of GPS module a serial to USB cable can be used to connect it to Pi's USB Port. After assembling all the components the below figure shows the Brain-Bot (Fig. 6).

Fig. 6. Brain-Bot

4 Software Implementations

After connecting all the components to the Raspberry Pi the next step is to set up a client-server model [1] and in order to do so standard java socket server methodology is used. Here, Raspberry Pi will act as a server which will open a socket on a specified port which will wait for the incoming connection from the client machine once the connection is established it will send and receive messages and the connection will terminate only when the client side application exits. As mentioned earlier it is similar to a simple chat server where the client machine will send some instructions as messages and the Pi will send acknowledgment or error message as message only. One thing that should be kept in mind here is that in the case of an error the server side code should not terminate. Now from here code can be further divided into following five parts.

4.1 Sever Side Code

Server side code will include the portion of opening a socket on a specific port as discussed earlier and in addition to it there will be some if-else construct or a switch case implementation that will interpret the incoming instructions from the client machine and will call the related method associated with the instruction received.

In order to setup the camera to get the live stream motion library for the Pi is used, after installing the motion library the next thing to do is turn on the http stream on a specified the port on which the live stream would be available in the motion.config file located in/etc. directory.

4.2 Client Side Code

On the client side, all that has to be done is to design an interactive interface through which normal user interact. First of all one should design a login screen so that the user with right credentials will be able to access the Brain-Bot if the provided credentials are correct then only the connection box will appear where the IP and the port on which the Pi is available and the socket is opened also the control method will be asked from the user.

The second step is to design a secondary interface which will enable the user to control the Brain-Bot, control the camera movement, plotting the current position of the Brain-Bot on the map and viewing and saving the live stream (Fig. 7). In order to view the live stream, the VLCJ library [8] is used which enables us to use the VLC player in java swings GUI.

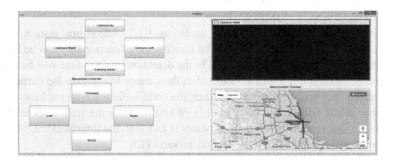

Fig. 7. Secondary interface

4.3 Brainwaves Based Motion Control

MindWave does not provide any official SDK for development of JAVA applications for MindWave mobile hence the methods of retrieving the values and parsing have to be implemented by ourselves only.

The EEG sensor comes with a software which when launched creates a socket server on local IP: "127.0.0.1" and Port: "13854" (by default) on which the raw as well as the eSense meter values, are streamed through the sensor in form of JSON when a client socket is connected to it. In order to control Brain-Bot using brainwaves Eye-Blink strength and strength of the attention is used. (eSense values)

The same secondary Interface will launch but with few modification that as soon as the GUI is launched a separate thread will connect to the MindWave's socket server and in case of an Eye-Blink event i.e. if Eye-Blink strength crosses a specified threshold, the direction will change in clockwise order and in case no Eye-Blink event has occurred the attention level is checked and if it is beyond set threshold value the bot will moved in the selected direction by sending predefined commands to the server. In case the value of the "signalLevel" greater than or equal to 150 (which means the headset is not worn properly or disconnected) the application and the thread should terminate/logout immediately.

4.4   Real Time Face Detection and Tracking

When talking about image processing face recognition/detection comes under the category of one of the oldest [7] and most implemented functionality using the concept of image processing. There are a lot of algorithms present for face identification where each and every one of them differs in their approaches but still new algorithms are being developed in order to increase the efficiency level [7]. The process of face detection/identification generally considers some of the parameters like light illumination, skin tone, geometry of the face, etc. Face detection and Tracking can be implemented via many open source programming language that sometimes are accompanied with their irrespective Integrated Development Environment (IDE) such as MATLAB, OPENCV, SIMPLECV, etc.

In this case a standard algorithm name as KLT Algorithm also known as Kanade-Lucas-Tomasi feature tracking. The face tracking functionality can be in one of the two modes: detection or tracking [12]. In the detection mode, a face will be detected in the current frame and if a face is detected in the current frame then the corner points of the detected face will be derived and then the code will switch to tracking mode in which these points will be tracked [11, 13]. While tracking the points some of them may be lost in that case if the number of points is less than the threshold the face is lost and the code will again switch to detection process [13].

4.5   Real Time GPS Tracking

GPS tracking has become a much-needed necessity since the last decade. In order to implement this functionality in the proposed system the code can be further divided into two parts on the basis of where it will be running i.e.: on the raspberry pi on the Brain-Bot (server-side) or on the controlling end (client side). The algorithm for the server side is as follows.

Step 1: Setup up a .html file in any of the directory in the pi.

Step 2: Open a socket on a port on the pi. This port should be different from that which is being used to control the Brain-Bot.

Step 3: Using the GPS library in python access the GPS module and if its status is "fix" then access the values of latitude and longitude.

Step 4: Store the values of latitude and longitude in the variable and append it to the values stored in latitude and longitude array in the .html file which will also contain a JavaScript code to plot the array on Google map.

Step 5: Write the change to the .html file and close it.

Step 6: Repeat Step 3, 4 and 5 after a specified time interval again and again.

The second part is to access the .html file available on the pi and load this file into a Javafx Web view based browser which will reload the file again and again after a specified interval.

5   Conclusion and Further Scope

Though adding of few components and sensors were discussed above but the procedure for connecting and interacting with them will be same as mentioned above no matter what type of component/sensor it is.

Now, talking about the further scope of Brain-Bot there is a lot of it as Raspberry Pi which is the heart of the Brain-Bot is a fully fledged computer therefore, anything can be achieved with it what a normal computer can achieve, only limitation of it is it's processing speed which it increasing with every new version of Raspberry Pi.

References

1. Ikhankar, R., Kuthe, V., Ulabhaj, S., Balpande, S., Dhadwe, M.: The raspberry pi controlled multi environment robot for surveillance & live streaming. IEEE Computer Society, May 2015
2. Budiharto, W.: Design of Tracked Robot with Remote Control for Surveillance. IEEE Computer Society, August 2014
3. Nguyen, H.-Q., Loan, T.T.K., Mao, B.D., Huh, E.-N.: Low Cost Real-Time System Monitoring Using Raspberry Pi. IEEE Computer Society, July 2015
4. Stephygraph, L.R., Arunkumar, N., Venkatraman, V.: Wireless Mobile Robot Control through Human Machine Interface using Brain Signals. IEEE Computer Society, May 2015
5. Bi, L.: Member, IEEE, Fan, X.-A., Liu, Y.: EEG-Based Brain-Controlled Mobile Robots: A Survey. IEEE Computer Society, March 2013
6. Jang, W.A., Lee, S.M., Lee, D.H.: Development BCI for individuals with severely disability using EMOTIV EEG headset and robot. IEEE Computer Society, February 2014
7. Joshila Grace, L.K., Reshmi, K.: Face Recognition in Surveillance System. IEEE Computer Society, March 2015
8. https://github.com/caprica/vlcj. Accessed 31 Aug 16
9. https://www.pi4j.com. Accessed 31 Aug 16
10. https://en.wikipedia.org/wiki/Electroencephalography. 31 Aug 16
11. http://www.brainworksneurotherapy.com/what-are-brainwaves. Accessed 31 Aug 16
12. http://store.neurosky.com/pages/mindwave. Accessed 31 Aug 16
13. http://in.mathworks.com/help/vision/examples/face-detection-and-tracking-using-live-video-acquisition.html. Accessed 31 Aug 16
14. http://www.zenlama.com/wp-content/uploads/2013/03/Brain_waves_large.jpg. Accessed 31 Aug 16

Contact Dynamics Emulation Using Leap Motion Controller

Akshat Bhardwaj[1(✉)], Akshay Grover[1], Praveen Saini[2],
and Mayank Singh[1]

[1] Krishna Engineering College, Ghaziabad, Uttar Pradesh, India
akshatbhardwaj16@gmail.com,
akshay.grover94@gmail.com, mayanksingh2005@gmail.com
[2] Moradabad Institute of Technology, Moradabad, Uttar Pradesh, India
praveensaini5@gmail.com

Abstract. Recent developments in Human-Computer Interaction technologies can be harnessed effectively to facilitate better cognitive learning and this is what this project aims to achieve in the field of Contact Dynamics. The project aims to enable a better comprehension of the concepts of Contact Dynamics to a layman through a technology that has been developed to foster interactive learning viz. the Leap Motion Controller. The project involves the usage of the Leap Motion Controller, a hand motion sensing device, to understand 'Dynamics' i.e., a branch of classical mechanics associated with the application of forces on bodies and the effect they have on their motion, along with the help of a conventional personal computer.

Keywords: Human-Computer Interaction · Leap Motion · Contact Dynamics · Hand-motion sensing · Newtonian Mechanics

1   Introduction

Theoretical knowledge pertaining to the concepts of Contact Dynamics is difficult to grasp at first glance. Also, for senior high school and varsity students, practical research and analysis in the field of Contact Dynamics are hard to conduct because of:

- High costs incurred in the construction of a physical prototype.
- Risks that involve collateral damage to people and property in the vicinity of the physical prototype due to erroneous calculations, unforeseen environmental conditions etc.

Therefore, a virtual model is not only instrumental but imperative for better understanding systems comprising of singular or multiple bodies upon which a variety of forces are applied. The goal is to study about the motion of these bodies under the application of various forces. So, the target of the project is to design a virtual simulation environment on the host computer which emulates the theoretical concepts of Contact Dynamics in particular and Newtonian Mechanics in general.

Another reason why various virtual prototypes are required because they assist in visuospatial constructive cognition [1]. Visuospatial constructive cognition is the

M. Singh et al. (Eds.): ICACDS 2016, CCIS 721, pp. 262–271, 2017.
DOI: 10.1007/978-981-10-5427-3_28

ability to visualize an object in the form of its constituent segments and build a model of the object using these segments. Hence, this project helps students conceptualize the prototypes and interact with them through hand gestures so as to promote both easy learning and a better understanding of the same while simultaneously providing them with a fun way to improve their visuospatial skills. Exploration into interactive learning through Leap Motion Controller has been explored in Australian Sign Language Recognition [2] to support the hearing impaired. This interactive framework can be used to treat, if not heal altogether, people afflicted by conditions like Attention Deficit Hyperactivity Disorder (ADHD) [3]. Also, it can be used to examine skeletal muscles using Electromyography (EMG) [4].

To achieve an interactive configuration, a sensor device called Leap Motion Controller is connected to a computer. This device is used to track the movements of a user's hands and fingers, in order to recognize the hand gestures being performed as the user glides their palm/fist/pointed finger(s) just over the Leap Motion device in a defined pattern. If the Leap Motion device is able to recognize a hand gesture, an operation corresponding to that gesture will be performed on the computer system to which the sensor device is connected. Several types of gestures can be customized using the device and operations corresponding to each gesture can be defined on the computer. By performing these hand gestures in the vicinity of the Leap Motion device, a user can operate a simulated virtual environment. For instance, the Leap Motion has been found to be rather dynamical in simulating musical instruments like piano as it has a vast gesture repertory [5]. The Leap Motion device is able to track the motion of hands hovering above it with the help of infrared radiation emitted by its sensors as well as with the help of 2 built-in cameras.

The Leap Motion Detector tracks the fingers and palm of the user when their hand moves within the range of the infrared radiation emitted by the device. This tracking data can be obtained from the Leap Motion API through an object called *frame*. The *frame* object contains data pertaining to the position of the user's hand like the velocity of the fingertip and its spatial position. This data can then be retrieved in the form of coordinates and manipulated upon to perform various operations like pushing a button, moving a static bar on the screen, taking input values on the host computer by the gestures of the fingers etc. In order for the operations to be performed on the computer through gestures, the gesture frames are fed to the LeapGesture library [6] which contains previously defined gesture recognition functions. If the frame data matches one of the previously defined gesture recognition functions in the LeapGesture library, then the operation corresponding to the gesture will be carried out on the computer. However, besides the use of predefined gestures, users may also be able to customize new gestures according to their convenience to interact with the framework, much like sensor gloves which have been used in applications involving the use of custom gestures [7]. But some additional pattern recognition functions may need to be incorporated into the project to recognize the new gestures. For instance, a 3D surface rendering software: OsiriX [8], which is used to process images produced by imaging techniques like MRI, CT, PET, Ultrasounds etc., makes use of gestures in which a circular motion is performed with the index finger of the right hand in clockwise and anti-clockwise motions to navigate through a data set.

Although other motion tracking devices that have depth sensors like Kinect from Microsoft could alternatively be used, a device is preferred that is compact, cost-effective, robust, and has high-resolution sensors. Kinect has been found to generate imprecise and low resolution depth maps [9]. This can cause discrepancies in the measurement of the distances of fingertips from the depth sensor. Since the Leap Motion Controller was found to be better in all the aforementioned parameters than Kinect, the former was incorporated in the project. Also, only the utility of hand gesture recognition suffices for the project as opposed to full-body motion detection that is provided by Kinect. Another alternative to the use of the Leap Motion Controller could be the Data Glove which was developed by Zimmerman [10]. The Data Glove has a major limitation, i.e., it is equipped with tactile switches, optical goniometer and resistance sensors besides a variety of other sensors to detect flexion of the fingers [11] which makes it a cumbersome device to use lest one forgets that the device comes with a hefty price tag which is several times the price of the Leap Motion Controller.

2   Project Configuration

A brief description of the tools and the technologies utilized in the project are given as follows:

2.1   Leap Motion Controller

Leap Motion Hardware. Leap motion controller is a cuboidal hand-motion gesture detection device (dimensions: 13 mm × 13 mm × 76 mm). It consists of 3 infrared sensors and 2 cameras which simultaneously detect the movements of a user's hand(s) in general and the fingers in particular in a 3-Dimensional conical space above the device [12] with sub-millimeter accuracy [13] for up to 10 fingers. The area in the vicinity of the Leap Motion device in which the hand gestures are accurately detected is 2 feet above the device, by 2 feet wide on each side along the length of the device covering an angle of 150°. And up to 4 feet across the device covering an angle of 120°. The fingers' position, velocity and direction coordinates are recorded by the device at a rate of up to 200 fps [14] (Fig. 1).

The below figure shows that the Leap Motion device has the best frame rate from among other popular gesture detection devices. Hence our predilection for the Leap Motion Controller.

Leap Motion Software. Leap Motion software comprises of the Leap Motion Software Development Kit (SDK). This SDK consists of the LeapGesture library which, in turn, provides the developers with the Application Programming Interfaces (API) of Leap Motion Controller. The Leap Motion API is a set of functions, classes and objects which allow the developer to use predefined gestures as well as standard commands from the Leap Motion library in order to interact with the system using the Leap Motion Device. The following figure explains the process through which hand gestures are recognized by the Leap Motion device (Fig. 2).

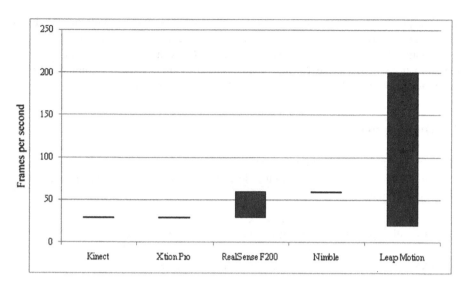

Fig. 1. Frame rates of different gesture recognition devices

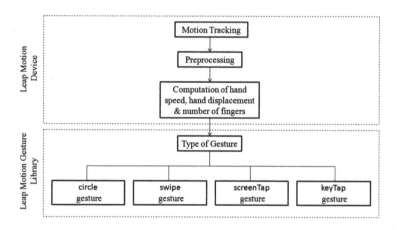

Fig. 2. A diagram presenting the recognition process implemented in the LeapGesture library

2.2 Programming Languages Used

HTML5 and CSS3. The <canvas> element of HTML5 is most extensively used in this project because not only does it allow for differentiating multiple objects like buttons on a webpage, but also facilitates easy interaction of hand gestures with those objects. Besides, this element of HTML5, along with CSS3, can also be used to draw graphics and 2D pictures on a webpage [15].

JavaScript. JavaScript is best suited for developing projects involving the Leap Motion device. This language is particularly used to extract as well as manipulate the coordinates of fingers/hands to interact with the objects in the webpage and to design the animations of the project. These animations provide a visually stimulating experience for students to learn the concepts of Contact Dynamics.

3 Methodology

The user opens the HTML file of the project through a web browser and is presented with an interface that prompts them to select one case from among four different cases of Contact Dynamics, namely:

- LM (linear motion) of a single block
- SMIP (sliding motion along an inclined plane) of two blocks
- DMHP (dragging motion along a horizontal plane) of two blocks
- FPVL (fixed pulley with vertical loads) (Fig. 3, Table 1)

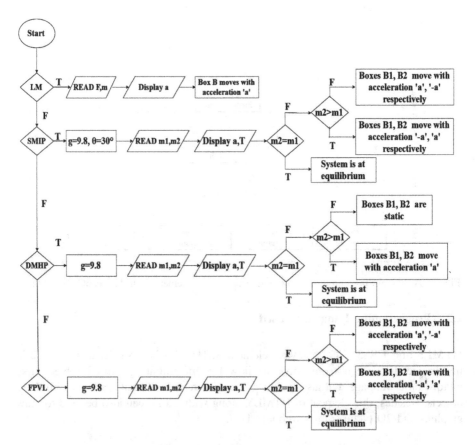

Fig. 3. Procedure to select and run a case of Contact Dynamics

Table 1. Abbreviations of the terminology used and their corresponding definitions

Abbreviation	Definition
F	Force acting on a block
m	Mass of a block
a	Acceleration with which a block moves
T	Tension in the rope connected to a box
g	Acceleration due to gravity (9.8 m/s$^{2)}$

Initially, the user needs to perform a *screenTap* gesture to select a case. The *screenTap* gesture is a pointing movement which is equivalent to a mouse-click. This gesture is recognized when the index finger rapidly prods forward and draws backward into its original position with a velocity of at least 40 mm/s [16]. Then, the user must move their finger over to the *Input* button and perform the same gesture again. This opens up a new HTML page which prompts the user to input several values corresponding to the case that the user selected, via a numeric keypad. The numeric keypad allows a user to input values, by performing the *screenTap* gesture, into the text fields that appear on the webpage of the browser's window (Table 2).

Table 2. The input requirements and outputs of different cases of Contact Dynamics taken in this project

Case	Prerequisite data	Input	Output
LM	Nil	Mass of the block and force applied on the block	Block moves with acceleration 'a'
SMIP	G (acceleration due to gravity) = 9.8 m/s^2 and Θ (angle of inclination of wedge) = 30°	Masses of both the blocks	Both blocks move along the direction of the block, the net force acting on which is greater, with acceleration 'a'. If the net force acting on each block is equal, the system remains stationary
DMHP	G = 9.8 m/s^2	Masses of both the blocks	Both blocks move along the direction of the suspended block, if the net force acting on the suspended block is greater, with acceleration 'a'. Otherwise, the system remains stationary
FPVL	G = 9.8 m/s^2	Masses of both the blocks	Both blocks move along the direction of the block, the net force acting on which is greater, with acceleration 'a'. If the net force acting on each block is equal, the system remains stationary

Upon entering the values in the requisite text fields, the net acceleration 'a' with which the system must move is calculated on the basis of the entered values and displayed. After a delay of about 4 s, the output is generated in the form of an animation which corresponds to the case that the user had previously selected. The animation shows the system moving with an acceleration of 'a' m/s^2. The animation was made using HTML5, CSS3 and JavaScript.

4 Results

The *screenTap* gesture is performed to select a case from among 4 different cases of Contact Dynamics taken in this project. To implement the *screenTap* gesture, *Pointable* class method *touchDistance* of Leap Motion API is used. This method creates an adaptive touch plane at the central axis of the device. The *touchDistance* values range from −1 to +1 on the transverse axis of the Leap Motion device. The adaptive touch plane is at value 0. If the fingertip position coordinates lie within the range [+1, 0), then this implies that the fingertip is hovering over the object. As soon as the fingertip position coordinates come within the range (0, −1], then the *screenTap* gesture will be performed and the case will be selected.

To select a single object out of multiple objects on a webpage, *pointable* and *interactionBox* objects of class *Frame,* and *normalizePoint()* method of class *InteractionBox* are used. These objects and the *normalizePoint()* method help map the finger coordinates to the canvas. These mapped coordinates are then displayed in the textual form on the canvas using the method *strokeText()*.

The following algorithm shows how the retrieved positional data coordinates of the fingertip can be manipulated to interact with the objects on a webpage that lie within different grids of the HTML canvas:

```
SELECT_CASE(case,X,Y)
if canvasX > x1 & canvasX > x2 & canvasY > y1 & canvasY >
y2
   thenimgChange("image.png")
   if touchDistance < 0
   then    canvas.strokeText(case,X,Y);
                        imgtype ←"image"
```

Following images depict the results of implementing the previously described methodology (Fig. 4).

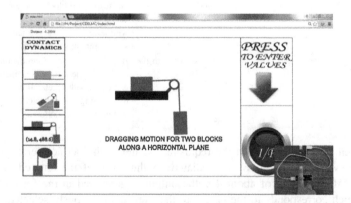

Fig. 4. Selecting a case of Contact Dynamics through *screenTap* gesture

The above image shows the 'DMHP' case being selected from the left menu (3rd from top) (Fig. 5).

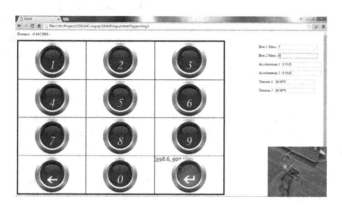

Fig. 5. A keypad to enter values into the requisite text fields through *screenTap* gesture in order to calculate the net acceleration of the blocks in the system

The above image shows the use of a virtual keypad to input values such as masses of the boxes, for the previously selected case, in the text fields by performing the *screenTap* gesture (Fig. 6).

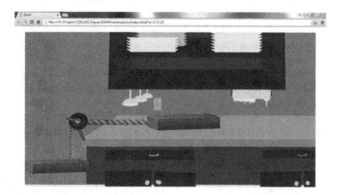

Fig. 6. The resultant animation of the selected case of Contact Dynamics showing the acceleration of the blocks in the system

An animation pertaining to the selected case of Contact Dynamics will be played wherein the boxes may move with a certain acceleration depending upon the values which were input by the user in the antecedent stage using a keypad.

5 Conclusion

In this paper, we have attempted to establish a novel approach to discerning, comprehending, analyzing and evaluating a very small portion, viz., Contact Dynamics, of a Brobdingnagian field, viz., Newtonian Mechanics. This project has the potential to be a viable and plausible alternative to the orthodox 'black-board' teaching methodology which, apparently, is insufficient to elucidate intricate concepts. This project has tremendous scope in academics as it can be used to incorporate concepts pertaining to various fields including, but not limited to: Defense, Automotive, Aeronautics and Biomechanics. This new alternative has already begun showing promise, so much so that the Leap-Motion SDK which comes with the Leap-Motion Controller shows the working of the human heart in 3-D and the process of pumping of blood through all 4 valves of the heart in a way that can easily be understood by a layman.

Acknowledgements. The authors are grateful to Birendra Singh for providing insight into the working of the Leap Motion device and for his invaluable contribution to the revision of this paper. The authors are also indebted to the faculty members of the Department of Computer Science and Engineering, Krishna Engineering College, for guiding the authors through various stages of the development of the project.

References

1. Mervis, C.B., Robinson, B.F., Pani, J.R.: Visuospatial construction. Am. J. Hum. Genet. **65** (5), 1222–1229 (1999). doi:10.1086/302633
2. Potter, L.E., Araullo, J., Carter, L.: The leap motion controller. In: Proceedings of the 25th Australian Computer-Human Interaction Conference on Augmentation, Application, Innovation, Collaboration, OzCHI 2013 (2013). doi:10.1145/2541016.2541072
3. Vinkler, M., Sochor, J.: Integrating motion tracking sensors to human-computer interaction with respect to specific user needs. In: Central European Seminar on Computer Graphics (2014). https://cescg.org/
4. Kainz, O., Jakab, F.: Approach to hand tracking and gesture recognition based on depth-sensing cameras and EMG monitoring. Acta Inform. Prag. **3**(1), 104–112 (2014). doi:10.18267/j.aip.38
5. Silva, E.S., de Abreu, J.A. O., de Almeida, J.H.P., Teichrieb, V., Ramalho, G.L.: A preliminary evaluation of the leap motion sensor as controller of new digital musical instruments (2013)
6. Nowicki, M., Pilarczyk, O., Wasikowski, J., Zjawin, K., Jaskowski, W.: Gesture recognition library for Leap Motion controller. Bachelor Thesis. Poznan University of Technology, Poland (2014)
7. Mehdi, S.A., Khan, Y.N.: Sign language recognition using sensor gloves. In: Proceedings of the 9th International Conference on Neural Information Processing, ICONIP 2002 (2002). doi:10.1109/iconip.2002.1201884
8. Ebert, L.C., Flach, P.M., Thali, M.J., Ross, S.: Out of touch – a plugin for controlling OsiriX with gestures using the leap controller. J. Forensic Radiol. Imaging **2**(3), 126–128 (2014). doi:10.1016/j.jofri.2014.05.006

9. Arkenbout, E., de Winter, J., Breedveld, P.: Robust hand motion tracking through data fusion of 5DT data glove and nimble VR kinect camera measurements. Sensors **15**(12), 31644–31671 (2015). doi:10.3390/s151229868
10. Zimmerman, T.G.: US Patent 4,542,291, U.S. Patent and Trademark Office, Washington, DC (1985)
11. Premaratne, P.: Human computer interaction using hand gestures. Cogn. Sci. Technol. (2014). doi:10.1007/978-981-4585-69-9
12. Beattie, N., Horan, B., McKenzie, S.: Taking the LEAP with the Oculus HMD and CAD - plucking at thin air? Procedia Technol. **20**, 149–154 (2015). doi:10.1016/j.protcy.2015.07.025
13. Weichert, F., Bachmann, D., Rudak, B., Fisseler, D.: Analysis of the accuracy and robustness of the leap motion controller. Sensors **13**(5), 6380–6393 (2013). doi:10.3390/s130506380
14. Zaiţi, I.-A., Pentiuc, Ş.-G., Vatavu, R.-D.: On free-hand TV control: experimental results on user-elicited gestures with leap motion. Pers. Ubiquit. Comput. **19**(5–6), 821–838 (2015). doi:10.1007/s00779-015-0863-y
15. Mowery, K., Shacham, H.: Pixel perfect: fingerprinting canvas in HTML5. In: Proceedings of W2SP (2012)
16. Bachmann, D., Weichert, F., Rinkenauer, G.: Evaluation of the leap motion controller as a new contact-free pointing device. Sensors **15**(1), 214–233 (2014). doi:10.3390/s150100214

Dynamic Two Level Threshold Estimation for Zero Motion Prejudgment: A Step Towards Fast Motion Estimation

Shaifali M. Arora[1] and Kavita Khanna[2(✉)]

[1] MSIT, Janakpuri, New Delhi, India
shaifali04@yahoo.co.in
[2] The NorthCap University, Gurugram, Haryana, India
kvita.khanna@gmail.com

Abstract. In most video sequences, especially containing slow motion, a large number of blocks are stationary. Early determination of these blocks may save large number of computations in any motion estimation (ME) algorithm. The decision for declaring a block to be stationary can be made by comparing the block distortion with a predetermined threshold whose large or small values may affect the speed and accuracy of a ME algorithm. Accurate prediction of this threshold proposes a challenging problem. In this manuscript, a dynamic two level threshold estimation technique has been proposed. This two level scheme not only detects constant variations in the neighboring blocks but is also capable of detecting stationary blocks with abrupt variations. Performance of the proposed technique is evaluated by implementing ZMP before ME process in adaptive rood pattern search (ARPS) algorithm. Simulation results show better performance of proposed technique in comparison to single level dynamic threshold predictor and fixed threshold predictor.

Keywords: Video compression · Motion estimation · Zero motion prejudgment · Search window · Spatial correlation

1 Introduction

Motion estimation is a very significant but time consuming component of a video encoder. Block based motion estimation techniques are simple in hardware implementation and hence extensively used in most of the exiting video standards like MPEG-X and H.264x. Full search motion estimation [1] is the most straight forward and global optimal algorithm among the various block matching algorithms (BMAs). However, its high computational load prohibits its use in real time applications. A large number of fast BMAs have been given in the past to reduce this computational burden. Most popular of these are three step search (TSS) [2], New three step search (NTSS) [3], Four step search (FSS) [4], Block based gradient descent search (BBGDS) [5], Diamond search (DS) [6] and Cross diamond search (CDS) [7]. These fast BMAs are based on the hypothesis that block distortion reduces monotonically as the search proceeds towards the global minima. These fast BMAs pursue different search patterns to speed up the search process. Sub sampling the current block pixels have been used

© Springer Nature Singapore Pte Ltd. 2017
M. Singh et al. (Eds.): ICACDS 2016, CCIS 721, pp. 272–281, 2017.
DOI: 10.1007/978-981-10-5427-3_29

by Wang et al. [8] in order to increase the search speed. Another way to speed the search process is by predicting the MV for the candidate blocks by exploring the correlation of the spatial and temporal neighboring blocks [8, 9]. All the above proposed algorithms go through all the search steps without considering the type of motion activity in a sequence. However, in applications like video telephony, video conferencing etc. few blocks show displacement between successive frames which indicates the presence of a large number of zero motion blocks in a frame. The detection of these stationary blocks before starting the MDP search would lead to large savings in computations.

It has been found that block distortion for the stationary blocks is small in comparison to the surrounding neighbouring blocks [10]. Therefore, the decision for detecting a block to be stationary or not depends on the distortion measure of the candidate block with the collocated block in reference frame. If the calculated distortion is below a predetermined threshold than that block is categorized as stationary block and search process is terminated thereafter. However, the threshold may change from block to block and frame to frame. So determination of this threshold plays a key role in achieving high compression rate without compromising much with the video quality.

In this manuscript a new two level dynamic threshold prediction technique to decide whether a block is stationary or not has been proposed. Distortion measure of the previous zero motion blocks is used for adaptively determining the threshold for the current block. This paper is subdivided in to five sections. An overview of zero motion prejudgment is given in Sect. 2. The proposed technique is detailed in Sect. 3. Section 4 presents a comparison of the presented technique to other state of art techniques for zero motion prejudgment (ZMP). Conclusion of the entire paper is given in Sect. 5.

2 Review of Zero Block Prejudgment

As discussed above, in various multimedia applications like video conferencing very few blocks possess motion. Threshold value plays a key role in determining such type of zero motion blocks. High T_s value will inappropriately determine moving blocks whose block distortion is below Ts as stationary, resulting in deteriorated video quality. On the other hand, low T_s will not accomplish the objective.

Threshold with which the block distortion is compared plays a crucial role in ZMP. Concept of using a threshold value for detection of stationary blocks is given in [11]. Ming et al. suggested to use fixed threshold [12] for early detection of stationary blocks, but didn't propose a global value for fixed threshold. Yao et al. in [10] found by experimentation that the block distortion for stationary blocks varies in the range 300 to 1300 and used a fixed threshold value of 512 to detect stationary blocks. Fixed threshold has been used extensively in various researches [11–14] because of its simplicity and ease of implementation. But this fixed threshold based ZMP prediction could not be applied to every situation as the prediction error may vary in different parts of a frame and also for different frames in a single sequence. It is therefore difficult to select an appropriate fixed threshold which is applicable in all situations. This need led to the development of the concept of adaptive thresholding. De Hann [15], Shi et al.

[16], Yang et al. [17], Ahmed et al. [18] and Ismail et al. [19, 20] have proposed different dynamic threshold estimation techniques which perform better than the fixed threshold estimation techniques but at the same time these techniques require large computation time and memory for estimating the threshold.

In general block distortion may vary from block to block and frame to frame over a very wide range. The distortion pattern of zero motion blocks in five sample test sequences have been plotted and compared in Fig. 1. It can be observed from the figure that neighboring blocks have similar block distortion because of the fact that these blocks may be part of same stationary segment of a frame. On the other hand this distortion varies abruptly for different segments of the frame. In a sequence like Clair maximum distortion for stationary blocks is observed as 2000 whereas it is less than 200 for most of the blocks. Also in sequences like hall and highway, block distortion for most of the stationary blocks is more than 512 but it is very small for sequences like news. So it can be concluded that instead of using a fixed threshold, dynamic threshold will enhance the probability of accurately finding zero motion blocks. The process of determining dynamic threshold is discussed in next section.

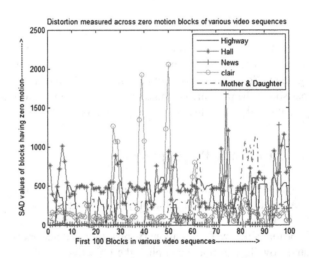

Fig. 1. Distortion measured for stationary blocks in different video sequences.

3 Proposed Dynamic Threshold Estimator

The proposed technique describes the prediction of threshold for ZMP. Average distortion measure of previous stationary blocks is utilized for predicting threshold for the current block. This threshold is varied so as to follow the changes in characteristics of video sequences. Further, It has been investigated that the difference between the average intensities of two matching blocks is very small. Therefore for enhancing the accuracy of prediction, difference between the average intensities of the current block and the reference block is considered as another important parameter for ZMP.

The overall process of determination of stationary blocks is divided into two levels - level A and level B. Whereas Level B identifies the stationary blocks with irregular and large distortions. Details pertaining to each of the levels are given in the subsequent subsection.

3.1   Level A

This level is designed to identify the stationary blocks with small constant distortion which are part of same stationary segment in a frame and have almost same distortions as that of neighbouring blocks. To identify these stationary blocks, block distortion is compared with the calculated dynamic threshold; if it is less than this threshold then block is declared as stationary block and search is terminated, otherwise Level B is executed to refine the checking process.

If $SADc < T1 + \alpha$, then block is stationary otherwise go to level B.

Here $SADc$ is block distortion between the current block and its collocated reference block, $T1$ is the dynamic threshold for level A. Initial value of $T1$ is taken as 384 and α is taken as 128 which makes the total sum 512. These values are taken to attain minimum acceptable video quality and are based on the fixed threshold value of 512 given by Nie and Ma [10]. Distortion pattern of various test sequences has been observed (a sample of which is shown in Fig. 1) which inspired to decide α as 128. This factor takes care of the small variations in distortions in neighbouring blocks. The value of $T1$ is updated by assigning the SAD value of first stationary block encountered. This is done so as to reduce the possibility of decision error. Thereafter $T1$ is dynamically updated by taking the average of SAD values of all the previous stationary blocks. A buffer is used to store the sum of SADs of all the previous stationary blocks and a counter is used to store the number of previously detected stationary blocks. The ratio of the two values, in buffer and counter gives the average variations of SAD of previous stationary blocks which is used for updating $T1$. Further it has been observed from Fig. 1 that some highly matching stationary blocks have very small SAD values say 60 whereas the average variation is nearly 280. The small distortion of this stationary block would reduce the average distortion such that consecutive neighbouring blocks with SAD 265 will remain undetected. Therefore this special feature is introduced in this manuscript to avoid very small SAD values to affect the average SAD, these small SADs are not considered in average SAD calculations. If the difference between $T1$ and distortion of current stationary block is more than 128 than its SAD is not considered for average calculation. If a stationary block goes undetected at level A, then level B is designed in a way so that there is high probability of its detection at level B.

3.2   Level B

This level attempts to identify the stationary blocks with abrupt variations which have been left in Level A. For example as shown in Fig. 1, for "hall" sequence, normal stationary blocks have variations around 500, i.e. $SAD_{avg} = 500$ and nearly this would be the threshold value at level A. But the stationary blocks between 28 and 34 have large SADs (more than 800) and that will remain undetected at level A. The single level threshold equation as given in [10] is:

$$T_s = \min(\max(\text{SADavg}, 512), \text{SADc}) * 0.75 + 128.$$

As per this equation the threshold for "hall" sequence will be:

$$T_s = \min(\max(500, 512), 800) * 0.75 + 128 = 512,$$

This clearly indicated that the stationary blocks with large variation will remain undetected with this single threshold.

But level B presented in the current work will be able to detect majority of stationary blocks with large distortions. Large threshold at level B would result in large decision errors which is defined as incorrect determination of moving blocks as stationary and vice versa. Therefore to handle this situation and to reduce the possibility of decision error, difference between average intensities of current and reference blocks is taken as another parameter in level B. This difference should be less than a fixed constant K for both the blocks to be similar. Parameter K controls the decision errors at Level B. If small values of K are chosen, decision error increases because in this case large numbers of stationary blocks remain undetected. On the other hand, higher values of K increases the decision errors by considering all the blocks as stationary blocks whose block distortions are below the threshold T_2. Figure 2 shows the effect of changing the value of K on both the video quality in terms of PSNR and computational complexity in terms of average number of search points required per frame. It can be clearly observed from the curves in the Fig. 2 that K is inversely proportional to PSNR and computations (search points) involved. This value is selected experimentally to be 1.5 that provides good and acceptable PSNR with small computations compared to larger and smaller values of K.

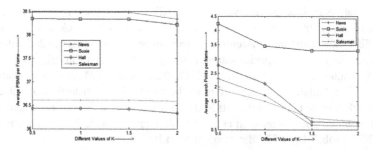

Fig. 2. Deviation inaverage PSNR per frame and average search points for different values of K

At Level B, the block distortion is compared with dynamic threshold T_2 and difference between average intensities is compared with K. Also difference between (T_1 and T_2) is taken to actually detect the stationary blocks with large variations. If the three parameters are below the predetermined values, block is detected as stationary block and search is terminated. Otherwise MVs for the block are calculated by using any fast motion estimation algorithm.

Check if $T_1 - T_2 > \beta$ AND SADc $< T_2 * \delta + \beta$ AND abs $(\mu c - \mu r) < K$

Else Implement Fast motion estimation algorithm to find MVs of non - stationary blocks

Initially T_2 is declared as 512. It is updated either when stationary blocks go undetected at Level A & B, but are found in the MV estimation process in fast BMA or stationary blocks are detected at Level B. T_2 is updated by assigning it the SAD value of the previous stationary block.

3.3   Proposed Algorithm

Once a block is found to be moving or stationary, the next step is to estimate the MVs of the block if it is moving. The proposed dynamic zero motion detection technique and motion vector estimation using ARPS algorithm is given in following steps:

1. Calculate the sum of absolute difference (block distortion) of the current block with its collocated block in the search window.
2. If it is less than the predicted threshold T_1 as in Level A, declare the block as zero motion block, update the threshold T_1 and go to step 6 otherwise go to next step.
3. Find the difference between the average intensity of the current block and its collocated block as M.
4. Compare the block distortion, difference between T1 & T2 and difference between average intensities with thresholds $(T_2*\delta + \beta$ & K) at Level B. If these are less than the specified thresholds in Level B, declare it as zero motion block and go to step 6 otherwise to next step.
5. Estimate the MVs using ARPS algorithm.
6. Exit.

4   Simulation Results

To evaluate the efficiency of proposed technique, simulations have been performed on various test video sequences with search window size of ±7, block size of 16×16 and 15 fps. The effectiveness of the algorithm can be checked by comparing the quality of the reproduced frames in terms of PSNR and SSIM, speed of transmission or memory required by number of bits per pixel required to store a residual frame and accuracy of zero motion detection by decision errors. Higher the PSNR and SSIM, with small search points and small decision errors proves the superiority of any fast ME algorithm. Performance of the proposed dynamic threshold estimator for ZMP is evaluated and compared with fixed threshold suggested in [10, 21] and single level dynamic threshold in [20]. To compare the efficiency of all three ZMP techniques, these are embedded before ARPS algorithm for fast motion estimation. All simulations have been performed using MATLAB Version 7.6.0.324 (R2008a).

4.1   Quality Comparison on the Basis of PSNR and SSIM

A comparison of the PSNR values for full search [1], ARPS without ZMP [10], ARPS with fixed threshold [10], ARPS with single level threshold named as dynamic early search stop termination (DESSTA) [20] and ARPS with the proposed two level dynamic threshold (PDT) have been given in Table 1.

Table 1. Performance comparison in terms of average PSNR per frame for different test video sequences.

	FS	Fast BMA without ZMP	Fast BMA with ZMP using threshold value as		
			Fixed	Dynamic [21]	Proposed
Mdaughter (144 × 176)	39.8915	39.7650	39.7276	39.7275	39.7418
Clair (144 × 176)	43.1733	43.1721	43.1698	43.1698	43.1709
Foreman (144 × 176)	28.6952	28.5424	28.5414	28.5414	28.5418
Susie (240 × 352)	38.1102	37.4837	37.3671	37.4104	37.4801
News (288 × 352)	37.7431	37.6314	37.6150	37.6150	37.6270
Hall (288 × 352)	36.6354	36.4514	36.4448	36.4203	36.4193
Highway(288 × 352)	35.4498	34.3847	34.3787	34.3786	34.3811
Football (288 × 352)	20.5633	22.2664	22.2663	22.2663	22.2664
Amelia (720 × 1280)	28.9998	28.7058	28.6891	28.6680	28.6773
River (720 × 1280)	29.9787	29.6996	29.6921	29.5761	29.6606

FS algorithm always gives the best possible matching results and therefore the best PSNR. It can be clearly observed from Table 1 that there is small degradation in video quality by estimating the zero motion blocks early. This degradation is because of the small number of moving blocks being determined as stationary blocks. Average PSNR degradation is 0.1884 dB w.r.t FS and 0.0153 dB w.r.t ARPS algorithm. The proposed method is able to produce better average PSNR compared to fixed threshold in [21] and DESSTA in [20].

Table 2 shows the performance of above stated algorithms in terms of structural similarity index measurement (SSIM) that measures similarity between two images [21]. Simulation results show the better SSIM produced by proposed dynamic technique as compared to DESSTA in [20] by .001. Small quality deterioration by 0.0024 and 0.0012 compared to FS and ARPS is because of the small errors involved in ZMP.

4.2   Comparison of Search Speed

Table 3 shows comparison of the proposed technique in terms of average search points required per block. It also shows the percentage savings in computations using various threshold techniques. It can be clearly observed that with ARPS algorithm the computations are reduced by 70–95% for slow motion sequences by using ZMP. Also for these sequences dynamic threshold provides 3 to 4 times more savings in computations than fixed threshold with negligible degradation in video quality. Moreover it is clear from the Table 3 that DESSTA results in better savings in computations (search points) compared to proposed technique but this is at the cost of deteriorated video quality in terms of PSNR, SSIM, also more bit rate and decision error as can be seen from Tables 1, 2, 3 and 4. The reason is enhanced accuracy in detection of zero motion blocks by the proposed technique.

Table 2. Performance comparison in terms of verage Structural Similarity Index Measurement per frame.

Sequence	FS	Fast BMA without ZMP	Fast BMA with ZMP using threshold value as		
			Fixed	Dynamic [21]	Proposed
Mdaughter (144 × 176)	0.9669	0.9664	0.9659	0.9659	0.9661
Clair (144 × 176)	0.9907	0.9907	0.9907	0.9907	0.9907
Foreman 144 × 176)	0.9082	0.9077	0.9076	0.9076	0.9076
Susie (240 × 352)	0.9640	0.9638	0.9630	0.9622	0.9628
News (288 × 352)	0.9835	0.9830	0.9829	0.9829	0.9829
Hall (288 × 352)	0.9469	0.9469	0.9467	0.9463	0.9464
Highway (288 × 352)	0.9055	0.8993	0.8991	0.8991	0.8992
Football (288 × 352)	0.7020	0.7020	0.7020	0.6948	0.7000
Amelia (720 × 1280)	0.9308	0.9308	0.9284	0.9268	0.9288

Table 3. Performance comparison in terms of average search point computations per block in a frame

Sequence	FS	Fast BMA without ZMP	Fast BMA with ZMP using threshold value as		
			Fixed	Dynamic [21]	Proposed
Mdaughter (144 × 176)	204.2828	6.5038	2.4863	1.4843	2.3299
Clair (144 × 176)	184.5500	4.9498	1.3218	0.3199	0.4013
Foreman (144 × 176)	184.5500	5.7704	3.9665	2.9662	3.1427
Susie (240 × 352)	202.0485	8.2886	5.1552	4.1453	5.0027
News (288 × 352)	204.2828	5.3948	1.8416	0.8407	1.0499
Hall (288 × 352)	204.2828	5.7705	4.1173	0.9045	0.7741
Highway (288 × 352)	204.2828	8.1913	6.8125	5.7981	6.2722
Football (288 × 352)	204.2828	11.8493	11.7755	10.7751	10.7826
Amelia (720 × 1280)	217.2486	14.2713	6.1300	3.0882	4.6422
River (720 × 1280)	217.2486	8.4870	6.3293	3.8544	5.0360

4.3 Comparison of Threshold Prediction Accuracy

Decision error is one of the important parameters to judge the performance of a motion estimation algorithm using ZMP and is given by equation

Table 4. Performance comparison in terms of percentage improvement in decision errors of proposed tech. over fixed and DESST.

Sequence	Improvement of proposed technique over	
	Fixed Th	DESST
Mdaughter (144 × 176)	15.8915	15.8915
Clair (144 × 176)	0.0000	0.0000
News (288 × 352)	2.1505	2.1505
Foreman (144 × 176)	77.7546	71.9892
Susie (240 × 352)	57.3409	57.4393
Hall (288 × 352)	44.3243	4.4723
Highway (288 × 352)	3.0647	3.2153
Football (288 × 352)	−5.9718	17.1731
Amelia (720 × 1280)	30.2807	24.3447

$$DecisionError = \frac{N_{sm} + N_{ms}}{N_s}$$

where N_{sm} is number of stationary blocks incorrectly determined as moving blocks, N_{ms} is total number of moving blocks incorrectly determined as stationary blocks, N_s is actual total number of stationary blocks determined using full search. From Table 4 it is clear that the proposed technique produces least decision error compared to fixed threshold in Luo et al. [21] and DESST in Ismail et al. [20] for prediction of stationary blocks. Further it can be seen that the proposed technique reduces decision errors by 50% in comparison to dynamic technique in Ismail et al. [20].

5   Conclusion

A two level dynamic threshold based zero motion prejudgment technique has been proposed in this manuscript which enhance the accuracy in determination of stationary blocks. The results clearly show that the proposed threshold prediction technique is able to estimate stationary blocks with better accuracy than the fixed threshold in [21]. Further the proposed technique can produce better video quality in terms of PSNR, SSIM with smaller decision error compared to dynamic early stop search termination technique [20]. Although there is slight increase in the number of search points due to computations involved in both the levels of threshold estimation with the proposed technique in comparison to [20] but then no compromise has been made with the video quality.

References

1. Jain, J., Jain, A.: Displacement measurement and its application in interframe image coding. IEEE Trans. Commun. **29**(12), 1799–1808 (1981)

2. Koga, T.: Motion-compensated interframe coding for video conferencing. In: Proceedings NTC 1981, p. C9-6 (1981)
3. Li, R., Zeng, B., Liou, M.L.: A new three-step search algorithm for block motion estimation. IEEE Trans. Circuits Syst. Video Technol. 4(4), 438–442 (1994)
4. Po, L.M., Ma, W.C.: A novel four-step search algorithm for fast block motion estimation. IEEE Trans. Circuits Syst. Video Technol. 6(3), 313–317 (1996)
5. Liu, L.K., Feig, E.: A block-based gradient descent search algorithm for block motion estimation in video coding. IEEE Trans. Circuits Syst. Video Technol. 6(4), 419–422 (1996)
6. Zhu, S., Ma, K.K.: A new diamond search algorithm for fast block-matching motion estimation. IEEE Trans. Image Process. 9(2), 287–290 (2000)
7. Lam, C.W., Po, L.M., Cheung, C.H.: A new cross-diamond search algorithm for fast block matching motion estimation. In: Proceedings of the 2003 International Conference on Neural Networks and Signal Processing, 14 December 2003, vol. 2, pp. 1262–1265. IEEE (2003)
8. Wang, Y., Wang, Y., Kuroda, H.: A globally adaptive pixel-decimation algorithm for block-motion estimation. IEEE Trans. Circuits Syst. Video Technol. 10(6), 1006–1011 (2000)
9. Chalidabhongse, J., Kuo, C.C.: Fast motion vector estimation using multiresolution-spatio-temporal correlations. IEEE Trans. Circuits Syst. Video Technol. 7(3), 477–488 (1997)
10. Nie, Y., Ma, K.K.: Adaptive irregular pattern search with zero-motion prejudgement for fast block-matching motion estimation. In: 7th International Conference on Control, Automation, Robotics and Vision, 2 December 2002, ICARCV 2002, vol. 3, pp. 1320–1325. IEEE (2002)
11. Zeng, B., Li, R., Liou, M.L.: Optimization of fast block motion estimation algorithms. IEEE Trans. Circuits Syst. Video Technol. 7(6), 833–844 (1997)
12. Hang, H.M.: Motion estimation for video coding standards. In: Standards and Common Interfaces for Video Information Systems, vol. 1, pp. 149–177, December 1995
13. Ren, R., Shi, Y., Zheng, B.: A Fast Block Matching Algorithm for Video Motion Estimation Based on Particle Swarm Optimization and Motion Prejudgment. arXiv preprint cs/0609131, 24 September 2006
14. Tourapis, A.M., Au, O.C., Liou, M.L.: Predictive motion vector field adaptive search technique (PMVFAST): enhancing block-based motion estimation. In: Photonics West 2001-Electronic Imaging, 29 December 2000, pp. 883–892. International Society for Optics and Photonics (2000)
15. De Haan, G.: Motion estimation and compensation: an integrated approach to consumer display field rate conversion. Delft University of Technology, TU Delft (1992)
16. Shi, Y.G., Zhang, Y., Wu, L.N.: Adaptive thresholding for motion estimation prejudgement. Electron. Lett. 34(21), 2016–2017 (1998)
17. Yang, J.F., Chang, S.C., Chen, C.Y.: Computation reduction for motion search in low rate video coders. IEEE Trans. Circuits Syst. Video Technol. 12(10), 948–951 (2002)
18. Ahmad, I., Zheng, W., Luo, J., Liou, M.: A fast adaptive motion estimation algorithm. IEEE Trans. Circuits Syst. Video Technol. 16(3), 420–438 (2006)
19. Ismail, Y., Elgamel, M., Bayoumi, M.: Adaptive techniques for a fast frequency domain motion estimation. In: 2007 IEEE Workshop on Signal Processing Systems, 17 October 2007, pp. 331–336. IEEE
20. Ismail, Y., McNeely, J.B., Shaaban, M., Mahmoud, H., Bayoumi, M.A.: Fast motion estimation system using dynamic models for H. 264/AVC video coding. IEEE Trans. Circuits Syst. Video Technol. 22(1), 28–42 (2012)
21. Luo, J., Yang, X., Liu, L.: A fast motion estimation algorithm based on adaptive pattern and search priority. Multimed. Tools Appl. 74(24), 11821–11836 (2015)

Emerging Technologies, Applications and Futuristic Scope of Cognitive Vehicular Network for 5G Wireless Systems

Zain Hashim[1](✉) and Nishu Gupta[2]

[1] Department of Electronics and Communication Engineering, Amity University, Noida, Uttar Pradesh, India
zainhashim64@gmail.com
[2] Department of Electronics and Communication Engineering, Motilal Nehru National Institute of Technology Allahabad, Allahabad, Uttar Pradesh, India
rel0513@mnnit.ac.in

Abstract. Research and study on fifth generation (5G) wireless communication systems is growing at a massive rate and has the potential to provide enhanced quality-of-experience (QoE), high spectral availability, less power utilization and less end-to-end latency to the wireless system designers. New wireless applications demand high data rates and mobility thereby urging for a deep excavation on 5G wireless systems. This article presents a heterogeneous network system based framework for 5G wireless systems. It proposes a potential cellular architecture that discusses various emerging and promising schemes for 5G wireless network such as cognitive radio oriented network, massive multiple-input multiple-output (MIMO), effective and energy-efficient communication systems, and visible light communication. The focus of the proposed prototype is on making the most effective use of quality of service (QoS), energy efficiency and spectral efficiency in heterogeneous wireless network and is expected to facilitate the interpretation of critical technical challenges towards spectrum efficient 5G wireless network.

Keywords: 5G communication · Cognitive radio · CR-VANET · Heterogenous network · MIMO

1 Introduction

In order to facilitate economic growth around the globe, effective and efficient utilization of information and communication technologies (ICT) is gaining popularity [1]. As far as global ICT strategy is concerned, wireless communication network proves to be the most critical element thereby providing a solid foundation to many other industries. It proves to be one of the highly effective and swiftly rising sectors. The fundamental requirements of fifth generation (5G) systems can be met by integrating smaller cells to existing cellular systems; providing peer-to-peer (P2P) communication; facilitating multi-tier heterogeneous network (*HetNet*) based device-to-device (D2D) communication; machine-to-machine (M2M) communication; millimeter-wave communication; virtualization of

© Springer Nature Singapore Pte Ltd. 2017
M. Singh et al. (Eds.): ICACDS 2016, CCIS 721, pp. 282–289, 2017.
DOI: 10.1007/978-981-10-5427-3_30

wireless resources; energy efficient enabled energy-aware communication; massive multiple-input multiple-output (massive-MIMO); and cloud-enabled radio access network (C-RAN). Thus, the 5G technology will surely have the potential to meet the essential requirements in terms of network efficiency and performance of the system.

1.1   Massive MIMO

MIMO system is a multiple-input multiple-output system which consists of multiple antenna elements ranging from 80–100 or even more elements at the transmitting as well as the receiving section. in order to accommodate larger data, effective communication in wireless medium can be achieved through multiple antennas. Hence, significant enhancement in the performance of the system can be deduced through various parameters viz. spectral efficiency, reliability, data transmission rate and energy efficiency. Both energy as well as spectral efficiency can be enhanced with the massive MIMO systems besides inheriting the advantages of the conventional system [2]. The interference that arisses due to intracell communication can be mitigated by using simple linear pre-coding and detection methodologies. Furthermore, the consequence of fast fading, distortions and noise can be significantly reduced by using massive MIMO systems. The base station can transmit separate signals using the same time-frequency resource to individual users by using multiuser MIMO.

The research paradigm has now shifted towards simplifying the medium access control layer. When the multiuser MIMO is efficiently used in massive MIMO systems, it will improve the performance of the wireless systems thereby mitigating various complicated scheduling schemes [3]. Hence now the researchers are moving towards using massive MIMO system because of its superiority over the conventional schemes and various added advantages.

1.2   Cognitive Radio

Since its inception, the concept of cognitive radio (CR) has gained tremendous interest among the researchers in industries as well as academia. In today's world, CR is considered as one of the most promising technology in the field of wireless communication systems [4–6] including its standardizations [7]. Utilization of the spectrum in a dynamic way in the network is the framework behind the CR technology. Hence, there has been considerable improvement and enhancement in the performance of the overall system where sensing, analyzing, computing, and adapting to the environment is concerned. CR has two main characteristics [8]; (a) Capturing the necessary data by adapting to the environment; by using this feature of CR technology, the unused part of the spectrum can be easily spotted. It helps the system to opt for optimized spectrum and efficient operating parameters, (b) the property of reconfiguring as per the environment. Software defined radio (SDR) has the potential to provide this feature which is the basic framework of CR technology [9]. Figure 1 presents spectrum band occupancy status in CR vehicular network scenario where nodes presented by cars are CR-enabled. It shows the frequency band occupancy status for CR node at a particular

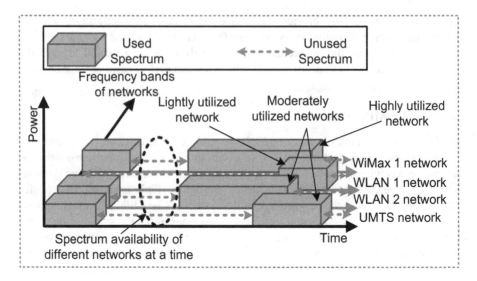

Fig. 1. Spectrum band occupancy status in CR vehicular network

location in four different available access network. It is shown that one network has highly utilized frequency band, two network have moderately utilized frequency bands and one network has a frequency band which is very lightly utilized. Hence, it is observed that there exists large number of spectrum holes in different access network with largely different characteristics in terms of multiple attributes [10].

The aim of this paper is to present a novel framework for *HetNet* as a promising solution towards 5G wireless communication and networking by using cooperative nodes. We study and discuss cooperative and dynamic radio resource allocation in *HetNet*.

2 Related Works

In this section, we review the existing wireless research activities and discusses the significance of the new *HetNet* framework. Recently, many researches and publications are carried out in the domain of spectrum efficiency (SE), energy efficiency (EE), and quality of service (QoS) in the conventional wireless network. EE will help to have an efficient performance of the system by conserving the energy of the battery of the MS along with the BS transmission energy. Since the optimized and enhanced utilization of the radio resource is mostly difficult to obtain in almost every wireless communication systems so to achieve this, it is required that the mobile station (MS) should connect itself with the access node that will be helpful in providing effective and enhanced radio services [11]. In [12], a multihop cellular network is considered along with static RN deployment, wherin a heuristic algorithm is given for suboptimal resource allocation scheme. The authors in [8] have explored the effect of the dimensions of the cell within the network on the capacity of the system and power consumption and henceforth proved that the EE involved in small cells which will proved to be the upcoming cellular communication system. Hence, the research orientation has moved towards using small cells in the network which will be the promising and efficient cellular communication system and hence will establish an effective and promising solution to the users using high transmission rate since energy consumed will be lesser than the traditional scheme in a green radio environment [13]. The authors in [14] have showed the effect of some factors viz. minimum power utilization and smaller cells on the overall performance of the system which showed an enhancement in the capacity as well as the coverage area of the wireless network. In the recent literatures and researches, it is clearly evident that mostly EE researchers have targeted the area of reducing the cell size and minimizing the power utilization of the battery of the mobile and hence the researchers have moved forwarded with the recent studies in which they have concentrated more on the cross-layer design and architecture of the network while studying about the energy efficiency (EE) [15].

It is realized that wireless network suffers from spectrum scarcity. In this connection, DSA is seen as an interesting technology to address the spectrum scarcity. Recent works over TV White Space [16] have proven the feasibility of this approach, usually referred as Cognitive Radio VANET (CR-VANET) [17]. A plenty of research works in recent years [18–23] highlight the importance of this technology. Existing research studies on CR focus on different problems including investigation techniques for spectrum management [24], MAC protocols [25], and routing [26].

3   System Model and Proposed Work

By using the scheme of dynamic allocation of the radio resource in the *HetNet*, a promising and efficient solution has been obtained by increasing cell-edge user and average cell *SE*. This scheme will also enhance the power utilization when the cell-edge communication is concerned. It is found that the cooperation in the *HetNet* will increase when there is a timely exchange of data and enough attention is given in choosing those nodes. A system has several baseband units and so these can coordinate among themselves in order to provide a promising solution viz. sharing the data information of user, scheduling information and the status of the channel whether occupied or unoccupied so as to enhance the *SE* and *EE*. In case of distributed architecture where there is no centralized unit, the rate of transmission that takes place in cooperative *HetNet* system tends to rise the overall complexity of the system. When a centralized architecture of a baseband unit connected with several remote radio heads is concerned, collaborative processing as well as systematized beam forming scheme can be applied efficiently in the baseband unit pool. For separate layers, cooperative transmission is especially beneficial among the nodes. For example, a user located at the edge of the cell within the node falls under the layer. Now the cooperative transmission that will take place within that node which comes under layer say 1' with 1' < 1 could help greatly eliminate the interferences which are dominant in characteristic. In the proposed system model, every node is assumed to be attached to a single antenna. Hence there are 'X' nodes which are cooperative in nature and 'Y' mobile stations which also have the same cooperative property. Together they will form a X × Y MIMO system. Moreover, a pre-coding algorithm in this MIMO system will prove to be a promising solution. It would help in obtaining an effective throughput of the system by efficiently choosing 'Y' mobile stations which are linked with the 'X' nodes [27]. This approach can alleviate the interferences occurring in the almost same radio resource due to the 'X' mobile stations which are catching from the same nodes.

We suppose that as the value of 'X' which is the cooperative set of nodes increases, there is a sharp increase in both the energy as well as spectrum efficiencies but to a certain value of 'X' which will be called as the threshold value of 'X' and as soon as the value of 'X' rises above its threshold value, there will be a saturation found in the performance of the system but at the same time there will be sudden rise in the complexity in coordination as well as the capacity requirement in the backhaul. With the cooperative *HetNet*, there is a close dependency of the cooperative set of nodes 'X' on the overall performance of the dynamic resource allocation scheme. So there should be a promising and effective approach which will form a trade-off between the complexity balancing and the performance gain of the system.

4 Performance Evaluation

In order to evaluate the performance of the mobile association and the impact of the dynamic radio resource allocation scheme in a *HetNet*, a simple network configuration is shown in Fig. 2. Simulations are performed using ns-2 simulator version ns-2.34. We consider varying node speed in the range of 20–50 m/s. Simulation time is set to 150 s. To facilitate the simulation in a reliable environment, we use two-ray ground fading model as the signal propagation model for vehicular communication. To analyse the effect of the proposed spectrum allocation scheme on the overall network, the network configuration incorporates a CR vehicular node that integrates four access network interfaces: WiMax, WLAN, UMTS, and LTE. For the performance evaluation, a single CR vehicular node scenario is considered which is assumed to be moving in the direction of LTE with variable velocity.

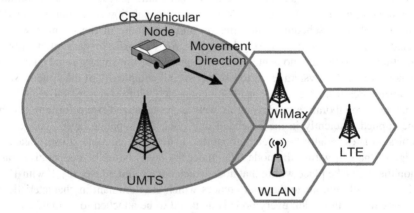

Fig. 2. Network configuration

4.1 Simulation Results

Table 1 shows the parameter value of considered access network at the time of network selection for the cognitive decision. The attributes considered are delay (D), data rate (DR), packet loss ratio (PLR), jitter (J) and traffic load (TL).

Table 1. Different parameters under consideration with respect to different network

Network	Parameters				
	D (ms)	DR (Mbps)	PLR (per 10^6 byte)	J (ms)	TL (% number of user)
Network 1: WiMax	60	45	45	7	35
Network 2: WLAN	57	53	30	11	15
Network 3: UMTS	15	3	25	6	60
Network 4: LTE	20	70	35	7	88

Figure 3 presents the graphical representation of weights of multiple attributes without considering CR vehicular node preferences. These are known as objective weights whose sum is 1. It shows that SAW and proposed cost-I based method select LTE and GRA selects WLAN as an optimal network for spectrum handoff. These selected network are not optimal for all types of non-safety services for CR vehicular network. Table 1 shows that the traffic load is highest in LTE network. Hence, LTE is not optimal network for spectrum handoff in busy hour. Similarly, WLAN is not optimal network for spectrum handoff for voice service in comparison with LTE and UMTS network. The delay in WLAN is high compared with LTE and UMTS network. Hence, user preferences need to be considered to select the optimal network for the spectrum handoff decision. It provides the dynamic approach to select the optimal network for the spectrum handoff decision based on CR vehicular node context aware information for different types of non-safety services.

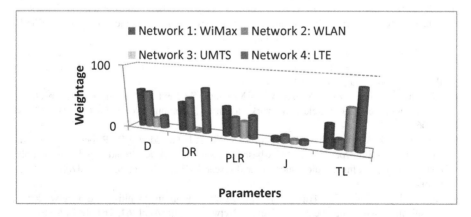

Fig. 3. Weights generated for different parameters without considering CR vehicular node preferences

5 Conclusion and Future Work

This paper presented a novel framework for *HetNet* as a promising solution towards the 5G wireless network by using cooperative nodes. A new heterogeneous 5G cellular architecture is proposed with applications using massive MIMO and CR technology. It is concluded that factors like cooperative capacity in a *HetNet* as well as the multi-hop property of RNs form promising and effective solution for the future wireless communication system by reducing the overall overhead of the system and providing high transmission rates within the network. It is also concluded that technologies like mm-wave communication, WiFi, WiMax, VLC and usage of femtocell within the network can be seen as promising approaches for future wireless communication systems. In future, we shall move towards research domains like remote radio heads, pico node and femto node which will further enhance the performance of *HetNet*.

References

1. Bangerter, B., Talwar, S., Arefi, R., Stewart, K.: Network and devices for the 5G era. In: IEEE Communications Magazine: 5G Wireless Communication Systems: Prospects and Challenges (2014)
2. Rusek, F., Persson, D., Lau, B.K., Larsson, E.G., Marzetta, T.L., Edfors, O., Tufvesson, F.: Scaling up MIMO: opportunities and challenges with very large arrays. IEEE Signal Process. Mag. **30**(1), 40–60 (2013)
3. Wang, C.X., Haider, F., Gao, X., You, X.H., Yang, Y., Yuan, D., Aggoune, H.M., Haas, H., Fletcher, S., Hepsaydir, E.: Massive MIMO channel measurements and modeling: advances and challenges. In: IEEE Communications Magazine: 5G Wireless Communication Systems: Prospects and Challenges (2014)
4. Wang, B., Liu, K.J.R.: Advances in cognitive radio network: a survey. IEEE J. Sel. Top. Sign. Process. **5**(1), 5–23 (2011)
5. Marinho, J., Monteiro, E.: Cognitive radio: survey on communication protocols, spectrum decision issues, and future research directions. Wirel. Netw. J. **18**(2), 147–164 (2011)
6. Kumar, S., Sahay, J., Mishra, G.K., Kumar, S.: Cognitive radio concept and challenges in dynamic spectrum access for the future generation wireless communication systems. Wirel. Pers. Commun. **59**(3), 525–535 (2011)
7. Harada, H., Alemseged, Y., Filin, S., Riegel, M., Gundlach, M., Holland, O., Bochow, B., Ariyoshi, M., Grande, L.: IEEE dynamic spectrum access network standards committee. IEEE Commun. Mag. **51**(3), 104–111 (2013)
8. Akyildiz, I.F., Lee, W.-Y., Vuran, M.C., Mohanty, S.: Next generation/dynamic spectrum access/cognitive radio wireless network: a survey. Comput. Netw. **50**(13), 2127–2159 (2006)
9. Gonzalez, C.R.A., Dietrich, C.B., Sayed, S., Volos, H.I., Gaeddert, J.D., Robert, P.M., Reed, J.H., Kragh, F.E.: Open-source SCA-based core framework and rapid development tools enable software-defined radio education and research. IEEE Commun. Mag. **47**(10), 48–55 (2009)
10. Kumar, K., Prakash, A., Tripathi, R.: Spectrum handoff in cognitive radio networks: a classification and comprehensive survey. J. Netw. Comput. Appl. **61**, 161–188 (2016)

11. Lopez-Benitez, M., Gozalvez, J.: Common radio resource management algorithms for multimedia heterogeneous wireless network. IEEE Trans. Mob. Comput. **10**(9), 1201–1213 (2011)

12. Liu, Y., Hoshyar, R., Yang, X., Tafazolli, R.: Integrated radio resource allocation for multihop cellular network with fixed relay stations. IEEE J. Sel. Areas Commun. **24**(11), 2137–2146 (2011)

13. Leem, H., Baek, S.Y., Sung, D.K.: The effects of cell size on energy saving, system capacity, and per-energy capacity. In: IEEE Wireless Communications and Networking Conference (WCNC) (2010)

14. Li, Q., Apostolos, H.N., Papathanassiou, Wu, G.: 5G network capacity, key elements and technologies. In: IEEE Vehicular Technology Magazine. Digital Object Identifier 10.1109/MVT.2013.2295070 (2014)

15. Hu, R.Q., Qian, Y.: An energy efficient and spectrum efficient wireless heterogeneous network framework for 5G systems. In: IEEE Communications Magazine: 5G Wireless Communications Systems: Prospects and Challenges (2014)

16. Nakao, H., Tsukamoto, K., Tsuru, M., Oie, Y.: A database driven data channel selection scheme for V2V communication over TV white space. In: 7th International Conference on New Technologies, Mobility and Security (NTMS), pp. 1–5. IEEE (2015)

17. Chen, J., Liu, B., Zhou, H., Wu, Y., Gui, L.: When vehicles meet TV white space: a QoS guaranteed dynamic spectrum access approach for VANET. In: International Symposium on Broadband Multimedia Systems and Broadcasting (BMSB), pp. 1–6. IEEE (2014)

18. Gupta, N., Prakash, A., Tripathi, R.: Clustering based cognitive MAC protocol for channel allocation to prioritize safety message dissemination in vehicular ad-hoc network. Veh. Commun. **5**, 44–54 (2016)

19. Bozkaya, E., Canberk, B.: Robust and continuous connectivity maintenance for vehicular dynamic spectrum access networks. Ad Hoc Netw. **25**, 72–83 (2015)

20. Baraka, K., Safatly, L., Artail, H., Ghandour, A.J., El-Hajj, A.: An infrastructure-aided cooperative spectrum sensing scheme for vehicular ad hoc networks. Ad Hoc Netw. **25**, 197–212 (2015)

21. Atallah, R.F., Khabbaz, M.J., Assi, C.M.: Vehicular networking: A survey on spectrum access technologies and persisting challenges. Veh. Commun. **2**(3), 125–149 (2015)

22. Gupta, N., Prakash, A., Tripathi, R.: Medium access control protocols for safety applications in Vehicular Ad-Hoc Network: a classification and comprehensive survey. Veh. Commun. **2**(4), 223–237 (2015)

23. Campolo, C., Molinaro, A., Scopigno, R.: From today's VANETs to tomorrow's planning and the bets for the day after. Veh. Commun. **2**(3), 158–171 (2015)

24. Lee, W.Y., Akyildiz, I.F.: Spectrum-aware mobility management in cognitive radio cellular networks. IEEE Trans. Mob. Comput. **11**(4), 529–542 (2012)

25. Ghandour, A.J., Fawaz, K., Artail, H., Di Felice, M., Bononi, L.: Improving vehicular safety message delivery through the implementation of a cognitive vehicular network. Ad Hoc Netw. **11**(8), 2408–2422 (2013)

26. Cesana, M., Cuomo, F., Ekici, E.: Routing in cognitive radio networks: challenges and solutions. Ad Hoc Netw. **9**(3), 228–248 (2011)

27. Wang, B., Li, B., Liu, M.: A novel precoding method for joint processing in CoMP. In: International Conference on Network Computing and Information Security (ICNCIS) (2011)

Intuitionistic Fuzzy PROMETHEE Technique for Multi-criteria Decision Making Problems Based on Entropy Measure

Pratibha Rani and Divya Jain[✉]

Jaypee University of Engineering and Technology, Guna, India
pratibha138@gmail.com, divya.jain@juet.ac.in

Abstract. Entropy measures play an important role in the field of fuzzy set theory and generalized by various authors for different purposes. In the present communication, intuitionistic fuzzy entropy measure based on sine function is developed. Further, the modified intuitionistic fuzzy PROMETHEE (IF-PROMETHEE) technique for multi-criteria decision making problems is discussed with the help of proposed entropy measure and the intuitionistic fuzzy preferences. Finally, the effectiveness of the technique is illustrated through a problem of selection of the antiretroviral drugs for HIV/AIDS to reduce the infection of HIV.

Keywords: Fuzzy set · Intuitionistic fuzzy set · Entropy measure · PROMETHEE · Multi-criteria decision making

1 Introduction

To circumvent the scarcity of fuzzy systems, Atanassov [1] originated the idea of intuitionistic fuzzy sets (IFSs), which deal better results in the decision of inaccurate and hesitant information. IFSs are the generalized content of fuzzy sets which are characterized by the membership function, non-membership function and hesitancy function. Due to the complexity in real life situation, the use of IFSs has gained more concentration from researchers in the field of decision making, image processing, medical diagnosis, pattern recognition etc. [10, 16].

Entropy and similarity measures are fundamental concepts in the fuzzy set theory as well as intuitionistic fuzzy set theory [9]. The idea of entropy on interval-valued fuzzy sets and intuitionistic fuzzy sets has been discussed by Burillo and Bustince [8] to determine the degree of intuitionism. Szmidt and Kacprzyk [25] generalized the axiomatic definition of De Luca and Termini entropy on IFSs with a geometrical explanation of IFSs. Thereafter, numerous entropies on FSs, IVFSs and IFSs have been developed and applied in the various fields [14, 21–26, 28, 31, 33].

There are various techniques to solve the multi-criteria decision making (MCDM) problems which can be classified into utility theory based techniques such as Analytic Hierarchy Process (AHP), Technique for Order Preference by Similarity to Ideal Solution (TOPSIS), VlseKriterijuska Optimizacija I Komoromisno Resenje (VIKOR) and outranking techniques such as Elimination Et Choice Translating Reality

© Springer Nature Singapore Pte Ltd. 2017
M. Singh et al. (Eds.): ICACDS 2016, CCIS 721, pp. 290–301, 2017.
DOI: 10.1007/978-981-10-5427-3_31

(ELECTRE), Preference Ranking Organization Method for Enrichment Evaluations (PROMETHEE) [19, 20]. In 1982, Brans [4] developed the concept of PROMETHEE to obtain the partial or complete ranking of the alternatives on the basis of positive outranking flow, negative outranking flow and net outranking flow. There are numerous types of PROMETHEE techniques that have been developed for different situations with crisp and fuzzy input data [2–7, 11, 12, 17, 18, 32]. These extensional forms of PROMETHEE technique can't be applied to represent the support and opposition information of decision maker. Therefore, to shirk the disadvantages of this technique with fuzzy values, Liao and Xu [20] developed the PROMETHEE technique for intuitionistic fuzzy set which is more valid in managing uncertain information. In this article, the authors have extended the work on intuitionistic fuzzy PROMETHEE technique based on the intuitionistic fuzzy entropy measure and the intuitionistic fuzzy preferences with calculated weight vector.

This paper is organized as: In Sect. 2, a few facts of IFSs, intuitionistic fuzzy entropy and construction theorem to convert fuzzy values into intuitionistic fuzzy values are discussed. Intuitionistic fuzzy entropy measure based on sine function is developed in Sect. 3. In Sect. 4, the extended PROMETHEE technique is generalized for IFSs by using proposed entropy measure and is applied to grade the antiretroviral drugs for HIV/AIDS in a real case study.

2 Preliminaries

In this section, fundamental ideas of intuitionistic fuzzy sets (IFSs), intuitionistic fuzzy entropy, construction method of IFSs from fuzzy sets and the basic idea of PRO-METHEE technique are discussed.

2.1 Intuitionistic Fuzzy Sets

Definition 2.1 [4]. Let U be a universe of discourse. An intuitionistic fuzzy set A in U is an object having the form:

$$A = \{\langle u, \mu_A(u), \upsilon_A(u) \rangle : u \in U\},$$

where $\mu_A : U \to [0, 1]$ and $\upsilon_A : U \to [0, 1]$ are the degree of membership and degree of non- membership of $u \in U$, respectively and for every $u \in U$,

$$0 \leq \mu_A(u) + \upsilon_A(u) \leq 1.$$

For each IFS A in U, we call $\pi_A(u) = 1 - \mu_A(u) - \upsilon_A(u)$ be the intuitionistic index of an element $u \in U$ in A, which denotes hesitancy degree of u to A. It is evident that $0 \leq \pi_A(u) \leq 1, \forall u \in U$. FSs can also be represented using the notation of IFSs. A FS A defined on U can be represented as the following IFS:
$A = \{\langle u, \mu_A(u), 1 - \mu_A(u) \rangle : u \in U\}$, with $\pi_A(u) = 0, \forall u \in U$.

Definition 2.2 [27]. A function $E : IFS(U) \rightarrow [0, 1]$ is said to be intuitionistic fuzzy entropy if it satisfies the following properties:

(P1) $E(A) = 0$ (minimum) if and only if A is a crisp set;
(P2) $E(A) = 1$ (maximum) if and only if $\mu_A(u_i) = \upsilon_A(u_i)$ for every $u_i \in U$;
(P3) $E(A) = E(A^c)$;
(P4) If $A \leq B$, then $E(A) \leq E(B)$ i.e., $\mu_A(u_i) \leq \mu_B(u_i)$ and $\upsilon_A(u_i) \geq \upsilon_B(u_i)$ for $\mu_B(u_i) \leq \upsilon_B(u_i)$ or $\mu_A(u_i) \geq \mu_B(u_i)$ and $\upsilon_A(u_i) \leq \upsilon_B(u_i)$ for $\mu_B(u_i) \geq \upsilon_B(u_i)$.

Definition 2.3 [23]. Let $\hat{A} \in FSs(U)$, where $FSs(U)$ represent the set of all fuzzy sets in the universal set U and $\pi, \eta : U \rightarrow [0, 1]$ be two mappings. Then, $I_{IFS} = \left\{ \left\langle u_i, g(\mu_{\hat{A}}(u_i), \pi_{\hat{A}}(u_i), \eta_{\hat{A}}(u_i)) \right\rangle : u_i \in U \right\}$ is an Atanassov IFS [4], where the mapping $g : [0, 1]^2 \times [0, 1] \rightarrow T$ is given as

$$g(\mu, \upsilon, \eta) = (g_\mu(\mu, \upsilon, \eta), g_\upsilon(\mu, \upsilon, \eta)),$$

where $g_\mu(\mu, \upsilon, \eta) = \mu(1 - \eta\upsilon)$, $g_\upsilon(\mu, \upsilon, \eta) = 1 - \mu(1 - \eta\upsilon) - \eta\upsilon$ and $T = \{(\mu, \upsilon) : (\mu, \upsilon) \in [0, 1] \times [0, 1]$ and $\mu + \upsilon \leq 1\}$ satisfies the following conditions:

  (i)   If $\upsilon_1 \leq \upsilon_2$ for every $\mu, \upsilon_1, \eta \in [0, 1]$, then $\pi(g(\mu, \upsilon_1, \eta)) \leq \pi(g(\mu, \upsilon_2, \eta))$;
 (ii) $g_\mu(\mu, \upsilon, \eta) \leq \mu \leq 1 - g_\upsilon(\mu, \upsilon, \eta)$ for all $m \in [0, 1]$;
(iii) $g(\mu, 0, \eta) = (\mu, 1 - \mu)$;
 (iv) $g(0, \upsilon, \eta) = (0, 1 - \eta\upsilon)$;
  (v) $g(\mu, \upsilon, 0) = (\mu, 1 - \mu)$;
 (vi) $\pi(g(\mu, \upsilon, \eta)) = \eta\upsilon$.

3   Information Measures for Intuitionistic Fuzzy Sets

In this section, entropy measure for IFSs based on sine function is introduced and compared with existing entropy measures. For every $A \in IFS(U)$, intuitionistic fuzzy entropy $E(A)$ is constructed as follows, which is based on Huang and Liu entropy [13]:

$$E(A) = \frac{1}{n} \sum_{i=1}^{n} \sin\left(\frac{1 - |\mu_A(u_i) - \upsilon_A(u_i)| + \pi(u_i)}{1 + |\mu_A(u_i) - \upsilon_A(u_i)| + \pi(u_i)}\right). \tag{1}$$

4   Intuitionistic Fuzzy PROMETHEE Technique

In this section, the intuitionistic fuzzy PROMETHEE (IF-PROMETHEE) technique is developed and applied to solve MCDM problems in intuitionistic fuzzy environment. An algorithm for proposed intuitionistic fuzzy PROMETHEE technique is as follows:

Step I. For multi-criteria decision making problem, generate a set of alternatives $A = \{\alpha_1, \alpha_2, \ldots, \alpha_p\}$ and a set of criteria $C = \{\beta_1, \beta_2, \ldots, \beta_q\}$. In this step, the evaluation values of the alternatives over the criteria are in fuzzy values.

Step II. In this step, create a decision matrix of intuitionistic fuzzy values from fuzzy values by using construction theorem [15, 16].

Step III. Using entropy (1), calculate the information of each intuitionistic fuzzy value in the intuitionistic fuzzy assessment matrix and the information matrix of this assessment matrix is $M = (E_{ik})_{p \times q}$, where $E_{ik} = E_1(\bar{r}_{ik})$.

Normalize the information values in the above decision matrix by using

$$\bar{E}_{ik} = \frac{E_{ik}}{\max E_{ik}}, \quad i = 1, 2, \ldots, p; k = 1, 2, \ldots, q. \tag{2}$$

The normalized information matrix is expressed as $\bar{M} = (\bar{E}_{ik})_{p \times q}$.

Step IV. Calculate the weight vectors $w = (w_1, w_2, \ldots, w_q)^T$, where $w_i \geq 0$ and $\sum_{k=1}^{q} w_k = 1$, using the formula

$$w_k = \frac{1 - \sum_{i=1}^{p} \bar{E}_{ik}}{q - \sum_{k=1}^{q} \sum_{i=1}^{p} \bar{E}_{ik}}; i = 1, 2, \ldots, p; k = 1, 2, \ldots, q. \tag{3}$$

Step V. Compute the deviations of each pair of alternatives over different criteria $\beta_k (k = 1, 2, \ldots, q)$ via

$$D_k(\alpha_i, \alpha_j) = \beta_k(\alpha_i) - \beta_k(\alpha_j). \tag{4}$$

Identify the decision maker's preference function, i.e., establish the parameters Ω as a strict preference threshold and Ξ as an indifference threshold. Then, calculate the preferences $\mu_{ij}^{(k)}$ for the alternative α_i against alternative α_j with respect to the criterion β_k by using V-shape indifference criterion

$$\mu_{ij}^{(k)} = \begin{cases} 0, & D_k(\alpha_i, \alpha_j) \leq \Xi \\ \frac{D_k(\alpha_i, \alpha_j) - \Omega}{\Omega - \Xi}, & \Xi \leq D_k(\alpha_i, \alpha_j) \leq \Omega. \\ 1, & D_k(\alpha_i, \alpha_j) > \Omega \end{cases} \tag{5}$$

Thereafter, the preference matrix $U^{(k)} (k = 1, 2, \ldots, q)$ can be created with the use of

$$U^{(k)} = (\mu_{ij}^{(k)})_{p \times p} = \begin{bmatrix} - & \mu_{12}^{(k)} & \cdots & \mu_{1p}^{(k)} \\ \mu_{21}^{(k)} & - & \cdots & \mu_{2p}^{(k)} \\ \cdots & \cdots & \cdots & \cdots \\ \cdots & \cdots & \cdots & \cdots \\ \mu_{p1}^{(k)} & \mu_{p2}^{(k)} & \cdots & - \end{bmatrix}. \tag{6}$$

Step VI. Calculate the intuitionistic fuzzy preference relation $I_R^{(k)} = (r_{ij}^{(k)})_{p \times p}$ over the criteria $\beta_k (k = 1, 2, \ldots, q)$.

Step VII. Construct the collective intuitionistic fuzzy preference relation $I_R = (r_{ij})_{p \times p}$ by using

$$r_{ij} = r(\alpha_i, \alpha_j) = (\mu_{ij}, v_{ij}) = \left(\sum_{k=1}^{q} w_k \mu_{ij}^{(k)}, \sum_{k=1}^{q} w_k v_{ij}^{(k)} \right), \tag{7}$$

where w_k is the calculated weight of the criterion $\beta_k (k = 1, 2, \ldots, q)$.

Thus, the global or overall intuitionistic fuzzy preference relation can be established as:

$$I_R = (r_{ij})_{p \times p} = \begin{bmatrix} - & (\mu_{12}, v_{12}) & \cdots & (\mu_{1p}, v_{1p}) \\ (\mu_{21}, v_{21}) & - & \cdots & (\mu_{2p}, v_{2p}) \\ \cdots & \cdots & \cdots & \cdots \\ \cdots & \cdots & \cdots & \cdots \\ (\mu_{p1}, v_{p1}) & (\mu_{p2}, v_{p2}) & (\mu_{p3}, v_{p3}) & - \end{bmatrix}. \tag{8}$$

Step VIII. Compute the intuitionistic fuzzy positive outranking flow $\varphi^+(\alpha_i)$ and the intuitionistic negative ranking flow $\varphi^-(\alpha_i)$ for the alternative α_i by using

$$\varphi^+(\alpha_i) = \frac{1}{(p-1)} \sum_{\delta \in U} \Pi(\alpha_i, \delta) \tag{9}$$

$$\varphi^-(\alpha_i) = \frac{1}{(p-1)} \sum_{\delta \in U} \Pi(\delta, \alpha_i), \tag{10}$$

Step IX. To compare the intuitionistic fuzzy values $\varphi^+(\alpha_i)$ and $\varphi^-(\alpha_i)$, Schmidt and Kacprzyk's method [29] is easy to use and is given as

$$\rho(\varphi(\alpha)) = 0.5(1 + \pi_{\varphi(\alpha)})(1 - \mu_{\varphi(\alpha)}). \tag{11}$$

The intuitionistic fuzzy net outranking flow cannot be directly calculated because the intuitionistic fuzzy set doesn't have subtraction operation. Therefore, the deviation between the Szmidt and Kacprzyk's function of the intuitionistic fuzzy positive outranking flow and the intuitionistic fuzzy negative outranking flow is computed by using

$$\rho(\varphi(\alpha_i)) = \rho(\varphi^+(\alpha_i)) - \rho(\varphi^-(\alpha_i)). \tag{12}$$

In this step, a partial ranking will be creating by comparing $\varphi^+(\alpha_i)$ and $\varphi^-(\alpha_i)$ of the alternatives through (12). Otherwise, a complete ranking will be obtained according to the deviation between the score values of the intuitionistic fuzzy positive outranking flow and that of the intuitionistic fuzzy negative outranking flow (Fig. 1).

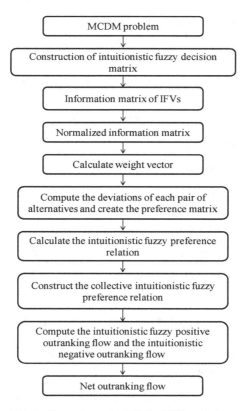

Fig. 1. Flow chart of PROMETHEE technique

4.1 Application of IF-PROMETHEE Technique

To rank the performance of ARV drugs, we have taken the set of drugs for HIV/AIDS that are Didanosine (α_1), Nevirapine (α_2), Zidovudine (α_3) and Lamivudine (α_4). These drugs $\{\alpha_1, \alpha_2, \alpha_3, \alpha_4\}$ are applied on their performance with respect to the (i) market price (β_1); (ii) effect on patients (β_2); (iii) viral load (β_3); (iv) side effects (β_4); (v) growth of the virus (β_5). Now, the procedural steps for IF-PROMETHEE technique are as follows:

Step I. The alternatives $\{\alpha_1, \alpha_2, \alpha_3, \alpha_4\}$ are to be appraised under the above five criteria as listed as in Table 1.

Table 1. Fuzzy decision matrix

	β_1	β_2	β_3	β_4	β_5
α_1	0.2846	0.75	0.234	0.23	0.24
α_2	0.318	0.248	0.766	0.097	0.76
α_3	0.759	0.75	0.315	0.32	0.278
α_4	0.241	0.437	0.41	0.155	0.394

Step II. From Table 1, Intuitionistic fuzzy decision matrix is created in Table 2 with the help of definition 2.3.

Table 2. Intuitionistic fuzzy decision matrix

	β_1	β_2	β_3	β_4	β_5
α_1	(0.23, 0.587)	(0.61, 0.2)	(0.192, 0.63)	(0.22, 0.75)	(0.196, 0.62)
α_2	(0.26, 0.554)	(0.2, 0.61)	(0.63, 0.192)	(0.094, 0.875)	(0.62, 0.196)
α_3	(0.62, 0.197)	(0.61, 0.2)	(0.259, 0.56)	(0.31, 0.66)	(0.227, 0.59)
α_4	(0.197, 0.62)	(0.36, 0.454)	(0.337, 0.484)	(0.15, 0.82)	(0.322, 0.50)

Step III. By using the formula (1), the information measure of each intuitionistic fuzzy value of the above decision matrix is computed and we obtained the following information matrix:

$$M = (E_{ij})_{4\times5} = \begin{bmatrix} 0.7464 & 0.6931 & 0.6588 & 0.4824 & 0.6760 \\ 0.8115 & 0.6931 & 0.6588 & 0.2151 & 0.6760 \\ 0.6767 & 0.6931 & 0.8033 & 0.6991 & 0.7401 \\ 0.6767 & 0.9735 & 0.9400 & 0.3266 & 0.9162 \end{bmatrix}.$$

The above information matrix is altered into the normalized information matrix by using (2), is given as follows:

$$\bar{M} = (E_{ij})_{4\times5} = \begin{bmatrix} 1.0000 & 0.9286 & 0.8826 & 0.6463 & 0.9057 \\ 1.0000 & 0.8541 & 0.8118 & 0.2651 & 0.8330 \\ 0.8424 & 0.8628 & 1.0000 & 0.8703 & 0.9213 \\ 0.6951 & 1.0000 & 0.9656 & 0.3355 & 0.9411 \end{bmatrix}.$$

Step IV. Calculate the criterion weight vectors by using (3) in normalized information matrix. Then, the weight vector of all the decision attributes are obtained as $W = (0.2195, 0.2288, 0.2301, 0.0966, 0.2250)^T$.

Step V. The deviations of each pair of alternatives over different criteria can be computed with the help of Eq. (4). The preferences $\mu_{ij}^{(k)}$ for the alternative α_i against the alternative α_j are obtained by using V-shape indifference criterion (5), where the indifference threshold Ξ is taken as zero for all criteria and the strict preference threshold Ω are considered as $\Omega = 53$ for first criterion β_1, $\Omega = 9.5$ for second criterion β_2, $\Omega = 23$ for third criterion β_3, $\Omega = 2.5$ for fourth criterion β_4 and $\Omega = 25$ for fifth criterion β_5. Then, the preference matrices $U^{(k)}(k = 1, 2, 3, 4, 5)$ are evaluated as follows:

$$U^{(1)} = \begin{bmatrix} - & 0 & 0 & 0.0687 \\ 0.0530 - & 0 & 0.1217 \\ 0.7464 & 0.6934 - & 0.8151 \\ 0 & 0 & 0 & - \end{bmatrix}, \quad U^{(2)} = \begin{bmatrix} - & 0.8421 & 0 & 0.5263 \\ 0 - & 0 & 0 \\ 0 & 0.8421 - & 0.5263 \\ 0 & 0.3158 & 0 & - \end{bmatrix},$$

$$U^{(3)} = \begin{bmatrix} - & 0 & 0 & 0 \\ 0.9778 - & 0.8283 & 0.6522 \\ 0.1496 & 0 - & 0 \\ 0.3257 & 0 & 0.1761 - \end{bmatrix}, \quad U^{(4)} = \begin{bmatrix} - & 0.5320 & 0 & 0.3000 \\ 0 - & 0 & 0 \\ 0.3680 & 0.9000 - & 0.6680 \\ 0 & 0.2320 & 0 & - \end{bmatrix},$$

$$U^{(5)} = \begin{bmatrix} - & 0 & 0 & 0 \\ 0.8880 - & 0.8200 & 0.6240 \\ 0.0680 & 0 - & 0 \\ 0.2640 & 0 & 0.1960 - \end{bmatrix}.$$

Step VI. The intuitionistic fuzzy preference relations $I_R^{(k)} = (r_{ij}^{(k)})_{p \times p}$ are obtained by using the equations $v_{ji} = \mu_{ij}$ and $v_{ij} = \mu_{ji}$ over the criteria $\beta_k (k = 1, 2, 3, 4, 5)$, which are given as

$$I_R^{(1)} = \begin{bmatrix} - & (0, 0.0530) & (0, 0.7464) & (0.0687, 0) \\ (0.0530, 0) - & (0, 0.6934) & (0.1217, 0) \\ (0.7464, 0) & (0.6934, 0) - & (0.8151, 0) \\ (0, 0.0687) & (0, 0.1217) & (0, 0.8151) & - \end{bmatrix},$$

$$I_R^{(2)} = \begin{bmatrix} - & (0.8421, 0) & (0, 0) & (0.5263, 0) \\ (0, 0.8421) - & (0, 0.8421) & (0, 0.3158) \\ (0, 0) & (0.8421, 0) - & (0.5263, 0) \\ (0, 0.5263) & (0.3158, 0) & (0, 0.5263) & - \end{bmatrix},$$

$$I_R^{(3)} = \begin{bmatrix} - & (0, 0.9778) & (0, 0.1496) & (0, 0.3257) \\ (0.9778, 0) - & (0.8283, 0) & (0.6522, 0) \\ (0.1496, 0) & (0, 0.8283) - & (0, 0.1761) \\ (0.3257, 0) & (0, 0.6522) & (0.1761, 0) & - \end{bmatrix},$$

$$I_R^{(4)} = \begin{bmatrix} - & (0.5320, 0) & (0, 0.3680) & (0.3000, 0) \\ (0, 0.5320) - & (0, 0.9000) & (0, 0.2320) \\ (0.3680, 0) & (0.9000, 0) - & (0.6680, 0) \\ (0, 0.3000) & (0.2320, 0) & (0, 0.6680) & - \end{bmatrix},$$

$$I_R^{(5)} = \begin{bmatrix} - & (0, 0.8880) & (0, 0.0680) & (0, 0.2640) \\ (0.8880, 0) - & (0.8200, 0) & (0.6240, 0) \\ (0.0680, 0) & (0, 0.8200) - & (0, 0.1960) \\ (0.2640, 0) & (0, 0.6240) & (0.1960, 0) & - \end{bmatrix}.$$

Step VII. With the use of formula (7) in above intuitionistic fuzzy preference relations, the overall intuitionistic fuzzy preference relation can be established as below:

$$I_R = \begin{bmatrix} - & (0.2441, 0.4364) & (0, 0.2491) & (0.1645, 0.1343) \\ (0.4364, 0.2441) & - & (0.3751, 0.4318) & (0.3172, 0.0947) \\ (0.2491, 0) & (0.4318, 0.3751) & - & (0.3639, 0.0846) \\ (0.1343, 0.1645) & (0.0947, 0.3172) & (0.0846, 0.3639) & - \end{bmatrix}.$$

Step VIII. According to the formula (9) and (10), the intuitionistic fuzzy positive outranking flows are obtained as:

$$\varphi^+(\alpha_1) = (0.1420, 0.2444), \varphi^+(\alpha_2) = (0.3781, 0.2153),$$
$$\varphi^+(\alpha_3) = (0.3526, 0.0000), \varphi^+(\alpha_4) = (0.1048, 0.2668)$$

and the intuitionistic fuzzy negative outranking flows are given as follows:

$$\varphi^-(\alpha_1) = (0.2844, 0.0000), \varphi^-(\alpha_2) = (0.2701, 0.3731),$$
$$\varphi^-(\alpha_3) = (0.1699, 0.3395), \varphi^-(\alpha_4) = (0.2867, 0.1025).$$

Step IX. With the use of formula (12), we get

$$\rho^+(\varphi(\alpha_1)) = 0.6922, \rho^+(\varphi(\alpha_2)) = 0.4374,$$
$$\rho^+(\varphi(\alpha_3)) = 0.5333, \rho^+(\varphi(\alpha_4)) = 0.7289,$$
$$\rho^-(\varphi(\alpha_1)) = 0.6138, \rho^-(\varphi(\alpha_2)) = 0.4952,$$
$$\rho^-(\varphi(\alpha_3)) = 0.6187, \rho^-(\varphi(\alpha_4)) = 0.5745.$$

Thus, by using (12), we have

$$\rho(\varphi(\alpha_1)) = 0.0784, \rho(\varphi(\alpha_2)) = -0.0578,$$
$$\rho(\varphi(\alpha_3)) = -0.0854, \rho(\varphi(\alpha_4)) = 0.1544.$$

Since $\rho(\varphi(\alpha_3)) < \rho(\varphi(\alpha_2)) < \rho(\varphi(\alpha_1)) < \rho(\varphi(\alpha_4))$, therefore, we obtain

$$\varphi(\alpha_3) > \varphi(\alpha_2) > \varphi(\alpha_1) > \varphi(\alpha_4).$$

Hence, the ranking of the four ARV drugs by IF-PROMETHEE is $\alpha_3 \succ \alpha_2 \succ \alpha_1 \succ \alpha_4$.

The ranking of these four alternatives is also compared with existing TOPSIS method and the comparison results are shown in Table 3. From Table 3, it can be concluded that α_3 is the optimal choice and the preference order of the remaining three options shows some diversities.

Table 3. Comparison with existing technique

Technique	Ranking	Optimal choice
IF-TOPSIS proposed by Joshi and Kumar [15]	$\alpha_3 \succ \alpha_1 \succ \alpha_4 \succ \alpha_2$	α_3
IF-TOPSIS proposed by Wei and Zhang [30]	$\alpha_3 \succ \alpha_1 \succ \alpha_4 \succ \alpha_2$	α_3
Proposed IF-PROMETHEE technique	$\alpha_3 \succ \alpha_2 \succ \alpha_1 \succ \alpha_4$	α_3

5 Conclusion

In this work, new entropy measure based on sine function is developed in the intuitionistic fuzzy environment. This paper deals with one of the outranking based techniques, PROMETHEE, for MCDM problems in intuitionistic fuzzy environment and applied the proposed IF-PROMETHEE to rank the antiretroviral drugs for HIV/AIDS disease on the basis of their performance. In this technique, the proposed entropy measure is used to construct the intuitionistic fuzzy decision matrix and derive the weight of each criterion. After that, the preference matrices are established with the use of V-shape indifference criterion. Later on, the intuitionistic fuzzy preference relations and overall intuitionistic fuzzy relation are calculated to acquire the positive and negative outranking flows for partial outranking of all alternatives. To obtain the complete ranking of the alternatives, the net outranking flows are computed for each alternative. Further, the ranking attained by proposed technique with the existing technique are discussed. Consistency of the proposed technique is also improved by calculating the weight vector, which was formerly assumed by few of the researchers.

Acknowledgements. The authors gratefully acknowledge the helpful comments and suggestions of the reviewers, which have improved the paper.

References

1. Atanassov, K.T.: Intuitionistic fuzzy sets. Fuzzy Sets Syst. **20**, 87–96 (1986)
2. Behzadian, M., Kazemzadeh, R.B., Albadvi, A., Aghdasi, M.: PROMETHEE: a comprehensive literature review on methodologies and applications. Eur. J. Oper. Res. **200**, 198–215 (2010)
3. Bilsel, R.U., Buyukozkan, G., Ruan, D.: A fuzzy preference ranking model for a quality evaluation of hospital Web sites. Int. J. Intell. Syst. **21**, 1181–1197 (2006)
4. Brans, J.P.: L'ingenierie de la decision; Elaboration d'intruments d'aide a la decision. La methode PROMETHEE. In: Nadeau, R., Landry, M. (eds.) L'aide a la decision: Nature, Instruments et Perspectives d'Avenir, pp. 183–213. Presses de l'Universite Laval, Quebec (1982)
5. Brans, J.P., Mareschal, B.: PROMETHEE methods. In: Figueira, J., Greco, S., Ehrgott, M. (eds.) Multiple Criteria Decision Analysis: State of the Art Surveys, vol. 78, pp. 163–195. Springer, New York (2005)
6. Brans, J.P., Mareschal, B.: PROMETHEE V - MCDM problems with segmentation constraints. INFOR **30**, 85–96 (1992)

7. Brans, J.P., Mareschal, B.: The PROMETHEE VI procedure: how to differentiate hard from soft multicriteria problems. J. Decis. Syst. **4**, 213–223 (1995)
8. Burillo, P., Bustince, H.: Entropy on intuitionistic fuzzy sets and on interval-valued fuzzy sets. Fuzzy Sets Syst. **118**, 305–316 (2001)
9. De Luca, A., Termini, S.: A definition of a non-probabilistic entropy in the setting of fuzzy sets theory. Inf. Control **20**, 301–312 (1972)
10. De, S.K., Biswas, R., Roy, A.R.: An application of intuitionistic fuzzy sets in medical diagnosis. Fuzzy Sets Syst. **117**, 209–213 (2001)
11. Goumas, M., Lygerou, V.: An extension of the PROMETHEE method for decision making in fuzzy environment: ranking of alternative energy exploitation projects. Eur. J. Oper. Res. **123**, 606–613 (2000)
12. Halouani, N., Chabchoub, H., Martel, J.M.: PROMETHEE MD-2T method for project selection. Eur. J. Oper. Res. **195**, 841–849 (2009)
13. Huang, G.S., Liu, Y.S.: The fuzzy entropy of vague sets based on non-fuzzy sets. Comput. Appl. Softw. **22**, 16–17 (2005)
14. Hung, W.L., Yang, M.S.: Fuzzy entropy on intuitionistic fuzzy sets. Int. J. Intell. Syst. **21**, 443–451 (2006)
15. Joshi, D., Kumar, S.: Intuitionistic fuzzy entropy and distance measure based TOPSIS method for multi-criteria decision making. Egypt. Inform. J. **15**, 97–104 (2014)
16. Jurio, A., Paternain, D., Bustince, H., Guerra, C., Beliakov, G.: A construction method of Atanassov's intuitionistic fuzzy sets for image processing. In: Proceedings of the Fifth IEEE Conference on Intelligent Systems, vol. 1, pp. 337–342 (2010)
17. Le Teno, J.F., Mareschal, B.: An interval version of PROMETHEE for the comparison of building products' design with ill-defined data on environmental quality. Eur. J. Oper. Res. **109**, 522–529 (1998)
18. Li, W.X., Li, B.Y.: An extension of the PROMETHEE II method based on generalized fuzzy numbers. Expert Syst. Appl. **37**, 5314–5319 (2010)
19. Liao, H., Xu, Z.S.: A VIKOR-based method for hesitant fuzzy multi-criteria decision making. Fuzzy Optim. Decis. Making **12**, 373–392 (2013)
20. Liao, H., Xu, Z.S.: Multi-criteria decision making with intuitionistic fuzzy PROMETHEE. J. Intell. Fuzzy Syst. **27**, 1703–1717 (2014)
21. Mishra, A.R.: Intuitionistic fuzzy information measures with application in rating of township development. Iran. J. Fuzzy Syst. **13**, 49–70 (2016)
22. Mishra, A.R., Jain, D., Hooda, D.S.: Intuitionistic fuzzy similarity and information measures with physical education teaching quality assessment. In: Satapathy, S.C., Raju, K.S., Mandal, J.K., Bhateja, V. (eds.) Proceedings of the Second International Conference on Computer and Communication Technologies. AISC, vol. 379, pp. 387–399. Springer, New Delhi (2016). doi:10.1007/978-81-322-2517-1_38
23. Mishra, A.R., Hooda, D.S., Jain, D.: Weighted trigonometric and hyperbolic fuzzy information measures and their applications in optimization principles. Int. J. Comput. Math. Sci. **3**, 62–68 (2014)
24. Mishra, A.R., Hooda, D.S., Jain, D.: On exponential fuzzy measures of information and discrimination. Int. J. Comput. Appl. **119**, 01–07 (2015)
25. Mishra, A.R., Jain, D., Hooda, D.S.: On fuzzy distance and induced fuzzy information measures. J. Inf. Optim. Sci. **37**, 193–211 (2016)
26. Mishra, A.R., Jain, D., Hooda, D.S.: On logarithmic fuzzy measures of information and discrimination. J. Inf. Optim. Sci. **37**, 213–231 (2016)
27. Szmidt, E., Kacprzyk, J.: Entropy for intuitionistic fuzzy sets. Fuzzy Sets Syst. **118**, 467–477 (2001)

28. Verma, R., Sharma, B.D.: Exponential entropy on intuitionistic fuzzy sets. Kybernetika **49**, 114–127 (2013)
29. Xu, Z.S., Liao, H.C.: Intuitionistic fuzzy analytic hierarchy process. IEEE Trans. Fuzzy Syst. **22**, 749–761 (2014)
30. Wei, C.P., Zhang, Y.: Entropy measures for interval-valued intuitionistic fuzzy sets and their application in group decision making. Math. Prob. Eng. **2015**, 1–13 (2015)
31. Ye, J.: Two effectives measures of intuitionistic fuzzy entropy. Computing **87**, 55–62 (2010)
32. Zhang, K.J., Kluck, K.J., Achari, G.: A comparative approach for ranking contaminated sites based on the risk assessment paradigm using fuzzy PROMETHEE. Environ. Manage. **44**, 952–967 (2009)
33. Zhang, Q.S., Jiang, S.Y.: A note on information entropy measures for vague sets and its application. Inf. Sci. **178**, 4184–4191 (2008)

Ku Band Microstrip Rectangular Patch

Praful Ranjan[(✉)]

Department of Electronics and Communication Engineering,
THDC Institute of Hydropower Engineering and Technology,
Bhagirathipuram, Tehri, India
prf98354@rediffmail.com

Abstract. This Paper presents a microstrip rectangular patch antenna for satellite communication. This antenna resonates at 15.88 GHz which comes under Ku band. The advantage of this antenna is 5.5 dBi gain and the antenna size is reduced up to 15% to conventional antenna. This microstrip antenna size reduced by Optimization technique. The proposed antenna design has good directivity and sharp narrow band. VSWR of the antenna is almost equal to 1. Impedance matching is perfect and it is almost 50 Ω. Edge side cut Feeding technique is used in this paper which is simple to design. Simulation has been performed by HFSS software.

Keywords: Microstrip patch antenna · Ku band · Bandwidth · HFSS

1 Introduction

Microstrip patch antenna is very simple to design planar structure of the antenna. Fabrication of the microstrip antenna is very easy [1–3]. It can be fit everywhere according to application. Currently these antennas are being increasingly used in every sector due to the less cost of substrates. Most of other antennas are bulky and size is too much large. In comparisons microstrip antenna is very small size and less weight. Its advantage is narrow bandwidth. Microstrip antenna is highly demanded in today's scenario [4, 5]. This antenna is fit for any type planar structure array type and many more structure. It is also used as array for gain improvement.

This paper presented Ku band application for satellite communication where range of Ku band is 12–18 GHz [6, 7]. This antenna resonates at 15.88 GHz. The advantage of this antenna is high gain. Gain of this antenna is 5.5 dBi. The size of the antenna is reduced compare to conventional antenna. In this paper microstrip antenna size is reduced by Optimization technique [8–10]. The feeding technique in this paper is edge side cutting feed. Proposed antenna has designed in HFSS software which is based on FEM method. Purpose of this antenna is to achieve high gain and perfect impedance matching. Return loss of this antenna is good which is almost equal to −30 dB.

© Springer Nature Singapore Pte Ltd. 2017
M. Singh et al. (Eds.): ICACDS 2016, CCIS 721, pp. 302–308, 2017.
DOI: 10.1007/978-981-10-5427-3_32

2   Description of the Antenna

The basic rectangular microstrip patch antenna simulated for Ku band application. HFSS software is used to simulate Ku band antenna. Structure of the antenna is very thin, conducting rectangular shape on dielectric substrates another side is ground plane [4].

All parameters are formulated from conventional rectangular microstrip antenna Eqs. (1)–(5). Where w is width of antenna. ε is dielectric permittivity. L is length of antenna and ΔL is change in small length. ε_{eff} is effective dielectric constant. In this paper dielectric substrate RT duroid is used where permittivity (ε = 2.2) and height of the substrate is 0.254 mm, which is very thin.

$$W = \frac{1}{2\mathrm{fr}\sqrt{\mu_0 \varepsilon_0}} \sqrt{\frac{2}{\varepsilon_r + 1}} \tag{1}$$

$$\varepsilon_{eff} = \frac{\varepsilon_r + 1}{2} + \frac{\varepsilon_r - 1}{2} \left(\frac{1}{\sqrt{1 + \frac{12h}{w}}} \right) \tag{2}$$

$$L = L_{eff} - 2\Delta L \tag{3}$$

$$L_{eff} = \frac{C}{2f_r\sqrt{\varepsilon_{eff}}} \tag{4}$$

$$\frac{\Delta L}{h} = 0.412 \frac{\left(\varepsilon_{eff} + 0.3\right)\left(\frac{w}{h} + 0.264\right)}{\left(\varepsilon_{eff} - 0.258\right)\left(\frac{w}{h} + 0.8\right)} \tag{5}$$

The top view of rectangular microstrip patch antenna is shown in Fig. 1 and simulated structure of the antenna in HFSS software is in Fig. 2.

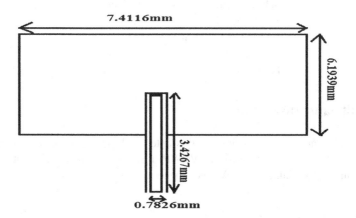

Fig. 1. Size of antenna

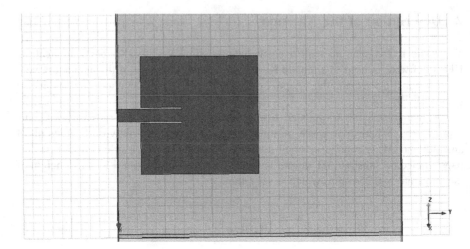

Fig. 2. Simulated structure of antenna

All the specification and parameter of this antenna is tabulated in Table 1. Substrate size is 15×15 mm^2. Length of the patch antenna is 7.4116 mm, Width of the patch antenna is 6.1939 mm. Height of substrate is 0.254 mm. Permittivity of the substrate is 2.2 which is RT Duroid. Feed length and feed width of side age feeding is 0.7826 mm and 3.4267 mm respectively.

Table 1. Specification of antenna

Parameters of the antenna	Unit (mm)
Length of patch antenna (l)	7.4116 mm
Width of patch antenna (w)	6.1939 mm
h (height of substrate)	0.254 mm
Substrate length	15 mm
Substrate width	15 mm
Permittivity of substrate (ε)	2.2
Feed length	0.7826 mm
Feed width	3.4267 mm

3   Results and Discussion

Proposed and simulated Return loss of this antenna (S_{11}) is shown in Fig. 3. Return loss of antenna achieved up to -30 dB. VSWR of rectangular microstrip patch antenna is already in Fig. 4. Value of VSWR is near to 1.

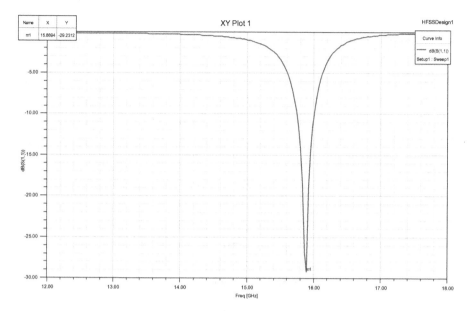

Fig. 3. S_{11} of simulated antenna

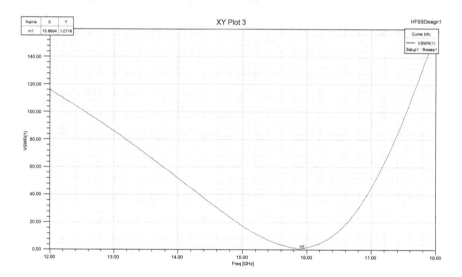

Fig. 4. VSWR of simulated antenna

Impedance of this antenna is also shown in Fig. 5. Impedance of this antenna is around 50 Ω and it is already mark in Fig. 5. It is clearly shows that the Impedance matching is perfect and it full fill the maximum power theorem. So that efficiency of this antenna is perfect.

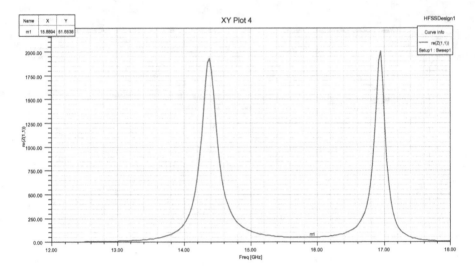

Fig. 5. Impedance of antenna

In Fig. 6 shows gain of the Ku band microstrip patch antenna and Fig. 7 represent directivity of the antenna. It shows in single rectangular patch antenna is good gain and the result of directivity is also perfect. In Fig. 8 shows axial ratio verses theta graph when phi is equal to 0.

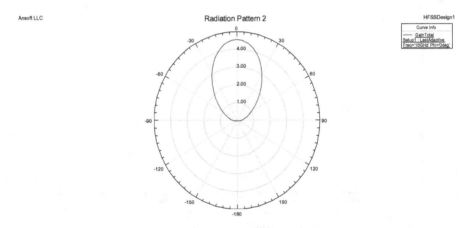

Fig. 6. Simulated gain result of the antenna

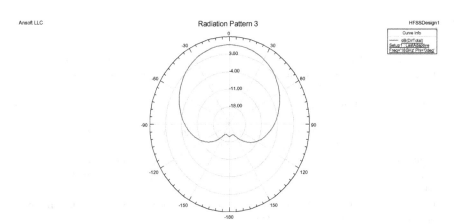

Fig. 7. Simulated directivity of the antenna

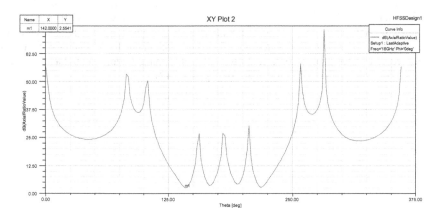

Fig. 8. Axial ratio of simulated antenna

4 Conclusions

This paper presents high gain, high directive and reduced size. Gain is achievable up to 5.5 dBi. Size of the antenna is reduced up to 15% by generalized antenna. Return loss of Ku band rectangular is achieved up to −30 dB. This antenna can be applicable for security region for future. Antenna proposed in this paper is very suitable for satellite application Gain may be improved by array structure of antenna. For future scope of antenna to improve or high gain, introducing number of similar antenna in similar fashion. This is another task of the antenna for achieving high gain and high return loss in Future.

References

1. Balanis, C.A.: Antenna Theory, Analysis and Design. Wiley, New York (1997)
2. Garg, R., Bartia, P., Bahl, I., Ittipiboon, A.: Microstrip Antenna Design Handbook. Artech House Inc., Norwood (2001). pp. 1–68, 253–316
3. Pozar, D.M., Schaubert, D.H. (eds.): The Analysis and Design of Microstrip Antennas and Arrays. IEEE Press, New York (1996)
4. Schellenberg, J.M.: CAD models for suspended and inverted microstrip. IEEE Trans. Microw. Theory Tech. **43**(6), 1247–1252 (1995)
5. Bahl, I.J., Bhartia, P.: Microstrip Antennas. Artech House, Boston (1980)
6. Huynh, T., Lee, K.F.: Single-layer single-patch wideband microstrip antenna. Electron. Lett. **31**(16), 1310–1312 (1995)
7. Çalışkan, K., Özkul, S.H., Sarıgül, H.C., Özmen, Y.E., İmeci, T.: Ku band microstrip patch antenna, pp. 1154–1157. IEEE (2015)
8. Ranjan, P.: Design of circularly polarized rectangular patch antenna with single cut. In: CAC2S 2013, pp. 174–177. Atlantis Press (2013)
9. Ranjan, P., Prashanti, N.: Design of double sided metamaterial antenna for mobile handset applications. In: SPIN 2014, pp. 675–678. IEEE (2014). 978-1-4799-2866-8/14
10. Ranjan, P., Aghwariya, M.K., Pandey, P.S., Prasanthi, N.: Cylindrical metallic pin structure microstrip patch antenna for wideband application. In: Singh, R., Choudhury, S. (eds.) Proceeding of International Conference on Intelligent Communication, Control and Devices. AISC, vol. 479, pp. 471–477. Springer, Singapore (2017)

Least Time Based Weighted Load Balancing Using Software Defined Networking

Karamjeet Kaur[1(✉)], Sukhveer Kaur[1], and Vipin Gupta[2]

[1] Arjan Dass College, Dharamkot, Moga, Punjab, India
bhullar1991@gmail.com, bhullarsukh96@gmail.com
[2] U-Net Solutions, Moga, Punjab, India
vipin2411@gmail.com

Abstract. The network is changing very rapidly due to Software Defined Networking. To properly implement networks, we need many network devices like routers, switches, load balancers, firewalls and intrusion detection (IDS)/ prevention (IPS). In traditional networking, these devices are very costly, inflexible & vendor specific. All these devices are made up of data plane & control plane. These planes are tightly coupled. You cannot force the vendors to sell you only the data plane so that you can use control plane of your choice. But SDN is changing this by separating the data plane & control plane. Now you can ask for the data plane from the vendor & can use open source control planes such as POX, RYU & Opendaylight. By writing network applications such as load balancer, firewall on top of these control planes, your data plane will start behaving like load balancer or firewall. Thus SDN offers us networking programmability. In our case, we created one load balancing application based on least time based Weighted Round Robin strategy. Load balancers devices are basically used for distributing large amount of client traffic among several servers depending upon load balancing strategy. The various strategies can be round robin, random, weighted round robin or server load balancing. We compared our new load balancing strategy with round robin strategy. For our experimental setup, we used Mininet Emulator Tool & POX Controller as our control plane.

Keywords: SDN · OpenFlow · Controller · Load balancer · LTWRR algorithm · Round-robin algorithm

1 Introduction

In traditional networks, network management is very difficult. Any type of modification and configuration in traditional network is very difficult and error prone task. In traditional networking, user cannot modify the product as per the network requirements because traditional network devices are non-programmable. Any type of modification, fixing error is done by only specific vendor. So the time required for introducing new services and features is very long. The cost for building even small network is very high because software and hardware is bundled together in network devices. As visible in Fig. 1, SDN removes these limitations of traditional networks by separating the forwarding plane that is also called data plane from the control plane.

© Springer Nature Singapore Pte Ltd. 2017
M. Singh et al. (Eds.): ICACDS 2016, CCIS 721, pp. 309–314, 2017.
DOI: 10.1007/978-981-10-5427-3_33

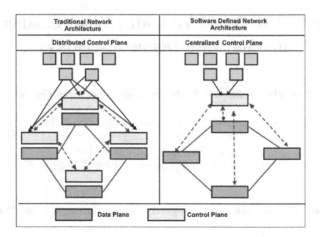

Fig. 1. Traditional network vs software defined network

SDN is rapidly emerging networking architecture, using this architecture network management is very easy [1]. It is also adopted by number of companies, organization and individuals. The main benefit of this type of network architecture is that it removes the need of vendor dependence because now network device become programmable. Now our data plane is simply dumb device that does not perform anything on its own. This data plane can behave as a firewall, load balancer according to the application written on the control plane [2]. The control plane inserts the flow rules into the data plane according to the application that are written on top of control plane. The SDN Controller is another name for control plane. Now we can build a large network with very low cost because hardware is available at very low cost and configuration of software is modified according to our choice by simply writing applications in different programming languages [3].

Openflow protocol is most used protocol to provide secure connection between the controller and the openflow switch. Each openflow switch maintains a flow table that contains number of flow entries that define what to do with the incoming packet [4]. These flow rules are inserted by the controller according to the logic of application as shown in Fig. 2. There are number of controllers are available: NOX [5], POX [6], Opendaylight [7], Ryu [8], Floodlight [9] etc. These controllers are written in different languages like NOX is written in C++, Opendaylight and Floodlight in Java language. In our case POX Controller was used which is based on Python language. Our main contributions in this paper are:

- Implemented Least Time based Weighted Round-Robin Load Balancing algorithm (LTWRR).
- Tested this algorithm on mininet emulation tool.
- Compared LTWRR algorithm with our already implemented Round-Robin load balancing algorithm. The Siege utility was used for load testing.

In this paper background and related work is covered in Sect. 2. The experimental setup is explained in Sect. 3.The experimental evaluation is described in Sect. 4 and last Sect. 5 discusses about future work & conclusions.

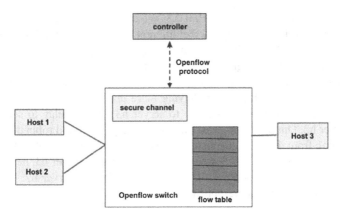

Fig. 2. Openflow protocol

2 Background and Related Work

Today network traffic is very large, therefore single server can not handle large number of requests. Load balancer solves these problems by distributing large number of requests to the number of replica servers. But the biggest drawback of load balancers based on traditional networks is that they are non-programmable and use dedicated, expensive hardware. Software defined networking solves these problems by converting simple openflow device into programmable load balancer. This load balancer does not use dedicated hardware, because we can convert dumb openflow based device into powerful and flexible load balancer by bringing programmability to the control plane.

Kaur et al. [10] implemented round robin load balancing strategy. The main problem with this technique is that it does not take into account the server load, link delay. This technique assumes that that all the servers have equal load and all the link have equal speed. But in reality, this does not happen. Generally, almost all link have different capacity and speed. Wang et al. [11] implemented Load balancing method, that divide the client traffic according to the weight assigned to the server. This method also does not take into account the link delay parameter.

Therefore we extend our previous work to solve these problems. In this paper we implemented least time based weighted round robin load balancing technique. In this technique we consider that each link has different speed, therefore we assign different delay to each link. Therefore the server that is attached to fastest link can handle more number of request than other servers.

3 Experimental Setup

To test our least time based weighted round robin load balancing application we created a network topology using Mininet emulation tool [12]. The topology consists of 1 host, 3 servers, 1 Openflow switch and one POX controller. The IP address of host h4 is 10.0.0.4. At host h4 we installed load testing tool "siege". The IP addresses of servers h1, h2, h3 are 10.0.0.1, 10.0.0.2 and 10.0.0.3. We also implemented python based web server on h1, h2 and h3. We assigned the different delay on every link that is between the servers and Openflow switch. We also assigned different weight (request ratio) according to delay. We assigned more weight to server that is connected to the openflow switch with least delay. Therefore server with least delay can handle more number of requests than other servers having more delay.

In Fig. 3 we assigned a 10 ms delay to server h3, 20 ms delay to server h1 and 30 ms to server h2. Our algorithm least time based weighted round robin distributes the requests coming from different clients to the servers according to weight. We can easily observe from the figure that first 5 requests are forwarded to server h3, next 3 requests are forwarded to server h1 and next 1 request is handled by server h2. This process continues till all the requests are not finished.

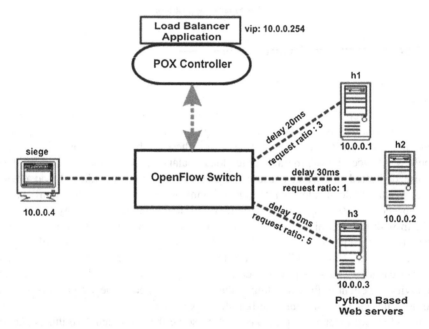

Fig. 3. Network topology

4 Experimental Evaluation

We compared our least time based weighted round robin algorithm with our already implemented round robin load balancing techniques on the basis of Transaction rate per seconds and response time in seconds. For testing we used the load testing tool "siege" [13]. The total number of requests is equal to number of concurrent users multiplied by the number of requests that each user send that is 5 in our case. If the number of concurrent users is 10, each user sends 5 requests then total numbers of requests are 50. After that 20 concurrent users, each send 5 requests then total number of requests are 100 and so on.

Figure 4 shows the response time of server. The y-axis represented the Response Time (sec). The x-axis represented the concurrent users. We can observed from the graph that response time in least time based weighted round robin load balancing is better than our already implemented round robin load balancing strategy.

Figure 5 shows the transaction rate of server. The y-axis represented the Transaction Rate (trans/sec). The x-axis represented the Concurrent Users. We can observe from the graph that transaction rate in least time based weighted round robin load balancing is better than previous round robin load balancing strategy. This means our least time based weighted round robin algorithm handles more number of request than previous round robin load balancing strategy.

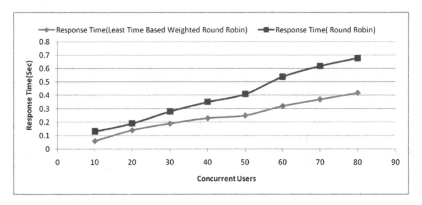

Fig. 4. Response time in least time based weighted round robin and round robin based load balancing strategy

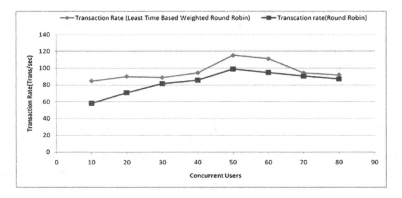

Fig. 5. Transaction rate in least time based weighted round robin and round robin based load balancing strategy

5   Conclusion and Future Work

Our least time based weighted round robin load balancer was successfully implemented using POX controller. We also conclude that our algorithm is better in performance than the previous round robin algorithm. Our load balancer is a software based load balancer that help to reduce cost as compared to traditional hardware based load balancer. We can reducing the period of time required to deploy new algorithms in SDN based load balancer.

In this paper we randomly assigned weights to servers according to link delay. But there should be some mechanism to calculate weight that should be assigned to the server accord to delay. We also do not take into account server load parameter. In future, we want to build some mechanism that automatically assigns weight to server according to load on server and link delay.

References

1. Xie, J., Guo, D., Zhiyao, H., Ting, Q., Lv, P.: Control plane of software defined networks: a survey. Comput. Commun. **67**, 1–10 (2015)
2. Xia, W., Wen, Y., Foh, C.H., Niyato, D., Xie, H.: A survey on software-defined networking. IEEE Commun. Surv. Tutorials **17**(1), 27–51 (2015)
3. Wickboldt, J.A., De Jesus, W.P., Isolani, P.H., Both, C.B., Rochol, J., Granville, L.Z.: Software-defined networking: management requirements and challenges. IEEE Commun. Mag. **53**(1), 278–285 (2015)
4. Ramos, F.M.V., Kreutz, D., Verissimo, P.: Software-defined networks: on the road to the softwarization of networking. Cutter IT J. (2015)
5. Tootoonchian, A., Gorbunov, S., Ganjali, Y., Casado, M., Sherwood, R.: On controller performance in software-defined networks. In: Presented as Part of the 2nd USENIX Workshop on Hot Topics in Management of Internet, Cloud, and Enterprise Networks and Services (2012)
6. Khondoker, R., Zaalouk, A., Marx, R., Bayarou, K.: Feature-based comparison and selection of Software Defined Networking (SDN) controllers. In: 2014 World Congress on Computer Applications and Information Systems (WCCAIS), pp. 1–7. IEEE (2014)
7. Reina Fuente, E.: How to control a new network paradigm: an overview of OpenDaylight SDN Platform (2015)
8. Wang, S.-Y., Chiu, H.-W., Chou, C.-L.: Comparisons of SDN OpenFlow controllers over EstiNet: Ryu vs. NOX. In: ICN 2015, p. 256 (2015)
9. Wen, X., Chen, Y., Hu, C., Shi, C., Wang, Y.: Towards a secure controller platform for openflow applications. In: Proceedings of the Second ACM SIGCOMM Workshop on Hot Topics in Software Defined Networking, pp. 171–172. ACM (2013)
10. Kaur, S., Kumar, K., Singh, J., Ghumman, N.S.: Round-robin based load balancing in Software Defined Networking. In: 2015 2nd International Conference on Computing for Sustainable Global Development (INDIACom), pp. 2136–2139. IEEE (2015)
11. Wang, R., Butnariu, D., Rexford, J.: OpenFlow-based server load balancing gone wild. In: Hot-ICE 2011, p. 12 (2011)
12. Keti, F., Askar, S.: Emulation of software defined networks using mininet in different simulation environments. In: 2015 6th International Conference on Intelligent Systems, Modelling and Simulation, pp. 205–210. IEEE (2015)
13. Prajapati, J.B.: Significance of testing through testing tools (2015)

QoS and QoE in Wireless Multicast Communication

Mahendra Kumar Jangir and Karan Singh[✉]

Jawaharlal Nehru University, New Delhi 110067, India
jangirnawalgarh@gmail.com, karancs12@gmail.com

Abstract. During last decade the deployment of multimedia and real-time applications over the network has grown with large interest. There are some parameters like service level agreements and quality of service such as delay, jitter, and packet loss on which the progress of these multimedia and real time applications depend. Though Multicasting is UDP based, but it is a very efficient group communication technique, it enhances efficiency by controlling network traffic and by reducing server and CPU load. Multicast optimizes performance by eliminating traffic redundancy and it is also helpful in distributed applications as well. Multicasting is a novel area of research in which broad scope of development is possible. In this paper, we are working on Quality of Services and Quality of Experiences and will provide an adaptive approach for data packet in terms of jitter by using the queuing mechanism. Our goal is to improve the performance of Multicast communication. The performance of the Multicast communication is calculated in terms of the throughput, packet loss, link utilization, delay and mean opinion score.

Keywords: Multicast · Wireless · Quality of services · Quality of experience

1 Introduction

Technically communication is defined as the exchanging the data or information between the sending and receiving machines either by means of wired or wireless. Initially, only two persons or machines were able to communicate each other, it was Unicast communication, nowadays we are able to transmit the same message to a group of machines, it names as Multicast communication. Similarly, there are other ways by which one can communicate are like Broadcast, Anycast, Geocast, Concast, Multipeer or Multipoint communication etc.

Multicast communication is used as a wired or wireless medium. Our concern is Quality of Services (QoS) [1] and Quality of Experience (QoE) [2] in Wireless Multicast communication. QoS is defined as the deterministic network behavior where it is assumed that the transmitted data should be with minimum packet loss, minimum delay and maximum bandwidth. It is difficult to measure QoS and, as well deployment of Multicast in WLAN. Some researchers used layered concept to enhance the QoS where as we try to enhance the same by keeping jitter and queuing delay as a center point. There are some services like broadcasting of news, real time data, budgetary information and some other multimedia applications are provided over a network, which

© Springer Nature Singapore Pte Ltd. 2017
M. Singh et al. (Eds.): ICACDS 2016, CCIS 721, pp. 315–325, 2017.
DOI: 10.1007/978-981-10-5427-3_34

consume large amounts of bandwidth and they also push back the network and service provider into a corner. Multicast transmission is one solution of this difficulty; this allows broadcasting of data and information without a rise in data traffic. Multicasting controls the escalation of data traffic by sending a unique packet to receivers and replicates only if, it is very necessary. Some other benefits of Multicasting are distributed applications, enhanced efficiency and optimized performance.

For scalable and reliable Multicast communication, there are some interrelated issues which need to be addressed is as follow.

Provision of Feedback: Just like broadcasting scheme, Multicasting mechanism also does not make use of feedback, i.e. Acknowledge (ACK) frames [3]. Due to lack of ACK frames, Multicasting services are highly affected by collision and other problems. We can also say that without ACK it is not possible to recover the errors.

Multi-rate Transmissions: In case of Unicast communication MAC protocol makes available the concept of physical layer which is multi-rate capable. Auto Rate Fallback (ARF) [4] mechanism is responsible here to make use of this feature possible. By using ACK packet, and considering channel conditions, ARF protocol selects the data rates. As above mentioned, there is an absence of ACK packet in Multicasting so it makes ARF mechanism impractical to implement. So in the case of Multicasting the highest rate of data communication is selected from one of the rates among the basic rate set by considering the channel conditions so that all receivers in that group can receive the data successfully.

Congestion: Due to large amount of data traffic there will be congestion in the network. Congestion [5] in network and quality of services are important issues which exploit video applications.

Throughput: Lack of ACK packet in Multicasting leads to congestion and because of congestion throughput will be less.

Demand for More Bandwidth: Demand of bandwidth is directly proportional to the demand of applications, so increasing with the demand of application in limited bandwidth cause increases the maximum throughput and it may lead to the failure of communication system because of congestion.

Security: Security is a very serious challenge. In [6], it is discussed that how to make our system very secure form the unauthorized access so that our data and information can be protected.

Quality of Service: For the different receivers it should be good and acceptable.

2 Related Work

We review related work to understand about the Multicast Services, QoS and IEEE 802.11 WLANs. There are many services and techniques that are used before to improve the quality of services or wireless Multicast communication.

Kuri *et al.* suggested the Leader Based Protocol Automatic Repeat-reQuest (LBP ARQ) technique [7]. ARQ was the most recent effort made to improve the reliability of Multicast services. In LBP one of the receivers is selected as a Group Leader (GL). The Access Point (AP) first send RTS to all MRs and then only GL sends a CTS frame to the AP, after receiving the CTS frame Access Point is ensured that the channel is clear and then it begins transmission of data frames. If data is received correctly, then GL will send ACK otherwise GL will do nothing. If any non leader gets any error, NACK will be sent by them. And if AP receives an ACK, implies that it is successful transmission, otherwise AP will repeat the whole process.

LBP has two main problems, First, when RTS and CTS frames are not used for small data frames and if the whole data frame gets lost, then non leader MRs can't send NACK because they don't know how or when to send as the target is not known, as a result LBP becomes unreliable. Second, if channel is more erroneous, then LBP reflects poor performance. RTS/CTS frame for Multicast structure does not contain data frame sequence number so if there is any received frame which is erroneous, then the non leader receiver sends NACK, regardless of whether that erroneous frame already received rightly or not. So it must retransmit the frame until all receivers successfully receive the correct frame, this cause many numbers of unnecessary retransmission that's why in case of lossy channel LBP is not efficient.

Li *et al.* Proposed Beacon-driven LBP (BLBP) [8] to overcome the problems of LBP scheme. It suggests the beacon frames, which are used to provide the sequence number to the data frames so that it can avoid unnecessary retransmission of data frames. Beacon frame contains the Frame Control, Duration, Receiver Address, Transmitter Address, Sequence Control and Frame Control Status as the frame fields. BLBP also faces two problems one BLBP modifies the beacon packet making it incompatible with 802.11 standards and second changing and selecting GL is an additional problem as like in LBP.

Gupta *et al.* proposed 802.11MX [9] which is a reliable Multicast MAC protocol and it solves the problem of selection of Group Leader (GL). 802.11 MX uses an ARQ mechanism with busy tone indicator. Multicast Receivers send NACK tone instead of NACK packet if it receives the corrupt packet. If the sender node gets NACK tone, then it retransmits otherwise it is assumed that the transmission is successful. It performs better than LBP and BLBP in terms of throughput because it does not require a leader receiver. 802.11 MX falls short when it occurs collision and if some Multicast receivers could not properly receive packets. Another problem in 802.11MX is that it doesn't adapt Multicast PHY rate to channel conditions between sender and MRs.

Basalamah *et al.* introduced Rate Adaption Multicasting (RAM) Mechanism [10]. It was proposed for reliable Multicast communication with rate adaptation. RAM scheme also uses the concept of RTS and CTS as like LBP. Here all MRs also use RTS to convey Receiver Signal Strength (RSS) to the sender or access point. Dummy CTS frame of varied length, which depends on the chosen PHY transmission mode is sent by each Multicast receiver. Then channel is sensed by AP to calculate the collision duration and hence it adapts the transmission rate for Multicast communication.

Villalon *et al.* defined the Auto Rate Selection for Multicasting Mechanism (ARSM) [11] whose objective is to identify the MR which exhibit worst channel condition in terms of Signal Noise Ratio (SNR) and this MR is then assigned as group leader, which is responsible for sending ACK packet on the behalf of all MRs, while other MRs can issue NACK when they find any error in transmission. Multicast Channel Probe Operation is the name of mechanism of discovering the GL.

Santos *et al.* proposed Dynamic Multicast Data Transmission (DMDT) [12] to diminish the processing carried out by the Multicast receivers. Under this scheme MCPO is kept deactivated till sender transmits a Multicast frame successfully and sender adapts the data rate based on the SNR value of ACK which is sent by the group leader. If a sender node detects N consecutive NACKs then it initiates MCPO. The Multicast receiver which has lowest SNR value, its data rate is adapted by the ARSM so that all MRs can receive data packet successfully, but it makes penalize those MRs which are capable to receive data at higher rates. HARSM is proposed to counter this.

Villalon *et al.* have proposed Hierarchical Auto Rate Selection for Multicasting Mechanism (HARSM) [13] where video encoding follows the Hierarchical fashion, *i.e.* in two layers named Base Layer and Enhanced Layer. BL video packets are transmitted to all Multicast Receivers and the operating mode of ELs is almost similar to ARSM but the difference is that it selects the receiver which has highest SNR. The HARSM selects the EL rate for transmission of packets.

Drawbacks: ARSM and HARSM both have 2 drawbacks.

1. Not compatible with 802.11 standards, they use two new packets making inter-operability with legacy IEEE802.11 unfeasible.
2. HARSM and ARSM use SNR threshold which requires compromise between signal overhead and best rate of data transmission.

Santos *et al.* proposed Adaptive Multicast Mechanism with Collision Prevention [12] in which Multicast Collision Prevention (MCP) is designed by slightly modification of 802.11 MAC Protocol. It has three major objectives. First one is to reduce the collision probability drastically of Multicast packets; second objective is to ensure that the Unicast and Multicast services access the channel according to the standards and finally it should keep the backward compatibility according to the standards.

Adaptive Multicast Mechanism with Collision Prevention (AMM/CP) considerable improve QoS of Multicast services in terms of delay and reliability and it also avoids Multicast collision, but not able to recover those packets which are delivered with some error because of channel conditions. There are some solutions, (a) Dynamically adapt data rate transmission (b) Collision prevention (c) Negative feedback for Multicast packet (d) Slow adaptation.

3 Network Model

How to enhance the Quality of Services and experience in terms of delay and jitter is the sole of our proposed model. The proposed model contains sending and receiving Multicast nodes and router. Layered concept is also imposed in our model which contains Layers; say Base layer (BL) and Enhancement layers (ELs). The joining and leaving of the nodes in the layers is taken care by the protocol called IGMP on the basis of the End to End packet delay and Jitter.

There are three components in the proposed model say Sender, Multicast Router and receivers. The sender is a device which sends data and packets to the intermediate device called Multicast Router which further transmits the message to the destination receivers. The sending device sends data in multiple layers say Base Layer (BL) and Enhancement Layers (EL1, EL2... ELn). Base Layer contains the minimum transmission rate of data, i.e. worst quality data, but the beauty of this layer is that, the all Multicast receivers can successfully receive data or in other words, it gives guarantee of receiving data to each and every receiver node (Fig. 1).

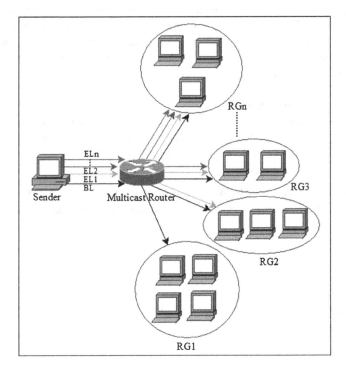

Fig. 1. Multilayer multicast model

On the second part of this model the Multicast Router is connected to the Multicast receivers. Multicast receivers are divided into n groups say RG1, RG2... RGn. The group is formed according to the receiving capacity of the nodes. If the capacity of any receiver is least or very low, then it will join the group RG1, which receives data as per the Base Layer (BL) capacity. Means the quality of data this group receives is worst. Similarly RG2, RG3 and so on are associated to the EL1, EL2 and so on, respectively, and gradually the Quality of the services is increasing as the receiver gets the data by enhanced layer.

3.1   Jitter and Buffer

We know that in wireless communication the channel conditions change rapidly because of mobility, interference, noise, and so many other reasons, so the capacity of the receiver may also changes and hence receiver may switch from one group to another or in other words Multicast receivers adapt their receiving rates. In this proposed model the rate is adapted automatically on the basis of jitter. Variation in the delay of the received packet is called Jitter. Data packets are transmitted in a continuous flow by keeping the even inter packet space, but at the receiving end this steady flow gets disturbed and the delay between the packets can vary because of the improper queuing, network congestion and other configuration errors. The quality of the Real Time Protocol (RTP) audio stream for Voice over IP (VoIP) will degrade due to jitter encountered. To handle this, we add playout delay buffer which will buffer these packets and then once again play these packets in steady flow. Playout buffer is also known as de-jitter buffer.

3.1.1   Jitter Mathematically

An end-to-end delay process $\{Dn, n \geq 1\}$ is an ordered sequence of packet end to end delays from the 1st packet; and it is a stochastic process. Consider a realisation $\{d_1, d_2, d_3,..., d_N\}$ of an end-to-end delay process with N samples. A realisation is a single instance of a stochastic process.

Average End-to-End Delay: The Average end-to-end delay is expressed as the sum of all delays $\{d_1, d_2, d_3,...,d_N\}$, divided by the total number of all measurements (N) and is denoted by μ_D.

$$\mu_D = \frac{\sum_{i=1}^{N} di}{N}$$

Jitter: The Jitter represents the average deviation of delays from the average delay and it is denoted by σ_D

$$\sigma_D = \sqrt{\frac{1}{N-1} \sum_{i=1}^{N} (di - \mu D)^2}$$

4   Proposed Work

To measure the Quality of services in wireless Multicast communication we have developed an algorithm which is based on the jitter. The name of the algorithm is "Jitter based Quality of Services Measurement" (JQSM). The steps and flow diagram of this algorithm is given in the next section.

4.1   Algorithm 1.1: J_QSM

The steps of algorithm 1.1 are as follows

```
Step 1. Initialize Parameters and set Number of
Iterations, (i) =10
Step 2. Source send i^th stream to receivers
Step 3. Intermediate nodes receive data packets
Step 4. Apply Algorithm 1.2 (L-QSM) to measure the
quality of service
Step 5. Repeat steps 1 to 4 depending on the number of
iterations.
```

4.2   Algorithm 1.2: L_QSM

This algorithm 1.2 is known as Layered Based Quality of Service Measurement (L_QSM) which is designed to measure the quality of services in wireless Multicast communication. It uses jitter and the number of layers to measure quality of services. Initially, it detects the queue status by using actual and expected jitter. If the queue is not overflowing, then apply join mechanism otherwise perform leave operation. The complete procedure of our algorithm is shown below.

Input: Actual Jitter (J_A), Expected Jitter (J_E), Capacity (C), Number of layers (N_L), layer threshold (δ_L) = k, Number of iterations (i) = 10.

Output: Quality of service status
```
1. If (J_A ≥ J_E)
2.      Then queue is not overflow
3.         if (queue is not overflow)
4. then apply Join mechanism
5.          if (N_L ≥ 70% of δ_L)
            Then high quality
            else if (50 % of  δ_L ≤ N_L && N_L ≤ 70% of δ_L)
                Then medium quality
            else if (N_L < 50% of δ_L)
                Then poor quality
6. Else queue overflow
7. If (queue overflow)
8.        Then apply Leave mechanism
9. If (N_L ≥ BL)
10. Then Go to Algorithm 1.1
11. Else Leave the group
12. Repeat step 1 to 11 until i ≤ 10
13. End
```

For better understanding, we have a flow diagram of the proposed algorithm, which is shown in Fig. 2. Where there are three switches cases each will tell the Quality of services depending on the threshold value of layers. It is well known that if the layer will BL, then its quality is poor and when it is ELs then its quality is good.

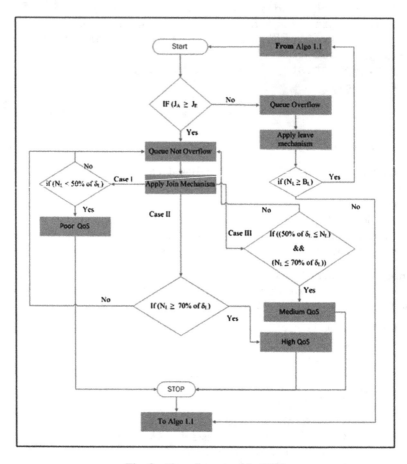

Fig. 2. Flow diagram of L_QSM

5   Simulation

The Proposed model has been simulated by creating the simulation topology on OPNET simulation.

This is the topology of administration and the department where the administration will behave like sender and department will like receivers. Department section has three departments say Polymer, Mechanical and Civil department, all the nodes in these departments are wireless equipped. There are certain parameters which have been taken to create and simulate the scenario for the proposed work. We selected the network scale as campus whose area is 10 * 10 km. A uniform Packet size of 500 and 1500 bits, Queue size of 4608000 bits is taken in our scenario. Link delay is 10 ms to 50 ms. Priority queue and Weighted fair queue are also used here.

6   Performance Evaluation

The Performance of the proposed method, J_QSM is evaluated in the terms of packet end to end delay, WLAN traffic dropped, traffic dropped in queue, video conferencing traffic, queue jitter, media access delay and mean opinion score. Mean opinion score is the method to evaluate the QoE. The quality of experience is a subjective in nature and it is defined as the overall satisfaction of end user towards the services and applications. The MOS is calculated by considering the human perception, dimension and experience for the performance of the network and applications.

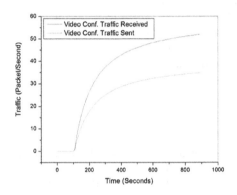

Fig. 3.   Video conferencing traffic

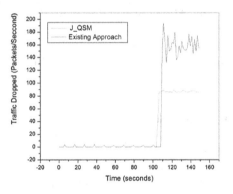

Fig. 4.   Traffic dropped in packet/Sec.

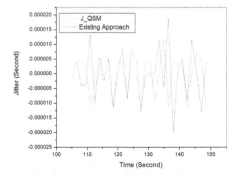

Fig. 5.   Jitter variation

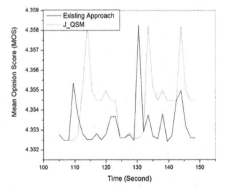

Fig. 6.   Mean opinion score

324   M.K. Jangir and K. Singh

The traffic sent and received in wireless Multicast video conferencing is shown in Fig. 3. It shows that all sent packets will not receive; some packets will loss during communication. The traffic is in terms of packet per second. Figure 4 shows the traffic dropped in terms of packet per second. In this case, two queues are used, one is Priority Queue (PQ) and another one is Weighted Fair Queue (WFQ). According to graph packet dropped in WFQ is less than the PQ. Our approach uses WFQ for simulation. Jitter is the time difference between two consecutive packets. Here in Fig. 5 we can see that, jitter of existing approach is more than our J_QSM. The X and Y axis have time in seconds and Jitter respectively. MOS is shown in Fig. 6.

7 Conclusion

Proposed algorithm is based on jitter and has the layered concept, which provides the Multicast receivers to select the layers. There is one base layer and many enhanced layers. Shifting of layers is completely based on the jitter, which really facilitate the wireless Multicast communication. Although we have improved the Multicast communication, but still there are many issues such as scalability, security, congestion control and fairness which can be further explored as a future work.

References

1. Fiedler, M., Hossfeld, T., Tran-Gia, P.: A generic quantitative relationship between quality of experience and quality of service. IEEE Netw. **24**(2), 36–41 (2010)
2. ITU: Definition of Quality of Experience (QoE). Reference: TD 109rev2 (PLEN/12), ITU, January 2007
3. LAN MAN Standards Committee of the IEEE Computer Society, ANSI/IEEE Std 802.11: Part 11: Wireless LAN Medium Access Control (MAC) and Physical Layer (PHY) Specifications, June 2007
4. Kamerman, A., Monteban, L.: WaveLAN-II: a high-performance wireless LAN for the unlicensed band. Bell Labs Tech. J. **2**(3), 118–133 (1997)
5. Katabi, D., Handley, M., Rohrs, C.: Congestion control for high bandwidth-delay product networks. ACM SIGCOMM Comput. Commun. Rev. **32**(4), 89 (2002)
6. Kruus, P.S.: A survey of multicast security issues and architectures. In: Proceedings of 21st National Information Systems Security Conference, pp. 5–8 (1998)
7. Kuri, J., Kasera, S.K.: Reliable multicast in multi-access wireless LANs. ACM Wireless Netw. **7**(4), 359–369 (2001)
8. Li, Z., Herfet, T.: Beacon-driven Leader Based protocol over a GE channel for MAC layer multicast error control. Int. J. Commun. Netw. Syst. Sci. **1**, 144–153 (2008)
9. Gupta, S., Shankar, V., Lalwani, S.: Reliable multicast MAC protocol for wireless LANs. In: IEEE International Conference on Communications (ICC03), vol. 1, pp. 93–97, May 2003
10. Basalamah, A., Sugimoto, H., Sato, T.: Rate adaptive reliable multicast MAC protocol for WLANs. In: IEEE 63rd Vehicular Technology Conference, VTC 2006-Spring, vol. 3, pp. 1216–1220, May 2006

11. Villalón, J., Cuenca, P., Orozco-Barbosa, L., Seok, Y., Turletti, T.: ARSM: a cross-layer auto rate selection multicast mechanism for multi-rate wireless LANs. IET Commun. 1(5), 893–902 (2007)

12. Santos, M., Villalon, J., Ramırez-Mireles, F., Orozco-Barbosa, L.: A novel QoE-aware multicast mechanism for video communications over IEEE 802.11 WLANs. IEEE Commun. Lett. 30(07), 1205–1214 (2012)

13. Villalon, J., Cuenca, P., Orozco Barbosa, L., Seok, Y., Turletti, T.: Cross-layer architecture for adaptive video multicast streaming over multirate wireless LANs. IEEE J. Sel. Areas Commun. 25(4), 699–711 (2007)

Signed Social Networks: A Survey

Nancy Girdhar[(✉)] and K.K. Bharadwaj

School of Computer and Systems Sciences, Jawaharlal Nehru University,
New Delhi 110067, India
nancy.grl991@gmail.com, kbharadwaj@gmail.com

Abstract. People hold both sorts of emotions-positive and negative against each other. Online social media serves as a platform to show these relationships, whether friendly or unfriendly, like or dislike, agreement or dissension, trust or distrust. These types of interactions lead to the emergence of Signed Social Networks (SSNs) where positive sign represents friend, like, trust, agreement and negative sign represents foe, dislike, distrust and disagreement. Although an immense body of work has been dedicated to the field of social networks; the field of SSNs remains not much explored. This survey first frames the concept of signed networks and offers a brief discourse on the two most prevalent theories of social psychology applied to study them. Then, we address the various state-of-the-art issues which relates the real world scenarios with signed networks. Grounded along the network attributes, this survey talks about the different metrics used to analyze these networks and the real world datasets used for observational purposes. This paper, makes an attempt to follow the contours of research in the area to provide readers with a comprehensive understanding of SSNs elaborating the open research areas.

Keywords: Signed social networks · Structural balance theory · Status theory · Modularity · Frustration

1 Introduction

One of the intrinsic potential benefits of social media is that one can take a deep insight in one's life as people are using it as a platform to open up with their opinions, emotions, thoughts and their beliefs on various topics on the web. They can express their views in various forms by liking or disliking as different people have different opinions on a particular topic. So, in addition to the concept of trust, support and friendship, these social interactions can also reflect disagreements and conflicts among the people on the social media sites. Thus, it is significant to take into consideration the hostile relations (negative links) along with the friendly associations (positive links) between the users. The social networks having information about the type of links (positive or negative) among the users besides the links itself are termed as Signed Social Networks (SSNs).

Although, a plethora of approaches is dedicated for the analysis of social networks (SNs); however most of them consider these networks as having only friendly (positive) relationships while ignoring the hostile (negative) ones entirely. The increase in the number of users on social networking sites as well as information about the positive

© Springer Nature Singapore Pte Ltd. 2017
M. Singh et al. (Eds.): ICACDS 2016, CCIS 721, pp. 326–335, 2017.
DOI: 10.1007/978-981-10-5427-3_35

and negative relationships among them has driven the researchers towards investigating the accountabilities of these relationships in the mining of social network data. Many research works [18, 20] have encountered a significant change in the nature and complexity of social graph, once the negative links are introduced in the networks. This lays the foundation for utilizing the negative links in various applications such as link prediction [19, 21, 28, 30, 33], recommender systems [16, 29] and community detection [1, 2, 18, 32]. Therefore, these SSNs are recently grabbing inexorable attention from the research community. This article reviews the various state-of-the-art issues of SSNs.

The rest of the article is organized as follows: Sect. 2 gives a brief on the background details of SSNs. Section 3 describes the state-of-the art and Sect. 4 discusses the datasets and evaluation metrics used for analyzing signed networks. Finally, the Sect. 5 presents some future research directions along with the conclusion.

2 Background

According to Moshirpour [23], Signed Networks are defined as the extension of networks that include the additional information about positive and negative links.

Signed Social Network: Mathematically, [19] a directed signed social network represented as signed graph can be defined as $G = (V, E, \delta)$ where, V is the vertex set representing nodes of the network, $E \subseteq V \times V$ is the edge set that represents the links of the network and $\delta : E \rightarrow \{-1, 0, +1\}$ is a function which assigns $+1$ value if there is a positive link (friend/trust) from node u to node v, -1 is assigned if there is a negative link (foe/distrust) from node u to node v and 0 if there is no link between the two nodes [6].

For example: Let a signed network having 5 users $V = \{U1, U2, U3, U4, U5\}$ is represented by a directed graph G and A is the corresponding adjacency matrix as shown in Fig. 1. Here, a friend (positive) relation is shown with a green color edge and a foe (negative) relation is represented with a red color edge.

$$A = \begin{pmatrix} & U_1 & U_2 & U_3 & U_4 & U_5 \\ U_1 & 0 & 0 & 0 & +1 & 0 \\ U_2 & +1 & 0 & +1 & 0 & 0 \\ U_3 & +1 & 0 & 0 & 0 & +1 \\ U_4 & 0 & -1 & -1 & 0 & 0 \\ U_5 & +1 & -1 & 0 & +1 & 0 \end{pmatrix}$$

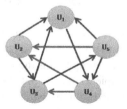

Fig. 1. Graphical representation of a directed SSN (Color figure online)

Ignoring the direction of the signed links, the network can be converted into undirected network assuming the links between the nodes as bidirectional and thus, the adjacency matrix representation of the undirected network will be symmetric in nature.

2.1   Theories of Signed Networks

To analyze these online SSNs, there are two different theories [20]. A brief description of each of these theories is given as follows.

Structural Balance Theory is the fundamental theory formulated by Heider in 1946 [14]. Based on the concept of *Friend-of-a-Friend* (FOAF), this theory is a notion to understand the structure, cause of tensions and conflicts between the two sentiments (positive and negative) in a network of actors (users). Further, Cartwright and Harrary in 1956 [5] modeled it in terms of signed graphs. This theory rests on the assumption that certain configurations of positive and negative edges are socially more probable than others. Ignoring the identities of the actors, four configurations are possible: *"my friend's friend is my friend", "my friend's enemy is my enemy", "my enemy's friend is my enemy", "my enemy's enemy is my friend"*.

According to the structural balance theory, a balanced triad is one with either one or three positive links (i.e., odd number of positive links) among three people. In Fig. 2, the first two triads are balanced as they have an odd number of positive links while later two are unbalanced as they have even number of positive links. This theory is pertinent on undirected networks only.

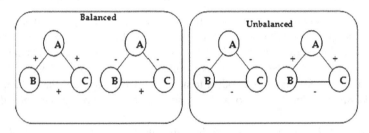

Fig. 2. Various configurations of social triads

Social Status Theory suggested by Guha et al. [12] and further developed by Leskovec et al. [20] proposes to use status of a person as the factor to decide whether a person will make a link (positive or negative) with another person in the network. Status can be in terms of social status (popularity, fame) or it can be economical status (money, power). Pagerank is one of the most popular ways to calculate status score in social networks.

According to this theory, if individual A(creator) makes a positive link to individual B (recipient), then A believes that B has higher status than him, whereas a negative link originated from individual A to B indicates that A considers status of B lower than him. It is evident that the status theory is more suitable for directed networks. To check whether triads of a network satisfy status theory, take each negative link in a triad, inverse its direction and the flip the sign of the link (positive sign) then the resultant triad should be acyclic in nature.

Computation of Status of a Node: The status of a node x in a directed network can be computed [19] as follows:

$$\xi(x) = d_{in}^+(x) + d_{out}^-(x) - d_{out}^+(x) - d_{in}^-(x) \qquad (1)$$

where, $d_{in}^+(x)$ and $d_{in}^-(x)$ denotes the number of positive and negative links received by the node x from other nodes in the network respectively. Similarly, $d_{out}^+(x)$ and $d_{out}^-(x)$ is the number of positive and negative links generated by the node x in the network, respectively.

Balance Theory vs Status Theory: In order to sense the difference between balance theory and status theory, assume the case that node A connects negatively to node B, further node B connects negatively to node C. Now what will be the sign of the link connecting node A to node C? Considering balance theory's configuration "My enemy's enemy is my friend", predicts the sign of the link between A and C as positive, whereas, the status theory predicts the sign of the link from A to C as negative. In other words, the result of balance theory differs from the results of status theory in this case.

3 State-of-the-Art

Link Prediction in SSNs: Traditional link prediction approaches used for social networks are massively based on the concept of "friendship". Thus, neglecting the other side of relationships viz., antagonism. Users in these networks find it difficult to decide among the people they trust from those they don't. Thus, they find it vague and obscure to distinguish between a friend and an acquaintance [4, 33]. Therefore, these approaches are not well suitable for analyzing and predicting links in SSNs.

Recently, researchers have begun to investigate on how to turn an unsigned acquaintances network into signed trust/distrust network [19, 30, 33]. A variety of available networks like Epinions, Slashdot, Wikipedia etc. have also started labeling links explicitly either as friend/foe [17] or trust/distrust [11, 26]. A number of theories in sociology [3, 20] provide deeper insight into the fundamental principles which explain how the patterns of negative and positive links resulted into different kinds of relationships. According to structural balance theory [5, 14], people in signed networks [12, 20] tend to follow the notion of FOAF whereas, status theory is based on the concept of social status which people possess in a society.

Thus, the sign inference problem, which aims to infer the unknown relationship between two entities, can be achieved by learning from balance or status information of signed networks.

Community Detection (CD) in a social network is identification of set of nodes that are more densely connected to each other than to the rest of the network [2, 24].

Different approaches in the literature are proposed to tackle the problem of community detection in social networks. Some traditional clustering algorithms assume communities as disjoint structure, where as some approaches assume communities as overlapping structures in the real-world networks [18]. Graph partitioning algorithms [8], hierarchical clustering algorithms [18] have also been used for CD in social networks etc. As CD in signed social networks is a bit different from the CD in social networks, its definition should take into account the extra information about the type of links among the users besides the links itself which is stated as follows:

Community Detection in SSNs attempts to partition the network in such a way that each partition should have dense positive intra-connections and sparse negative intra-connections. One way to do such optimization is by using the concept of modularity introduced by Newman [24].

Trust, Distrust and Reputation in Community Detection: In recent few years a lot of work is done on trust and reputation. Trust and distrust are personal characteristics while reputation is a public characteristic of a person/organization. Trust and reputation are very necessary components in real world social networks and these are incorporated in most of the domains like recommender systems [16, 26], e-learning, e-commerce, semantic web and so on.

Recently, researchers have begun to scrutinize on how to transform an unsigned social network into signed trust/distrust network [12, 19, 30, 33]. A variety of existing networks have also started tagging links explicitly either as friend/foe [17] or trust/distrust [12] (like Epinions, Slashdot, Wikipedia). To bring any online model or network more near to the physical world, it is inevitable to incorporate trust and reputation in it.

Social Recommender Systems: The principle intent of Social Recommender Systems (SRSs) is to ease information overload over social media users by delivering the most attractive and relevant content/items they are looking for. SRSs that suggest content, people and communities often used personalization techniques [7] to adapt the needs and interests of an individual user or a group of users. There is a lot of work done both in industry and academia for developing new approaches in recommender systems over the last decade.

In SSNs, not only the information about the relationships, but also the type of relationships are given which can be used to make better recommender systems than existing as it will be easy to recommend things to a group of people having similar likings.

4 Datasets and Evaluation Metrics Used for Signed Social Networks

In this section we have provided a list of publicly available real world signed datasets and benchmark datasets used for observational purposes:

4.1 Datasets

Epinions[1] website which is a *"who-trust-whom"* online social network of a general consumer review site on which users can post reviews about the various products and

---

[1] https://snap.stanford.edu/data/soc-sign-epinions.html.

services. The rating of reviews is done on the scale of 1 to 5 by different reviewers who label them by like/dislike based on their trust/distrust on the review.

Slashdot[2] is a tech-based news website which enables users to tag other users as *"friends"* or *"foes"*. On this site, users can also tag other users negatively. Here, a *friend* tag is considered as a positive link and a *foe* tag is considered as a negative link.

Wikipedia[3] network is an adminship election dataset in which users cast their votes to promote individuals for admin post. A positive vote is considered as a positive link and a negative vote is viewed as a negative link.

Slovene Parliamentary Party Network [10] represents the relations among 10 political parties of Slovene Parliamentary. The weights on the links assessed are based on the scale of −3 to +3, where the positive and negative weight shows similarity and dissimilarity between the pair of parties respectively.

Gahuku-Gama Subtribes Network [27] describes the positive and negative alliances among 16 Gahuku-Gama Subtribes. Since, it is an unsigned network, which can be converted by assuming links between same community as positive and between different communities as negative.

Table 1 shows the different datasets that are used for analysis of SSNs.

Table 1. Description of the datasets.

Attributes	Datasets				
	Real-world			Benchmark	
	Epinions	Slashdot	Wikipedia	Slovene parliamentary party	Gahuku-Gama subtribes
Nodes	131828	82144	10835	10	16
Edges	841372	549202	159388	90	116
Type	Directed	Directed	Directed	Undirected	Undirected
Ground truth available	No	No	No	Yes	Yes
Used in articles	[19, 20]	[19, 20]	[19, 20]	[32]	[1, 32]

4.2   Evaluation Metrics for SSNs

Let a signed network $G = (V, E, \delta)$ be partitioned into k communities $\{C_1, C_2, \ldots, C_k\}$ and A is the adjacency matrix corresponding to G i.e., $A_{ij} = \delta(i,j)$. Given a node $i \in V$, d_i^+ and d_i^- are the positive and the negative degrees of node i respectively.

Modularity [24] measures how good the partition of the network is, by taking into account the degree distribution. In signed networks, a division of the network should be done such that it takes into account the contribution of binary links (positive or neg-

---

[2] https://snap.stanford.edu/data/soc-sign-Slashdot090221.html.

[3] https://snap.stanford.edu/data/wiki-RfA.html.

ative links) available among the nodes in the network. Thus, modified definition of modularity [1, 2, 18] is given by the Eq. (2).

$$Q_{signed} = \frac{1}{2E} \sum i,j \left[A_{i,j} - \left(\frac{d_i^+ d_j^+}{2E} - \frac{d_i^- d_j^-}{2E} \right) \right] \delta(c_i, c_j) \tag{2}$$

$\forall i, j \in G$ $\delta(c_i, c_j) = 1$ when both the nodes i and j belong to the same community c else 0 and c_i denotes the community to which the node i belongs.

For signed overlapping communities, O_i is the number of communities which include vertex v_i, modularity Q_{ov} [22] is computed as given in the Eq. (3).

$$Q_{ov} = \frac{1}{2d^+ + 2d^-} \sum i,j \frac{1}{O_i O_j} \left[A_{i,j} - \left(\frac{d_i^+ d_j^+}{2E} - \frac{d_i^- d_j^-}{2E} \right) \right] \delta(c_i, c_j) \tag{3}$$

Frustration [8] measures the unstability in the network. Frustration is the sum of number of inter-positive links between the communities and the number of intra-negative links within the [1, 2] communities which is given in the Eq. (4).

$$F(C_1, C_2, \ldots, C_k) = \sum i,j \frac{|A_{i,j}| - A_{i,j}}{2} \delta(c_i, c_j) + \frac{|A_{i,j}| + A_{i,j}}{2} \left(1 - \delta(c_i, c_j)\right) \tag{4}$$

Frustration implies mutually antagonistic or hostile groups with few imbalances. Therefore, to detect communities frustration minimization can serve as an objective function [1, 2].

Social Balance Factor: To determine whether a network is structurally balanced or not, social balance factor (β) [25] can be used. A network with number of balanced triads and total number of triads given by $T_{balance}$ and T_{total} respectively, the social balance factor of the network is computed as follows:

$$\beta = \frac{T_{balance}}{T_{total}} \tag{5}$$

Error Rate: It is based on the concept of frustration, which is used to measure the partitioning quality of a signed network. The error rate of a partition C can be defined [1, 32] as follows:

$$error(C) = \frac{F(C)}{\sum i \sum j |A_{i,j}|} \times 100\% \tag{6}$$

where, $F(C)$ is defined in Eq. (4). It is obvious that the smaller the value of the $error(C)$ better will be the partition quality.

5 Conclusion and Future Challenges

In this paper, we presented a survey of Signed Social Networks (SSNs) and discussed trends and perspectives of further research. We have discussed signed network theories and different metrics used to analyze and evaluate these networks. Signed networks mimic the real world scenarios, grabbing the attention of many researchers and thus emerging as a popular research field. There are many research challenges which are yet to be addressed in this area. Some of them are briefly listed as follows:

- It would be interesting to integrate users' tastes and their trusted friends' into collaborative filtering techniques for more accurate recommendations [7, 15].
- The role of positive and negative links in online settings can be exploited in the field of community detection to discover overlapping communities, hierarchical structures and analysis of time evolving communities which are not yet much explored in the context of SSNs [6, 15, 19, 22].
- Fusion of trust-distrust and trust-reputation mechanisms into formulation of techniques can enhance the strength and effectiveness of the schemes for SSNs [9, 11, 12, 31].
- Although, a lot of work is done in the field of link prediction, but monolithically considering links as positive [21], which is far from the case of real world networks as they consist of negative links too. So, development of new procedures to identify relevant parameters for link prediction using the information obtained from the SSNs could be a future research direction [19, 25, 28, 33].
- Other promising research direction would be incorporation of trust in recommender systems and utilization of trust inference mechanism in sparse SSNs to handle the sparsity problem [26, 28].
- Discovering new schemes for similarity computation between various profile features in SSNs and incorporation of social trust and reputation for quality social recommendations [26, 28].
- Information entropy describes the uncertainty associated with a given probability distribution. The applications of entropy concept in complex networks are widely and deeply applied. Nevertheless, the application of entropy in signed networks is currently limited and challenged [13].
- Percolation is one of the best studied processes in statistical physics and serves as a conceptual framework to treat more factual problems such as collective behavior, robustness of networks. This concept is still very less dealt in the view of signed networks [13].
- Along with the positive and content-centric interactions, the user generated content is pervasively available in social media that can be used to investigate, whether user generated content is useful and can be helpful in negative link prediction problem [30].
- Both the theories, social balance and status are applicable only when a link participates in some triads, which is not always true in the case of real world networks which are sparse and links may or may not participate in the triads [15]. Hence, the prediction accuracy will be compromised in these cases. Thus, new psychology social theories like Emotional Information, Diffusion of Innovations and Individual Personality could be very helpful for studying the problem of signed link formation [3].

- Another interesting research direction is to study link analysis in dynamic signed networks by deploying the social theories [3].
- Due to the dearth of publicly available datasets with ground truth information it is difficult to analyze and comprehend the performance of various algorithms on SSNs for different tasks [15]. Furthermore, the signed directed dataset having integration of users attributes with links is also not available. Thus, the focus of research community can also be concentrated on development such datasets.

References

1. Amelio, A., Pizzuti, C.: Community mining in signed networks: a multiobjective approach. In: International Conference Proceedings of IEEE/ACM on ASONAM, pp. 95–99 (2013)
2. Anchuri, P., Magdon-Ismail, M.: Communities and balance in signed networks: a spectral approach. In: International Conference Proceedings of IEEE/ACM on ASONAM, pp. 235–242 (2012)
3. Beigi, G., Tang, J., Liu, H.: Signed link analysis in social media networks. arXiv preprint arXiv:1603.06878 (2016)
4. Brzozowski, M.J., Hogg, T., Szabo, G.: Friends and foes: ideological social networking. In: Conference Proceedings of SIGCHI on Human Factors in Computing Systems, pp. 817–820 (2008)
5. Cartwright, D., Harary, F.: Structural balance: a generalization of Heider's theory. Psychol. Rev. **63**(5), 277 (1956)
6. Chen, J., Wang, H., Wang, L., Liu, W.: A dynamic evolutionary clustering perspective: community detection in signed networks by reconstructing neighbor sets. Phys. A: Stat. Mech. Appl. **447**, 482–492 (2016)
7. Costa, G., Ortale, R.: Model-based collaborative personalized recommendation on signed social rating networks. ACM Trans. Internet Technol. **16**(3), 20 (2016)
8. Doreian, P., Mrvar, A.: A partitioning approach to structural balance. Soc. Netw. **18**(2), 149–168 (1996)
9. Falher, G.L., Cesa-Bianchi, N., Gentille, C., Vitale, F.: On the troll-trust model for edge sign prediction in social networks. arXiv preprint arXiv:1606.00182 (2016)
10. Ferligoj, A., Kramberger, A.: An analysis of the slovene parliamentary parties network. In: Ferligoj, A., Kramberger, A. (eds.) Developments in Statistics and Methodology, pp. 209–216. FDV, Ljubljana (1996). Metodološki zvezki 12
11. Gangal, V., Narwekar, A., Ravindran, B., Narayanam, R.: Trust and distrust across coalitions: shapley value based centrality measures for signed networks. In: AAAI, pp. 4212–4219 (2016)
12. Guha, R., Kumar, R., Raghavan, P., Tomkins, A.: Propagation of trust and distrust. In: International Conference Proceedings of WWW, pp. 403–412 (2004)
13. Guo, L., Gao, F.: How do signs organize in directed signed social networks? arXiv preprint arXiv:1606.00228 (2016)
14. Heider, F.: Attitudes and cognitive organization. J. Psychol. **21**(1), 107–112 (1946)
15. Javari, A., Jalili, M.: Cluster-based collaborative filtering for sign prediction in social networks with positive and negative links. ACM Trans. Intell. Syst. Technol. **5**(2), 24 (2014)
16. Kant, V., Bharadwaj, K.K.: Fuzzy computational models of trust and distrust for enhanced recommendations. Int. J. Intell. Syst. **28**(4), 332–365 (2013)

17. Kunegis, J., Lommatzsch, A., Bauckhage, C.: The slashdot zoo: mining a social network with negative edges. In: International Conference Proceedings on WWW, pp. 741–750 (2009)
18. Lancichinetti, A., Fortunato, S., Kertész, J.: Detecting the overlapping and hierarchical community structure in complex networks. New J. Phys. **11**(3), 033015 (2009)
19. Leskovec, J., Huttenlocher, D., Kleinberg, J.: Predicting positive and negative links in online social networks. In: International Conference Proceedings on WWW, pp. 641–650 (2010)
20. Leskovec, J., Huttenlocher, D., Kleinberg, J.: Signed networks in social media. In: Conference Proceedings of SIGCHI on Human Factors in Computing Systems, pp. 1361–1370 (2010)
21. Liben-Nowell, D., Kleinberg, J.: The link-prediction problem for social networks. J. Am. Soc. Inf. Sci. Technol. **58**(7), 1019–1031 (2007)
22. Liu, C., Liu, J., Jiang, Z.: A multiobjective evolutionary algorithm based on similarity for community detection from signed social networks. IEEE Trans. Cybern. **44**(12), 2274–2287 (2014)
23. Moshirpour, M., Chelmis, C., Prasanna, V., Saravanan, M., Karthikeyan, P., Arathi, A., Mohammad, H.: Advances in social networks analysis and mining. In: International Conference Proceedings of IEEE on ASONAM (2013)
24. Newman, M.E.: Modularity and community structure in networks. Proc. Natl. Acad. Sci. **103**(23), 8577–8582 (2006)
25. Patidar, A., Agarwal, V., Bharadwaj, K.K.: Predicting friends and foes in signed networks using inductive inference and social balance theory. In: International Conference Proceedings of IEEE on ASONAM, pp. 384–388 (2012)
26. Pitsilis, G., Knapskog, S.J.: Social trust as a solution to address sparsity-inherent problems of recommender systems. arXiv preprint arXiv:1208.1004 (2012)
27. Read, K.E.: Cultures of the central highlands, New Guinea. Southwest. J. Anthropol. **10**(1), 1–43 (1954)
28. Symeonidis, P., Tiakas, E.: Transitive node similarity: predicting and recommending links in signed social networks. WWW **17**(4), 743–776 (2014)
29. Tang, J., Aggarwal, C., Liu, H.: Recommendations in signed social networks. In: International Conference Proceedings on WWW, pp. 31–40 (2016)
30. Tang, J., Chang, S., Aggarwal, C., Liu, H.: Negative link prediction in social media. In: International Conference Proceedings of ACM on Web Search and Data Mining, pp. 87–96 (2015)
31. Wu, Z., Aggarwal, C.C., Sun, J.: The troll-trust model for ranking in signed networks. In: International Conference Proceedings of ACM on Web Search and Data Mining, pp. 447–456 (2016)
32. Yang, B., Cheung, W., Liu, J.: Community mining from signed social networks. IEEE Trans. Knowl. Data Eng. **19**(10), 1333–1348 (2007)
33. Yang, S.H., Smola, A.J., Long, B., Zha, H., Chang, Y.: Friend or frenemy? Predicting signed ties in social networks. In: International Conference Proceedings of ACM SIGIR on Research and Development in Information Retrieval, pp. 555–564 (2012)

Text Document Clustering Based on Neural K-Mean Clustering Technique

Daljeet Kaur[✉] and Jagpuneet Kaur Bajwa

Department of Computer Science, Punjabi University, Patiala, India
daljeet.pawra@gmail.com, jagpuneetbajwa@gmail.com

Abstract. Data clustering is a significant tool for applications like search engines and document browsers. It gives the user an overall vision of the information contained in the data sets. The well-known techniques of data clustering do not look for exact problems of clustering like high dimensionality of the dataset, large size of the datasets and to understand the ability of the cluster description. The work done before does not have the inbuilt property of clustering, so, here for extracting the features from the document, the clusters of different classes present in the document are taken. In the proposed work, this problem can be solved by using similarity technique on neighbors in addition to K- means method.

Keywords: Document clustering · Similarity · K-Means Clustering · Accuracy

1 Introduction

Data Clustering divides the documents into groups such that the closeness among the documents of the same gathering is augmented and the comparability among the data of various groups is minimized. Document clustering idea is utilized as a part of different regions like data recovery, content mining and so on. At first, it was explored to enhance the accuracy in the data recovery frameworks and finishes it up as an effective approach to discover the closest neighbor of a document. Despite the fact for a drawn out stretch of time, examination has been completed in Document Clustering. It is still entangled to tackle the issue. The current data recovery frameworks like Boolean model functions estimated when the growth of information is exactly known for exact documents. In Boolean model, a data is spoken to as an arrangement of catchphrases. Inquiries are spoken to as Boolean articulations of catchphrases.

They are associated by the administrators AND, OR, and NOT to show the extent of these administrators including the sections [1]. The Boolean model is extremely inflexible internet searcher model. The positioning of data is extremely troublesome on the grounds that the coordinated documents fulfill just the question to the same degree. The development of inquiry for the vast majority of the clients are additionally troublesome and if the extent of the data gathering is expanded, the intricacy for recovering the data will likewise be expanded. The difficulties confronted in the Document Clustering are: selecting fitting components of the data that ought to be utilized for grouping, selecting the suitable likeness measure among the documents, selecting the proper clustering technique using the aforementioned comparability measure,

© Springer Nature Singapore Pte Ltd. 2017
M. Singh et al. (Eds.): ICACDS 2016, CCIS 721, pp. 336–344, 2017.
DOI: 10.1007/978-981-10-5427-3_36

actualizing the clustering calculation in a productive approach to make it straightforward regarding required CPU and memory assets to discover a route for surveying the nature of the performed clustering. In this work, K-Means Clustering is utilized for grouping the documents with high measurements (Fig. 1).

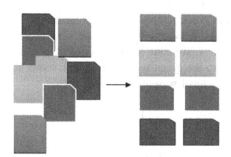

Fig. 1. Document clustering having same properties

2 Literature Survey

In Erk and Padó [2] "An organized Vector Space Model for word significance in connection", the registering vector space representations for the importance of word events are considered. It is suggested that the current models for this assignment don't consider syntactic structure adequately and shown a novel organized Vector Space Model that addresses the above issues by fusing the selectional inclinations for words contention positions. So, linguistic structure is incorporated into the calculation of word significance in setting the model that performs best in class for demonstrating the logical ampleness of rewords. Mitchell and Lapata [3] "Vector-based models of semantic arrangement" proposed a system for speaking to the importance of expressions and sentences in vector space. The exploratory results exhibit that the multiplicative models are better than the added substance choices when thought about against human judgments. Erk [4] "A basic, comparability based model for selectional inclinations" given another, straightforward model for the programmed incitement of selectional inclinations, utilizing corpus-based semantic likeness measurements. Concentrating on the errand of semantic part marking, the authors have figure selectional inclinations for semantic parts. Last result demonstrates that the comparability based model gives lower mistake rates. Steinbach et al. [5] "A Comparison of Document Clustering strategies" looked at the two fundamental ways to deal with Document Clustering, Agglomerative Hierarchical Clustering and K-Means. The outcomes shows that the bisecting K-Means method is superior to the standard K-Means approach and on a par with or superior to the various leveled approaches that have tried for an assortment of group assessment.

3 Ranking of Documents

There are s distinct terms and are denoted by the vocabulary or index terms. The vector space is formed by these "orthogonal". Dimension = s = | vocabulary | Each term, x, in a document or query, y, is given a real valued weight, wxy. Queries and documents are represented as s-dimensional vectors: $dy = (w1y, w2y,...,wsy)$. In the Vector Space Model [2], a collection of n documents can be represented by a term-document matrix. The "weight" of a term in the document is corresponding to an entry in the matrix. If it is zero, the term has no significant in the document else it does not exist in the document. With respect to the given weighting model, terms are weighted which may include global weighting, local weighting or both [6].

$$
\begin{array}{cccc}
 & T1 & T2 & T3 \\
D1 & w11 & w21 & w31 \\
D2 & w12 & w22 & w32 \\
D3 & w13 & w23 & w33 \\
\end{array}
$$

With local weights, the term weights are represented as term frequencies, sf. On using global weights, the term's weight is given by IDF values. In this work, Salton's Vector Space Model [3] is used which incorporates both global and local weights. So, it is called as sf * IDF weighting a term's weight = sf * IDF.

4 K Means Algorithm

K-Means [7] is one of a partitional clustering algorithm. It performs iterative relocation to partition a dataset into clusters, locally minimizing the average squared distance between the cluster centers and the data points. The objective of K-Means is to reduce the sum of distance from every data point to its closest center. Let $\{cx\}kx = 1$ be the centroids of k clusters. Let $\eta(.)$ be the assignment function. Then $\eta(x) = y$ means the xth item is assigned to the yth cluster. K-Means reduces the following objective.

$$
n2n(x) = \mathop{\mathrm{argmin}}_{c,n} \sum_{x=1} \left| e_x - c_{n(x)} \right|
$$

Lowering the objective function leads to more compact clusters, where each item gets closer to its cluster centroid. Finding the global optima for the K-Means objective function is an NP-complete problem [GJW82].

5   Simulation Model

The whole simulation is being done in MATLAB 2010a environment in which for document clustering [6] k means and neural network has been utilized.

Similarity Algorithm: 1

```
loadalldata
total_documents=get(handles.popupmenu1,'Value');
SimilarityFound = [];
a = 0;
fori=1:total_documents
try
for j = i+1 : 6
a = a+1;
SimilarityFound(a,1) = i;
SimilarityFound(a,2) = j;
SimilarityFound(a,3)= Similar(Data{1,i},Data{1,j});
end
fori = 1 : numel(Variables)
    b = 0;
    c = 1;
CheckPoint = 0;
    Point = 0;
while b~=r && c~=2
  if b ==r
c = c+1;
b = 0;
end
b = b+1;
if Variables(i)==SimilarityFound(b,c)
CheckPoint = CheckPoint+ SimilarityFound(b,3);
 Point = Point+1;
end
end
 Match = CheckPoint/Point;
if Match>Val
 y = y+1;
Cluster(1,y) = Variables(i);
else
z =z+1;
Cluster(2,z) = Variables(i);
End
end
```

Above method describes the similarity method for document clustering based on checkpoints.

Feature Extraction Algorithm: 2

```
Extracted = generator(Data2);
NewData = generator(Data1);
Values = 0;
for j = 1 : numel(NewData)
value = 0;
for k = 1 : numel(Extracted)
ifNewData(j)==Extracted(k)
value = 1;
end
end
if value == 1
Values = Values +1;
end
end
end
```

Above algorithm describes the method to find the features of clustered documents.

Feature Vector Generator Algorithm:3

```
fori = 1 : numel(docs)
   Words = docs(i);
WordsAscii = cell2mat(Words);
WordAscii = double(WordsAscii);
number = 0;
GeneratedWeight = '';
    Value = 1;
    a =1;
for j = 1 : numel(WordAscii)
  WordChar = char(WordAscii(j));
  for k = 1 : numel(caps)
  ifstrcmp(caps(k),WordChar)
  number = k;
  end
  end
  for l = 1 : numel(small)
  ifstrcmp(small(l),WordChar)
  number = l;
  end
  end
  New = num2str(number);
  GeneratedWeight = strcat(GeneratedWeight,New);
  end
  Check = 0;
  for d = 1 : numel(GeneratedWeight)
  Ch = str2double(GeneratedWeight(d));
   Check = Check+Ch;
  end
  Weight(i) = Check
```

Above method describes the process of feature vector generation.

6 Simulation Flowchart

Flowchart shows the working model of proposed work in which document clustering has been done using k means clustering in MATLAB environment. Firstly document uploading will be doe then feature extraction will be done on various features. After that similarity will be found using proposed method and in the end FRA, FRR and accuracy will be measured (See Fig. 2).

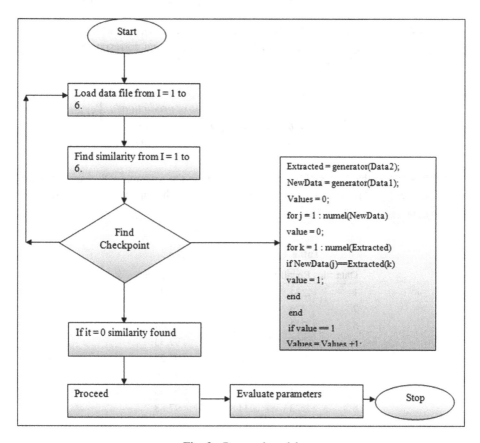

Fig. 2. Proposed model

7 Results and Discussion

The whole simulation is being done in MATLAB 2010a environment and the performance measurement is being done using Recall rate, precision rate and accuracy.

i. **Accuracy:** Accuracy is the whole correctness of the model. It is calculated as the sum of correct classifications of class x divided by the total number of classifications of class x. It is defined as:

$$Accuracy(x) = \left(\frac{sum\ of\ correct\ classification}{total\ number\ of\ classification} \right) \times 100$$

ii. **Precision:** Precision is the proportion of the examples which truly have class x among all those which are classified as class x. This is defined as:

$$Precision(x) = \left(\frac{number\ of\ correctly\ classified\ instances\ of\ classx}{number\ of\ instances\ classified\ as\ belonging\ to\ classx} \right) \times 100$$

iii. **Recall:** It is a measure of the ability of a prediction model to select instances of a certain class from a data set also called as sensitivity and corresponds to the true positive rate. It is defined as:

$$Recall(x) = \left(\frac{numbers\ of\ true\ positive\ predictions}{numbers\ of\ true\ positive\ predictions + numbers\ off\ alse\ negative\ predictions} \right) 100$$

Table 1 shows the values of the parameters used in the research with respect to data files. The average of recall rate is 0.243278. Precision rate has an average of 0.1325 and accuracy has 97.49 as average.

Table 1. Parameter comparison

Data file	Recall rate	Precision rate	Accuracy
1	.254	.11	97.34
2	.276	.14	97.66
3	.222	.16	97.44
4	.235	.12	97.33
5	.234	.15	97.22
6	.245	.18	97.66
7	.2345	.11	97.55
8	.222	.11	97.88
9	.267	.12	97.33

Figure 3 shows the graphical representation of Recall rate and the Precision rate. Blue line is for recall rate and red shows the precision rate. Recall rate values lies from 0.254 to 0.267 whereas the values of precision rate lies from 0.11 to 0.12. Recall rate and Precision rate should be less for the reliable work. The values obtained in the research for precision and recall clearly shows the improvement as compare to the previously implemented work.

Recall and Precision Rate Graph

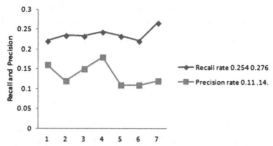

Fig. 3. Recall and precision comparison graph (Colour figure online)

Figure 4 is for the accuracy. The value of accuracy lies from 97.34 to 97.33. Betterment in the accuracy is shown in the implemented work.

Methods	Accuracy
Proposed	97%
Traditional [8]	91%

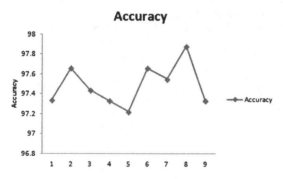

Fig. 4. Accuracy graph

8 Conclusion and Future Scope

Classification of documents into predefined categories has become the crucial topic in digital world. This paper discussed the implementation details of a document classification system based similarity measures and k means algorithm. This is a new technique having advantages over the other clustering systems as it can handle vague and imprecise queries of user very well. Similarity measure technique based on neural network is better for handling vague, uncertain and imprecise queries. From result simulation, it has been seen that proposed methodology has provided good results on the basis of proposed metrics. Future scope of this work lies in the comparison of proposed work with other clustering methods like fuzzy clustering, PSO based clustering etc.

References

1. Donoho, D.L.: High dimensional data analysis: the curses and blessings of dimensionality. In: American Math. Society Conference: Mathematical Challenges of the 21st Century, Los Angeles, CA, pp. 6–11, August 2000
2. Erk, K., Padó, S.: A structured vector space model for word meaning in context. In: Proceedings of the Conference on Empirical Methods in Natural Language Processing (EMNLP-08), Honolulu, pp. 897–906 (2008)
3. Mitchel, J., Lapata, M.: Vector-based models of semantic composition. In: Proceedings of ACL, pp. 236–244 (2008)
4. Erk, K.: A Simple, similarity-based model for selectional preferences. In: Proceedings of ACL, pp. 216–223 (2007)
5. Steinbach, M., Karypis, G., Kumar, V.: A comparison of document clustering techniques. Technical report, Department of Computer Science and Engineering, University of Minnesota (2010)
6. Jajoo, P.: Document clustering. Thesis, Department of Computer Science & Engineering Indian Institute of Technology Kharagpur (2008)
7. Jaganathan, P., Jaiganesh, S.: An improved K-means algorithm combined with particle swarm optimization approach for efficient web document clustering. In: 2013 International Conference on Green Computing, Communication and Conservation of Energy (ICGCE). IEEE (2013)
8. Sudha, A.: Text document clustering using dimension reduction technique. Int. J. Appl. Eng. Res. **11**, 4770–4774 (2016). ISSN 0973-4562

Informatics

An Accelerated Approach for Generalized Entropy Based MRI Image Segmentation

Anushikha Jain[✉], Maninder Singh Nehra, and Manoj Kuri

Department of Computer Science, Government Engineering College Bikaner,
Bikaner, India
jainanushikha@gmail.com

Abstract. Image segmentation, a major research class is frequently governed by the way of two foremost parameters, associated with a specified segmentation procedure: threshold decision and seed-point determination. Various methods such as the histogram based processes, entropy headquartered process, business measure approaches and so on. These are well recognized for threshold choice within the image segmentation issues. In this article, threshold determination is done on the basis of extraordinary entropy measures on each of grey scale and color images. Comparative analysis of the Shannon and non-Shannon entropies (Renyi, Havrda-Charvat, Kapur and Vajda) is done to receive an appropriate threshold worth for the perfect image segmentation. It's concluded via the simulation experiments performed on MRI images, that the role of the smallest minima obtained within the entropy versus grey-degree plot is different for every entropy measure. The threshold values received from these plots is accordingly elegant on the specific definition of the entropy chosen, which in flip influences segmentation outcome. It's further observed that the segmentation results acquired, making use of Havrda-Charvat entropy measure is healthier than other entropy measures.

Keywords: Entropy · Image segmentation · Renyi · Havrda · Vajda · Kapur

1 Introduction

Image segmentation entails the division or separation of the image into areas of equivalent attributes and is a vital step in a series of processes aimed toward working out a given picture [1–10]. The intention of segmentation is to simplify and change the representation of a photo into anything that's more meaningful and easy to analyze. Photo segmentation is as a rule used to find objects and limits (traces, curves, and so on.) in pics. More precisely, the picture segmentation is the procedure of assigning a label to every pixel in a snapshot such that pixels with the identical label share specific visible traits [11]. The outcomes of photo segmentation is a collection of segments that at the same time cover the entire picture, or set of contours extracted from the image. Each and every of the pixels in vicinity is similar with respect to some characteristic or computed property like color, depth or texture. Adjacent regions are tremendously specific with recognize to the equal attribute(s). Functions of photograph segmentation include identification of objects, feature extraction and so on [1–10]. Segmentation of

© Springer Nature Singapore Pte Ltd. 2017
M. Singh et al. (Eds.): ICACDS 2016, CCIS 721, pp. 347–356, 2017.
DOI: 10.1007/978-981-10-5427-3_37

simple grey-level photos additionally presents valuable information about the surfaces in the scene [1].

This paper discusses an introduction to MRI (Magnetic Resonance imaging) and photo segmentation systems. Part II shares a short introduction on MRI, Sect. 3 discusses the necessity and methodology of Segmentation and part IV deals with outcome retrieved for MRI image segmentation using entropy founded process.

2   Magnetic Resonance Imaging (MRI)

In the beginning it's described how magnetic resonance can also be established with a pair of magnets and a compass. The level of abstraction already raises toward the end of this primary section, but despair thee not: as the complexity rises, so shall it fall once more. Complete working out of previous sections will not be a prerequisite for future reap.

If a compass occurs to search out itself close a robust magnet, the compass needle will align with the area. In an ordinary pocket compass, the needle is embedded in liquid to dampen its oscillations. Without liquid, the needle will vibrate via the north course for a period before coming to relaxation. The frequency of the oscillations is dependent upon the magnetic discipline and of the strength of the magnetic needle. The extra powerful these are, rapid the vibrations might be. In an MR scanner, the powerful magnet is totally robust for factors in an effort to be defined under. The magnetic field across is fairly susceptible in comparison.

Magnetic resonance is just not a quantum phenomenon, it's generally offered, although such. It may be described with quantum mechanics, however method necessitates giant heritage competencies. MR can replacement be described classically, for the reason that it may be shown that classical description of magnetic dipoles behavior within the magnetic discipline is an instantaneous outcome of quantum mechanics.

2.1   Imaging

To this point, it has been mentioned how physique can also be dropped at emit radio waves, however it has now not been mentioned how radio waves from one position in the body will also be distinct from radio waves emitted at yet another function, which is instead essential for imaging.

The most apparent ways for MR imaging could be purported to be projection or the utilization of antennas that may notice where within the physique the radio waves are emitted. The x-ray and natural microscopy are examples of such "optical" science, and it's going to be naturally obvious to enlarge this form of imaging to the MR. Optical science are, nonetheless, "wavelength limit", it can't be used to, which means that collect pix more certain than approximately one wavelength. In different words: as a result of primary explanations, one can't be localize the supply of radio waves extra precisely than about one wavelength when using lenses or different course-sensitive antennas. The radio waves utilized in MR scanning are generally a number of meters long, so with optical systems we are able to infrequently assess whether or not the sufferer is in or external the scanner. Optical systems from binoculars, eyesight, CT, X-ray, ultrasound and microscopes, are therefore nearly vain for MR-imaging, and fundamentally special precept is required. This precept was offered through Paul Lauterbur in 1973, and it resulted in the Nobel Prize in medicine in 2003. In actual fact, Lauterbur made protons provide their possess areas away through making the frequency of the emitted radio waves reflect the function. Lauterbur shared the prize with Sir Peter Mansfield, who additionally contributed to the development of systems utilized in magnetic resonance imaging (MRI).

2.2 Principles

A requirement for MR imaging is that the scanner is geared up with further electromagnets referred to as "gradient coils" that rationale linear discipline variant. Path and strength will also be altered as favored. The spatial localization happens consistent with unique standards, of which the simplest is slice determination. Other types of coding involve the so-called k-space algorithms.

2.3 Extension to More Dimension – k-Space

Viewed a crisis with hydrogen nuclei positioned as pearls on a string. We will now extend to 2 dimension and remember the concern in a slice of tissue with uniform water content material after a gradient has been applied (Fig. 1):

Fig. 1. Phase roll of MRI

The figure exhibit a phase roll in the gradient course (upwards and correct). The "thick arrow" on the middle of the drawing suggests the web magnetization, that is, the sum of all the small magnetization vectors (a vector is an arrow). It's seen that the quantity is relatively small, in view that there is a roughly equally many arrows pointing in all guidelines. As in the one-dimensional case, there should be a gigantic internet magnetization even after a gradient has been applied. This occurs if there, as proven in following figure, is structure in the article that suits the section roll (the dots mark places where there aren't any protons) (Fig. 2).

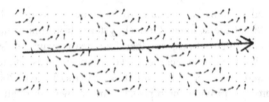

Fig. 2. Spin pattern of MRI

For the sake of clarity, spin patterns in the following can be proven in two exceptional approaches.

Instead than displaying arrows pointing in quite a lot of instructions, segment rolls will likely be proven as an intensity variant as in the figure in the middle, the place color displays the course of the arrows2 (Fig. 3):

Fig. 3. Gradient pattern in MRI

For each and every such pattern, vector k is assigned, whose course suggests the path of alternate and whose size shows the density of stripes as proven to the proper.

Through applying gradients, we "draw" patterns in the sufferer, one at a time, in a predetermined order special for the chosen sequence. All recommendations of the stripes and all densities of stripes are drawn up unless a designated limit. As said, lower back radio wave signal depends upon the similarity between object and pattern and it's registered as an operate of k.

3 Entropy Based Image Segmentation

The easiest method of photo segmentation is known as the thresholding procedure. This method is headquartered on threshold worth to convert in to a gray-scale snapshot into a binary image. Optimum threshold separates one of a kind objects from historical past [15].

Threshold resolution in a picture segmentation is an extraordinarily difficult undertaking. It provides foremost expertise about image and play principal function in segmentation of photo. A couple of one of a kind methods for opting for a threshold exist; users can manually choose a threshold value, or thresholding algorithm can compute a value routinely, which is called as automated thresholding [11–15]. A simple approach could be to decide on the mean or median worth, intent being that if the thing pixels are brighter than the history, they must even be brighter than natural [11]. An extra subtle method possibly to create a histogram of the photograph pixel intensities and valley factor is used as a threshold [15].

Various threshold selection techniques are well known in the literature.

(a) Basic Global Thresholding.
(b) Clustering methods.
(c) Histogram-based method.
(d) Region growing method.

Right here in this work we will have a foremost discussion on Entropy situated photo segmentation approaches.

3.1 Entropy Based Image Segmentation

The methodology of photograph segmentation utilizing the gray level co-occurrence matrix and Shannon entropy measure is discussed in [5]. On this work we lengthen this system utilizing the co-incidence matrix with non- Shannon entropy measures (reminiscent of Renyi, Havrda-Charvat, Kapur and Vajda entropy) on MRI portraits. The fundamental steps of the algorithm are reproduced here for the sake of convenience [5]:

(a) To start with, the co-occurrence matrix [5] of the image to be segmented is computed for each color channel.
(b) The probability distribution is then calculated from its co-occurrence matrix.
(c) Entropy operate for each and every entropy definitions, as outlined beneath, are then calculated for every given image to be segmented utilizing the probability distribution.
(d) The numbers of minima points are decided from the entropy function versus gray degree plot. The grey and color element stage comparable to the smallest minima could also be taken as a threshold for snapshot segmentation issues.

Subsequent, we talk about unique entropy measures [8–11], which can be used on this work for a comparative study in photo segmentation issues.

3.2 Different Entropy Measures

(1) Shannon Entropy

Shannon's entropy measure presents an absolute limit on the pleasant viable lossless compression of a signal beneath special constraints [3]. It's outlined as:

$$H_s\left(p_{m_1,m_2}\right) = -\sum_{m_1}\sum_{m_2} p_{m_1,m_2} \log p_{m_1,m_2}$$

Where p is the probability distribution associated with the two-D random variable. On this work, we've computed the values from the entries of the gray stage co-occurrence matrix [5, 6] of the given image as given through the relation where, represents the picture dimensions along x and y directions respectively. The entropy perform for purpose of the calculation of threshold for image segmentation is then computed from the expression given in Table 2, which represents the maximum number of gray level present in a particular image.

(2) Kapur Entropy

Kapur's entropy of order and type defined as [3, 8]:

$$H_s p(m1, m2) = \left(\frac{\sum_{m1} \sum_{m2} p_{m1,m2}^{\alpha+\beta-1}}{\sum_{m1} \sum_{m2} p_{m1,m2}^{\beta}} - 1 \right)(2^{1-\alpha} - 1)^{-1}$$

And, corresponding Functional Representation is given in Table 1 and entropy function in Table 2.

Table 1. Functional representation

Entropy function	Functional representation
Shannon	$\sum_{\forall m2} \sum_{\forall m1} p_{m1,m2} * \log(p_{m1,m2})$
Renyi	$H_s p(m1, m2) = \frac{1}{1-\alpha} \log \sum_{m1} \sum_{m2} (pm1m2)^{\alpha}$
Havrda	$H_s p(m1, m2) = \frac{1}{2^{\alpha-1}} \sum_{m1} \sum_{m2} p_{m1m2}^{\alpha} - 1$
Kapur	$H_k p(m1, m2) = \left(\frac{\sum_{m1} \sum_{m2} p_{m1,m2}^{\alpha+\beta-1}}{\sum_{m1} \sum_{m2} p_{m1,m2}^{\beta}} - 1 \right)(2^{1-\alpha} - 1)^{-1}$
Vajda	$Hv(p_{m1m2}) = \left(\frac{\sum_{m1} \sum_{m2} p_{m1,m2}^{\alpha}}{\sum_{m1} \sum_{m2} p_{m1,m2}} - 1 \right)(2^{1-\alpha} - 1)^{-1}$

(3) Vajda Entropy

Vajda entropy measure is a distinct case of Kapur's entropy the place is taken. It provides the expertise of rapid calculations over Kapur's entropy measure.

And, corresponding Functional Representation is given in Table 1 and entropy function in Table 2.

(4) Renyi Entropy

The Renyi entropy which is a generalization of Shannon entropy is considered one of a household of functional for quantifying the diversity, uncertainty or the randomness of a process. It's outlined as [3, 10]:

$$H_s p(m1, m2) = \frac{1}{1-\alpha} \log \sum_{m1} \sum_{m2} (pm1m2)^{\alpha}$$

Table 2. Entropy function

Entropy function	Entropy at grey level t
Shannon	$-\sum\limits_{m1=0}^{t}\sum\limits_{m2=t+1}^{L-1} p_{m1,m2}\log(p_{m1,m2}) - \sum\limits_{m1=t+1}^{L-1}\sum\limits_{m2=0}^{t} p_{m1,m2}\log p_{m1,m2}$
Renyi	$Entropy(t) = -\dfrac{\log(\sum\limits_{m1=0}^{t}\sum\limits_{m2=t+1}^{L-1}(pm1,m2)^{\alpha})}{1-\alpha}$
Havrda	$H_{hc}(pm1,m2) = \dfrac{\sum\limits_{m1}\sum\limits_{m2} p_{m1,m2}^{\alpha} - 1}{2^{1-\alpha}-1}$
Kapur	$Entropy(t) = \sum\limits_{m1=0}^{t}\sum\limits_{m2=t+1}^{L-1}\left(\dfrac{p_{m1,m2}^{\alpha+\beta-1}}{p_{m1,m2}^{\beta}}-1\right)\left(2^{1-\alpha}-1\right)^{-1} +$ $\sum\limits_{m1=t+1}^{L-1}\sum\limits_{m2=0}^{t}\left(\dfrac{p_{m1,m2}^{\alpha+\beta-1}}{p_{m1,m2}^{\beta}}-1\right)\left(2^{1-\alpha}-1\right)^{-1}$
Vajda	$Entropy(t) = \left(\dfrac{\sum\limits_{m1=0}^{t}\sum\limits_{m2=t+1}^{L-1} p_{m1,m2}^{\alpha}}{\sum\limits_{m1=0}^{t}\sum\limits_{m2=t+1}^{L-1} p_{m1,m2}}-1\right)\left(2^{1-\alpha}-1\right)^{-1} +$ $\left(\dfrac{\sum\limits_{m1=t+1}^{L-1}\sum\limits_{m2=0}^{t} p_{m1,m2}^{\alpha}}{\sum\limits_{m1=t+1}^{L-1}\sum\limits_{m2=0}^{t} p_{m1,m2}}-1\right)\left(2^{1-\alpha}-1\right)^{-1}$

(5) Havrda-Charvat Entropy

The Havrda–Charvát entropy of degree introduced through Havrda and Charvát and in a while modified by using Daróczy is more commonly utilized in statistical physics and is outlined as follows [3]:

$$H_s p(m1,m2) = \frac{1}{2^{\alpha-1}}\sum_{m1}\sum_{m2} p_{m1m2}^{\alpha} - 1$$

And, corresponding Functional Representation is given in Table 1 and entropy function in Table 2.

4 Results and Simulation

Right here, we gift the simulation outcome performed in MATLAB on the "MRI" photos. The entropy of those portraits are computed using 2, 4, 6, 8, 10 and entropy versus grey stage plot is obtained for different definition of entropy and the plots are depicted for ease of reference. The snapshot is then segmented by smallest minima acquired from the entropy function versus grey degree plot. Bought simulation outcome are shown as beneath.

Here it is apparent that satisfactory extraction is performed by using Havrda established entropy method as shown by using Fig. 4b.

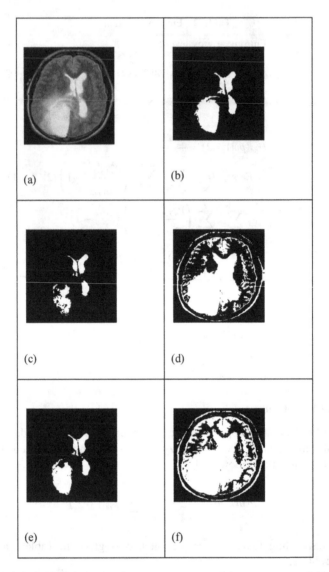

Fig. 4. (a) Original MRI image and rest are segmented images extracted by (b) Havrda (c) Kapur (d) Renyi (e) Shannon (f) Vajda entropies

5 Accelerated Approach

Code conversion method is utilized here, that is supported via MATLAB Coder unit. Generated C codes are re-simulated in Matlab atmosphere whose execution time was 0.102450 s at the same time in common matlab code execution time is 0.164932 s as shown in Figs. 5 and 6. Figure 7 indicates the code iteration report.

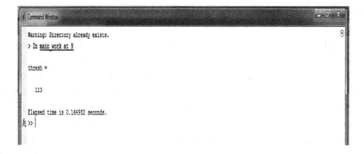

Fig. 5. Execution time of matlab code

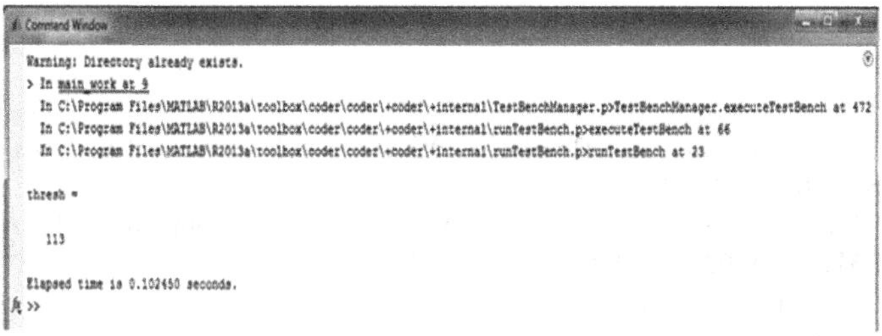

Fig. 6. Execution time of C code based matlab simulation

Fig. 7. C-code generated from MATLAB code

6 Conclusion and Future Scope

On this work, we now have investigated the problem of threshold resolution in picture segmentation hindrance, and quantitative evaluation of the pleasant of the improved photos using extraordinary entropy measures. Appropriate threshold choice is a problematic project in photo segmentation issues. A number of entropy measures for threshold decision reason in grey and color photograph segmentation problems are studied. Threshold resolution is done on the groundwork of one of a kind entropy measures on both grey scale and color images. Comparative be trained of the Shannon and non-Shannon entropies (Renyi, Havrda-Charvat, Kapur and Vajda) is done to obtain an appropriate threshold value for the reason of snapshot segmentation. And influence consequently retrieved proves that Havrda established image segmentation approach is exceptional for Tumor detection in MRI photos.

References

1. Weszka, J.S., Rosenfeld, A.: Threshold evaluation techniques. IEEE Trans. Syst. Man Cybern. **8**(8), 622–629 (1978)
2. Otsu, N.: A threshold selection method from gray-level histograms. IEEE Trans. Syst. Man Cybern. **SMC-9**(1), 62–66 (1979)
3. Patni, G.C., Jain, K.C.: Axiomatic characterization of some non-additive measures of information. Metrika **24**, 23–34 (1977)
4. Pavan, K.K., Rao, A.A., Rao, A.V.D., Sridhar, G.R.: Single pass seed selection algorithm. J. Comput. Sci. **6**(1), 60–66 (2010)
5. Chanda, B., Majumdar, D.: Digital Image Processing and Analysis. Prentice-Hall of India, New Delhi (2011)
6. Chanda, B., Majumder, D.D.: A note on the use of the gray level co-occurrence matrix in threshold selection. Sig. Process. **15**, 149–167 (1988). North-Holland
7. Jain, A.K.: Fundamentals of Digital Image Processing. Prentice- Hall of India, New Delhi (2010)
8. Kapur, J.N.: Generalized entropy of order α and type β. In: Mathematical Seminar, Delhi, pp. 78–94 (1967)
9. Sahoo, P.K., Arora, G.: Image thresholding using two-dimensional Tsallis–Havrda–Charvat entropy. Pattern Recogn. Lett. **27**, 520–528 (2006)
10. Sahoo, P.K., Wilkins, C., et al.: Threshold selection using Renyi's entropy. Pattern Recogn. **30**, 71–84 (1997)
11. Shapiro, L.G., Stockman, G.C.: Computer Vision, pp. 279–325. Prentice-Hall, New Jersey (2001)
12. Pham, D.L., Xu, C., Prince, J.L.: Current methods in medical image segmentation. Annu. Rev. Biomed. Eng. **2**, 315–337 (2000)
13. Mobahi, H., Rao, S., Yang, A., Sastry, S., Ma, Y.: Segmentation of natural images by texture and boundary compression. Int. J. Comput. Vis. (IJCV) **95**(1), 86–98 (2011)
14. Rao, S.R., Mobahi, H., Yang, A.Y., Sastry, S.S., Ma, Y.: Natural image segmentation with adaptive texture and boundary encoding. In: Zha, H., Taniguchi, R.-I., Maybank, S. (eds.) ACCV 2009. LNCS, vol. 5994, pp. 135–146. Springer, Heidelberg (2010). doi:10.1007/978-3-642-12307-8_13
15. Gonzalez, R.C., Woods, R.E., Eddins, S.L.: Digital Image Processing using MATLAB. McGraw-Hill, New Delhi (2011)

Automatic Face Naming Using Image Processing: A Review Study Based on Face Name Detection in Images or Videos

Pragya Baluni[1(✉)], S.K. Verma[2], and Y.P. Raiwani[3]

[1] Department of Computer Science and Engineering, THDC IHET,
Tehri Garhwal, India
pragyabaluni@ymail.com
[2] Department of Computer Science and Engineering, GBPEC, Pauri, India
skverma.gbpec@rediffmail.com
[3] Department of Computer Science and Engineering, HNBGU, Srinagar, India
yp_raiwani@yahoo.com

Abstract. Automatic character identification in images is essential for semantic image analysis such as indexing, summarization and retrieval. Face identification, however greatly characteristic to individuals, is an enormously troublesome errand in modernized vision. Structure is enthused about modified naming of people in different images or montage material with their character. A noteworthy testing issue due to the extensive assortment in intrapersonal appearance assortments in light of the fact that photometric variables, for instance, distinctive lighting tints, viewpoint point, and scale, or due to changes in expressions, or impediments, hairstyles, so appearances of each characters and the inadequacy vulnerability of available comment. The objective of this paper is to clarify the characteristics required in programmed face naming procedure and to review some of their recent studies.

Keywords: Automatic face naming · Face identification · Character recognition · Review · Feature extraction

1 Introduction

Recent studies on the area, propose not to utilize just the graphic or literary substance alone, yet to consolidate them both. With this methodology, face acknowledgment issue is disentangled to a face-name affiliation issue. Taking after these methodologies, in our strategy literary and visual data is joined to name faces. A directed algorithm is utilized for naming a predetermined number of classes having a place with all the more often showing up appearances. We partition the issue into 2 sub issues; one the more habitually seeming confronts the less-much of the time showing up countenances on the web images are named. Another the countenances that are not coordinated with any classification are then thought to be the less-as often as possible showing up appearances and named utilizing the literary substance. We extricated every one of the names from printed substance, and after that wipe out the ones used to name as often as

© Springer Nature Singapore Pte Ltd. 2017
M. Singh et al. (Eds.): ICACDS 2016, CCIS 721, pp. 357–368, 2017.
DOI: 10.1007/978-981-10-5427-3_38

possible showing up countenances some time recently. The rest of the names are the competitor classes for less as often as possible showing up countenances.

Face identification is a procedure that decides the area of a human face in a computerized image. In this venture, face recognition is the initial step. It includes catching images continuously from a camera and after that figuring out if or not the image contains facial elements. On the off chance that a face is distinguished in an image it is then highlighted in the image and went on to face acknowledgment. Fingerprints, hand geometry, iris checks, DNA examination and to some degree individual marks are all biometric identifiers. In any case, the stand out that does not defer or meddle with access is face acknowledgment. People distinguish others by their face and voice and in this manner are liable to be more alright with a framework that utilizations face and voice acknowledgment [2].

This makes face acknowledgment perfect for high activity regions which are interested in the overall population for e.g. airplane terminals and railroad stations, ATM's, open transportation and organizations of numerous types. Face acknowledgment gives a record of who was there. Since the record is stored in a database, known persons can be detected automatically and unknown persons checked quickly.

Face tracking and face clustering procedure as shown in Fig. 1 might fizzle because of impediment, low determination video, substantial movement, changed foundation and different conditions. Face identification of image is more simple than video. The circumstance is more terrible in video. This conveys commotions to the character identification in video. Additionally different performing artists assuming part for various periods of the same character name. There might be different represents, a ton of expression and light impact, dressing, wearing, even roll out up and hairstyle changes [3]. The significant intra-class difference, the similar individual name relates to the characteristics of massive variation presences. The assurance for the quantity of indistinguishable appearances is not trivial.

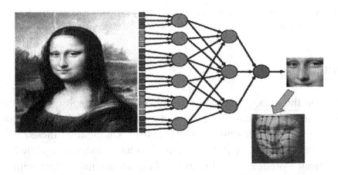

Fig. 1. Example of face recognition [1]

1.1 General Attributes for Face Naming

Choosing face tracker can be a troublesome assignment due to the accessibility of numerous face trackers. The application supplier must choose which face tracker is most appropriate to his/her individual needs and, obviously, the kind of video that he/she needs to use as the objective. As a rule, the critical issues are the tracker's velocity, vigor, and precision. Like the instance of numerous preparing apparatuses for communicate video, velocity is not the most basic issue on the grounds that disconnected handling is allowed in most video organizing and ordering exercises. Be that as it may, an ongoing face tracker is vital if the objective document depends on too huge an amount of video, say, 24 h of consistent video recording that requirement day by day organizing [15]. Additionally, the pace of the tracker is basic in most non-communicate video applications, e.g. HCI. There is dependably a tradeoff amongst velocity and execution related issues, for example, robustness and accuracy.

1.2 Image-Based Features

The aforementioned degradations manifested in biometric tests can be surveyed utilizing image highlights that are computationally inexpensive to compute. Automatic QA is basically tended to by breaking down spatial and temporal components that are demonstrative of the image content [16]. Highlights that are utilized widely as a part of current writing can be extensively isolated into four classifications:

- Orientation elements are acquired from edges in the image. If there should be an occurrence of the iris and face, edge data is generally utilized as elements for acknowledgment. Obscuring, brightening, and commotion corrupt edge data along these lines influence execution. Subsequently, introduction data can give a decent sign of the nature of a biometric sample.
- Power range is a transient measure of the force of the image signal. This measure means that the measure of data present in image area. Thus, otherworldly vitality is frequently registered for various image areas to acquire nearby evaluation of value.
- Intensity statistics are immediate measurable assessment of powers of pixels in the image. Normally, a factual measure, for example, Kurtosis or point spread function (PSF) estimation is utilized to evaluate obscuring or enlightenment corruption in the image. The measure can then be contrasted with the reference values got from perfect images to figure the degree of degradation.
- Wavelet transform gives both spatial and recurrence comprehension of the data content in every sub-band of the image. These are especially suited to learn the nearness of fine miniaturized scale edges in the iris area and to acquire nearby examination of value in various areas of image.

1.3 Facial Features

It's hard to accomplish a good precision rate of naming appearances for images caught under abandoned situation. Not just brightening, posture, center resolution of images source to bad naming in face acknowledgement systems, but too eye-classes, make-up, facial hairs, hairstyle a few other individual and atmosphere associated changes on the face, create acknowledgment troublesome for analysts of the range. With a specific end goal to lessen the impacts of such issues, highlight vector choices on facial depictions are essential. Two unique techniques for face representations are connected for this study. A novel methodology presented by Kumar et al. [13], and the another is the SIFT [17] descriptors extricated for 9 particular facial focuses, as its label shows a measure- invariant technique vigorous to stance, enlightenment, measure and so forth.

2 Background of the Study

As such, it is a significant requirement for mechanical accomplishments particularly in business and law implementation applications. Individuals have a tendency to enhance techniques for applications that need security and protection as opposed to utilizing passwords. Though diverse types of particular biometric identification are present, for example, iris or retinal or fingerprints, are expressed in the investigation of Duygulu et al. [4], these techniques depend on the support of the issue of individual. In this way, with the growing interest on innovative change, face acknowledgment is about to become an integral part of our lives.

The prominent individuals, for example, big names or government officials seem all the more often on the internet, consequently; gathering image testers for them is a moderately less demanding errand contrasted with the assignment of gathering image tests for individuals seem less-as often as possible on the web. With respect to certainties, in this study we concentrate on naming less every now and again showing up individuals who are seen alongside all the more as often as possible showing up individuals on the web. The procedure will be just to name the all the more as often as possible showing up individuals to start with, then name the less-regularly seeming ones by them, utilizing the textual content [5–7].

Ozkan and Duygulu in [8] relate a graphics based technique for naming appearances. Dissimilar to present face depictions with concern focuses, not just specific focuses on the face are utilized, additionally identified interest focuses are considered. Then again, the utilization of all recognized interest focuses on a face, instead quite compelling focuses; don't generally give the best result. At long last, utilizing their closeness diagram, the most comparative images are discovered by means of delivering the deepest subsection on that chart that drives the insignificant images to be removed.

Guillaumin et al. in [9] proposed a strategy of naming the faces from their database that comprises of newscast photographs with inscriptions by considering two situations, one is to discover faces for a solo query. The main methodology is a kNN technique with an edge and the additional method is to separate among the neighbors. With the utilization of nine specific facial elements, they beat the coordinating attention point's issue experienced in [10].

Le and Satoh in [11] present an unverified technique for explanations of countenances on the internet. Their technique comprises of 2 stages. The first stage is to source the information from the web and locate the deepest set by means of positioning the conveyance of visual likenesses and the 2nd stage is the grouping of the output query where coupled naming of appearances as craved individual or non-sought individual is resolved. This strategy is enhanced utilizing SVM alleged Lib-SVM [12].

Kumar et al., in [13], propose a technique for relationship of names to confront utilizing better reasonable dataset that is not the same as current face acknowledgment dataset in the feeling of countenances being caught "in nature". Their dataset comprises of 30.281 images identified from half a million captioned images.

Le et al. in [14] additionally centered on name-face affiliation; though as opposed to the overall methodology of doling out names to the countenances on the images, they intend a strategy which plans to accomplish a coordinated task for names and faces. They concoct this thought taking into account the case that not every one of the names extricated from literatures, or not every one of the countenances separated from images, have the same probability for being critical as far as having a relating face-image in light of the fact that the name is said, imagedness, or having a comparing name in light of the fact that the image contains the face, namedness. The tabular analysis of different face acknowledgment studies is appeared underneath in Table 1.

Table 1. Tabular analysis of different face acknowledgment studies.

Author name/year	Technique name	Methodology used	Results
Duygulu et al. (2002)	Object recognition as machine learning	Diverse types of particular biometric identification are used, for example, iris or retinal or fingerprints	To enhance techniques for applications that need security and protection as opposed to utilizing passwords
Ozkan and Duygulu (2006)	Graphics based technique	Utilization of all recognized interest focuses on a face, instead quite compelling focuses	The most comparative images are discovered by means of delivering the deepest subsection on that chart that drives the insignificant images to be removed
Guillaumin et al. (2008)	Automatic face naming with caption-based supervision	Proposed a strategy of naming the faces from their database that comprises of newscast photographs with inscription	With the utilization of nine specific facial elements, they beat the coordinating attention point's issue
Le and Satoh (2008)	Unsupervised face annotation by mining the web	Proposed strategy is enhanced utilizing SVM alleged Lib-SVM	Present an unverified technique for explanations of countenances on the internet
Kumar et al. (2009)	Attribute and simile classifiers for face verification	Propose a technique for relationship of names to confront utilizing better reasonable dataset	Dataset comprises of 30.281 images identified from half a million captioned images
Le et al. (2007)	Finding important people in large news video databases using multimodal and clustering analysis	A strategy which plans to accomplish a coordinated task for names and faces	Centered on name-face affiliation; though as opposed to the overall methodology of doling out names to the countenances on the images

3 Methodologies

3.1 Phase-Only Correlation (POC)

Phase-Only Correlation (POC) has been likewise called stage relationship, which has one of the image coordinating methods and has been effectively actualized to biometric confirmation and PC vision challenges. The POC capacity has been characterized as reverse Discrete Fourier change of the standardized cross force range. The tallness and location of the relationship top has been shown the likeness and translational development between images, individually. The algorithm utilizing POC has been proposed for the face acknowledgment [18]. The POC-based face acknowledgment algorithm has been taken after exceptionally basic methodology. To begin with, the face image has been standardized and additionally the rest venture of the LBP-based face acknowledgment algorithm. Following, an arrangement of the position focuses has been situated on the face image to assess the neighborhood piece similitude. The stage based correspondence coordinating has been utilized; the comparing point sets are acquired, where the relating point pair having low closeness esteem has been disposed of as an anomaly. At last, the coordinating score has been computed as the quantity of right relating point sets. In the event that the image has blocked district, the coordinating score of the POC coordinating has been diminished notwithstanding for the certified pair [19].

3.2 Local Binary Pattern (LBP)

Basically, the local binary pattern (LBP) had been intended for surface portrayal. It has expanded increasingly researchers "and faculties" consideration for its computational adequacy and high separation property additionally it has been invariant to monotonic dark scale changes which are essential for surface investigation. Other than that, the likelihood of preparing image continuously has been empowered by its computational straightforwardness which beats numerous other surface descriptors [20]. LBP is a standout amongst the best nearby component extractors, which removes surface elements of the photo by contrasting every pixel and nearest in a little neighborhood. Besides, there is no preparation necessity, which makes it quick and simple to incorporate into the new information sets. Besides, in light of the utilization of histograms as the capabilities, it has vigorous against revolution and scaling [18].

Additionally, the sample-image size measurement can be decreased to the quantity of histogram canisters. As the dim estimations of neighbors have been thought about, it is strong beside monotonic changes in the face image. Accordingly, LBP is one of the splendor obtuse descriptors. The strategy of the LBP based face acknowledgment algorithm is exceptionally straightforward. Initially, the face district has been recognized, the component focuses on the face have identified, and after that the scale, revolution and interpretation have standardized by position of highlight focuses. Next, LBP has been computed for every nearby piece image. At last, the coordinating score has been computed utilizing the weighted Chi square separation between histograms of LBPs [21] Different strides of LBP

i. Radius of 2 neighboring windows and total count of neighbors.
ii. Binary designs acquired by correlation among the middle pixel and its neighbors.
iii. Utilizing parallel ciphers to create the histograms and link them for every image sub-piece LPQ [20].

3.3   Local Phase Quantization (LPQ)

LPQ is a well-known histogram-based component extractor which has a place with the group of nearby surface descriptors, and played out the evaluation of stage in a neighborhood window at the pixel position. In recurrence space, Local stage investigation has been directed to a point by point shine coldhearted surface depiction of face images. LPQ has been additionally uncaring against image debasement, obscure impact, which happens for the most part in true applications, for example, video reconnaissance, which has been created by out of center of camera or item movement. LPQ has a typical splendor and obscure heartless component extractor. To utilize nearby stage quantization for face portrayal, it can be connected for the methodology of face acknowledgment [21]. To begin with the face image has been named with the LPQ administrator. At that point, the name image has been separated into non-covering rectangular areas of equivalent size and a histogram of marks has been figured autonomously inside every district. At last, the histograms from various districts have been connected to fabricate a worldwide depiction of the face. LPQ strategy has been given below [20]

   i. STFT at four particular frequencies incorporated a little space at the pixel location.
   ii. Based on the indication of genuine and nonexistent qualities, Binary quantization has been finished.
   iii. A histogram has been directed taking into account the 8-bit stream.
   iv. Finding the genuine and nonexistent coefficients for the four frequencies.

3.4   Local Binary Patterns & Nearest Feature Space (LBP&NFS)

The simple and efficient Nearest Feature Space (NFS) and Local Binary Patterns (LBP) technique classifiers that the great speculation capacity has joined to build another methodology for fulfilling the ongoing and power choice execution. The face image database got from web has been utilized for analyses. The handy results demonstrate that the model technique performs superior to anything conventional approaches as far as continuous productivity (0.7 s for each sample) and precision (72.5% Average Recognition Rate) NFS was initially shown by Jen Tzun and actualized in face acknowledgment. Basically, it has been an augmentation of nearest neighbor (NN) in light of the fact that it has been suited a bigger ability of model components by amplifying the geometrical parts of indicate point and space. Essentially, it has been tackle with separation between testing highlight point and its forecast highlight point in extended component space as per the geometrical ideas. As NFS demonstrations need than closest component plane (NFP) and closest element line (NFL) by Chien presumed that it has been just centered on the NFS-related strategies. The work has been utilized Local Binary Pattern (LBP) and NFS which has been an augmentation of multi choice level blend in light of consolidated elements for face acknowledgment procedures.

   For pre-processing of images, the histogram equalization (HE) strategy has been utilized to dispose of enlightenment impact since utilizing the current ways to deal with face acknowledgment. The light standardization has been performed independent of the lighting up conditions then the two components are joined, the LBP has been utilized to remove further element on DCT-Scharr-image. At that point Nearest Neighborhood (NN) classifier has been to discovering N quantities of the ideal applicants. The course-to acceptable structure has been separated into the rough and the fme stages. In this way, before the termination of this stage the rough stride can wipe out a ton of no-great examples in the Training Databases and diminishing the extension to character the test image of the N ideal applicants. At long last, the utilization of all the more capable progressed LBP again and the extra powerful speculation capacity of Nearest Feature Space (NFS) to get the personality of the test image. The NFS not just broaden the model of NN, and increment the limit of speculation additionally the reasonable set number of applicants circumstance is ideal for occupied in concert the execution of the NFS. The NN expansion of the NFS broadens the model limit from looking the closest component opinion to the closest separation amongst question and model space.

Indisputably, addition to this part choice level combination part, we join both component level combination and choice level combination successively to frame the new compelling and continuous face acknowledgment strategy. Exploratory consequences with average response rate (ARR) of seventy six percentage and 0.7 s for every image of constant productivity output in light of the Luminary Database [22].

3.5   Local Binary Pattern & Local Phase Quantization (LBP&LPQ)

A local-based brightness insensitive algorithm has been generally utilized for face acknowledgment which has the course of action of image standardization and invariant descriptors. The Lighting unfeeling show of picture has been acquired in view of the proportion of inclination sufficiency to the first image force and isolated into littler sub-squares. Neighborhood stage quantization and Multi-scale nearby paired example, separate the sub-pieces qualities. Separation of nearby closest neighbor classifiers has been measured and melded at the score level to locate the finest match and choice level combination consolidates the aftereffects of two coordinating systems joining highlight extractors can bring about preferable execution over utilizing one descriptor. Amongst the nearby descriptors with huge execution, LPQ and LBP have recognized not computationally quickly with basic estimations which are inhumane beside monotonic image corruption [20]. The examination of different face acknowledgment algorithms on the premise of their exactness and diverse arrangement of information base is appeared underneath in Table 2.

Table 2. Comparison of algorithms using different database based on accuracy.

Algorithm	Database	Accuracy (%)
POC	FERET	96%
LBP	YALE	96.97%
LPQ	YALE	95.3%
LBP & NFS	ORL	72.5%
LBP & LPQ	YALE	98.3%

4   Review Summary

There are some conclusions that could be drawn after reviewing the different face identification methods of recent research developments that are as follows:

State-of-the-Art
The effective techniques are the model-based which coordinate point of interest proofs from nearby fixes with a worldwide shape requirement. The coordination of the neighborhood and worldwide data or Ist-and 2nd-level processes is acknowledged with differing qualities of techniques extending from Bayesian forecast to SVR. The two-level methodologies are techniques that in the primary level concentrate fiducially historic points, and in the second level anticipate and merge milestones with less enlightening elements under direction of a face shape model are more fruitful. It gives the idea that the execution of algorithms in the most recent five years have enhanced to a point where for the m 17, it is on a standard with manual area stamping. Truth be told, on the off chance that we constrain our perceptions to the distributed results in the articles this implies a couple rate focuses, as 2–3% of IOD. External the m 17 set, the exactness stays inside 5–8%. In any case, our tests on the seven most conspicuous area detecting algorithms have uncovered that these outcomes are not generally reproducible.

Identification Under Adverse and Realistic Conditions
Face identification methods, being regularly neighborhood in nature, can be made heartier to characteristic inconsistency and securing circumstances. It is conceivable to express that light impacts can be for the most part remunerated by such preprocessing ventures as Laplacian of Gaussian (LoG) separating or histogram balance. Additionally, outward appearances and unobtrusive stance varieties can be compensated for by a wealthier arrangement of preparing occurrences. The most despicable aspect of area stamping stays serious stance varieties, i.e., past 20° yaw edges and tilts, particularly when self-impediments happen. We expect that in-plane revolutions can be revised after discovery of the face and of the eyes. It creates the impression that half and half techniques like appearance-helped geometry-based strategies [21, 22], 3D-helped strategies [23, 24] or an associated battery of neighborhood layouts as in [25] hold a decent guarantee for achievement.

Ground-Truthed, Robust and Databases
The positive outcomes of various algorithms may vary emphatically from one database to another database. Actually, the over database execution of the early approaches, as they were ready on one database and then afterward tried on another database, demonstrated a shortcoming i.e. causing severe descents in execution. It is urging to observe those later approaches, quite [24, 26] have vigorous execution over various distinctive databases. The test comes about, however very broad in aim, has not yet uncovered a definitive and most reasonable correlation, in that techniques have not been offered opportunities to be prepared on self-assertive blends of databases. Truth be told, for a reasonable correlation, we recommend that strategies ought to be tried in the Leave One Database Out style (LODBO), where algorithms are prepared with different databases aside from one and after that tried on the prohibited one. To conclude, this review of procedural examinations and the point of interest databases ought to be

stretched out to element acts to assess the attendant issue of historic point following algorithms [27]. Truth be told, the historic point following issue itself justify a distinct review work.

Methods to be Reconnoitered
It could be promising examination ways in area stamping strategies are the accompanying: (i) Sparse word references: The worldview of acknowledgment beneath sparsity limitation and working of prejudicial lexicons appears to be one reasonable technique. The discriminative scanty word reference can be developed per milestone [28, 29] or by and large as in [30]; (ii) Adaboost chose highlights for multi-view land-stamping: Gabor or Haar wavelet highlights chose through adjusted Adaboost plan where shared characteristic and geometric setup of historic point appearances is misused [31]; (iii) Multi-outline land-detecting: Determination of point of interest positions abuses the data in ensuing casings of a video, utilizing, for instance, a spatio-transient depictions [32, 33].

Data Mining in Related to Gesture and Facial Expression
At present web contains no less than two lakhs face recordings [34], as a rule clarified with logical data, and this number is quickly expanding. This abundance of information gives an intriguing chance to investigate human outward appearances; it could be said, to information mine demeanors crosswise over societies, sexual orientations, features and ages. This wellspring of face information is essential since it has to know as attention to that absence of naturalistic, unconstrained demeanor information was a noteworthy barricade in PC examination of outward appearances. It has been called attention to those pretending expressions that is outward appearances carried on as incited by a controller contrast in their progression and assortment when contrasted with unconstrained articulation of the same feelings. We accept strong area detecting will be involved for appointing this exceptionally rich web wellspring of honest to goodness hominoid expressions [35].

5 Conclusion

This paper gives an itemized depiction of different face expectation models by utilizing image preparing from which specialist can get a thought for a productive face forecast procedures considering maturing consequences for human appearances. This paper has examination made between existing models on the premise of exactness, velocity, utilized strategies, and database size. There are prospects extents of enhancements in present approaches as no model certification hundred percent precision and are limited to particular element. Present philosophies can be extended by joining face forecast and acknowledgment, so that a hearty acknowledgment based expectation model can be created keeping in domain the impacts of maturing, facial qualities, environment and so on that is fit for perceiving current info image that is not present in the image database by anticipating it on the premise of already put away images that comparing to current information image.

Taking everything into account, facial area detecting has progressed significantly from its small starting toward the end of 80. The issue can be thought to be understood for close forward countenances with impartial to gentle facial signs, and sufficient determination. It creates the impression that a portion of the effective approaches can be keep running at images rates at moving conditions. Then again, for uncontrolled conditions including subjective postures and expressions, the issue can't yet be considered as completely tackled. Late research comes about, be that as it may, however, give us a positive outlook.

References

1. Berg, T., Berg, A., Edwards, J., Maire, M., White, R., Teh, Y., Learned Miller, E., Forsyth, D.: Names and faces. Technical report, University of California Berkeley (2007)
2. Bicego, M., Lagorio, A., Grosso, E., Tistarelli, M.: On the use of sift features for face authentication. In: CVPRW 2006: Proceedings of 2006 Conference on Computer Vision and Pattern Recognition Workshop, p. 35. IEEE Computer Society, Washington, DC (2006)
3. Chang, C.-C., Lin, C.-J.: LIBSVM: a library for support vector machines (2001). Software: http://www.csie.ntu.edu.tw/cjlin/libsvm
4. Duygulu, P., Barnard, K., de Freitas, J.F.G., Forsyth, D.A.: Object recognition as machine translation: learning a lexicon for a fixed image vocabulary. In: Heyden, A., Sparr, G., Nielsen, M., Johansen, P. (eds.) ECCV 2002. LNCS, vol. 2353, pp. 97–112. Springer, Heidelberg (2002). doi:10.1007/3-540-47979-1_7
5. Everingham, M., Sivic, J., Zisserman, A.: Taking the bite out of automatic naming of characters in TV video. Image Vis. Comput. 27(5), 545–559 (2009)
6. Huang, G.B., Ramesh, M., Berg, T., Learned-Miller, E.: Labeled faces in the wild: a database for studying face recognition in unconstrained environments. Technical report 07-49, University of Massachusetts, Amherst (2007)
7. Friedman, J.H.: Another approach to polychotomous classification (2006)
8. Ozkan, D., Duygulu, P.: A graph based approach for naming faces in news photos, vol. II, pp. 1477–1482 (2006)
9. Guillaumin, M., Mensink, T., Verbeek, J., Schmid, C.: Automatic face naming with caption-based supervision, pp. 1–8 (2008)
10. İkizler, N., Duygulu, P.: Person search made easy. In: Leow, W.-K., Lew, Michael S., Chua, T.-S., Ma, W.-Y., Chaisorn, L., Bakker, Erwin M. (eds.) CIVR 2005. LNCS, vol. 3568, pp. 578–588. Springer, Heidelberg (2005). doi:10.1007/11526346_61
11. Le, D.-D., Satoh, S.: Unsupervised face annotation by mining the web. In: ICDM, pp. 383–392 (2008)
12. Kre, U.H.-G.: Pairwise classification and support vector machines. pp. 255–268 (1999)
13. Kumar, N., Berg, A.C., Belhumeur, P.N., Nayar, S.K.: Attribute and simile classifiers for face verification. In: IEEE International Conference on Computer Vision (ICCV) (2009)
14. Le, D.-D., Satoh, S., Houle, M.E., Nguyen, D.P.T.: Finding important people in large news video databases using multimodal and clustering analysis. In: ICDEW 2007: Proceedings of 2007 IEEE 23rd International Conference on Data Engineering Workshop, pp. 127–136. IEEE Computer Society, Washington, DC (2007)
15. Miller, T., Berg, A.C., Edwards, J., Maire, M., White, R., Teh, Y.-W., Learned-Miller, E., Forsyth, D.: Faces and names in the news. In: IEEE Conference on Computer Vision and Pattern Recognition (CVPR) (2004)
16. Lu, K., Dong, L.: Using LBP histogram for face recognition on Android platform, pp. 266–268. IEEE (2011)

17. Tajima, Y., Ito, K., Aoki, T.: Performance improvement of face recognition algorithms using occluded-region detection. IEEE (2013)
18. Nikan, S., Ahmadi, M.: Local gradient-based illumination invariant face recognition using local phase quantization and multi-resolution local binary pattern fusion. Inst. Eng. Technol. (IET) Image Process. 9(1), 12–21 (2014)
19. Ahonen, T., Hadid, A., Pietikäinen, M.: Face description with local binary patterns: application to face recognition. IEEE T-PAMI 28(12), 2037–2041 (2006)
20. Haixu, W.L., Li, C.X.: A new face recognition algorithm using LBP and NFS. In: International Conference on Computer Design and Applications (ICCDA), vol. 1, no. 6, pp. 323–327. IEEE (2010)
21. Wiskott, L., Fellous, J.M., Kruger, N., von der Malsburg, C.: Face recognition by elastic bunch graph. IEEE Trans. Pattern Anal. Mach. Intell. 7, 775–779 (1997)
22. Salah, A.A., Çınar, H., Akarun, L., Sankur, B.: Robust facial land marking for registration. Ann. Telecommun. 62(1–2), 83–108 (2006)
23. Lu, X., Jain, A.K.: Automatic feature extraction for multi-view 3D faces recognition. In: Proceedings of International Conference on Automatic Face and Gesture Recognition, Southsampson, UK (2006)
24. Dibeklioğlu, H., Salah, A.A., Akarun, L.: 3D facial landmarking under expression, pose and occlusion variations. In: Proceedings of IEEE International Conference on Biometrics: Theory, Applications and Systems, Washington DC (2008)
25. Zhu, X., Ramanan, D.: Face detection; pose estimation, and landmark localization in the wild. In: Proceedings of Conference on Computer Vision and Pattern Recognition, Providence, RI, USA, pp. 2879–2886 (2012)
26. Martinez, B., Valstar, M.F., Binefa, X., Pantic, M.: Local evidence aggregation for regression based facial point detection. IEEE Trans. Pattern Anal. Mach. Intell. 99, 1 (2012)
27. Cao, X., Wei, Y., Wen, F., Sun, J.: Face alignment by explicit shape regression. In: Process of Conference on Computer Vision and Pattern Recognition, Providence, RI, USA, pp. 2887–2894 (2012)
28. Tie, Y., Guan, L.: Automatic landmark point detection and tracking for human facial expressions. J. Image Video Process. 2013, 8 (2013). doi:10.1186/1687-5281-2013-8
29. Mairal, J., Bach, F., Ponce, J., Sapiro, G., Zisserman, A.: Discriminative learned dictionaries for local image analysis. In: Proceedings of Conference on Computer Vision and Pattern Recognition, Anchorage, Alaska, pp. 1–8 (2008)
30. Yang, M., Zhang, L., Feng, X., Zhang, D.: Fisher discrimination dictionary for sparse representation. In: Process of International Conference on Computer Vision, Barcelona, Spain, pp. 543–550 (2011)
31. Salakhutdinov, R., Torralba, A., Tenenbaum, J.: Learning to share visual appearance for multiclass object detection. In: Process of Conference on Computer Vision and Pattern Recognition, Colorado Springs, USA, pp. 1481–1488 (2011)
32. Torralba, A., Murphy, K.P., Freeman, W.T.: Sharing visual features for multiclass and multiview object detection. IEEE Trans. Pattern Anal. Mach. Intell. 29(5), 854–869 (2007)
33. Black, M., Yacoob, Y., Jepson, A., Fleet, D.J.: Learning parameterized models of image motion. In: Process of Conference on Computer Vision and Pattern Recognition, San Juan, Puerto Rico, pp. 561–567 (1997)
34. Wang, H., Ullah, M.M., Kläser, A., Laptev, I., Schmid, C.: Evaluation of local spatio-temporal features for action recognition. In: Proceedings of British Machine Vision Conference, London, UK, p. 127 (2009)
35. McDuff, D., el Kaliouby, R., Picard, R.W.: Crowdsourcing facial responses to online videos. IEEE Trans. Affect. Comput. 99, 456–468 (2012)

Directional Contourlet Based Multi-resolution Image Fusion Method for INSAT Images

P. Santhi, G. Thirugnanam[(⊠)], and P. Mangaiyarkarasi

Department of Electronics and Instrumentation Engineering,
Annamalai University, Chidambaram, Tamil Nadu, India
ggtt_me@yahoo.com

Abstract. Among the accessibility of multi-detector information in numerous fields, image fusion has received growing consideration in the researchers for a extensive spectrum of applications. Image fusion is the procedure to merges statistics from various images of the identical view. These pictures perhaps taken from various detectors, obtained at dissimilar times. In this paper, an image fusion technique rely on Directional Contourlet transform is proposed to improve the quality of image and meet the needs of application of vision. Two or more images to be fused should be decomposed using Contourlet with multi-resolution frequencies. The resulting sub-images are fused using Directive Contrast rule to obtain the combined image. As the wavelet transform has several special features in evaluation with scalar wavelets on image processing, but it flushes it to keep the inherent information. The efficacy of the proposed scheme has been explained using various image sets such as the multi-focus pictures, multi-detector satellite image. The proposed Directional Contourlet transform based fusion method has compared with wavelet transform image fusion method qualitatively and quantitatively. Experimental results concluded that the proposed scheme performs superior for image fusion in comparison with wavelet transform.

Keywords: Directional contourlet transform · INSAT images · Wavelet transform · Image fusion

1 Introduction

Image fusion is a method of integrating the significant data from a set of pictures of the same sight into an exclusive image, and the ensuing fused image is more revealing and inclusive than the input images. Input images could be the multi-sensor, multimodal or multi-focal point [1]. The fused image is supposed to keep all significant facts from the input images. The image fusion avoid introducing artifacts that contribute to an incorrect analysis. One of the imperative basic steps of the fusion process is image registration. Image registration is the procedure of transforming various sets of data into one organize system. Image fusion finds application in the field of navigation guidance, target detection, and recognition, medical diagnosis, satellite imagery for remote sensing, military, and civilian surveillance, etc. [2]. Image fusion techniques are classified into pixel, feature, and decision points.

© Springer Nature Singapore Pte Ltd. 2017
M. Singh et al. (Eds.): ICACDS 2016, CCIS 721, pp. 369–376, 2017.
DOI: 10.1007/978-981-10-5427-3_39

Pixel fusion works straight on the pixels of source images while feature fusion techniques function on features taken out from the source images. The wavelet grasp the phantom and time, where the former system failed. Discrete wavelet transform (DWT) is unrivaled of the extensively applied tools [5]. The DWT fusion strategy is selecting the maximum sub-bands in every elevated enormity. The demerits of wavelet is sensitive in the vicinity of the information. In this work, the Multi-Resolution Analysis (MRA) is achieved by directional non-subsampled Contourlet transform.

From the literature, it is inferred that pixel level fusion leads to unwanted side effects such as reduced contrast. In the recent years, many image fusion techniques have been proposed, such as arithmetical and numerical methods, hue-saturation-intensity (HSI) method, principal component analysis (PCA) method, image gradient pyramid and multiresolution methods. These methods involve huge computation using floating point arithmetic and hence these are time and memory consuming. In the recent years, fusion methods based on pyramid and multiresolution analysis turn out to be most popular. Li et al. also used DWT for decomposition area based activity measure and maximum selection rule for fusion [3]. Hence in this paper, Directional Contourlet transform is implemented for decomposition.

In this paper, the fusion scheme based on Directive Contrast using Directional and Nonsubsampled Contourlet transform (CT) domain. The Directive contrast method integrates with the sum-modified-Laplacian to get more accurate salient features [4]. Hence, the Directive contrast method is implemented for fusion in this projected work. The work is structured as follows. The CT and image fusion are explained in Sects. 2 and 3. In Sect. 4, proposed directive contrast fusion rule is presented. The simulation results are presented in Sect. 5. Finally, the conclusion is given in Sect. 6.

2 Directional Contourlet Transform

Directional Contourlet transform is a multidirectional Nonsubsampled renovation technique used in image investigation for capturing contours and superior details in images. The CT is a collection of basis task leaning in dissimilar ways in numerous scales with stretchy feature ratios. This framework should form a foundation with little idleness unlike other transform proficiencies in image analysis. Contourlet representation contains basic elements leaning in an assortment of directions that are provided by other separable transform technique [6].

Among this imminent, it is able to create a double filter bank arrangement shown in Image 1, filter is employed to get the spot break, followed by a Directional Filter Bank (DFB). The whole effect is extension of image using elements like contours, so called contourlet transform.

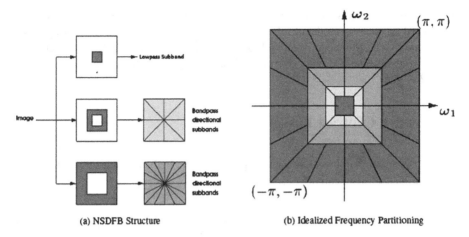

(a) NSDFB Structure   (b) Idealized Frequency Partitioning

Fig. 1. Contourlet filter bank

3   Image Fusion

Image fusion is combining pertinent information from two or more source images into a single image such that it contains most of the data from all the source images [8]. In this work, Image fusion is employed for integrating an INSAT-3D vegetation information across India as Image 1 and INSAT- 3A shows rainfall information in India as Image 2. The resulting fused image contains both the vegetation and rainfall data. A Directive contrast, fusion process with CT approach is done.

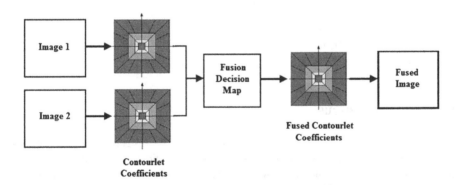

Fig. 2. Systematic process of contourlet based image fusion

The block diagram of a generic Contourlet-based image fusion system is presented in Image 2. INSAT 3D is considered as Image 1, and INSAT 3A is taken as Image 2. Directional Nonsubsampled Contourlet Transform is applied on Image 1 as well as applied on Image 2 separately. Eight sub-bands are generated in each output of Images 1 and 2. In this eight sub-band coefficients, one is a low pass approximation coefficient and remaining seven subsets are high pass detail coefficients. The Directive Contrast Fusion rule is used on each seven detail sub-sets [9]. For the fusion of low-frequency approximation coefficient, the mean is applied to two pictures. Finally, fused Contourlet coefficients image is obtained, and inverse CT is done to get the fused image as shown in Image 2.

4 Directive Contrast Fusion Rule

(i) For the fusion of low-frequency approximation coefficient, mean is applied to blend instead of averaging [7].

$$A_i(new) = mean(A_1, A_2) \tag{1}$$

(ii) For fusing high-frequency detail coefficients of corresponding pixels in all source images,

$$H_i(new) = \begin{cases} H_i^1 & if \ |C_iH^1| \geq |C_iH^2| \\ H_i^2 & otherwise \end{cases} \tag{2}$$

$$V_i(new) = \begin{cases} V_i^1 & if \ |C_iV^1| \geq |C_iV^2| \\ V_i^2 & otherwise \end{cases} \tag{3}$$

$$D_i(new) = \begin{cases} D_i^1 & if \ |C_iD^1| \geq |C_iD^2| \\ D_i^2 & otherwise \end{cases} \tag{4}$$

Where C_iH is Horizontal contrast
       C_iV is a Vertical contrast
       D_iV is Diagonal contrast

5 Result and Discussion

The RGB of INSAT 3D of size 256×256 highlights the vegetation in India is considered as Image 1, and INSAT 3A of size 256×256 indicates the rainfall in India is taken as Image 2 and as shown in Image 3 and in 4. Images 1 and 2 is converted to YUV components, and Y component is considered for fusion. The Y component of INSAT 3D and INSAT 3A are shown in Images 5 and in 6, respectively. INSAT 3D and INSAT 3A images are decomposed to two levels using Directional Nonsubsampled Contourlet transform. The resulting sub-bands are shown in Images 7 and in 8. The Contourlet transform decomposes the image in a multidirectional way and generates more directional sub-bands whereas wavelets are directionally sensitive.

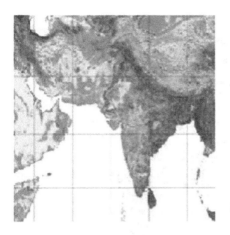

Fig. 3. Image 1 (INSAT 3D)

Fig. 4. Image 2 (INSAT 3A)

Fig. 5. Y component of Image 1

Fig. 6. Y component of Image 2

The Directive Contrast Fusion rule is used on each seven detail sub-sets in two images. For the fusion of approximation coefficient, the mean is calculated between low-frequency components in two images. After fusing, fused Contourlet coefficients image is obtained, and inverse CT is called for to get Y component of the merged image as depicted in Image 9. Then this Y component fused image is changed into an RGB fused image as depicted in Image 10 (Tables 1 and 2).

Fig. 7. Two level Contourlet transform decomposition for Image 1

Fig. 8. Two level Contourlet transform decomposition for Image 2

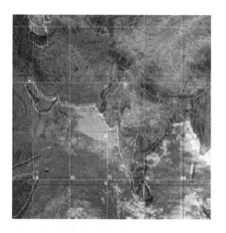

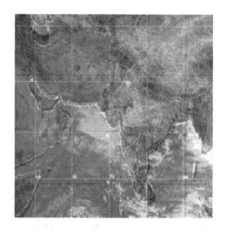

Fig. 9. Y component of fused image

Fig. 10. Fused image

Table 1. Evaluation indices of PSNR for wavelet transform and contourlet transform.

Images	Wavelet transform	Contourlet transform
Proposed INSAT	39.6732	46.8139
LANDSAT	37.5982	45.7403
PAN-MS	38.0267	45.9634

Table 2. Evaluation indices of normalized correlation for wavelet transform and contourlet transform

Images	Wavelet transform	Contourlet transform
Proposed INSAT	0.8917	0.9667
LANDSAT	0.8745	0.9512
PAN-MS	0.8864	0.9588

6   Conclusion

The paper has presented a Directional Contourlet Transform based INSAT colour image Directive contrast fusion method. This method maintains both INSAT 3D and INSAT 3A details of satellite pictures. Simulation results confessed the pre-eminence of the proposed Contourlet method to wavelet-based satellite image fusion techniques. The proposed method shown to be effective for the fusion in the existence of interference.

References

1. Nikolov, S., Hill, P., Bull, D., Canagarajah, N.: Wavelets for image fusion. In: Petrosian, A.A., Meyer, F.G. (eds.) Wavelets in Signal and Image Analysis, pp. 213–241. Springer, Heidelberg (2001)
2. Vekkot, S., Shukla, P.: A novel architecture for wavelet based image fusion. World Acad. Sci. Eng. Technol. **57**, 372–377 (2009)
3. Li, H., Manjunath, B.S., Mitra, S.K.: Multisensor image fusion using the wavelet transform. Graph Models Image Process. **57**(3), 235–245 (1995)
4. Pu, T., Ni, G.: Contrast based Image fusion using the discrete wavelet transform. Opt. Eng. **39**(8), 2075–2082 (2000)
5. Xiong, Z., Ramchandran, K., Orchad, M.T.: Wavelet packet image coding using space-frequency quantization. IEEE Trans. Image Process. **7**, 160–174 (1998)
6. Qiguang, M., Baoshul, W.: A novel image fusion method using contourlet transform. In: Proceedings of 2006 International Conference on Communications, Circuits and Systems, vol. 1, pp. 548–552 (2006)
7. Chandana, M., Amutha, S., Kumar, N.: A hybrid multi-focus medical image fusion based on wavelet transform. Int. J. Res. Rev. Comput. Sci. **2**, 1187–1192 (2011)
8. Tu, T., Huang, P.S., Hung, C., Chang, C.: A fast intensity-hue-saturation fusion technique with spectral adjustment for IKONOS imagery. IEEE Trans. Geosci. Remote Sens. **1**(4), 309–312 (2004)
9. Saleta, M., Catala, J.L.: Fusion of multispectral and panchromatic images using improved IHS and PCA mergers based on wavelet decomposition. IEEE Trans. Geosci. Remote Sens. **42**(6), 1291–1299 (2004)

Feature Extraction Methods for Human Gait Recognition – A Survey

Sugandhi K.[(✉)], Farha Fatina Wahid, and Raju G.

Department of Information Technology,
Kannur University, Kannur, Kerala, India
sugandhikgs@gmail.com, kurupgraju@gmail.com,
farhawahid@yahoo.co.in

Abstract. Human gait recognition opens a wide variety of challenging problems for research community. Feature extraction has a significant role in designing human gait recognition systems. Numerous features have been defined based on gait video frames. Spatial as well as temporal descriptors have equal importance within gait features. In this paper, we present a survey of prominent feature extraction methods incorporated in human gait recognition systems and their respective recognition accuracies are reported. Also, a description of popular gait databases is presented.

Keywords: Biometric techniques · Gait · Silhouette · Subject · Covariates

1 Introduction

Biometric systems emerged as an efficient authentication technique in the present scenario. As the name shows, biometric systems ensure that a unique physiological or behavioral trait of an individual is sufficient for identification/recognition. The idea of biometric authentication systems dates back to 1891 and it was purposefully used first for identifying criminals based on their fingerprints [1]. Due to the wide applicability of the biometric technique, several physiological characteristics, other than fingerprint such as face, iris, retina, palm, DNA, etc. as well as behavioral characteristics such as gait, voice, typing rhythm, etc. have emerged.

From the dictionary definition, gait is the manners of walking. Despite humans have the same walking styles, researchers showed that each person has unique characteristics in their walking [2]. As a biometric trait, gait has some attractive features for uniquely identifying a person. The major reason for using gait is its unobtrusive nature. i.e., it can be captured at a distance without the prior consent of the person under observation. It is very difficult to hide, steal or fake, the gait. Also it is non-invasive. i.e., it does not force the person to walk in a specific manner. Another specialty is that it is hard to disguise. The possibility of varying gait of a person is much less unless the extreme physical changes caused by carrying a load or change in footwear, etc. In the context of gait capturing process, a low resolution camera is sufficient. Due to these unique characteristics of gait, Gait recognition systems started playing a significant role in the biometric authentication process.

© Springer Nature Singapore Pte Ltd. 2017
M. Singh et al. (Eds.): ICACDS 2016, CCIS 721, pp. 377–385, 2017.
DOI: 10.1007/978-981-10-5427-3_40

Though the research based on gait started several decades back, it has come into limelight quite recently. Human motion analysis was the major topic in early researches and in 1973, Johansson et al. [3] is the first to introduce the concept of gait in front of the public as a subset of the human motion analysis. There are many challenges being faced by the researchers on gait recognition. A good number of published works [9–11, 13, 14] have emerged recently which open a variety of research problems.

Gait is being used in various applications including medical diagnostics of diseases such as Parkinson gait disorders, recognition of distracted pedestrians in airports, border crossings and other public access areas. Gait recognition is also used for the design and construction of robotics, creation of computer animated images in game and film industry, gender classification, prediction of different stages of human life such as childhood, youth and aged conditions, etc.

As gait recognition is done without the consent of the person being considered, there are many challenges for the same. The main challenge is related to covariate factors, ranging from external factors to internal factors. People walk wearing different types of cloths at different point of time, with different foot wears, on different surfaces like concrete, mud, grass etc., at different time spans. These constitute the major external factors affecting gait recognition. Another external factor is the camera position leading to different walking view angle at which the image is captured. The internal factors are the physiological change in body due to aging, drunkenness, pregnancy, gaining or losing weights and so on as well as any sickness due to foot injury or disorder in lower limbs. Another important aspect is in terms of variation in gait speed, in the temporal point of view. Broadly speaking, extraction of relevant features that characterizes the gait and the classification strategies that will be adopted for accurate recognition are the major concern of any human gait recognition system.

In the current scenario, human gait recognition methods are roughly divided into two categories, namely model free approach and model based approach [4]. Literatures showed that model free approaches are simple and have less computational burden. In this approach, gait is considered to be made up of a static component based on the size and shape of a person and a dynamic component which reflects the actual movement. Model free approach operates directly on the gait sequences without considering any prior model. In model based approach, there should be a prior model of the human body and features are extracted based on this model. Features have a significant role in any recognition system as it quantifies what is being observed. The success of recognition task depends on how accurately the extracted features represent the observed thing. Due to the complexity of gait recognition systems, extraction of appropriate feature is a great challenge. In a broad sense, gait features are mainly categorized into two; static features and dynamic features. Static features include height, stride length, silhouette bounding box length, etc. and dynamic features include frequency domain parameters such as frequency and phase of the movements.

In this paper, we present prominent as well as contemporary feature extraction techniques employed in gait recognition. The paper is articulated as follows: Sect. 2 deals with basic concepts behind human gait followed by discussion of standard gait databases. Section 3 gives an overview of prominent feature extraction techniques employed for human gait recognition. Discussions and conclusion are explored in Sect. 4.

2 Basics of Gait and Standard Gait Databases

2.1 Basics of Gait

As gait is an emerging biometric trait, it is essential to know the basic characteristics of human gait [5]. Some of the commonly used terms of human gait recognition systems are as follows:-

Subject   : The term subject indicates the person under consideration.
Silhouette   : The outline of the walking subject is considered as the silhouette.
Covariate   : Natural potential variations of the subject as well as the factors affecting the performance of the subject are referred to as the covariates. e.g., carrying conditions, change in view angles, etc.
Gait Cycle   : It is the time period or sequence of events or movements during locomotion in which one foot contacts the ground to when the same foot again contacts the ground.
Stride   : A single gait cycle is referred to as stride.

Each Gait cycle or stride has mainly two phases, namely stance phase and swing phase [6]. The phase in which the foot remains in contact with the ground is known as stance phase while in swing phase, the foot is not in contact with the ground as illustrated in Fig. 1. During one gait cycle, 60% remains in stance phase and 40% in swing phase. During stance phase, reference foot (shaded foot in the Fig. 1) undergoes five movements such as initial contact, loading response, mid stance, terminal stance and pre-swing respectively. When it is in initial contact, heel touches the ground. Then body weight is transferred on to the referenced leg during loading response. At mid stance, balancing and alignment of the body weight on referenced leg takes place. Heel of the referenced foot rises, but toe remains in contact with the ground in terminal stance. At last toe rises and swings in the air and is known as pre-swing step. Three movements undergoes during swing phase such as initial swing, mid swing and terminal swing respectively. Initial swing begins the moment the foot leaves the ground and continues until maximum knee flexion occurs, when the swinging extremity is directly under the body and directly opposite the stance limb. Mid swing phase begins following maximum knee flexion and ends when the tibia is in a vertical position. The tibia passes beyond perpendicular, and the knee fully extends in preparation for heel contact in terminal swing [7].

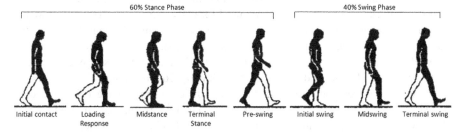

Fig. 1. Different steps during a gait cycle

2.2   Standard Gait Databases

Table 1 shows some of the well-known gait databases used in most of the works and its basic information. Several gait databases are publicly available [8] or permitted with a little formality for comparative performance evaluation. Due to the lack of sufficient subjects in early databases, researcher's made an effort to create their own databases. Considering the availability of less number of samples and variations, creating human gait database for validation and verification of recognition algorithm is a promising area.

Table 1. Some of the well-known gait databases used in most of the works and its basic information.

Sl. no	Database		Subjects	Covariates	Year
1	CASIA gait database	A	20	View	2001
		B	124	View	2005
		C	153	Speed, carrying condition	2005
2	Human ID challenge gait database		122	View, surface, shoe, carrying conditions	2002
3	CMU moBo database		25	View, speed, carrying condition, surface incline	2001
4	SOTON database	Small	12	View	2001
		Large	115		
		Temporal	25	View, time	2012
5	OU-ISIR database	A	34	Speed	2007–
		B	68	Clothing	2012
		D	185	Gait fluctuations	

3   Gait Feature Extraction Techniques

One of the crucial steps in any gait recognition system is the feature extraction. We have carried out a survey of research papers on gait recognition. Based on the survey, about 12 recent works were identified for a detailed study. A brief summary of the chosen papers focusing on the feature extraction method are given below.

Frieze feature and wavelet feature are used for gait recognition for their substantial discriminative nature. It is showed that these features are mainly contributed for the dynamic motion characterization of a human gait. Chen et al. [9] came up with an improved dynamic Bayesian network to model the dynamic image sequences. Instead of extracting frieze feature and wavelet feature directly from the gait cycle, here a novel gait representation scheme known as frame difference energy image (FDEI) is constructed. This is a combination of well-known Gait Energy Image (GEI) and frame difference representation. Training is carried out by Viterbi algorithm thereby finds the similarity between the probe sequence and the training sequence. Two databases were used for experiments–CMU MoBo gait database and CASIA-B multi view gait database. They reported 95.7% accuracy.

An alternative approach to feature extraction is to extract features directly from the raw gait video. This approach is followed in several recent works. An interesting work is discussed in [10], where gait features are recognized directly from the video on a spatio-temporal feature domain. Histogram of Spatio-temporal interest points Descriptors (HSD) are used as gait feature. First, Spatio-temporal Interest Points (STIP) are detected from each gait video individually. Authors claimed that STIP is an interest point of a dominant walking pattern which can be used to represent characteristics of each individual gait. Second, histogram of STIP descriptors is determined. SVM classifier was adopted for classification. Experiments were carried out by using CASIA-B, CMU MoBo and OU-ISIR databases. 99.2%, 98% and 92% of accuracies were obtained respectively for these gait databases.

Another work in [11], present a framework to construct a gait feature directly from raw gait video. Firstly, STIP, that represent significant movements of human body along both spatial and temporal directions, are detected from a raw gait video sequence. Then, histogram of oriented gradients (HOG) and histogram of optical flow (HOF) are employed to describe each STIP. Finally Bag of words (BoW) model is applied on each set of STIP descriptors to construct a gait feature for representing and recognizing individual gait. Authors claimed that this feature can explore local motion information for walking variations than global shape information used in most existing gait recognition tasks. CASIA gait database B is used for experimentation and widely adopted Euclidean distance is used to measure the gait dissimilarity. The proposed method reported 61% of accuracy.

Many image processing applications deals with image histograms. By looking at the histogram for a specific image, a viewer will be able to judge the entire tonal distribution at a glance [12]. The authors in [13], represented gait by combining histogram of oriented gradients and Gait Gaussian Image (GGI), and resulted Gradient Histogram Gaussian Image (GHGI). Feature extraction is done using Gaussian membership function and histogram of oriented gradients. The extracted features are Gaussian features for each pixel, local distribution of gradients and edge parameters. Nearest neighbor classifier is used for classification. It is a gait period dependent approach and Treadmill A and B databases are used for conducting experiments. The observed results are really appreciative. Authors got correct classification rate of 94.1% on treadmill gait database A.

Another method [14] is employed on histogram of Transient Binary pattern (TBP). It is a combination of spatio-temporal approach and texture descriptors. Gait is represented directly from the silhouette images of the database. Feature extraction is carried out by Transient Binary Patterns (TBP). Pixel wise TBP is first extracted. This pixel wise TBP is grouped into regional blocks from which they construct regional TBP histograms. These regional TBP histograms collectively form the local TBP histogram that represents both temporal as well as spatial location. They have used majority voting with Euclidean distance as the distance measure. Three standard databases are employed namely - OU-ISIR gait database, CASIA-B gait database and CMU MoBo gait database. They disclosed that TBP method outperforms other approaches such as PSA, FD based method, GEI, AEI and GPI. The proposed TBP method showed 99%, 90.8% and 96% accuracy for the OU-ISIR, CASIA B and CMU MoBo Databases respectively.

Gait Energy Image (GEI) introduced by Kusakunniran et al. [15], has a great deal of importance in recent gait related works. It is one of the spatio-temporal gait representations and has wide acceptance nowadays. It is easy to construct GEI, just by taking the average of sequence of gait templates within a gait cycle. GEI represents human motion in a single image while preserving the temporal information. The problem of gait recognition across different viewing angle is discussed in [16]. GEI is used as the gait feature. According to the authors, GEI provides a substantial correlation across views which are naturally bridged by the spatial information. Also their assumption is that a pixel with higher intensity in GEI corresponds to a body part that moves less during walking cycle while a pixel with lower intensity corresponds to a body part that moves constantly. Based on this assumption, authors proposed a gait partitioning model using bipartite graph modeling to co-cluster the GEI into segments across views. This model contains most of the correlated gait information. Then Canonical Correlation Analysis (CCA) is applied to maximize linear correlation among segments. Sum of cosine similarities are used for similarity measurement and experiments were carried out using CASIA B multi-view gait database. Nevertheless, the experimental analysis showed that the method outperforms for multi-view gait recognition than cross view gait recognition. The proposed method achieves appropriately 87%, 62% and 40% accuracies for the view angles of 18°, 36° and 54° respectively.

A view transformation model (VTM) is proposed in [17] to solve view variation difficulty facing for human gait recognition. In this paper, Gait Energy Image (GEI) is considered as gait feature. According to authors, GEI varies on different views. Therefore, they construct a VTM from multiple regression processes for transforming GEI into a common view. The regression model is trained by multilayer perceptron to predict a pixel in GEI for target view from Region of Interest (ROI) on a source view. The authors used Euclidean distance to measure gait similarity and experiments were carried out using CASIA B multi-view gait database. Their analysis shows that using the proposed VTM, average accuracies of 99%, 98% and 93% are achieved using 5, 4 and 3 cameras respectively.

Modifications to GEI are further developed. Yogarajah et al. [18] proposed a methodology for gait recognition under different covariate conditions. The authors focused mainly on increasing the gait recognition rate by concentrating more on feature selection. In their work, they proposed human identification through Joint Sparsity Model (JSM) and L1 norm minimization approach. According to the authors, GEI can attain better gait recognition rate under normal conditions. So in order to increase the gait recognition rate on different covariate conditions, GEI feature vectors are submitted to JSM thereby separated the common and innovation components. From these components, a new gait feature is proposed, known as GEI_{JSM}. Sparse representation based classification method is the generalization of Nearest Subspace method and is used for classification purpose. Experiments were conducted using CASIA database B and the analysis shows that approximately 85% of recognition accuracy can be obtained using this approach and provides statistically significant better results than that of the existing individual identification approaches.

Active Energy Image (AEI) is another recent gait representation method proposed in [19]. Authors claimed that existing gait representation methods usually suffer from low quality human silhouette and insufficient dynamic characteristics. Hence, extracting only the active regions by calculating the difference of two adjacent silhouettes provide more desirable results. This is to be termed as Active Energy Image (AEI). Also, AEI representation is almost similar to Frame Difference Energy Image (FDEI) proposed in [9]. Even though AEI concentrate more on dynamic regions to reflect the walking manner of an individual. Euclidean distance is used for similarity computation and approximately 98% of recognition rate is obtained during normal walking condition on CASIA B database.

Two novel gait representation methods, known as Shifted Energy Image (SEI) and gait structural profile (GSP) were proposed in [20]. Existing gait representation methods may get erroneous results due to this variation. Hence in order to remove the effect of structural differences while retaining the useful gait information, SEI and GSP were introduced. Identification is performed by fusing the two features - distance among SEI templates and the GSP vectors. The resultant distance is used for taking recognition decisions. Experiments were conducted using CASIA, CMU MoBo and ACTIOBIO databases and obtained 99%, 90% and 89% of accuracies, respectively.

4   Discussion and Conclusions

In this paper, we have reviewed a set of contemporary and prominent works in the area of human gait recognition with special emphasis on feature extraction. The reviewed feature extraction methods are broadly categorized as follows –methods utilizing binary silhouette directly from databases, methods for extracting features from raw gait video rather constructing gait frames, histogram based methods, methods used for frieze features and wavelet features, Fourier descriptor based methods, methods using different gait representation schemes such as GEI, FDEI, AEI, SEI, GSP, and finally geometric gait features with soft biometric techniques. The observations based on the feature extraction techniques, database used and accuracy reported are given below:

Out of the feature extraction methods discussed, performance evaluation were mostly done on CASIA B multi view gait database and shows relatively better results. About 99.2% of recognition rate is achieved by extracting histogram of STIP descriptors when classification is done using SVM classifier. But when introducing BoW models for same feature sets with Nearest Neighbour classifier can attain only 61% of accuracy. Out of different gait representation schemes, GEI and SEI with GSP can attain 99% of accuracy on CASIA B gait database. Both the methods used distance measures for similarity computation. Nearest Neighbour classifier can be adopted for majority of the gait features discussed so far and can attain better recognition rate.

Being a very dynamic and challenging area, in depth study is required to implement the various feature extraction methods and comparing the performance with some latest and computational environments would definitely lead the researchers to go beyond what is being achieved in the area of human gait recognition. This survey has no aim to discover a best method; rather it presents a comprehensive catalogue of significant works on human gait recognition, concentrating more on feature extraction. Features are highly dependent on the problem domain. It is evident that researchers in this era come up to overcome the challenges for better gait recognition performance (Table 2).

Table 2. Some of the prominent works of human gait recognition

Paper reference	Gait representation	Feature extraction	Classification (classifier, similarity/ dissimilarity measurement)	Accuracy	Database
Chen et al. [9]	Frame Difference Energy Image (FDEI)	Dynamic Bayesian network LTSM	Viterbi algorithm	95.7%	CASIA B
Kusakunniran [10]	Raw gait video	Histogram of STIP descriptors (HSD)	SVM classifier	99.2%	CASIA C
				98%	CMU MoBo
				92%	OU-ISIR
Kusakunniran [11]	Raw gait video	BoW models for describing STIP descriptors	Nearest Neighbor (NN) classifier	61%	CASIA B
Arora et al. [13]	Gradient Histogram Gaussian Image (GHGI)	Gaussian membership function with histogram of oriented gradients (HOG)	Nearest Neighbor classifier (NN)	94.1%	Treadmill A and B databases
Lee et al. [14]	Binary silhouette image	Transient binary patterns (TBP)	Majority voting with Euclidean distance	99%	OU-ISIR
				90.8%	CASIA B
				96%	CMU MoBo
Kusakunniran et al. [16]	Gait Energy Image (GEI)	Canonical Correlation Analysis (CCA)	Sum of cosine similarity	87%	CASIA B
Kusakunniran et al. [17]	Gait Energy Image (GEI)	View Transformation Model (VTM)	Euclidean distance	99%	CASIA B
Yogarajah et al. [18]	GEI_{JSM}	Joint Sparsity Model	Sparsity based classification method	85%	CASIA B
Zhang et al. [19]	Active Energy Image (AEI)	Active descriptors with 2DLPP projection	Euclidean distance	98.39%	CASIA B
Xiaxi et al. [20]	Shifted energy image and gait structural profile	Shape and dynamic descriptors	Distance among SEI templates and the GSP vectors	99%	CASIA B
				90%	CMUMoBo
				89%	ACTIBIO

Acknowledgement. The authors would like to acknowledge Department of Science and Technology (DST), New Delhi, India for the financial support extended under the INSPIRE Fellowship scheme.

References

1. Biometrics. https://en.wikipedia.org/wiki/Biometrics
2. Cutting, J., Kozlowski, L.: Recognizing friends by their walk: gait perception without familiarity cues. Bull. Psychon. Soc. **9**, 353–356 (1977)
3. Johansson, G.: Visual perception of biological motion and a model for its analysis. Percept. Psychophys. **14**, 201–211 (1973)
4. Lee, T., Belkhatir, M., Sanei, S.: A comprehensive review of past and present vision-based techniques for gait recognition. Multimedia Tools Appl. **72**, 2833–2869 (2013)
5. Gait. http://medical-dictionary.thefreedictionary.com/gait
6. Gait - Physiopedia, universal access to physiotherapy knowledge. http://www.physio-pedia. com/Gait
7. Normal human locomotion, part 1: basic concepts and terminology. J. Prosthet. Orthot. http://www.oandp.org/jpo/library/1997_01_010.asp
8. Reyländer, S.: Scientific Databases for Gait Analyses. AV Akademikerverlag, Saarbrücken (2015)
9. Chen, C., Liang, J., Zhu, X.: Gait recognition based on improved dynamic Bayesian networks. Pattern Recogn. **44**, 988–995 (2011)
10. Kusakunniran, W.: Attribute-based learning for gait recognition using spatio-temporal interest points. Image Vis. Comput. **32**, 1117–1126 (2014)
11. Kusakunniran, W.: Recognizing gaits on spatio-temporal feature domain. IEEE Trans. Inform. Forensic Secur. **9**(9), 1416–1423 (2014). http://dx.doi.org/10.1109/tifs.2014.2336379
12. Image Histogram. https://en.wikipedia.org/wiki/Image_histogram
13. Arora, P., Srivastava, S., Arora, K., Bareja, S.: Improved gait recognition using gradient histogram Gaussian image. Procedia Comput. Sci. **58**, 408–413 (2015)
14. Lee, C., Tan, A., Tan, S.: Gait recognition with transient binary patterns. J. Vis. Commun. Image Represent. **33**, 69–77 (2015)
15. Han, J., Bhanu, B.: Individual recognition using gait energy image. IEEE Trans. Pattern Anal. Mach. Intell. **28**, 316–322 (2006)
16. Kusakunniran, W., Wu, Q., Zhang, J., Li, H., Wang, L.: Recognizing gaits across views through correlated motion co-clustering. IEEE Trans. Image Process. **23**, 696–709 (2014)
17. Kusakunniran, W., Wu, Q., Zhang, J., Li, H.: Cross-view and multi-view gait recognitions based on view transformation model using multi-layer perceptron. Pattern Recogn. Lett. **33**,882–889 (2012)
18. Yogarajah, P., Chaurasia, P., Condell, J., Prasad, G.: Enhancing gait based person identification using joint sparsity model and l_1-norm minimization. Inf. Sci. **308**, 3–22 (2015)
19. Zhang, E., Zhao, Y., Xiong, W.: Active energy image plus 2DLPP for gait recognition. Sig. Process. **90**, 2295–2302 (2010)
20. Huang, X., Boulgouris, N.: Gait recognition with shifted energy image and structural feature extraction. IEEE Trans. Image Process. **21**, 2256–2268 (2012)

Modeling the Decline of Orkut with Popularity in Facebook

Tanuja Jha[✉], Shilpi Burman Sharma,
and Shubham Krishna Chaturvedi

Computer Science and Engineering, Amity University, Noida, India
tanujatannul@gmail.com, ssharma22@amity.edu,
shubh201994@gmail.com

Abstract. Social networking services are gaining popularity at a very fast rate. Social networking websites like Facebook, Twitter, Myspace and many more have been active among people for a long time, thus providing users many features to enjoy online. Apart from great success of these networking websites, there have been various reasons for the downfall of a known website- Orkut. This paper concludes various reasons for the downfall of Orkut and helps in understanding the popularity of Facebook. The outcome of this paper will help in understanding whether Facebook will have a downfall like Orkut or there may be some other reasons for its downfall.

Keywords: Orkut · Facebook · Social networking site · Downfall

1 Introduction

A social networking website works with a plan to construct social networks or social relations among people sharing similar interests, backgrounds, activities or real life relations. It helps in the representation of each user, their social connections and provides various additional features. It is a web-based service that provides user with an opportunity to create social profile, list of users to share connections and helps in searching new people around the world [1].

Orkut, a social networking website was launched by Google. It was named after its creator Orkut Büyükkökten, a Google employee.

In 2004, Mark Zuckerberg along with his fellow student launched a social networking service called as Facebook. Presently, Facebook has more than 1.65 billion monthly active users [2].

These networking sites have a distinct popularity among people in the world but apart from great success, there had been some drawbacks which resulted in the downfall of popular social networking site- Orkut while Facebook is still popular.

This paper presents various reasons for the downfall of Orkut and comparison between Orkut and most popular social networking site Facebook, their features and addiction to the users. Apart from this, various aspects of Facebook growth and its increasing demand in the market have been discussed. User being an essential part of the social networking sites provided an addition observation on rise of Facebook and downfall of Orkut. This paper also details about different phases or era of Facebook and

© Springer Nature Singapore Pte Ltd. 2017
M. Singh et al. (Eds.): ICACDS 2016, CCIS 721, pp. 386–392, 2017.
DOI: 10.1007/978-981-10-5427-3_41

its future status in the social networking site market. This paper can be beneficial for the networking websites to keep themselves in safe hands.

2 Related Work

Reference [3] analysis indicates the popularity of social networking websites among the people of all age groups around the world. The paper contains the reasons for the downfall of Orkut and also concludes that same reasons benefitted Facebook in marketing itself all around the world.

The study reveals that the fall of Myspace and the Rise of Facebook was due to either the way site was associated with its user or the way site implemented the technology and its marketing scheme [4]. In the paper, the researcher made use of "Real Software Abstraction" which includes the Marxian Concept of real abstraction. The study also analyzes that Myspace failed to market itself to the users while Facebook is still improving.

Reference [5] includes the privacy concern in social networking sites. The paper illustrates that after the evolution of various social networking sites namely Facebook, Myspace, Twitter there has been issues related to the cybercrimes mainly phishing, identity theft and stalking. The paper also concerns about the data storage, data management, and data security. Security concern has always been raised when hackers gain an unauthorized access over the account of user as it may lead to potential harm to the user. The paper concludes with the focus on preventive measures that could be taken to reduce the cybercrime and increase the safety of user information.

The study shows the influence of social network on users in present era [6]. The paper provides a descriptive study about the privacy policies of the networking sites and about the disclosure of personal information.

3 Methodology

3.1 Downfall of Orkut

Orkut was a social networking platform which connected users with the whole world. In the times when people had to wait for months and years to meet their dear ones, Orkut served as a saviour and a friend by connecting people anytime, anywhere. It was designed with an aim to help users to meet their friends and relatives. Orkut was an active website for people to chat and reached its golden era in 2010 [2] but due various reasons it had gone a drastic setback and suffered a downfall [7].

If we compare various stats between Facebook and Orkut, we represent reasons for the downfall of Orkut [8, 9] (Table 1).

Table 1. Comparison between Facebook and Orkut

Characteristics	Facebook	Orkut
Nature of user interface	Facebook has simple and professional user interface	Orkut had an amateurish interface
Security	Facebook provides more user security and privacy [8]	Orkut provided less user security and privacy
Online games	Facebook provides high speed games which increase the interest of the users	Orkut provided low speed games which bored the users
Bugs in user interface	The user interface of Facebook is not buggy	The user interface of Orkut was buggy
Promotion	Facebook is successful in advertising itself	Orkut was not successful in advertising itself
Network flooding	There is no network flooding with new sign ups on Facebook [9]	Network always flooded with new sign ups on Orkut
Hacking of accounts	The rate of hacking Facebook account is less	The rate of hacking an Orkut account was high
Webpages	Webpages do not crash in case of Facebook	Webpages crashed in case of Orkut [8]

4 Observation

Both Facebook and Orkut were launched in the year 2004. After some years, Orkut gained more popularity than Facebook. By January 2009, Orkut had more number of visitors than Facebook [10]. Orkut maintained this popularity for nearly 1 year. By the end of April 2010, Orkut leaded the social networking market with 19.7 million unique

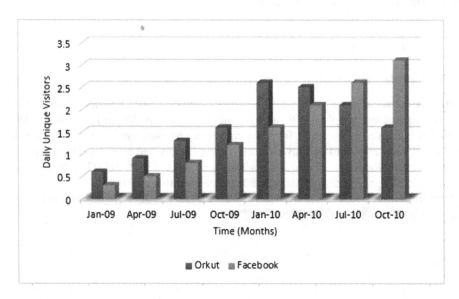

Fig. 1. Chart showing comparison between Facebook users and Orkut users [10].

visitors in comparison to Facebook which has 18 million unique visitors [10]. After April 2010, there came a phase when the number of visitors on Orkut and Facebook became equal. This happened due to downfall of Orkut and raise of Facebook as illustrated in Fig. 1. Facebook gained more popularity and number of visitors increased. Facebook grabbed number one position in July 2010 for the first time with 20.9 million visitors showing a growth of 179% while Orkut showed only 16% growth in the same period of time. From here, Facebook took the market thus becoming a reason for downfall of Orkut [10].

5 Discussion

A. Product Life Cycle of Facebook and Orkut

Product Life cycle of social networking sites has been discussed with respect to the graph in Fig. 2. The social networking site has to go through each phase of the Product Life Cycle. Every social networking site is first introduced, advertised and brought into the market [11]. New registration is done in this phase and usually new users are the early adopter and addictive user of social networking sites. Second phase is the growth phase in which a site grows and sets up itself in the market. Users get attracted towards the new website and give a look over the features of the website. There is an increment in the number of users. In this phase, the website reaches enough mass in such a way that sponsors and marketers take a note of the growth of the company. Its popularity is defined in maturity phase where it is most used and its features are exploited. It is the phase where website has maximum number of users. It is the period where website has to be very careful as after the features are used by the users and result in boredom, the website owner should keep adding new features in the website to reduce the chance of decrease in the number of users. Every cycle reaches its end in the decline phase.

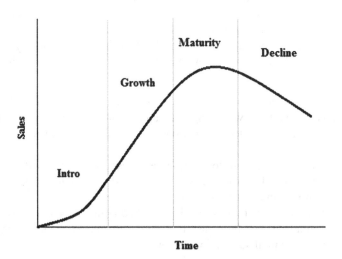

Fig. 2. Illustrates product life cycle of social networking sites [10]

As per product life cycle, both the networking sites have gone through the intro phase. In the intro phase, Facebook had a slow growth as it was limited to Boston Universities till 2005 [12] while Orkut being a Google product had a speedy growth in comparison to Facebook. In the first six months, Orkut entered its growth phase and became popular in North America with an exponential growth in Brazil [13]. Orkut apart from Brazil and North America, became famous in European countries and also in India. There was spike growth in Orkut Popularity in countries like Brazil and India. Yahoo! CEO, Marissa Mayer who was the product manager of Orkut in 2009 said that the people of countries like India and Brazil think that Orkut owns Google. According to people in Brazil, Google is a subsidiary of Orkut [13]. This proved that Orkut was a big success in its growth period while Facebook too entered the growth phase of product life cycle and by the time of August 2005, Facebook was spread worldwide and was available for all the users with valid email account. Facebook gained trust of the people for sharing their identifying information in their profile [14]. By the end of year 2009, Orkut and Facebook both entered the maturity period of product life cycle. Orkut, in the year gap of 2010 and 2011 was ripping maturity period as it was the most used social networking site while Facebook had an exponential growth in the year 2011 of its maturity period [15]. Thus, the exponential growth of Facebook and some changes in policy and user interface of Orkut led to sudden downfall of Orkut. Orkut didn't have gradual downfall but a steep downfall and was officially shut down in the year 2014 while Facebook is still in the maturity phase of the product life cycle and is trying to continue this period as long as possible. Considering the frequent up gradation in the last few years by Facebook, the growth of Facebook in its maturity period is stable thus leading itself to decline period at a very slow pace.

B. Can We Say that Facebook May Have Downfall like Orkut?

Considering the product life cycle of Facebook, we can say that Facebook will be able to maintain its growth for a long period of time. In future, Facebook may not face the circumstances faced by Orkut which lead to its downfall.

If in future, some other social sites come into existence then Facebook has made sure that it remains the part of human life for social sharing. Though the other social networking sites may come into use, but Facebook is the base. Some key points have been mentioned below which shows that Facebook may not have downfall like Orkut as illustrated in reference [11].

- Facebook is not localized in popularity as Orkut was. It has become a big sensation.
- Facebook is the platform where big companies contact with the customers, companies advertise their products, promotions of social moments are done, and news is published.
- Facebook is a single platform for sharing happiness, status of an individual, joyful moments, contacting lost friends, making new friends, sharing ideas, thoughts, studying in groups and much more.
- Though the new social networks may be launched in the market but this would not lead to downfall of Facebook as it is very difficult to launch such a better replacement to downfall such a popular site.

6 Conclusion

Unlike Orkut, Facebook may have its own way of downfall. Facebook was one of the alternative social networking sites when Orkut was active. During the decline period of Orkut, Facebook was very popular and maximum number of users shifted to Facebook. There are many applications like snapchat, Hike etc. which may attract the users. But, it may not be easy to compete with Facebook as it is dynamic and is continuously adding up new features which do not allow the users to stop using it.

There may be some other cause which may result in the downfall of Facebook. Now a days, people share videos and pictures more than the genuine thoughts. Whatever is shared can be accessed by all those who are in the friend list of which many of them are not close. So, people don't prefer to share texts on Facebook. Facebook is more used by the people who are new to it. But, with time people get bored and find Facebook less attractive. Facebook is 10 years old and the users prefer to use something innovative. Also, there are many fake profiles on Facebook which are created by stalkers or marketers. There can be any possibility for which Facebook may come to ground. With changing time there might comes the existence of need of users which cannot be fulfilled by Facebook. Thus, we get the conclusion that Facebook may have downfall but not in the way Orkut had.

References

1. Issa, T., Pedro, I., Piet, K.: Social Networking and Education. LNSN, pp. 3–13. Springer International Publishing, Cham (2016). doi:10.1007/978-3-319-17716-8
2. https://en.wikipedia.org/wiki/Facebook. Accessed 20 June 2016
3. Priyanka, G.: Death of Orkut = Rise of Facebook: a new era of social networking in cyber world. MyReaseachJournals 3(9) (2014)
4. Gehl, R.W.: Real (software) abstractions on the rise of Facebook and the fall of Myspace. Soc. Text (2012). doi:10.1215/01642472-1541772
5. Sharma, S.: Awareness on confidentiality in social networking site. Int. J. Sci. Eng. Res. 4(4) (2013)
6. Sharma, S.: Social network analysis & information disclosure: a case study. Int. J. Comput. Electr. Autom. Control Inf. Eng. 9(2) (2015)
7. Kaur, M., Singh, S.: Analyzing negative ties in social networks: a survey. Egypt. Inform. J. 17(1), 21–43 (2016)
8. Reasons for the downfall of Orkut Social Networking site, 15 June 2012. http://thethingstoknow19.blogspot.in/2012/06/reasons-for-downfall-of-orkut-social.html. Accessed 08 June 2016
9. TricksMachine: 3 Examples of Failed Social Network Leaders, Who's Next? (2011). http://www.tricksmachine.com/2011/05/3-examples-of-failed-social-network-leaders-whos-next.html. Accessed 13 July 2016
10. Nrusinha: Who Killed Orkut: Facebook Or Google Itself? DAZEINFO. http://dazeinfo.com/2012/07/10/who-killed-orkut-facebook-or-google-itself-study. Accessed 10 July 2016
11. QUORA: Will Facebook have a downfall like Orkut? https://www.quora.com/Will-Facebook-have-a-downfall-like-orkut. Accessed 18 July 2016

12. The Guardian: A brief history of Facebook (2007). https://www.theguardian.com/technology/2007/jul/25/media.newmedia. Accessed 22 July 2016
13. Live Mint: The rise, fall and subsequent death of Orkut (2014). http://www.livemint.com/Consumer/zAYIirsyDYC2ZVcNxGkXcJ/The-rise-fall-and-subsequent-death-of-Orkut.html. Accessed 27 June 2016
14. Dwyer, C., Hiltz, S.R., Passerini, K.: Trust and privacy concern within social networking sites: a comparison of Facebook and MySpace. In: Americas Conference on Information Systems, AMCIS 2007 Proceedings. Paper 339 (2007)
15. Acquisti, A., Gross, R.: Imagined communities: awareness, information sharing, and privacy on the Facebook. In: Danezis, G., Golle, P. (eds.) PET 2006. LNCS, vol. 4258, pp. 36–58. Springer, Heidelberg (2006). doi:10.1007/11957454_3

Optimizing Support Vector Machines for Multi-class Classification

J.K. Sahoo$^{(\boxtimes)}$ and Akhil Balaji

Department of Mathematics, BITS Pilani-K.K Birla Goa Campus,
NH-17B, Bye Pass Road, Zuarinagar, Goa, India
{jksahoo, f2012363}@goa.bits-pilani.ac.in

Abstract. The accuracy obtained when classifying multi-class data depends on the classifier and the features used for training the classifier. The parameters passed to the classifier and feature selection techniques can help improve accuracy. In this paper we propose certain dataset and classifier optimization to help improve the accuracy when classifying multi-class data. These optimization also help in reducing the training time.

Keywords: Support Vector Machines · Bagging · Ensemble · Training · Multi-class classification

1 Introduction

In machine learning, sample data is classified as a particular class based on the values of its different parameters. However in most datasets a particular attribute can have multiple classes. Hence the classifier needs to be able to classify the data under a specific class. This types of classification is known as multi-class classification. Methods such as Support Vector Machines (SVM), Decision Trees and Bagging are widely used to classify such data. These methods normally use transformation methods and classification techniques such as one-against-one (OAO) or one-against-rest (OAR) to convert the multi-class classifier into a single class classifier. To improve accuracy, attributes from the dataset were modified using techniques like scaling and normalization. Certain noisy and unnecessary features were removed from the dataset to improve the training time and also helped in improving the accuracy.

In this paper, we propose a way to optimize the parameters and the dataset that is used by Support Vector Machine classifier to classify multi-class data. These optimizations lead to higher accuracy of the predicted class value of the testing dataset. Also Ensemble methods such as Bagging which use Support Vector Machines as the base classifier can be used to obtain a higher accuracy.

In [1], the author introduced a new variant of Support Vector Machines (SVM) namely Fuzzy Support Vector Machines (FSVM) which introduces the fuzzy membership functions to classify multi-label data. He also used two other strategies namely One Against One (OAO) and One Against All (OAA) to train the classifier on the multi-label data. The accuracy obtained in [1] for the yeast dataset using the FSVM technique was 52.08%. Whereas for textual datasets like BIBTEX and TMC2007 the

M. Singh et al. (Eds.): ICACDS 2016, CCIS 721, pp. 393–398, 2017.
DOI: 10.1007/978-981-10-5427-3_42

accuracy obtained was 38.69% and 58.96% respectively. The author used the complete datasets to train the classifiers and no feature selection techniques were used. Preprocessing techniques like scaling and normalizing of the dataset instances were also not performed.

We use the same datasets from [1] by transforming it from multi-label data to multi-class data. We were also able to use feature selection techniques to scale down the number of features by removing the noisy features. To improve the classifier, data instances were scaled according the respective attributes mean and then normalized. The accuracy obtained after training a single classifier like SVC with the optimized dataset was far high than the accuracy obtained in [1]. We obtain even higher accuracy by using ensemble classifiers like Bagging.

2 Support Vector Machines

Support Vector Machines are extremely useful in multi class classification as they are very effective in high dimensional spaces. They can even be used in cases where the number of dimensions is greater than the number of samples [2]. SVM machines are also efficient in terms of memory in comparison with other classifiers such as KNN as they make use of subset of training points in the decision function known as support vectors [3]. The kernel used by the decision function can be varied as well to suit the application and the dataset.

However as the number of features becomes greater than the number of samples (Curse of Dimensionality), the accuracy of the classifier tends to reduce because the data becomes sparse [4]. To overcome this problem feature selection techniques like CfsSubsetEval (which is a method in Weka) and chi-squared are used. In CfsSubsetEval a subset of features are selected based on their correlation values with the class and with each other [5].

3 Bagging

Bootstrap aggregating also known as Bagging involves having a collection of classifiers being trained on a particular dataset. When it comes to predicting on a test dataset each classifier casts a vote for a particular class and depending on the number of votes received, the class with the maximum number of votes is selected. Every classifiers vote has equal weight, this helps in improving the stability and accuracy of the results [7].

Given a standard training set D of size n, bagging generates m new training sets, each of size n', by sampling from D uniformly and with replacement. By sampling with replacement, some observations may be repeated in each D_i. If $n' = n$, then for large n the set is expected to have the fraction $(1-1/e)$ ($\approx$63.2%) of the unique examples of D, the rest being duplicates [8]. This kind of sample is known as a bootstrap sample. The m models are fitted using the above m bootstrap samples and combined by averaging the output (for regression) or voting (for classification).

Bagging helps to reduce the variance of a single base estimator by introducing randomization into its construction procedure and then making an ensemble out of it. It also helps in avoiding over fitting. It helps improve the accuracy with respect to a single model, without making it necessary to change the underlying base algorithm. Bagging methods work best with strong and complex models. Whereas Boosting methods usually work best with weaker models.

Mostly Bagging is used with decision tree models, however Bagging can also be used with other classifiers like SVC. As part of our experiments to improve accuracy we used the Bagging ensemble method. The numbers of classifiers used were varied based on the application.

4 Multi-class Classification

In machine learning, Multi-Class classification is used to classify instances of a multi-class dataset into one of multiple classes. This is different from Multi-label classification, wherein multiple labels are predicted for each instance. We can convert a multi-class classifier into binary classifiers using certain strategies such as One Against Rest and One Against All.

The One Against Rest (OAR) strategy involves training a single classifier (ensemble in case of Bagging) per class, with the sample of that class as positive samples and all other samples as negatives. This strategy requires the base classifiers to produce a real-valued confidence score for its decision [6]. However the method faces some shortcomings like the scale of confidence values may differ between the binary classifiers.

In the One Against One (OAO) strategy, $K(K-1)/2$ binary classifiers are trained to obtain K classifiers, each of these classifiers receives a pair of classes from the original training set and must learn to distinguish between these two classes. For classification, a voting scheme is used and each classifier is applied to a particular sample and the class that gets the highest number of votes gets selected as the predicted class. However ambiguity can arise if more than two or more classes gets the same number of votes. In such cases, strategies such as picking the one with the smallest average error can solve the ambiguity.

5 Computer Experiments

We considered 3 benchmark datasets downloaded from [1]. They are from biology and text categorization and are widely used for evaluating multi-class classification methods. These datasets were preprocessed and were used to compare different multi-class classification methods.

For the One Against One (OAO) strategy, we considered the SVC classifier whereas for the One Against Rest (OAR) strategy Linear SVC which is similar to SVC with parameter kernel = 'linear', but implemented in terms of liblinear rather than libsvm, so it has more flexibility in the choice of penalties and loss functions and should scale better to large numbers of samples. Ensemble methods like Bagging were used to improve the accuracy of obtained results.

(A) **Feature Selection.** Each Dataset was first passed through a feature selection algorithm to select which attributes would be used for training the classifier. We used the CfsSubsetEval algorithm; it evaluates the worth of a subset of attributes by considering the individual predictive ability of each feature along with the degree of redundancy between them. The features selected are selected such that they are highly correlated with the class while having low inter-correlation between them.

(B) **Standardization.** Each attribute from the dataset needs to be standardized before the dataset can be passed to a classifier. Normally the data is transformed to centre it on the mean value of each feature. This is done using Scaling, wherein each non-constant feature is divided by its standard deviation. After scaling, each instance is normalized to unit norm.

(C) **Training.** Each of the dataset sets were passed to three classifiers. To test the One Against Rest (OAR) strategy the data was passed to the SVC classifier. The kernel used was linear, the decision function used was 'ovr' (One vs Rest). To test the One Against One (OAO) strategy the data was passed to the Linear SVC classifier with the kernel as linear and 'ovo' (One vs One) as the decision function. The ensemble classifier Bagging was used which each of the prior base classifiers to help improve the accuracy and reduce variance in the results.

(D) **Testing.** In the experiments 70% of the dataset sets was passed to train the classifier whereas 30% was used to test the trained classifier. The classifier was used to predict the class label given the test data instances. The accuracy was measured as the total number of test instances whose class label was successfully predicted by the classifier.

YEAST is a multi-label dataset from the Biology category. It consists of in total 103 attributes for each instance. The total number of class labels per instancewas 14 (Table 1 and Fig. 1).

Table 1. Experimental results for YEAST dataset (Biology category)

Classifier	Instances	Features	Classes	Train	Test	Accuracy
SVC (OAO)	1484	7	10	70%	30%	60.98%
LinearSVC (OAR)	1484	7	10	70%	30%	59.86%
Bagging (SVC)	1484	7	10	70%	30%	61.43%
Bagging (Linear SVC)	1484	7	10	70%	30%	61.65%

BIBTEX is a multi-label dataset from the Text category. It consists of in total 1972 attributes for each instance. The total number of class labels per instance was 23 (Table 2 and Fig. 2).

Table 2. Experimental results for BIBTEX dataset (Text category)

Classifier	Instances	Features	Classes	Train	Test	Accuracy
SVC (OAO)	7395	26	4	70%	30%	94.99%
LinearSVC (OAR)	7395	26	4	70%	30%	95.10%
Bagging (SVC)	7395	26	4	70%	30%	95.58%
Bagging (LinearSVC)	7395	26	4	70%	30%	95.17%

TMC2007 is a multi-label dataset from the Text category. It consists of in total 508 attributes for each instance. The total number of class labels per instance was 14 (Table 3 and Fig. 3).

Table 3. Experimental results for TMC2007 dataset (Text category)

Classifier	Instances	Features	Classes	Train	Test	Accuracy
SVC (OAO)	28596	58	2	70%	30%	94.74%
LinearSVC (OAR)	28596	58	2	70%	30%	94.74%
Bagging (SVC)	28596	58	2	70%	30%	94.91.%
Bagging (LinearSVC)	28596	58	2	70%	30%	94.74%

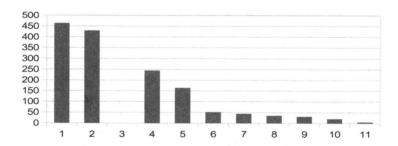

Fig. 1. Frequency wise distribution of each class in YEAST dataset.

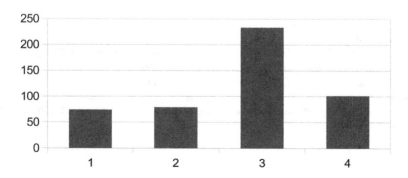

Fig. 2. Frequency wise distribution of each class in BIBTEX dataset.

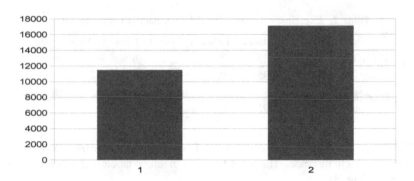

Fig. 3. Frequency wise distribution of each class in TMC2007 dataset.

6 Conclusion

In this paper we proposed an easy way to optimize the use of SVM on multi-class data. We have shown that the strategy required for multi-class classification varies as per dataset. We have seen that the OAO strategy was superior when it came to a single classifier whereas for ensemble methods OAR was a superior method. We also have shown that applying feature selection and standardization techniques dramatically helped in improving the accuracy of the classifier. The use of the Bagging as an ensemble classifier was gives higher accuracy than simple classifier.

References

1. Abe, S.: Fuzzy support vector machines for multilabel classification. Elsevier Pattern Recogn. **48**(6), 2110–2117 (2015)
2. Boser, B.E., Guyon, I.M., Vapnik, V.N.: A training algorithm for optimal margin classifiers. In: Proceedings of the Fifth Annual Workshop on Computational Learning Theory (1992)
3. Raikwal, J.S., Saxena, K.: Performance evaluation of SVM and k-nearest neighbor algorithm over medical data set. Int. J. Comput. Appl. **15**(14) (2012). ISSN 0975-8887
4. Hughes, G.F.: On the mean accuracy of statistical pattern recognizers. IEEE Trans. Inf. Theory **14**, 55–63 (1968)
5. Hall, M.A.: Correlation-based Feature Subset Selection for Machine Learning, Hamilton, New Zealand (1998)
6. Platt, J.C.: Probabilistic Outputs for Support Vector Machines and Comparisons to Regularized Likelihood Methods. Microsoft Research (1999)
7. Leo, B.: Bagging predictors. Mach. Learn. **24**(2), 123–140 (1996)
8. Aslam, J.A., Popa, R.A., Rivest, R.L.: On estimating the size and confidence of a statistical audit. In: Proceedings of the Electronic Voting Technology Workshop (EVT 2007), Boston, MA (2007)

Scalable Online Analytics on Cloud Infrastructures

Jyoti Sahni[1,2(✉)] and Deo Prakash Vidyarthi[2]

[1] Department of CSE & IT, The NorthCap University, Gurugram, India
jyotika.sahni@gmail.com
[2] School of Computer and Systems Sciences, Jawaharlal Nehru University,
New Delhi, India
dpv@mail.jnu.ac.in, jyoti92_scs@jnu.ac.in

Abstract. The need for low latency analysis of high velocity real time continuous data streams has led to the emergence of Stream Processing Systems (SPSs). Contemporary SPSs allow a stream processing application to be hosted on Cloud infrastructures and dynamically scaled so as to adapt to the fluctuating data rates. However, the run time scalability incorporated in these SPSs are in their early adaptations and are based on simple local/global threshold based controls. This work studies the issues with the local and global auto scaling techniques that may lead to performance inefficiencies in real time traffic analysis on Cloud platforms and presents an efficient hybrid auto scaling strategy *StreamScale* which addresses the identified issues. The proposed *StreamScale* auto-scaling algorithm accounts for the gaps in the local/global scaling approaches and effectively identifies (de)parallelization opportunities in stream processing applications for maintaining QoS at reduced costs. Simulation based experimental evaluation on representative stream application topologies indicate that the proposed StreamScale auto-scaling algorithm exhibits better performance in comparison to both local and global auto-scaling approaches.

Keywords: Stream Processing Systems (SPS) · Scalability · Online analytics · Cloud computing · Internet of Things (IoT)

1 Introduction

The emergence of IoT, involving a network of virtually ubiquitous sensors, has led to a scenario where huge amounts of continuous data streams are generated that needs to be processed in real time. As a result, data stream processing has recently surfaced as a new computational paradigm. It involves real time analysis of 'data in motion' so as to extract actionable information and intelligence for productive decision making. Examples of streaming applications may be found in diverse domains e.g. real time traffic analysis for congestion predictions, security intelligence for fraud detection, QoS monitoring for end user services and continuous trend analysis in social networking models. Over the past few years, a number of SPSs have been developed to support continuous analytics of data streams. Examples include commercial solutions e.g. StreamBase [12], InfoSphere [3]; open source solutions e.g. Apache Storm [4], S4 [8] and academic solutions e.g. STREAM [2] and Borealis [1].

© Springer Nature Singapore Pte Ltd. 2017
M. Singh et al. (Eds.): ICACDS 2016, CCIS 721, pp. 399–408, 2017.
DOI: 10.1007/978-981-10-5427-3_43

Streaming applications are structured as directed graphs where vertices are the processing elements (PEs) and edges are the data streams. A classical SPS [1, 2] allows these applications to be executed on fixed size clusters with PEs distributed among different nodes. The cluster size is generally chosen to meet the expected maximum workload. However, since peak loads occur occasionally, the amount of resources needed is rarely static and varies as a result of workload fluctuations on multiple time scales. Further, workload at times may exceed the maximum expected workload due to unexpected traffic surges. A static resource deployment therefore results in performance inefficiencies. Under provisioning of resources leads to QoS (Quality of Service) violations inducing financial penalties while overprovisioning results in resource wastage. To cater to this problem, stream processing frameworks such as StreamCloud [6] and Esc [10] allows an application to grow or shrink its resource pool automatically to adapt to the fluctuating data rates. However, the run time scalability incorporated in these SPSs are in their early adaptations and are based on simple threshold based controls on machines/PEs. They do not accurately suggest the best potential PEs to be scaled and the capacity by which they need to be scaled for improved performance. Also, these scaling approaches assume consistent performance of the underlying resource set and hence are not suitable in Cloud environments which display substantial performance variability [7]. The proposed work aims to address this gap by presenting an efficient auto scaling strategy for real time traffic analysis on Cloud platforms.

The rest of this paper is organized as follows. Section 2 discusses the data stream application model and Cloud resource model used in this work. The need for hybrid auto-scaling mechanism for stream applications is discussed in Sect. 3. Section 4 describes the proposed *StreamScale* auto-scaling algorithm. Section 5 reports the experimental results. Finally, Sect. 6 concludes the work.

2   System Model

This section briefly explains the data stream application model and the Cloud resource model used in this work.

2.1   Data Stream Application Model

This work targets data stream processing applications that may be defined using a Directed Acyclic Graph (DAG) of PEs where data dependencies between them is characterized by streaming dataflow edges. Formally, a stream application is defined as a Continuous dataflow as follows [9].

Continuous Dataflow: A continuous data flow G is a quadruple $G = (P, E, I, O)$ where $P = \{P_1, \ldots P_n\}$ is a set of vertices representing the PEs and $E = \{\langle P_i, P_j \rangle\}$ is a set of directed dataflow edges without cycles representing the message flow from P_i to P_j. $I \neq O$ is the set of input PEs also called as source PEs which receive messages only from external sources and $O \neq \varnothing$ is the set of output PEs (sink PEs) that emit output messages only to the external entities. Each PE represents a long running user defined task which executes continuously accepting and consuming messages from incoming edges and producing messages on outgoing edges. Figure 1 shows an example data stream application.

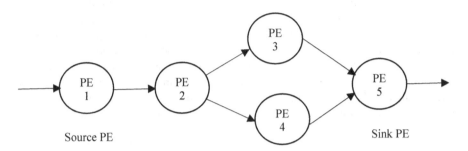

Fig. 1. Example data stream application

2.2 Application Deployment on Cloud Infrastructure Model

For hosting stream applications, an Infrastructure as a Service (IaaS) cloud resource model is assumed. An IaaS cloud service provider offers different VM instances comprising of varied combinations of CPU, memory, storage and networking capacity at different prices. The pricing model is based on a pay-as-you-go billing scheme similar to the current commercial Clouds and the users are charged for the number of time intervals they lease a VM, even if the leased VMs have not been completely used in the last time interval. The time interval is specified by the Cloud provider. A SPS middleware enables streaming applications to be deployed on a cluster of homogeneous VMs. Data parallelism is achieved by allowing each PE of an application to have replicated instances distributed across VMs in the cluster and the incoming traffic at the PE load balanced among them. The number of instances of a PE thus defines its degree of parallelism and scaling an application therefore involves identifying the appropriate degree of parallelism for the constituent PEs based on the incoming load.

3 Need for a Hybrid Scaling Technique

The auto-scaling techniques employed in existing data stream processing systems [6, 10] use the performance of individual PEs (or a group of PEs) to identify the locations where scaling actions are required. Such approach (henceforth referred to as a local scaling) considers each processing unit as an independent entity and thus may lead to inefficient scaling decisions. For example, consider a simple pipeline data stream application with three processing elements PE1, PE2 and PE3 of processing capacities 1000 tuples/sec, 1000 tuples/sec and 3500 tuples/sec respectively as shown in Fig. 2. Let the input data rate be 3200 tuples/sec. It is clear that if individual PEs make independent scaling decisions, bottleneck processing element, PE1, (with less processing capacity in comparison to its input data rate) needs a scale-out operation while PE3 (with very high processing capacity compared to its input data rate) needs a scale-in operation. Further, no scaling is required for PE2. However, it may be observed that these scaling decisions will result in the bottleneck shifted first to PE2 and then to PE3 thus requiring scale-out operation at PE2 and subsequently at PE3. Another approach is to consider the entire application as a black box and make scaling decisions based on the overall performance of the application (henceforth referred as a global scaling). In this, by observing the ratio of the output data rate of an application to its input data rate, one can identify when a scale-out action is required. However, identifying the appropriate locations and the associated scale size is an important issue in such a situation. Also, in cases as depicted in Fig. 3, this approach suggests that the application is running efficiently and no scaling actions are needed. However, it may be observed that both PE1 and PE2 are overprovisioned with atleast three times the capacity in comparison to their input rates and hence need a scale-in operation.

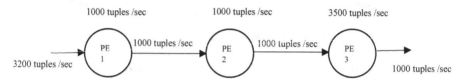

Fig. 2. Example data stream application depicting problems with *local* scaling approach

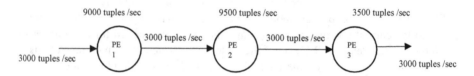

Fig. 3. Example data stream application depicting problems with *global* scaling approach

It is evident that both pure local and pure global approaches fail to capture the significance of the intermediate PEs in the overall application's performance and hence are not be able to make appropriate scaling decisions. This motivates the need for a hybrid scaling approach which considers the performance of the individual PEs and the overall performance of the application w.r.t to the incoming load so as to identify appropriate scaling actions.

4 The Proposed Approach

This section discusses the details of the hybrid auto-scaling approach *StreamScale* proposed in this work. *StreamScale* combines the local and global technique so as to reap the benefits of both in making appropriate scaling decisions.

4.1 Proposed QoS Metrics

This work proposes two metrics: *Global relative throughput* and *Local deviation need* for making scaling decisions.

Global Relative Throughput: To measure the application's overall performance w.r.t the input data rate, this work defines a global metric *global relative throughput* as the ratio of the processing capacity of the least performing PE of the application to the application's input data rate (Eq. 1).

$$Global\,relative\,throughput = \min\left(\min_{p \in P}\left(\frac{(Processing\,Capacity(p)}{(\sum_{i \in I} input\,data\,rate(i)) \times s(p)} \times 100\right), 100\right)$$

(1)

where $s(p)$ is the fraction of the overall input processed by p and is defined as the ratio of the number of input messages consumed by p to the overall number of messages input to the application.

Local Deviation Need: Whenever a scaling operation is triggered, the size by which a PE p ought to be scaled is decided by the *local deviation need* metric. It is defined as the difference between the processing capacity of p and its expected input rate (Eq. 2).

$$Local\,deviation\,need(p) = \left|Processing\,capacity(p) - \left(\sum_{i \in I} input\,data\,rate(i)\right) \times s(p)\right|$$

(2)

4.2   Problem Formulation

This work assumes that a data stream application is hosted on a base set B of VMs, where $B = \{VM_1, VM_2, \ldots, VM_n\}$ is the application's stable resource pool specified by the user. The application, at any point of time, will have atleast B set of VMs in its underlying resource pool. It is required that the application meets a desired QoS requirement specified in terms of the target relative throughput - *global relative throughput*. The goal of the auto-scaling system is to maintain the relative throughput of the application by supporting a flexible auxiliary set A of VMs that are dynamically provisioned depending upon the current workload. Formally, if $\bar{t}$ denotes the target relative throughput of the application and t denotes the observed mean relative throughput, the auto-scaler should identify the PEs that needs to be scaled-out/scaled-in and by what amount such that the observed relative throughput t is no less than $\bar{t}$.

4.3   The Hybrid Approach

The proposed auto-scaling approach, *StreamScale*, uses a MAPE (Monitor, Analyze, Plan and Execute) control loop which runs continuously until the application is stopped by the user. The entire process is described in Algorithm 1. When the control loop observes that a scale-out operation is required (line 2), it uses a routine *IdentifyCongestedPEs* (Algorithm 2) to identify the PEs that needs to be scaled-out (line 3). Next, for each congested PE, the routine *Evaluatediffinst* (Algorithm 4) is used to identify the excess instances required and the corresponding VM share to be added (lines 5–10). Finally, the total number of VMs required for all the congested PEs are provisioned and the application topology is balanced accordingly (lines 11–12). Similarly, when a scale down operation is required (line 13), the auto-scaler uses the routine *IdentifyOverProvisionedPEs* (Algorithm 3) to identify the PEs that needs to be scaled-down (line 14). For each over provisioned PE, the routine *Evaluatediffinst* (Algorithm 4) is used to identify the number of excess instances that needs to be removed and their corresponding VM share (lines 16–21). Finally, the auto-scaler de-provisions the total number of VMs occupied by the overprovisioned PEs and rebalances the topology (lines 22–27).

Algorithm 1 *StreamScale*

Input: Data Stream application A

      Base Pool size B_size

      Target *global relative throughput* $\bar{t}$

      Observed *global relative throughput* t

      Observation period for scale-out t_up

      Observation period for scale-in t_dn

1. While application A is running
2.   If $t < \bar{t}$ continuously for t_up time units
3. $PEstoScaleup = IdentifyCongestedPEs(A, t\_up)$
4. $N\_VMs\_scaleup = 0$
5.   For each $PE\ p$ in $PEstoScaleup$
6. $N\_instances = Evaluatediffinst(p, t\_up) \times 1.2$
7. $AvgVMshare = mean(\%VM\ share\ of\ p\ instances)$
8. $VMshare = N\_instances \times AvgVMshare$
9. $N\_VMs\_scaleup = N\_VMs\_scaleup + VMshare$
10.   End For
11.   Provision $\lceil N\_VMs\_scaleup \rceil$ VMs
12.   Rebalance topology as identified by step 6
13.   Else If $t > 100$ continuously for t_dn time units
14. $PEstoScaledn = IdentifyOverProvisionedPEs(A, t\_dn)$
15. $N\_VMs\_scaledn = 0$
16.   For each $PE\ p$ in $PEstoScaledn$
17. $N\_instances = Evaluatediffinst(p, t\_dn,) \times 0.8$
18. $AvgVMshare = mean(\%VM\ share\ of\ p\ instances)$
19. $VMshare = N\_instances \times AvgVMshare$
20. $N\_VMs\_scaledn = N\_VMs\_scaledn + VMshare$
21.   End For
22.   If $Pool\_size - \lfloor N\_VMsscaledn \rfloor \geq B\_size$
23.   De-provision $\lfloor N\_VMsscaledn \rfloor$ VMs
24.   Else
25.   De-provision $Pool\_size - B\_size$ VMs
26.   End if
27.   Rebalance topology as identified by step 17
28.   End if
29. End While

Algorithm 2. $IdentifyCongestedPEs(A, ob\_tup)$

---

1. $CongestedPEs = \emptyset$
2. $MaxRateInput = \max input \, rate \, of \, the$
   $\quad\quad application \, in \, the \, last \, ob\_tup \, minutes$
3. For each $PE \, p \, in \, A$
4. $\quad$ If$(Processing \, capacity(p) < s(p) \times MaxRateInput).$
5. $\quad\quad CongestedPEs = CongestedPEs \cup p$
6. $\quad$ End if
7. End For
8. Return $CongestedPEs$

Algorithm 3. $IdentifyOverProvisionedPEs(A, ob\_tdn)$

---

1. $OverProvisionedPEs = \emptyset$
2. $MaxRateInput = \max input \, rate \, of \, the$
   $\quad\quad application \, in \, the \, last \, ob\_tdn \, minutes$
3. For each $PE \, p \, in \, A$
   $\quad\quad$ If$(Processing \, capacity(p) > s(p) \times MaxRateInput)$
4. $\quad\quad\quad OverProvisionedPEs = OverProvisionedPEs \cup p$
5. $\quad\quad$ End if
6. End For
7. Return $OverProvisionedPEs$

Algorithm 4. $Evaluatediffinst(p, ob\_t)$

---

1. $MaxRateInput = \max input \, rate \, of \, the$
   $\quad application \, in \, the \, last \, ob\_t \, minutes$
2. $local\_deviationneed = |\sum_{k=1:m} Processingrate(p_k) - MaxRateInput \times s(p)| \quad ,$
   m is the number of instances of PE p
3. $average\_instance\_capacity = (\sum_{k=1:m} Processingrate(p_k))/m$
4. $Required\_instances = (local\_deviationneed \, / \, average\_instance\_capacity)$
5. Return $Required\_instances$

---

5 Performance Evaluation

The proposed auto-scaling heuristic has been evaluated and compared with two baseline algorithms through a simulation. A discrete event simulator was developed that emulates the real-world cloud characteristics based on the benchmarking results obtained in [7, 11]. Also, in accordance with the latest pricing schemes a per-minute billing scheme with a minimum billing period of 10 min was assumed [5]. The experimental setup of a base VM cluster consisting of 2 homogeneous VMs each with a configuration of 512 MB memory and processing capacity of 100 MIPS was emulated. In order to analyze and compare the performance of the proposed auto-scaling heuristic with other scaling implementations, three representative topologies: linear, star and diamond topologies depicting different scenarios were studied. The layout of these topologies are shown in Fig. 4.

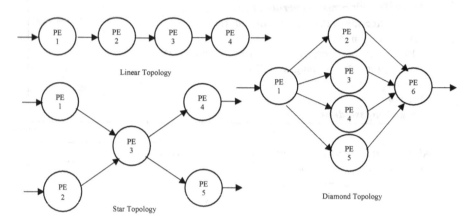

Fig. 4. Layout of topologies used for the experiments

Further, to simulate traffic variations in continuous data flows the input to each topology was implemented by mimicking a random walk of tuples with the initial value of 250 tuples/sec, step length of ±25 and size of ~100 Kbytes/tuple. For each topology, the experiments were run for 12 h on the simulated resources exhibiting temporal and spatial performance variations as observed in real cloud environments [7, 11].

Each experiment was repeated 5 times and the average values reported. In order to evaluate the efficacy of the proposed auto-scaling heuristic, it has been compared with two other baseline scaling approaches:

(a) a global approach implemented with brute force mechanism which examines the topology using a DFS traversal rooted at the input PEs and increases the number of instances at congested PEs by one until the observed relative throughput reaches the target relative throughput.

(b) a local approach where each PE makes local scaling decisions based on its input data rate.

The evaluation of the different algorithms were made on the following two parameters: (a) global relative throughput (b) cost.

Figures 5 presents the comparative results of the different scaling algorithms on linear, star and diamond topologies respectively. It can be observed that across all the topologies Local scaling approach is outperformed by the Global scaling and *StreamScale* algorithms both in terms of the global relative throughput and cost. Further, it may be noted that since Global scaling approach uses a DFS traversal to increases the number of instances at congested PEs until the observed relative throughput reaches the target defined, it takes some time to converge to the required resource configurations for the different PEs. On the other hand, the proposed StreamScale algorithm is able to systematically calculate and provision the right amount of resources required resulting in improved performance at approximately the same (or less) cost.

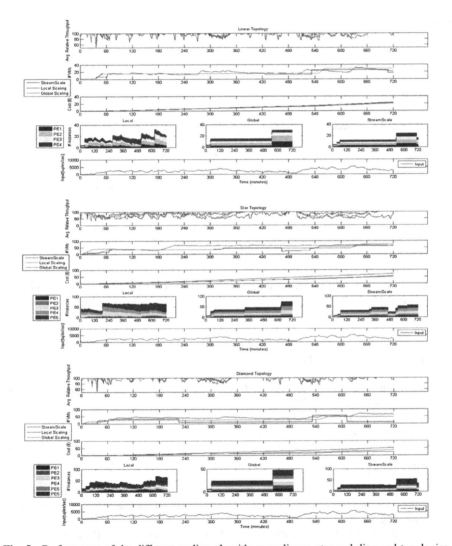

Fig. 5. Performance of the different scaling algorithms on linear, star and diamond topologies

Overall for all the topologies, the proposed StreamScale auto-scaling algorithm delivers an improvement of 20% and 8% in the overall relative throughput and incurs 21% and 7% lesser costs in comparison to the local and global scaling approaches respectively.

6 Conclusion

This paper identifies the need for a *global* performance metric that measures the overall performance of a data stream application with respect to the input data rates and proposes a performance metric *global relative throughput* for the same. A target *global relative throughput* threshold based *hybrid* auto-scaling algorithm *StreamScale* that effectively identifies the locations where (de)scaling operations are required and the corresponding scaling sizes so as to maintain the target performance is also proposed.

References

1. Abadi, D.J., Ahmad, Y., Balazinska, M., Çetintemel, U., Cherniack, M., Hwang, J.-H., Lindner, W., Maskey, A., Rasin, A., Ryvkina, E., Tatbul, N., Xing, Y. and Zdonik, S.B.: The design of the Borealis stream processing engine. In: CIDR, pp. 277–289 (2005)
2. Arasu, A., Babcock, B., Babu, S., Datar, M., Ito, K., Motwani, R., Nishizawa, I., Srivastava, U., Thomas, D., Varma, R., Widom, J.: STREAM: the stanford stream data manager. IEEE Data Eng. Bull. **26**, 19–26 (2003)
3. Biem, A., Bouillet, E., Feng, H.: IBM infosphere streams for scalable, real-time, intelligent transportation services. In: SIGMOD 2010: Proceedings of the 2010 ACM SIGMOD International Conference on Management of Data, pp. 1093–1103 (2010)
4. Toshniwal, A., Donham, J., Bhagat, N., Mittal, S., Ryaboy, D., Taneja, S., Shukla, A., Ramasamy, K., Patel, J.M., Kulkarni, S., Jackson, J., Gade, K., Fu, M.: Storm@twitter. In: Proceedings of the 2014 ACM SIGMOD International Conference on Management of Data - SIGMOD 2014, pp. 147–156 (2014)
5. Google Compute Engine. https://developers.google.com/compute/pricing
6. Gulisano, V., Jiménez-Peris, R., Patiño-Marínez, M., Soriente, C., Valduriez, P.: StreamCloud: an elastic and scalable data streaming system. IEEE Trans. Parallel Distrib. Syst. **23**(12), 2351–2365 (2012)
7. Iosup, A., Yigitbasi, N., Epema, D.: On the performance variability of production cloud services. In: Proceedings - 11th IEEE/ACM International Symposium on Cluster, Cloud and Grid Computing, CCGrid 2011, pp. 104–113 (2011)
8. Jain, N., Amini, L., Andrade, H., King, R.: Design, implementation, and evaluation of the linear road benchmark on the stream processing core. In: Proceedings, pp. 431–442 (2006)
9. Kumbhare, A.G., Member, S., Simmhan, Y., Member, S.: Reactive resource provisioning heuristics for dynamic dataflows on cloud infrastructure. IEEE Trans. Cloud Comput. **3**(2), 105–118 (2015)
10. Satzger, B., Hummer, W., Leitner, P., Dustdar, S.: Esc: towards an elastic stream computing platform for the cloud. In: Proceedings - 2011 IEEE 4th International Conference on Cloud Computing, CLOUD 2011, pp. 348–355 (2011)
11. Schad, J., Dittrich, J., Quiané-Ruiz, J.-A.: Runtime measurements in the cloud observing analyzing and reducing variance. Proc. VLDB Endow. **3**(1–2), 460–471 (2010)
12. StreamBase Complex Event Processing – Overview—TIBCO: 2013. http://www.tibco.com/products/event-processing/complex-event-processing/streambase-complex-event-processing

User Search Intention in Interactive Data Exploration: A Brief Review

Archana Dhankar$^{(\boxtimes)}$ and Vikram Singh

Computer Engineering Department, National Institute of Technology,
Kurukshetra, Kurukshetra 136119, Haryana, India
archana19dhankar@gmail.com, viks@nitkkr.ac.in

Abstract. Data exploration finds relevant data efficiently even if a user doesn't know exactly what he/she is aiming for. These exploratory search paradigms are not well-supported in traditional database systems, thus interactive data exploratory (IDE) system evolved. A naïve data user exhibits various kinds of search behavior while formulating exploratory queries. In IDE system, each user interaction leads to more relevant results, due to its highly interactive and user-centric approach. To understand why and what user is searching for, more efficient data exploration systems need to be designed. This paper aims to discuss various factors affecting the user search behavior, how an IDE system support user. Various practices for measuring system support's effectiveness are also highlighted. Finally, proposed a strategy for modeling the user search intentions for exploratory queries in IDE systems.

Keywords: Exploratory search · Interactive Data Exploration · User search intention

1 Introduction

Humans are information seeker by nature, thus aims to achieve never ending desires of amalgamation with real world openly as well as passionately. Primarily, he applies his natural instincts to extract the information to enhance his knowledge and develop complex intellectual skills. This intent of information seeking is the main motivation for the evolution of search engines or exploratory systems. These systems are designed by considering the naive user inability or limited capability of forming his request of data/information and mainly based on recall-oriented search. A naïve user applies his data request via interfaces in search systems. User search queries are often ill-phrased and rarely fetch the desired results in initial search trails, leads to the multiple trails by a user over the search system. After each trial, user reviews retrieve the result and move ahead for the further information seeking task, if found unsatisfactory. This query-result-review paradigm serves primarily two objectives first, it helps in the formation of improved data request query and second it helps to a user in developing more clarity in his requirement. As most of the search trials fail due to user uncertainty of data need, which a naïve user often fails to comprehend. Figure 1, shows the growing modularity of user search query in leading search engine (Google) in the span of 1999–2012 [19].

© Springer Nature Singapore Pte Ltd. 2017
M. Singh et al. (Eds.): ICACDS 2016, CCIS 721, pp. 409–419, 2017.
DOI: 10.1007/978-981-10-5427-3_44

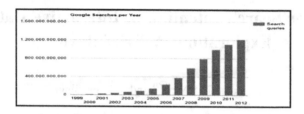

Fig. 1. Number of user searches (in Google, Y: 1999–2012).

A wealth of information will fail to capture the required attention of users [32]. Existing search systems no longer meet the desired criteria. The existing approach of searches such as keyword based and look up search is inadequate to develop new complex intellectual skills. The evolving type of information seeking is known as exploratory search. Exploratory search is an emerging discipline that encompasses information domains via three facets: "Lookup," "Learn" and "Investigate." [4].

To build more effective IR systems we need to get to the roots of the fundamental information seeking behavior. User interaction plays a deciding role in defining the search system effectiveness. The Cranfield methodology [20] used by TREC [21] has been doing groundbreaking research on IR systems considering all the factors. Since TREC-3 it has become mandatory to realize the importance of user interaction. The Interactive Track [23], and High Accuracy Retrieval of Documents (HARD) track [22] have both focused on the user in IR systems. These tracks have succeeded in emphasizing the importance of user but often fail in drawing experimental inferences.

Human information interaction (HII) is the new evolving research area, which tries to encapsulate the user interaction with information. Even after establishing the obvious importance of user, there is no impact on the fundamental design of the existing IR systems. Primarily, due to several challenges related to the inherent contextual complexity of human cognitive interaction and the difficulty in mapping real life scenarios into structured tools. There are various remedial solutions like Auto Complete, Query Recommendations [24], and personalized search [25] etc. However, these remedial solutions are limited in processing well-structured and exact queries. For exploratory queries where the query itself is imprecise and the response is not clear, existing search approaches fail to meet desired ideals. This class of applications is referred as Interactive Data Exploration (IDE) applications that try to model user interaction with efficient exploratory searches.

IDE is a crucial element for a variety of discovery-based applications such as scientific computing and financial studies. IDE is fundamentally a multi-step, non-linear process with imprecise end-goals. For example, data-driven scientific discovery through IDE often requires non-expert users to iteratively interact with the system to make sense and to identify interesting patterns and relationships in large data sets. IDE suffers from severe challenges than traditional web searches. Here, the typical user usually lacks the fundamentals of query formulation. The queries are imprecise and intent is normally vague. In Data Exploration (DE) Systems exploratory queries are asked when very little of it is known to the user. A single exploratory task consists of a stream of queries aimed at learning more about the topic and then analyzing the information gathered. These topics are often open-ended. Many studies are also done in the case of IDE Systems, where the system customizes itself *on-the-fly*.

To further increase the efficiency and accuracy of IDE systems, it is critical that relevant information should reach the naïve user. This scenario leads in shifting from the traditional lookup search to *useful search* [35]. Establishing usefulness as the criteria according to which any specific aspect of interactive information retrieval should be evaluated could lead to principled research. Consider the demands like what triggered the user to initiate the search session; what support the search system can provide the user in order to meet the information needs of the user; what factors affect the searcher's intention during the session. Answering these "what's" will bring us closer to build effective and much more useful search systems. The goal is to support the user's ability to build relationships among discovered information items [26]. In the design of search interfaces for browsing rich information, we need to design a certain degree of elasticity into the product to give users more control over the results.

1.1   Contribution and Outline

This paper primarily investigates notions of data exploration and further highlights the importance of user search intention. In this process, we reviewed traditional search system and observed search behaviors. The final contribution is a strategy, which encapsulates the various search behaviors for modeling the user intention in the exploratory search. Section 2 discusses the nature of exploratory queries and the models on information behavior. In Sect. 3 we will discuss the support provided by IDE systems to the users to develop clarity on his data interests and requirements Sect. 4 details the aspects affecting the user search behavior during an exploration seeking session. Section 5 discusses the evaluation of the usefulness of IDE systems to support the user in achieving his exploration goals. We propose a modified model after incorporating the exploratory nature of queries and high system-user interaction in Sect. 6. Lastly, we conclude by emphasizing the need of understanding the user behavior in order to move from mere finding to understanding.

1.2   Related Work

Several theoretical conducts have been proposed to illustrate this complex cognitive process of human mind. Belkin's Anomalous States of Knowledge (ASK) framework was an early attempt to model the cognitive state of the [27]. User studies like [28] have been performed in the past to understand the fundamentals of how to do user search. Nevertheless, these studies are limited to web related searches. In the case of dedicated IDE systems, the behavior of the user changes. The user might start with a different intent at the beginning of the search session but might end up searching something else. These factors must be mapped accurately while drawing inferences from the search system and user interaction. Marchionini [4] provides a detailed description of the nature of exploratory queries and how they differ from normal lookup queries. Recently much research has been conducted to develop high-quality interaction tools to provide the user the continuous control over the search session. [29] Also discusses the new insights for search evaluation based upon the exploratory nature of posed queries.

[17] Provides an extensive research work over the decades related to the changing trends in information needs. Similarly, White [5] discussed a hypothetical paradigm of exploratory search and how the user can move beyond the traditional query-response paradigm. He also gives valuable insights on the interactions with search systems [3]. In the recent times, the involvement of humans interacting with search systems has led to the emergence of new fields like HII (Human Information Interaction). Fidel [30] provides an ecological approach to information behavior, which helps in understanding the gap that exists in the system design and the user search intentions.

[32] Compares the exploratory searching behavior on one group only using web search engines, while the other used social media sites to search. The results indicate that smaller amount of data is found on social media site while web search engines give diverse relevant documents. [31] Implements search system based on the user histories. In this paper, we briefly review the fundamentals of user search behavior.

2 Exploratory Search and User Behavior

For effective IDE systems, the human search behavior must be observed carefully. A typical user employs a number of strategies in an exploratory search session.

2.1 Exploratory Search

A typical exploratory search comes in between simple lookup search and complex analytical search. As, [4] straightaway distinguish a user conducted the search in three complementary activities, such as lookup, learn and investigate. Lookup is the fundamental search, supported mostly by web-based search engines. The result of lookup search is well structured, thus known as item search. Learning activity of search consists of multiple steps and the results set require intense interpretation and handling. The investigation activity of search is the most complex of all activities. It takes place over long period of time and the results are usually imprecise.

Exploratory search is the integration of "learn" and "investigate" activities of search more deeply. Both activities are recall-oriented, that is maximizing the number of relevant responses received than precision, which is minimizing the number of irrelevant responses. Hence, it becomes critical to retrieve relevant results as much as, rather exact results. Although, a typical web search system is keyword based and highly inclined towards precision. Because of this reason today's search services augmented various methods on top of basic search to meet the needs of users more efficiently. Exploratory search demands strong human participation in an iterative manner. Hence, data exploration systems are required which incorporate user participation. Interactive Data Exploration (IDE) systems are one such application.

2.2   User Search Behavior Models

Researchers have classified models into separate but complementary areas of information behavior [16, 17]: *information-seeking behavior* and *information searching behavior*. Both represent same aspects but with different views. Research in the field of information behavior would suggest the various models as nested fields (Fig. 2) [14]. Information behavior being is the most general form. Information seeking behavior is defined as the subset since it consists of the various methods used to collect information sources. The Information search behavior is defined at the third level that comprises of the user and system interactions to gain as many insights as possible. At last Exploratory Search behavior is placed, as it narrows original scope.

Fig. 2. Nested models of information behavior.

There are mainly two popular models for information seeking behavior, proposed by Wilson [14] and Ellis [33]. In Wilson's model information need arises from fundamental needs of the daily routine. While, Ellis model states, that a user search experience is divided into many subtasks, e.g. browsing, extracting and verifying.

3   User Support in IDE System

Search systems are proactive, hence provides automatic support or variable amount of assistance can be given to the user. Modern search systems have the capability to provide real-time support and progressively analyzing user logs to provide efficient search strategies. We observed that IDE system user support can be at various levels, as shown in Fig. 3. Integrating these dimensions ensure a seamless experience.

Fig. 3. 3-Levels of user support

Fig. 4. System supports for exploratory queries

3.1   System Support

An efficient IDE search system must provide a holistic support environment (Fig. 4). They mainly involve the definition of the tasks, understands the already available information, provide progress updates, handles ambiguity and confusion, the conclusion of the search and provides the explanation of the system actions.

Approaches, such as Relevance feedback [15], understanding User Behavior through Log Data Mining [42], User Experience through Crowdsourcing and gathering user reflections [40] clearly encouraged construction of revised search strategies. Similarly, Trails [10] as mined from user logs are very effective in identifying search patterns. Tools offering scripted documents [9] help users to observe effective search results that are best matched. Integrating user behavior information can considerably improve ordering of results [7]. Metro maps capture the relationships between the available set of information and visualizes the space [8].

Approaches, such as Query Refinement, Query Expansion [13], Interactive Query Expansion (IQE) [12], Real-Time Query Expansion (RTQE) and Automatic Query Expansion (AQE) [11] has proven to be very effective in improving the search experience. Studying Short and Long Term Behavior during personalized search [41] helps to gain deep insights in user Behavior. Additional support to naïve users can be provided by providing informed navigation and steering operators [34, 35]. As, while initiating search session, the user does not know *how to begin* and *form a search path*.

3.2   User Interface Support

Better user interface and better visualization have a direct impact on user behavior [18]. As it is said a picture says a thousand words. It is easier for the human brain to get more information from pictures then a lengthy piece of text. [6] Introduced the notion of exploratory search systems (ESS) evaluation strategies that support the advanced exploratory interface for user search queries. Much research has been conducted lately to develop innovative interfaces to support exploratory search.

3.3   Knowledge Base/Database Support

A knowledge base (KB) is a technology used to store complex structured and unstructured information used by a computer system. By providing better resources of data that are complete and unambiguous, the system can draw more refined results.

4   Factors Affecting User Search Intention

Information seeking is a distinctive case of problem-solving. It includes recognition and interpretation of the information problem, creating a plan of search, assessing the results, and if necessary, iterating through the process again [1]. The *expertise of the user* making a search plays a definitive role [2]. A naive user tends to stray from the exploratory path. On the contrary, an expert user knows the domain beforehand; hence more precise queries are posed. The *cognitive viewpoint* is complex hence IDE systems becomes inherently complex if modeled by focusing on human interactions.

The standard model of the information gathering process makes the assumption that the user's *information need is static*. However, careful analysis finds that user's information needs are dynamic and they may change as they interact with the IDE system. Various aspects related to retrieved results, such as *how much relevant result retrieved, how much is newly retrieved, already viewed results set* plays important role in shaping the user intention. A *task motive* also plays an important role.

Additionally, in IDE user submit *feedback on* reviewed database objects, hence it is critical to incorporate feedback into search model. Similarly, factors like *eye-tracking* are also considered to investigate how users interacted with the system. The motive was to gain insights into *how users searched* information. This includes *the total number of search results viewed* and measures of how users evaluated the results set.

5 Evaluation of IDE System Support

Most of the metrics do not involve the role of the user, although a range of ranking algorithms has been published for effective evaluation of the search systems. Some classic measures are recall and precision. In [36] user's perspectives towards search is given importance. Information presentations and the challenges discussed in [37]. User friendliness and responsiveness are highlighted in [38]. Many measures are based on the relevancy of information retrieved and user satisfaction [39]. Information visualization [3] also plays a determining role in the evaluation.

Over the years, while evaluating IDE systems support, four fundamental areas of measurement of the performance of IDE systems have been identified. The first set is based on contextual measures. This type of measure differentiates among the searchers based on demographics such as age. The second area is the interaction of the user with the system. The third area of measurement is focused on the performance of the system. The final area is based on the usability of the search system. It consists of the feedback generated by the system. However, all these measures fail to capture the essence of user involvement. While evaluating an IDE system should measure user satisfaction, task outcomes, and interaction behaviors.

The evaluating strategy must be clearly defined across two domains. One is the metrics that contains precise definitions of what needs to be measured and the other is the policies which state the process of measuring the identified metrics.

6 Proposed Model for Modelling Exploratory Search Behavior

Many information seeking and searching models [14] has been proposed to gain a better understanding of user intentions. These models of information behavior do not describe the same set of singularities. Also, these models are not devised keeping the exploratory nature of queries. The existing models do not give any explanation on the causing factors of search session and do little in mapping the search scope for the user.

The aim is to help the user find the best match results, keep track of the information already found and any updates regarding information change. The new model will help us understand the relationship between user and search session.

6.1   System Model

We propose, an intention model for exploratory queries, in which exploratory session is based upon five steps, shown in Fig. 5.

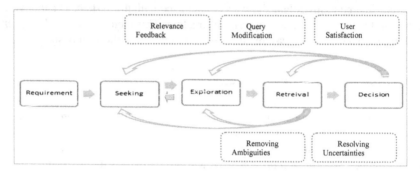

Fig. 5.   Modeling exploratory search behavior.

The first stage is the information *requirement phase*, in which user feels the *need of information gain* due to curiosity aroused to satisfy and develop the human intellect. This phase will result in the *information seeking phase*, in which user *initiates the search process* by simply gathering the resources available to search. The *exploration phase* marks the beginning of the *information retrieval phase*, as the user is able to formulate queries and come up with definitive search options. After this phase, IDE system retrieves share first set of outputs for review, now user reformulates the previous search query for relevant result sets. In this reformulation, IDE system assists to the user via relevance feedback and query recommendations. The results are integrated into the Retrieval phase. The user can navigate from the initial search path by selecting and deselecting the samples generated by the IDE system. Lastly *decision phase*, in which gathered information is consumed and utilized for further processing.

7   Conclusion

Understanding the user *actual search intentions* and *how the search motives changes* as the search session progress will help to the systems more precisely and effectively. Hence, it becomes evident to IDE system to provide necessary support, assistance as well as guidance to the naïve user. This paper investigated various factors affecting the user search intention and how an IDE system assists this user in improving the clarity. Also discussed, how to evaluate the effectiveness of IDE system's support, which helps to bridge the gap in user needs and retrieved information. We proposed a new strategy for modeling search behavior for exploratory search, integrating various fundamental activities of an information seeking behavior.

References

1. Marchionini, G.: Information-seeking strategies of novices using a full-text electronic encyclopedia. J. Am. Soc. Inf. Sci. **40**(1), 54 (1989)
2. Li, Y., Belkin, N.J.: An exploration of the relationships between work task and interactive information search behavior. J. Am. Soc. Inf. Sci. Technol. **16**(9), 1771–1789 (2010)
3. White, R.: Interactions with Search Systems. Cambridge University Press, Cambridge (2016)
4. Marchionini, G.: Exploratory search: from finding to understanding. Commun. ACM **49**(4), 41–46 (2006)
5. White, R., Resa, R.: Exploratory Search: Beyond the Query-Response Paradigm. Morgan and Claypool, San Rafael (2009)
6. White, R., Gheorghe, M., Marchionini, G.: Report on ACM SIGIR 2006 workshop on evaluating exploratory search systems. ACM SIGIR Forum **40**(2), 52–60 (2006). ACM
7. Agichtein, E., Brill, E., Dumais, S.: Improving web search ranking by incorporating user behavior information. In: Proceedings of the 29th Annual International ACM SIGIR Conference on Research and Development in Information Retrieval, pp. 19–26 (2006)
8. Shahaf, D., Guestrin, C., Horvitz, E.: Metro maps of science. In: Proceedings of the 18th ACM SIGKDD International Conference on Knowledge Discovery and Data Mining, pp. 1122–1130 (2012)
9. Zellweger, P.T.: Scripted documents: a hypermedia path mechanism. In: Proceedings of the Second Annual ACM Conference on Hypertext, pp. 1–14 (1989)
10. Bilenko, M., White, R.W.: Mining the search trails of surfing crowds: identifying relevant websites from user activity. In: Proceedings of the 17th International Conference on World Wide Web, pp. 51–60 (2008)
11. Mitra, M., Singhal, A., Buckley, C.: Improving automatic query expansion. In: Proceedings of the 21st Annual International ACM SIGIR Conference on Research and Development in Information Retrieval, pp. 206–214 (1998)
12. Harman, D.: Towards interactive query expansion. In: Proceedings of the 11th Annual International ACM SIGIR Conference on Research and Development in Information Retrieval, pp. 321–331 (1988)
13. White, R.W., Marchionini, G.: Examining the effectiveness of real-time query expansion. Inf. Process. Manag. **43**(3), 685–704 (2007)
14. Wilson, T.D.: Models in information behaviour research. J. Doc. **55**(3), 249–270 (1999)
15. Ruotsalo, T., et al.: Directing exploratory search with interactive intent modeling. In: Proceedings of the 22nd ACM International Conference on Conference on Information and Knowledge Management. ACM (2013)
16. Saracevic, T., Paul, K.: A study of information seeking and retrieving searchers, searches, and overlap. J. Am. Soc. Inf. Sci. **39**(3), 197 (1988)
17. Case, D.O.: Looking for Information: A Survey of Research on Information Seeking, Needs and Behavior. Emerald Group Publishing, Bingley (2012)

18. Fekete, J.-D., van Wijk, J.J., Stasko, J.T., North, C.: The value of information visualization. In: Kerren, A., Stasko, J.T., Fekete, J.-D., North, C. (eds.) Information Visualization. LNCS, vol. 4950, pp. 1–18. Springer, Heidelberg (2008). doi:10.1007/978-3-540-70956-5_1
19. http://www.internetlivestats.com/google-search-statistics/
20. Cleverdon, C.W., Keen, M.: Cranfield research project-factors determining the performance of indexing systems, vol. 2, Test results (1966)
21. Harman, D.: Overview of the first text retrieval conference. In: Proceedings of the 16th Annual ACM SIGIR Conference on Research and Development in Information Retrieval, pp. 36–47 (1993)
22. Allan, J.: HARD track overview in TREC 2003: high accuracy retrieval from documents. In: Proceedings of the Text Retrieval Conference, pp. 24–37 (2003)
23. Dumais, S., Belkin, N.J.: The TREC interactive track: putting the user into search. In: Voorhees, E., Harman, D. (eds.) TREC: Experiment and Evaluation in Information Retrieval. MIT Press, Cambridge (2005)
24. Chatzopoulou, G., Eirinaki, M., Polyzotis, N.: Query recommendations for interactive database exploration. In: Winslett, M. (ed.) SSDBM 2009. LNCS, vol. 5566, pp. 3–18. Springer, Heidelberg (2009). doi:10.1007/978-3-642-02279-1_2
25. Speretta, M., Gauch, S.: Personalized search based on user search histories. In: The 2005 IEEE/WIC/ACM International Conference on Web Intelligence. IEEE (2005)
26. Belkin, N.J.: People, interacting with information. ACM SIGIR Forum 49(2), 13–27 (2016). ACM
27. Belkin, N.J., Oddy, R.N., Brooks, H.M.: ASK for information retrieval: part I. Backgr. Theory J. Doc. 38(2), 61–71 (1982)
28. Stohn, C.: How Do Users Search and Discover? Findings from Ex Libris User Research. EX Libris, Jerusalem (2015). http://www.exlibrisgroup.com/files/Products/Primo/HowDoUsers SearchandDiscover.pdf. [cited 23 Aug 2015]
29. White, R.W., Marchionini, G., Muresan, G.: Evaluating exploratory search systems: introduction to special topic issue of information processing and management. Inf. Process. Manag., 433–436 (2008)
30. Fidel, R.: Human Information Interaction: An Ecological Approach to Information Behavior. MIT Press, Cambridge (2012)
31. Golovchinsky, G., Diriye, A., Dunnigan, T.: The future is in the past: designing for exploratory search. In: Proceedings of the 4th Information Interaction in Context Symposium. ACM (2012)
32. Choi, D., Ziad Matni, Z., Shah, C.: Switching sources: a study of people's exploratory search behavior on social media and the web. Proc. Assoc. Inf. Sci. Technol. 52(1), 1–10 (2015)
33. Ellis, D.: A behavioural model for information retrieval system design. J. Inf. Sci. 15(4-5), 237–247 (1989)
34. Cetintemel, U., et al.: Query steering for interactive data exploration. In: CIDR (2013)
35. Dimitriadou, K., Olga Papaemmanouil, O., Diao, Y.: Explore-by-example: an automatic query steering framework for interactive data exploration. In: Proceedings of the 2014 ACM SIGMOD International Conference on Management of Data. ACM (2014)
36. Salton, G.: Evaluation problems in interactive information retrieval. Inf. Storage Retr. 6(1), 29–44 (1970)
37. Cleverdon, C.W.: User evaluation of information retrieval systems. J. Doc. 30(2), 170–180 (1974)
38. Tague, J., Schultz, R.: Evaluation of the user interface in an information retrieval system: a model. Inf. Process. Manag. 25(4), 377–389 (1989)
39. Kelly, D.: Methods for evaluating interactive information retrieval systems with users. Found. Trends Inf. Retr. 3(1–2), 1–224 (2009)

40. Bateman, S., Teevan, J., White, R.W.: The search dashboard: how reflection and comparison impact search behavior. In: Proceedings of the SIGCHI Conference on Human Factors in Computing Systems, pp. 1785–1794 (2012)
41. Bennett, P.N., et al.: Modeling the impact of short-and long-term behavior on search personalization. In: Proceedings of the 35th International ACM SIGIR Conference on Research and Development in Information Retrieval, pp. 185–194 (2012)
42. Dumais, S., et al.: Understanding user behavior through log data and analysis. In: Olson, J.S., Kellogg, W.A. (eds.) Ways of Knowing in HCI, pp. 349–372. Springer, New York (2014)

Internet of Things

A Novel Ultra Low Power Current Comparator

Veepsa Bhatia[1(✉)] and Neeta Pandey[2]

[1] Department of ECE, Indira Gandhi Delhi Technical University for Women,
Delhi, India
veepsa@gmail.com
[2] Department of ECE, Delhi Technological University, Delhi, India
neetapandey06@gmail.com

Abstract. A novel ultra low power current comparator has been proposed in this paper. The current comparator utilizes Dynamic Threshold Metal Oxide Semiconductor (DTMOS) technique to reduce the power dissipation, by reducing the supply voltage. The circuit is capable of working at a supply voltage as low as ±0.2 V. The circuit has been implemented in 0.18 μm (Taiwan Semiconductos Manufacturing Company) TSMC technology parameters.

Keywords: Current comparator · Delay · DTMOS · Monte Carlo · PDP · Power dissipation

1 Introduction

The ever increasing requirement of smaller feature size for transistors in the CMOS technology, demands for lower supply voltages [1]. Further, many applications in the fields of biomedical devices, hearing aids etc. requires that these circuits be operated with a minimum sized battery. This has forced analog circuit designers to devise low-voltage, low-power circuit design techniques. Reducing the supply voltage in analog circuits is one option but supply voltage reduction in analog circuits reduces its dynamic range thereby degrading the signal quality. Further, with downward CMOS technology scaling, the output resistance of MOS transistors also deteriorates, which in turn reduces, the maximum achievable gain from a MOS amplifier. Thus, there is a continuous quest for analog designers to find low-voltage circuit techniques that meet the latest technology trends. In order to serve this purpose, many LVLP (low voltage low power) techniques have been devised in CMOS technology [2–6]. One such LVLP technique is Dynamic Threshold Metal Oxide Semiconductor (DTMOS) transistor. The dynamic threshold MOS (DTMOS) technique was originally devised for digital circuits but can be extended to enhance the performance of a low voltage analog circuit. A DTMOS transistor is characterized by its ability to modulate the threshold voltage of the MOS transistor dynamically, using body bias technique. DTMOS transistor was first proposed by [7, 8]. Since the inception of the DTMOS concept, various circuits applying this technique have been proposed [9–15].

© Springer Nature Singapore Pte Ltd. 2017
M. Singh et al. (Eds.): ICACDS 2016, CCIS 721, pp. 423–432, 2017.
DOI: 10.1007/978-981-10-5427-3_45

A very important circuit a current comparator is popularly used in various applications of current mode circuits such as data convertors and other front-end signal processing applications. A current comparator operates by comparing two currents, commonly called an input current and a reference current and outputs the result in the form of a voltage. In last few decades, numerous current comparator structures have been reported in the literature, each offering some benefit over the other [16–18]. The first well known structure of a fully functional current comparator was proposed in [16]. This structure implements a current comparator trio that compares an input current and a reference current and using the current mirroring technique, generates a trio of proportionately related currents, whose proportions are evaluated by the aspect ratio of the output transistors of the current mirrors used in the design. However, this structure suffers from a high propagation delay and large power dissipation [17]. Further, some high speed current comparators have been proposed in [18–28]. These structures operate on a pre-calculated current difference between the input and the reference current and compare this difference with a threshold, set using various techniques, and producing the corresponding output level. Thus, for these structures to be fully functional current comparators, it is highly necessary to precede the same with a current differencing unit.

In this paper, a novel wholesome current comparator complete with a capability to calculate the difference between the two currents, offering a very high speed operation, along with low power dissipation has been proposed. The current differencing capability has been implemented by the means of current mirrors while low power operation has been achieved by using DTMOS in the current mirror.

2 DTMOS Technique

The concept of DTMOS was first introduced in [8]. By connecting together the gate to the body of a simple MOS transistor, the threshold voltage of the derived DTMOS is reduced upon forward biasing the body. This significantly increases the current drive of the DTMOS [29, 30]. However, a limitation arises with the significant reduction in the threshold voltage (Vt) of the MOS transistor due to standby power considerations in static circuits and possibility of failure in dynamic circuits which in turn leads to result in reduction of the gate overdrive and hence, the speed of operation of the overall circuit. A remedy to this limitation can be achieved by implementing a dynamic threshold MOS wherein, the Vt is low when the MOS turns on and vice versa. This exact behaviour is exhibited by a DTMOS by connecting the gate to the body of a MOS transistor [29]. The reduced Vt of DTMOS is the result of reduction in the depletion charge which causes an increase in the inversion charge and hence higher current drive [31].

Figure 1 illustrates a simple n type DTMOS in which body terminal (B) is directly connected to the Gate terminal (G) of an NMOS.

In a DTMOS, the bias voltage at the body terminal changes with input signal as per the relation in (1). This in turn dynamically changes the Vt of the transistor [32].

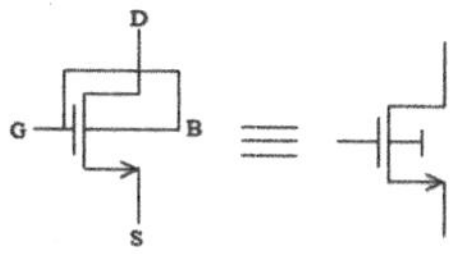

Fig. 1. MOS transistor using DTMOS

$$V_{th} = V_{th0} + \lambda.\left(\sqrt{|2\phi_B - V_{BS}|}\right) \tag{1}$$

where symbols have their usual meaning. In DTMOS technique, gate to source voltage VGS equals body to source voltage VBS and is equal to applied input voltage. Hence, VBS increases with increase in the input voltage while Vt decreases as per the relation in (1).

2.1 Small Signal Model of a DTMOS

In a DTMOS, the body terminal acts as a second gate and gives rise to a drain-current component (I_d) [33] given by

$$I_d = gmb.V_{BS} \tag{2}$$

where gmb is the body transconductance. The increase in I_d can be used to model gmb as

$$gmb = \frac{dI_d}{dV_{BS}} \tag{3}$$

Since I_d depends V_{SB} on through the dependence of V_t on V_{SB}, it can be obtained

$$g_{mb} = \chi g_m \tag{4}$$

where

$$\chi = \frac{\partial V_t}{\partial V_{SB}} = \frac{\gamma}{2\sqrt{2\emptyset_f + V_{SB}}} \tag{5}$$

The value of x lies in the range of 0.1–0.3. This dependent current source can be included in the small signal model of conventional MOS as shown in the Fig. 2 to come up with the small signal model of a DTMOS. Since in DTMOS body and gate are connected together, hence they can be a common terminal as shown in the Fig. 2.

This body bias technique has several advantages over other low voltage techniques namely, high transconductance gain, larger bandwidth etc. As rise time is inversely proportional to bandwidth, hence this technique results in lower delay i.e., faster circuit operation [34].

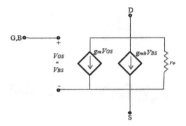

Fig. 2. Small- signal equivalent circuit of MOS transistor with dynamic body bias technique

3   Proposed DTMOS Based Current Comparator

A current comparator compares an input current (I_{in}) to a reference current (I_{ref}) and produces a resulting output voltage [35, 36], it can be formulated as

$$V_{out} = \begin{cases} 1, \, for \, I_{in} > I_{ref} \\ 0, \, for \, I_{in} < I_{ref} \end{cases} \tag{6}$$

The proposed current comparator employing DTMOS technique is shown in the Fig. 3.

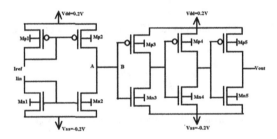

Fig. 3.   DTMOS based current comparator

3.1   Working Principle

The circuit consists of two simple DTMOS based current mirrors. An N-type current mirror comprising Mn1 and Mn2 and a P-type current mirror comprising Mp1 and Mp2 DTMOS connected as shown in Fig. 3. Iin is applied at the input node of N-type current mirror while Iref is is applied at the input node of P-type current mirror. In coherence with the operating principle of a current mirror, I_{in} applied at the drain of Mn1is mirrored at the drain of Mn2. Similarly I_{ref} applied at the drain of Mp1 is mirrored at the drain of Mp2. From the very basic law of circuit theory (KCL), applied at node A, a resulting voltage V_A is obtained at A as per the postulates of Eq. (6), i.e. when $I_{in} < I_{ref}$, then $I_{ref} - I_{in}$ leads to a high output voltage at the output node A, while when when $I_{in} > I_{ref}$, $I_{in} - I_{ref}$, leads to a very low voltage at A. Hence the node voltage at A reflects the result of the comparison between the two currents.

Further, three inverters are cascaded at the output node B in order to obtain full rail to rail output swing. The inverters employed are also DTMOS based inverters operating at the same supply voltage as the current mirrors.

3.2   Input and Output Impedance of Proposed Current Comparator

Figure 4 depicts the small signal model of the proposed current comparator for computing its input and output impedances. Input impedance (R_{in}) is the ratio of input voltage and input current, written as

$$R_{in} = \frac{V_{in}}{I_{in}} \tag{7}$$

From Fig. 4, equation for current at node Dn1 is given by

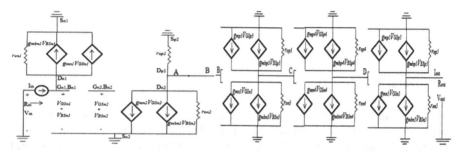

Fig. 4. Small-signal model for calculating input and output impedance of proposed current comparator

$$I_{in} = g_{mn1} V_{GSn1} + g_{mbn1} V_{BSn1} + \frac{V_{GSn1}}{r_{on1}} \tag{8}$$

Since,

$$V_{GSn1} = V_{BSn1} = V_{in} \tag{9}$$

Substituting (9) in (8) we get,

$$I_{in} = g_{mn1} V_{in} + g_{mbn1} V_{in} + \frac{V_{in}}{r_{on1}} \tag{10}$$

$$I_{in} = \left[g_{mn1} + g_{mbn1} + \frac{1}{r_{on1}} \right] V_{in} \tag{11}$$

$$\frac{V_{in}}{I_{in}} = \frac{1}{\left[g_{mn1} + g_{mbn1} + \frac{1}{r_{on1}} \right]} \tag{12}$$

Therefore, from Eqs. (7) and (12) input impedance of the proposed current comparator is

$$R_{in} = \cfrac{1}{\left[g_{mn1} + g_{mbn1} + \cfrac{1}{r_{on1}} \right]} \tag{13}$$

Output impedance (R_{out}) of any complex circuit can be calculated using test voltage method [33]. In this method, first input signal is made zero, then an output voltage source V_{out} is applied at the output terminal which leads an output current I_{out} into in the circuit. This gives Rout as the ratio of output voltage to output current as

$$R_{out} = \frac{V_{out}}{I_{out}} \tag{14}$$

On solving using KCL at nodes B, C, D and output node, the output impedance of proposed comparator is obtained as

$$R_{out} = r_{on5} || r_{op5} \tag{15}$$

4   Simulation Results

The functionality of the proposed circuit is verified through SPICE simulations. The power supply of ±0.2 V is used as suggested in [37]. The DC and Transient response have been obtained and the results are illustrated in the Figs. 5, 6 and 7. Figure 5(a) shows the DC analysis of the circuit for input current I_{in} in the range of 0 to 20 μA while reference current I_{ref} is fixed at 10 μA. As can be seen that when $I_{in} < I_{ref}$, the output voltage of the current comparator is −0.2 V, switching occurs at the point where $I_{in} = I_{ref}$, after which the output voltage rises to 0.2 V, thus verifying the operation of the circuit. Figure 5(b) illustrates the DC gain exhibited by the proposed current comparator. I_{in} is varied from −20 μA to 20 μA and I_{ref} is stepped for each simulation from −5 μA to 5 μA in steps of 0.5 μA. The DC gain is 24 V/μA.

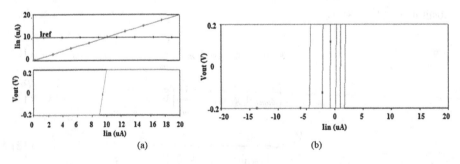

Fig. 5. (a) DC Analysis of the proposed current comparator (b) DC Gain plot of proposed current comparator

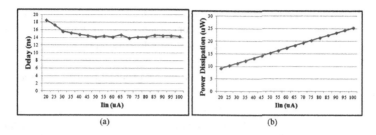

(a)   (b)

Fig. 6. (a) Delay Vs I_{in} (b) Power Dissipation Vs I_{in}

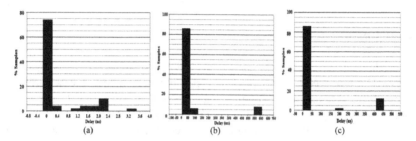

(a)   (b)   (c)

Fig. 7. Monte Carlo Simulations for (a) I_{ref} = 10 μA and I_{in} = 20 μA (b) I_{ref} = 15 μA and I_{in} = 30 μA (c) I_{ref} = 20 μA and I_{in} = 40 μA

Further, the circuit performance was measured for different values of I_{in}, at a fixed value of I_{ref} = 10 μA. The results are enlisted in Table 1 below. It can be seen that as I_{in} increase, the delay decreases, owing to faster switching at higher currents. However,

Table 1. Delay, Power and PDP of the proposed current comparator for different values of input current and fixed value of reference current

Input current (μA)	Delay (ns)	Power dissipation (μW)	PDP (pJ)
20	18.5415	9.27	.17187
25	17.3445	10.3	.17864
30	15.64	11.3	.17673
35	15.189	12.3	.18682
40	14.836	13.3	.19731
45	14.55	14.3	.20735
50	14.174	15.3	.21686
55	14.468	16.3	.23582
60	14.1495	17.3	.24478
65	14.762	18.3	.27014
70	13.8735	19.3	.26775
75	14.1595	20.3	.28743
80	14.1965	21.3	.30238
85	14.6445	22.3	.32657
90	14.567	23.3	.33941
95	14.578	24.3	.35424
100	14.334	25.3	.36265

as expected, power dissipation increases with rise in I_{in}. Power delay product (PDP) has also been calculated in the Table 1. The curves showing the variation of delay and power dissipation with respect to I_{in} have been graphically represented in the Fig. 6(a) and (b) respectively.

Monte Carlo analysis was also carried out on the proposed current comparator. The parameters Tox, Nch, Vth0, and Cj are varied according to DEV/GAUSS = 0.05% LOT/UNIFORM = 1% for both nmos and pmos. (This means device parameter has Gaussian variation of 0.05% and the variation between the transistors in different lots of wafer is 1% in uniform distribution.) Figure 7 represents the effect of Monte Carlo on delay with (a) $I_{in} = 20\ \mu A$ and $I_{ref} = 10\ \mu A$ (b) $I_{in} = 30\ \mu A$ and $I_{ref} = 15\ \mu A$ (c) $I_{in} = 40\ \mu A$ and $I_{ref} = 20\ \mu A$.

5 Conclusion

A power efficient current comparator has been reported implemented using DTMOS technique. The proposed current comparator provides a commendable performance in terms of power dissipation as compared to the similar MOS based structure. The proposed structure has been simulated on 180 nm technology and operates at a very low supply voltage of ±0.2 V making it a preferred structure of choice for low voltage analog and mixed mode circuit applications.

References

1. Khateb, F., Dabbous, S.B.A., Vlassis, S.: A survey of non-conventional techniques or low-voltage low-power analog circuit design. Radioengineering 22, 415–427 (2013)
2. Yan, S., Sanchez-Sinencio, E.: Low voltage analog circuit design techniques: a tutorial. IEICE Trans. Analog Integr. Circ. Syst. E00-A(2) (2000)
3. Khateb, F., Khatib, N., Koton, J.: Novel low-voltage ultra-low power DVCC based on floating-gate folded cascade OTA. Microelectron. J. 42, 1010–1017 (2011)
4. Farshidi, E., Keramatzadeh, A.: A new approach for low voltage CMOS based on current-controlled conveyors. IJE Trans. B: Appl. 27, 723–730 (2014)
5. Ramirez-Angulo, J., Lopez-Martin, A.J., Carvajal, R.G., Chavero, F.M.: Very low-volatge analog signal processing based on quasi-floating gate transistors. IEEE J. Solid-State Circ. 39, 434–442 (2003)
6. Fallah, M., MiarNaimi, H.: A novel low voltage, low power and high gain operational amplifier using negative resistance and self cascode transistors. IJE Trans. C: Aspects 26, 303–308 (2013)
7. Assaderaghi, F., Sinitsky, D., Parke, S.A., et al.: Dynamic threshold-voltage MOSFET (DTMOS) for ultra-low-voltage VLSI. IEEE Trans. Electron Devices 44, 414–422 (1997)
8. Assaderaghi, F., Parke, S.A., Sinitskyd, D., Bokor, J., Ko, P.K., Hu, C.: Dynamic threshold-voltage MOSFET (DTMOS) for very low-voltage operation. IEEE Device Lett. 15, 510–512 (1994)
9. Maymandi-Nejad, M., Sachdev, M.: DTMOS Technique for low-voltage analog circuits. IEEE Trans. Very Large Scale Integr. VLSI Syst. 14, 1151–1156 (2006)

10. Li, Z., Yu, M., Ma, J.: A novel input stage based on DTMOS for low-voltage low-noise operational amplifier. In: IEEE Asia Pacific Conference on Circuits and Systems, pp. 1591–1594 (2006)
11. Achigui, H.F., Fayomi, C.J.B., Sawan, M.A.: 1-V low-power low-noise DTMOS based class AB opamp, In: The 3rd International IEEE-NEWCAS Conference, pp. 307–310 (2005)
12. Shen, E., Kuo, J.B.: A novel 0.8 V BP-DTMOS content addressable memory cell circuit derived from SOI-DTMOS techniques. In: Proceedings of IEEE Conference on Electron Devices and Solid-State Circuits, pp. 243–245 (2003)
13. Liu, J., Han, Y., Xie, L., Wang, Y., Wen, G.: A 1-V DTMOS-based fully differential telescopic OTA. In: Proceedings of IEEE Asia Pacific Conference on Circuits and Systems, pp. 49–52 (2014)
14. Chouhan, S.S., Halonen, K.: The DTMOS based UHF RF to DC conversion. In: IEEE 20th International Conference on Electronics, Circuits, and Systems, pp. 629–632 (2013)
15. Chouhan, S.S., Halonen, K.: The design and implementation of DTMOS biased all PMOS rectifier for RF energy harvesting. In: IEEE 12th International Conference on New Circuits and Systems, pp. 444–447 (2014)
16. Freitas, O.A., Current, K.W.: CMOS current comparator circuit. Electron. Lett. **19**, 695–697 (1993)
17. Traff, H.: Novel approach to high speed CMOS current comparators. Electron. Lett. **28**, 310–312 (1992)
18. Tang, A.T.K., Toumazou, C.: High performance CMOS current comparator. Electron. Lett. **30**, 5–6 (1994)
19. Min, B.M., Kim, S.W.: High performance CMOS current comparator using resistive feedback network. Electron. Lett. **34**, 2074–2076 (1998)
20. Chen, L., Shi, B., Lu, C.: Circuit design of a high speed and low power CMOS continuous-time current comparator. Analog Integr. Circ. Sig. Process **28**, 293–297 (2001)
21. Kasemsuwan, V., Khucharoensin, S.: High speed low input impedance CMOS current comparator. IEEE Trans. Fundam. **E88-A**(6), 1549–1553 (2005)
22. Chavoshiani, R., Hashempour, O.: Differential current conveyor based current comparator. Int. J. Electron. Commun. (AEÜ) **65**, 949–953 (2011)
23. Chavoshiani, R., Hashempour, O.: A high-speed current conveyor based current comparator. Microelectron. J. **42**, 28–32 (2011)
24. Tang, X., Pun, K.P.: High performance CMOS current comparator. Electron. Lett. **45**(20), 1007–1009 (2009)
25. Dominguez-Castro, R., Rodriguez-Vazquez, A., Medeiro, F., Huertas, J.L.: High resolution CMOS current comparators. In: Eighteenth European Solid State Circuits Conference, Denmark, pp. 242–245 (1992)
26. Ravezzi, L., Stoppa, D., Dallabetta, G.F.: Simple high-speed CMOS current comparator. Electron. Lett. **33**, 1829–1830 (1997)
27. Banks, D., Toumazou, C.: Low-power high-speed current comparator design. Electron. Lett. **44**, 171–172 (2008)
28. Fernandez, R., Cembrano, G., Castro, R., Vazquez, A.: A mismatch-insensitive high-accuracy high-speed continuous - time current comparator in low voltage CMOS. In: IEEE Proceedings of the Analog and Mixed Signal IC Design, pp. 303–306 (1997)
29. Shieh, M.S., Chen, P.S., Tsai, M.J., Lei, T.F.: A novel dynamic threshold voltage MOSFET (DTMOS) using heterostructure channel of Si1 yCy interlayer. IEEE Electron Device Lett. **26**, 740–742 (2005)
30. Kang, S.M., Leblebici, Y.: CMOS Digital Integrated Circuits: Analysis and Design. TMH, (2008)

31. Assaderaghi, F.: DTMOS: its derivatives and variations, and their potential applications. In: The 12th International Conference on Microelectronics, pp. 9–10 (2002)
32. Tsividis, Y.P.: Operation and Modeling of the MOS Transistor. Mc-Graw Hill, New York (1987)
33. Sedra, A., Smith, K.: Microelectronics Circuits. Oxford University Press, Oxford (1998)
34. Gupta, M., Aggarwal, P., Singh, P., Jindal, N.K.: Low voltage current mirrors with enhanced bandwidth. Analog Integr. Circuits Sig. Process. **59**, 97–103 (2009)
35. Sridhar, R., Pandey, N., Bhatia, V., Bhattacharyya, A.: High speed high resolution current comparator and its application to analog to digital converter. Springer J. Inst. Eng. India, Ser. B, 2250–2106 (2015). doi:10.1007/s40031-015-0189-1
36. Sridhar, R., Pandey, N., Bhatia, V., Bhattacharyya, A.: On improving the performance of Traff's comparator. In: IEEE 5th India International Conference on Power Electronics, pp. 1–4 (2012)
37. Uygur, A., Kuntman, H.: An ultra low-voltage, ultra low- power DTMOS-based CCII design for speech processing filters. In: The 8th International Conference on Electrical and Electronics Engineering, pp. 31–35 (2013)

A Secure Multi-owner Multi-copy Facility with Privacy Preserving on Public Storage Cloud Dynamic Data

Priya Sontakke$^{(\boxtimes)}$ and Amrita Manjrekar$^{(\boxtimes)}$

Department of Computer Science, Department of Technology,
Shivaji University, Kolhapur, India
priyavsontakke@gmail.com, aam_tech@unishivaji.ac.in

Abstract. Most of the organization produced huge sensitive data and uses expensive applications. Both of these are quite expensive due to requirements of high storage capacity and installing the same application on different computers. Cloud Service Providers (CSP's) offered paid Storage-as-a-service (SaaS) and Platform-as-a-service (PaaS) services that enable to store large data and uses many applications by less amount. Sometimes organizations need to be replicated data on multiple servers for increasing levels of scalability, availability, and durability and need to verify the intactness and consistency of dynamic multiple data copies. Implemented system provides evidence that all data copies are actually stored and remain intact. Moreover, implemented system supports dynamic behavior on cloud data, where the data owners are capable of archiving, accessing, updating and scaling the data copies stored by CSP. In addition, the system allows owners to appoint third party verifier and used to identify corrupted copies and reconstructs them.

Keywords: Cloud computing · Dynamic data · Cloud Service Provider (CSP) · Provable data possession (PDP) · Multi-copy · Multi-owner

1 Introduction

Cloud computing is a general term for anything that involves delivering hosted services, scalable services like data sharing, accessing etc., over the internet on demand basis [17]. Cloud server is used to maintain data and applications. A customers can use applications without installing in own computer and access own files from anywhere any other computer with internet access. Cloud computing is broken down into three segments: application, storage, and connectivity. Each segment serves a different purpose and offers different products around the world.

In cloud computing, the CSPs, such as google, Amazon is able to deliver various services to cloud users CSP allows storing more data than a private computer. Once data stored in the cloud, authorized user can access all data from any geographical location using internet access [1]. Let us consider a practical data application; a company has a different type of departments. The company allows its employee in the same department to store and share files using the cloud. The company saves significant investment by utilizing the cloud instead of creating local infrastructure. This data

© Springer Nature Singapore Pte Ltd. 2017
M. Singh et al. (Eds.): ICACDS 2016, CCIS 721, pp. 433–447, 2017.
DOI: 10.1007/978-981-10-5427-3_46

application poses some risk regarding security issues. Data leakage is the main issues because cloud providers are not fully trusted. Especially, when customer store highly sensitive and confidential data in the cloud such as medical records, bank details, business plans etc. cloud offered by CSP may not be trustworthy due to losing control of data [19]. It is important to ensure whether data is not corrupted or not altered. In a result security and privacy have always been very important factor in cloud computing system. Data security can be achieved by encrypting sensitive data before storing to the cloud servers [11, 18].

Sometimes organizations need to improve availability of data and application due to increasing demands of customers and failure of sensitive data. Organization create number of copies for easily available to the customers. Suppose all copies are stored in single server still all copies can simultaneously fail by server down. To avoid these simultaneously failure needs to store each copy in different cloud server [12]. To remove inconsistency of all copies need to check integrity. Where check all copies are actually stored in a recently updated form and remain intact [13, 15]. Up till now hash operations, signature schemes, and many more other traditional cryptographic technique are used for checking data integrity. These techniques are fails for cloud data because each time for checking integrity needs to download all data from cloud and compare with the stored local copy of same data in computer. Due to downloading and storing all data each time need high communication overhead in network. Therefore, now days need an efficient technique to verify the integrity of cloud data with minimum computation, communication cost, and storage overheads [4].

Provable data possession (PDP) [2] is a technique used for checking data integrity of cloud data. In this model, data owners create metadata information for each file before storing into the cloud. Data owner is store metadata of file into the local computer instead of storing the whole copy of file for checking data integrity. PDP model used both *static data* and *dynamic data* depending upon various data applications. Basic PDP scheme is helpful for storing static data like some invention information, company's history, and yearly profit loss etc. data. In this basic PDP scheme authorized used able to access data but unable to scale by the data owner. For dynamic data, DPDP [5] schema used to perform an update operation by data owner on stored cloud data. This DPDP scheme is mostly used when currently working data stored in cloud like weather information, new invention, employee details etc. Both Basic PDP and DPDP technique are used single copy of data file. Due to failure and scalability issues, DPDP uses multiple copy of file. Secure and efficient technique are need to verify integrity of multiple copies. Secure and efficient PDP [3] schema are used cryptographic hash function with symmetric key encryption. In multiple data copies, the overall system integrity fails if there are one or more corrupted copies found. Multiple-Replica PDP (MR-PDP) [16, 20] scheme used to reconstruct corrupted data copy using duplicate copies on other cloud servers.

This paper *Multi-Owner Multi-Copy facility on Dynamic Data in Cloud Computing* proposes a solution to overcome issues regarding cloud data integrity, security, and availability. This system provides a multi-owner facility where data owner shares authentication of the file with other owners. Data owner stores multiple copies of the single file on different cloud servers at different geographical locations to achieve availability and scalability. Here, Layershift cloud offered by Jelastic is used to provide

SaaS services to the client for storing the data. In this system, data owner appoints third party verifiers. Verifier checks the integrity of data stored in layershift cloud once a day. Verifier recognizes corrupted copy and reconstructs them. Here, data owner also provides secure sharing facility with multiple owners and authorized users.

1.1   Checking the PDF File

Kindly assure that the Contact Volume Editor is given the name and email address of the contact author for your paper. The Contact Volume Editor uses these details to compile a list for our production department at SPS in India. Once the files have been worked upon, SPS sends a copy of the final pdf of each paper to its contact author. The contact author is asked to check through the final pdf to make sure that no errors have crept in during the transfer or preparation of the files. This should not be seen as an opportunity to update or copyedit the papers, which is not possible due to time constraints. Only errors introduced during the preparation of the files will be corrected.

This round of checking takes place about two weeks after the files have been sent to the Editorial by the Contact Volume Editor, i.e. roughly seven weeks before the start of the conference for conference proceedings, or seven weeks before the volume leaves the printer's, for post-proceedings. If SPS does not receive a reply from a particular contact author, within the timeframe given, then it is presumed that the author has found no errors in the paper. The tight publication schedule of LNCS does not allow SPS to send reminders or search for alternative email addresses on the Internet.

In some cases, it is the Contact Volume Editor that checks all the pdfs. In such cases, the authors are not involved in the checking phase.

2   Related Work

Deswarte et al. [6] proposed an RSA-based secure hash function which is holomorphic. This system is based on the hash function which prevents cheating in a data transfer transaction while placing a little burden on the trusted third party. This system is very flexible and simple to implement, but the low performance may prevent their widespread adoption. The limitation of these algorithms lies in the computational complexity at the cloud server.

Ateniese et al. [2] proposed first PDP schema which provide public auditability for ensuring possession of data files on untrusted storages. This schema allows to verifying data possession without having access/retrieving to the actual data file. This schema utilizes the RSA based homomorphic linear authenticator for auditing outsourced data files. By minimizing the access block, reduced the overhead at server side and required small constant amount of communication per challenges. The public audibility schema demands the linear combination of sampled few data set of block. This PDP schema is not more privacy preserving and this may leak user information to the external auditor.

Erway and Tamassia [5] proposed a dynamic version of the PDP scheme based on cryptographic hash function and symmetric key encryption. This scheme is efficient but allows only a fixed number of challenges due to the fact that through the scheme setup they come up with all future challenges and store pre-computed responses as tokens. These tokens can be stored verifier side in a plain form or sometimes stored at the server side in an encrypted form. This model is unsuitable for public verification with the help of third party. Here, Data owner has burden to check the data integrity.

Z. Hao [7] proposed the system which supports both the dynamic nature of data and public verifiability. Public verifiability allows to all, who knows the owner's public key. This system supports the dynamic operation at a block level. Here, still need to extend the system to support data level dynamics. The difficulty is that there is no clear mapping relationship between the data and the tags. In the current construction, data level dynamics operation can be performed using block. When small piece of data is modified, only the corresponding blocks and tags are updated instead of modifying whole data file. However, this can bring unnecessary computation and communication costs.

R.C. Merkle [8] proposed Tree based- dynamic multi-copy provable data possession (TB-DMCPDP) scheme. The proposed work is based on using Merkle hash trees (MHTs) [9]. TB-DMCPDP uses a structure of binary tree. To verify the integrity of the data schema used binary tree. The MHT is a tree of hashes where the leaves of the tree are represented with the hashes of the data blocks which are used for performing dynamic operation properly. This system supports multiple copies of dynamic data with the help of directory in MHT. This system needs more setup cost for the preparation of the MHTs which generate metadata for all file copies.

Curtmola et al. [16] proposed a multiple replica PDP (MR-PDP) system. This is helpful for ensuring multiple replicas of the data. In this schema all replica of data are stored at the cloud server. Data availability is improved by storing multiple replicas. All replicas are stored in single cloud server. Sometime all replicas of file are unavailable due to failure of cloud server. MR-PDP model is needed to store each replica in distributed cloud server. This model can generate further replicas on demand, at little expense, when some of the existing replicas are failed. MR-PDP is not efficient in data integrity issue.

Ayad F. Barsoum and M. Anwar Hasan [10] proposed provable multi-copy dynamic data possession (PMDDP) system. This system provides evidence to the customer that CSP stores all copies of the file. Data owner performs a full block level dynamic operation using map version table. Map version table is used to store metadata information about the updated file copies. PMDDP system discussed to identify a list of the corrupted copies. But unable to recover corrupted copies. This system need to be more storage space to store MVT table.

3 Proposed System

The proposed system consists of different components which are illustrated in Fig. 1:

(i) Data owner is an organization or an individual originally store sensitive data on a cloud server. (ii) CSP handles different Cloud Servers (CSs) and provides paid storage space on its infrastructure to stores files. (iii) Authorized Users - A set of data owner's employee who has the right to access the cloud data. (iv) The verifier may be Data Owner or Third Party person or Authorized User.

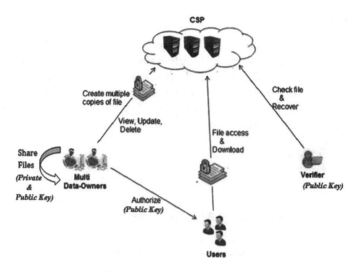

Fig. 1. Proposed system model

Implemented system allows the data owner to store sensitive files in the cloud. First, Data owner encrypt the file before storing into cloud server and creates an identical number of file copies. CSP receive all copies in encrypted form and store data in different cloud servers. The owner can be access stored cloud data and update from any geographical location. Data owner can increase and decrease copies of file at any time according to demands of clients. Data owner interacts with the registered user to authenticate users by checking identity. An authenticated user sends a request to CSP for data copy. After receiving request CSP send a data copy in an encrypted form. Authorized user can be decrypted using a public key shared with the data owner. Data owner has authority to appoint third party verifier whether verifier may be person or organization. The verifier is used to check data copies which are actually stored in appropriate cloud server and remain intact. Once in a day, verifier checks that all copies are stored an updated with most recent modification. If any copy of a file is corrupted, the verifier identifies that copy and recovers the corrupted file copy using existing duplicate copy of a file.

In this system, Jelastic used to provides a Platform-as-a-Service (PaaS), with Layershift's global hosting services. Layershift used to runs Java application and provide a platform to store files. Layershift is a public cloud which is available to all by paying fees.

Here, data owner used sensitive data to store in the cloud server, which is essential in many applications such as business plans, patient's medical records, and government security agent's information

Implemented system consists of following module, which is formed on the basis of the functionalities.

3.1   Key Generations

Data owner runs key generation algorithm to generate the private and public key. Key generation algorithm is used for each file before storing into the cloud server. Each file has generates its own unique keys which are used to decrypts file and performing operations. All file data owners have private and public keys. Authorized user and verifier can access file and decrypt using public key shared by any one of the file owner. Public Key is only used for decrypting file but unable to modify data without private key (Table 1).

$(\mathbf{pk}, \mathbf{sk}) \leftarrow \mathbf{KeyGen}()$

Public key *pk* and a private key *sk*.

Table 1. Private and public key algorithm

$e^{\wedge} : G_1 \times G_2 \rightarrow G_T$ is a bilinear map.
g is a generator for G_2,
Private Key is $x \in Zp$
Public Key is $y = g^x \in G_2$

3.2   Generating Multiple Copies

Data owner store multiple copies of the file to improve availability, scalability of single copy system. Sometimes all copies may fail simultaneously, if all copies are stored in the same geographical location or cloud server. Geographical diversity can ensure this failure so; here each copy of the file is stored in the different geographical location.

Data owner uses CopyGen algorithm to create a number of copies in encrypted form. Algorithm creates a number of distinct identical copies by adding randomly generated a number in each copy. Identical data copies enable the CSP to simply deceive the owner by storing only one copy and pretending that store's multiple copies of the file. Data owner encrypts all copies of the file EK, i.e. Ek(i||F) (Table 2).

$\tilde{F} \leftarrow \mathbf{CopyGen}(CN_i, F)_{1 \leq i \leq n}$

This algorithm takes as input a copy number CN_i and a file F, and generates unique differentiable n copies $\tilde{F} = \{\tilde{F}_i\}_{1 \leq i \leq n}$.

Table 2. Copies generators algorithm

Single i^{th} no. of Copy Generate: $\tilde{F}_i = E_k(i\|F)_{1 \leq i \leq n}$.
Where, i= no. of copy, F= file, E_k= encryption
All File Copies: $\tilde{F} = \{\tilde{F}_i\}_{1 \leq i \leq n}$

$\Phi \leftarrow \textbf{TagGen}(sk, \tilde{F})$

Once copies are created, data owner generate the tag for each file copy to make a identical copy. TagGen algorithm takes as input the private key sk and the file copies $\tilde{F}$, and outputs tags Φ. The owner sends Φ to the CSP to be stored along with the copies $\tilde{F}$ (Table 3).

Table 3. Tag generator's algorithm

Copies of File $\tilde{F} = \{\tilde{F}_i\}$ Tag for i^{th} copy of File: $\quad \sigma_i = (H(ID_F\|\|i))$ Tag ϕ is : $\qquad\qquad\qquad \phi = \prod_{i=1}^{n} \sigma_i$ Send $\{\tilde{F}, \phi, ID_F\}$ to the CSP to store File with Copies.

After creating copies of file and tag for each copy. Data owner sends all copies with the tag to CSP to store in the cloud server.

3.3   Generating Multiple Owners

Multiple-owner facility is more flexible than the single owner. Multiple owner systems allow every owner to alter data instead of a burden on the single owner. In single owner system can't perform operation if owner is not available [14]. In this system, Data owner have authentication to share the authority of file with the other trusted registered owners. Each file has multiple different owners. All owners of the file have permission to access the file, modify data, and delete the file. At a time only one file owner have authentication to perform modification operation. When oner is access file copy for performing modification, all other copies of file are disable or not available to access. Once modification performed to all copies then file copies are access by the other data owner, authorized user, and verifier. But, multiple authorized users can access file at a time. Advantages of this module are below:

- No central authority of data owner is required in this system.
- The burden of work for altering data will be distributed to all owners.
- Any one of data owner can appoint as an authority before performing any operation.

Multiple data owners can perform various operations on data files. The list of operation given below:

1. (*UpdateReq*) $\leftarrow$ **PrepareUpdate(F, *UpdateInfo*)**

This algorithm is run by the data owner to update the stored file copies in a cloud server. Here, data owner sends an update request to CSP with file copy and update information to modify data.

2. $(\tilde{F}, \Phi') \leftarrow$ **ExecUpdate** $(\tilde{F}, \Phi', UpdateReq)$

This algorithm is run by the CSP, where the input parameters are the file copies $\tilde{F}_i$, the tags set Φ', and the request UpdateReq send by the data owner. This algorithm stores an updated version of the file copies $\tilde{F}$ along with an updated tags set Φ'.

A. **Upload:** All registered data owner have authority to upload new file F with requiring copies of the file. Firstly, the owner runs PrepareUpdate algorithm and send a request to the CSP, then CSP executes the ExecUpdate algorithm to upload all copies of the file with tag (Table 4).

Table 4. File upload algorithm

PrepareUpdate()
1.   Create n copies of File $F_i = E_k(i\|F)_{1 \le i \le n}$
2.   Create tag for all copies
$\quad \sigma_i = (H(ID_F\|i)) \qquad \phi = \prod_{i=1}^{n} \sigma_i$
3.   Send update request to the CSP
$\quad \{\tilde{F}, \phi, ID_F, \mathbf{Insert}\}$
ExecUpdate()
1.   Store copies of file F_i.
2.   Store tag ϕ

B. **Update:** Data owner updates the single copy of file then CSP updates all copies of that file. Data owner sends a request to the CSP with file and updated information by running the PrepareUpdate algorithm. CSP receive all information and execute an ExecUpdate algorithm to make changes on all copies of the file (Table 5).

Table 5. File update algorithm

PrepareUpdate()
1.   Create n copies of File $F'_i = E_k(i\|F)_{1 \le i \le n}$
2.   Create new tag for all copies
$\quad \sigma'_i = (H(ID_F\|i)) \qquad \phi' = \prod_{i=1}^{n} \sigma_i$
3.   Send update request to the CSP
$\quad \{\tilde{F}', \phi', ID_F, \mathbf{Update}\}$
ExecUpdate()
1.   Replace copies of file F_i to the F'_i.
2.   Replace tag ϕ to ϕ'.

C. **Delete:** Data owner has authority to delete the single copy of file or all copies of the file. Data owner can send a request to the CSP to delete specific file copy from the cloud server. CSP receive a request with file copy and tag. After receiving request CSP run ExecUpdate() algorithm to remove file copy from cloud storage (Table 6).

Table 6. File delete algorithm

ExecUpdate()
1. Delete copies of file F_i.
2. Delete tag ϕ to ϕ'

D. **Add Copies:** Sometimes data owner need to increase copies of the file to improve performance. Owner sends a request to the CSP for accessing the file. Once copy of file received, owner generates new copies of a file by the CopyGen algorithm and sends a request to the CSP to store file copies on a different cloud server. CSP run Upload algorithm to store new copies on a cloud server.

3.4   Identify Corrupted Copy

Verifier is an entity appointed by the data owner, to check the consistency of all data copies once in a day. Firstly, verifier sends a request to CSP then CSP sends the copy of a file. Using this copy verifier check which copies of file it is by removing a tag or randomly used the number. Then verifier checks if it is a correct copy or not. If a copy is not corrupted, it ignores but if corrupted copy found then verifier uses identifying

Table 7. Identifying corrupted copy

Input:
  • σ List- Generated by the data owner. σ is a tag
  • μ List- Generated by CSP. $\mu = \{\mu_{ik}\}_{1\leq i\leq n\ 1\leq k\leq}$
  • start- indicate the start index of the currently working lists.
  • end- indicate the last index of this lists.
Output:
  • invalidList- The invalid indices are stored in invalidList.
  • Recovered File Copy Stored.
Procedure:
  Step1: Data owner generates σList and sends to the CSP.
  Step2: CSP receives σList and generates μ List.
  Step3: CSP runs Prove algorithm and sends $P = \{\sigma\mu\}$ to the verifier.
  Step4: Verifier runs Verify algorithm and check.
  If all copies intact and consistent then return 1
  Go to: Step8,
  Otherwise return 0 **Go to: Step5.**
  Step5: Verifier uses divide & conquer algorithm to σList & μ List.
  Step6: Identified indices of corrupted copies & store into invalidList.
  Step7: Repeat step 5 & 6.
  Step8: Return invalidList.
  Step9: CSP Send Request for File Copy F_i to other CSP
  Step10: CSP Receive F_i and Store.

corrupted copy algorithm to check which copy has been corrupted and reconstruct that copy using existing duplicate file copy. This module verifies data integrity, Public Verifiability, and Possession-free verification. Table 7 gives an algorithm for identifying corrupted copies.

3.5   Sharing Access Authority

This module is used for secure data sharing facility in cloud computing. Sometimes data owner want to access data from another data owner in secure manner. If two companies are going to work in different part of the same product at that time company need to share files with each other for understanding what they are working. For example, Dell, Sony, Apple companies uses NVDI, Intel companies' graphics card. So, each company wants to know features of updated version of graphics card. But, this can be happen only if both data owner/company have trust about each other. In this process initially, data owner 1 send a request to the data owner 2. Then,

1. Data owner 2 REJECTS its request if he/she does not want to share data.
2. Data owner 2 ACCEPT its request if he/she does want to share data.

If the request is rejected then owners are unable to share files. If the request is accepted, owners can access files but unable to perform modification on shared files. In this sharing facility, each owner shares only those file which are important to opponent of owner to improve the performance of the system.

4   Experimental Evaluation

Implementation of the presented scheme consists of different modules like Owner Module, User Module, CSP Module and Verifier Module. Owner Module runs on the Data owner side that includes KeyGen, CopyGen, TagGen, and PrepareUpdate algorithm. User module runs on the Authorized user side. CSP module runs on the Layershift cloud with including an ExecuteUpdate algorithm. Verifier module runs on verifier side and includes Verify algorithm.

The Owner, User, and Verifier modules are run on the different desktop computer. Each computer has 3 GB RAM, Intel i3 core processor running windows 10 operating system for development. For program writing, NetBean IDE is used. The entire program is written in the java language. The CSP module runs on the Layershift's Jelastic instance. Through this instance, data owner gets 10 GB free memory size. Jelastic's is a unique pay-per-use model with dynamic scalability means owner only charges the actually used size of memory. Layershift is a public cloud. Layershift provides space to store files and used to run java program by providing global hosting service.

4.1   Result Analysis

1. **Storage Computation Time**
I. **Single Copy of File:**
Computation time is measured while data owner uploads a single file in the cloud server. Here, computation time can be calculated by adding time requires for generating

keys, tag, encrypting the file and to store single data file in a cloud server. The graph is generated when the single owner is used for storing the different size of the single file in cloud storage.

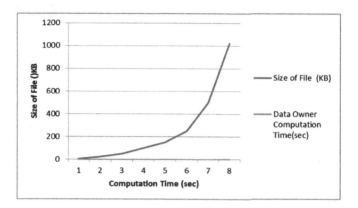

Fig. 2. Storage computation time for single copy.

As observed from Fig. 2, computation time grows with increasing size of the file to store, because the large size of a file required more time to encrypt.

II. Multiple Copies of File:

Computation times are calculated for storing multiple copies of the file in different server. Here, 1 MB file size is taken for performing. Each copy of the file is stored in different cloud server to improve availability with improving performance of system. Layershift cloud is used to store each copy of the file in distributed environment.

As observed from Fig. 3 computation times remain approx. with an increasing number of copies of the file to the store because pre-computation cost for the single and multi-copy file are same and need few seconds time to store each copy in different cloud server.

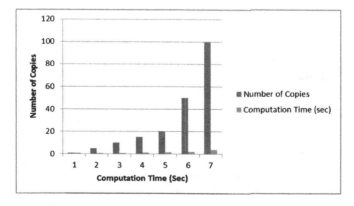

Fig. 3. Storage computation time for multiple copy.

2. Dynamic Operation Performing Time

Computation time is calculated when data owner modifies data in all copies. Here, data owner used 1 MB file size for performing modification operation on a different number of copies. Modification is performed by inserting new data, deleting some data or changing data.

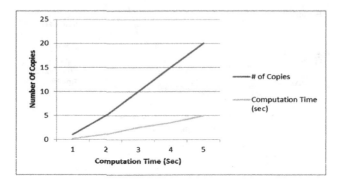

Fig. 4. Dynamic operation computation time for multiple copies

As observed from Fig. 4, computation time grows with increasing number of copy because each copy needs time to perform the modification.

3. Verification Computation Time

This graph shows the verification time (in seconds) with different corrupted percentages data on single copy file. Here, percentages ranging from 1% to 25% of data in files are randomly corrupt. The verification time is about 0.031 s when 1% of the data are corrupted. Here, the file is taken 1 MB size to calculate verification time.

As observed from Fig. 5, our scheme has very small ratio of increasing in verification and reconstruction time with increasing percentage of corrupted data. The

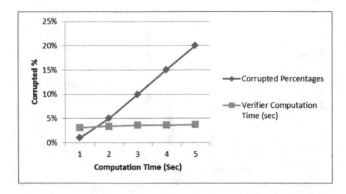

Fig. 5. Verification times with different percentages of single copy corrupted file

verification of time is changed with size of file copy, number of file copies etc. factor. Suppose the number of copies is increased, BS algorithm is used to verification time which is more efficient than individual verification of each copy.

4.2 Comparison with Existing System

1. Storage Computation Time

In Fig. 6 present the computation time (in sec) graph of the TB-DMCPDP and our proposed system. Computation time required a confirmation that the file copies are actually stored on the different cloud server in an updated and consistent state. For storing multiple copies of the file, implemented system require less time than TB-DMCPDP. For 50 copies, the computation time for the TB-DMCPDP and our system scheme are 13.5084 and 1.8654 s respectively. Our implemented system reduced approximately 86% of computation time with previous system. The speed up of our system with respect to the TB-DMCPDP is presented in Table 8. The

$$\textbf{Speed Up} = \frac{Computation\ Time\ of\ TBDMCPDP - Computaion\ Time\ of\ our\ system}{Computation\ Time\ of\ TBDMCPDP} \times 100$$

As observed from the timing curve of the TB-DMCPDP scheme grows with a number of copies compare to this scheme, because TB-DMCPDP scheme contains more terms which are linear with each copy of file.

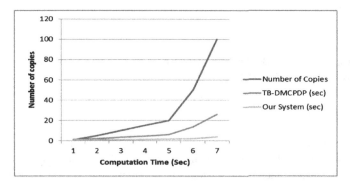

Fig. 6. Comparison with TB-DMCPDP system to compute computation time for storing multiple copies

Table 8. Speed-Ups of computation time

Number of copies	Speed up
1	20%
5	51.37%
10	64.5%
15	70.23%
20	74.16%
50	82.93%
100	86.49%

2. Dynamic Operation Computation Time

Data owner have rights to perform dynamic operation like update, delete, append etc. Here, single data owner are used to perform update operation on number of file copies. For different number of copies, graph shows the computation time (sec) for dynamic operations performed.

Computation time for both schemes is approximately equal. But, the slight increase of the TB-PMDDP scheme is due to additional hash operation requires regenerating a new directory root that constructs a new metadata. But, both of the system, data owner performs operation on single copy of file and CSP perform changes in all copies of file (Fig. 7).

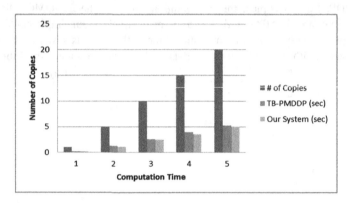

Fig. 7. Comparison with TB-DMCPDP system to compute computation time for performing dynamic operation on multiple copies

5   Conclusion

This implemented system handles the problem of creating multiple file copies. Confidentiality is handled by encrypting the data files before uploading into the cloud server. In this system, each copy is stored in different cloud server to improve availability and scalability. All data owner allows dynamic operation. Moreover, the implemented system supports public verifiability, where the third party verifies whether data is corrupted or not without losing private information. Additionally, Data owner can securely share files with other data owners and authorized users by considering security and privacy. In future, the verifier will perform operation parallel on multiple copies of a file and this will improve the performance of a system.

Acknowledgments. The research presented in the paper has been supported by Department of Technology, Computer Science and Technology, Shivaji University, Kolhapur.

References

1. Buyya, R., Yeo, C.S., Venugopal, S., Broberg, J., Brandic, I.: Cloud computing and emerging IT platforms. Future Gener. Comput. Syst. **25**(6), 599–616 (2009)

2. Ateniese, G., Burns, R., Curtmola, R., Herring, J., Kissner, L., Peterson, Z., Song, D.: Provable data possession at untrusted stores. In: Proceedings of the 14th ACM Conference on Computer and Communications Security (2007)
3. Ateniese, G., Pietro, R.D., Mancini, L.V., Tsudik, G.: Scalable and efficient provable data possession. In: Proceedings of the 4th International Conference on Security and Privacy in Communication (2008)
4. Sebé, J.D.-F., Martinez-Balleste, A., Deswarte, Y., Quisquater, J.-J.: Efficient remote data possession checking in critical information infrastructures. IEEE Trans. Knowl. Data Eng. **20**(8), 1034–1038 (2008)
5. Erway, C.P., Tamassia, R.: Dynamic provable data possession, USA, pp. 213–222 (2009)
6. Filho, D.L.G., Barreto, P.S.L.M.: Demonstrating data possession and uncheated data transfer (2006)
7. Hao, Z., Zhong, S., Yu, N.: A privacy-preserving remote data integrity checking protocol with data dynamics and public verifiability. IEEE Trans. Knowl. Data Eng. **23**(9), 1432–1437 (2011)
8. Barsoum, A.F., Anwar Hasan, M.: On verifying dynamic multiple data copies over cloud servers (2011)
9. Merkle, R.C.: Protocols for public key cryptosystems. In: IEEE Symposium on Security and Privacy, p. 122 (1980)
10. Barsoum, A.F., Anwar Hasan, M.: Provable multi-copy dynamic data possession in cloud computing systems. IEEE Trans. Inf. Forensics Secur. **10**(3), 485–497 (2015)
11. Wang, Q., Wang, K.R., Lou, W.: Ensuring data security in cloud computing (2009). http://eprint.jacr.org/
12. Zhu, Y., Hu, H., Ahn, G.-J., Yu, M.: Cooperative provable data possession for integrity verification in multi-cloud storage. IEEE Trans. Parallel Distrib. Syst. **23**(12), 2231–2244 (2012)
13. Zeng, K.: Publicly verifiable remote data integrity. In: Chen, L., Ryan, M.D., Wang, G. (eds.) ICICS 2008. LNCS, vol. 5308, pp. 419–434. Springer, Heidelberg (2008). doi:10.1007/978-3-540-88625-9_28
14. Liu, X., Zhang, Y., Wang, B., Yan, J.: Mona: secure multi-owner data sharing in cloud. IEEE Trans. Parallel Distrib. Syst. **24**(6), 1182–1191 (2013)
15. Barsoum, A.F., Anwar Hasan, M.: Integrity verification of multiple data copies over untrusted cloud servers. In: 12th IEEE/ACM International Symposium on Cluster, Cloud and Grid Computing (2012)
16. Curtmola, R., Khan, O., Burns, R., Ateniese, G.: MR-PDP: multiple-replica provable data possession (2009)
17. Armbrust, M., Fox, A., Griffith, R., Joseph, A.D., Katz, R.H., Konwinski, A., Lee, G., Patterson, D.A., Rabkin, A., Stoica, I., Zaharia, M.: A view of cloud computing. Comm. ACM **53**(4), 50–58 (2010)
18. Singh, G., Supriya: A study of encryption algorithms (RSA, DES, 3DES and AES) for information security. Int. J. Comput. Appl. **67**(19) (2013). (0975–8887)
19. Kasunde, D.S., Manjrekar, A.A.: Verification of multi-owner shared data with collusion resistant user revocation in cloud. In: 2016 International Conference on Computational Techniques in Information and Communication Technologies (ICCTICT), New Delhi, pp. 182–185 (2016). doi:10.1109/ICCTICT.2016.7514575
20. Chavan, A.S., Manjrekar, A.A.: Data embedding technique using secret fragment visible mosaic image for covered communication. In: 2015 International Conference on Information Processing (ICIP), Pune, pp. 260–265 (2015). doi:10.1109/INFOP.2015.7489390

A Technique to Reduce Problem of Delay in Key Rekeying in Mobile Networks

Rajwinder Kaur[✉] and Karan Verma[✉]

Department of Computer Science and Engineering,
Central University of Rajasthan, Ajmer, India
rajwinderkaur.rk04@gmail.com, karan.cse@curaj.ac.in

Abstract. With the recent advancement in technology, necessary enhancement in communication speed is needed as well. Automatic key management plays an expressive role in large virtual private networks (VPNs). Establishment of VPN occurs when a Secured Gateway and an End User negotiate security association (SA) in mobile networks. In this paper we first describe the basic concept of IPsec, Internet Key Exchange (IKE) and then describe the mechanism to decrease time delay during re-keying when communication starts after intrusion. A Secured Gateway is used during negotiation between peers on an untrusted network. The path between end user and secured gateway should be minimum as possible for better communication. Here, we are proposing a methodology in which there are multiple secured gateways where one gateway sends its whole VPN session information to the next secured gateway in order to create the backup before occurrence of failure and thus avoid the re-keying and re-authentication after any interruption in running communication.

Keywords: Internet key exchange · Mobile networks · Gateway · VPN · IPsec · IKEv1 · IKEv2 · Security association · Security parameter database

1 Introduction

IPsec is a framework that provides security in peer-to-peer or gateway-to-peer or gateway-to-gateway communication and responsible for data integrity and access control [1]. It operates in two modes: Transport Mode (for end-to-end) and Tunnel Mode (for VPN) in order to provide security. End users commonly use IKEv2 protocol to negotiate security association and then IPsec security association towards the secured gateway [2]. It protects the confidentiality of user data to make transmission safe and provides quick handoff to node. To reduce the time delay during communication after any crash, different SGs can perform an important task by sending information of VPN sessions to other gateways present in the cluster within the network. A VPN act as a trusted network domain over an untrusted network [20]. Signature hash algorithm [16] can be used in VPN session to provide the assurance of genuine peer in communication. It provides cryptographic security and high quality to IPv4 and IPv6 [3]. IPsec is a suite of IETF protocol which provides Internet protocol security.

Security Association (SA) is one of the key concepts in IKE and IPsec. IKE is responsible for creation and management of Security Association [4]. SA is an

© Springer Nature Singapore Pte Ltd. 2017
M. Singh et al. (Eds.): ICACDS 2016, CCIS 721, pp. 448–456, 2017.
DOI: 10.1007/978-981-10-5427-3_47

agreement between two peers which provide set of services and it defines the security parameters during exchange of messages. In addition, IKEv2 protocol used to ensure the dynamic management of SA in IPsec. IPsec uses two databases: Security Association Database and Security Policy Database in order to store security policies and four messages in two pairs are used to arrange the security association between entities.

Basically, IKE is a protocol set used to commit two functions which are creation of secured environment and management of security association between authenticated peers [5]. It ensures the security and services also. First of all, a peer is configured with an initial protection Security Parameter Database (SPD) and when a packet is to be sent by a peer, it examines the SPD, then IPsec searches for if there is an existing SA. If IPsec does not find any IKE, then it sends request to local IKE and available IKE creates an SA and if needed, it updates the SPD. Now packet will be transmitted. IKE acts as a heart of IPsec. ISAKMP, OAKLEY, SKEME are the three protocols on which IKE's architecture is based [1]. It operates in two phases: Phase 1 and Phase 2.

A. Overview of IKEv1 and IKEv2
The first generation, Internet Key Exchange version 1(IKEv1) has two phases of communication: Phase 1 and Phase 2. Phase 1 includes Main Mode and Aggressive Mode. This version of IKE used digital signature for authentication and session keys. It also provides perfect forward secrecy to the user. But the flaw of this version are: complexity, security association (SA) life is fixed and authentication failure in Aggressive Mode [1].

IKEv2 version is proposed to replace Internet Key Exchange to overcome its loopholes. IKEv2 is simple, efficient, secure and secure key exchange protocol [4]. IKEv2 is used to provide mutual authentication between two peers. It also assures authentication services from the starting of negotiation. The SAs lifetime is not fixed here, it can be decided by either peer.

B. IKE process consists of two different phases
Management tunnel also called as an ISAKMP tunnel build in Phase 1 of IKEv2. There is no any user traffic in ISAKMP and it is used to carry out secure negotiation of the IPSEC tunnel which will be established during IKEv2 phase 2. In phase1, VPN starts its establishment [2]. In this phase, two peers negotiate the encryption and authentication methods to secure the next traffic which is required to substantiate the VPN. Peers also validate each other by using encryption and authentication with the help of some keying parameters. Main Mode and Aggressive Mode are the two modes used to carry out in first phase. To establish VPNs Main Mode is usually used. In phase 1, Main Mode protocol mainly consists of six messages (i.e. three 2-way messages exchange between two peers) [6]. The second mode i.e. the Aggressive Mode acts as an organized version of Main Mode. In contrast, this mode does not provide any identity protection but it can exchange the security parameters with peers before authentication and it consists of only three messages as shown in Fig. 1.

INITIATOR   **RESPONDER**

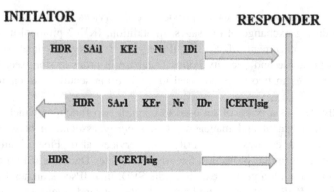

Fig. 1. IKEv2 phase 1 exchange

Phase 1: The phase 1 includes keying parameters like peer authentication method, Diffie-Hellman group, hash algorithm, data encryption algorithm and session key lifetime. ISAKMP tunnel is obtained by using these features and secret keys created in first phase, are used in phase 2 to create and update session keys in IPsec tunnel. Thus it is used to secure and protect the traffic in second phase.

Phase 2: After completion of phase 1, only then phase 2 can start. In this phase, initiator sends request (IKE_AUTH) and responder replies with IKE_AUTH response as shown in Fig. 2. In the duration of phase 2, unacknowledged notification messages and new security parameters (if needed) can be sent [7]. IPsec SAs decide encryption key lifetime authentication attributes which are used to protect user data through VPN.

INITIATOR   **RESPONDER**

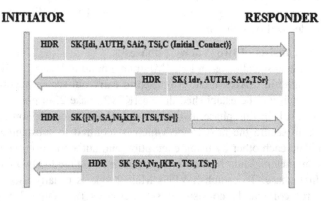

Fig. 2. IKEv2 phase 2 exchange

2   Related Work

An overview of techniques to reduce the delays in communication and to overcome the problem of key resetting is given in this section. Then related work presented in this section is mainly concentrated on delay in key rekeying during communication. After that it was realized, different gateways interfaces through VPN tunnel mode scheme can be a more suitable approach to resolve this problem. In data transmission, content size of the headers [18] in IPv4 and IPv6 may be of size as given below in Table 1.

Table 1. Header size of content

Internet protocol versions	Header size	UDP header size	Non - ESP size	IKE header size	Padding size
IPv4	20 Bytes	8 Bytes	4 Bytes	28 Bytes	At least 1 Byte
IPv6	40 Bytes	8 Bytes	4 Bytes	28 Bytes	At least 1 Byte

Do Hyeon Lee and Jeom Goo Kim [8] have designed the network on a real time mobile node. They found that key re-exchange is affected by less bandwidth to overcome this problem they created multi-interface of a node. The experimental setup showed that re-authentication of a key is very much difficult to obtain. Also, the multi-interface of the node can reduce key latency that was happened by quick hand-off for IPsec transmission. They have presented the IPsec/IKE Simulation Tool (NIIST), and showed outcomes of its use to examine and also characterized relative performance of Virtual Private Network environments based upon IPsec/IKE technologies. Basically this framework gives detailed packet level models of Internet Key Exchange protocols. On TCP as the VPN application, their study applies simple and fixed size file transfers (i.e., FTP).

K. Okhee and D. Montgomery [9] observed the behavior of Internet Key Exchange in a huge scale Virtual Private Network (VPN) through various experiments performed by the network simulator NIIST. They found many routing problems for a VPN simulation of more than 50 secured gateways. In this paper they also have mentioned four re-keying implementation techniques and impacts of dynamic SA establishment.

Daniel Palomares Velasquez [2] has proposed a technique in which different gateways avoid re-authentication while transferring VPN session and reduce CPU consumption. By using this technique, redistribution of the load and better network performances can be achieved which can maintain the same security level that was at the starting of communication.

Allard [10] has proposed a method to update IP addresses in IPsec/IKEv2 context transfer and also has given the way out to avoid collision after transfer of context with the help of MOBIKE. It is mentioned in this paper that IKEv2 parameters should be single handed which have to be transferred for continue IKEv2 sessions after any handover. Then they implemented a module which handled the SAs of IPsec and IKE.

Yu [11] proposed a solution to resolve the problems on IPsec by giving a cluster mechanism by simulation for IPsec gateways. They have stated that if cluster is not used in implementation, it does not affect seamless switching mechanism. High availability link is not suggested by author between the gateways during the communication of SAs. But it is mentioned in this paper that clusters can be installed (deployed) in distinct network segments. All results in this paper is not a real implementation but a simulation.

Yong Lee and Goo Yeon Lee have mention in their paper that MMR i.e. Mobile Multi-hope Relay network is not difficult to deploy and easy to manage because of its characteristics of self-healing and organizing in [12]. They have proposed an authentication method which is hybrid and also proposed a distribution algorithm for IEEE 802.16j MMR service and defined the strategy for proposed scheme applied to MMR networks and also mentioned its useful functionalities. This method can be used in controlling traffic and it is more powerful method of authentication, which also assure less and small delay swing during hand-off which is a better scheme for mobile multimedia communication.

Sen Xu and Chin-Tser Huang [13] illustrated the security problems in the standard and possible strikes to the authentication of different parties and key management protocols. Some solutions are also presented to halt these strikes. At last they have given a security handover protocol that also can be sustained in the future 802.16e for mobile communication. In this paper it is also indicated that Multicast is another problem in some new standard, where authentication and key management protocols should be reconsidered to facilitate the multicast activities.

Table 2. Comparison between IKEv1 and IKEv2

IKE versions	Internet Key Exchange version 1 (IKEv1)	Internet Key Exchange version 2 (IKEv2)
Modes of Exchange	Two Modes: 1. Main mode 2. Aggressive mode	In IKEv2, only one exchange procedure is defined Exchange modes were outdated
Messages Exchange for Establishment of VPN	Main mode: 9 messages Aggressive mode: 6 messages	Only four messages need to establish VPN
Authentication Method	Authentication method should be same for both parties	Different authentication methods can be used by the parties [17]. Asymmetrical authentication is used. (For e.g. Initiator: PSK and Responder: RSA-Sig)
SAs Lifetime	Requirement of Agreement	SAs can be deleted by any party at any time by exchanging DELETE payloads. No negotiation before
Mechanism of Rekeying	Mechanism is not defined here in IKEv1	Mechanism is defined here in IKEv2
Multi-homing and Mobile Clients	NOT supported in IKEv1	Supported by MOBIKE
Methods of Authentication	Four Methods: 1. Pre-Shared Key (PSK) 2. Public Key Encryption 3. Digital Signature (RSA Sig) 4. Revised Mode of Public key Encryption	Two Methods: 1. Pre-Shared Key 2. Digital Signature

The work of Safdar Hussain Shaheen and Yousaf [14] provide main key points of IKEv1 and IKEv2 in means of security in their paper. And then comparative analysis IKEv1 and IKEv2 is stated. This analysis indicated that IKE2 is less complicated, more reliable, less complex than version 1 of IKE. It also assessed that IKEv2 needs less round trips for exchange of messages to form IKE SA and IPsec SA in contrast to IKEv1. Also rekeying mechanism, aliveness detection, NAT traversal, remote access VPN, multi-hosting and multi-homing services are inbuilt in IKEv2 already. In Table 2, a very concise overview of IKE versions: IKEv1 and IKEv2 is given.

Chiung-Ying Wang and Hsiao-Yun Huang [15] have proposed the method in which mobility management mechanism appraises the Wi-Fi environment only with distinct wireless networks. For instance bluetooth, and mobile handset and WiMAX carriers, such as GPRS, CDMA. These all are still under examination. In this paper, they have also proposed a mechanism for management of mobility which comprises of context management unit (U-gate), UbiPaPaGo and UbiHandoff mechanisms in order to decrease handoff number and to satisfy Quality of Services restraints like signal strength indication, ratio of packet loss, availability of bandwidth, jitter, optimized path and service available to the each user etc.

3   Proposed Work

In mobile networks, the chances of interruption during communication are more which can create a problem of peer re-authentication and re-keying. If we talk about IKEv2, the rekey time in IKEv2 is much faster than that of IKEv1 because the occurrence of loss of packets is less in IKEv2 which leads to less need of rekey SAs. We proposed a mechanism to reduce the delay in key re-keying during communication. Here, we are considering scenario in which there are number of gateways used in communication between peers. When a peer sends request, SG_ip1 will give the access to that node by using its interface and communication will be done with the help of old IPsec tunnel. For the purpose of security and verification to ensure that IKE SAs established between the intended peer, digital signature can be used. Peer will send its digital signature in VPN session i.e. in message exchange to next peer. After receiving the digital signature in message exchange, the responder will verify the sender by using its public key. Now, Secured Gateway (SG_ip1) will send its all information that came from peer to SG_ip2, that is IKEv2/IPsec transfer will be done at this step. With VPN sessions details, all the IKEv2/IPsec context will be transfer to SG_ip2 in order to avoid re-authentication. If we don't send the IKEv2/IPsec context at this step, re-authentication against SG_ip2 would interrupt the communication which could be worst situation in real-time based applications. Now if SG_ip1 fails or crashes, then without consuming time in re-keying process, SP_ip2 will resume the process where it was halted (that is information exchange will be resumed) because of failure. SG_ip2 has all information of peer, because SP_ip1 has already sent to SP_ip2. As old IPsec tunnel is crashed, now new IPsec tunnel will serve its services to the communication process. Each message exchange will hold a nonce as a cryptographic functions. These nonce values are used to show the freshness of the message which also append originality to the key derivation technique used to get the keys from Diffie-Hellman (DH) key. Nonce are the randomly chosen bits which should be of size at least 128 bits or half of the key size of negotiated pseudo-random function (prf). Flow Chart of proposed methodology is given in Fig. 3.

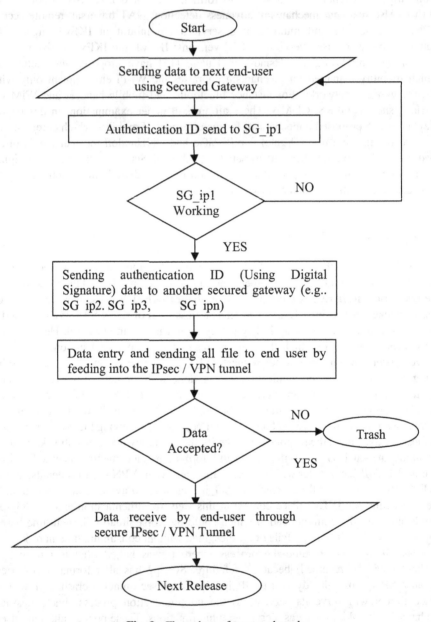

Fig. 3. Flow chart of proposed work

4 Conclusion

In this paper, we have given the comparative details of IKEv1 and IKEv2. Also we have presented VPN solutions to decrease time delay during re-keying and introduced overview of versions of internet Key Exchange (IKE). Dynamic behavior of VPN environments based upon IPsec/IKE technologies is key mechanism in this paper. The remaining goal is to make gateways more secure to protect communication. As a next step we intend to implement the present mechanism. Furthermore, in order to speed up and protect the communication two hash algorithm can be used: Message Digest Algorithm 5 (MD5) or Secure Hash Algorithm (SHA). But MD5 is more appropriate for reducing the time delay because it is quicker than other algorithms. MD5 algorithm constructs of hash of size 128-bit and it is a one way hashing algorithm. This hash algorithm also strengthen the security, check for the data integrity and used for authentication within the framework of IPSec.

References

1. Cremers, C.: Key exchange in IPsec revisited: formal analysis of IKEv1 and IKEv2. In: Atluri, V., Diaz, C. (eds.) ESORICS 2011. LNCS, vol. 6879, pp. 315–334. Springer, Heidelberg (2011). doi:10.1007/978-3-642-23822-2_18
2. Palomares, D., Migault, D., Laurent, M.: Failure preventive mechanism for IPsec gateways. In: 2013 Third International Conference on IEEE Communications and Information Technology (ICCIT) (2013)
3. Zhou, P., et al.: Security investigation and enhancement of IKEV2 protocol. In: 3rd IEEE International Conference on IEEE Broadband Network and Multimedia Technology (IC-BNMT) (2010)
4. Soussi, H., et al.: IKEv1 and IKEv2: a quantitative analyses. In: Proceedings of World Academy of Science, Engineering and Technology. Citeseer (2005)
5. Taral, M.P.P., Gadicha, V.B.: Secure key exchange over internet (2014)
6. Kaufman, C., et al.: Internet key exchange protocol version 2 (IKEv2). RFC 5996 (2010)
7. Kasraoui, M., Cabani, A., Chafouk, H.: Collaborative key exchange system based on Chinese remainder theorem in heterogeneous wireless sensor networks. Int. J. Distrib. Sens. Netw. **501**, 159518 (2015)
8. Kim, O., Montgomery, D.: Behavioral and performance characteristics of IPsec/IKE in large-scale VPNs. In: Proceedings of the IASTED International Conference on Communication Network and Information Security (2003)
9. Lee, D.H., Kim, J.G.: IKEv2 authentication exchange model and performance analysis in mobile IPv6 networks. Personal Ubiquit. Comput. **18**(3), 493–501 (2014)
10. Allard, F., et al.: IKE context transfer in an IPv6 mobility environment. In: Proceedings of the 3rd International Workshop on Mobility in the Evolving Internet Architecture. ACM (2008)
11. Yu, L., et al.: An IPSEC seamless switching mechanism with high availability and scalability by extending ikev2 protocol. In: International Conference on Advanced Intelligence and Awareness Internet. IETF (2011)
12. Lee, Y., et al.: Performance analysis of authentication and key distribution scheme for mobile multi-hop relay in IEEE 802.16 j. Personal Ubiquit. Comput. **16**(6), 697–706 (2012)

13. Xu, S., Matthews, M., Huang, C.-T.: Security issues in privacy and key management protocols of IEEE 802.16. In: Proceedings of the 44th Annual Southeast Regional Conference. ACM (2006)
14. Shaheen, S.H., Yousaf, M., Majeed, M.Y.: Comparative analysis of internet key exchange protocols. In: International Conference on Information and Communication Technologies (ICICT). IEEE (2015)
15. Wang, C.-Y., Huang, H.-Y., Hwang, R.-H.: Mobility management in ubiquitous environments. Personal Ubiquit. Comput. 15(3), 235–251 (2011)
16. Kivinen, T., Snyder, J.: Signature authentication in the internet key exchange version 2 (IKEv2) (2015)
17. Sheffer, Y., Fluhrer, S.: Additional Diffie-Hellman tests for the internet key exchange protocol version 2 (IKEv2) (2013)
18. Kaufman, C., et al.: Internet key exchange protocol version 2 (IKEv2) (2014)
19. Jo, M., et al.: A survey of converging solutions for heterogeneous mobile networks. IEEE Wirel. Commun. 21(6), 54–62 (2014)
20. Alshalan, A., Pisharody, S., Huang, D.: A survey of mobile VPN technologies. IEEE Commun. Surv. Tutor. 18(2), 1177–1196 (2016)

Automated Learning Based Water Management and Healthcare System Using Cloud Computing and IoT

Punit Gupta[(⊠)], Dilpreet Singh[(⊠)], Anuj Purwar[(⊠)], and Mohit Patel[(⊠)]

Department of Electronics and Communication Engineering,
Department of Computer Science Engineering,
Jaypee University of Information Technology, Solan, India
punitg07@gmail.com, anujpurwar201296@gmail.com,
mohitpatel2314@gmail.com, dilpreet.singh.in@ieee.org

Abstract. Utilization of Water is increasing day-by-day in Homes, factories, Schools, Universities, Industries etc. which are consuming water on regular basis. Today, most of the places are suffering from the scarcity of water which is becoming the most imperative issue for human being because water is one of the most important natural resource present on earth. About 70% of the earth's surface is covered with water out of which only 1% is available as fresh water. In that case there is a need to use water efficiently. A vast amount of water is being wasted without being consumed anywhere due to existing ineffective water supply system. Unnecessary leakage of large amount of water during supply, unsystematic supply to various regions i.e. not according to consumption, need or requirement, degraded water quality, time taking process to find the fault and then fixing it are the major drawbacks in the existing supply system. In this research we are designing and implementing an efficient water management system based on smart wireless sensor technology, using IOT, automatic learning with multiple modules and cloud computing to enhance the water supply system.

Keywords: IOT · Embedded system · Automatic learning · Ultrasonic depth sensor · GSM shield · Microcontroller · Cloud computing

1 Introduction

India's population has reached beyond 1.2 billion and is increasing day by day. Due to overpopulation the demand of food, water and other daily life necessities is also increasing continuously leading to decreased supply which results in scarcity of water, unavailability of foods and inefficient supply of daily life necessities. One cannot survive without water which is the most important natural resource in this world. So efficient utilization of water becomes very important in our day to day life. Drinking water supply and sanitation in India continues to be inadequate, in spite of long lasting efforts by the various levels of government and communities at improving coverage. Meanwhile, government agencies in charge of operating and maintaining the infrastructure are seen

© Springer Nature Singapore Pte Ltd. 2017
M. Singh et al. (Eds.): ICACDS 2016, CCIS 721, pp. 457–470, 2017.
DOI: 10.1007/978-981-10-5427-3_48

as weak and deprived the financial resources to carry out their work. Therefore, the aim of our research is to design an efficient Water Utilization Supply System, which can ensure a continuous supply of water to various places, by notifying our respective Government Department 24 h.

The solution focuses on developing an efficient system that gives real time data for the quantity of water passed form main supply and received by consecutive sub tanks, whether there is any kind of leakage anywhere in the supply lines and also gives feedback about how much of water was supplied from reservoir and how much is delivered. Figure 1 shows the interfacing of entire system i.e., sensor-nodes with master nodes surveillance and then casting of data by master node to the cloud for accessibility of data instantly. Here, each sensor-node is in itself under the surveillance of MCU.

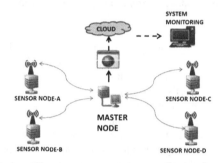

Fig. 1. Diagram of sensor nodal network

System uses IoT (Internet of things). The internet of things is the internetworking of physical devices like sensors, embedded with electronics, actuators, and network connectivity that enable these objects to collect and exchange data. The IoT provides an access to the data remotely across existing network infrastructure. The IoT provides a platform resulting in improved efficiency, accuracy and economic benefit.

We investigate the microcontroller based water level measurement and controlling in a wired and wireless environment [1]. Water Level management approach would help in reducing the home power consumption and as well as water overflow. Furthermore, it can indicate the amount of water in the tank.

WSN [2] has become one of the basic technological needs as it solves the inconvenience of wiring. It has wide perspective in area of remote sensing, various automation controls and domestic appliances. Through WSN easy collection, transmission and processing of data takes place. We have used this technology in order to reduce complexity, power consumption and cost [3].

The sensors interfaced with microcontroller, present on subsequent tank, sends data to its subsequent microcontroller which inturn collects data and pushes it on the microprocessor present at the main supply (Hub) through GSM shield. The entire data processing of raw data is done here at the main HUB by the microprocessor unit.

The processed data is pushed into cloud where the database is made and stored in real time so that it can be used and accessed at any time.

System make a database by collecting the raw data in real time. Future prediction of water consumption by subsequent node is then done on the basis of previous values of volume of water present in the data base. This then determines at what time and how much of water should be supplied to the subsequent nodes, this helps in efficient utilization and cuts off the access supply of water to the nodes by delivering the access amount to the node where it is required.

This kind of design will be of great welfare to our society & daily use. Water-efficiency improvements offer multiple benefits.

- Some of the water saved represents new supply that can be dedicated to other uses, and efficiency improvements that do not produce new supply provide other important co-benefits.
- The system can be used in various spheres of daily life individually in residential complex, Smart cities, Government complex, Schools, Campus, private sectors.
- This will help us to predict beforehand if there is any shortage of water, so that necessary measures can be taken.

2   System Architecture and Basic Modelling

Figure 2 includes overall working and representation of all the components used in our system design. The modeling and architecture includes the components as listed:

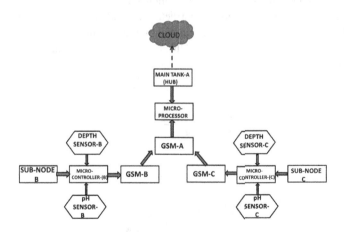

Fig. 2. Block diagram of system model

A. Water Supply Node

Each water tank is acting a single node which stores and supply water for utilization purpose. These nodes supply water to its consecutive sub-tanks (outlets) through pipelines and sub-tanks also supply water to various other outlets connected to it. Each water tanks consists of ultrasonic depth sensors and microcontroller in it. The main water node (Tank) is the main HUB and supervises the entire system. Each tank acts as a node for the nodal sensor placements and establishes a wireless sensor network (Fig. 3).

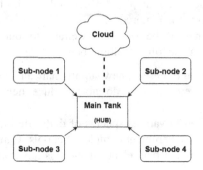

Fig. 3. Block diagram of nodal network

B. Water Level Measurement

Measuring of water level consists of a ultrasonic depth sensor which produces a measurable response signal. Here, the sensor measures the water level at every instant of time. Each Depth sensor is interfaced with the microcontroller. All the sensors are connected in such a way that they form a Wireless sensor network. Ultrasonic sensors are basically distance measuring sensors which measures the water level by use of ultrasonic waves. It is a microphones that detect ultrasonic noise that is present under certain conditions, convert it to an electrical signal, and send it to a microcontroller. It consists of Transmitter which sends the Ultrasonic waves(echo) and Receiver receives the Ultrasonic waves.

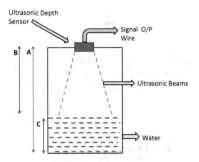

Fig. 4. Working of ultrasonic sensor

Figure 4 shows, the working of ultrasonic sensor, Ultrasonic waves which in turn strikes at the water level of the tank and return back. The time lapse between sending and receiving the signal is recorded and the level of water at any instant is then calculated by the microcontroller through the program using Eq. 1

$$Distance = Speed\ of\ Ultrasonic\ waves$$
$$* Time\ lapse\ between\ sending\ and\ receiving\ signal/2 \qquad (1)$$

With measured distance we will be able to measure the level of water in each tank.

C. Microcontroller

Microcontroller is a computer on a chip that is programmed to perform almost any control, sequencing, monitoring and display the function. Here in our case, the data sent by ultrasonic depth sensor is received by the microcontroller and the water level is determined through the algorithm existing in the microcontroller. After calculating the depth it will send the data to the main controlling tank (Tank A) through GSM Module.

D. Internet of Things (IOT)

Internet of Things is one of the major development in technology [4]. The Internet of Things (IOT) is concerned with interconnecting communicating objects that are installed at different locations that are possibly distant from each other [5]. Internet of Things represents a concept in which, network devices have ability to collect and sense data from the world, and then share that data across the internet where that data can be utilized and processed for various purposes. The internet of things describes a vision where objects become part of internet: where every object is uniquely identified and access to the network [6].

E. Cloud Computing

Cloud computing is an Internet-based computing that provides shared computer processing, resources and data to computers and other devices on demand. In more general terms, it is a computing platform where the entire information is stored casted by various integrated networks or systems i.e., computers, to it. Here, in our case whatever raw data received by the main HUB after processing is pushed into the cloud so that it can be accessed remotely at any instant.

F. Water Leakage Control System

The principle used in the determination of any leakage in any pipeline or tank is just by finding the difference in initial and final water level of tank. These levels are obtained through the data stored in the server. It is measured by the finding the difference between quantity of water delivered from the main water tank through outlet and the amount reached to the sub-tank. This difference then gives the leakage amount.

The Fig. 5 depicts the initial water level of the tank which is equal. After delivering L liters of water from one tank to another, let water level decreased by X1 amount. As

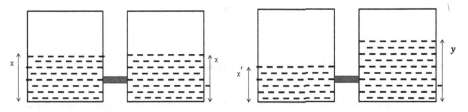

Fig. 5. Tanks with equal level   **Fig. 6.** Tanks with unequal level

seen in Fig. 6, L liters of water is received by the another tank. So, then water decreased in one should almost be equal to another.

$$Volume\ decreased\ in\ one\ tank \approx Volume\ increased\ in\ another\ tank \pm 5-10\ L \quad (2)$$

As we are dealing in gallons of water so five to ten liters of water can be ignored.

G. GSM Module Sim 900A

GSM (Global System for Mobile Communication) is a digital mobile telephony system. GSM is a cellular network which means that cell phones connect to it by searching for cells in the immediate vicinity. It works on +5v which can be provided from Arduino Uno. With the help of AT commands GSM shield is able to send data to another GSM.

The GSM module present in our design having a connection with microcontroller and to the GSM module of the main HUB (Tank A). It makes use of IOT to send the data collected from microcontroller to other GSM in run time. The main GSM shield installed at the main HUB is also interfaced with microprocessor i.e. raspberry pi in our case. GSM collects raw data and pushes to raspberry pi which in turn push full fledged data to the server by means of IOT and make a proper usable data base.

H. pH Sensor

pH scale measures the acidity or basicity of given aqueous solution and tells us whether respective water is suitable for drinking or not by indicating a numeric value from 0–14. If the indicated value is between 0–6 then the solution is acidic, if 8–14 then Alkaline (basic) and if exactly 7 then solution is neutral, as can be seen in Fig. 8.

We are using it for the same purpose i.e. checking of water quality supplied to tanks from various nodes.

If the value read by pH scale comes out to be different from pH range which is suitable for drinking i.e. 6.5 to 8.5 then data from the respective tank will be send to main hub indicating water supplied to respective tank is not suitable for drinking so that further measures can be taken to improve its quality (Fig. 7).

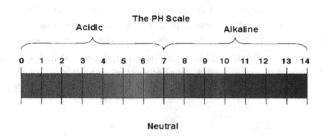

Fig. 7. pH Scale

In this way we are able to monitor quality of water in a efficient way.

I. Microprocessor

The main processing unit of our system is microprocessor. The main GSM shield is interfaced with it and entire processing of our system is carried out by microprocessor.

The data received by main GSM Module is casted to the microprocessor which in turn pushes the data to the cloud. The prediction algorithm also runs on microprocessor which does future prediction of amount of water to be supplied to the corresponding tanks.

3 Design and Implementation

A. Measurement of Tank Parameters

In Fig. 8, Tank A is the main supply from where water is delivered to different regions or divisions of the system. It is also the HUB of our system where whole data will be accessed and after the processing data will be stored in the cloud (server). Main tank is also acting like a supervisor for the sub nodes. "For the sake of simplicity we have considered that there are only three nodes connected with each other and one node main tank (Tank-A).

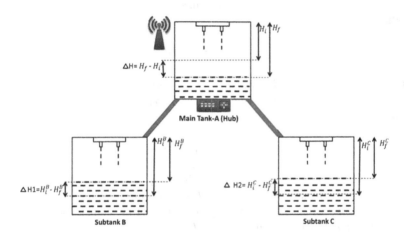

Fig. 8. Demonstration of flow and calculation of water

B. Formulae and Calculations for Water Level

Initial height of each tank can be known with the help of Water level Sensor which is already there in Tanks. Sensor continuously sense the water and measures the height till the water level reached to at any instant say H', then the difference in the two height gives the actual change in water level (Table 1).

Change in height of water in Tank A = Initial Height − Final height

$$\Delta H = H_f - H_i \qquad (3)$$

When $\Delta H > 0$, positive i.e. Water level is decreasing
When $\Delta H < 0$, negative i.e. Water level is rising

Table 1. Abbreviation for height of water

Abbreviation	Description
H_i	Initial height of water in **Main Tank A**
H_f	Final height of water in **Main Tank A**
H_i^B	Initial height of water in **Sub Tank B**
H_f^B	Final height of water in **Sub Tank B**
H_i^c	Initial height of water in **Sub Tank C**
H_f^c	Final height of water in **Sub Tank C**
ΔH	Change in water level in **Main Tank A**
$\Delta H1$	Change in water level in **SubTank1**
$\Delta H2$	Change in water level in **SubTank2**

Conventionally Tank A is supplying the water to Tank B and Tank C. Similarly, is the case for Sub nodes, Tank B and Tank C. Height will be known with the help of the Sensors which are connected inside these tanks.

Tank B:

$$\Delta H1 = H_i^B - H_f^B \tag{4}$$

When $\Delta H1 > 0$, positive i.e. Water level is rising
When $\Delta H1 < 0$, negative i.e. Water level is decreasing

Tank C:

$$\Delta H2 = H_i^c - H_f^c \tag{5}$$

When $\Delta H2 > 0$, positive i.e. Water level is rising.
When $\Delta H2 < 0$, negative i.e. Water level is decreasing.

This is how we will get actual readings of height of the corresponding tanks.

C. Measurement of Volume of Water in Tanks

This water level is assigned as the initial water level and the data is sent to the cloud. The ultrasonic sensor continuously sends the signal and as it encounters any change in the water level it again records it and sends data to microcontroller, when it become stable which in turn calculates the new water level i.e., change of water level from initial level is computed. This change in water level is then used to compute the volume of water delivered by the tank to other sub-tanks.

Measurement of the water level takes place at each node, will send the data to main HUB using GSM Shield. Capacity of main tank is V_i gallons and is filled with water to some of its capacity. Two sub-tanks connected to it are of capacity V_i^B gallons and V_i^C gallons. Tank A delivers some gallons of water to each nodes (Table 2).

Similar, in case for volume, Change in Volume of water in Tank A = Initial Height − Final height

Table 2. Abbreviation for volume of water

Abbreviation	Description
V_i	Initial volume of water in **Tank A**
V_f	Final volume of water in **Tank A**
V_i^B	Initial volume of water in **Tank B**
V_f^B	Final volume of water in **Tank B**
V_i^C	Initial volume of water in **Tank C**
V_f^C	Final volume of water in **Tank C**
ΔV	Change in volume in **Tank A**
$\Delta V1$	Change in volume in **Tank B**
$\Delta V2$	Change in volume in **Tank B**

$$\Delta V = V_f - V_i \tag{6}$$

Similarly, Is the case for Sub-nodes, Tank B and Tank C. Volume will be known with the help of the Sensors which are connected inside these tanks.

Tank B:

$$\Delta V1 = V_i^B - V_f^B \tag{7}$$

When $\Delta V1 > 0$, positive i.e. Water level is rising
When $\Delta V1 < 0$, negative i.e. Water level is decreasing

Tank C:

$$\Delta V2 = V_i^c - V_f^c \tag{8}$$

When $\Delta V2 > 0$, positive i.e. Water level is rising.
When $\Delta V2 < 0$, negative i.e. Water level is decreasing.

Change in volume of water in tank A = Change in volume of water in subtank B + Change in volume of water in subtank C

$$\Delta V \approx \Delta V1 + \Delta V2 \tag{9}$$

To keep an eye on how much water is delivered to each tank we have used ultrasonic depth sensors in each of the tanks which in turn measures the water level in each of the tank.

3.1   Volume Measurement

$$V = height * Area\ of\ cross\ section \tag{10}$$

Considering initially the sub-tanks are empty. We know the maximum height of sub-tanks A and B. Let us say, H_i^B and H_i^C. The water is delivered from the main tank to each of the tank. The ultrasonic sensor again measures the water level (as described above) and sends the data to the microcontroller.

Let us say the data (height) sent by the ultrasonic sensors ds_1 and ds_2 is hs_1 and hs_2.

Change in water level from initial of sub-tank B $= h_i^B - hs_1$.

Change in water level from initial of sub-tank C $= h_i^C - hs_2$.

The above two heights are then used to compute the volume of water in each of the two sub-tank. V1 and V2 be the volume of water in each of the sub-tanks. The sum of volumes V1 and V2 is equal to the volume of water delivered by the main tank.

D. Circuit Diagrams

Figure 9 shows a circuit diagram which consists of Ultrasonic Depth Sensor, pH sensor and GSM Module interfaced with MCU (Arduino Uno R3).

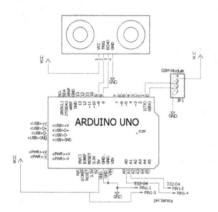

Fig. 9. Circuit diagram at sub-node

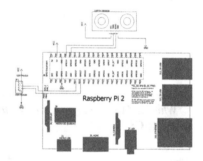

Fig. 10. Circuit diagram at main hub

Ultrasonic Depth sensor has four pins VCC, GND, TRIG, ECHO. The TRIG and ECHO pin is connected to the pin 9 and 8 analogue pin of MCU (Arduino UNO R3). The VCC and GND pins are connected to VCC and GND of MCU. Depth sensor is collecting raw data i.e., the water level measurement, and is sending it to the MCU in analogue signals form.

GSM Module has four pins TX(2), RX(3), VCC(1),GND(2). TX and RX are connected to RX and TX of MCU. The TX of Arduino is transmitting the data to RX pin of GSM Module and TX of GSM module is sending acknowledgement to RX of MCU.

pH sensor has four pins 1, 2, 3, 4. Pin no. 1 and 2 are VCC and GND and pin no. 3 and 4 are connected to MCU. The entire data is processed by MCU which is then sent to main HUB shown in Fig. 10 through GSM module connected to the node side as well as Hub side.

Figure 10 shown consists of Ultrasonic Depth Sensor and GSM Module interfaced with microprocessor (Raspberry Pi). The entire data of system is collected in main HUB and is processed by the microprocessor unit which is then pushed in cloud.

E. Analysis of Data

The analysis of data has come into play. All the data received by HUB is pushed into server. Figure 11 shows the data transfer from sub-nodes to main HUB. Hub consisting of an Intelligent machine which will process the data according to the command we provided. Figure also showing the analysis table which shows the water level content in each tank A and B, pH values of water in sub-tanks and consumption of water by each of the tank.

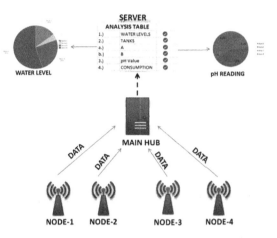

Fig. 11. Demonstration of flow of data

For the research, we made a web application which is telling the output. Figure 12 shows that application of our project where the entire data analysis is taking place. It consists of three tanks corresponding to which the data of each tank is received. Two attempts for data analysis on web application are shown.

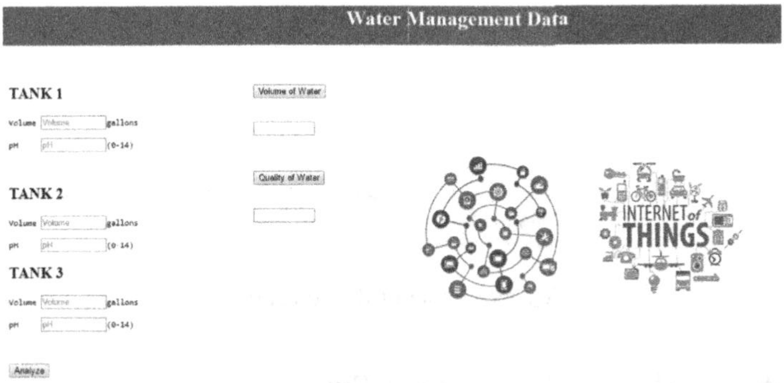

Fig. 12. Application of water management data

In Figs. 13 and 14, three tanks rows in which volume of water of each tank appearing after stabilization. pH row depicts the pH of water present in each of the tank i.e., the quality. The volume of water dialog box shows the entire water level content in tanks.

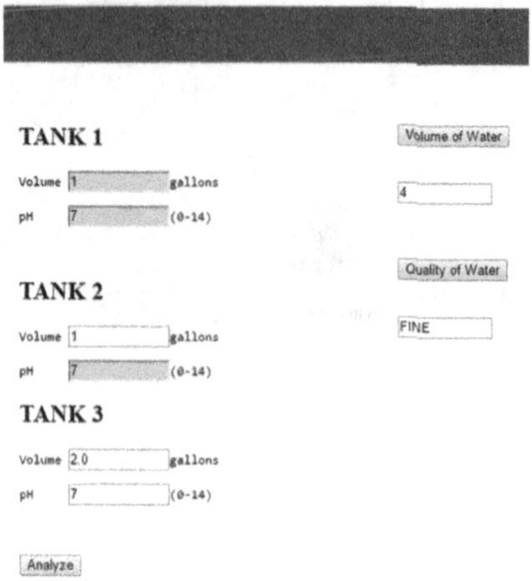

TANK 1

Volume 1   gallons

pH 7   (0-14)

TANK 2

Volume 1   gallons

pH 7   (0-14)

TANK 3

Volume 2.0   gallons

pH 7   (0-14)

Analyze

Volume of Water

4

Quality of Water

FINE

TANK 1

Volume 2   gallons

pH 6   (0-14)

TANK 2

Volume 2   gallons

pH 6   (0-14)

TANK 3

Volume 3   gallons

pH 7   (0-14)

Analyze

Volume of Water

7

Quality of Water

FINE

Fig. 13. Data calculation attempts [1] 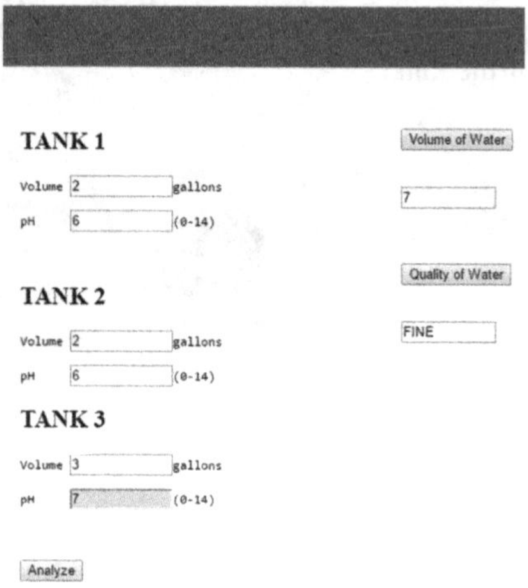   **Fig. 14.** Data calculation attempts [2]

Figure 15 is showing the back end data, the values of water and ph are received, table is formed with the help of Data base management (SQL) and according to the values analysis is done.

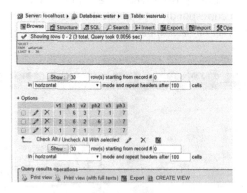

Fig. 15. Table of data on server

4   Benefits of Water Management System

1. Minimal human intervention.
2. Supply sufficient amount as per the demand.

3. Simple and easy to configure.
4. Saving energy and resources so that they can be utilized in proper way and amount.
5. Leakage detection.
6. Tank level monitoring to avoid or flow and intimate the level of water at any time in the tank.

5 Conclusion

There has been already various research conducted regarding this issue but most of them has some shortness in practice. In our research we have tried to overcome these problems and come with a more efficient automated water level monitoring and controlling system. The main issue that is being addressed in this project is developing a wireless sensor network model which can ensure minimum wastage of water during supply from various reservoirs.

Our intension of this research work is to establish easily configurable, economical and flexible system which can solve our water losing problems and can ensure proper supply of water to respective tanks. It focuses on the regular basis check of water level of the main water supply as well as cisterns and to estimate the consumption of water through each outlet so that efficient controlling of water supply could be made as per the usage of consumer. Main water tank supplies water to various intake pipes which will supply water to various other cisterns i.e. sub-node. Main supply tank integrates information it receives from various sub-nodes, coordinates and influences the working of entire system and casts it to the server i.e., cloud, for to make the information collected accessible instantly and remotely. Our paper gives the whole data about how much quantity of water is being supplied to respective nodes, based on this data our project performs calculations and through machine learning its tells the respective consumption and requirement of supply to various nodes. Moreover it also performs a quality check of water which is supplied at various nodes and indicates the whether it is suitable for drinking or not. We have successfully implemented this project in our lab and therefore proposed a web based water level monitoring and controlling network which would offer us to control this system from any place via internet even with different types of devices. This could have a substantial benefit from this research work for efficient management of water.

References

1. Reza, S.M.K., Tariq, S.A.M., Reza, S.M.M.: Microcontroller based automated water level sensing and controlling: design and implementation issue. In: Proceedings of the World Congress on Engineering and Computer Science 2010 (WCECS 2010), 20–22 October 2010, vol. 1, San Francisco (2010)
2. Shaikh, A., Pathan, S.: Research on wireless sensor network technology. Int. J. Inf. Educ. Technol. 2(5), 476 (2012)

3. Lambrou, T.P., Anastasiou, C.C., Panayiotou, C.G., Polycarpou, M.M.: A low-cost sensor network for real-time monitoring and contamination detection in drinking water distribution systems. IEEE Sens. J. **14**(8), 2765–2772 (2014)

4. Bhatt, J., Patoliya, J.: IoT based water quality monitoring system. Int. J. Ind. Electron. Electr. Eng. **4**, 44–48 (2016)

5. Gazis, V., Sasloglou, K., Frangiadakis, N., Kikiras, P.: Wireless sensor networking, automation technologies and machine to machine developments on the path to the Internet of Things. In: 16th Panhellenic Conference on Informatics, pp. 276–282 (2012)

6. Gadallah, Y., Tager, M., Elalamy, E.: A framework for cooperative Intranet of Things wireless sensor network applications. In: Eight International Workshop on Selected Topics in Mobile and Wireless Computing, The American University in Cairo, pp. 147–154 (2012)

7. Coetzee, L., Eksteen, J.: The Internet of Things – promise for the future? An introduction. In: Cunningham, P., Cunningham, M. (eds.) ISTAfrica 2011 Conference Proceedings. IIMC International Information Management Corporation, pp. 1–9 (2011)

8. Wang, J., Cao, Y., Yu, G., Yuan, M.: Research on application of IOT in domestic waste treatment and disposal. In: Proceeding of the 11th World Congress on Intelligent Control and Automation, Shenyang, 29 June–4 July 2014, pp. 4742–4745 (2014)

9. Gong, C., Liu, J., Zhang, Q., Chen, H., Gong, S.: The characteristics of cloud computing. In: 39th International Conference on Parallel Processing Workshops, Changsha, pp. 275–279 (2010)

10. Mahmood, Z.: Cloud computing: characteristics and deployment approaches. In: 11th IEEE International Conference on Computer and Information Technology, UK, pp. 121–126 (2011)

11. Lakhe, R.R.: Wireless network using zigbee for water monitoring. Int. J. Eng. Res. Appl. (IJERA) (2008)

Challenging Issues of Video Surveillance System Using Internet of Things in Cloud Environment

Dileep Kumar Yadav[1,2(✉)], Karan Singh[1], and Swati Kumari[3]

[1] SC and SS, Jawaharlal Nehru University, New Delhi, India
dileep252000@gmail.com, karan@mail.jnu.ac.in
[2] Department of CSE, Krishna Engineering College, Ghaziabad, UP, India
[3] Department of ECE, Ambedkar Institute of Advanced Communication
Technologies and Research, New Delhi, India
swatisamastipur@gmail.com

Abstract. In video surveillance system, traditional systems are susceptible to environmental variation i.e. change in light, motion in the background due to water, fluctuation or reflection of light *etc.* This paper focuses on the challenging issues, application areas, freely available resources (dataset, tools) and benefits of video surveillance system, risk occurred in visual surveillance system. Here, we are exploring the study of major challenges along with application area. This paper also presents some basic steps of proposed framework using Internet of Things in cloud (IoTC) environment. Such surveillance systems can be developed according to suitability and requirement of society, army, navigation, robotics, healthcare, transportation, social media, *etc.*

Keywords: Video surveillance system · Cloud environment · Internet of things · IoTC · Security system

1 Introduction

The visual surveillance system involves in the observation of moving object using electronic cameras. Presently this system is considered as an effective tool for surveillance and security. The visual surveillance system is used to detect, identify, and monitor changing information for managing, protecting, and directing the object [1–4]. This system is extremely economical and valuable that provides strength to the security of buildings, people, vehicles and other valuables things [3–5]. In the area of computer vision, there is currently a growing demand for the motion based object detection, which enables immersive visual surveillance and consumer electronic based security applications [11–14]. It can be applicable in multimedia, computer vision systems, traffic analysis and monitoring, artificial intelligence and automatic computer algorithm development. In general, the object detection is simply a concept of evaluating the state of motion based pixel in the video frames [6–12].

The main aim of this work in visual surveillance system is to detect the moving object from video which is captured through (CCTV, IP, etc.). It strengthens the

© Springer Nature Singapore Pte Ltd. 2017
M. Singh et al. (Eds.): ICACDS 2016, CCIS 721, pp. 471–481, 2017.
DOI: 10.1007/978-981-10-5427-3_49

security of concerned areas such as indoor-outdoor, banks, offices, open market, shops, shopping malls, hospitals, fields, road, garden, restricted zones, railway platforms, houses, river, sea, defence, army, navy, maritime, behaviour or activity analysis, games, etc. [12–15]. At port, sea-bay, coastal areas are vulnerable to different critical hazardous scenarios due to the intrinsically complex traffic. Due to the diversity in functionalities of ships or human visual inspection are error-prone as well as highly laborious. So, the automatic ship, human, traffic detection are emerging research areas in the field of sea or port surveillance [16–19].

The moving object can be detected using frame differencing method, background subtraction method, kernel based background subtraction, differential method, and optical-flow based methods [25–29]. In this paper, we are exploring the study of major challenges along with application area along with a suggested framework using Internet of Things in cloud (IoTC) environment. It also focuses benefits, risks, and IoTC based video surveillance based suitability for society, army, navy, navigation, robotics, healthcare, transportation, social media *etc.*

1.1 Organization of the Paper

First section has covered the brief overview, application area and major issues of surveillance system. Second section explored about major challenges. Third section focuses on the application relevant areas. In section four, this paper describes resources such as datasets, programming tools. Fifth and sixth section emphasis on benefits and risk involved in the video surveillance system. The seventh section provides an algorithmic steps of proposed work. Finally, eight section explore conclusion and give direction for future work.

2   Major Challenges

In this section, we have explored the following major issues has generated due to dynamic nature of background.

- *Dynamic Background:* The dynamic nature can cause vacillate the background that which represents a periodic or irregular and able to generate more complex background. The dynamic background in video scenes can be generated due to the following issues: (i) moving tree leaves, branches, or flag, (ii) flowing river water, sea, canal *etc.*, (iii) spouting water or fountain water, rain in the background.
- *Illumination Variation:* The illumination has a significant impact on the appearance as light changes on the surface. The pixel brightness varies in an image sequence depends on the objects' surface reflectance and illumination due to some external issues [13, 16, 17, 27]. The illumination variation can be categorized in two ways as discussed below [4, 14, 15, 27, 29].

  i. *Gradual illumination Variation*: Due to the cloud covering sun light, mist, dust *etc.*
  ii. *Sudden illumination Variation*: Due to sudden change in intensity due to switch off or switch on of light source. It strongly effect the appearance.

- *Environmental Effect:* In practical situations [4, 27, 29], due to various kind of environmental issues such as sunny-day, foggy-day, mist, snow-fall, and dust-particles *etc.* the pixel intensity may vary from one frame to another. During winter season, moving fog may introduce motion in background.
- *Camouflage:* In some video sequences, the object color may be poorly differ from background or almost similar [17–19, 27, 29]. In such case, it is very difficult to distinguish the foreground and background pixel [31–33]. Such sequences are available with wallflower dataset [17].
- *Bootstrapping:* In many video sequences, the background frames are not available such as bootstrap, osu-padestrian, *etc.* [15–19, 27, 29]. Such sequences are available with wallflower, change detection, and I2R datasets [17–19].
- *Foreground Aperture:* In video sequence, if moved foreground object has the uniform color region then any change inside such region may not be completely detected [15–17, 27, 29]. This kind of video sequence is available with wallflower dataset [17].
- *Noise in Video Fame:* Generally video signals are superimposed with the noise, here, due to such signals different types of noise has been generated such as sensor noise, camera hardware noise, or compression artefacts *etc.* [12, 13, 17–20, 27].
- *Shadow:* In video surveillance system, shadows cast by moving foreground object also moved with the object [27, 34–37]. The overlapping shadows of object's region needs to be separation and classification. This kind of datasets have been available in [18].
- *Camera Jitter:* In some situations, due to wind the camera can be sway back and forth. So, this can create nominal motion in video sequence [12, 18, 27]. The foreground mask shows many false alarms due to such motion in the absence of a robust background maintenance mechanism.
- *Automatic Adjustment of Camera:* Now a days, modern cameras have automatic white balance, automatic focus, automatic gain control, and auto brightness control [12, 13, 18, 19, 27]. Such kind of auto adjustment may modify or change the dynamic of the color levels in different video frames.
- *Moved background Object:* In some situations, background object also moved but in practice, such object should not able to become part of foreground [18].
- *Beginning of Moving Object:* When any object initially part of background and then moves in the background. In case of detection of such kind of object revealed as part of background and [18, 30] known as "ghost".
- *Inserted background Object:* During object detection process, if a new background object has inserted or entered. Such kind of object can be considered as part of background only if these are different from bootstrapping [4].
- *Sleeping Foreground Object:* A moving foreground object may become motionless [12, 13, 25, 27]. Such objects cannot be distinguished from the object of background and finally incorporated in the background.

Apart from above challenges, some other challenges may arise during data transmission or data capturing. These critical challenges are briefly summarized here.

- Failure of hardware device.
- Technical problem due to internet problems such as allocation of incorrect IP address, or incorrect data transmission *etc.*
- Space problem on server or cloud.
- Failure of connection from client machine to cloud server or IoT device to cloud server *etc.*

In this paper, we have considered those datasets which consist of dynamic background, illumination variation, camouflage, bootstrapping, and foreground aperture in colored video sequences [17–23]. Some sequences are also available in literature and collection of computer vision related datasets. Apart from these, this work also focused on thermal video sequences because the thermal imaging has the ability to penetrate gradual illumination variation, dynamic nature (slow movement or minor change) in the background scene.

3 Application Areas

The detection and segmentation of moving object from video sequence is the fundamental step of visual surveillance system in computer vision. It is also very active research area that is useful for real-time applications which are explored as shown in Fig. 1.

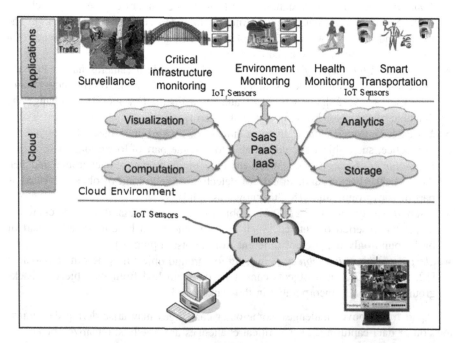

Fig. 1. Basic architecture of video surveillance in cloud environment

- IoTC in Intelligent Video Surveillance: The visual surveillance is the main application of computer vision. The main goal of IoT and cloud based visual surveillance is to detect and track the moving object from video using security cameras (CCTV, IP, etc.). It also governed in the transportation, robotics, manufacturing, GIS system, and police and law-enforcement system *etc*. It strengthens the security of concerned areas such as indoor-outdoor, defence, navy, army, maritime, offices, shopping malls, open market, shops, fields, road, garden, railway platforms, houses, restricted zones, river, sea, behaviour or activity analysis, games, *etc*. [12, 13, 19, 27, 29]. The visual surveillance is more specific and interesting for shopping malls, stores, indoor-outdoor, and offices surveillance [19, 22]. It can also be useful for shoplifting applications to study the consumer behaviour and some of the surveillance related applications are show in Fig. 2.

Fig. 2. Various applications of IoTC based Video Surveillance System

The IoTC based surveillance system can also be installed to observe the sea, traffic or other meterological hazard warning system in order to manage the traffic within a port or waterway.

- IoTC in Intelligent Visual Surveillance of Animals and Insects: The IoT and cloud based visual surveillance system can also detect and observe the activities of animal in protected areas such as zoo, river, sea, shore, coastal area, ocean, forest, etc. In these areas, the object of interest are animals such as birds, fish, hinds or honeybees.
- IoTC in Healthcare Surveillance: Now a days, the healthcare organization can reduce the cost of patient observation IoT devices. The healthcare facilities required to observe patients at risk for falls, in harmful situations, and specially the patients who are agitated or confused. It is also able to provide better facility using IoT and cloud and supports BigData. Various services can be combines with video, advanced analytics and IoT sensor integration with cloud.

- IoTC in Human Computer Interaction: Now a days several real-time IoT and cloud based based applications of computer vision needs interaction between human and computer through a video that is acquired by static camera. These are helpful in games (i.e. Microsoft's Kinect) or Ludo-applications (i.e. Aqu@theque).
- IoTC in Biometric Identification and Recognition: In recent years, the development of content-based video data management is acting as a spur to the development of content-based video data management tasks such as object motion prediction, detection of suspicious activities, moving object recognition, behaviour classification and recognition [4, 12, 13, 25, 27, 29]. In far-field surveillance, the IoTC is more appropriate.
- IoTC in Optical Motion Capture: The aim of optical motion is to compute a full and precise capturing of optical flow of a object with the help of camera [25]. Generally, the silhouette is extracted in each view using background subtraction technique and finally visual hull is obtained in 3-dimension.
- IoTC in Video Indexing and Retrieval: In a surveillance system, the videos data coming from surveillance cameras will be processed and interpreted by the video analysis module, sometime may be stored on cloud or accessed through cloud from IoT devices.
- IoTC in Content based Video Coding: The video content can be generated by segmenting the video into video objects and tracked. Then transverse across all video sequences. Here, the registered background and objects are encoded separately. Thus, the content based video coding utilized for object detection in static or dynamic environment.

4 Resources and Datasets

Several datasets are publicly available for moving object detection from video sequences. These datasets also provides realistic frames with accurate ground-truth. This paper simply, explored the existing datasets which are captured using static cameras and data has not used IoT or cloud. But in real-time examples and its need for society IoTC is used for video surveillance. These applications can be implemented in MATLAB or OpenCV environment. Some researchers are now a days using Python. Various frame sequences with challenging issues are discussed in Table 1.

Each sequence shows a different kind of problem likely to encounter as dynamic background, illumination variation, camouflage, foreground aperture, light switch on or off and bootstrapping. This dataset consists of one ground truth frame per video sequence.

Table 1. Description of publicly available datasets

Data set	Color format	Challenging issues
Microsoft's Wallflower dataset [17]	Color	Dynamic background, illumination variation, camouflage, foreground aperture, light switch on or off, bootstrapping. (https://www.microsoft.com/en-us/research/project/test-images-for-wallflower-paper/#)
Change detection dataset [18]	Color; Thermal	Camera Jitter, dynamic background, intermittent object motion, shadow. (http://changedetection.net/)
I2R dataset [19]	Color	Dynamic background or illumination variation. (http://perception.i2r.a-star.edu.sg/bk_model/bk_index.html)
CSIR-CSIO dataset [20]	Gray: Thermal	Background motion, illumination variation. (http://www.vcipl.okstate.edu/otcbvs/bench/)
OTCBVS dataset [21]	Gray: Thermal	Moving person with moving background in thermal imaging. (http://www.vcipl.okstate.edu/otcbvs/bench/)
Zoo dataset [22]	Gray: Thermal	Motion of background. (http://www.cvc.uab.es/~ivanhc/ObjDect/huertaDect.html)
PETS dataset [23]	Color	Background motion, illumination variation. (http://ftp.pets.rdg.ac.uk/pub/)
Background Models Challenge (BMC-2012) dataset [24]	Color: Gray	Dynamic background, illumination variation, bootstrapping, camouflage, foreground aperture. (http://clickdamage.com/sourcecode/cv_datasets.php)
SABS dataset [25]	Color	Illumination Changes, Camouflage, Dynamic Background, Boot Strapping. Shadows, Video Noise. (http://www.vis.unistuttgart.de/en/research/information-visualisation-and-visual-analytics/visual-analytics-of-video-data/sabs.html)
SBMI 2015 dataset [26]	Color	Illumination Variation, Dynamic Background. http://sbmi2015.na.icar.cnr.it/
SBMnet 2016 dataset [27]	Color	Intermittent Motion, Jitter, Clutter, Illumination Changes, Background Motion, Very Long and Very Short. http://scenebackgroundmodeling.net/
UCSD dataset [28]	Color	Motion saliency, Contrast, Motion in Background Scene. http://www.svcl.ucsd.edu/projects/background_subtraction/ucsdbgsub_dataset.htm

Apart from above lots of contents and resources are available at [29, 30]

5 Benefits of Video Surveillance System

The IoTC based visual surveillance system is designed for surveillance and security personnel. These systems support the monitoring, recording, transmission, management, law-enforcement, associated legal and constitutional implications whether the surveillance technology. It also provide a flexible, standards solutions through a broad range of surveillance devices. The key benefits of visual surveillance system is presented in Table 2.

Table 2. Benefits of IoTC based visual surveillance system

Benefit	Description
Continuous real-time monitoring	Allows authorized person to monitor and visualize the critical areas, restricted or suspicious zones continuously along with activity of a person
Remote video monitoring	Monitoring people of remote areas for medical facilities using IoTC, Visualizing geographical region. The hospitality and medical facility can be achieved using IP based video surveillance in IoTC environment
Increase security and safety	To watch suspicious situations/activities, unauthorized visitor/vehicle and track those using IoTC surveillance systems in given premises or restricted areas. It may be helpful to prevent crimes and break-ins
Improve productivity	Such system could improve communication between buildings, departments, and allowing for the heightened productivity. It also improves the productivity of manufacturing, automobile, even in small scale industries to monitor the activities of employees
Prevent dishonest claims	To disprove the assertion of false reports such as loan for property, criminal offences, misbehave
Resolve disputes	The surveillance system can resolve disputes by providing clear visual proof
Visual evidence for investigations	To collect and utilize the invaluable visual evidence for investigations of criminal activity. Such video/footage acts as a secondary proof for investigation
Digital storage	IoT devices can also be used and enable us to store the recorded video on cloud, network servers, or NVRs
Cost	The cloud environment provides plenty of resources, the cost of processing/service is a major key in cloud-based video surveillance system

6 Risks of Visual Surveillance System

In real-time system, various kind of risk factors can be seen in the system due to following issues.

- Weather: Monitoring cameras or sensor may be damaged due to heat, wind, snow, rain etc.
- Accidents: Installed cameras can capture and analyze traffic and each incident on the road.
- Privacy: The surveillance cameras may detect and track privacy of any patient in hospital.
- Tampering: If camera is tampered or damaged then the video signal may be degraded or lost.

7   Working Steps of Suggested Framework

In this section, we are proposing video surveillance in very few and basic steps. These working step of IoT based cloud video surveillance system can be described as given below.

- Install IoT devices such as sensors, camera etc.
- Assign an IP address to each device.
- Connect with the cloud using internet of Wi-Fi technology.
- Connect end user device such as laptop or computer with the cloud.
- After installing and setup of above mentioned system perform the processing.
- Transmit the data to the cloud.
- Access the data from cloud to end user device through internet.
- Now execute the required program for performing surveillance.
- Store the processed data in hard drives or cloud environment.
- Collect the required processed data.

8   Conclusion and Future Directions

This paper work has explored the major challenges of video surveillance system and its applications. IT also focuses on benefits and risk factors involved with the IoTC based video surveillance system. The video surveillance system with IoT in cloud environment can be utilized for capturing data through IoT devices which can be stored on cloud. The suggested framework explored about the processing of this data and again store the processed data on cloud environment or hard drives for future use. Such system is highly recommended for surveillance of border, sea traffic, or various indoor-outdoor activities as mentioned in applications.

In future work, we will try to use some hardware such as camera, Raspberry-Pi, *etc.* to capture some information from video. By capturing we will apply cloud to store of retrieve data from cloud for processing. We will perform some tasks from IoT & cloud environment.

References

1. Akula, A., Khanna, N., Ghosh, R., Kumar, S., Das, A., Sardana, H.K.: Adaptive contour based statistical background subtraction method for moving target detection in infrared video sequences. J. Infrared Phys. Technol. **63**, 103–109 (2013). Elsevier
2. Shah, M., Deng, J., Woodford, B.: Video background modeling: recent approaches, issues and our solutions. Mach. Vis. Appl. **25**(5), 1105–1119 (2014). Springer
3. Popovic, G., Arsic, N., Jaksic, B., Gara, B., Petrovic, M.: Overview, characteristics and advantages of IP camera video surveillance systems compared to systems with other kinds of camera. Int. J. Eng. Sci. Innovative Technol. **2**(5), 356–362 (2013)
4. Sharma, S., Chang, V., Tim, U.S., Wong, J., Gadia, S.: Cloud based emerging services systems. Int. J. Inf. Manage. 1–12 (2016). Elsevier

5. Sharma, S.: Expanded cloud plumes hiding big data ecosystem. Future Gener. Comput. Syst. **59**, 63–92 (2016)
6. Song, B., Hassan, M.M., Tian, Y., Hossain, M.S., Alamri, A.: Remote display solution for video surveillance in multimedia cloud. Multimedia Tools Appl. **5**, 13375–13396 (2015). Springer
7. Gubbi, J., Buyya, R., Marusic, S., Palaniswami, M.: Internet of Things (IoT): a vision, architectural elements, and future directions. Future Gener. Comput. Syst. **29**(7), 1645–1660 (2013). Elsevier
8. Buyya, R., Yeo, C.S., Venugopal, S., Broberg, J., Brandic, I.: Cloud computing and emerging IT platforms: vision, hype, and reality for delivering computing as the 5th utility. Future Gener. Comput. Syst. **25**(6), 599–616 (2009). Elsevier
9. Sharma, S., Tim, U.S., Gadia, S., Wong, J.: Growing Cloud Density and as-a-Service Modality and OTH-Cloud Classification in IOT Era (2015, unpublished)
10. Dong, X., Huang, X., Zheng, Y., Bai, S., Xu, W.: A novel infrared small moving target detection method based on tracking interest points under complicated background. J. Infrared Phys. Technol. **65**, 36–42 (2014). Elsevier
11. Bao, X., Zinger, S., Wijnhoven, R., de Peter, H.N.: Ship detection in port surveillance based on context and motion saliency analysis. In: Proceeding SPIE, Video Surveillance and Transportation Imaging Applications, vol. 8663, pp. 1–8 (2013)
12. Cristani, M., Farenzena, M., Bloisi, D., Murino, V.: Background subtraction for automated multisensor surveillance: a comprehensive review. Eurasip J. Adv. Sign. Process **43** 1–24 (2010). Springer
13. Gao, G., Wang, X., Lai, T.: Detection of moving ships based on a combination of magnitude and phase in along-track interferometric SAR-Part I: SIMP metric and its performance. IEEE Trans. Geo Sci. Remote Sens. **53**(7), 3565–3581 (2015)
14. Stauffer, C., Grimson, W.E.L.: Adaptive background mixture models for real-time tracking. In: IEEE Computer Society Conference on Computer Vision and Pattern Recognition, vol. 2, pp. 246–252. IEEE Computer Society, Fort Collins (1999)
15. Haque, M., Murshed, M., Paul, M.: On stable dynamic background generation technique using gaussian mixture models for robust object detection. In: 5th International Conference on Advanced Video and Signal Based Surveillance, pp. 41–48. IEEE, New Maxico (2008)
16. Jung, C.R.: Efficient background subtraction and shadow removal for monochromatic video sequences. IEEE Trans. Multimedia **11**(3), 571–577 (2009)
17. Toyama, K., Krumm, J., Brumitt, B., Meyers, B.: Wallflower: principles and practice of background maintenance. In: 7th International Conference on Computer Vision, pp. 255–261. IEEE Computer Society Press, Greece (1999)
18. Goyette, N., Jodoin, P.M., Porikli, F., Ishwar, P.: Change detection—a new change detection benchmark database. In: Proceedings of IEEE Workshop on Change Detection at CVPR USA, pp. 1–8 (2012)
19. I2R Dataset. http://perception.i2r.a-star.edu.sg/bk_model/bk_index.html
20. CSIR-CSIO Moving Object Thermal Infrared Imagery Dataset (MOTI-ID). CSIR Dataset 09. http://www.vcipl.okstate.edu/otcbvs/bench/
21. OTCBVS Benchmark Dataset: OSU-Pedestrian. http://www.vcipl.okstate.edu/otcbvs/bench/
22. Huerta, I., Pedersoli, M., Gonzalez, J., Sanfeliu, A.: Combining where and what in change detection for unsupervised foreground learning in Surveillance. Pattern Recogn. **48**(3), 709–719 (2015). Elsevier
23. PETS Dataset. http://ftp.pets.rdg.ac.uk/pub/
24. BMC-2012 Dataset. http://clickdamage.com/sourcecode/cv_datasets.php
25. SABS Dataset. http://www.vis.uni-stuttgart.de/en/research/information-visualisation-and-visual-analytics/visual-analytics-of-video-data/sabs.html

26. SBMI Dataset. http://sbmi2015.na.icar.cnr.it/
27. SBMnet Dataset. http://scenebackgroundmodeling.net/
28. UCSD-Dataset.   http://www.svcl.ucsd.edu/projects/background_subtraction/ucsdbgsub_dataset.htm
29. Computer Vision Datasets. http://clickdamage.com/sourcecode/cv_datasets.php
30. Bouwmans, T., Porikli, F., Hörferlin, B., Vacavant, A.: Background Modeling and Foreground Detection for Video Surveillance. Publisher CRC Press, Taylor and Francis Group, Cogent (2014)
31. Zivkovic, Z., Heijden, V.D.F.: Efficient adaptive density estimation per image pixel for the task of background subtraction. Pattern Recogn. Lett. **27**(7), 777–780 (2006). Elsevier
32. Hati, K.K., Sa, P.K., Majhi, B.: Intensity range based background subtraction for effective object detection. IEEE Sig. Process. Lett. **20**(8), 759–762 (2013)
33. Lee, S., Lee, C.: Low complexity background subtraction based on spatial similarity. Eurasip J. Image Video Process. **30**, 2–16 (2014). Springer
34. Aggarwal, J.K., Cai, Q.: Human motion analysis: a review. Comput. Vis. Image Underst. **73** (3), 428–440 (1999). Elsevier
35. Prati, A., Mikic, I., Trivedi, M., Cucchiara, R.: Detecting moving shadows: algorithms and evaluation. IEEE Trans. Pattern Anal. Mach. Intell. **25**(4), 918–923 (2003)
36. Al-Najdawi, N., Bez, H., Singhai, J., Edirisinghe E.: A survey of cast shadow detection algorithms. Pattern Recogn. Lett. **33**(6), 752–764 (2012). Elsevier
37. Sanin, A., Sanderson, C., Lovell, B.: Shadow detection: a survey and comparative evaluation of recent methods. Pattern Recogn. **45**(4), 1684–1689 (2011). Elsevier

Dynamic Orchestration Model for Complex Business Processes: An Application to e-SCMS

Reena Gupta$^{(\boxtimes)}$, Raj Kamal, and Ugrasen Suman

School of Computer Science and Information Technology,
Devi Ahilya University, Indore, India
gupta.reena865@gmail.com, dr_rajkamal@hotmail.com,
ugrasen123@yahoo.com

Abstract. Design and development of an efficient and trustworthy e-business application using orchestration has number of issues. Some of them considered here are reducing complexity, higher flexibility and improving efficiency, quality attributes, ensuring trust, and processing over large datasets. The present paper considers the application of dynamic orchestration in e- Supply Chain Management System (SCMS), which is based on hybrid approach. An orchestration enabled e-SCMS process model is also proposed. The paper considers (a) layered-system architecture and (b) Quality of Service (QoS) attributes. The attribute enables an optimal web service selection scheme and takes into account the trust parameter of the service providers. The scheme also reduces the complexity. The results show reduced complexity, improved efficiency, and higher flexibility. An evaluation when considering the different criteria shows that the presented orchestration architecture offers an improved solution than existing approaches for designing a complex e-SCMS business process.

Keywords: Service-oriented architecture · Web services orchestration · QoS enabled · Trustworthy · Business process · e-SCMS

1 Introduction

Business processes are the result of interoperable atomic services. Distributed system is a way to achieve interoperability of services over a local network [1]. As the business grows and becomes electronic, the interoperability is required for collaboration among more and more services over the web. Service Oriented Architecture (SOA) is an architectural way to create applications which are made up of interoperable services [2]. A SOA enables design and development of e-business processes using IT enabled services [3]. This concept becomes real with the help of web services.

Web services avail the interoperability over the web on the basis of the web protocols such as XML, WSDL, SOAP, and UDDI [2]. A single component service can have a bound on number of functionalities. A complex business process creation requires various functionalities to perform collectively. Component services needs to be composed to create a complex process [4]. Web Services Orchestration (WSO) is the most popular industrial trend used for the composition. Orchestration is a way of

© Springer Nature Singapore Pte Ltd. 2017
M. Singh et al. (Eds.): ICACDS 2016, CCIS 721, pp. 482–494, 2017.
DOI: 10.1007/978-981-10-5427-3_50

coordinating and controlling the execution of the web services. An orchestrator is responsible for deciding the execution sequence of the web services. Web services can communicate with each other via an orchestrator [5].

A widely used orchestration language is Business Process Execution Language (BPEL). It is widely used industrial standard that makes such communication possible. It deals with Web Service Description Language (WSDL) for the formatting purpose. A feature of BPEL is support for elementary operations such as receive, terminate, invoke, and constructors such as empty, switch, while, scope, pick, and flow [6]. There are two ways available for the composition: static and dynamic. Static composition does not consider the run-time user requirements. Dynamic composition handles runtime requirements [4]. Therefore, the composition needs to be dynamically managed [7]. Quality of Service (QoS) attributes facilitates dynamically adaptable composition [8].

An existing literature presented the solutions for the dynamically orchestrated business process and business integration [9–18]. Mittal et al. [9] designed an orchestration based engine for supply chain management. Eclipse BPEL designer was used for the designing. Meli et al. [10] proposed an approach for dynamic re-orchestration of patient workflow. The focus was to reduce hospital waiting time. Singh and Shrinivasan [11] proposed an Extended Service Oriented Architecture model for Supply Chain Management (ESOASCM) based on supply chain scenario. It included Work Flow Management System (WFMS), Petri Nets, Orchestration Engine (OE), and SOA. It helped in reduction of time and cost of material manufacturing.

Rouhi and Mahdavi [12] reduced network traffic by introducing semi-central orchestration model. It found more scalable as compared to central orchestrator but low scalable than distributed orchestrator. Lins et al. [13] proposed a SOA based solution BPM-SOA to automate the business process. Virtual travel agency scenario was used to evaluate the solution BPM-SOA. BPMN and WS-BPEL were the standard used to achieve the solution. Esfahani et al. [14] introduced a decentralized orchestration of a business process with runtime-adaptability. It tried to uncover the issue of scalability which is available in the centralized orchestration. It considered runtime circumstance such as available bandwidth. It demonstrated decentralization of a loan approval process.

Cheng and Law [15] developed a prototype based SC Collaborator system for collaboration and integration of web services. Model driven service orchestration was used to compose web services of SC Collaborator. It demonstrated the use of SC Collaborator with the help of construction supply chain scenario. Cheng et al. [16] presented a prototype system SC collaborator of portal based orchestrated framework for supply chain. A case study was given for bus manufacturing scenario. Tewolde-berhan and Janseen [17] reviewed the literature and found that the reliable and efficient orchestration and experimentation are the key requirements of web services orchestration in supply chains. Experiment is conducted for both the sequential and parallel invocation. It simulated web service orchestration for supply chain using java based simulation building blocks. These building blocks were based on the BPEL4WS. Wang and Lee [18] proposed an integrated BPM-SOA layered framework. It used loan approval process for the experiment. BPEL was the implementation language for orchestration.

Some of the major issues identified in most of them are lack of experiment on larger business process, quality attributes, trustworthy environment and the needs of higher flexibility, efficiency, and reduced complexity. Therefore, a solution is needed to cover such identified issues. The proposed approach covers the above discussed problems. Our solution is considering different quality attributes such as response time, throughput, availability, reliability, and execution cost. Our approach is experimented for a complex business process of electronic Supply Chain Management System (e-SCMS). Proposed solution is more flexible and efficient as it is reducing the time complexity exponentially. It also works in a trustworthy environment.

The paper is organized as follows. Section 2 describes the concept of hybrid orchestration model and hybrid approach. Section 3 introduces an application of e-SCMS. Its subsection represents the basic overview of e-SCMS, overall system architecture for e-SCMS, demonstrates orchestration supported process model of e-SCMS, sequence diagram, and user interface design. Section 4 describes the implementation and experimentation method. Section 5 discusses the derived conclusion.

2 Hybrid Approach

Present paper considers a QoS attribute based optimal web service selection scheme. This scheme ensures trust and reduces complexity [19]. Further, an orchestration mechanism has been adopted to compose web services. Figure 1 shows the use of hybrid orchestration model in composition. A hybrid orchestration model is the combination of basic orchestration models such as: sequence, parallel, loop, and conditional. Consider that there are 13 web services involved in the Fig. 1. WS_1, WS_2, WS_6, WS_7, WS_8, WS_{12}, and WS_{13} perform sequential orchestration. WS_3, WS_4, and WS_5 executes in parallel. The WS_7 performs repeated execution for specified condition K. Conditional model will allow the execution of only one service among WS_9, WS_{10}, or WS_{11} which satisfies the condition C_1, C_2, or C_3 respectively.

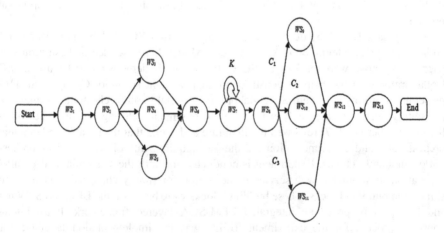

Fig. 1. Hybrid orchestration model

The above described hybrid orchestration model is based on hybrid approach which uses the concept of QoS-aware optimization. It is the combination of local optimization and global optimization based approaches. The Hybrid approach uses user's runtime functional preferences to achieve dynamic results. It uses five QoS attributes such as response time, throughput, availability, reliability, and execution cost for optimization. The approach defines constraints for each QoS attribute at both local and global level. The constraint defines that the response time and execution cost should be minimized and throughput, availability, and reliability should be maximized.

Local optimization is responsible for the selection of an optimal service for every task at the component level. It also ensures the composition in a trusted environment and reduces complexity exponentially. The idea of optimization is to calculate QoS attributes for each component service and to select one optimum component service for each task which also satisfies the QoS constraints. Locally optimize component services can easily optimize composite service at the global level. Global optimization calculates the aggregated QoS at the composition level only for the optimal services selected at the component level. This collective concept maximizes the overall utility of the composition and produces efficient results. It reduces the time complexity of composition exponentially as it reduces the complexity at the component level. The reduced time complexity of hybrid model is $O(m * t * logs + t * logs * k)$.

A business process is a collaboration of multiple atomic web services. The process of collaboration can be performed with the help of two models namely, orchestration or choreography [20]. The present paper considers the use of widely used industrial standard i.e., orchestration [5]. A complex business process design can use hybrid orchestration model. A complex process of e-SCMS is the combination of various basic business functionalities such as searching, order, payment, and shipment. Any business functionality can have multiple web services. Web services execution of e-SCMS can be a combination of sequence, parallel, conditional, and loop models. Hence, hybrid orchestration model is needed to collaborate various basic orchestration models. The present paper shows orchestration enabled dynamic solution for the presented scenario of e-SCMS based on the hybrid orchestration model. It ensures that proposed solution is QoS enabled, efficient, flexible, less time complex, with large dataset, and trustworthy.

3   An Application to e-SCMS

The present solution considers an Application to e-SCMS and the design of orchestration enabled dynamic business process. Following subsections describes the adopted methodology to achieve the designing goals and covers the basic introduction of the legacy system, system architecture, orchestration based process model of the system, sequence diagram, and user interface.

3.1   An Overview of e-SCMS

Today's digital world and competitive edge needs the business over the web. Composition of atomic web services facilitates e-business. E-business leads to a powerful impact on supply chain management [21]. A supply chain process is made up of various business functionalities. Dynamic selection of an appropriate service to complete a business process is becoming a challenging issue [22]. An effective integration of different business functions is the key requirement of a supply chain process [23]. The e-SCMS provides better integration approach and gains improved performance than the traditional supply chain management.

Table 1 gives the formal requirement specifications in designing e-SCMS. Table 1 includes aim of designing the system, basic technologies that are used to design the system, the key functionalities that the system will provide, and benefits of the system.

Table 1. System specifications summary

Key specifications	Description
Aim	Ensure trust, reduced complexity, QoS enabled solution, more flexibility, improved efficiency, testing over large dataset
Technical specification	JSP, Web services, XML, WSDL, SOAP, UDDI, JAVA, Axis2, MySQL, Eclipse, orchestration
Functional specification	Authentication, search, trust, purchasing, payment, shipment
Benefits	Enhancing user friendliness, enhancing business, saving time, customer satisfaction

3.2   System Architecture

Figure 2 shows architecture of e-SCMS. It is a four layered architecture. The layers are: communication layer, operational layer, business process layer, and presentation layer. Every layer performs a specific function to create a business process.

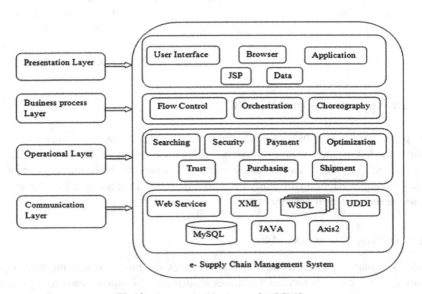

Fig. 2. System architecture of e-SCMS

Communication layer represents various tools and technologies used in e-SCMS. The e-SCMS uses JAVA as a logic development platform. Axis2 server is used to create web services. These services are described in WSDL, published and deployed in UDDI, and accessible through SOAP protocols [24]. XML is the general format for all other web service standards [2]. MySQL database server is used to store and retrieve user and product information of the system. *Operational layer* is responsible for various functions involved in the system. Our e-SCMS business process is the integration of following services: security service, trust service, searching service, optimization service, purchasing service, payment service, and shipment service. *Business process layer* is responsible to integrate individual functionalities discussed in the operational layer. There are two ways to integrate web services: orchestration and choreography. Orchestration composes the services on the basis of a controller service whereas choreography based on multiparty collaboration [20]. The presented approach is based on the orchestration. The *presentation layer* of e-SCMS covers user interface designing in JSP.

3.3   Orchestration Enabled Process Model for e-SCMS

As described above, the orchestration facilitates the web service integration solution. Figure 3 shows orchestration process in e-SCMS. Process begins with the UDDI registry of functionally identical services of different service providers or suppliers. Selection of a desired supplier is an important aspect. Mubeen and Subramanya [25] introduced the selection method of the best supplier based on the parameters such as throughput and delivery time. The proposed approach uses reliability to select trustworthy suppliers.

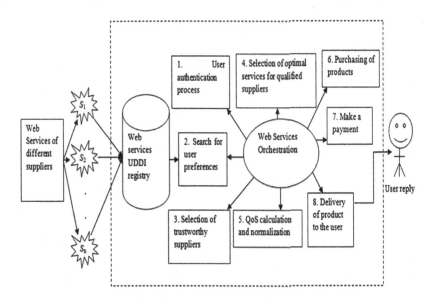

Fig. 3. A process model of e-SCMS

A user who wishes to enter into the system can register via filling the registration detail. Registered user can login into the system via entering its login detail. Then authenticated user proceeds to search its preferences. The search process will apply only on the trustworthy service provider's services.

QoS attributes calculation and normalization is the key components responsible for optimum web service selection among qualified supplier's services. The QoS attributes are response time, throughput, availability, reliability, and execution cost. Furthermore, user will purchase its searched product for the required quantity. User will make the payment for the total generated cost. Finally, purchased product will be delivered to the user. Orchestration is the central coordinator that will combine all these functionalities. Orchestrator will monitor the execution sequence throughout the service integration process.

3.4   Sequence Diagram

Figure 4 shows e-SCMS sequence diagram model. The diagram represents a sequence of activities involved in the system. A detailed description of various activities is as follows:

1. Any new user wants to access the system will interact with the user registration interface. The interface will ask for the registration detail. A user will get the message "Registered successfully" for a successful registration.
2. A registered user can logged in into the system by feeding its login information. A user acknowledged with a message "Login successfully" for a successful login.
3. An authenticated user initiates the search process by feeding its choice via user interface.
4. The search process proceeds only for the qualified trustworthy supplier's web services.

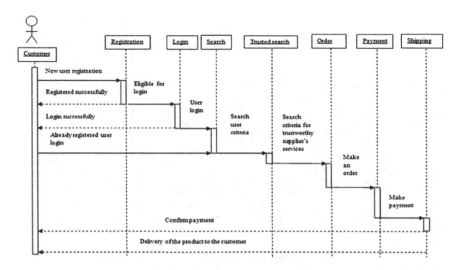

Fig. 4. Sequence diagram of e-SCMS

5. User placed an order for the resultant search.
6. Make a payment for the purchased items.
7. e-SCMS system will notify to the user for their payment confirmation and deliver purchased items.

3.5 User Interface Design

This subsection enhances the user interactivity of e-SCMS by introducing a prototype of the system. User interface designing comes under the presentation layer as discussed in the previous Sect. 3.2. User interface designing of e-SCMS is supported by JSP. Figure 5 illustrates the login interface for the users to login into the system. Figure 6 shows the user registration interface for the users who want to get registered into the system. Searching interface is depicted in the Fig. 7 from where user can feed its requirements.

Fig. 5. User login interface

Fig. 6. New user registration

Fig. 7. Searching interface

4 Implementation and Experimentation

4.1 Implementation Detail

An e-SCMS business process is designed and developed on the widely used advance JAVA development platform. It uses eclipse as an editing tool. Axis2 server has been used to create web services. The proposed approach is tested in a LAN over a large dataset of more than 100 web services. The web services are created for various tasks such as login, register, raw materials, searching, order, and payment. Windows 8.1 is used as simulation OS. An experimentation has performed on the 64 bit Intel (R) Core (TM) based i3-3217U Processor 1.80 GHz and 4.00 GB RAM with 500 GB Hard Disk.

4.2 Performance Measure

The performance of presented approach is measured by comparing with existing approaches [9, 11, 15–17] based on various performance criteria. The performance criteria are QoS enabled, ensuring trusted environment, complexity measure, testing over large dataset, more efficient, and flexible result. Table 2 illustrates the overall description of e-SCMS performance evaluation based on different criteria. It results that presented approach gains an improved performance as it is flexible, efficient, quality enabled, trustworthy, less time complex, and fully experimented.

Further, time complexity of our approach is measured in LAN environment. The time complexity of e-SCMS solution is $O(m * t * logs + t * logs * k)$ with the m number of QoS constraints, t number of tasks, s number of services associated with each task t, and k number of occurrences of trust rate. Here, $t * logs * k$ is the time complexity of optimum services selection at the component level [19] and $m * t * logs$ is the time complexity of optimum services composition. It shows that the time complexity of the system reduces exponentially. The time complexity O $(m * t * logs + t * logs * k)$ for e-SCMS is measured under the following criteria:

Table 2. Overall result of performance measure based on different criteria

Performance criteria	Mittal et al. [9]	Singh and Srinivasan [11]	Cheng and Law [15]	Cheng et al. [16]	Tewoldeberhan and Janseen [17]	Proposed solution for e-SCMS
QoS enabled	No	No	No	No	No	Yes, e-SCMS solution considers QoS attributes such as: Response time, throughput, availability, reliability, and execution cost
Ensuring trusted environment	No	No	No	No	Yes	Yes, e-SCMS calculates trustworthiness of its suppliers or service providers based on its reliability to ensure trust
Time complexity measure	No	No	No	No	No	Yes, The proposed solution reduces the time complexity exponentially i.e., O ($m * t * logs + t * logs * k$)
Testing over large dataset	No	No	Yes	Yes	Yes	Yes, Performance of e-SCMS is evaluated over 100 web services
More efficient, and flexible result	Efficient but less flexible	Efficient but less flexible	Flexible but less efficient	Flexible but less efficient	Efficient and flexible	Yes, System is more efficient and flexible as it selects optimum services dynamically based on user preferences

Variable Number of Tasks (*t*). Table 3 measures the time complexity of presented solution in terms of variable number of tasks (*t*), fixed number of web services (100), fixed number of occurrences of trust rate (10), and fixed number of QoS constraints (5). Figure 8 represents the graph related to the Table 3. The evaluation shows that the time complexity is reduced exponentially.

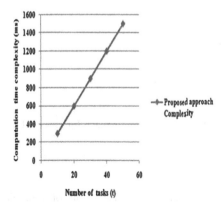

Fig. 8. Time complexity graph of proposed approach for specified number of tasks (*t*)

Table 3. Time complexity measure of proposed approach for variable number of tasks (*t*)

Time complexity of proposed approach	Web services (100), tasks (*t*), occurrences (10), QoS(5)				
	10	20	30	40	50
O(*m* * *t* * *logs* + *t* * *logs* * *k*)	300	600	900	1200	1500

Variable Number of Web Services (*s*). Table 4 measures the time complexity of presented solution in terms of variable number of web services (*s*), fixed number of tasks (10), fixed number of occurrences of trust rate (10), and fixed number of QoS constraints (5). Figure 9 illustrates the graph corresponding to the Table 4. The study shows that the there is an exponential reduction in the time complexity.

Table 4. Time complexity measure of proposed approach for variable number of web services (*s*)

Time complexity of proposed approach	Web services (*s*), tasks (10), occurrences (10), QoS(5)				
	20	40	60	80	100
O(*m* * *t* * *logs* + *t* * *logs* * *k*)	195.15	240.315	266.73	285.465	300

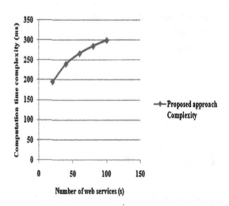

Fig. 9. Time complexity graph of proposed approach for specified number of web services (*s*)

5 Conclusion

The proposed approach brings an improved solution for dynamic orchestration enabled complex business process integration. The approach is based on the hybrid orchestration model, which uses the concept of local optimization and global optimization. The approach is applied to design a complex e-SCMS business process application. The contributions given to achieve this solution are defining of the problem domain, system architecture, orchestration enabled process model, sequence diagram, and user interface design of e-SCMS scenario. The approach enlightens a development and experimentation scenario.

An observation is performed based on criteria, such as reduced time complexity, improved efficiency, more flexibility, quality attribute, ensuring trusted environment, and fully experimented over large dataset. It results that the proposed solution is better than the existing approaches. An extension of the current work in different domain of e-business and reliability improvement can be an integral part of the future work.

References

1. Tanenbaum, A.S., Steen, M.V.: Distributed Systems: Principles and Paradigms. Prentice Hall, NJ (2006)
2. Josuttis, N.M.: SOA in Practice: The Art of Distributed System Design. O'Reilly Media, Sebastopol (2007)
3. Baun, C., Kunze, M., Nimis, J., Tai, S.: Cloud Computing: Web-Based Dynamic IT Services. Springer, Heidelberg (2011). doi:10.1007/978-3-642-20917-8
4. Rathore, M., Suman, U.: A quality of service broker based process model for dynamic web service composition. J. Comput. Sci. 7(8), 1267–1274 (2011)
5. Kamal, R., Agrawal, S.: A design framework of orchestrator for computing systems. In: International Conference on Computer Information Systems and Industrial Management Applications (CISIM), pp. 410–413. IEEE, Gwalior, India (2010)
6. Saab, C.B., Coulibaly, D., Haddad, S., Melliti, T., Moreaux, P., Rampacek, S.: An integrated framework for web services orchestration. Int. J. Web Serv. Res. 6(4), 1–29 (2009)
7. Immonen, A., Pakkala, D.: A survey of methods and approaches for reliable dynamic service compositions. SOCA 8, 129–158 (2014)
8. Lin, K.J., Zhang, J., Zhai, Y., Xu, B.: The design and implementation of service process reconfiguration with End-to-End QoS constraints in SOA. SOCA 4, 157–168 (2010)
9. Mittal, A., Sharma, K.K., Dalal, S.: Approach of BPEL in supply chain activities for managing bullwhip effect of SCM system. Int. J. Res. Asp. Eng. Manag. 1(2), 26–30 (2014)
10. Meli, C.L., Khalil, I., Tari, Z.: Load-sensitive dynamic workflow re-orchestration and optimisation for faster patient healthcare. Comput. Methods Programs Biomed. 113, 1–14 (2014)
11. Singh, S.K., Shrinivasan, S.: Extended service oriented architecture using work flow management system and petri nets (ESOASCM). Int. J. Comput. Appl. 77(7), 28–31 (2013)
12. Rouhi, S., Mahdavi, M.: Providing a semi-central model for web service composition. Int. J. Inf. Technol. Converg. Serv. 2(2), 1–9 (2012)
13. Lins, F., Damascenom, J., Souza, A., Silva, B., Aragão, D., Medeiros, R., Sousa, E., Rosa, N.: Towards automation of SOA-based business processes. Int. J. Comput. Sci. Eng. Appl. 2(2), 1–17 (2012)
14. Esfahani, F.S., Murad, M.A.A., Sulaiman, M.N., Udzir, N.I.: Run-time adaptable business process decentralization. In: The Third International Conference on Information, Process, and Knowledge Management, pp. 76–82 (2011)
15. Cheng, J.C.P., Law, K.H.: A portal-based web service framework for construction supply chain integration and collaboration. In: Proceedings of 2009 NSF Engineering Research and Innovation Conference, Honolulu, Hawaii (2009)

16. Cheng, J.C.P., Law, K.H., Jones, A., Sriram, R.: Service Oriented and Orchestrated Framework for Supply Chain Integration. In: Proceedings of the ASME 2009 International Design Engineering Technical Conferences & Computers and Information in Engineering Conference IDETC/CIE 2009, August 30-September 2, 2009, San Diego, California, USA (2009)

17. Tewoldeberhan, T., Janssen, M.: Simulation-based experimentation for designing reliable and efficient web service orchestrations in supply chains. Electron. Commer. Res. Appl. **7**, 82–92 (2008)

18. Wang, N., Lee, V.: An integrated BPM-SOA framework for agile enterprises. In: Nguyen, N.T., Kim, C.-G., Janiak, A. (eds.) ACIIDS 2011. LNCS, vol. 6591, pp. 557–566. Springer, Heidelberg (2011). doi:10.1007/978-3-642-20039-7_56

19. Gupta, R., Kamal, R., Suman, U.: A QoS-aware optimal selection scheme for web services with a trusted environment. CSIT **3**(1), 13–21 (2015)

20. Karande, A., Karande, M., Meshram, B.B.: Choreography and orchestration using business process execution language for SOA with web services. Int. J. Comput. Sci. Issues **8**(2), 224–232 (2011)

21. Lee, M.C., Han, M.W.: E-business model design and implementation in supply-chain integration. In: Proceedings of the 2009 International Symposium on Web Information Systems and Applications (WISA 2009), Nanchang, P. R. China, 22–24 May, pp. 001–004. Academy Publisher (2009)

22. Huang, X., Chen, X., Xu, J., Yang, J.: Dynamic supplying desired web service for e-business. In: Second International Symposium on Electronic Commerce and Security, ISECS 2009, pp. 369–373. IEEE (2009)

23. Akyuz, G.A., Rehan, M.: Requirements for forming an 'E-Supply Chain'. Int. J. Prod. Res. **47**(12), 3265–3287 (2009)

24. Grolinger, K., Capretz, M.A.M., Cunha, A., Tazi, S.: Integration of business process modeling and web services: a survey. SOCA **8**, 105–128 (2014)

25. Mubeen, S., Subramanya, K.N.: Selection of supplier in B2B e-commerce using work flow petri net. Int. J. Manag. Value Supply Chain **5**(3), 91–101 (2014)

Efficient Vehicle Detection and Classification for Traffic Surveillance System

Vijay Ukani[✉], Sanjay Garg, Chirag Patel, and Hetali Tank

Department of Computer Science and Engineering, Institute of Technology,
Nirma University, Ahmedabad, India
{vijay.ukani,sgarg,11FTPHDE05,13mcen35}@nirmauni.ac.in

Abstract. Video surveillance systems is a key component of any security system. Making an intelligent system that can detect and track multiple moving objects from video and also deals with dynamic backgrounds, illumination problem and environment conditions is a challenging task. The proposed system is designed for real-time vehicle detection and classification. The traffic is increasing day by day due to increase in number of vehicles. Vehicle detection, classification, and counting is a very important application by which highway monitoring, traffic planning, analysis of the traffic flow, etc. can be easily done. In this paper, vehicle detection is done by background subtraction and from each detected vehicles Scale-Invariant Feature Transform (SIFT) features is extracted. Vehicles are classified using the neural network and Support Vector Machine (SVM). SVM showed better generalization than Artificial Neural Networks.

Keywords: Video surveillance · Vehicle detection · Vehicle classification · Background subtraction · Neural network · SVM · SIFT

1 Introduction

Nowadays it is very common to deploy video surveillance camera at public places and highway for monitoring the events and objects. With the help of traffic surveillance cameras that are installed on highways, live monitoring of the traffic scenarios is possible. Manual monitoring of the traffic feeds may be error-prone and includes human dependency. There is an immediate need to automatize the tasks such as the detection of a dangerous situation, license plate recognition, information about traffic flow, recognition of vehicles that passes from the highways, finding over-speeding vehicles, information about accidents, traffic congestion etc. Vision-based traffic surveillance system helps to alert about these situations. Vehicle classification and their count can serve as an important ingredient in controlling traffic and designing traffic policies. With an assumption of a single static camera mounted on the highways, the proposed system is able to detect vehicles as they move through cameras view and classify each individual object in several categories.

This work was supported by GUJCOST under Grant No. MRP/2014-15/2217.

M. Singh et al. (Eds.): ICACDS 2016, CCIS 721, pp. 495–503, 2017.
DOI: 10.1007/978-981-10-5427-3_51

2 Related Work

2.1 Object Detection

Object Detection is a very important task for video surveillance system. It is the first step in automation of video surveillance system as it finds moving objects from the background. Objects in a video are defined by the moving objects that have information and maximum attention in the video sequences. Various approaches have been proposed for detecting objects from video streams. The methods of detection are divided into 2 class: Temporal differencing, Background subtraction.

In temporal differencing, video is captured using a static camera and moving objects are identified by the difference between two frames or difference between current frame and the reference frame. When any difference is found, the pixel is classified as a moving object pixel. In background subtraction, the background model is estimated by mathematical equations and probability distribution. This background is subtracted from the current frame and moving objects are segmented. The background model is also updated. Background subtraction methods are divided into 2 classes: Recursive and non-recursive methods [1, 2]. This method can be further classified as median method [3], min-max method, approximated median method, mixture of Gaussian, fuzzy color histograms [4], and codebook generation [5].

Several attempts were made to detect moving objects. Pineau et al. [6] discovered moving objects by demonstrating pixel gray level distribution with time using Gaussian mixture model and Markov regularization. The method performed in real time but the problem of illumination variation still persisted. Zheng et al. in [7] detected moving objects by frame difference algorithm and region combination. The algorithm is able to detect fast moving object efficiently but sometimes failed to detect objects with slow motion as they are classified as background. A background removal technique based on DCT was presented by Sagrebin et al. in [8] which was robust to illumination changes and had low computational complexity.

A new technique is introduced in [8–10], where the foreground is extracted by improved GMM and chromaticity-gradient background subtraction method. The algorithm eliminates the impact of illumination changes and shadows. The slow moving objects are also detected. The problem with this method is that it expects the background model to be initialized. Detection of multiple objects under multiple cameras in real time is demonstrated by Kumar et al. in [11]. Cameras are arranged in such a way that the entry and exit of the objects can be covered in the video. Algorithm uses frame difference for background subtraction and finds centroid features for object representation. The algorithm is not robust as it did not use any classifier. Detection of moving objects by improved background subtraction algorithm and feature-based approach was introduced in [12]. The problem of initiating the background model still persisted with this method.

The approaches discussed earlier takes time for computation, building and updating background model. These approaches do not work if the background is not initialized. In case of sudden changes in illumination, generated background model may not work. So it needs to be accurate and efficient for finding moving object.

2.2 Vehicle Detection and Classification

Detection and tracking are preliminary steps for classification of vehicles. A real-time system for measuring traffic parameters was described in [13]. Vehicles were tracked in traffic sequences using features that can handle occlusion. The system did not track entire vehicle but only used subfeatures of the vehicle so that occlusions could be handled. But the approach used was computationally expensive. An adaptive background subtraction method was used to separate vehicles from the background. The background was modeled in such a way that it can adapt to illumination and weather conditions.

A 3D model based vehicle classification was proposed in [14] which was based on the shape of the vehicle. Gaussian mixture model (GMM) for background removal and Haar wavelet for noise removal was proposed in [15]. The extracted features were used to classify the detected objects as vehicle and non-vehicle using support vector machine (SVM). Vehicles were detected using background subtraction method then it is classified as car and non-car in [16]. The system provided location and velocity information for detected vehicle. But it was not capable of classifying vehicles into further categories.

A general active learning framework for vehicle detection was described in [17]. The system worked for real time video and recorded video images. Using Adaboost classifier, the objects were classified into vehicles and non-vehicle. A vehicle detection technique using high-resolution satellite images was proposed in [18]. Due to being satellite image, vehicles were seen as spots, thus, making it difficult to segment it from the background. The approach did not work efficiently for high-density traffic. Vehicles were classified as cars and truck only. A comparitive summary of object detection techniques could be found in [19].

Open Issues: The approaches discussed above take more time for execution and sometimes it becomes tedious. Issues like illumination, occlusion and scale variance still remains and in many cases vehicles are not classified into a number of classes.

3 Proposed Approach

3.1 System Framework

Detection of vehicles can be implemented by different methods. Here the main problem is changing in light and traffic flow. In the proposed system, traffic video (recorded/live) is given as an input to the system and by converting it into frames, the background can be extracted and then detection of the vehicle is performed. The overall system framework is shown in Fig. 1.

The detected vehicles segmented from the video sequences. Classification is performed using neural network and support vector machine by its type (Car, Bike, Truck, Mini truck, Bus and three wheeler).

Occlusion is an important problem in vehicle detection even if camera resolution is high. Obtaining individual vehicles from blobs are difficult when they are occluded. Here, it is handled by using edge detection. Using the edges of detected vehicles it is separated individually. Another problem is vehicle scale changes when it enters and

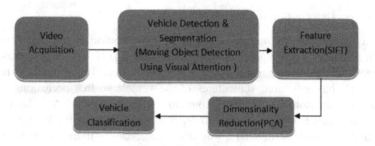

Fig. 1. System framework

leaves from camera frame. For obtaining accurate classification the scale change issue is handled by using the SIFT features that are invariant to scale.

3.2   Vehicle Detection and Segmentation

Vehicle detection is performed by using moving object detection approach. Visual attention means the portion of a scene which will attract attention of all eyes. In vehicle surveillance, the vehicles are a part of the scene which forms the area with visual attention.

The approach proposed in [21] was used for vehicle detection. Apply average filter on video sequence I(x, y, t), having size N × M for particular time t,

$$I_{avg} = I(x,y,t) \otimes A(N,M)$$

Where A is averaging filter, having mask size N × M, and $\otimes$ is defined as a convolution between two images. Employ Gaussian filter [22] on image

$$I_{Gaussian} = I(x,y,t) \otimes G(h,\sigma)$$

Where G is Gaussian low-pass filter, having mask size 11, and σ is 5. The mask size and σ is determined empirically. The saliency value at each pixel position (x, y) is given by

$$S(x,y) = d\left[I_{Gaussian}(x,y), I_{avg}(x,y)\right]$$

Where d is the distance between two pixels in the respective images. The distance used in the proposed approach is taken from [22]. The labeled objects are tracked in the current frame. If new objects found then it is given the new label and segmented. The same procedure is applied to the entire video sequence. From all the video sequence, 6097 vehicles are segmented and stored in terms of images with a different view like side view, front view, and rear view.

3.3   Feature Extraction

SIFT features are used because various issues like change in illumination, occlusion, and change in scale came across. SIFT is invariant to scaling and partially invariant to illumination and occlusion. Hence it is well suited for defined approach.

SIFT contains two parts: (1) SIFT detector and (2) SIFT descriptor. In the first step, key points are detected. With the original image, progressively 5 blurred images are obtained using Gaussian kernel. Then original image is resized into half. This step is repeated 4 times. This is called scale space. After that difference of Gaussian (DOG) over different octave is calculated using the formula given in [20]. The maxima and minima of the DOG image stack are determined by comparing a pixel to its 26 neighbors in the 3 × 3 region with current and adjacent scale. In the second step, descriptors are made. The orientation and magnitude is derived from equations given in Sect. 5 of [20]. The descriptor is made by sampling magnitude and orientations around the keypoint location. Finally, local image descriptor (size of 128 elements) is calculated for each image. The flowchart for feature extraction is elaborated in Fig. 2.

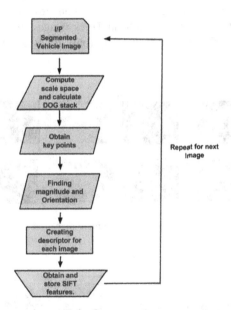

Fig. 2. Flow chart for feature extraction

3.4   Vehicle Classification

Vehicles are classified into 6 classes as bike, bus, car, mini truck/van, truck and 3 wheeler. Two approaches are used for classification: Neural network and SVM. For training the neural network gradient descent with momentum activation function with 1 and 2 hidden layer is used. Gradient descent with momentum allows the network to react when minima occur. It will slide through this minima with the help of momentum. This function works with two parameters which are learning rate, lr and momentum constant, mc. The value of lr and mc is in between 0 and 1. Learning rate is important for finding minimum error. Training with too small learning rate, progress is very slow and with too large progress is very fast. So it is large enough that converges to minimum solution. Momentum constant is helpful in speeding convergence and avoiding minima. By changing the momentum constant and learning rate performance of the classifier is evaluate.

4 Experimental Setup and Results

The experiments are performed on an Intel(R) Core(TM) i3-3227U CPU 1.90 GHz with 4 GB RAM and the algorithms are implemented in MATLAB 8.3 64 bit.

4.1 Vehicle Detection and Segmentation

Various types of vehicles are segmented from ongoing video and stored as an image. There are total 6097 vehicle images. The dataset contains 1109 Motor Bike images, 150 Bus images, 4009 Car images, 453 Mini Truck images, 16 Auto rickshaw images and 360 truck images. The results of this step (only for Bike and Bus) are shown in Figs. 3, 4 and 5.

Fig. 3. Results of vehicle detection

Bike   Bus

Fig. 4. Results of vehicle segmentation

Fig. 5. Results of vehicle classification

4.2 Classification of Vehicles

The vehicles were classified using neural networks for various values of learning rate and using SVM. The parameters have been used here are based on experiments. Various combinations of learning rate and momentum constant were tried and the best pair was selected for the experiments.

The recognition accuracy of the approach is summarized in following tables.

(1) Neural Network with 1 Hidden Layer

Learning rate = 0.01, Momentum Constant = 0.9

	Motor bike	Bus	Car	Mini truck/van	Auto rickshaw	Truck
Motor bike	58	–	4.5	9.5	28	–
Bus	–	60	7	13.5	0.5	19
Car	2	10	54	30	3	1
MiniTruck/van	–	12	28	57	2	1
Auto rickshaw	23	5	9	8	51	4
Truck	–	35	12	3	2	48

(2) Neural Network with 2 Hidden Layer

Learning rate = 0.01, Momentum Constant = 0.9

	Motor bike	Bus	Car	Mini truck/van	Auto rickshaw	Truck
Motor bike	63	–	4	8	23	2
Bus	–	68	5.3	11.7	0.8	14.2
Car	0.8	10.2	63	22	2.8	1.2
MiniTruck/van	0.2	13.4	22.6	63	0.5	0.3
Auto rickshaw	19.8	7.6	6.4	5.83	54	6.36
Truck	–	29.6	11.4	1.9	2.3	54.8

(3) Support Vector Machine (RBF kernel)

	Motor bike	Bus	Car	Mini truck/van	Auto rickshaw	Truck
Motor bike	91.84	–	5.8	–	1.46	0.9
Bus	–	90.89	0.9	3.4	–	4.81
Car	1.8	0.63	88.6	5.4	2.8	0.77
MiniTruck/van	0.3	1.13	7.7	84.54	6.33	–
Auto rickshaw	0.45	0.89	3.78	1.2	93.58	0.1
Truck	–	6.9	0.8	0.4	0.2	91.7

The results were recorded for other values of learning rate and number of hidden layer but for brevity, they are excluded here.

5 Conclusion

An efficient technique for preparation of the feature descriptor is proposed in the paper. PCA is used to reduce computational complexity as the data set used were of the traffic video sequences. The artificial neural network as well as support vector machine was tried for classifying the vehicles. ANN by varying the number of hidden layer and SVM by various kernels were implemented but the result of the radial basic network (SVM) is reported in the paper. Performance analysis of various techniques suggests that the support vector machine gives better generalization than ANN.

References

1. Cheung, S., Kamath, C.: Robust techniques for background subtraction in urban traffic video. In: Visual Communications and Image Processing, vol. 5308 (2004)
2. Parks, D., Fels, S.: Evaluation of background subtraction algorithms with post-processing. In: IEEE Fifth International Conference on Advanced Video and Signal Based Surveillance (2008)
3. Melli, R., Prati, A., Calderara, S., Cucchiara, R.: Reliable background suppression for complex scenes. In: 4th ACM International Workshop on Video Surveillance and Sensor Networks (2006)
4. Kim, W., Kim, C.: Background subtraction for dynamic texture scenes using fuzzy color histograms. IEEE Signal Process. Lett. 19(3), 127–130 (2012)
5. Bove, V., Butler, D., Sridharan, S.: Real-time adaptive background segmentation. In: International Conference on Acoustics, Speech, and Signal Processing, ICASSP, Hong Kong, China (2003)
6. Carminati, L., Pineau, J.B.: Gaussian mixture classification for moving object detection in video surveillance environment. In: IEEE International Conference on Image Processing, ICIP 2005, vol. 3, pp. 113–116, September 2005
7. Li, N., Wu, H., Zheng, X., Zhao, Y.: An automatic moving object detection algorithm for video surveillance application. In: International Conference on Embedded Software and Systems, ICESS 2009, pp. 541–543, May 2009

8. Pauli, J., Sagrebin, M.: Real time moving object detection for video surveillance. In: Sixth IEEE International Conference on Advanced Video and Signal Based Surveillance, pp. 31–36, September 2009
9. Patel, C., et al.: Gaussian mixture model based moving object detection from video sequence. In: Proceeding ICWET 2011. MUMBAI Conference Proceeding Published by ACM digital library, February 2011. ISBN 978-1-4503-0449-8
10. Bin, Z., Liu, Y.: The improved moving object detection and shadow removing algorithm for video surveillance. In: International Conference on Computational Intelligence and Software Engineering (CiSE), pp. 1–5, December 2010
11. Saroj, P., Tripathi, R., Kumar, K.S., Prasad, S.: Multiple cameras using real time object tracking for surveillance and security systems. In: 3rd International Conference on Emerging Trends in Engineering and Technology (ICETET), pp. 213–218, November 2010
12. Ramesh Babu, D.R., Gopala Krishna, M.T., Ravishankar, M.: Automatic detection and tracking of moving object in complex environment for video surveillance application. In: 3rd International Conference on Electronics Computer Technology (ICECT), vol. 1, pp. 234–238, April 2011
13. Coifman, B., Beymer, D., McLauchlan, P., Malik, J.: A real-time computer vision system for measuring traffic parameters. In: IEEE Conference on Computer Vision and Pattern Recognition, pp. 496–501 (1997)
14. Papanikolopoulos, N.P., Masoud, O., Kwon, E.: Vision-based monitoring of weaving sections. In: Proceedings of the IEEE Conference on Intelligent Transportation Systems, pp. 770–775, October 1999
15. Fujiyoshi, H., Lipton, A.J., Patil, R.S.: Moving target classification and tracking from real-time video. In: Proceedings of the IEEE Workshop Applications of Computer Vision, pp. 8–14 (1998)
16. Koller, D.: Moving object recognition and classification based on recursive shape parameter estimation. In: Proceedings of 12th Israel Conference on Artificial Intelligence, Computer Vision, 27–28 December 1993
17. Sivaraman, M., Trivedi, S.: A general active learning framework for on-road vehicle recognition and tracking. IEEE Trans. Intell. Transp. Syst. 11(2), 267–276 (2010)
18. Sasikumar, M., Abraham, L.: Vehicle detection and classification from high-resolution satellite images. ISPRS Ann. Photogramm. Remote Sens. Spat. Inf. Sci. II, 1 (2014)
19. Patel, C.I., Garg, S.: Comparative analysis of traditional methods for moving object detection in video sequence. Int. J. Comput. Sci. Commun. 6(2), 309–315 (2015)
20. Lowe, D.G.: Distinctive image features from scale invariant keypoints. Int. J. comput. vis. 60, 91–110 (2004)
21. Patel, C.I., et al.: Top-down and bottom-up cues based moving object detection for varied background video sequences. Adv. Multimed. 2014, 13 (2014). Hindawi Publishing Corp.
22. Patel, C.I., Garg, S., Zaveri, T., Banerjee, A., Patel, R.: Human action recognition using fusion of features for unconstrained video sequences. Comput. Electr. Eng., 1–18 (2016)

Graphical and Theoretical Approach of Thermodynamics in Cyclic Theory of Universe

Nitin Chandola[1(✉)], Mayank Chaturvedi[2], Rohit Singh Rawat[1],
and Yogesh Dhami[1]

[1] Department of Mechanical Engineering, Graphic Era University,
Dehradun, India
nitinchandola7@gmail.com,
rohitsinghrawat276@gmail.com,
yogeshdhami007@gmail.com
[2] Department of Electrical Engineering, Graphic Era University,
Dehradun, India
mayankchaturvedi.geit@gmail.com

Abstract. In cyclic theory of universe the scenario is just inverse of the theory of inflation. The cyclic theory model almost solves the problem of homogeneity, isotropy and flatness. It also has relevant cause and effect scenarios of different phenomenon like reheating, contraction of branes and it also shows the thermodynamic relevance. The basic approach of the paper is to satisfy the thermodynamics laws and to formulate the situation of ultimate fate of universe. Each and every phenomena that has been described in cyclic theory of universe has been taken into account while drawing the hypothetical graphs of thermodynamics. While treating thermodynamics with cosmology and astrophysics, many factors have been neglected like shape of universe, the cosmological constant, invariant scalar factor and factors related to the depth of cosmology. The paper also shows the behaviour of pressure, volume and temperature by using arbitrary values. The time and space has been neglected in graphical representation.

Keywords: Cyclic theory of universe · Ekpyrotic phase · Black holes · Thermodynamics

1 Introduction

Challenging the big bang or inflationary picture [20] the Cyclic Theory of Universe (CTU) seems to be relevant because it solves the problem of flatness, homogeneity and isotropy [2]. In inflation theory [20] the universe's ultimate fate is heat death whereas CTU describes that the heat death may not be the end of universe. The ekpyrotic phase or the ultra- slow contraction of brane plays an important role in reheating the universe. The microwave background detected that the tensor perturbations of inflation exists in two widely separated scales. [12] This can be due to the regular contraction and

© Springer Nature Singapore Pte Ltd. 2017
M. Singh et al. (Eds.): ICACDS 2016, CCIS 721, pp. 504–515, 2017.
DOI: 10.1007/978-981-10-5427-3_52

expansion of the universe and may be equivalent to CTU. The CTU was based on three major assumptions:

1. The big bang is not the beginning of space and time but rather the transition from earlier phase of evolution.
2. The big bang occurred periodically and will continue to occur in future.
3. The main factor that shaped the structure of universe was ekpyrotic phase occurred before big bang.

The behaviour of CTU appears as a pendulum structure in which the conversion of energy takes place from potential to kinetic and vice versa [17]. Like the pendulum, cyclic universe also loses its energy after each oscillating cycle. Universe stores entropy, such that the outside observer will not be able to observe the disappeared entropy during the contraction. It will be the black hole which will absorb the entropy and will grow event horizon and the system will be swallowed [14]. The matter which exhibits the cosmological and thermodynamic properties such as contraction and reheating after the degradation of radiation and matter is assumed as 'Λ matter' also known as quintessence constant [15]. Another important objective for considering the CTU as a favourable theory for understanding the universe is due to its capability of solving the cause of quantum stability, quantum fluctuations and thermal fluctuations [17]. This serve as a motivation for addressing the issues related to the thermodynamics in the theory [21].

2 Big Bang Phase

The CTU supports the big bang theory and gives more significant information about the behaviour of universe. The big bang leads to an exponentially fast expansion of universe Where Mp ≈ 1019 GeV is the Planck Mass [20]. The model proposes in heat death of the universe in which the maximum entropy will be reached.

$$H = \sqrt{\left[\frac{8\pi}{3M_p^2}\right] V(\emptyset)} \tag{1}$$

3 Cyclic Model of Universe

The model believes in existence of the two branes which is separated by a distance and consists a hidden dimension [16]. It supports the M- theory in which the six extra dimensions does not play any active role and hence the theory is created as in 5-D or 4-D [22]. The dark energy is considered to be the potential form of energy which after the spontaneous action banged again and caused the second phase of big bang which further caused the expansion of universe till present [6]. The futuristic behavior of CTU shows that there is a way to go again to that level where the universe will start a new cycle again, which might be the explanation of problems of inflationary model [10]. In this theory the gravitational energy, the kinetic and potential energy of existing universe and the inter-brane forces plays an important role while the conversion and degradation of energy will takes place [9, 22]. The 5-D brane picture is complex for thermodynamic analysis hence the effective 4-D picture is used for the further analysis of CTU. Few theories are available in literature to curb the questions related to reheating of the universe while in the ekpyrosis phase. According to the holographic principle, there must be ghost condensate energy which would have turned to matter and radiation, to reheat the universe. The inter-brane forces during the phenomena of collision of branes which is elastic in nature (due to thermodynamics), also causes reheating [3, 14, 18]. Another reason of ekpyrosis of CTU can be described by the asymmetries generated by primordial black holes causing the reheating of universe and collision of brane [19]. The microwave background has shown that the detection of inflationary, tensor, perturbations are at two different scales [8]. Hence, it may be possible that a number of cycles of contraction and expansion could have taken place and which supports the CTU [12]. The dark energy scenario is easily explained in the CTU and seems to be analogical with the oscillating pendulum in which potential energy converts into kinetic energy and vice versa [9].

4 Motivation

CTU utilises thermodynamic approach to explain both first and second law of thermodynamics [22]. By No Hair theorem [14], the work that has been converted to heat will be stored in black holes and will cause the outside observer to lose the sight of entropy whereas the event horizon of the black hole will grow. Bekenstine proposed that the second law holds good to sum of all black holes and matter entropy [14].

$$ds_{(total)} \geq 0 \tag{2}$$

At last the whole entropy will be

$$S_{overall} = S_{matter} + S_{blackhole} \tag{3}$$

The concept of gravity explains the second law of thermodynamics in cyclic nature of the universe. The another kind of power has been induced to the subject when Friedmann and Tolman [11] discovered that the overall entropy does not show any cyclic appearance in fact it increases from cycle to cycle. It also explains how the cycle become longer due to the extrapolation into the past, leading to initial singularity. Hence it is clear that ekpyrosis was the phenomena due to which the cyclic behaviour of universe took place in past and will also going to happen in future. The cyclic nature of entropy:

$$S(t) = S(t + \tau) \tag{4}$$

Where S(t) is the total entropy at any point of time and $S(t + \tau)$ is increase in entropy in one cycle [11]. Another factor that supports the thermodynamic nature of universe is Brane Scale factor that varies from cycle to cycle which is the main reason for increase in entropy and black holes too. [22] The microwave backgrounds and non-Gaussian [7] study showed the multi inflationary model detection [8] in universe. Hence, the thermodynamics plays vital role in defining the ultimate fate of the universe [12]. The gravity is taken as the energy and heat source, in CTU, which will provide the external work done to the universe such that the first law of thermodynamics is followed and second law must not be violated. The 4-D approach [18] to Brane theory made it possible to construct the outer structure of basics of thermodynamics [3]. Hence, in actual form the thermodynamics is not cyclic as to be expected from cyclic process, which validated the statement, "Entropy of universe is increasing" [21, 22].

5 Methodology

Depending upon its reliability and futuristic approach, a particular mechanism of universe has to be selected. As the CTU does not exhibits the problem related to flatness, homogeneity and isotropy [2]. It makes it easy to believe in the evolution of matter and energy. The CTU has major part related to energy (even dark energy) due to which the thermodynamics has significant role in this theory, where reheating is a phenomena that defines the future of space and time. The macroscopic view of the universe is considered and also the system is open [21, 22]. Due to complex behaviour of volume of the universe CTU considered the volume of the universe negligible at first, whole density and volume change is calculated according to the continuum chart. The validity of time, space and laws of thermodynamics is then checked mathematically and thermodynamically. Further study in the graphical representation shows the behaviour of CTU in P-V (Pressure-Volume) and T-S (Temperature-Entropy). The conclusion is taken after discussing the results and behaviour obtained.

6 Thermodynamic Approach to Cyclic Theory

6.1 Approach

Big Bang theory proposes the ultimate fate of universe is heat death and deals in a single cycle mechanism of universe. Whereas, CTU describes the cyclic nature of universe. Hence, the macroscopic view of the thermodynamics is determined. It is assumed initially that the macroscopic view has high pressure to energy density ratio ($\omega \gg 1$) [22]. Initially, the availability was at its peak but the spontaneous expansion of universe caused the entropy to increase, hence, heat caused the formation of space and time. The initial version of singularity after the spontaneous degradation and Infinite time scale is the cause of considering macroscopic views, as well as in reheating of branes. The oscillating motion of the universe like pendulum, converts the potential energy into kinetic energy at every point of peak of motion. Energy loss in between the cycles can be taken as the defects in medium to which the bob is tied. The loss of energy in oscillating universe is also like the pendulum.

6.2   First Law of Thermodynamics

6.2.1   Concept of Continuum [21]

The macroscopic approach considers the large volume of the universe whereas the sub atomic and microscopic factors are neglected. The volume of universe was in contract and continuous form. Hence, with degradation of it caused the formation of space and time. The phenomenon can be understood by Fig. 1. As per continuum chart at the end $\frac{\delta m}{\delta v} = 0$ and $\delta v = \infty$. As per cyclic theory in the ekpyrotic phase the slow contraction between branes shows the degradation in volume as $\omega \gg 1$, so the graph denotes it as point (1) and (2) [18]. It indicates that the volume will continue to increase over the cycles, the pressure will degrade and so does the mass to volume ratio or average density ratio.

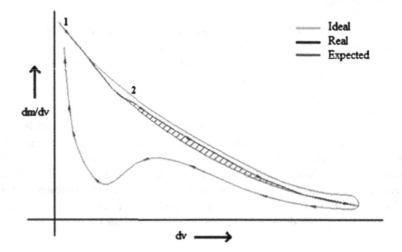

Fig. 1. Continuum chart

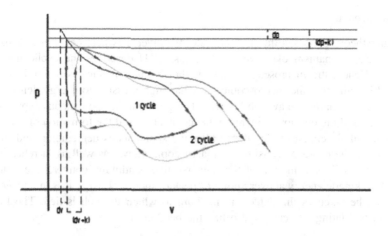

Fig. 2. P-V chart for cyclic theory

6.2.2   Work Transfer for Cyclic Theory of Universe

The work transfer in this theory is directly related to the reheating of the universe. As the continuum chart exhibits that with increasing volume per cycle of the universe can cause deceleration of each cycle, which has direct relation with momentum of colliding Branes. By CTU the external work done on the universe in ekpyrotic phase between branes is due to Inter-brane forces and gravity. So,

$$W_{system} = \text{interbrane force} + \text{gravitation force} \tag{5}$$

Hence, the work transfer between the branes takes place due to inelastic collision and distribution of momentum in different directions. The difference between the inter-brane collisions [19] is due to the potential developed between them $V(\varphi)$ [4].

$$V(\varphi) = -V_0 e^{-\varphi/L} \tag{6}$$

In the Time dependent scenario the work done by Brane in mechanical sense can be given by:

$$W = F \times L \tag{7}$$

Where F is the force of attraction between forces and L is the distance between them.

6.2.3   Path Function or Point Function

Being cyclic in nature doesn't mean that the system will reach the same point of initiation every time, due to the path disturbances [13]. The study in P-V charts shows that the theory though is depicting a cyclic behaviour of universe but the events are not cyclic. This may be due to entropy which is discussed in further part of the work. Hence the equation used here are inexact differentials [21]. Hence it is assume that-

$$\oint dv \neq 0 \tag{8}$$

$$\oint dp \neq 0 \tag{9}$$

$$\oint dT \neq 0 \tag{10}$$

This gives the base to the assumption that the cyclic universe will observe change in volume, temperature, and pressure. Where as per the continuum chart volume will increase and, temperature and volume can be concluded with observance of P-V and T-S charts.

As far as the quasi-static process in the universe is considered, it depends upon the reference of observing it, for a long period of time the universe is assumed to be an anti-quasi-static process [21].

6.2.4   Heat Transfer

Neglecting the Multiverse theory the universe seems to be an isolated system. Hence, the heat dissipated by the system will be absorbed by the black holes that were primordial and still forming [19] such that the external observer will feel complete absence of heat [14]. Therefore the cyclic theory will be able to produce micro systems in the universe for heat transfer [21].

$$\oint dQ \neq 0 \tag{11}$$

6.2.5   Concept of Energy in Universe

The macro system like universe is majorly composed of gravitational energy [5]. According to Newton the Static Universe is impossible until it is all empty, however according to the ekpyrotic phase the universe at each cycle's end will consist of radiation and matter [22].

Hence

$$\frac{a''}{a} = -\frac{4\pi Gv}{3a^3} \tag{12}$$

Cyclic theory emphasizes the gain of lost heat of the universe from the gravitational energy [22]. If n is number of cycles of universe and t is time then:

$$At n = 1, \ and \ t = 0$$
$$TotalEnergy = PotentialEnergy \tag{13}$$

$$At n = 1, \ and \ t = \lambda$$
$$TotalEnergy = KineticEnergy - heatloss \tag{14}$$

$$At n = 1, \ and \ t = \infty \ (end \ of \ cycle)$$
$$TotalEnergy = KineticEnergy - heatloss \tag{15}$$

Now the term heat loss will be compensated by the gravity [1]. If mass of branes are m and M respectively hence the gravitational force will be at distance x are:-

$$F = -\frac{GmM}{x^2} \tag{16}$$

So,

$$Total \ Energy = Kinetic \ Energy + \frac{GmM}{x^2} - heatloss \tag{17}$$

$$TotalEnergy_{(a)} = \frac{1}{2}mv^2 + \frac{1}{2}Mv^2 + \frac{GmM}{x^2} - heat \ loss_{(a)} \tag{18}$$

But according to path function the energy change will not be zero [21]. So, some heat will get lost in the black holes [14].

6.2.6   First Law of Thermodynamics

The study of cyclic universe inside an isolated system is complex and hence can cause the uncomprehensive way of explaining its thermodynamics. Hence the universe is considered here to be isolated, with black holes, as its internal systems or microsystem. Here the heat dissipated by the work done per cycle by the branes, are compensated by gravity and the heat left in the system can be given

$$\sum W_{cycle} = \sum Q_{cycle} + KineticEnergy + GravitationalEnergy \qquad (19)$$

The internal energy of system [21] i.e. for the universe can be given by:

$$Q - W = \Delta E \qquad (20)$$

Where Q-W is the difference between heats dissipated and work done by the universe. Hence, from this we can determine that the branes were not 100% contracted, which may be due to black holes and potential difference at different locations at branes. Hence, the universe in cyclic term, did not show the static behaviour.

6.2.7   Perpetual Motion Machine of Kind 1 (PPM-1) [21, 22]

The gravity provides the external energy to the system of branes for its reheating and expansion. Hence, the whole energy will not get converted to work.

6.2.8   P-V Chart [21]

The p-v chart can be drawn on the basis of the continuum chart as by the relation that, the volume decrease cycle to cycle. According to the p-v chart:

The initiation of the CTU was at high pressure and temperature, but as the Big Bang took place, the pressure decreased gradually but volume increased in exponential manner and was driven by perturbations [1]. The second big bang caused further contraction at 'a' when the ekpyrosis (semi) was formed and further increased till present scenario 'c'. At last at point 'd' the radiation and matter will remain. The reverse cycle of physical universe will start from 'd' by the interbrane force till 't' where 'e' will be the primordial black holes helping the contraction, reheating and increasing pressure with decreasing volume simultaneously [14, 22]. The gravity at point 'g' will actively take part in defining the ekpyrotic phase of the universe for Big Crunch to form Big Bang, hence the pressure will rise rapidly such that the ekpyrosis takes place before next cycle [22]. The graph of work done on first cycle to second cycle is the heat dissipation stored in or trapped in black holes [14]. Hence from cycle to cycle, the overall pressure will decrease with density and the volume will increase to infinite space [21].

6.3   Second Law of Thermodynamics

By the Kelvin- Planck statement [21], "It is impossible to construct a device which operating in a cycle will produce no effect other than the transfer by heat from a cooler to a hotter body". Hence, the same relies with the universe, it is impossible that the reheating of universe without any external work, so the external work is to be done by the gravity that will impart the capability of reheating of the universe [22]. By the holographic principle, the heat will disappear for external observer whereas the event horizon of the black hole will increase in size [14]. Hence the equation gives the compensation of heat loss:

$$\sum Q_{cycle} = GravitationForce + InterbraneForce \qquad (21)$$

As per the cyclic theory, the process may be cyclic in physical level, but in the thermodynamics, the process seems to be irreversible. This may be due to the loss of heat which is not compensated neither by the gravity nor by the inter-brane force. Hence the loss of work will cause the change in thermodynamic state of the system [21]. Figure 3 shows the heat engine diagram for one cycle of CTU.

$$W_1 - W_2 \approx n \times k \qquad (22)$$

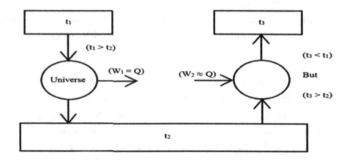

Fig. 3. Heat engine diagram for one cycle of CTU

Where k is constant of heat loss at first cycle and n is the variable of heat loss. Hence by this, we can conclude that irreversibility influenced the spontaneity of the universe as well as the entropy is the main cause of the universe's present scenario [22]. We can also determine that, "Gravity is the energy reservoir of universe".

6.3.1   Perpetual Motion Machine of Kind 2 (PPM-2)

The PPM2 model gets abolish when the gravity factor is imparted to do work on the degraded system [22]. In the PPM-2 model for cyclic theory of universe, there will still remain a loss of work in the form of heat loss, trapped in form of potential between the two branes [6].

6.3.2   Concept of Entropy

By the Clausius entropy law is

Energy of the world is constant.

Entropy of the world tend towards a maximum.

As per the P-V diagram shown by Fig. 2, some part of the cycle lacks in the work done, that must be due to heat production entrapped inside the black holes [14]. So, the degradation of energy takes place at each cycle, which give rise to the entropy. Which implies that per cycle degradation is the cause of irreversibility in the cyclic theory. The irreversibility is only caused when the behaviour of universe is spontaneous [21]. Thus this provides contradiction to the realization by Friedmann and Tolmanthat the second law of thermodynamics is the obstacle to CTU. The concept of long cycle, for each cycle holds true. But the initial singularity will not be obtained in each cycle because of the irreversibility. So, it may be possible that at the end of each cycle the only remains of universe will be black holes, dust and darkness [11]. By the Clausius theorem, for a reversible process [21].

$$\oint \frac{dQ}{T} = 0 \tag{23}$$

But, the CTU in thermodynamics perspective is not a cyclic or reversible process, so

$$\oint \frac{dQ}{T} \neq 0 \tag{24}$$

As far as consideration of universe as an isolated system is considered then by entropy principle,

$$dS \geq \frac{dQ}{T} \tag{25}$$

And, as far as the possibility is assumed the process in the cyclic theory is seemed to be thermodynamically irreversible. Hence,

$$dS_{(iso)} > 0 \tag{26}$$

So, in this process, the entropy of the universe is continuously increasing [21] and according to the second law of thermodynamics. The CTU is macroscopic viewpoint. In the combination of system and surrounding i.e. the universe as whole is irreversible.

$$dS_{(univ)} > 0 \tag{27}$$

As per the Holographic principle the heat will be stored in the black holes [14]. Hence, the universe will be disintegrate to a system and inner surrounding i.e. black hole.

$$dS_{(sys)} + dS_{(blackholes)} \geq 0 \tag{28}$$

6.3.3 Graphical Representation of T-S Chart

The CTU shows the behaviour for temperature and entropy as per the thermodynamic laws as shown by Fig. 4. According to the temperature chart the heating condition of the initial or primordial universe must be infinite Kelvin, but the spontaneous degradation caused entropy generation. Hence, the temperature at point A will get decreased till point C. Due to second bang in universe [8] cause increase in temperature that must be less than temperature at point A and at point B. The expansion stops for the reversible action of ekpyrosis [9]. In cycle 2 the overall entropy will get conserved in black holes [14] hence the ds represent the change in entropy and the temperature will also decrease as [21].

$$dS = \frac{dQ}{T} \; i.e. \; S \propto \frac{1}{T} \tag{29}$$

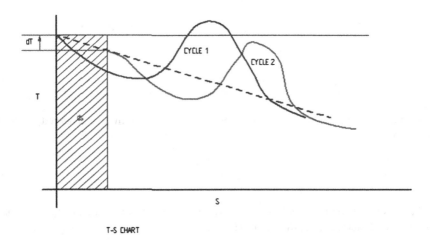

T-S CHART

Fig. 4. T-S chart for the cyclic theory of universe

7 Conclusion

From the above analysis we can conclude that hypothetically the graphs drawn can be much dissimilar to the real values but, there is no law that has been exploited by the charts drawn according to the CTU. It infers that the cyclic theory can be justified with the law of thermodynamics. This can also ensure a better field of research to understand the behaviour of thermodynamics of universe.

References

1. Copeland, E.J., Lidsey, J.E., Wands, D.: Axion perturbation spectra in string cosmologies. Phys. Lett. B **443**(1), 97–103 (1998)
2. Albrecht, A., Dimopoulos, S., Fischler, W., Kolb, E.W., Raby, S., Steinhardt, P.J.: New inflation in supersymmetric theories. Nucl. Phys. B **229**(2), 528–540 (1983)
3. Battefeld, T.: Modulated perturbations from instant preheating after new ekpyrosis. Phys. Rev. D **77**(6), 063503 (2008)
4. Buchbinder, E.I., Khoury, J., Ovrut, B.A.: Non-Gaussianities in new ekpyrotic cosmology. Phys. Rev. Lett. **100**(17), 171302 (2008)
5. Turok, N., Craps, B., Hertog, T.: From big crunch to big bang with AdS/CFT. arXiv preprint arXiv:0711.1824 (2007)
6. Marvel, K., Turok, N.: Horizons and tunneling in the euclidean false vacuum. arXiv preprint arXiv:0712.2719 (2007)
7. McEwen, J.D., Hobson, M.P., Lasenby, A.N., Mortlock, D.J.: A high-significance detection of non-Gaussianity in the WMAP 5-yr data using directional spherical wavelets. Mon. Not. R. Astron. Soc. **388**(2), 659–662 (2008)
8. Kaplan, D.B., Nelson, A.E.: Inflationary axion cosmology beyond our horizon. arXiv preprint arXiv:0809.1206 (2008)
9. Lehners, J.-L.: Diversity in the phoenix universe. Phys. Rev. D **84**(10), 103518 (2011)
10. Lehners, J.-L., Steinhardt, P.J.: Planck 2013 results support the cyclic universe. Phys. Rev. D **87**(12), 123533 (2013)
11. Frampton, P.H., Ludwick, K.J.: Cyclic cosmology from the little rip. Mod. Phys. Lett. A **28** (29), 1350125 (2013)
12. Caligiuri, J., et al.: Constraining the history of inflation from microwave background polarimetry and laser interferometry. Phys. Rev. D **91**(10), 103529 (2015)
13. Lehners, J.-L., Wilson-Ewing, E.: Running of the scalar spectral index in bouncing cosmologies. J. Cosmol. Astropart. Phys. **2015**(10), 038 (2015)
14. Bousso, R.: The holographic principle. Rev. Mod. Phys. **74**(3), 825 (2002)
15. Yurov, A.V.: Complex field as inflaton and quintessence. arXiv preprint arXiv:hep-th/0208129 (2002)
16. Khoury, J.: A briefing on the ekpyrotic/cyclic universe. arXiv preprint arXiv:astro-ph/0401579 (2004)
17. Erickson, J.K., Gratton, S., Steinhardt, P.J., Turok, N.: Cosmic perturbations through the cyclic ages. Phys. Rev. D **75**(12), 123507 (2007)
18. Buchbinder, E.I., Khoury, J., Ovrut, B.A.: New ekpyrotic cosmology. Phys. Rev. D **76**(12), 123503 (2007)
19. Baumann, D., Steinhardt, P.J., Turok, N.: Primordial black hole baryogenesis. arXiv preprint arXiv:hep-th/0703250 (2007)
20. Linde, A.D.: A new inflationary universe scenario: a possible solution of the horizon, flatness, homogeneity, isotropy and primordial monopole problems. Phys. Lett. B **108**(6), 389–393 (1982)
21. Nag, P.K.: Basic and Applied Thermodynamics, 2nd edn. Tata McGraw Hill Education Private Limited, New Delhi (2002)
22. Steinhardt, P.J., Turok, N.: A cyclic model of the universe. Science **296**(5572), 1436–1439 (2002)

Supplier Performance Evaluation for Manufacturing Industries: Re-exploring with Big Data Analysis

Purnima Matta[✉] and Akash Tayal

Indira Gandhi Delhi Technical University for Women, Delhi, India
purnima.matta@gmail.com, akashtayal@yahoo.com

Abstract. In the present era of globalization, every industry needs to explore methods for effective supplier selection. This paper re-defines the supplier selection problem in industries as a big-data problem and reviews the pre-existing approaches for supplier ranking. The major focus is on introducing Big-Data for supplier selection problem in industries. The approaches used are majorly looked for its implementation time and importantly, processing big-data in a way to prevent error tendencies and discrepancies in results. This article reviews AHP and PCA-based methods for supplier ranking problem re-defined as a real-time big-data problem. It also proposes further solutions and methodologies for better results.

Keywords: Big-data · PCA (Principal Component Analysis) · AHP (Analytical Hierarchy Process) · Clustering · Correlation analysis

1 Introduction

"The term "big data" has been regarded historically as a terminology used by "softer" industries to keep track of people's behaviors, buying tendencies, sentiments, etc." However, the "big data" concept quite goes with manufacturing industries as well. Supplier Selection in manufacturing domain can be considered to be a big data problem satisfying the three V's of Big Data. It is well observed that number of sensors grow based on the complexity of the used devices and tasks [1]. In manufacturing firms, the component parts, sensors, raw materials, actuators can equal up to 70%–80% of production cost [2]. In such circumstances, the purchase department has a major role in supplier selection by periodically evaluating the suppliers in terms of several performance criteria [5]. With the globalization of market, the number of potential suppliers and the number of factors or criteria to consider for supplier evaluation increases. Therefore, an effective and efficient evaluation of supplier is important for the success of any manufacturing firm [35].

"Supplier selection is a multi-criteria problem." Cost, quality, on time delivery, and flexibility are major factors that have been used in supplier selection literature [20]. Among the multiple criteria for supplier selection, green factor has also been considered. Supplier selection is mostly focused on environmental aspect and; thus, a firm's ecological performance can be demonstrated by its suppliers.

© Springer Nature Singapore Pte Ltd. 2017
M. Singh et al. (Eds.): ICACDS 2016, CCIS 721, pp. 516–526, 2017.
DOI: 10.1007/978-981-10-5427-3_53

Supplier selection has been a major topic with consideration of manufacturing industries and environment in literature. As stated in [5, 10]; Timmerman proposed linear weighing models for supplier selection based on AHP (Analytical Hierarchy Process). But, as big-data comes into picture, AHP is considered to be a tedious method and tendency of errors is more with huge data. Petroni and Braglia [5] proposed vendor ranking based on PCA (Principal Component Analysis) results. Handeld [6] studied the relevance of environmental criteria for supplier assessment. Robak et al. [3] considers supply chain management as a big data concept. Kaisler et al. [11] stated in his article that "big data can support value creation for organizations". Ghosh [13] defined big data in logistics and supply chain as "a rethinking step" and it helps in effective decision-making in businesses. Tayal and Singh [22] proposed PCA for data reduction and clustering in big-data.

However, while many firms have noted the tremendous potential of Big Data for supplier selection yet not integrated it into their operations. As time passes, those firms who have integrated Big-Data will likely have a decisive competitive advantage. This article describes supplier selection to be a big-data problem. The existing methodologies for evaluation of the suppliers' rank are reviewed in context with the selection criteria including the measuring criteria for green supplier selection [5, 14]. The multivariate statistical technique, PCA-based methodology and AHP are implemented on same data-set for supplier selection by a manufacturing firm. The article discusses the outcomes of these ranking procedures and the effectiveness of generated ranks for the considered big-data problem.

2 Supplier Evaluation: A Big-Data Problem

2.1 Defining Big-Data

"Within a computational architecture, big-data is something difficult to capture, manage, store, analyze and visualize. It is somewhat misnomer just to characterize big-data with the size of data" [23].

Big Data refers not only to very large data sets but are high-volume, velocity, and variety information assets. It requires new forms of processing for enhanced decision-making, insight discovery and process optimization.

"Big Data creates "value" – both within and across domains and disciplines. Value arises from the ability in analyzing the data to obtain actionable information" [11].

2.2 Three Main Aspects of Big-Data

Volume. With the growing globalization, the tremendous growth in number of suppliers in market and analysis of numerous criteria for supplier selection makes supplier selection analysis data-set huge. Also, the manufacturing firms require good quantities of instruments, actuators, spare parts etc. The supplier criteria which relate to this V depends on volume whether in terms of cost, quantity, time, etc.

Velocity. It refers to anything that varies over time. The supplier selection includes transportation time, vendor's geographical location, and certain other criteria which depend on time. If, for a particular instrument, there are 10 distributers with different location and transportation times, it would increase the data entry for that product by ten times in our data-set. Also, the time consumed to commission a manufacturing plant is tremendous. The technology which is changing at a much faster pace keeps adding onto much better options in the similar price range for each product. Supplier evaluation for any manufacturing firm thus, requires frequent processing of growing data for analysis.

Variety. It refers to the most important aspect of big data [1]. The supplier selection data is highly unstructured. It may consist of numerous formats like GPS data for location, text etc. Even when it may seem that in case of supplier selection for an instrument or device, the data is more structured, but the integration is one of the most important challenges. This may be due to different measuring units, range, size, etc. of the considered criteria.

2.3   Criteria Mapping on Big-Data Aspects

Table 1 maps the criteria considered for supplier ranking to the 3 V's of big-data defining it to be a big-data problem.

Table 1. Criteria mapping with big-data

Volume	C3: Service period/warranty period
	C4: Minimum order quantity
	C6: Additional requirements
	C7: Overall cost
	C21: Geographical location of vendors
	C17: Number of vendors
	C16: Transportation & storage cost
Velocity	C5: Cash-to-cash cycle time
	C8: Fuel spent
	C15: Claim policies
	C18: Lifetime of asset
	C20: Emissions
	C12: Performance history
Variety	C1: Accuracy
	C2: Size of instrument
	C10: Range
	C19: Transportation means
	C9: Technology/innovation
	C11: IP rating
	C14: Management & organization
	C13: Precision

3 Supplier Ranking for Manufacturing Firm: The Implementation

In big manufacturing industries, uncountable instruments and devices are used for the process and right suppliers for such products need to be targeted by the industries. The article aims at obtaining supplier scores implementing the AHP approach and PCA-ranking approach separately for the same data-set; post obtaining criteria clusters from PCA and analyzing the results. The ranking has been obtained using MS Excel (Fig. 1).

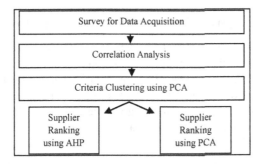

Fig. 1. Implementation flowchart

3.1 Survey for Acquiring Data

In this application, a questionnaire was prepared for survey for a steel manufacturing firm and was submitted to technical team leads of the target suppliers. The data is based on that survey keeping into view the suggestions of buying organization. The 21 criteria were considered and segregated in terms of volume, velocity, and variety and provided to suppliers' teams (Table 1) to rate as per Likert scale. Factor importance like accuracy, instrument size, etc. (all 21 criteria) has been asked for in the survey. For example, "How much per-cent weight-age is given to instrument size by supplier?" The survey included 235 suppliers. Since the data grows into big-data; currently, 235 × 21, therefore, our first aim was in making the data concise. As proposed by Tayal and Singh [22], PCA was implemented for the purpose of reducing the dimensions (criteria) for big-data analysis. The analysis has been done using SPSS 23.0 software package. Table 2 shows the collected information fetched to data view of SPSS.

Table 2. Data view of SPSS: a glimpse

	Accuracy	Size_Of_Instrument	Service_Period	Minimum_Quantity	Average_Collection_Period	Requireme...	Overall_Cost	Fuel_Spent	Technology
1	90.00	80.00	70.00	20.00	50.00	70.00	60.00	88.00	74.00
2	75.00	95.00	100.00	50.00	55.00	40.00	65.00	60.00	95.00
3	80.00	15.00	20.00	85.00	40.00	30.00	50.00	88.00	92.00
4	100.00	70.00	50.00	30.00	75.00	60.00	80.00	64.00	74.00
5	75.00	10.00	25.00	35.00	30.00	35.00	45.00	65.00	70.00
6	50.00	90.00	100.00	30.00	90.00	75.00	100.00	58.00	74.00
7	45.00	15.00	15.00	75.00	20.00	10.00	25.00	59.00	65.00
8	65.00	30.00	35.00	60.00	80.00	60.00	90.00	61.00	73.00
9	95.00	95.00	100.00	86.00	80.00	70.00	95.00	84.00	60.00
10	85.00	80.00	70.00	40.00	60.00	50.00	65.00	64.00	83.00
11	95.00	88.00	20.00	30.00	80.00	90.00	100.00	82.00	76.00
12	10.00	25.00	10.00	100.00	50.00	40.00	60.00	60.00	78.00
13	80.00	70.00	50.00	50.00	40.00	20.00	50.00	69.00	89.00
14	80.00	35.00	30.00	40.00	45.00	30.00	65.00	91.00	73.00

3.2   Correlation Analysis and Criteria Clustering Using PCA

PCA, a multivariate statistical method, is a data-reduction technique used in identifying a smaller set of variables that account for a large portion of total variance in the larger original variable-set [5]. PCA, a statistical linear transformation method that is used in analysis and compression of data [2], projects original data sets into new orthogonal space. Covariance analysis of the data-set gives the coordinate directions called principal components in new space. Principal components represent the direction of maximum variance of original data sets. Steps for clustering using PCA include:

- **Step 1.** To test for a sufficient level of correlation amongst variables.
  For this purpose, KMO (Kaiser Meyer Olkin) and Bartlett's test of Sphericity is analyzed. KMO gives an MSA value i.e., Measure of Sampling Adequacy, the value for which should be close to 1 for better results. MSA indicates the extent of correlation that holds between variables. Bartlett's test is required for testing the null hypothesis for the correlation matrix to be an identity matrix. In this case, the null hypothesis is rejected at 0.000 levels and Overall KMO-MSA is 0.543, which is acceptable. Thus, we can proceed to dimension reduction by implementing PCA.
- **Step 2.** To identify the number of important components present in data.
  The "Scree Plot" and "Total Variance Explained" helps in identification. The rule is "to cover maximum of the total variability in the data" and "to consider eigenvalues greater than 1". In scree plot (Fig. 2), "scree" represents the components that are at the bottom (below knee) of the sloping plot of eigenvalues versus component number. Components 1–9 account for 58% of the total variance (Table 3). Here, component-9 forms the knee (Fig. 2).

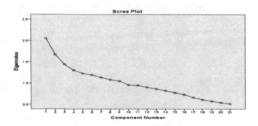

Fig. 2. Scree plot

Table 3. Total variance explained

Component	Initial eigenvalues			Extraction sums of squared loadings			Rotation sums of squared loadings		
	Total	% of variance	Cumulative %	Total	% of variance	Cumulative %	Total	% of variance	Cumulative %
1	2.050	9.760	9.760	2.050	9.760	9.760	1.657	7.892	7.892
2	1.666	7.935	17.695	1.666	7.935	17.695	1.434	6.828	14.720
3	1.435	6.832	24.527	1.435	6.832	24.527	1.390	6.618	21.338
4	1.300	6.189	30.716	1.300	6.189	30.716	1.381	6.575	27.913
5	1.225	5.835	36.551	1.226	5.835	36.551	1.305	6.215	34.128
6	1.190	5.666	42.217	1.190	5.666	42.217	1.285	6.117	40.245
7	1.131	5.384	47.601	1.131	5.384	47.601	1.252	5.961	46.206
8	1.076	5.126	52.727	1.076	5.126	52.727	1.233	5.871	52.077
9	1.045	4.976	57.703	1.045	4.976	57.703	1.182	5.626	57.703
10	.954	4.543	62.246						
11	.944	4.496	66.742						
12	.900	4.286	71.028						
13	.860	4.096	75.125						
14	.821	3.909	79.034						
15	.775	3.692	82.725						
16	.729	3.470	86.195						
17	.660	3.144	89.340						
18	.610	2.907	92.247						
19	.574	2.733	94.980						
20	.541	2.578	97.558						
21	.513	2.442	100.000						

Extraction Method: Principal Component analysis.

- **Step 3.** To determine the clusters of criteria formed by thus obtained principal components.

  The initial component extraction by the "loading matrix doesn't always give interpretable results. Therefore, Varimax rotation has been incorporated to make the large loadings of relevant variables on each component larger than before to bring-in its impact and smaller loadings smaller to nullify its relevance completely (Table 4).

  As per Table 5, IP Rating, Range, Precision and Accuracy are the variables that load on Principal Component 1. The clusters obtained are shown in Table 5.

3.3   Supplier Ranking

The Suppliers are ranked on the basis of the criteria clusters by implementing both AHP and PCA-based approach and the results are analyzed.

AHP-Based Ranking. The AHP was introduced by Saaty [7] to handle complex decision making. The AHP inputs include evaluation criteria set, and alternative options in a set to decide from. A weighing factor for each evaluation criterion is

Table 4. Rotated component matrix

	Component								
	1	2	3	4	5	6	7	8	9
IP_rating	.678	−.095	.183	−.150	.111	−.010	−.071	−.090	.123
Range	.614	−.040	−.157	.045	.144	.098	−.051	.103	−.160
Precision	−.514	−.025	.451	.031	.333	.190	−.023	−.002	−.014
Accuracy	.380	−.009	.018	.285	.046	.233	.266	.286	−.057
Emissions	−.096	.771	.046	.000	.067	.152	.003	−.137	.051
Transportation_means	−.087	.596	.196	−.024	−.081	−.042	−.163	.218	−.064
Fuel_spent	.293	.458	−.173	.222	.234	−.187	.260	.166	−.177
Geographical_location_of_vendors	.072	.074	.669	−.022	−.050	.036	.279	−.074	.203
Number_of_vendors	−.053	.100	.657	.040	−.096	−.099	−.255	.082	−.183
Lifetime_of_asset	−.090	.114	−.060	−.807	.065	.027	.013	−.074	.010
Transportation_storagecost	−.200	.183	−.088	.472	−.011	.203	.056	−.105	.048
Overall_cost	.104	−.037	−.250	−.386	.108	.310	.131	.269	−.234
Technology	.137	.024	−.079	−.079	.783	−.068	.051	−.063	.038
Requirements	−.054	.029	−.051	.011	−.066	.738	.085	.146	.028
Size_of_instument	.366	.048	.109	.173	.005	.574	−.189	−.263	.107
Claim_plicies	−.072	−.062	−.044	.047	.080	.054	.792	−.043	.094
Servies_period	.074	.019	−.252	.357	.294	.136	−.481	.047	.290
Management	−.111	.005	.034	.047	−.304	.113	−.036	.671	.111
Performance_history	.219	.072	−.035	−.094	.342	−.058	−.071	.572	.084
Minimum_quantity	−.082	−.132	.057	.109	.146	.144	.065	.220	.738
Average_collection_period	−.093	−.412	.108	.094	.352	.194	−.004	.114	−.545

Extraction Method: Principal Component Analysis.
Rotation Method: Varimax with Kaoser Normalization.
a. Rotation converged in 11 iterations.

Table 5. Clusters obtained

Cluster	Cluster name	Criteria included
CC1	Quality	C1: Accuracy
		C10: Range
		C11: IP rating
		C14: Precision
CC2	Green	C8: Fuel spent
		C19: Transportation means
		C20: Emissions
CC3	Logistics	C17: Number of vendors
		C21: Geographical location of vendors
CC4	Cost	C7: Overall cost (Initial + Running + Scrap Value)
		C16: Transportation & storage cost
		C18: Lifetime of asset
CC5	Technology/innovation	C9: Technology/innovation
CC6	Complexity	C2: Size of instrument
		C6: Additional requirements (skills and softwares)
CC7	Reputation	C3: Service period/warranty period
		C15: Claim policies
CC8	Service	C12: Performance history
		C13: Management & organization
CC9	Order flexibility	C4: Minimum order quantity
		C5: Cash-to-cash cycle time

obtained as per decision maker's pair-wise criteria comparisons. "The higher the weight, the more relevant is the corresponding criterion." Next, for each criterion, a score is assigned to every option as per the decision maker's pair-wise comparisons of the options based on that criterion. The higher option scores denote the better performance of the option with respect to the considered criterion. Finally, the options scores and the criteria weights are combined in AHP to determine a global score for each option, and a consequent rank [7]. The AHP implementation steps are as follows:

- To compute the criteria weights' vector (Fig. 3).
- To compute option scores matrix.
- To rank the options (Table 6).

- Quality
- Green
- Logistic
- Cost
- Tech/Innovation
- Complexity
- Service
- Reputation
- Order Flexibility

Fig. 3. Criteria cluster weights as obtained by AHP (Color figure online)

Table 6. Supplier ranking by AHP

RANK	SUPPLIER	RANK	SUPPLIER	RANK	SUPPLIER	RANK	SUPPLIER	RANK	SUPPLIER	RANK	SUPPLIER	RANK	SUPPLIER	RANK	SUPPLIER
1	210	31	127	61	205	91	211	121	152	151	112	181	87	211	98
2	49	32	54	62	111	92	171	122	212	152	119	182	201	212	177
3	52	33	20	63	220	93	37	123	60	153	133	183	109	213	34
4	150	34	169	64	140	94	76	124	134	154	231	184	233	214	118
5	75	35	213	65	58	95	186	125	196	155	204	185	187	215	38
6	155	36	56	66	129	96	103	126	21	156	224	186	225	216	46
7	199	37	189	67	227	97	78	127	72	157	97	187	13	217	181
8	163	38	173	68	40	98	86	128	82	158	139	188	57	218	5
9	74	39	77	69	83	99	125	129	230	159	108	189	102	219	92
10	51	40	217	70	167	100	126	130	185	160	206	190	148	220	207
11	53	41	79	71	88	101	67	131	141	161	99	191	214	221	26
12	95	42	85	72	132	102	175	132	30	162	2	192	208	222	25
13	166	43	197	73	63	103	159	133	235	163	157	193	8	223	61
14	50	44	42	74	154	104	107	134	215	164	142	194	176	224	160
15	106	45	80	75	65	105	190	135	221	165	188	195	143	225	32
16	222	46	202	76	138	106	174	136	193	166	158	196	147	226	9
17	122	47	184	77	120	107	104	137	17	167	10	197	136	227	33
18	81	48	114	78	7	108	64	138	223	168	4	198	209	228	84
19	91	49	219	79	130	109	29	139	194	169	234	199	100	229	22
20	55	50	71	80	68	110	179	140	144	170	18	200	180	230	153
21	48	51	105	81	137	111	11	141	162	171	41	201	161	231	24
22	182	52	226	82	145	112	69	142	59	172	16	202	44	232	31
23	218	53	94	83	124	113	89	143	110	173	115	203	192	233	14
24	73	54	117	84	93	114	229	144	36	174	203	204	6	234	101
25	12	55	156	85	113	115	3	145	168	175	200	205	15	235	27
26	149	56	23	86	172	116	128	146	43	176	35	206	70		
27	164	57	123	87	165	117	96	147	195	177	47	207	39		
28	170	58	146	88	118	118	1	148	19	178	151	208	121		
29	131	59	116	89	66	119	45	149	178	179	198	209	90		
30	216	60	232	90	191	120	228	150	28	180	135	210	62		

PCA-Based Ranking. PCA ranking method, practically implemented by Petroni and Braglia [5], aims at finding the weighing coefficients first, and then to get supplier score based on which ranking is done. PCA-based ranking is obtained as:

$$w_i = x_1 v_1 + x_2 v_2 + \ldots\ldots\ldots\ldots\ldots\ldots + x_{21} v_{21} \, for \, i = 1 \, to \, 9. \qquad (1)$$

where x: denotes absolute values of loadings greater than 0.1

v: denotes the percentage of variance explained by the component to obtain weighing coefficients.

These weighing coefficients are multiplied by the value of corresponding variable for each supplier to get supplier score.

Using Formula (1), weighing coefficient for C1, w1 = 0.097; for C2, w2 = 0.11; and so on for all 21 criteria.

4   Discussions and Observations

From Tables 6 and 7, it can be noted that the supplier ranks obtained by both AHP and PCA-based methods are different (as per AHP, supplier-210 is ranked 1st and PCA-ranking ranks supplier-14 as the best). Both the methods possess certain shortcomings which need to be overcome while handling big-data problem for supplier selection.

Table 7. Supplier ranking by PCA

RANK	SUPPLIER	RANK	SUPPLIER	RANK	SUPPLIER	RANK	SUPPLIER	RANK	SUPPLIER	RANK	SUPPLIER	RANK	SUPPLIER	RANK	SUPPLIER
1	14	31	160	61	194	91	188	121	166	151	129	181	134	211	50
2	9	32	108	62	34	92	96	122	28	152	233	182	36	212	91
3	46	33	230	63	95	93	115	123	75	153	170	183	167	213	130
4	147	34	175	64	142	94	169	124	104	154	97	184	57	214	58
5	141	35	173	65	118	95	121	125	21	155	20	185	110	215	219
6	31	36	64	66	191	96	226	126	133	156	65	186	145	216	227
7	90	37	33	67	35	97	74	127	140	157	232	187	83	217	126
8	192	38	67	68	195	98	84	128	85	158	222	188	146	218	81
9	26	39	198	69	76	99	143	129	102	159	156	189	88	219	18
10	8	40	107	70	181	100	48	130	200	160	174	190	224	220	223
11	231	41	229	71	180	101	106	131	165	161	73	191	105	221	212
12	41	42	5	72	161	102	182	132	6	162	23	192	215	222	63
13	15	43	40	73	206	103	193	133	205	163	29	193	135	223	42
14	78	44	109	74	53	104	162	134	168	164	59	194	17	224	79
15	89	45	54	75	209	105	184	135	71	165	119	195	94	225	125
16	25	46	203	76	148	106	69	136	82	166	30	196	154	226	114
17	101	47	27	77	187	107	43	137	61	167	99	197	197	227	56
18	138	48	7	78	176	108	157	138	163	168	103	198	13	228	122
19	92	49	144	79	68	109	216	139	207	169	211	199	51	229	199
20	87	50	70	80	149	110	177	140	112	170	60	200	120	230	217
21	38	51	225	81	22	111	220	141	204	171	111	201	186	231	210
22	44	52	24	82	77	112	12	142	98	172	55	202	80	232	213
23	47	53	32	83	62	113	214	143	185	173	16	203	1	233	150
24	196	54	158	84	45	114	86	144	39	174	183	204	127	234	218
25	228	55	4	85	3	115	136	145	49	175	37	205	124	235	52
26	153	56	139	86	72	116	2	146	172	176	221	206	137		
27	159	57	235	87	151	117	234	147	10	177	164	207	202		
28	178	58	93	88	155	118	190	148	171	178	19	208	131		
29	201	59	11	89	128	119	116	149	132	179	189	209	117		
30	152	60	208	90	100	120	123	150	113	180	179	210	66		

4.1   Shortcomings of the AHP-Based Ranking Approach

- The method is quite complex and thus, inconvenient to deal with voluminous data. The complexity of method makes it a cumbersome and time-consuming methodology.

- AHP criteria weighing is based on expert-knowledge and judgment which is subjective as per decision-maker and can't deal with vagueness or fuzziness in data.

4.2 Shortcomings of the PCA-Based Ranking Approach

- PCA-based approach may not provide a generalized consensus. The criteria being situation and firm-specific cannot be always weighed in terms of relative relevance.
- Each criteria is weighed separately and the cluster is not utilized which is irrelevant and time-consuming for big-data problem.

Apart from the above shortcomings, it is observed that the ranks obtained may not be always same for one problem as expert-reviews may vary each time in case of AHP; and PCA-ranking by relative weighing cannot be accepted as a generalized approach for every manufacturing firm.

5 Conclusions

The article describes supplier ranking and thus, selection problem in manufacturing firm as a big data problem. A review on supplier ranking methods (AHP and PCA-based approach) is done considering the nature and type of data. Since, the big data problem is voluminous and highly un-structured; the approach primarily takes into view the amount of processing, time consumption in the analysis.

PCA has the advantage of evaluating multidimensional data with different units and ranges. Also, its effectiveness in bringing out clusters of variables helps in data reduction for better and faster processing but PCA-ranking approach doesn't utilizes the criteria clusters and criteria weights are relative.

PCA obtained clusters reduces computation in AHP-ranking approach but it is still a highly-complex method for big-data handling.

In the future work, the following may be looked into:

- Since the rank evaluated in each method is different, an integrated ranking approach is required to obtain supplier ranks on common grounds.
- An optimization model should be proposed by manufacturing firms; considering the complexity of big-data for cost and time-effective ranking of suppliers. Linear regression analysis can be implemented for the purpose.
- Meta-heuristics can be implemented for obtaining an optimal solution to deal with a level of fuzziness in the data-set.

References

1. Jirkovský, V., Obitko, M., Novák, P., Kadera, P.: Big data analysis for sensor time-series in automation. IEEE (2014)
2. Bei-lin, L., Yong-chao, S.: Research on strategic supplier selection of supply chain based on PCA. IEEE (2009)

3. Robak, S., Franczyk, B., Robak, M.: Applying big data and linked data concepts in supply chain management. IEEE (2013)
4. Krumeich, J., Werth, D., Loos, P., Jacobi, S.: Big data analytics for predictive manufacturing control – a case study from process industry. IEEE (2014)
5. Petroni, A., Braglia, M.: Vendor selection using principal component analysis. Spring (2000)
6. Tahriri, F., Osman, M.R., Ali, A., Rosnah, M.Y.: A review of supplier selection methods in manufacturing industries (2008)
7. Saaty, T.L.: The Analytic Hierarchy Process. McGraw-Hill, New York (1980)
8. Adamcsek, E.: The analytic hierarchy process and its generalization (2008)
9. Khatri, J., Dash, A.: Sustainable metal recycling supply chains: prioritizing success factors applying combined AHP & PCA techniques. IJMVSC (2015)
10. Sarode, A.D., Khodke, P.M.: Performance measurement of supply chain management: a decision framework for evaluating and selecting supplier performance in a supply chain. Vol I, IJAMT (2008)
11. Kaisler, S., Armour, F., Espinosa, J.A., Money, W.: Big data: issues and challenges moving forward. IEEE (2012)
12. Zong, W., Zhao, G.: Application of SPSS for evaluation the curriculum designing and analysis the teaching in food engineering speciality. IEEE
13. Ghosh, D.: Big data in logistic and supply chain management – a rethinking step. IEEE (2013)
14. Shianghau, W., Jiannjong, G.: The trend of green supply chain management research (2000–2010)
15. Dongxiao, N., Jie, T., Ling, J.: Research on Chinese cities comprehensive competitiveness based on PCA and FA in SPSS. IEEE (2011)
16. Qiang, B., Jingjuan, G.: Evaluation model of supply chain risk based on principle component analysis. IEEE (2010)
17. Liu, Z., Xu, Q.: Comparison and prioritization among evaluation models with principal component analysis in supplier selecting. IEEE (2011)
18. Krumeich, J., Schimmelpfennnig, J., Jacobi, S.: Advanced planning and control of manufacturing processes in steel industry through big data analytics. IEEE (2014)
19. Sumei, Z.: The comprehensive evaluation of teaching quality based on principal component analysis. IEEE (2010)
20. Odum, M.: Factor scores, structure and communality coefficients: a primer (2011)
21. Paula, A., Dias, F., Póvoa, B., Miranda, J.L.: Operations research and big data: IO2015-XVII congress of Portuguese
22. Tayal, A., Singh, S.P.: Integrating big-data analytics & hybrid fire-fly simulated annealing approach for facility layout problem. Ann. Oper. Res. (2016). 10.1007/s10479-016-2237-x
23. Eaton, C., Deroos, D., Deustch, T., Lapis, G., Zikopaoulos, P.: Understanding Big Data. McGraw Hill/IBM

Data Sciences

A Distributed, Scalable Computing Facility for Big Data Analytics in Atmospheric Physics

Reena Bharathi$^{(\boxtimes)}$, S.C. Shirwaikar, and Vilas Kharat

Department of Computer Science, Savitribai Phule Pune University,
Pune, Maharastra, India
reena_b06@yahoo.com, scshirwaikar@gmail.com,
laddool@yahoo.com

Abstract. Technological advancements in computing and communication have led to a flood of data from different domains like healthcare, social networks, Internet commerce and finance. Over the past few years a larger chunk of data comes from the domain of scientific applications, using simulated experiments or collected using sensors. This development calls for new architectural models for data acquisition, storage, and large-scale data analytics.

In this paper, we present a distributed and scalable computing facility, using low cost machines, which support analytics of large scientific data sets, constituting three sequential modules, namely data pre-processing, data analytics and data post-processing. These three modules together form a big data value chain which is illustrated through a case study related to Atmospheric physics.

Keywords: Data analytics · Big data · MapReduce · Clustering · Hadoop · Atmospheric physics

1 Introduction

Data analytics is the science of examining a raw data set with the purpose of drawing some meaningful information from it which can be used to support high level decisions. "Big Data" refers to huge volumes of data, both structured and unstructured, produced by high-performance applications falling in a wide and heterogeneous group of application scenarios from scientific computing to social networks, from e-governance to medical information systems [1].

Big data Analytics refers to the tools and techniques used to acquire, store, analyze and generate intelligence from big data. The different analytical platforms for big data analytics are Enterprise data warehouses, traditional data warehouses and data marts, distributed file system platforms like Hadoop, Cloud based analytical platforms etc.

Scientific applications can be categorized as data intensive applications, or compute intensive applications, or a combination of both. Data-intensive applications process huge volumes of data, to the size of terabytes and petabytes arriving in real time from arrays of sensors, or as the outputs from simulated experiments. Compute Intensive Applications involve heavy and complex data analysis, over increasingly large data sets. These compute intensive algorithms are iterative in nature and are implemented using a parallel distributed processing architecture.

© Springer Nature Singapore Pte Ltd. 2017
M. Singh et al. (Eds.): ICACDS 2016, CCIS 721, pp. 529–540, 2017.
DOI: 10.1007/978-981-10-5427-3_54

There are various challenges faced in performing analytics on scientific data sets, some of which are listed below:

- Data acquisition from different sources, leading to different data formats.
- Accumulating chunks of data, when the data acquired is time bound, leading to the need to combine different chunks into a single big data set.
- Data acquisition when done as big chunks of data, some type of pre processing will be required on it, thus leading to the need for data preprocessing in the form of aggregations, removing irrelevant data etc.

Two approaches can be defined for dealing with the above mentioned challenges.

- Design a Big data analytics set up, that integrates pre processing with analytics, when the data chunks are huge. Various pre-processing techniques like aggregations, removal of meaningless and redundant data etc., are applied so as to reduce the volume of the big data sets, thus making it suitable for processing by various data analysis algorithms.
- When the data chunks are small, normal Analytics tools can be used to perform both pre-processing and analytics. The analyzed outputs collected over a period of time tend to become big data sets. Design a Big data analytics set up to performs analytics on this big data set.

In this paper, we present a framework that implements the first approach and is used to meet some of the above mentioned challenges in the domain of scientific data analytics. In the next section background and existing work related to big data analytics in scientific environment is presented. Section 3 describes our experimental setup comprising of both hardware and software. The various algorithms designed and implemented as required for pre-processing and analytics are presented in Sect. 4 which mainly includes the k-mean clustering algorithm. Section 5 presents experiments carried out on data sets related to Atmospheric Physics. The paper ends with conclusion and presents some future directions.

2   Background and Related Work

2.1   Big Data

Given the current popularity of big data sets, arriving at a concise definition of big data is difficult. The three dimensions used in deciding how big data is viewed are as follows: [2]

a. With respect to the technology dimension, the Big data technologies define a new generation of technologies and architectures, designed to economically extract intelligence from very large volumes of a wide variety of data, by enabling high-velocity capture, discovery, and/or analysis.
b. With respect to the Volume dimension, datasets whose size cross the limits of typical database software tools, to capture, store, manage, and analyze are defined as Big data sets.

c. With respect to the Architectural Dimension, Big data is a data set that limits the performance ability of traditional relational approaches for data analytics and hence requires a scaling approach for efficient analytics.

2.2 Big Data Analytics

Data analytics can be viewed as a framework, that is a combination of software techniques, and hardware technologies, that analyze raw data sets, to generate information [3]. Big data analytics heavily relies on the hypotheses that large data sets offer a higher form of intelligence and knowledge and requires larger amount of efforts which can be handled through integration of Technology with parallelization of algorithms [4].

Architecture for big data analytics should basically include a set of tools and mechanisms to load extract process and analyze dissimilar data while taking into account the massively parallel processing power to perform complex transformations and analysis. These types of architectures are generally scalable and easy to understand.

2.3 Big Data Analytics System Architecture

The architectural model for big data analytics can be designed with respect to the four stages namely: the data generation, data acquisition, data storage and data processing.

Data acquisition refers to the process of collecting data using specific data collection technologies. Data pre-processing is applied on the raw data sets, to remove meaningless data, and thereby provide efficient storage. Data processing and analysis is an integration of analytical methods or tools to identify, transform, and model data to extract valuable information.

Based on the above four stages, an architectural model for big data analytics, can be designed as a layered architecture as illustrated in Fig. 1.

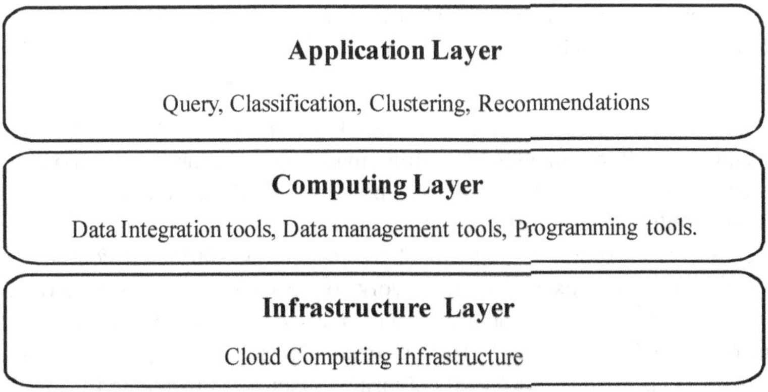

Application Layer

Query, Classification, Clustering, Recommendations

Computing Layer

Data Integration tools, Data management tools, Programming tools.

Infrastructure Layer

Cloud Computing Infrastructure

Fig. 1. A layered architecture for big data analytics

Big Data Analytics in the Domain of Scientific Applications: The ever increasing advances in hardware and software have largely affected the way scientific research is conducted leading to distributed experimentation and realistic simulations. The Scientific domain is full of Data intensive applications that deals with processing of increasingly large and complex data sets as also compute intensive applications requiring high performance distributed computing [5]. Data/compute-intensive applications provide a high degree of computational power to process very huge datasets.

Some of the challenges faced by these scientific applications include: [5]

- The need for new algorithms/updates in existing algorithms that can scale to big data analytics.
- The need for new metadata management technologies to handle complex and distributed data sources.
- The need for HPC platforms to provide uniform high-speed memory access to terabyte data structures.
- Specialized architectures to process and filter huge data streams coming from sensors and instruments.
- Distributed file systems which exhibits high performance, reliability and fault tolerance.
- New approaches to software agility, so that algorithms can execute on nodes where the data resides.

Thus there is a growing need for an architecture, that can be defined as an integration of tools and technologies to support data federation and collaboration for data analytics, data visualization and exploration of big data sets, for scientific data analytics.

Architectural frameworks for Scientific data Analytics

The Hardware Architecture: The scalability and performance requirements of a scientific data analytics application can be achieved through parallel/concurrent algorithms and frameworks. Earlier methods of dealing with massive data such as MPIs and Cluster computing were replaced by distributed processing on the cloud [6]. Various scientific cloud computing projects like Nebula, Cumulus, Magellan [9], open science cloud [10] are being undertaken in the recent years, the details of which are described in [7].

The Software Architecture: Clouds aid in efficiently using its cluster computing infrastructure for solving intensive scientific, mathematical problems by reducing them to software frameworks that can successfully exploit the cloud resources, like the Hadoop MapReduce framework [8].

MapReduce is a programming model for designing distributed computations on massive data sets and an execution framework for massive data processing on a bunch of commodity servers [11]. Scientific data analysis can be thought of as a Single Program Multiple Data (SPMD) algorithm or as algorithms that possess the composable property [11]. Most of the SPMD algorithms can be implemented using the MPI technique; but when the execution of SPMD is targeted in the cloud, where hardware failures are common, reliability is achieved through Map Reduce implementations such as Hadoop [12]. Hadoop uses a disseminated file system called the Hadoop Distributed File System (HDFS) to store data as well as the transitional results across all the data/computing nodes. Resiliency to node failures is handled by data replication on multiple nodes. The MapReduce computation tasks are scheduled based on the principle of data locality, thereby improving the overall I/O bandwidth.

3   Experimental Setup

This section describes about an experimental setup that supports Scientific data analytics in the domain of Atmospheric Physics, which we have implemented using the Hadoop and MapReduce framework.

3.1   Hardware Setup

With the objective of having a setup for experimenting with MapReduce based applications, the authors have set up a dynamically configurable Hadoop cluster, of 5 nodes using low cost computers, LAN and wired internet connection setup. The cluster is composed of one master and 4 slave nodes and can be configured to extend to more nodes. Each node has a configuration of 2 GB RAM. The HDFS, for the cluster, has a configured capacity of 250 GB.

3.2   Data Acquisition and Recording

The data sets used in experimentation is Live atmospheric data of Pune district consisting of various parameters, recorded every minute/every second. There were two types of data sets: the Weather data set and Air trajectory data set.

The Weather Data Set: Data is obtained through a sensor that gives a per minute or per second recording of the various parameters of Weather, throughout the day and is periodically flushed to the collection centre. A one year data set, spans across 800 files and consists of the set following parameters: the air temperature, humidity, air pressure, wind speed, wind direction, solar radiation, date & time. A sample of the recording of the weather attributes, done per second is also shown below in Fig. 2.

```
Date      ,Time  , WS ,WD ,Temp ,Humidity ,Pressure ,Rain Accu. ,Rain Duration. ,Radiation
4/1/2015 , 09:43:02 , 0.0 , 0.0 , 35.5 , 11.8 ,950.1 , 0.00 ,  0 , 0748
4/1/2015 , 09:43:03 , 0.0 , 0.0 , 35.5 , 11.8 , 950.1 , 0.00 , 0 , 0748
4/1/2015 , 09:43:04 , 0.0 , 0.0 , 35.5 , 11.8 , 950.1 , 0.00 , 0 , 0748
4/1/2015 , 09:43:05 , 0.0 , 0.0 , 35.5 , 11.8 , 950.1 , 0.00 , 0 , 0748
4/1/2015 , 09:43:06 , 0.0 , 0.0 , 35.5 , 11.8 , 950.1 , 0.00 , 0 , 0748
4/1/2015 , 09:43:07 , 0.0 , 0.0 , 35.5 , 11.8 , 950.1 , 0.00 , 0 , 0748
4/1/2015 , 09:43:08 , 0.0 , 0.0 , 35.5 , 11.8 , 950.1 , 0.00 , 0 , 0748
4/1/2015 , 09:43:09 , 0.0 , 0.0 , 35.5 , 11.8 , 950.1 , 0.00 , 0 , 0748
4/1/2015 , 09:43:10 , 0.0 , 0.0 , 35.5 , 11.8 , 950.1 , 0.00 , 0 , 0748
```

Fig. 2. Sample weather data recorded per second

Air Trajectory Data Set: Backward trajectory analysis is a commonly used tool to identify synoptic scale atmospheric transport patterns and/or determine the origin of air pollutants. The transport of atmospheric compounds and aerosols from a source to receptor sites can be easily understood with the help of back trajectories, as they trace the path of a polluted air parcel backward in time and space and have been used to track the history/pathways of air parcels arriving at a specific location [13]. The backward trajectories data was obtained from HYSPLIT model derived 5-day back-trajectories. The data was taken for last 5 years, 5 months each year. Further the authors have considered three height levels representing the topography of the observation site viz., 500 m (within Atmospheric Boundary Layer, ABL), 1500 m(above ABL) and 4000 m (in the lower free troposphere). The data is spread across 950 files approx. Figure 3 shows the sample Air trajectories data.

```
5          1
GDAS       9          3                    15          0          0
GDAS       9          3                    22          0          0
GDAS       9          3                    29          0          0
GDAS       9          4                    1           0          0
GDAS       9          4                    8           0          0
3 BACKWARD            OMEGA

9   4   1   12   18.53   73.817      500
9   4   1   12   18.53   73.817      1500
9   4   1   12   18.53   73.817      4000
6 PRESSURE THETA  AIR_TEMP MIXDEPTH  RELHUMID  TERR_MSLP Temp Mix_dep
              humidity       Terres_MSl
1             1 9 4 1 12 0 0 0 18.53 73.817 500 893 314.3 304.2 691.4 20.9         551.6
2             1 9 4 1 12 0 0 0 18.53 73.817 1500 797.4 315.4 295.6 691.8 28.3      552.6
3             1 9 4 1 12 0 0 0 18.53 73.817 4000 591 317.3 273 690.8 75.9          551.9
1             1 9 4 1 11 0 1 -1 18.563 73.831 358.4 908.7 314.2 305.7 1760 18.4    558
2             1 9 4 1 11 0 1 -1 18.578 73.934 1220.6 818.4 315.3 297.7 1881 24     617.8
3             1 9 4 1 11 0 1 -1 18.615 73.882 3820.5 601.4 316.6 273.7 1794.273    585
```

Fig. 3. Sample air trajectories data set

3.3 Data Pre-processing and Aggregation

Data cleaning to fill up or infer missing data, detect and remove outliers in data, were done using Map Reduce tasks, so as to facilitate cleaning as a distributed process. Irrelevant information in the data files, like data schemas/column headings were also removed during this process. After cleaning, mappers and reducers were applied on the cleaned data, to obtain Aggregations/Average/Max/Min of various attributes. Aggregation was also applied to obtain a reduction in data volume (aggregating per second data to per 15 min data).

3.4 Algorithms Developed

The authors have defined a set of classes for scientific algorithms based on their data processing capabilities (how many times they need to iterate over a data set). The algorithms are divided into different classes as follows [12]:

One pass Algorithms: These algorithms traverse through the data set only once, and can be adapted as a single execution of MapReduce model. These include zero level statistical analysis like finding the min/max/average, variance, and correlation analysis between a set of attributes. A summary of the algorithms developed as one pass algorithms is given in Table 1. These algorithms were tested on the Weather data set.

The Map phase iterates over the data set and generates partial output. The Reducer phase collects the partial outputs, and applies final aggregation/summarization, to generate the final value.

Table 1. One-pass algorithms implemented

	Algorithm types	Scope
1	Basic statistical functions	Max/Min/Average
2	Correlation analysis	Pearson's coefficient analysis
3	Matrix operations for big matrices	Addition, Multiplication, Transpose of a matrix, Row/Col Max/Min values, Max/Min with respect to entire matrix, Count of a value within a matrix

- Iterative/Multi pass Algorithms: These algorithms traverse through the data set multiple times, equivalent to the number of iterations. Algorithms such as K-Means, Fuzzy Cmeans etc. belong to this class. This paper focuses on the implementation of k-means algorithm, as a Map Reduce model, and further defines it as a workflow for the Atmospheric Physics domain.

3.5   MapReduce Implementation of K-Means Algorithm

K-means clustering assume a Euclidean space, and also assume the number of clusters, k, is known in advance. The authors have used Euclidean distance measure, to find the distance of a data point to the centroids. The outline of the K-means algorithm is as follows:

```
Initially choose k points that are likely to be in dif-
ferent clusters;
Make these points centroids of their clusters;
Do
Begin
For each remaining point p
 Do
 Begin
    Find the centroid that's closest to p;
    Add p to the cluster of that centroid;
 End;
Adjust the centroid of each cluster to account for all
points added to it;
End;
While (the distance between the old & new centroid > a
threshold value);
```

The implementation of the K-Means algorithm, as a Map Reduce Model, is given below in Fig. 4.

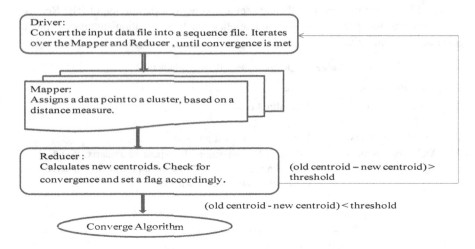

Fig. 4. KMeans as a MapReduce model

4   Case Study: Implementation and Customization of K-Means Clustering Algorithm for the Atmospheric Physics Domain

Clustering, a descriptive data mining algorithm is the process of examining a collection of "points," and grouping the points into "clusters" according to some distance measure.. There are many different methods for discovering clusters in data. Here we present a workflow of application of K-means clustering algorithm, to the Air Trajectories data set.

4.1   Air Trajectories Data Set from Atmospheric Physics

Our sample data file, consisting of information related to air trajectories (data spanning for 4 years (2008–2012), with data for 6 months/year) is as given in Fig. 3. The air trajectories data, with the destination location given as Pune, was obtained from the HySPLIT model. The first 11 records describe the data set. From 12th record, it's repetitive, where each data record has 18 attributes in it. The clustering is done based on the latitude and longitude attributes, in the data set.

4.2   The Workflow of Application of K-Means on Air Trajectory Data Set

Clustering analysis is been done on atmospheric trajectories, for studying the influence of atmospheric transport patterns on pollutant concentrations [14].The trajectories were separated into different clusters, to discover the primary pathways that favour advection of aerosol particles towards the city of Pune, that originated elsewhere.

A set of multiple Map Reduce jobs (6 MR jobs) were defined in order to customize KMeans, to include the pre processing, and post processing operations. The entire workflow is as shown in Fig. 5.

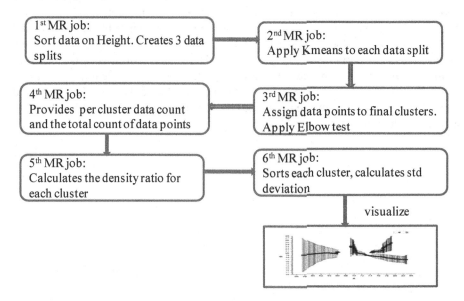

Fig. 5. Workflow for clustering air trajectories

Data pre-processing involved sorting the data set on the height attribute, thereby getting three splits of the data set, one of each height 1, 2, & 3 respectively. The pre processing was done as a Map Reduce job. The k-means algorithm was run on each height data set. In order to determine an optimal value of k, the number of clusters, the Elbow test was applied. The algorithm was run for different values of k: 2, 3, 4, 5, 6, 7 & 8. As per the values given in Table 2, the final number of clusters was set to 5, since the elbow bent/steep fall occurs at this point, as shown in Figs. 6, 7 and 8.

Table 2. Elbow test values

Height	No. of clusters: 2	No. of clusters: 3	No. of clusters: 4	No. of clusters: 5	No. of clusters: 6	No. of clusters: 7	No. of clusters: 8
Height 1	2.890	2.587	2.195	1.9064	0.4551	0.4301	0.357
Height 2	7.345	3.660	3.463	3.176	1.017	0.1221	0.190
Height 3	1.274	0.9353	0.862	0.846	0.3207	0.2984	0.2917

Once the data set is partitioned into clusters, the post processing for each cluster data involved sorting the data on the age attribute, averaging based on age attribute, and then deriving the standard deviation of latitude and longitude attributes. The final output is as shown in Fig. 9, is then plotted using the Origin software to show the different clusters, which is then superimposed onto the Map of India, as shown in Fig. 10. Once the clusters are superimposed onto the map, the domain expert can infer about the source location of the aerosol particles that are reaching Pune. From the Fig. 10, its clear that the clusters marked in purple (36%), greenish blue (20%) and red (5%) are touching the location Pune with lat long (18, 73.5). The source location for the cluster marked in purple is at lat long (12.40, 71.58) and is in the coastal region of Karnataka, in the Arabian Sea. The second cluster marked in greenish blue has its source location at lat long (24.87, 74.77) and is in the border between Rajasthan and Gujarat. The third cluster marked in red has its source location at lat long (24.50, 69.91) and is in Sahara desert region of Pakistan.

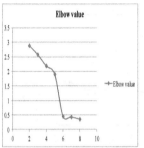

Fig. 6. Height 1 graph

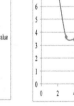

Fig. 7. Height 2 graph

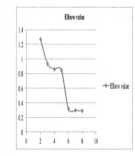

Fig. 8. Height 3 graph

Centroid		age	height	Latitude	Longitude	StdDev-Lat	StdDev-Long
20.05211926	75.72760659	1	1	18.5645142	73.75628835	0.054916257	0.11906467
20.05211926	75.72760659	10	1	18.69103267	73.68665767	0.539417516	0.950732188
20.05211926	75.72760659	100	1	21.65354094	79.00848246	3.924463396	4.693987726
20.05211926	75.72760659	101	1	21.66052059	79.07371471	3.91161655	4.709275752
20.05211926	75.72760659	102	1	21.6954	79.10022647	3.910472028	4.744656808
20.05211926	75.72760659	103	1	21.73288791	79.15704425	3.921842258	4.758435701
20.05211926	75.72760659	104	1	21.77208605	79.24094362	3.940764904	4.751606086
20.05211926	75.72760659	105	1	21.79022255	79.27288427	3.983490536	4.776932421

Fig. 9. Final output of KMeans workflow

The domain experts from the field of Atmospheric physics were also provided with the average values of the 6 output variables (pressure, theta, relative humidity, air pressure, terrestrial, and mix depth) as per the air trajectories data set (Fig. 3), within each cluster, for a detailed domain based interpretation and inference of the clusters.

The authors are working in close association with the domain experts from the Atmospheric physics to provide data pre processing and analytics as per their requirement.

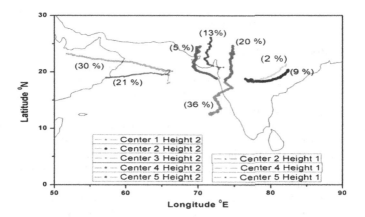

Fig. 10. Cluster plot superimposed on the map of India

5 Conclusion and Future Directions

Scientific applications such as Atmospheric physics generate big data sets, and need a big data analytics setup, for its data pre processing and data analytics. In this paper, an experimental setup for big data analytics, using Hadoop and Map Reduce framework has been presented. This paper clearly indicates that a low cost experimental setup, can be used for data analytics needs of a realistic scientific application, thus eliminating the need for any specialized, high cost computing environments requiring dedicated and high speed networks.

A similar experimental setup can be designed to support the second approach, where normal tools will be used for initial analytics, while the big data setup will be used for post processing of these analytical results, collected over a larger time period. The kmeans algorithm presented here is limited to use of Euclidean distance and can be further extended to support variations in proximity measure.

Acknowledgments. The experimental data sets for this work are obtained from the Atmospheric Physics research lab, Nowrosjee Wadia College, Pune. The authors would like to thank Dr. Gajanan Aher and his team for their enthusiastic support and guidance.

References

1. Cuzzocrea, A., Song, I.-Y., Davis, K.C.: Analytics over large-scale multidimensional data: the big data revolution!. In: Proceedings of the ACM 14th International Workshop on Data Warehousing and OLAP, pp. 101–104. ACM (2011)
2. Hu, H., Wen, Y., Chua, T.-S., Li, X.: Toward scalable systems for big data analytics: a technology tutorial. IEEE Access **2**, 652–687 (2014)
3. Chen, H., Chiang, R.H.L., Storey, V.C.: Business intelligence and analytics: from big data to big impact. MIS Q. **36**(4), 1165–1188 (2012)
4. Boyd, D., Crawford, K.: Critical questions for big data: provocations for a cultural, technological, and scholarly phenomenon. Inf. Commun. Soc. **15**(5), 662–679 (2012)
5. Gorton, I., Greenfield, P., Szalay, A., Williams, R.: Data-intensive computing in the 21st century. Computer **41**(4), 30–32 (2008)
6. Srirama, S.N., Jakovits, P., Vainikko, E.: Adapting scientific computing problems to clouds using MapReduce. Future Gener. Comput. Syst. **28**(1), 184–192 (2012)
7. Tudoran, R., Costan, A., Antoniu, G., Bougé, L.: A performance evaluation of azure and nimbus clouds for scientific applications. In: Proceedings of the 2nd International Workshop on Cloud Computing Platforms, p. 4. ACM (2012)
8. Wang, L., Tao, J., Kunze, M., Castellanos, A.C., Kramer, D., Karl, W.: Scientific cloud computing: early definition and experience. In: HPCC, vol. 8, pp. 825–830 (2008)
9. Ramakrishnan, L., Zbiegel, P.T., Campbell, S., Bradshaw, R., Canon, R.S., Coghlan, S., Sakrejda, I., Desai, N., Declerck, T., Liu, A.: Magellan: experiences from a science cloud. In: Proceedings of the 2nd International Workshop on Scientific Cloud Computing, pp. 49–58. ACM (2011)
10. Grossman, R.L., Gu, Y., Mambretti, J., Sabala, M., Szalay, A., White, K.: An overview of the open science data cloud. In: Proceedings of the 19th ACM International Symposium on High Performance Distributed Computing, pp. 377–384. ACM (2010)
11. Ekanayake, J., Pallickara, S., Fox, G.: Mapreduce for data intensive scientific analyses. In: IEEE Fourth International Conference on eScience, eScience 2008, pp. 277–284. IEEE (2008)
12. Dean, J., Ghemawat, S.: MapReduce: a flexible data processing tool. Commun. ACM **53**(1), 72–77 (2010)
13. Pawar, G.V., Devara, P.C.S., Aher, G.R.: Identification of aerosol types over an urban site based on air-mass trajectory classification. Atmos. Res. **164**, 142–155 (2015)
14. Jorba, O., Pérez, C., Rocadenbosch, F., Baldasano, J.: Cluster analysis of 4-day back trajectories arriving in the Barcelona area, Spain, from 1997 to 2002. J. Appl. Meteorol. **43**(6), 887–901 (2004)

Abstracting Communication Methodology in IoT Sensors to Eliminate Redundancy and Cycles

Sharad Saxena[✉]

Computer Science and Engineering Department, Thapar University, Patiala
147004, Punjab, India
sharad.saxena@thapar.edu

Abstract. Internet of Things is a huge collection of sensors or actuators that are interconnected either through fixed or dynamic networks. Fixed networks has nearly fixed location of sensors and are distantly placed, while dynamic networks are specialized as, inclusion of, the movement of the sensor objects. Information, when requested in these networks follows multi-path and observe cycles when reaching to the Requester Node (RN). This causes redundancy, slow networks and flooding of garbage packets in the networks. Therefore, in this article a methodology has been proposed for information requisition in IOT with the objective to eliminate cycle and redundancy.

Keywords: IoT · Data redundancy · Sensor objects · Information communication

1 Introduction

Internet of Things (IOT) is most hyped concept and growing very high in IT era. It has very widely projected the conception of a global platform of interconnected physical devices or objects sensors, actuators with a vision of anything, anytime and at anyplace availability of services [1]. IOT can also be taken as extended version of internet that permits conversation between human-things, things-things and human-human [2]. IOT featured a world where anything can be conneted either through wire or wireless in an intelligent way that has never been done before and with no additional cost of IP addressing and naming. These networks turns out the huge volume of data and distributed analysis in computers. The objects can sense and communicate, hence becomes a powerfull tool for understanding complexity. The important aspect is that these information systems are now under deployment and can work without the intervention of human being. The IOT referes to rigrous hard coding and interconnection of every day objects to make them every machine-understandable and identifiable on Internet [3–8]. Most of the contents on IOT are made possible thorough IP addressing and coded RFID tags, that are attached to an EPC (Electronic Product Code) network [9].

© Springer Nature Singapore Pte Ltd. 2017
M. Singh et al. (Eds.): ICACDS 2016, CCIS 721, pp. 541–549, 2017.
DOI: 10.1007/978-981-10-5427-3_55

2   IoT Graphical View and Problem Statement

With the growth of IoT, interconnected devices called sensors in internet generates large amount of information required for some special purposes. The information is flooded in to the network and is consumed by some other sensor(s). Information sharing in IoT needs to be properly indexed and must be processed in an effective manner. The network here comprise of fixed sensors and the mobile sensors. Every fixed sensor in the network has fixed multiple paths to other fixed sensors while moving sensors have no fixed paths. The information addressing in IoT thus can be classified in to four categories (1) fixed to fixed sensor (2) fixed to mobile sensor (3) mobile to fixed sensor and, (4) mobile to mobile sensor. The sensor that demands for some information is known as Requester Node (RN) and the node responding to the sensor is known as Correspondent Node (CN). The CN sends required information to all possible paths to reach *RN* and causing flooding of information into the network. Further, same information reaches to *RN* from multiple paths and some of the packets moves in cycle indefinitely.

The interconnection of sensors (*see* Fig. 1) in IoT can be considered as an interconnected graph (*see* Fig. 2) of sensor nodes having either fixed or dynamic objects (sensors). Here each sensor maintains two types of buffers: one for fixed sensors connected as spanning tree and buffer for mobile sensors that are in the range.

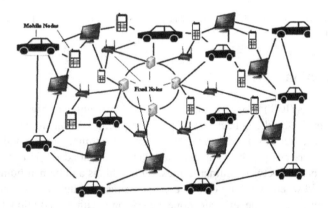

Fig. 1. IoT network sample view

3   Information Communication in IoT Graph

An IoT Graph *IOT(O, E)* is taken as ordered graph with *O* objects and *E* number of paths. Here, *O* is non empty and finite set of fixed (O_f) and moving (O_m) objects, and *E* is a set of unordered pairs of fixed (E_f) and dynamic (E_d) paths such that:

$$O = O_f \cup O_m \ and \ E = E_f \cup E_d \tag{1}$$

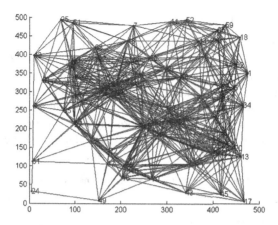

Fig. 2. IoT view as connected graph with 75 fixed sensors (sample)

Here, $O_f = \{f_1, f_2, f_3, \ldots, f_n\}$ and $O_m = \{m_1, m_2, m_3, \ldots, m_n\}$ are fixed sets of fixed and mobile objects, and $E_f = \{fe_1, fe_2, fe_3, \ldots, fe_n\}$, $E_d = \{de_1, de_2, de_3, \ldots, de_n\}$ are the fixed sets of fixed and mobile paths of objects respectively. The algorithm for creation of spanning tree for each fixed node can be stated as in Algorithm 1. The communication paradigm under four scenarios (1) fixed to fixed sensor (2) fixed to mobile sensor (3) mobile to fixed sensor and, (4) mobile to mobile sensor is discussed below.

Algorithm 1. Spanning Tree Creation for the Graph
1. Main(){
2. Requester_Node (RN) = f_m;
3. Other_Nodes = { f_1, f_2, f_3, ...,f_n};
4. Buffered_Sp_Tree {RN} = Sp_Tree (f_m);
//spanning tree stored at RN
5. }
6. Function Sp_Tree (f_m)
7. { Spanning tree = {};
8.   For each node m in Other_Nodes
9.   { Find link or edge fe_i = (f_m, m) // i=1, 2, 3, ..., n
// f_m ∈ Requester_Node
// m ∈ Other_Node
10.   If fe_i != NULL then
Spanning_tree=Spanning_tree ∪ {fe_i};
11. Requester_Node = Requester_Node ∪ {m};
12. Other_Node = Other_Node − {m};
13. }}

3.1   Fixed to Fixed Sensor (F-to-F)

Since fixed sensor are static in position the path from a fix sensor (*RN*) to any other fix sensor (*CN*) is known and is used to create a shortest path tree from *RN* to *CN*. Initially, when a fix sensor joins the network, it creates a shortest path table and store it in its' local buffer. The known and fix path enable avoiding of redundancy of packet and any cycle in the graph. The information travels from *CN* to *RN* in fixed shortest path route. The device are advised to have regular check for any change in the path. The algorithm for this communication is stated in Algorithm 2. The different shortest path tree with different *RN*s (samples) are depicted in Fig. 3(a), (b), (c) and (d).

Algorithm 2. Fixed to Fixed Sensor Communication
---
1. Find_Fix_Loc (CN)
2. {
3.   Path_Found = {};
4.   For each node N in Buffered_Sp_tree{}
5.   { if N = CN then
6.   Path_Found = Path from RN to CN;
7.   Break;
8. }
9. Return Path_Found;   }

3.2   Fixed to Mobile Sensor (F-to-M)

In this type of communication initially the fixed sensor (*RN*) sends a *Find_Mob_Loc (CN)* request to sensors on its fixed shortest path. The interconnected intermediate node checks for the availability of the mobile *CN* in their buffer for stored path of fixed sensors and for mobile sensors. Any of the sensor having location of *CN* works as the path to the mobile sensor (*see* Fig. 4). The communication algorithm is stated in Algorithm 3.

Algorithm 3. Fixed to Mobile Sensor Communication
---
1. Path_Found = {};
2. Find_Mob_Loc (CN)
3. {
4.   For each node N in Buffered_Sp_tree{}
5.   { Find CN in Wireless Buffer of N
6.   if FOUND then
7.   Path_Found = Path from RN to CN (de_i)
8.   //$i = 1, 2, 3, ... ,n$
9.   }
10.   Return Path_Found }

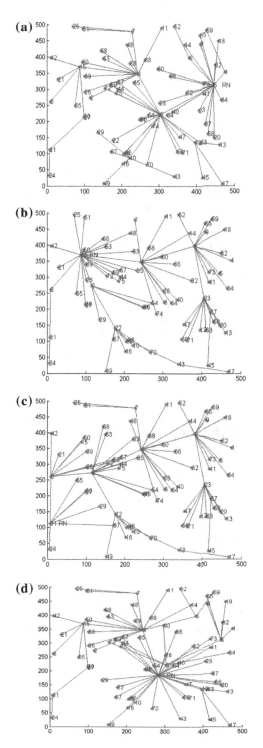

Fig. 3. (a) Spanning tree at RN = 5, (b) Spanning tree at RN = 15, (c) Spanning tree at RN = 31, (d) Spanning tree at RN = 74

Fig. 4. Fixed to mobile sensor communication

3.3   Mobile to Fixed Sensor (M-to-F)

Any mobile sensor send the request of communication to the nearby fixed sensor in range. The fixed sensor broadcast the information to all the nodes connected to it over to its spanning tree path. Hence information reaches to *CN* without creating a cycle or redundancy (*see* Fig. 5.). The communication algorithm is stated in Algorithm 4.

Algorithm 4. Mobile to Fixed Sensor Communication
1. Path_Found = {};
2. Find_Fix_Sensor_Loc (RN)
3. {
4.   Sensor_In_Range (s$_i$) = {s$_1$, s$_2$, s$_3$ ... s$_n$}; // i=1, 2, 3, .. n
5.   Find distance (*de$_i$*) of RN ⩝ s$_i$;
6.   Path_Found = MIN (*de$_i$* to RN) + Buffered_Sp_tree {} ;
7. Return Path_Found; }

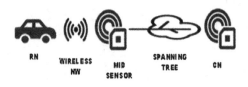

Fig. 5. Mobile to fixed sensor

3.4   Mobile to Mobile Sensor (M-to-M)

A mobile *RN* initially send communication request to the nearest fixed sensor in range. The fixed sensor broadcast the same information to all connected fixed nodes. Any of the node having information about mobile *CN* respond back to *RN*. Hence a path from mobile device to fix node and to mbile CN is created without redundancy and cycle (see Fig. 6). The communication algorithm is stated in Algorithm 5.

Algorithm 5. Mobile to Mobile Communication

1. Path_Found = {};
2. Find_Mob_to_Mob_Loc (RN)
3. {
4.   Sensor_In_Range (s$_i$) = {s$_1$, s$_2$, s$_3$ ... s$_n$}; // i=1, 2, 3, .. n
5.   Find Distance (de$_i$) of RN ⤚ s$_i$;
6.   Path_Found = MIN (de$_i$ to RN);
7. }
8.   Find_Fix_Loc (RN);
9.   Find_Mob_Loc (RN);
10.   Return Path_Found;
11. }

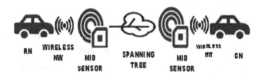

Fig. 6. Mobile to mobile sensor

4   Simulation and Results

For result analysis and comparison the energy consumption in sensor nodes have been compared with IoT graph and the spanning tree created at different RN (5, 15, 31, 74) for 75 nodes. The DSR protocol has been used for routing [10]. The simulation parameters and results are shown in Table 1 and Fig. 7 respectively.

Table 1. Simulation parameters

Paramters	Values
Simulator used	NS2
Sensor nodes	75
Requester nodes	5, 15, 31, 74
Simulation time	100 ms
Simulation area	500 × 500 m

From Fig. 7. It is evident that the energy consumption in IoT graph is more as compared to other methods of data communication, if a data packet is communicated from RN (5, 15, 31 or 74) to a selected destination node using multi-hop. Further the energy consumption order is F-to-F, F-to-M, M-to-F and M-to-M from lowest energy to the highest level. This shows that the proposed method for IoT communication is more energy efficient than the original IoT graph.

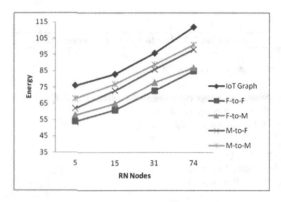

Fig. 7. Energy consumption in IoT graph and F-to-F, F-to-M, M-to-F, M-to-M communication

5 Discussion and Summary

Millions of interconnected devices in IOT communicate in terms of sensing, detecting and listening from the real world through the medium, called the Internet. The information is shared and used for several purposes by human and devices. With the development of cheap technologies and smartphones, an always-available, mobile and nearly free connectivity is possible. This causes several business firms, government agencies, companies and individual to search and use any kind of information in IOT. Information demanded by any entity is normally broadcasted on the internet and any device having replied for the information is sent back to the requesting entity. The process involves a large number of packet generation and communication on the internet either through wire or wireless. Thus, millions of packets travels through the internet and only some of them are matters of relevance and other are causing congestion, flooding and duplicacy on the internet. Therefore, in this article a new approach has been proposed for information communication in IOT. Here, the network is divided in two major concerns, namely fix and mobile. The fixed network is fixed network of static devices/sensors and is not changing while mobile network provides mobility to the sensors on the network. Every fixed sensor when connected to the networks stores a spanning tree path to all nearly connected sensors and always uses that fixed path for communication, while every mobile sensor first look for nearly available fixed sensor and uses their stored fix path for sending its information on to the network. The approach therefore helps in eliminating cycles and redundancy in the interconnected network of IOT.

References

1. Kosmatos, E.A., Tselikas, N.D., Boucouvalas, A.C.: Integrating RFIDs and smart objects into a unified internet of things architecture. Adv. Internet Things: Sci. Res. **1**, 5–12 (2011)

2. Aggarwal, R., Lal Das, M.: RFID security in the context of "Internet of Things". In: First International Conference on Security of Internet of Things, Kerala, 17–19 August, pp 51–56 (2012)
3. Biddlecombe, E., "Internet of Things". UN Predicts, Retrieved July 6 (2009)
4. Butler, D.: Computing: everything, everywhere. Nature **440**, 402–405 (2014)
5. Dodson, S.: The net shapes up to get physical. Guardian (2008)
6. Gershenfeld, N., Krikorian, R., Cohen, D.: The internet of things. Sci. Am. **291**, 76–81 (2014)
7. Lombreglia, R.: The Internet of Things, Boston Globe (2010)
8. Reinhardt, A.: A Machine-to-Machine Internet of Things (2004)
9. Graham, M., Haarstad, H.: Transparency and development: ethical consumption through web 2.0 and the internet of things. **7**(1), 1–18 (2011). Spring
10. Haraty, R.A., Kdouh, W.: SDDSR: sequence driven dynamic source routing for ad hoc networks. In: Proceeding of World Automation Congress, pp. 1–8 (2006)

Analysis of Application Layer Protocols in Internet of Things

S. Sasirekha[1]([✉]), S. Swamynathan[2], S. Chandini[1], and K. Keerthana[1]

[1] Department of Information Technology, SSN College of Engineering,
Chennai, India
sasirekhas@ssn.edu.in
[2] Department of Information Science and Technology, Anna University,
Chennai, India
swamyns@annauniv.edu

Abstract. In the vision of Internet of Things (IoT), everyday objects such as domestic appliances, actuators and embedded systems of any kind soon will be connected with each other using Internet. Especially, with the emerging trends and devices evolving in this technology, choosing an optimized communication protocol for a particular application scenario is highly essential. Hence, in this work an analysis of existing communication protocols namely IETF Constrained Application Protocol (CoAP), IBM Message Queuing Telemetry Transport (MQTT) and W3C HyperText Transfer Protocol (HTTP) was carried out to understand their significance and classify them based on the application scenario. To perform a real-time analysis of these protocols, a test environment for inventory management system is designed. It involves sensors and communication boards, which generates data about the availability status of the every product. Various test cases were executed on all the three protocols by varying the request types in the process of retrieving the sensor data. To justify the performance of each protocol, metrics such as response time, latency and throughput are determined and analyzed. Finally, using the obtained results the protocols were classified and justified that each protocol works optimized for particular request type.

Keywords: Internet of Things · Protocol metrics · Application layer protocols

1 Introduction

In the current state-of-art [1], Internet of Things (IoT) is a paradigm that envisions the world where everything is connected and can be remotely monitored and controlled [6]. The primary enabling factor of this promising paradigm is the integration of several technologies and communications solutions [2]. From forests to factories, it improves the efficiency and reduces costs if relevant data is collected and analyzed. However, to connect everything, devices that can run on batteries for years are needed, and this, in turn, requires optimized

© Springer Nature Singapore Pte Ltd. 2017
M. Singh et al. (Eds.): ICACDS 2016, CCIS 721, pp. 550–561, 2017.
DOI: 10.1007/978-981-10-5427-3_56

communication protocol to communicate efficiently as well. In the recent days, IoT application layer protocols are gaining popularity in a wide range of scenarios where low-cost, low-power or resource constrained devices are present. It serves as an enabling factor for the IoT devices to provide connectivity for everyone and everything. It is also evident from [8] that this application layer protocol will be considered for the future evaluation of the Internet that realizes machine-to-machine (M2M) learning. Hence in this work, an analysis of existing communication protocols namely IETF Constrained Application Protocol (CoAP) [9], IBM Message Queuing Telemetry Transport (MQTT) [12] and W3C HyperText Transfer Protocol (HTTP) [4] was carried out to understand their significance and classify them based on the application scenario. To perform this analysis, a generic architecture which serves as the platform for testing all the three protocols is proposed. Further, various test cases were also performed in analyzing its distinguishing features and possible future applications classifying based on the request type. The most diffused protocols are MQTT and the CoAP, and both are designed to reduce overhead and perform device friendly. HTTP is a stateless request/response protocol that operates by exchanging messages across a reliable Transmission Control Protocol/Internet Protocol (TCP/IP) connection and is widely used in IoT communication. MQTT is a publish/subscribe messaging protocol built on top of the Transmission Control Protocol and designed to be lightweight. MQTT has a client/server model, where every sensor is a client and connects to a server, known as a broker, over TCP. MQTT is message oriented whereas CoAP is a request/response protocol which loosely follows the Hypertext Transfer Protocol (HTTP), but over the User Datagram Protocol (UDP) instead of TCP. Like HTTP, CoAP is being standardized within the Internet Engineering Task Force (IETF). These protocols are being used as communication component in various applications. In this work, to carry out a real-time analysis, a test environment for Inventory Management was designed. Its purpose is to validate against the stock-out conditions. Various tests are done in this environment to identify a less overhead and the most optimized protocol helps to meet out the specified constraint.

Extending the analysis, in this work a comparative study of the protocols CoAP, MQTT and HTTP was also performed for the application Inventory Management system with a load sensor and communication boards. The load sensor checks for the weight (say for example in kilogram) of the product to which it is attached. Further, based the user defined threshold it provides the data about the availability of the product upon request. The data communication is monitored using a network analyzer like Wireshark, and the protocols are compared using various critical protocol metrics such as response time, network traffic and throughput. Upon comparison of metrics of application layer protocols, the protocol with optimized metrics is suggested. The proposed work involves sensor data collection, study and determination of protocol metrics and comparative analysis of the metrics.

In the remainder of the paper, Sect. 2 briefs about some of the related works carried out. In Sect. 3, a generic architecture for performing protocol analysis is illustrated. Then in Sect. 4, the implementation steps are discussed and in

Sect. 5, the test results obtained, and their inferences are elaborated. In Sect. 6, comparison of the IoT application protocols based on various request types is done. Finally, Sect. 7 concludes.

2 Background Study

Application layer protocols play a significant role in IoT communication, and protocol metrics are the important factor that determines the performance of the protocol for any real-time application. Therefore, a survey was done to justify the primary objective of this work in determining the optimized application layer protocol for handling efficient communication among the IoT devices based on the various protocol metrics.

In [5], the author predicts that by 2020, tens of billions of things will be deployed worldwide, collecting a wealth of diverse data. It also provides a picture of the main technological components needed to enable the interconnection of things to allow the interconnection of things. It mainly highlights that the communication protocols are the major influencing factor for handling this communication. Likewise, Singh in [13] proposes a Device to Device Communication (D2D) in IoT are envisaged through various protocols such as Constrained Access Protocol (CoAP), Message Queue Telemetry Transport (MQTT) and MQTT-SN. One of the major concerns in the deployment of IoT is to ensure the security of devices and D2D communications. According to Zhou in [15], IoT has experienced a booming development these years. Most of the current IoT applications are built in a highly vertical way, consisting of proprietary protocols and devices. This paper presents a unified design of message-centric architecture based on MQTT for IoT application and management, and target on some practical problems and optimization for an actual system.

Karagiannis in [7] discusses that the computational overhead and application size metrics are the major factors which influence the performance of the application layer protocol. In this paper, a comparative study for other protocol metrics like response time, network traffic, and throughput which are the critical metrics for determining protocol performance are also discussed. The author has also defined a common IoT architecture. It is represented by describing various parts where application layer protocols are needed to handle communication and suggests that IETF CoAP as the most lightweight and optimized protocol since it works over UDP layer. Similarly, Farokhmanesh in [3], the network protocols namely HTTP, MQTT and CoAP are compared and studied using hello-world instance data exchange using zolertia z1 [14] motes and a border RPL router. The paper suggested that CoAP is the optimized protocol among the three because it can enhance throughput and save more energy. Since these protocols were analyzed only based one metrics, in this proposed work, the same protocols were compared for few more metric including the throughput namely response time, traffic and latency to prove its efficiency. Here, cost efficient Arduino and Raspberry Pi are used for analysis which is used by Li in [11] and for a simple testing scenario, load sensor data is used which can also be helpful in maintaining the stock out conditions.

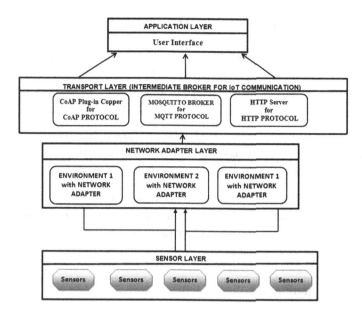

Fig. 1. A generic architecture for protocol analysis.

Other related works include the work of Rohokale in [10], who proposes that IoT enables the possibility of information discovery about a tagged object or a tagged person by browsing through internet addresses or database entry that corresponds to a particular active RFID with sensing capability. Hence, from the background study, it is inferred that CoAP, MQTT, and HTTP are the existing application layer protocols. Also, the protocol metrics such communication overhead and energy consumption are compared and analyzed using application layer protocols by various authors. The above metrics used for comparison can be used to estimate performance but are not enough for suggesting the optimized protocol. Some of the critical metrics that are required to identify most optimized protocols are response-time, network traffic and throughput which are analyzed and compared in this work for a real-time Inventory Management application scenario. In addition to the analysis based on the protocol metrics, also a comparative analysis of application layer protocols is done based on the architecture and security layer upon which the protocol works, but there haven't been any implementation work regarding the working of protocols and IoT. In this work, the implementation of the application layer protocols such as HTTP, MQTT, and CoAP are included, and the proposed testbed solution have been analyzed using various protocol metrics like response time, throughput, traffic which are all the key metrics which decides the performance of a protocol using Wireshark Network Analyzer.

3   Generic Architecture for Protocol Analysis

The generic architecture for the protocol analysis organized and categorized into four different layers as shown in Fig. 1. The four layer includes, the sensor layer, data collection layer, transport layer and application layer. The first layer of the design involves deploying the sensor nodes and collecting the data from the sensor nodes. The second layer is responsible for collecting those data with the help of network adapters. Next, the data obtained by network adapters are then transferred to the third layer which is the transport layer. In this layer, it consists of the intermediate brokers which hold standard methods associated with request/response model respectively to deliver the data to the end user. The intermediate brokers after verifying the client request send the response to the user interface which the client can view and retrieve. The request to the application data is sent from the application layer, which is the fourth layer of the proposed architecture design.

4   Implementation

The test environment was implemented for an inventory management scenario. The design begins with deploying load sensors and communication boards for collecting the data in the data collection layer. The load sensor data helps in checking the availability of the product in the inventory. The sensors were kept attached to each product for determining the quantity (in terms of weight (kg)) of the product. An user-defined threshold is also defined to notify the inventory manager about the stock out condition. As the implementation was tested only on a prototype model, so a 5 kg Micro-Load Cell is deployed to collect the data collection as shown in Fig. 2. The sensor data is processed using the communication boards Arduino (2 boards) for HTTP and MQTT request type and Raspberry Pi B+ for CoAP based request type.

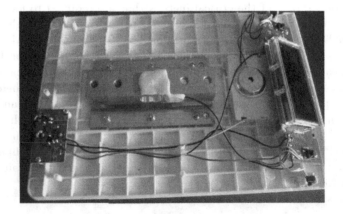

Fig. 2. Implementation sensor with arduino and load sensor.

These boards are stacked with network adapters the data gets transferred. Here, the network adapter Arduino Ethernet shield in case of protocols like HTTP and MQTT. Since, for processing the data using CoAP protocol, use of an adapter is optional, a direct connection to the transport layer is made using CoAP plug-in. The Ethernet Shield and Raspberry Pi B+ nodes sends the data to the intermediate interface between the Application layer or User Interface (UI) and the network nodes. The intermediate interface includes Mosquitto broker in case of MQTT message processing, Copper in the case of CoAP messages and HTTP server (80) in the case of HTTP request/response messages for the application layer protocols MQTT, CoAP, and HTTP respectively. The interface communicates with UI, which shows the processed results using which performance analysis is performed using network analyzer Wireshark, which helps in analyzing the network data based on various parameters namely throughput, response time and traffic. The step by step procedure carried out for analysis is depicted in Fig. 3.

Next, for processing application layer protocol HTTP request/response messages, an EthernetClient object is created using the Ethernet.h library files of Arduino and the connection request are sent from the client to the sender. On successful establishment of the connection, the sensor value is read from the load sensor node which acts the sender. After collecting the sensor data, the client sends the collected data to the HTTP server which is then displayed in UI. If the connection is not available or if the connection fails, the client, i.e., the Arduino Ethernet shield will keep on sending the request message to the load sensor, and polling takes place.

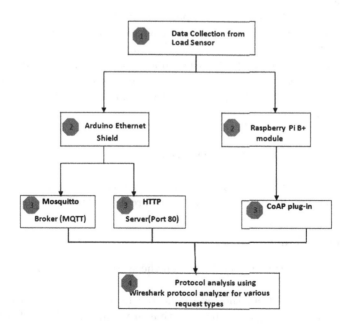

Fig. 3. Step-by-step procedure of analysis.

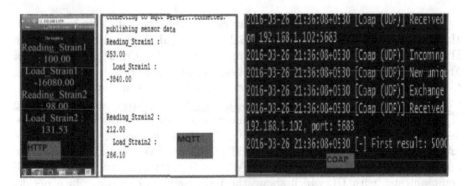

Fig. 4. Screenshot of output generated from HTTP, MQTT and COAP.

In the case of MQTT protocol, a Publish -Subscribe object is created and using the object the connection request was sent to the Mosquitto broker. The mosquito broker sends the request message to the sender, and if the sender is responding to the request using acknowledgment, the connection gets established, and the sensor value was collected and then displayed in the serial monitor that acts the user interface, and the connection remains intact. If the connection fails, then the Mosquitto broker stores the packets sent and received until connection failure by setting the KEEPALIVE flag for future connection requests. The Load Sensor value read using HTTP Request/Response Method, MQTT Publish/Subscribe method and using CoAP Get/Post method is generated as shown in the Fig. 4.

In the case of CoAP protocol, Copper acts as an interface between the client and the sender. The Copper is a plug-in which consists of the native methods namely GET, PUT, DELETE, POST, etc., used by CoAP for sending and processing messages obtained from the sender (sensor). The user interface used for monitoring the IoT communication is Cygwin, which is a Linux terminal and txthings (a CoAP library) for processing CoAP messages is installed and used for the request/response transfer.

5   Analysis Using Protocol Metrics

The analysis was carried out for the metrics such as response time, throughput and network traffic. Its results and inference are elaborated as follows.

5.1   Response Time

Response time is the time interval between the start of the conversation and the first response received.

Figure 5 is plotted from the data collected by the network analyzer Wireshark. The Wireshark captures the data that are being transferred between the

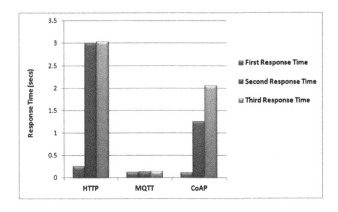

Fig. 5. Response time analysis of the protocols.

sender and the receiver. From Fig. 5, it clearly shows that HTTP has the highest response time because as soon as the connection fails, the client keeps on polling until successful connection establishment. The MQTT protocol has the least response time because, in MQTT, the broker remembers the connection request by setting the KEEPALIVE flag. The CoAP protocol has an optimized response time and is the most suitable for applications which has to deliver fast message, but it is not reliable since it works on the UDP layer rather than TCP which used by both HTTP and MQTT protocols.

Response time can be calculated for each protocol as follows:

- For HTTP
  http.request.method == "GET" || http.response.code = 200
- For MQTT
  Add a filter called MQTT and then monitor timedelx
- For CoAP
  Add a filter called UDP and then monitor timedelx

5.2 Throughput

Throughput is the number of packets passing per unit time through the network. The throughput is calculated using Wireshark data by using the formula (1).

$$Throughput = \frac{Size\ of\ the\ data\ (in\ bits)}{Transmission\ time\ (in\ sec)} \tag{1}$$

From the Fig. 6, it is clearly visible that CoAP has the highest throughput since it works on the UDP layer and there is no need for any connection establishment like TCP which takes more time. HTTP has the least throughput.

5.3 Network Traffic

Traffic or Network traffic or data traffic is the amount of data moving across the network at a given point of time. CoAP and MQTT have a better traffic rate

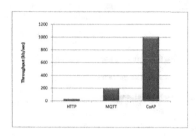

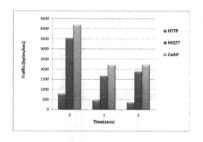

Fig. 6. Throughput analysis of the protocols.

Fig. 7. Network traffic analysis of the protocols.

as understood from the graph Fig. 7. Since CoAP works on UDP and MQTT has a facility of connection re-establishment, both has better rates compared to HTTP.

In addition to the above analysis done based on the protocol metrics, also a comparative analysis of application layer protocols is done based on the architecture and security layer which is summarized in the Table 1.

Table 1. Features of application layer protocols

Layer\ protocols	HTTP	MQTT	CoAP
Network layer	Works on TCP layer	Works on TCP layer	Works on UDP layer
Security layer	No security for the data shared	Built with SSL/TLS security mechanism and ensures data delivery	Built with SSL security but delivery is not assured since it works on UDP layer possibility of data loss is there
Transport layer	If the server does not responds the client keeps on polling until connection is established	Has retained messages mechanism and holds the connection for a longer time	Provides offline messaging facility
Application layer	Has no QoS messaging i.e. quality of service	Provided with QoS messaging mechanism	Provided with QoS messaging mechanism

Table 1 shows the differences and also summarizes features of various application layer protocols. From Table 1, it is seen that the HTTP and MQTT work with better reliability of message transfer on TCP layer and CoAP works on UDP layer which isn't more reliable since packet loss in UDP layer is higher. Moreover, MQTT and CoAP have security mechanism whereas HTTP lacks security. MQTT and CoAP also support offline messaging whereas HTTP doesn't support offline messaging and data transfer begins as a new connection.

6   Comparison Based on Various Request Types

The comparison of these application layer protocols helps to identify the most optimized protocol that can be used for the IoT communication rather than using a protocol which is less efficient for a given real-time application.

Table 2. Comparison of protocols based on application and type of request

Application	Request type	Suitable protocol(s)
Remote monitoring, weather monitoring, natural disaster,	Asynchronous	HTTP
Asset tracking, drug tracking	Synchronous	CoAP, MQTT (if single sensor node)
Smart homes, predictive maintenance, firmware updates	Event-based	MQTT
Traffic control, location and tracking	Hybrid	HTTP, COAP

The comparison was done for the various request types and the applications that classifies under their category. The request types such synchronous, asynchronous, event based and hybrid approach were analyzed. From the inferred results and Table 2, it can be seen that for the synchronous type of requests and large-scale management systems CoAP and MQTT protocol are used. For asynchronous response, HTTP is best suitable where it allows caching and delays. For event-based applications like Facebook where the data must keep on be updated for which protocol like MQTT is the most appropriate.

7   Conclusions

The analysis results obtained clearly shows that CoAP is the most optimized application layer protocol which can be used for an IoT application like Inventory Management System since it provides better throughput with higher traffic and optimized response time. MQTT are suitable for small scale applications which involves a single node since it has three-way handshake mechanism and takes more time for data transfer whereas in CoAP more than one node can be connected and the data transfer is quite higher since works in a UDP layer, and there is no need for any connection establishment. HTTP are appropriate when the application involves sensitive data which cannot be afforded to be lost since CoAP involves data loss as it works on UDP layer without any connection establishment and packet travels in all possible routes available. It is evident from the results obtained that the IoT application protocol are defined for a specific purpose. It is inferred from the results that it is clearly visible that CoAP has the highest throughput since it works on the UDP layer and there is no need for any connection establishment like TCP which takes more time. HTTP has the least throughput.

References

1. Atzori, L., Iera, A., Morabito, G.: The internet of things: a survey. Comput. Netw. **54**(15), 2787–2805 (2010)
2. Chen, S., Hui, X., Liu, D., Bo, H., Wang, H.: A vision of IoT: applications, challenges, and opportunities with China perspective. IEEE Internet Things J. **1**(4), 349–359 (2014)
3. Farokhmanesh, F.: Analyzing and evaluating network protocols in IoT. In: IEEE Ninth International Conference (2014)
4. Fielding, R., Irvine, U.C., Gettys, J., Mogul, J., Frystyk, H., Masinter, L., Leach, P., Berners-Lee, T.: HTTP-HyperText Transfer Protocol
5. Gazis, V., Görtz, M., Huber, M., Leonardi, A., Mathioudakis, K., Wiesmaier, A., Zeiger, F., Vasilomanolakis, E.: A survey of technologies for the internet of things. In: International Wireless Communications and Mobile Computing Conference, IWCMC 2015, Dubrovnik, Croatia, 24–28 August 2015, pp. 1090–1095 (2015)
6. Gubbi, J., Buyya, R., Marusic, S., Palaniswami, M.: Internet of Things (IoT): a vision, architectural elements, and future directions. Future Gener. Comput. Syst. **29**(7), 1645–1660 (2013)
7. Karagiannis, V., Chatzimisios, P., Vazquez-Gallego, F., Alonso-Zarate, J.: A survey on application layer protocols for the internet of things. Trans. IoT Cloud Comput. **1**(1) (2015)
8. Khan, R., Khan, S.U., Zaheer, R., Khan, S.: Future internet: the internet of things architecture, possible applications and key challenges. In: Proceedings of the 2012 10th International Conference on Frontiers of Information Technology, FIT 2012, pp. 257–260. IEEE Computer Society, Washington, D.C. (2012)
9. Hartke, K.: Observing resources in CoAP (2012)
10. Rohokale, V.M., Prasad, N.R., Prasad, R.: A cooperative internet of things (IoT) for rural healthcare monitoring and control. In: 2011 2nd International Conference on Wireless Communication, Vehicular Technology, Information Theory and Aerospace Electronic Systems Technology (Wireless VITAE), pp. 1–6, February 2011
11. Shakshuki, E.M., Ferdoush, S., Li, X.: The 9th international conference on future networks and communications (fnc 2014)/the 11th international conference on mobile systems and pervasive computing (mobispc 2014)/affiliated workshops wireless sensor network system design using raspberry pi and arduino for environmental monitoring applications. Procedia Comput. Sci. **34**, 103–110 (2014)
12. Shinde, S., Nimkar, P., Singh, S., Salpe, V., Jadhav, Y.: MQTT-Message Queuing Telemetry Transport protocol. Int. J. Res. **3**(3), 240–244 (2016)

13. Singh, M., Rajan, M.A., Shivraj, V.L., Balamuralidhar, P.: Secure MQTT for internet of things (IoT). In: 2015 Fifth International Conference on Communication Systems and Network Technologies (CSNT), pp. 746–751, April 2015
14. Uwase, M.-P., Long, N.T., Tiberghien, J., Steenhaut, K., Dricot, J.-M.: Poster abstract: outdoors range measurements with Zolertia Z1 Motes and Contiki. In: Langendoen, K., Hu, W., Ferrari, F., Zimmerling, M., Mottola, L. (eds.) Real-World Wireless Sensor Networks. LNEE, vol. 281, pp. 79–83. Springer, Cham (2014). doi:10.1007/978-3-319-03071-5_9
15. Zhou, C., Zhang, X.: Toward the internet of things application and management: a practical approach. In: Proceeding of IEEE International Symposium on a World of Wireless, Mobile and Multimedia Networks, WoWMoM 2014, Sydney, Australia, 19 June 2014, pp. 1–6 (2014)

Classification of Emotions from Images Using Localized Subsection Information

Abhishek Singh Kilak$^{(\boxtimes)}$ and Namita Mittal

Malaviya National Institute of Technology, Jaipur, India
{2012rcp9516,nmittal.cse}@mnit.ac.in

Abstract. Emotional intelligence has important social significance and literature indicates that facial features are an important factor in determining the emotional state. It has been an intense study field to build systems that are capable to recognize emotions automatically based on facial expressions. Various approaches have been proposed but still there is a scope of improvement in detection accuracy because of diverse form of expressions exhibiting the same emotion. A widely used approach in the object detection field is Histogram of Oriented gradients. In this paper extensive experiments are conducted using various subsection sizes of images of histogram of oriented gradients and also along with Local Binary Pattern to extract the features for classification of emotions from facial images. Quantitative analysis of the approach in comparison with others is done to show its applicability and effectiveness.

Keywords: Emotion detection · Local binary patterns · Histogram of oriented gradients

1 Introduction

Ever since the premodern times, face studies were greatly influenced by popular physiognomy theories that assumed that face and outer appearance could judge personality or character of a person [1]. It has been a point of debate always, but nevertheless literature supports that facial features respond in tandem to emotional state. Ekman [2] described six universal emotions of surprise, happiness, sadness, disgust, anger and fear that can be found across all cultures. Interpretation ability of recognizing emotions based on facial expressions is thus an important research issue. It has been an intense study field for the last three decades to build systems that are capable to recognize emotions automatically based on facial expressions. Machines that are emotionally intelligent have important social significance and the literature indicates that facial features are an important factor in determining the emotional state.

There is a need of intelligent systems that may react according to emotional state of humans. They can be applied in areas such as human-computer interaction, virtual reality, recommender systems and drive assistance. They can also be used for affective disorder detection like bipolar disorder, depression and anxiety. The steps involved in the detection of emotions from face expressions are shown in Fig. 1.

© Springer Nature Singapore Pte Ltd. 2017
M. Singh et al. (Eds.): ICACDS 2016, CCIS 721, pp. 562–571, 2017.
DOI: 10.1007/978-981-10-5427-3_57

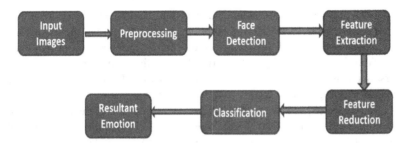

Fig. 1. Steps involved in Emotion detection

Various approaches have been proposed but still there is a scope of improvement in detection accuracy because of diverse form of expressions exhibiting the same emotion. Histogram of Oriented gradients has been used widely in the field of object detection. Extensive experiments are conducted using various subsection sizes of images in calculating histogram of oriented gradients combined with Local Binary Pattern variation for even lower level implementation to extract the features for classification of emotions from facial images, in the paper.

Accordingly, work done previously in emotion detection field is presented in Sect. 2, approach for facial expression detection is presented in Sect. 3, where extraction of features is also specified. The experimental results are provided in Sect. 4. Quantitative analysis of the approach in comparison with others is done to show its applicability and effectiveness. Finally, conclusion and expandable future work is presented in Sect. 5.

2 Related Work

The steps involved in this process of emotion detection from facial features include face recognition, pre-processing, extraction of features, feature selection and lastly classification. For all of the steps stated, there are different techniques suggested in literature. Many approaches have been proposed and experimented upon.

An approach to unwind Gabor features was done where Facial image cropped into upper and lower part [3] and then fiducial points were used and applied to the two parts to extract features. Neural network was used for classification and maximum accuracy of 86.6% accuracy was reported for upper face features.

Another use of Gabor filters was done for Expression recognition in relation to affection by aging. The lifespan [4] database was used by Guodong Guo. Manually labeled fiducial points followed by and Gabor filtering [5] was used to extract features. SVM classification using 10-fold cross validation for cross age group yielded 69.32% average accuracy. 64.04% average accuracy was acquired from the same setup when repeated for FACES [6] database.

Personalized classifiers have been proposed in many approaches as they argue that training pattern may have large difference when compared to the pattern extracted from an unseen person. The presence of moustache, wrinkled face or heavy eyebrows in an unseen person may provide different and can thus lead to erroneous results. Such approach is unrealistic to deal with emotion detection in real life scenarios. An approach to remove bias of person specific features has been proposed that uses Selective Transfer machine [7] for generic classification. This approach is different from personal bias and tends towards generic classifier. Labels are not required as unsupervised learning is used in this proposed method.

Viola and Jones [8] has been used for face detection and thereafter lip, nose and mouth regions were captured and classified using SDAM [9] approach by Yubo Wang and others [10]. Classification was performed on JAFFE [11] using SVM based classifier. The experiment was performed on images taken by them in laboratory as well as those taken from the web. Accuracy of 92.4% has been reported by them.

The difference between spontaneous and posed expressions was explored by Jiang et al. [12]. Cohn Kanade dataset was used for the posed images while International Affective Picture system [13] was used as display content to capture spontaneous reactions. Dataset acquisition on a set of 52 users was done in the experiment. All frame images were averaged to provide neutral frame for LDOS-PerAff-1 [14] dataset. Gabor Filtering was done and statistical were calculated. Feature vector reduction was done followed by classification and accuracy of 62% was reported for the spontaneous expression set.

Various approaches have been proposed but still there is a scope of improvement in detection accuracy because of diverse form of expressions exhibiting the same emotion. Histogram of Oriented gradients has been used widely approach in the field of object detection. In this paper extensive experiments are conducted using various subsection sizes of images for histogram of oriented gradients and also local binary pattern are applied for extracting features to classify emotions from facial images. Quantitative analysis of the approach in comparison with others is done to show its applicability and effectiveness.

3   Proposed Work

The phases involved for the classification of emotions in the approach are:

  (i)   Preprocessing
 (ii)   Extraction of Features
(iii)   Reduction of Feature Size
 (iv)   Classification
  (v)   LBPh feature extraction
 (vi)   Statistical moment and other feature calculation and appending
(vii)   Classification

3.1   Preprocessing

Facial part of the images was detected using Viola and Jones [8] from the images of CK + dataset [15]. Only first and last image I were taken as they represent neutral and extreme expression. Images are then cropped to contain only the face part. Some of the images in the dataset are colored. Therefore, to obtain uniformity, they are converted to gray scale. Example images are shown in Fig. 2.

Fig. 2. Cropped last frames samples

3.2 Extraction of Features

In this step Histogram of Oriented Gradients were extracted from the cropped face part of images as shown in Fig. 3. The logic behind the histogram of oriented gradients descriptor is that object's local appearance and it's shape can be described within an image by the edge direction distribution or gradient intensity. The image is divided into cells which are small connected regions. For the pixels within these cells, histogram of gradient directions is compiled. The cell size use in the experiments ranged from 10 by 10 pixels to 76 by 76 pixels. The feature vector is composed of HOG blocks where individual entries within a particular block are composed of cell histograms with orientation binning.

$$\text{Total Number of blocks} = \left(floor\left(\frac{Len}{Cell}\right) - 1 \right) * \left(floor\left(\frac{Bre}{Cell}\right) - 1 \right) \quad (1)$$

$$\text{Total no of cell parts in feature vector computation} = \text{Total Number of blocks} * 4 \quad (2)$$

$$\text{Total number of histograms per cell} = 9 \quad (3)$$

Fig. 3. Cropped image and its histogram visualization for cell size 32

3.3   Reduction of Feature Size

The HOG feature extraction was done for cell size of 10 to 72. Resultant feature vector was bulky and therefore feature reduction of the resultant HOGs of the images was done using principal component analysis (PCA) with variance coverage of 0.95.

3.4   Classification

The resultant vectors of the previous step were then subjected to classification. Different classifiers were used for this purpose which were linear discriminant, SVM (Linear, Quadratic and Cubic), Ensemble Subspace discriminant and Multilayer Perceptron. The results of these are shown in Tables 1, 2, 3 and 4.

3.5   Local Binary Pattern Half (LBPh) Feature Extraction

Continuing with the experiment, local patterns were extracted for only the left half face part of facial image (LBPh). This was done as it was assumed that the right part of facial image would convey redundant information of the left part. The resultant image is shown in Fig. 4.

Fig. 4. Local pattern image of cropped left part of face of S52

3.6   Statistical Moment and Other Feature Calculation and Appending

For each local pattern image mean and standard deviation (first two statistical moments) were calculated. This provided μ_f, σ_f for the initial frame and μ_l, σ_l for the corresponding last frame. These two moments were used to calculate six other dependent features. These dependent features included $\mu_f - \mu_l$, $\sigma_f - \sigma_l$, μ_f/μ_l, σ_f/σ_l, $(\mu_f - \mu_l)/\mu_f$ and $(\sigma_f - \sigma_l)/\sigma_f$. This resulted in a feature vector 10 elements. This was appended to the feature vector obtained in step 2.

3.7   Classification

The resultant vector was then subjected to PCA for feature reduction and thereafter classification. Classifiers used for this purpose were linear discriminant, SVM (Linear, Quadratic and Cubic) and Ensemble Subspace discriminant. The results of classification using (HOG + LBPh) at five fold cross validation is shown in Table 5 and in Fig. 6.

4 Results

The results in terms of obtained accuracy at 5 fold cross validation (HOG) is shown in the following tables.

Table 1. Results at various cell sizes

Classifier\Cell size	10	12	14	16	18	20	22	24
Linear discriminant	87.6	87.6	88.6	88.3	89.6	90.6	90.9	91.2
Linear SVM	59.6	61.9	67.4	69.1	70	75.2	79.8	81.8
Quadratic SVM	82.4	83.1	85	86.6	86.3	87.3	86.6	88.6
Cubic SVM	80.5	81.8	82.4	82.4	84	85.3	85.3	86.6
Ensemble subspace discriminant	89.6	89.3	89.9	88.9	89.3	90.9	90.6	92.8
Multilayer perceptron	80.2	80.9	81.1	83.4	83.4	81.4	85.3	85.7

Table 2. Results at various cell sizes

Classifier\Cell size	26	28	30	32	34	36	38	40
Linear discriminant	88.9	88.3	91.5	87	90.2	89.9	88.3	87.6
Linear SVM	83.7	84	86	84.7	85	85.7	87	87
Quadratic SVM	88.3	85	88.3	85.7	87.3	87.6	86.3	87.6
Cubic SVM	86	84	87.6	84.4	84.7	85	83.4	85.7
Ensemble subspace discriminant	88.6	89.9	91.5	89.6	91.9	89.3	89.3	88.9
Multilayer perceptron	85.3	85.3	87	85.3	85.3	85.3	85.3	87.9

Table 3. Results at various cell sizes

Classifier\Cell size	42	44	46	48	50	52	54	56
Linear discriminant	86.3	85.3	84.7	87	91.2	84	84.4	82.7
Linear SVM	85.7	83.7	84.4	85	87.6	82.7	84	82.7
Quadratic SVM	85	82.1	84	84.7	87.6	84.4	83.4	82.4
Cubic SVM	83.7	81.4	82.7	83.7	87.6	82.4	83.7	80.8
Ensamble subspace discriminant	87.6	86	85.3	86.6	89.6	84.7	85	85
Multilayer perceptron	86.3	84.7	82.4	85.3	87	81.8	83.4	86

Table 4. Results at various cell sizes

Classifier\Cell size	58	60	62	64	66	68	70	72
Linear discriminant	84	88.3	86.6	85.3	84.4	85	70	70.4
Linear SVM	84	86.3	84.7	85	83.4	82.4	69.1	67.4
Quadratic SVM	86	86.3	85.3	84.7	80.5	82.4	67.1	67.1
Cubic SVM	83.4	84.4	83.1	83.7	78.8	79.5	66.4	66.8
Ensamble subspace discriminant	84.7	87.6	86.6	86.6	85	83.7	70.7	70.4
Multilayer perceptron	87	84.4	83.7	84.4	81.1	81.8	65.1	65.1

By experimental results it was found that the best results were obtained for cell size 30*30 to 50*50 (Fig. 5).

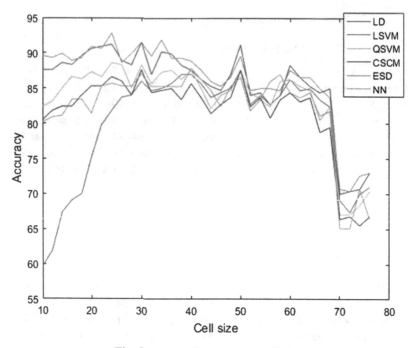

Fig. 5. Graph of accuracy vs. cell size

The results in terms of obtained accuracy at 5 fold cross validation (HOG + LBP) is presented in Table 5.

Table 5. Accuracy of (HOG + LBP) at different cell sizes

Classifier\cell size	30	32	34	36	38	40	42	44	46	48	50
Linear discriminant	89.9	88.3	90.2	88.6	88.9	87.6	85.7	83.7	85	87	89.9
Linear SVM	86	85.7	86.6	85.3	85.3	87	85.3	84.4	83.7	86	88.6
Quadratic SVM	87.6	87.9	87	88.6	86	88.9	83.4	84.4	84	84.4	86.6
Cubic SVM	87.3	87.6	85.7	87	83.4	85.3	82.7	81.4	82.7	83.7	86.3
Ensamble subspace discriminant	89.9	88.6	91.2	88.9	88.9	89.6	87.6	86.6	86.6	88.3	91.9

This can be viewed graphically as:-

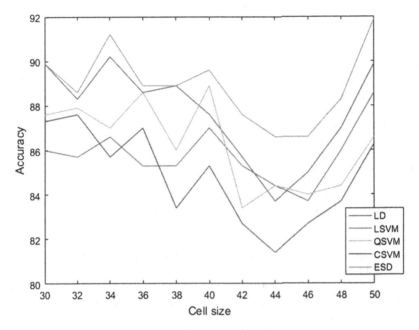

Fig. 6. Accuracy (HOG + LBP) at various cell sizes

Comparison of performance on CK + Database on different State of the art approaches can be seen in Table 6.

Table 6. Quantitative analysis of method proposed with state of the art methods

Approach	Uddin [20]	Ahmad [19]	Zhong [16]	Song [17]	Zhang [18]	Our approach
Average accuracy	93.33	90.38	88.26	89.56	93.14	91.9

5 Conclusion

High accuracy is obtained for the multiple classifications. By experimental results it was found that the best results were obtained for cell size 30*30 to 50*50 for HOG. This is attributed to window sizes that might actually capture features necessary for correct classification. Adding LBP features to the vectors obtained increases accuracy in many cases. Quantitative analysis of the approach in comparison with others is done to show its applicability and effectiveness. This comparison is illustrious only and results of the approach would be even better as the other approaches have not considered Contempt as a class which has the least number of samples in CK+dataset.

More extensive experiments can be conducted in future which involve other models for creation of hybrid vectors over different datasets that may further increase the accuracy of classification of emotions.

References

1. Highfield, R., Wiseman, R., Jenkins, R.: How your looks betray your personality. New Sci. **201**, 28–32 (2009)
2. Ekman, P.: An argument for basic emotions. Cogn. Emot. **6**(3–4), 169–200 (1992)
3. Guo, G., Guo, R., Li, X.: Facial expression recognition influenced by human aging. IEEE Trans. Affect. Comput. **4**(3), 291–298 (2013)
4. Minear, M., Park, D.C.: A lifespan database of adult facial stimuli. Behav. Res. Methods Instrum. Comput. **36**(4), 630–633 (2004)
5. Daugman, J.G.: Uncertainty relation for resolution in space, spatial frequency, and orientation optimized by two-dimensional visual cortical filters. JOSA A **2**(7), 1160–1169 (1985)
6. Ebner, N.C., Riediger, M., Lindenberger, U.: FACES—A database of facial expressions in young, middle-aged, and older women and men: development and validation. Behav. Res. Methods **42**(1), 351–362 (2010)
7. Chu, W.S., De la Torre, F., Cohn, J.F.: Selective transfer machine for personalized facial action unit detection. In: Proceedings of the IEEE Conference on Computer Vision and Pattern Recognition, pp. 3515–3522 (2013)
8. Viola, P., Jones, M.: Rapid object detection using a boosted cascade of simple features. In: Proceedings of the 2001 IEEE Computer Society Conference on Computer Vision and Pattern Recognition, CVPR 2001, Vol. 1, pp. I–511 (2001)
9. Wang, T., Ai, H., Huang, G.: A two-stage approach to automatic face alignment. In: Third International Symposium on Multispectral Image Processing and Pattern Recognition, pp. 558–563. International Society for Optics and Photonics (2003)
10. Wang, Y., Ai, H., Wu, B., Huang, C.: Real time facial expression recognition with adaboost. In: Proceedings of the 17th International Conference on Pattern Recognition, ICPR 2004, Vol. 3, pp. 926–929 (2004)
11. The Japanese Female Facial Expression (JAFFE). http://www.mis.atr.co.jp/~mlyons/jaffe.html
12. Jiang, B., Valstar, M., Martinez, B., Pantic, M.: A dynamic appearance descriptor approach to facial actions temporal modeling. IEEE Transactions Cybern. **44**(2), 161–174 (2014)
13. Lang, P.J., Bradley, M.M., Cuthbert, B.N.: International affective picture system (IAPS): affective ratings of pictures and instruction manual. Technical report A-8 (2008)
14. Tkalcic, M., Tasic, J., Košir, A.: The LDOS-PerAff-1 corpus of face video clips with affective and personality metadata. Multimodal Corpora: Advances in Capturing, Coding and Analyzing Multimodality, vol. 111 (2010)
15. Kanade, T., Cohn, J.F., Tian, Y.: Comprehensive database for facial expression analysis. In: Proceedings of Fourth IEEE International Conference on Automatic Face and Gesture Recognition, pp. 46–53 (2000)
16. Zhong, L., Liu, Q., Yang, P., Liu, B., Huang, J., Metaxas, D.N.: Learning active facial patches for expression analysis. In: IEEE Conference on Computer Vision and Pattern Recognition (CVPR), pp. 2562–2569 (2012)

17. Song, M., Tao, D., Liu, Z., Li, X., Zhou, M.: Image ratio features for facial expression recognition application. IEEE Trans. Syst. Man Cybern. Part B (Cybern.) **40**(3), 779–788 (2010)
18. Zhang, L., Tjondronegoro, D.: Facial expression recognition using facial movement features. IEEE Trans. Affect. Comput. **2**(4), 219–229 (2011)
19. Poursaberi, A., Noubari, H.A., Gavrilova, M., Yanushkevich, S.N.: Gauss-Laguerre wavelet textural feature fusion with geometrical information for facial expression identification. EURASIP J. Image Video Process. **1**, 1–13 (2012)
20. Uddin, M.Z., Lee, J.J., Kim, T.S.: An enhanced independent component-based human facial expression recognition from video. IEEE Trans. Consum. Electron. **55**(4), 2216–2224 (2009)

Comparative Study of Classification Techniques for Weather Data

Shweta Panjwani[1(✉)], S. Naresh Kumar[1], and Laxmi Ahuja[2]

[1] Centre for Environment Science and Climate Resilient Agriculture,
Indian Agricultural Research Institute, New Delhi 110 012, India
shweta.panjwani537@gmail.com
[2] Amity Institute of Information Technology,
Amity University, Noida, Uttar Pradesh, India

Abstract. Data mining techniques are widely used to analyze the large amount of data. Classification is an important technique which classifies data of various real world applications. This paper aims to compare the performance of classification algorithms for weather data using Waikato Environment for Knowledge Analysis (WEKA). Performance analysis done using cross fold and training set method. The best algorithm found was J48 Decision Tree classifier with highest accuracy and minimum error as compared to others.

Keywords: Weather data · Data mining · Classification · Performance evaluation J48 decision tree · Multi-layer Perceptron · Bayes network

1 Introduction

Data mining is also known as Knowledge Discovery in Databases (KDD) and is the major area of discovering useful information from huge amounts of data [1, 11]. Data mining applications play an important role in different disciplines such as health, biotechnology, climate science, e-business, etc. Various data mining techniques such classification, clustering, algorithms have been used by researchers and impact modelers for weather forecasting and prediction.

Long-term rainfall prediction has been done using Evolving Fuzzy Neural Network (EFuNN), Back Propagation and Scale Conjugate Gradient Algorithm for Kerala state [2]. Kotsiantis et al. [3] predicted daily average, maximum and minimum temperature using data mining algorithms such as Feed-Forward Back Propagation (BP), linear least-squares regression (LR), M5rules algorithm, Decision tree and instance based learning (IB3), k-Nearest Neighbor (KNN), for Patras city in Greek. The obtained results are evaluated by calculating parameters i.e. Correlation Coefficient and RMSE. Hayati and Mohebi [4] developed short-term temperature forecasting model using Multi-layer Perceptron for Kermanshah city, west of Iran. This model was evaluated using ten years of weather data and found minimum forecasting error. For robust forecasting of weather, choosing a suitable data mining technique becomes crucial. So, the main purpose of this research work is to perform the evaluation of different data

M. Singh et al. (Eds.): ICACDS 2016, CCIS 721, pp. 572–576, 2017.
DOI: 10.1007/978-981-10-5427-3_58

mining methods used in weather forecasting. Here we used different classification algorithms viz., Bayes Network, J48 Decision tree and Multi-Layer Perceptron, a software tool WEKA was used for performance evaluation.

2 Methodology

2.1 Classification Algorithms

Classification is a machine learning technique used to predict group membership for data instances. As an illustration, it may be used to forecast the weather on a particular day, whether it will be sunny, rainy or cloudy. Most commonly used classification techniques are decision trees and neural networks. We used the following classification techniques for comparative study.

Bayes Network
Bayes Network classifier is powerful probabilistic representation which is based on the Bayes theorem. Bayes Network is similar to the directed acyclic graph. To perform classification, Bayes rule can be used to calculate the probability of criteria for a given series of instances (I1.... In), and then by predicting the class with the highest posterior probability to eventually form a Bayesian Network [5]. Assumptions to be made while creating Network are that there are no missing values and all attributes are nominal, apart from any such value replaced globally. The output generated from Bayes network can be displayed in terms of a graph.

Multi-Layer Perceptron (MLP)
A MLP is a feed-forward neural network having one or more hidden layers and its neurons are called hidden neurons Fig. 1. Basically MLP has three layers: input, hidden and output layer. Each and every neuron (code) in every layer is linked to each and every neuron in the adjacent layers. The training vectors has been connected to the input layer which are further processed by the hidden and output layers [6].

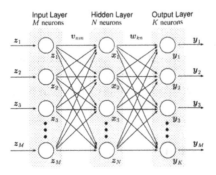

Fig. 1. MLP, a multilayer network

J48 Decision Tree

J48 algorithm is improved version of the C4.5 algorithms which generates output in the form of Decision tree. In order to classify a new item, it first creates a decision tree based on the attribute values of the available training data. To reach a particular end node of a decision tree, the attribute that discriminates various instances most clearly is used to split that portion of tree based on the training data. This feature becomes easy to know about the data instances so that they can be best classified to have the highest information gain [7, 10].

2.2 Experimental Setup

WEKA 3.8 is used as tool for performance evaluation of different classification techniques. The Waikato Environment for Knowledge Analysis (WEKA) is a most powerful data mining tool which works under JAVA environment and developed by the University of Waikato in New Zealand, WEKA is collection of machine learning algorithm (Classification, Clustering and Regression) which can be directly applied to real data mining applications. Apart from all these, WEKA also provides the facility of developing machine algorithm. WEKA supports the file format such as ARFF, CSV and C4.5 [8, 9] and has different interface mode (Explorer, Experimenter, Simple CLI) to work. We used Explorer for data pre-processing and experimenter for performing statistical tests between learning algorithms. Weather data of a single location (New Delhi) having 3 attributes (outlook, temperature, precipitation) were used to compare the classification techniques. In this dataset temperature and precipitation are independent attributes, while outlook attribute is dependent.

Classification techniques were applied using two different methods i.e. Training Set and Cross Fold method. Training set method uses percentage training set data to apply classification techniques. Cross fold method was used to divide data into 10-fold equal size samples and then uses single sample to validate the classification model and remaining subsamples are used as training data. This process is then repeated with rest of the subsamples. Cross fold method has lower variance, hence it can predict more accurate estimate of the model.

Kappa statistic is a metric to check the accuracy (the reliability and validity of the collected data) of any particular measuring case. Higher the Kappa statistics value means stronger the agreement/bonding. Mean Absolute Error (MAE) measures closeness between predicted model and actual model. Root Mean Square Error (RMSE) measures the error between model predicted value and actually observed value. Hence, minimum the values of RMSE and MAE better are the prediction and accuracy.

3 Result and Discussion

Result is presented in two parts so that the performance evaluation can be easily done. In the first part, classified instances i.e. correctly and incorrectly classified are shown and Kappa statistic, RMSE and MAE parameters are presented in the next part. Correct classification percentage obtained for Bayes Network, Multi-Layer Perceptron and J48 Decision tree using cross fold method are 62%, 65%, 66.5% respectively Fig. 2 and using training set method are 59%, 68%, 49% respectively Fig. 3. Correct classification percentage decreased in the training set method for J48 and Bayes Network but increased for Multi-Layer Perceptron.

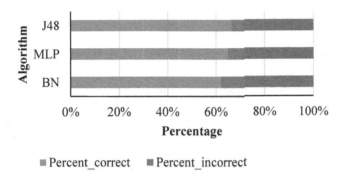

Fig. 2. Classification results using 10 cross fold method

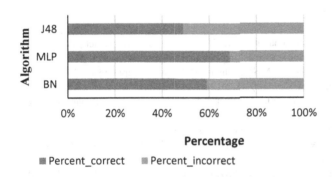

Fig. 3. Classification results using training set method

In the experiment, algorithms statistics were also compared using both methods and kappa statistics was found to be negative (−0.12) in case of training set method (Table 1). The MAE and RMSE values obtained were much higher which show error in prediction. Among the classification methods, cross fold method is found to be better than training set method.

To evaluate the overall performance of algorithms, classification results using cross fold method was examined and J48 algorithm was found to be maximum correct classifier with 66.5%. Comparison between different evaluation shows that J48 having minimum MAE (0.28) and RMSE (0.30). Kappa statistic of Multi-Layer Perceptron (0.52) and J48 Decision tree (0.50) were moderate (Table 1).

Table 1. Evaluation statistics for classification techniques

Classifier	Cross fold method			Training set method		
	MAE	RMSE	Kappa statistic	MAE	RMSE	Kappa statistic
Bayes network	0.42	0.43	0.43	0.42	0.48	0.03
Multi-layer perceptron	0.47	0.47	0.52	0.34	0.47	0.25
J48 Decision tree	0.28	0.30	0.50	0.51	0.59	−0.12

4 Conclusion

Different classification techniques are used in weather forecasting by climatologists. Performance evaluation of different classification techniques was done to select the best technique using Cross fold and training set method and their statistical parameter were compared. This analysis demonstrated that overall best classifier algorithm for weather data is J48 Decision tress with cross fold method. Accuracy level of weather forecast, an important component of decision making in various sectors including agriculture, is expected to be increased by employing this method.

References

1. Rushing, J., Ramachandran, R., Nair, U., Graves, S., Welch, R., Lin, H.: ADaM: a data mining toolkit for scientists and engineers. Comput. Geosci. **31**(5), 607–618 (2005)
2. Abraham, A., Philip, N.S., Mahanti, P.K.: Soft computing models for weather forecasting. Int. J. Appl. Sci. Comput. **11**(3), 106–117 (2004)
3. Kotsiantis, S., Kostoulas, A., Lykoudis, S., Argiriou, A., Menagias, K.: Using data mining techniques for estimating minimum, maximum and average daily temperature values. Int. J. Math. Phys. Eng. Sci. **1**(1), 16–20 (2008)
4. Hayati, M., Mohebi, Z.: Application of artificial neural networks for temperature forecasting. World Acad. Sci. Eng. Technol. **28**(2), 275–279 (2007)
5. Friedman, N., Geiger, D., Goldszmidt, M.: Bayesian network classifiers. Mach. Learn. **29**(2–3), 131–163 (1997)
6. Hassoun, M.H.: Fundamentals of Artificial Neural Networks. MIT Press, Cambridge (1999)
7. Vaithiyanathan, V., Rajeswari, K., Tajane, K., Pitale, R.: Comparison of different classification techniques using different datasets. Int. J. Adv. Eng. Technol. **6**(2), 764 (2013)
8. Solanki, A.V.: Data mining techniques using WEKA classification for Sickle Cell Disease. Int. J. Comput. Sci. Inf. Technol. **5**(4), 5857–5860 (2014)
9. Weka. http://www.cs.waikato.ac.nz/ml/weka/documentation.html
10. Dash, S.R., Dehuri, S.: Comparative study of different classification techniques for post operative patient dataset. Int. J. Innov. Res. Comput.Commun. Eng. **1**(5), 1101–1108 (2013)
11. Data Mining - Typical Data Mining Process for Predictive Modeling. BPB Publications, First Edition 2004 –REPRINTED 2007. ISBN 81-7656-927-5

Content Based Component Retrieval Based on Neural Network (NN) Classification Method

Rupali Garg[(✉)] and Jagpuneet Kaur Bajwa

Department of Computer Science, Punjabi University, Patiala, India
rupaligarg1992@gmail.com, jagpuneetbajwa@gmail.com

Abstract. With the development of multimedia data, there is urgent need of high bandwidth for retrieval process. Selection of extracted features play an important role in retrieval process. Good selection features also save time and enhance the accuracy rate. The main objective of this proposed work is to classify the reusable components using neural network (NN) and genetic algorithm (GA). From result analysis it has been seen that proposed work has provided good results in terms of recall and precision rate.

Keywords: Genetic algorithm · Neural network · Component based retrieval · Software engineering

1 Introduction

The issue of reusability of components is generally related to the efficient storage and retrieval of reusable components from software repository. The reusability of the component depends on the suitability and match of retrieved component with that of the user query. To further enhance the relevance of the retrieved component classification, clustering and ranking needs to be done before hand effectively. Component searching and retrieval are the main issues in CBSE [1].

Efficient searching as well as retrieval methods are needed to develop the quality of the software. Component retrieval process is needed to compare the documents for the purpose of regaining useful components [13, 14]. So, in this paper, utilization of neural network has been done to get reusable components [7, 9, 10].

To reuse the components, it is very important to have optimization technique. Retrieval process must have less time consumption and must be efficient. Genetic algorithm (GA) can be used for finding the best component [2]. As genetic algorithms generally reduce the feature set, so neural network in next step will classify the components on similar basis.

There are large number of features to get reusable components like Cyclometric complexity, regular metric, clustering, XNOR method [8], cluster selection [11] etc. But the main problem in these methods is that they have the problem of consistency between methods [15–17]. So, in proposed work, this problem will be solved using proposed algorithms (Fig. 1).

© Springer Nature Singapore Pte Ltd. 2017
M. Singh et al. (Eds.): ICACDS 2016, CCIS 721, pp. 577–584, 2017.
DOI: 10.1007/978-981-10-5427-3_59

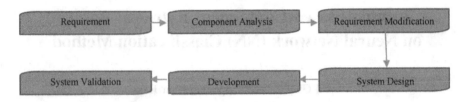

Fig. 1. Component based software engineering

2 Literature Survey

Kaur et al. [3], "Identification and Performance Evaluation of Reusable Software Components Based Neural Network", investigated auxiliary characteristics of capacity situated programming parts utilizing programming measurements and the measurements utilized are Cyclometric Complexity Using Mc Cabe's Measure, Halstead Software Science Indicator, Regularity Metric, Reuse recurrence metric, Coupling Metric. Neural Network Based Approach is utilized to set up the relationship between diverse traits of the reusability and serve as the programmed apparatus for the assessment of the reusability of the methodology by ascertaining the relationship taking into account its training. In Bakhshi [4], "Development of a Software Repository for the Precise Search and Exact Retrieval of the Components" a product segment archive is produced to store reusable component. Various look procedures are utilized to pursuit the obliged part and recovery of those parts. The procedures utilized for looking and recovering of parts are decisive word based hunt, mark based pursuit and Operational semantic catchphrase based recovery procedure is proposed. Yadav and Kaur [5], "Design of rank based reusable component retrieval algorithm" proposed a calculation which is the mix of two most mainstream recovery strategies i.e. Essential word based methodology and Semantics based segment recovery technique. After this the recovered parts are positioned by past client requests. Thus, this paper proposed a proficient model for recovering the reusable parts in more streamlined way. Gupta and Kumar [6], "Reusable software component retrieval system", presented a meta-information display and faceted order for capacity and recovery of programming parts that considers space semantic data in light of ontologies and texonomies. Rather than most existing stores, which just recover a constrained arrangement of parts, the proposed metadata model makes conceivable the suggestion of interrelated segments, as metaphysics and scientific classifications attributes were joined. Singh and Janhavi [12], "Development of Component repository", proposed a software repository for storage and recovery of programming reusable segments. This vault executes two sorts of pursuit methods Keyword based hunt In this decisive word is entered to store and pertinent parts which coordinate the catchphrases are retrieved. User Priority-Based Component Retrieval: Select Component Type, Select Component Language, Select Component Domain and Select Component Name and the definite coordinating segment is recovered.

3 Proposed Work Model

Retrieving the components considering these features becomes more difficult and time consuming. The purpose of this work is to select the best component from a repository that can be reused. In the proposed system one such component repository is developed. From repository best component has to be found. Best components are retrieved in a twostep process. The first step gives all the relevant components, and the second step gives the best component to the user. This enhances the chances of retrieval of best component from a repository. The first technique used is simple keyword based retrieval and second technique is neural network. Neural network give satisfactory results for those components which have attributes and weights. The neural network based technique is very effective when the repository size is very large (Fig. 2).

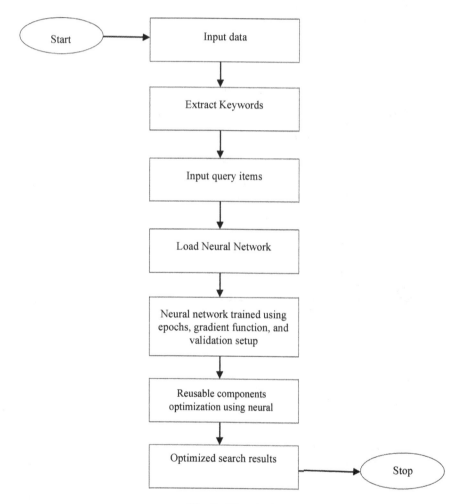

Fig. 2. Flowchart

4 Proposed Algorithms

Algorithm 1: Addition of Component Retrieval Process

```
Global component component2=[];
gen_fun=get(handles.edit2,'String');
gen_fun=double(gen_fun);
gen_fun=dec2bin(gen_fun);
spec_fun=get(handles.edit3,'String');
spec_fun=double(spec_fun);
spec_fun=dec2bin(spec_fun);
memory_utilization=get(handles.edit4,'String');
memory_utilization=double(memory_utilization);
memory_utilization=dec2bin(memory_utilization);
platform=get(handles.edit5,'String');
platform=double(platform);
platform=dec2bin(platform);
processor=get(handles.edit6,'String');
processor=double(processor);
processor=dec2bin(processor);
disk=get(handles.edit7,'String');
disk=double(disk);
disk=dec2bin(disk);
operating_system=get(handles.edit8,'String');
operating_system=double(operating_system);
operating_system=dec2bin(operating_system);
language=get(handles.edit9,'String');
language=double(language);
language=dec2bin(language);
encryption=get(handles.edit10,'String');
encryption=double(encryption);
encryption=dec2bin(encryption);
format=get(handles.edit11,'String');
format=double(format);
format=dec2bin(format);
ease_use=double(ease_use);
ease_use=dec2bin(ease_use);
binding=get(handles.edit18,'String');
binding=double(binding);
binding=dec2bin(binding); component{1,1}=gen_fun;
component{1,2}=spec_fun;
component{1,3}=memory_utilization;
component{1,4}=platform;
component{1,5}=processor;
component{1,6}=disk;
component{1,7}=operating_system;
component{1,8}=language;
component{1,9}=encryption;
component{1,10}=format;
component{1,11}=password;
component{1,12}=visibility;
component{1,13}=price;
component{1,14}=synchronization;
component{1,15}=ease_use;
component{1,16}=binding;
component1=component;
component2=component;
Save
```

Above algorithm describes the component retrieval process. Initially take the components as global. Then count their memory utilization, processors, prices, visibility and synchronization. After that get components based on various metrics like memory-utilization, platform, processor, disk, operating- system, language, encryption, format, password, visibility, price, synchronization and ease use.

Algorithm 2: Addition of Fitness Function using GA

```
[rs,cs]=size(component1);
For i=1:cs
Fs=component1{1,i};
Fs=bin2dec(Fs);
Fs=sum(sum(Fs));
for s=1:rows
Ft=component{s,i};
Ft=bin2dec(Ft);
Ft=sum(sum(Ft));
FitnessFunction = @(e)fitness_fn(e,Fs,Ft);
%calling
fitness function
numberOfVariables = 1;
[x(pk)                       fval]                       =
ga(FitnessFunction,numberOfVariables,[],[],[],[],[],[],[],opt
ions);
if x(pk)==1
cluster_chances(1,i)=cluster_chances(1,i)+1;
end
end
```

Above algorithm describes the process of optimization process using fitness function. Initially take the size of the components. Then find out the best component based on fitness function having best fitness value.

5   Results and Analysis

5.1   Computation Metrics

We have considered FN (False Negatives), FP (False Positives), r (recall rate), p (Precision rate) metrics and accuracy. False Negatives (FN) are that information that was actually the useful information but was not detected by algorithm in the cluster. False Positives (FP) are that information that was actually not the useful information but was detected by algorithm in the cluster. Recall rate (r) is the positives that has been detected by algorithm. Precision rate (p) is the negatives that have been recognized by the algorithm. The accuracy is the exactness of the true values obtained by implementation of proposed algorithm.

Recall rate is defined as:

$$Recall = \frac{Relavant\ Data - Retrieved\ data}{Relavant\ Data}$$

Precision Rate is defined as:

$$Precision = \frac{Relavant\ Data - Retrieved\ data}{Retrieved\ Data}$$

Accuracy is defined as:

$$Accuracy = \frac{t_p + t_n}{t_p + t_n + f_p + f_n}$$

5.2   Analysis of Result Values

(See Fig. 3, Table 1).

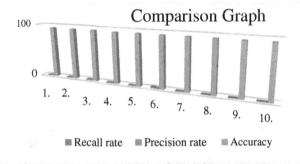

Fig. 3. Comparison graph

Table 1. Parameter evaluation

Components	Recall rate	Precision rate	Accuracy
1	.19	.201	93.94
2	.189	.198	93.45
3	.178	.203	93.77
4	.190	.189	93.22
5	.193	.187	93.66
6	1.98	.200	93.56
7	.198	.234	93.87
8	.193	.201	93.78
9	.189	.234	93.66
10	.179	.222	93.76

6 Conclusion and Future Scope

Getting reusable components for software development is very important to enhance the accuracy of the network. In proposed work, component retrieval system consists of two steps feature reduction and then classification. Feature selection reduction is done using genetic algorithm (GA) and then classification will be done using neural network (NN). In proposed work feature reduction is necessary to get obtained features in optimal values and classification is important to get accurate reusable components. The objective of this research lies in classifying the software components that can be reused, by using FFBPNN (Feed forward back propagation neural network). Neural network is used in the research for training the process quickly for achieving the solution. For the learning process, Sigmoid and hyperbolic tangent functions are used for the learning process. FFBPNN is used for the classification purpose for reusing the software components as per the needs of the attributes and the characteristics. From result simulations the obtained accuracy value is found out to be 93.94% of obtained reusable components. Future scope lies in the usage of other classification algorithms like SVM (Support vector machines), as it has good training rate, so that more accurate reusable components can be obtained.

References

1. Maxville, V., et al.: Intelligent component selection: computer software and applications conference. In: Proceedings of the 28th Annual International. IEEE (2004)
2. Pathak, P., et al.: Effective information retrieval using genetic algorithms based matching functions adaptation. In: Proceedings of the 33rd Annual Hawaii International Conference on. IEEE (2000)
3. Kaur, A., et al.: Identification and performance evaluation of reusable software components based Neural Network. Int. J. Res. Eng. Technol. 1(2), 100–104 (2012)
4. Bakshi, A.: Development of a software repository for the precise search and exact retrieval of the components. Int. J. Adv. Res. Comput. Sci. Softw. Eng. (2013)
5. Yadav, S., Kaur, K.: Design of rank based reusable component retrieval algorithm. Int. J. Adv. Res. Comput. Sci. Softw. Eng. (2013)
6. Gupta, S.C., Kumar, A.: Reusable software component retrieval system. Int. J. Appl. Innov. Eng. Manag. 2, 187–194 (2013)
7. Srinivas, C., et al.: Clustering software components for program restructuring and component reuse using hybrid XOR similarity function. AASRI Procedia 4, 319–328 (2013)
8. Srinivas, C., et al.: Clustering software components for program restructuring and component reuse using hybrid XNOR similarity function. Procedia Technol. 12, 246–254 (2014)
9. Srinivas, C., et al.: Clustering and classification of software component for efficient component retrieval and building component reuse libraries. Procedia Comput. Sci. 31, 1044–1050 (2014)
10. Sandhu, K., Gaba, T.: A novel technique for components retrieval from repositories. Int. J. Adv. Comput. Technol. 3, 912 (2014)
11. Madaan, N., Kaur, J.: A survey on selection techniques of component based software

12. Singh, A., Janhavi: Development of component repository. Int. J. Adv. Res. Comput. Sci. Softw. Eng. (2014)
13. Zaremski, A.M., Wing, J.M.: Signature matching: a key to reuse. In: Proceedings of 1st ACM SIGSOFT Symposium on the Foundations of Software Engineering, Los Angeles, 08–10 December 1993, pp. 182–190 (1993)
14. Hemer, D., Lindsay, P.: Specification-based retrieval strategies for module reuse. In: Proceedings of Australian Software Engineering Conference, Canberra, 27–28 August 2001, pp. 235–243 (2001)
15. Mittermeir, R.T., Pozewaunig, H.: Classifying components by behavioral abstraction. In: Proceedings of 4th Joint Conference on Information Sciences, North Carolina, 23–28 October 1999, pp. 547–550 (1999)
16. Mili, R., Mili, A., Mittermeir, R.T.: Storing and retrieving software components: a refinement based system. IEEE Trans. Softw. Eng. 23, 445–460 (1997)
17. Meng, F.C., Zhan, D.C., Xu, X.F.: A specification-based approach for retrieval of reusable business component for software reuse. World Acad. Sci. Eng. Technol. 15, 240–247 (2006)

Data Mining Classification Models for Industrial Planning

Ricardo Bragança[1], Filipe Portela[1(✉)], A. Vale[2], Tiago Guimarães[1], and Manuel Santos[1]

[1] Algoritmi Research Centre, University of Minho, Guimarães, Portugal
a51055@alunos.uminho.pt, {cfp,mfs}@dsi.uminho.pt
[2] Value Added Partners, Porto, Portugal

Abstract. The data mining models are an excellent tool to help companies that live from the sale of items they produce. With these models combined with Lean Production, it becomes easier to remove waste and optimize industrial production. This project is based on the phases of the methodology CRISP-DM. Several methods were applied to this data namely, average, mean and standard deviation, quartiles and Sturges rule. Classification Techniques were used in order to understand which model has the best probability of hitting the correct result. After performing the tests, model M1 was the one with the best chance to accomplish a great level of classification having 99.52% of accuracy.

Keywords: Data mining · Classification · CRISP-DM · DSR · Lean · WEKA

1 Introduction

Companies in industry are increasingly feeling the need to find a way to optimize their production to meet the adversities of the economic world. One of the best ways to do this is using the data mining models that allow, based on past sales, get an estimate of how much will sell the right time, production efficiently and reducing the waste of raw material and labor work. The rating models are a great tool to help businesses achieved success. Having said that, test yourself several models in terms of classification hoping to find models with higher accuracy than 90%.

This paper initially made an overview of the concepts inherent in the project including data mining, Lean Production and Decision Support ending with what exists today. Subsequently it is presented methodologies, CRISP-DM, DSR and at the level of the tools was used WEKA. Then the paper presents the results following the phases of the CRISP-DM. Finally, it created a little discussion about the project and concluding with the presentation of closing arguments.

© Springer Nature Singapore Pte Ltd. 2017
M. Singh et al. (Eds.): ICACDS 2016, CCIS 721, pp. 585–594, 2017.
DOI: 10.1007/978-981-10-5427-3_60

2 Background

2.1 Data Mining

In the world there is a vast amount of data stored, but these are only examined in a very superficial way, which leads to having a wealth of data and great poverty of knowledge [1]. In the last decades, data mining has been widely recognized as an powerful and versatile tool of data analysis and has made a significant contribution in the areas of information technology clinical medicine, sociology, physics, in the areas of management, economics and finance [2]. Data mining (DM) is the task that seeks to discover patterns in data sets by using methods of artificial intelligence, machine learning, statistics and database systems [3]. Wu [4] suggests a more complete definition for DM, he believes it is the integration of various subjects: (i) databases, (ii) databases technologies, (iii) statistic, (iv) machine learning, (v) math, (vi) neural networks and others. The DM was designed to use two techniques, predictive and descriptive. The predictive also known as supervised learning is characterized by obtaining examples and input data, predicting future values. In turn, descriptive also known as unsupervised learning is characterized by learning through data grouping with identical characteristics [5].

2.2 Lean Production (LP)

LP originates from the Toyota Company, started in the end of World War II with the implementation of the Toyota Production System (TPS) and aimed to increase productivity and reduce the cost of car production by eliminating any waste. The fact that this system allowed for Toyota leadership in the automotive market has led researchers at the Massachusetts Institute of Technology (MIT) dubs it Lean Production [6]. The LP is an organizational model that brings numerous benefits to the organization that implements it by reducing costs and eliminating waste [7]. There is a great difficulty to find the best setting for LP as the existing definitions and their focus differs from author to author, as well as the practices involved [8]. The Lean term comprises the establishment of a culture of continual improvement and organizational learning [9]. At the operating level, it reduces unnecessary production time, materials and manufacturing efforts, thus reducing the cost by reducing waste [10]. There are obstacles that must be taken into account when seeking the implementation of this methodology, namely the human factor, often brings the rejection of change by employees and that can cast doubt to the implementation of Lean [11]. The implementation of Lean is a lengthy process, thus requiring a well-defined strategy and must involve top management in the process so that there is real knowledge of the organization [6].

2.3 Decision Support

The Decision Support refers to applications involving broad analyses and exploration of current and historical data in organizations supporting the high-level

Decision-making. The decision Support requires the integration of two types of management:

- **Data management,** which includes the organization's databases that are managed by database management systems;
- **Knowledge management,** which handles tasks related to reasoning.

Due to various limitations existing in the processing of human Knowledge it is necessary to use other support. In the Simon's decision-making process there are three main phases [12]:

- **Intelligence,** at this stage the decision maker observes reality, identifies and defines the problems. The main requirement of decision support is the ability to observe internal and external sources of information in search of opportunities and problems interpreting being it discovered.
- **Design,** here is built the representative model of the system through assumptions that simplify the reality and describe the relationship between variables, then the model is validated. In the design phase, the support to decision involves generating alternatives, discussion of selection criteria, the importance of the chosen criteria, and forecasting consequences.
- **Choice,** at this stage it is made the choice of model of the proposed solution, following its assessment. Different scenarios are tested in order to select the option that reinforces the final decision in decision support.

2.4   Related Work

In the production context, new sensor technologies and the increased application of simulation and monitoring systems led to an enormous increase of manufacturing data. Additionally, a new approach for the assessment of manufacturing quality based on process signals from the machine tool is proposed, which provides current tool state and information for every manufacturing process. In order to reuse and evaluate this data for knowledge-based process planning, an approach to manufacturing data collection and evaluation using data mining methods was developed. An analysis and classification of manufacturing data has been carried out to identify input data for knowledge-based process planning [13]. Ming-Te et al. [14], suggest the use of DM, notably Genetic Programming, Artificial Neural Networks and Logistic Regression to improve the LP configuration for improved performance.

Groger et al. [15] presented a paper describing the optimization of manufacturing as a targeted approach to the DM. Based on a huge amount of data, previously defines the cases of DM use that will be applied to identify hidden data patterns to optimize the entire manufacturing process. By using Dashboards and Key Performance Indicators (KPI) it is possible to analyze in the depth the reasons for deviations and presented indication in order to improve processes.

Unver [16] indicates that there is an opportunity expressed in manufacturing industries for a concept denominated Intelligent manufacturing. This concept is used all the advantages of Lean: cost control; quality improvement and product and waste disposal, combined with business intelligence more precisely the dashboards presenting the processed data and KPI, which allow managers to determine the most appropriate options for applying Lean. Vazan et al. [17] indicates that there is an opportunity expressed in manufacturing industries for a concept denominated Intelligent manufacturing. This concept is used all the advantages of Lean: cost control; quality improvement and product and waste disposal, combined with business intelligence more precisely the dashboards presenting the processed data and KPI, which allow managers to determine the most appropriate options for applying Lean.

3 Methods and Tools

Throughout the project, we used two methodological approaches, Design Science Research (DSR) and Cross Industry Standard Process for Data Mining (CRISP-DM).

As the first methodology is in the field of Information Systems (IS), it was used for conducting the research process. As the second one is a project linked to data mining it will be used in carrying out the project. In the last years the DSR regained importance in the paradigm of research specifically in the field of IS [18]. In the IS area, DSR is used in the construction of artifacts in a countless number of areas from systems for decision support, Modeling tools, assessment methods and among others [19]. DSR is a set of techniques and synthetic and analytical perspectives to conduct research processes. The main objective of this approach is the creation of knowledge through the design of new and innovative artifacts and analysis of their use and performance along with reflection and abstraction [20]. DSR consists of six phases: (i) Identification of the problem and motivation, which defines the specific research problem and where the value of the solution is justified; (ii) Definition of the solution objectives and identification of goals for the problem definition and knowledge of what is possible; (iii) Development and Design of the solution, at this stage artifacts for the solution are created; (iv) Demonstration, is intended at this stage to demonstrate the efficacy of articles developed in the previous stage to solve the problem; (v) Evaluation, at this stage is intended to observe and measure how the artifact can actually support the solution of the problem; (vi) Communication, at this stage communication is made to the researchers and/or professionals interested, what is the found problem, its importance, which artifacts have been developed, as well as its usefulness and the fact of whether it is a novelty or not [21].

One of the main methods of data mining is the CRISP-DM and it was developed by a consortium comprised of NCR Systems Engineering Copenhagen, DaimlerChrysler AG, SPSS Inc. and OHRA Verzekering en Bank Groep B.V. [22]. The main objective of this methodology is to define a complete data mining process from Understanding the data for the implementation of developed models through the monitoring of improvements The main objective of this methodology consists in defining a complete data mining process from understanding the data to the implementation of developed models through the monitoring of improvements [23].

This approach consists of six main phases: (1) Business Understanding, (2) Data Understanding, (3) Data Preparation, (4) Modeling, (5) Evaluation and (6) Implementation [24]. The WEKA was the tool chosen to implement this project because despite being widely used in data mining projects is also open source.

Taking into account the circumstances of the project, it can be said that an investigation is centered on a problem, which leads to starting the investigation on the problem identification and motivation stage at the DSR level and finish in the communication phase. The problem that gave rise to this research is the existence, in the organization to be held, at the level of intervention, of a misfit production in the face of orders received as excess produce, which entails a series of costs. Through the development of the article, we intend to adjust the production to the reality of the company as well as the reduction/elimination of existing waste. Therefore, it is essential to use the CRISP-DM methodology in order to understand how the business works, understand the data, and prepare the data, eliminating what does not make sense, obtaining the models that were applied to the data and evaluation of models. The evaluation was performed using WEKA tool that helped get the results of each model.

4   Industrial Planning

As previously stated the entire project was developed following CRISP-DM methodology. The next section describes the stages of this methodology.

4.1   Business Understanding

This project is part of the need to eliminate all types of waste inherent in the process of a producer organization of textile labels and their role is to design, produce, manipulate and encode all types of labels for de leading companies of confection and sale of textile products and supplements worldwide. For this purpose, we developed data mining models that will be presented in subsequent points.

4.2   Data Understanding

The data used to carry out this project concern the quantity sold of a product from 09-11-2012 to 19-02-2016 and contain 4299 records. In Table 1 is found a description of the attributes that initially existed before proceeding to any kind of change. After performing a data analysis, it was denoted the existence of periods with no data because there was no data from the beginning to the end of the calendar year analysis.

Table 1. Description of the initial attributes

Attribute	Description	Example	Maximum	Minimum	Average
Article	Article nomenclature	REFXPTA	n.a.	n.a.	n.a.
Data	Day, month and year in which particular item has been sold	2014-01-06	19-02-2016	09-11-2012	n.a.
Quantity	Quantity sold by a particular article	47.350.692	199.000	−31.800	7.273.498

4.3 Data Preparation

In order to obtain results as reliable as possible the interval was shortened from 01-01-2014 to 30-12-2015, thereby obtaining 52 completed weeks in each of the years. Given the introduction of the number of weeks, in addition to changing the attributes, they were also performed calculations in the attribute of quantity sold, particular sum and medium, thus obtaining the classes to which the quantities belong. In Table 2 is a description of the attributes that will be used later in the models.

Table 2. Description of the attributes that have changed

Attribute	Description	Example
Article	Article nomenclature	REFXPTA
Year	Year in which a particular item has been sold	2014
Week	Number of the week a particular item has been sold	1
Quantity	Sold quantity of a certain item	196.745
Class	Class is inserted where the quantities	]0;196.745]

After completing the grouping, it was necessary to resort for methods able to identify the quantity sold interval, to perform predictions using the classification approach.

Taking into account the absence of a method able to determine these intervals, it was used: Average, quartiles, medium and standard deviation and Sturges rule.

The average was calculated using the mathematical expression $\overline{\chi} = \frac{1}{n}\sum_{i=1}^{n} xi$ where n is the number of weeks and xi is the quantity sold of given article. The intervals are $[min, \overline{x}]$ and $]\overline{x}, max]$. Another important method is the quartiles, a non- central measure of tendency, that in face of a sample, is intended to determine a set of four distinct classes. In the first instance, it was necessary to sort the data set in ascending order and then identify the maximum and minimum value. To determine the first class is necessary to identify the minimum quantity sold of article sample REFXPTA and the value of the sold amount corresponding to the first quartile to determine this amount was necessary to use the following calculation $xn = \frac{(25\%*n)}{100\%}$. The first class has defined as a range between two values, $[min, xn = \frac{25\%*n}{100\%}]$, the range determines the following class $]xn = \frac{25\%*n}{100\%}, xn = \frac{50\%*n}{100\%}]$, the third class is defined by the range $]xn = \frac{50\%*n}{100\%}, xn = \frac{75\%*n}{100\%}]$ and finally the fourth grade $]xn = \frac{75\%*n}{100\%}, max]$. The mean and standard deviation methods require the same calculation made in the first describe method, but it needs the value of the standard deviation. Once identified, its value was determined by:

$$s = \sqrt{\frac{\sum_{i=1}^{n}(xi - \overline{x})^2}{n-1}}$$

The variable xi is the quantity sold per week and n the number of weeks. From the determined values, the classes were defined. One of the intervals can be set by $]\overline{x}, \overline{x} + s]$, but it is important to note that the upper and lower values cannot exceed the *max* and *min* respectively. Finally, we determine the classes using the Sturges rule. The number of classes is determined from the expression $k = 1 + 3,322 * \log_{10} 208$ and the amplitude of each class was determined by reference to $amplitude = (max - \min)/k$. The first class corresponds to the range that is determined by the *min* value calculation and application $h1 = \min + amplitude$, The first range is obtained from $k1 = [min, h1]$. The second range will be obtained from $k2 =]h1, h1 + amplitude]$; the remaining intervals are calculated according to this process, sequentially to determine the set of class. In Table 3 is an example of dataset, which corresponds to the average data amount sold, by applying the Sturges rule.

Table 3. Example dataset

Class number	Class	Quantity
1	[0;59535875.13]	19
2	]59535875.13;119071750.3]	26
3	]119071750.3;178607625.4]	31
4	]178607625.4;238143500.5]	10
5	]238143500.5;297679375.625]	8
6	]297679375.625;357215250.75]	2
7	]357215250.75;416751125.875]	4
8	]416751125.875;476287000]	4

4.4 Modeling

While carrying out this project and having in consideration that it intends to build predictive models in order to foresee what it will produce, supervised learning techniques will be used, more precisely in this case the classification. In the classification, it was used as a target to classes obtained by applying the methods referenced from above. The techniques used in the models were classification Support Vector Machine (SVM), Decision Tree (DT), Naive Bayes (NB). The techniques used to the classification level were J48, Naive Bayes, MultyLayerPerceptron e LisbSVM (Table 4). The sampling method 10-folds Cross Validation was implemented to test mechanism for the models. At the level of NB, a default application was utilized.

Table 4. Description of models

Model	Description
M1	Average application to the average quantities sold
M2	Application quartile average of quantities sold
M3	Application average and standard deviation of the average quantities sold
M4	Application Sturges rule to the average quantities sold
M5	Average application to the sum of quantities sold
M6	Application of quartiles to the sum of quantities sold
M7	Application the mean and standard deviation to the sum of quantities
M8	Application Sturges rule to the sum of quantities sold

Regarding the SVM, a radial basis function at the level of the kernel was used. The DT's possessed a confidence factor of 0.25 and a number of folds equals to three.

4.5 Evaluation

In order to determine which is the best model for use in industrial planning, it was carried out their evaluation for the classification (Table 5). According to the accuracy, which is the ability of a classifier correctly predict the class of new data and the accuracy average, as its name indicates is the average of the classifiers applied to each model. The best models are those in which the percentage of accuracy is closer to 100%. Following this, the models M1 and M5 with a percentage of accuracy of 99.52% and 86.54% respectively, which means that these designs are more likely to achieve. At the other end of the standings, have the M2 and M4 models with 72.84% e 74.04% respectively. Note that the four algorithms tested in each model, the more times that obtained better result was J48 decision tree followed by Naive Bayes.

Table 5. Classification results

Model	Best algorithm	Accuracy	Accuracy average
M1	MultyLayer Perceptron; LisbSVM	100.00%	99.52%
M2	J48	97.12%	72.84%
M3	J48	94.23%	80.05%
M4	NaiveBayes	91.35%	74.04%
M5	J48	99.04%	86.54%
M6	J48	97.12%	75.96%
M7	J48; NaiveBayes	96.15%	82.21%
M8	NaiveBayes	96.15%	77.89%

5 Discussion

After completing the analysis of the obtained models, it could be perceived that on average the specimens had higher percentage of accuracy, in other words, those that are more likely to hit, are the models that have fewer classes as target. In this case, both the average the sum of the quantity sold as the average number of average sold. However, only the second can achieve accuracy higher than the acceptable values (95%). On the other end, the classification model that contained the average quantity sold per week, which was applied, to Sturges rule was what got worst rating with about 91% accuracy.

On the subject of acuity, the best designs are repeated with the model M1 on the lead followed by M5. Regarding the last classified, there were scrambled, being in last place also the average quantities sold, but this time it was applying the standard deviation. On average, the algorithm that obtained better result more often at the level of acuity was the one belonging to decision trees J48.

6   Conclusion and Future Work

To conclude, it is important to understanding how the data mining models are significant in industrial planning. Together with methodologies such as Lean Production, is a fundamental tool to combat waste and help the optimization of industrial production. Taking into account the data obtained and its modifications it can be shown that, at the level of classification, the best model is the M rating because it is what had the best percentage of accuracy meaning that it is more likely to hint.

When it comes to forecasting quantities sold, it is no enough just to look at the quantities sold in previous years it is also necessary to take into account the weather to realize the impact that it may have had on production.

In the future work, it is important to carry out the last phase of CRISP-DM, which is the phase of implementation, taking these models into practice, helping this way all organization to improve their production process.

Today there is a huge amount of production data (Big Data), and each time more, people want to get the necessary information in real time, which requires us to learn and adapt our technologies and techniques. Given this, it was interesting to explore these increasingly dominant options in the world of technology.

Acknowledgements. This work has been supported by Compete: POCI-01-0145-FEDER-007043 and FCT - Fundação para a Ciência e Tecnologia within the Project Scope UID/CEC/00319/2013.

References

1. Alsultanny, Y.: Labor market forecasting by using data mining. Procedia Comput. Sci. **18**, 1700–1709 (2013)
2. Xu, W., Zheng, T., Li, Z.: A neural network based forecasting method for the unemployment rate: prediction using the search engine query data. Presented at the 2011 Eighth IEEE International Conference on e-Business Engineering (2011)
3. Ramos, S., Duarte, J., Duarte, F.J., Vale, Z.: A data-mining-based methodology to support MV electricity customers characterization. Procedia Energy Build. **91**, 16–25 (2015)
4. Yan, W.: Application research of data mining technology about teaching quality assessment in colleges and universities. Procedia Eng. **15**, 4241–4245 (2011)
5. Ren, X., Yan, D., Hong, T.: Data mining of space heating system performance in affordable housing. Procedia Build. Environ. **89**, 1–13 (2015)
6. Maia, L., Alves, A., Leão, C.: Metodologias para Implementar Lean Production: Uma Revisão Crítica de Literatura. Presented at the 6º Congresso Luso-Moçambicano de Engenharia (CLME2011) A Engenharia no combate à pobreza, pelo desenvolvimento e competitividade (2011)
7. Maia, L., Alves, A., Leão, C.: Definition of a protocol for implementing lean production methodology in textile and clothing case studies. Presented at the ASME 2013 International Mechanical Engineering Congress and Exposition, San Diego, California, USA (2013)
8. Hasle, P., Bojesen, A., Jensen, P., Bramming, P.: Lean and working environment: a review of the literature. Int. J. Oper. Prod. Manag. **32**(7), 829–849 (2012)

9. Yamamoto, Y., Bellgran, M.: Fundamental mindset that drives improvements towards lean production. Assem. Autom. **30**(2), 124–130 (2010)

10. Hassan, K., Kajiwara, H.: Application of pull concept-based lean production system in the ship building industry. J. Ship Prod. Des. **29**(3), 105–116 (2013)

11. Balashova, E., Gromova, E.: Prospects and specifics of resource management in enterprises operating in different sectors of the Russian economy. Econ. Manag. Enterp. **216**(2), 102–108 (2015)

12. Turban, E., Sharda, R., Delen, D.: Decision Support and Business Intelligence Systems, 9th edn. Prentice Hall, Upper Saddle River (2011)

13. Denkena, B., Schmidt, J., Kruger, M.: Data mining approach for knowledge-based process planning. Presented at the 2nd International Conference on System-Integrated Intelligence: Challenges for Product and Production Engineering (2014)

14. Ming-Te, L., Kuo-Chung, M., Pan, W.-T.: Using data mining technique to perform the performance assessment of lean service. Neural Comput. Appl. **22**(7), 1433–1445 (2013)

15. Groger, C., Nidermann, F., Mitschang, B.: Data mining-driven manufacturing process optimization. Presented at the World Congress on Engineering 2012, London, UK (2012)

16. Unver, H.: An ISA-95-base manufacturing intelligence system in support of lean initiatives. Int. J. Adv. Manuf. Technol. **65**(5), 853–866 (2013)

17. Vazan, P., Tanuska, P., Kebisek, M.: The data mining usage in production system management. Int. J. Mech. Aerosp. Ind. Mechatron. Manuf. Eng. **5**(5), 922–926 (2011)

18. Myers, M., Venable, J.: A set of ethical principles for design science research in information systems. Procedia Inf. Manag. **51**, 801–809 (2014)

19. Gregor, S., Hevner, A.: Positioning and presenting design science research for maximum impact. MIS Q. **37**(2), 337–355 (2013)

20. Vaishnavi, V., Kuechler, B.: Design science research in information systems (2013). http://desrist.org/desrist/content/design-science-research-in-information-systems.pdf

21. Hain, S., Andrea, B.: Towards a maturity model for e-collaboration - a design science research approach. Presented at the 44th Hawaii International Conference on System Sciences (2011)

22. Erohin, O., Kuhlang, P., Schallow, J., Deuse, J.: Intelligent utilisation of digital databases for assembly time determination in early phases of product emergence. Procedia CIRP **3**, 424–429 (2012)

23. Hoe, A., et al.: Analyzing students records to identify patterns of students performance. Presented at the 2013 International Conference on Research and Innovation in Information Systems (ICRIIS) (2013)

24. Wallis, R., Erohin, O., Klinkenberg, R., Deuse, J., Stromberger, F.: Data mining - supported generation of assembly process plans. Procedia CIRP **23**, 178–183 (2014)

Designing a Smart-Contract Application Layer for Transacting Decentralized Autonomous Organizations

Alex Norta[(✉)]

Department of Software Systems, Tallinn University of Technology,
Akadeemia tee 15A, 12816 Tallinn, Estonia
`alex.norta.phd@ieee.org`

Abstract. This keynote paper addresses existing problems with traditional non-machine readable contracts that are based on trust. Such contracts have mostly a ceremonial purpose between transacting business parties and when conflicts occur, traditional contracts are often not enforcible. On the other hand, so called smart contracts that are machine readable and supported by blockchain-technology transactionalities, do not require qualitative trust between contracting parties as blockchain establish instead a quantitative notion of trust. However, currently existing smart-contract solutions that equip the protocol layer on top of blockchains with Turing-complete programming languages, lead to the false claim by industry practitioners they can manage smart contracts successfully. Instead, it is important to start considering the currently missing application layer for smart contracts.

Keywords: Decentralized autonomous organization · Smart contract · Blockchain · E-governance · Lifecycle management

1 Introduction

The traditional understanding of a contract is a written or spoken agreement enforceable by law. An important prerequisite for a contract is that the parties involved voluntarily engage to establish a consensus [10]. In most business cases, contracts are documents [22] that identify the contracting parties uniquely, a service that is offered for some form of compensation that is usually monetary, and a set of additional clauses such as service-delivery dates, penalties for delivery failure, compensation clauses, and so on. Subsequent transactions are trust-based and contracting parties usually consider contracts as a symbol for an existing business deal. Another problem with the traditional form of setting up and managing contracts is that they are often underspecified. Most importantly, traditional contracts do not provide sufficient details about the actual transaction process and consequently, frictions between the contracting parties are very likely, e.g., one party assumes a specific product certificate before delivering a partial compensation and the other party assumes the opposite. The resulting

© Springer Nature Singapore Pte Ltd. 2017
M. Singh et al. (Eds.): ICACDS 2016, CCIS 721, pp. 595–604, 2017.
DOI: 10.1007/978-981-10-5427-3_61

deadlocks lead to costly conflict resolutions, or even a collapse of the entire contract transaction. Also the enforcement of traditional contracts [14] proves to be either too complicated, time consuming, or impossible, certainly in international circumstances.

A solution for the listed issues pertaining to managing traditional contracts is to aim for an automation in the form of smart electronic contracts [26] that govern business transactions between decentralized autonomous organizations (DAO) [4]. A smart contract is a computerized transaction protocol [25] to execute contract terms and blockchain technology [15] is suitable for achieving non-repudiation with fact-tracking of a consensual smart-contract agreement. The blockchain is a distributed database for independently verifying the chain of ownership of artifacts [21] in hash values that result from cryptographic digests.

Recently, an experiment with a DAO [1] has been developed with the smart-contract technology of Ethereum[1]. This DAO served as a crowdfunding project[2] and was hacked because of security flaws, resulting in a loss of $50 million. The incident shows it is not enough to merely equip the protocol layer on top of a blockchain with a Turing-complete language such as Solidity[3] to realize secure smart-contract management. Instead, we propose in this keynote paper that it is crucial to address a gap for secure smart-contract management pertaining to the currently ignored application-layer development.

The remainder of this keynote paper is structured as follows. Section 2 gives a brief overview of the sociotechnical implications of smart contracts for DAOs. Section 3 commences with the setup phase of a lifecycle for a smart-contract management application. Next, Sect. 4 discusses the ad-hoc establishment of a distributed governance process for smart-contract enactment, semantic rollback and termination that Sect. 5 shows. Section 6 briefly discusses latest scholarly publications and blockchain-technology innovations that enable smart-contract management. Finally, Sect. 7 concludes this keynote paper and proposes future research directions.

2   Sociotechnical Implications

It is important to briefly point out the profound sociotechnical implications of blockchain-technology enabled machine-readable smart contracts. Traditional contract management comprises soft and fraudulent, qualitative decision making that requires enormous centralized-planning coercion for stateism-powered enforcement. On the other hand, smart contracts promise to achieve a transition of society [2,29] towards hard and objective, quantitative decision making based on trustless [24], disintermediated, decentralized and distributed organizational structures.

We next give some examples of those novel solutions that blockchain-technology enables beyond the initial crypto-currency inception of bitcoin [15].

---

[1] https://ethereum.org/.

[2] https://www.wired.com/2016/06/50-million-hack-just-showed-dao-human/.

[3] https://solidity.readthedocs.io/en/develop/.

These examples are free-market innovations that are superior to government solutions that stateist laws ignore and often criminalize. One example is a blockchain-based notary service[4] that cryptographically digests multimedia files and returns a uniquely identifying number at a specific timestamp. If only a single bit of the multimedia file changes, the identifying number changes resulting from a cryptographic digest.

Another notable example is a blockchain-technology based passport[5] that is more secure than traditional government-issued passports. The former can be instrumental for trading services on a Governance 2.0 platform termed Bitnation[6] that also serves as an e-notary for the Estonian e-Residency program[7].

Also state-of-the-art industrial applications employ blockchain technology. For example, cyber-physical systems use blockchains [5] to solve critical e-governance problems. Blockchains also enable new business models [32] in Internet-of-Things (IoT) applications. Even potential data-privacy violations in e-healthcare [31] can be tackled with the help of blockchains and there are many more sociotechnical application domains we can not list here due to page limitations.

For all the examples above, smart contracts are a means to enable e-governance for novel business models. Consequently, we next conceptually describe the secure application-level lifecycle management that industrial smart-contract solutions do not yet consider. Note that the respective lifecycle stages are conceptual summaries from published research papers that we reference in the sequel.

3   The Setup Phase

A peer-to-peer (P2P) smart-contract collaboration model Sect. 3.1 presents. Next, Sect. 3.2 gives the high-level structure of the academic smart-contract language termed eSourcing Markup Language (eSML) that we use as a proof of concept for an earlier ontology study [19]. Finally, Sect. 3.3 shows the smart-contract setup lifecycle.

3.1   P2P-Collaboration Model

Pertaining to DAO-collaborations, Fig. 1(a) conceptually depicts a configuration. The blueprint for an electronic-community formation is a so-called business-network model (BNM) [23]. The latter captures choreographies that are relevant for a business scenario and it contains legally valid template contracts that are service types with affiliated organizational roles. The BNMs are available in a collaboration hub that houses business processes as a service (BPaaS-HUB) [9] in the form of subset process views [9]. The latter enable a fast and semi-automatic discovery of collaboration parties for learning about their identity, services, reputation, and so on.

---

[4] https://proofofexistence.com/.
[5] https://www.youtube.com/watch?v=1iAg6BITPdc.
[6] https://bitnation.co/.
[7] https://cointelegraph.com/news/estonian-e-residency-and-bitnation-launch-new-public-notary-in-blockchain-jurisdiction.

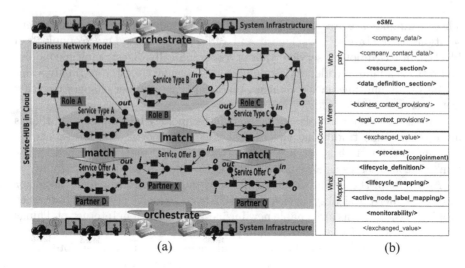

Fig. 1. P2P-collaboration using the eSourcing framework [17].

On the external layer of Fig. 1(a), service offers identically match with service types contained in the BNM with the contractual sphere of collaborating parties. Additionally, a collaborating partner must match into the specific partner roles associated with a respective service type. We refer the reader to [8,9] for details about the tree-based process-view matching to establish a DAO-configuration into a contract-based collaborations.

3.2 Smart-Contract Structure

Figure 1(b) shows the top-level structure of a smart-contract language termed eSourcing Markup Language (eSML) [19]. The core structure of a smart contract we organize according to the interrogatives *Who* for defining the contracting parties together with their resources and data definitions, *Where* to specify the business- and legal context, and *What* for specifying the exchanged business values. For achieving a consensus, we assume the *What*-interrogative employs matched process views that require cross-organizational alignment for monitorability. We refer to [19] for more information about the smart-contract ontology.

3.3 Conceptual Setup Lifecycle

The lifecycle of Fig. 2 commences with breeding collaboration inceptions that produce BNMs comprising service types and roles. The BNMs that emerge from the breeding ecosystem exist permanently for repeated use in the subsequent populating stage. The validation of BNMs matches the available inserted service offers of potential collaboration eCommunity partners against service types.

Fig. 2. Conceptual contracting setup-lifeycle for smart-contract establishment [17].

The *populate*-phase in Fig. 2, yields a proto-contract for a *negotiate* step that involves the collaborating partners. The negotiation phase has three different outcome options. An agreement of all partners establishes a smart contract for subsequent rollout of a distributed governance infrastructure (DGI); a counteroffer from a partner that results in a new contract negotiation; finally, a disagreement of an eCommunity partner results in a complete termination of the setup phase. Note that the setup-lifecycle is formalized and we refer the reader to [16] for further details.

4   Deducing a Distributed Governance Infrastructure

In a vertical time-line depicted in Fig. 3, we show the creation sequence for elements of a distributed governance infrastructure for enactment. If all eCommunity partners agree during the *negotiate* stage, a smart contract comes into existence that serves as a DGI-coordinating agent. In the *enterprise infrastructure distribution*, local smart-contract copies come into existence for every eCommunity-partner together with business network model agents (BNMA) and monitors. The *extract* stage creates sets of policies from the local smart-contract copies and assigns each a BNMA and monitor. Finally, the *prepare* stage populates the lowest technical DGI-level with matching services and corresponding endpoints for communication channels before *enactment*. For dismantling the DGI, the *termination* stage removes the entire infrastructure step by step.

Once the e-governance infrastructure is set up, technically realizing the behavior in the local copies of the contracts requires concrete local electronic services. After picking these services follows a creation of communication endpoints so that the services of the partners are able to communicate with each other. The final step of the preparation is a liveness check of the channel-connected services. The enactment by an engine carries out the tasks contained in the local electronic services and propels the eCommunity business collaboration technically.

5   Enacting, Rolling Back and Terminating

Three business-semantics rollback scenarios exist [12,20] that may either be disruptive or calming, and that govern the transition of an eCommunity from one configuration to another. A conceptual depiction of these rollbacks Fig. 4 shows. Briefly, disruptive rollbacks imply a smart-contract renegotiation must start from

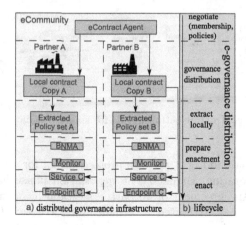

Fig. 3. Properties of a distributed governance infrastructure [12].

scratch again. Calming rollbacks imply that the DAOs of an eCommunity see scope to reconcile collaboration issues. In both cases, the eCommunity experiences configuration changes.

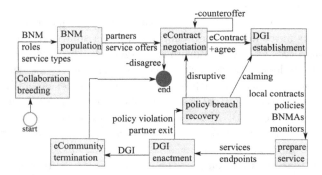

Fig. 4. A conceptual lifecycle for rolling back collaboration conflicts [20].

Pertaining to Fig. 4, there are one disruptive and three conflict calming business-semantics rollbacks. The first type of disruptive business-semantics rollback commences after the decision to replace a current eCommunity partner with the objective to set up a new DGI. Thus, the disruptive business-semantics rollback dismantles the existing DGI and rolls back to the *negotiation*-service. Such a business-semantics rollback implies it is possible to have multiple eCommunity partners choose to discontinue their involvement in a newly emerging smart contract. Note that a policy-violating partner may again be part of the new smart contract. We infer, the reason for a disruptive partner change is caused by a policy violation of a severity that does not permit an eCommunity to continue collaboration.

Of the remaining three conflict calming business-semantics rollbacks, one also replaces an eCommunity-partner in a way where it does not dismantle and recreate a DGI. Likewise, the other conflict calming business-semantics rollbacks equally leave the existing DGI intact. If the eCommunity-partners vote to ignore a respective policy violation, the related smart-contract enactment resumes without any modification. The third type of conflict calming business-semantics rollback allows the complete replacement of a local smart contract copy with a new one as part of the existing DGI that remains otherwise unchanged. Thus, the new local smart contract and related policies, BNMA and monitor must adhere to the main DGI-coordinating smart-contract agent.

6 Discussion

So far, blockchain-technology innovation stem from free-market, open-source initiatives. Only very recently, also traditional computer-science academia realizes that blockchain-technology can no longer be ignored. Thus, Sect. 6.1 gives recent academic related work and Sect. 6.2 discusses recent smart-contract innovation that employs blockchain technology.

6.1 Academic Related Work

The authors in [27] map a running case of a collaborative process onto a smart-contract scripting language. That approach addresses the trust-issue in collaborative processes in that no single third-party entity must monitor events. Instead, the blockchain enables trustless process collaboration because of no single entity being in control. The mapping from collaborative processes to blockchains enables the monitoring of process enactment and an auditing of related events.

The role of smart contracts supported by blockchains is also stressed in [30] for trust evaluation based on a diverse input of social-media facts. The authors present a proof-of-concept prototype that employs a blockchain ID for combining in a weighted way facts such as the amount of video feeds, number of likes and followers, online reputation, and so on, to calculate a reputation that diverse users may consider, e.g., future employers. The prototype helps to secure the identity of individuals from hijacking, from online character assassination and provides the real reputation of individual. For smart contracts, such a secure reputation system is important for evaluating the potential eCommunity partners during the setup phase and also during enactment-phase conflict resolutions.

Finally in [3], the authors stress that decentralized smart-contract validation requires formal methods. As a mentioned example, game theory is potentially useful to analyze the behavior of contracting parties under the assumption of perfect rationality and return maximization, which is not a realistic assumption given the nature of human action [13] that differs from trivial machines. Such game-theoretical verifications are only suitable when the contracting parties are fully automated software agents. Yet, it is important to formally check the soundness of decentralized smart contracts during the setup phase [18] to assure the enactment of a smart contract is sound to assure a desired termination state.

6.2 Latest Blockchain-Based Smart-Contract Innovation

We briefly discuss some notable blockchain-technology driven smart-contract innovations without claiming completeness. A very prominent example for a smart contract solution is Ethereum [28] that operates on top of a public blockchain-based distributed computing platform to execute peer-to-peer contracts using a crypto-currency called ether. Solidity[8] is the smart-contract language employed in Ethereum that is a statically typed object-oriented language resembling Java in its syntax.

Another smart-contract system is Lisk[9] that differs from Ethereum in that every blockchain application is on its own sidechain. Informally, sidechaining allows tokens from one blockchain to be securely used within a completely separate blockchain and still moved back to the original chain. Furthermore, Lisk also differs from Ethereum by using JavaScript for smart-contract specifications.

More recently, Synereo [11] emerged from a failed implementation of a censorship-free social media such as facebook using Ethereum. The failure reasons are a lack of Ethereum scalability because of the full replication of the blockchain into every node, combined with costly proof-of-work block validations. Synereo uses RChain[10] that is a concurrent and compositional blockchain. Furthermore, Synereo adopts as a smart-contract language Rholang[11] that is a concurrency-oriented programming language with a focus on message-passing and asynchrony.

7 Conclusion

This keynote paper investigates the benefits and existing gaps in the use of blockchain-technology supported smart contracts. Traditional contracts that are not machine-readable typically merely have a symbolic character and pose severe problems such as inherent ambiguity that inevitably leads to conflicts, lack of enforceability, and so on. As a solution, machine-readable smart contracts force contracting parties into more detailed specifications yielding a reduction of conflict causes that occur during the enactment stage.

While blockchain-technology driven solutions rapidly penetrate industry-domains such as finance, e-governance, cyber-physical systems solutions such as for Industry 4.0, traditional academia [6,7] only slowly considers blockchain-technology focused research. That is surprising given the interdisciplinary and

---

[8] https://github.com/ethereum/solidity.

[9] https://lisk.io/.

[10] https://blog.synereo.com/2016/09/05/meet-rchain-the-first-scalable-blazing-fast-turing-complete-blockchain/.

[11] https://github.com/synereo/rholang.

scientifically challenging application cases for disruptive concepts such as smart contracts. This paper points out the existing gap in industry solutions pertaining to the application layer for smart contracts, in particular smart-contract lifecycle management. Note that the presented application-layer smart-contract lifecycle is based on pre-existing scholarly literature.

Considering the state of industry solutions, it is evident that the lack of academic involvement is a reason for suboptimal solutions pertaining to achieving a scalable management of blockchains, finding less expensive but still secure means of validating blocks and transactions, developing suitable and expressive Turing-complete smart-contract languages, and so on. We hope this paper raises awareness and results in an enhanced engagement of academia in blockchain research and development.

References

1. Ammous, S.H.: Blockchain technology: what is it good for? Available at SSRN 2832751 (2016)
2. Atzori, M.: Blockchain technology and decentralized governance: is the state still necessary? Available at SSRN (2015)
3. Bigi, G., Bracciali, A., Meacci, G., Tuosto, E.: Validation of decentralised smart contracts through game theory and formal methods. In: Bodei, C., Ferrari, G.-L., Priami, C. (eds.) Programming Languages with Applications to Biology and Security. LNCS, vol. 9465, pp. 142–161. Springer, Cham (2015). doi:10.1007/978-3-319-25527-9_11
4. Butterin, V.: A next-generation smart contract and decentralized application platform (2014)
5. Dai, W., Vyatkin, V., Pang, C., Christensen, J.H.: Time-stamped event based execution semantics for industrial cyber-physical systems. In: 2015 IEEE 13th International Conference on Industrial Informatics (INDIN), pp. 1263–1268, July 2015
6. Dirk, D.: Smart Business Process Management, pp. 207–223. Workflow Management Coalition (2012)
7. Draheim, D.: Business Process Technology: A Unified View on Business Processes, Workflows and Enterprise Applications. Springer Science & Business Media, Heidelberg (2010). doi:10.1007/978-3-642-01588-5
8. Eshuis, R., Norta, A., Kopp, O., Pitkanen, E.: Service outsourcing with process views. IEEE Trans. Serv. Comput. 99(PrePrints):1 (2013)
9. Eshuis, R., Norta, A., Roulaux, R.: Evolving process views. Inf. Softw. Technol. **80**, 20–35 (2016)
10. Hamburger, P.A.: The development of the nineteenth-century consensus theory of contract. Law History Rev. **7**(2), 241–329 (2011)
11. Konforty, D., Adam, Y., Estrada, D., Meredith, L.G.: Synereo: the decentralized and distributed social network (2015)
12. Kutvonen, L., Norta, A., Ruohomaa, S.: Inter-enterprise business transaction management in open service ecosystems. In: 2012 IEEE 16th International Enterprise Distributed Object Computing Conference (EDOC), pp. 31–40. IEEE (2012)
13. von Mises, L.: Human Action. Ludwig von Mises Institute, Auburn (1949)
14. Olsen, M.: How firms overcome weak international contract enforcement: repeated interaction, collective punishment and trade finance. Collective Punishment and Trade Finance, 22 January 2015 (2015)

15. Nakamoto, S.: Bitcoin: a peer-to-peer electronic cash system. Consulted **1**(2012), 28 (2008)

16. Norta, A.: Creation of smart-contracting collaborations for decentralized autonomous organizations. In: Matulevičius, R., Dumas, M. (eds.) BIR 2015. LNBIP, vol. 229, pp. 3–17. Springer, Cham (2015). doi:10.1007/978-3-319-21915-8_1

17. Norta, A.: Establishing distributed governance infrastructures for enacting cross-organization collaborations. In: Norta, A., Gaaloul, W., Gangadharan, G.R., Dam, H.K. (eds.) ICSOC 2015. LNCS, vol. 9586, pp. 24–35. Springer, Heidelberg (2016). doi:10.1007/978-3-662-50539-7_3

18. Norta, A., Eshuis, R.: Specification and verification of harmonized business-process collaborations. Inf. Syst. Front. **12**, 457–479 (2010)

19. Norta, A., Ma, L., Duan, Y., Rull, A., Kõlvart, M., Taveter, K.: eContractual choreography-language properties towards cross-organizational business collaboration. J. Internet Serv. Appl. **6**(1), 1–23 (2015)

20. Norta, A., Othman, A.B., Taveter, K.: Conflict-resolution lifecycles for governed decentralized autonomous organization collaboration. In: Proceedings of the 2015 2nd International Conference on Electronic Governance and Open Society: Challenges in Eurasia, EGOSE 2015, New York, NY, USA, pp. 244–257. ACM (2015)

21. Panikkar, B.S., Nair, S., Brody, P., Pureswaran, V.: ADEPT: An IoT Practitioner Perspective (2014)

22. Roxenhall, T., Ghauri, P.: Use of the written contract in long-lasting business relationships. Ind. Mark. Manage. **33**(3), 261–268 (2004)

23. Ruokolainen, T., Ruohomaa, S., Kutvonen, L.: Solving service ecosystem governance. In: 2011 15th IEEE International Enterprise Distributed Object Computing Conference Workshops (EDOCW), pp. 18–25. IEEE (2011)

24. Schaub, A., Bazin, R., Hasan, O., Brunie, L.: A trustless privacy-preserving reputation system. In: Hoepman, J.-H., Katzenbeisser, S. (eds.) SEC 2016. IAICT, vol. 471, pp. 398–411. Springer, Cham (2016). doi:10.1007/978-3-319-33630-5_27

25. Swan, M.: Blockchain thinking: the brain as a DAC (decentralized autonomous organization). In: Texas Bitcoin Conference, pp. 27–29 (2015)

26. Szabo, N.: Formalizing and securing relationships on public networks. First Monday, **2**(9) (1997)

27. Weber, I., Xu, X., Riveret, R., Governatori, G., Ponomarev, A., Mendling, J.: Untrusted business process monitoring and execution using blockchain. In: La Rosa, M., Loos, P., Pastor, O. (eds.) BPM 2016. LNCS, vol. 9850, pp. 329–347. Springer, Cham (2016). doi:10.1007/978-3-319-45348-4_19

28. Wood, G.: Ethereum: a secure decentralised generalised transaction ledger. Ethereum Proj. Yellow Pap. (2014)

29. Wright, A., De Filippi, P.: Decentralized blockchain technology and the rise of lex cryptographia. Available at SSRN 2580664 (2015)

30. Yasin, A., Liu, L.: An online identity and smart contract management system. In: 2016 IEEE 40th Annual Computer Software and Applications Conference (COMPSAC), vol. 2, pp. 192–198, June 2016

31. Yue, X., Wang, H., Jin, D., Li, M., Jiang, W.: Healthcare data gateways: found healthcare intelligence on blockchain with novel privacy risk control. J. Med. Syst. **40**(10), 1–8 (2016)

32. Zhang, Y., Wen, J.: The IoT electric business model: using blockchain technology for the internet of things. Peer-to-Peer Netw. Appl. **4**, 983–994 (2016)

Digitization of Ancient Manuscripts and Inscriptions - A Review

N. Jayanthi$^{(\boxtimes)}$, S. Indu, Snigdhaa Hasija, and Prateek Tripathi

Electronics and Communication Engineering Department,
Delhi Technological University, Delhi, India
njayanthidce@yahoo.in, s.indu@rediffmail.com,
snigdhaahasija@gmail.com, prattrip@gmail.com

Abstract. The article describes the most recent developments in the field of enhancement and digitization of ancient manuscripts and inscriptions. Digitization of ancient sources of information is essential to have an insight of the rich culture of previous civilizations, which in turn requires the high rate of accuracy in word and character recognition. To enhance the accuracy of the Optical Character Recognition system, the degraded images need to be made compatible for the OCR system. So, the image has to be pre-processed by filtering techniques and segmented by thresholding methods followed by post processing operations. The need for digitization of ancient artefacts is to preserve information that lies in the ancient manuscripts and improve the tourism of our country by attracting more and more tourists. This article gives an analysis of the different methods used for the enhancement of degraded ancient images in terms of low resolution, minimal intensity difference between the text and background, show through effects and uneven background. The techniques reviewed include ICA, NGFICA, Cumulants Based ICA and a novel thresholding technique for text extraction.

Keywords: ICA · NGFICA · Cumulants Based ICA · Thresholding · Text extraction

1 Introduction

A notable amount of research has been conducted for the purpose of extracting the text from deteriorated ancient documents. Images taken from camera and scanned documents at times suffer from the issue of lower resolution, uneven background and minimal intensity difference between foreground and background. Several methods have been proposed for enhancing the document images [2–4, 13, 20] and palm leaf manuscripts [1, 14, 16, 17]. Not much work has been done on the enhancement of inscription images, however some enhancement methods have been addressed for these images in [7, 15, 19] using Independent Component Analysis and line-based decomposition.

The main stages of processing in a digitization system are: noise removal, segmentation and character recognition by OCR. This review focuses on these processing steps and describes the state-of-the-art in this field. It surveys the work on digitization systems for ancient manuscripts from the aspects of:

© Springer Nature Singapore Pte Ltd. 2017
M. Singh et al. (Eds.): ICACDS 2016, CCIS 721, pp. 605–612, 2017.
DOI: 10.1007/978-981-10-5427-3_62

Pre-processing - Filtering techniques for the removal of noise.

Segmentation - Various thresholding techniques to binarize the pre-processed image.

Character recognition by OCR- Converting the manuscripts into machine-readable format.

1.1 Evolution of Digitization of Ancient Documents

Evolution of this field started with the need to retrieve the traditional valuable knowledge on medical treatments (herbal medicines), stories of dynasties, Buddhist doctrine, astrology, astronomy and techniques of traditional massages. Camera held images were filtered, binarized and then digitized by OCR (Table 1).

Table 1. Summarises the different enhancement and binarization techniques outlining the main problems and current research in each of them.

Problems encountered in text extraction from the images	Enhancement techniques	Binarization techniques
Uneven background	Bilateral filtering + morphological operations and Curvelet transform	Contrast and adaptive binarization technique
Low resolution	Filtering in sobolev space, Interpolation based resolution enhancement and Wavelet + MRF approach	Thresholding using average grey values
Low contrast text region	MRF based post processing	Matched Wavelet based text extraction algorithm
Minimal intensity difference between foreground and background	Filtering on the HSV plane and ICA based techniques	Iterative global thresholding
Non uniform brightness	Mean and Median Filtering	Region based binarization method

2 Applications

- For the protection and preservation of cultural heritage.
- Retrieval of traditional valuable knowledge on medical treatments which has helped the field of herbal medicines expands.
- To acquire knowledge from the Buddhist doctrines.
- In the field of astronomy and astrology to discover the ancient method of sky-watching and knowing the position of stars.

- Improving tourism of our country by attracting more and more tourists.
- Preservation of documentary evidence of the past.
- Interpretation of the archived documents for further study and analysis.
- Combining the extracted information from the inscriptions with that from the existent monuments gives an insight into the world's dynastic history [19].

3 Techniques Used in Digitization of Documents

A typical configuration of processing modules is illustrated in Fig. 1

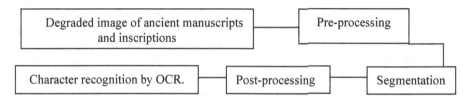

Fig. 1. Traditional flow of processing in digitization of ancient manuscripts and inscriptions.

3.1 Degraded Images of Old Manuscripts

Factors of deterioration of old manuscripts are Physical factors (sunlight, rain, pollution etc.), Biological factors (fungus, insects) and Human factors (improper handling). Such factors result in very low contrast between the foreground text and the background which makes thresholding hard. In order to enhance the legibility of the manuscripts, Digital Image Processing techniques are required.

3.2 Pre-processing

Often images must be made objective to remove parameters that if taken into consideration drastically affect the threshold values required for segmentation:

3.2.1 Use of Different Color Spaces
Using varied color spaces it is possible to obtain and reduce the factors of the environment on the subject image. It is known that RGB is the way the computer perceives color whereas HSV emphasizes more on how the human eye comprehends color [23]. It is thus advisable to create appropriate color maps for proper implementation of some particular filters which helps us achieve better results by making use of the HSV plane. Recently we proposed that filtering techniques on the image in the HSV plane have been used for text extraction from both manuscripts and inscriptions [20].

3.2.2 Noise Removal
Mean and median filtering for images with small letter size does not give good results [27]. Laplacian is generally used for highlighting the regions of rapid intensity change

and Laplacian of Gaussian filter, its improvement, is a better method. For handwritten documents bilateral filtering gives better results than Gaussian and average filtering [4]. In case of uneven background the use of low-pass Wiener filter gives better extraction of text from background [1]. Filtration in weighted sobolev space in comparison with L space enhances the image quality of the poor resolution text images.

3.2.3   Image Enhancement

Once we have removed the noise and have decided a color space based on usage, the enhancement of images can help discipline the threshold values to more stringent levels. Nadernejad et al. proposed simple edge-based approach to identify regions with high edge density and strength [8] which performed well only if there was no complex background. The capability of an image enhancement strategy for inscription images based on Independent components is exhibited in terms of enhancement of the precision of the OCR in comprehending the images as proposed by Garain et al. to enhance images using FastICA algorithm based on the contribution of text in them, resulting in three independent layers or components [7, 15]. Inscription images have minimal intensity difference between the background and the foreground and Fast-ICA based analysis fails in such procedures of text extraction. A suitable method that can minimize the dependency among the signals as it takes into account its slope is Natural gradient Flexible ICA (NGFICA). It is thus suitable for the separation of a mixture of extremely correlated signals [18]. Also we proposed a suitable method [21] to extract the text layer from the inscription images by considering the problem as blind source separation which aims to calculate the independent components from a linear mixture of source signals by maximizing a contrast function based on higher order cumulants, which in turn provides much faster result processing in case of data with high dimensionality as it is based on simultaneous handling of higher order cumulants.

3.3   Segmentation

If the document image contains printed text and handwritten text then hybrid approach (both global and local thresholding) is suitable for extracting information from the image [3]. In case of uneven background, segmentation using contrast adaptive binarization gives better text extraction from background [1]. It is being found that no particular binarization technique can be a fit for all images [16]. Variance based method proposed by Babu et al. - uses variance to separate the regions of text and non-text [6]. Text edges have high variance and vice versa and did not prove successful due to blurred edges of text and minimum distinction between text and non-text region. After using the above mentioned pre-processing techniques, the images become easier to segment and thus help us define stringent thresholding values as depicted in [19–21]. An improvement in past techniques is also possible as depicted in [22]. This method proposes the application of Difference of Gaussian as a second order derivative edge detector combined with Niblack's Thresholding for text extraction from slanted images achieving a precision of 74.8% and a recall of 76.2%.

3.4   Post Processing

In this phase, fundamental morphological operations such as opening, closing, erosion and dilation are generally used for further enhancement of binarised signal.

3.5   Character Recognition by OCR

OCR is amongst the most successful methods used for conversion of text into machine readable digital format [24]. Presents the evolution of OCR techniques. The character recognition capabilities of OCR work reasonably well with printed text but their text recognition capabilities deteriorate when used with ancient manuscripts and inscriptions due to several degradations. Thus, there is a requirement for preprocessing and enhancement techniques for OCR to work on ancient inscriptions and manuscripts [25]. Describes all the pre-processing, feature extraction and post-processing techniques for commercial OCR machines. There are several commercially available OCR packages. There has been a major change in the steps followed in OCR Research [26]. The focus has shifted from the accurate classification of isolated characters to the well-organized domain specific and typographic knowledge as many practical OCR techniques require an integrated understanding of the documents to convert the complex historical inscriptions and manuscripts to computer-readable form.

3.6   Some Robust Digitization Techniques

The following are the methods that combine all of the above to provide proper extraction techniques.

- Novel Method for manuscript and inscription text extraction [20]: In this method the property of the HSV map to isolate the chroma from the luma helps us in generating a method that can work on extracting text from both, inscriptions as well as manuscripts without the need to differentiate among the two types of documentations. Mapping to HSV also helps achieve correct implementation of filters and this further helps in achieving extraction with a precision of 89.6% and a recall of 78.2%. A comparison of the HSV plane processing method which takes into consideration the methodology mentioned above with other prominent method is shown in Table 2.
- Digitization of Historic Inscription Images using Cumulants based Simultaneous Blind Source Extraction [21]: This paper addresses the problem of binarization and enhancement of historic inscription images by considering it a problem of Blind Source Extraction thereby isolating the text layer from the inscription images to calculate the independent components from a linear mixture of source signals. It achieves an F-measure of 79.02% and a PSNR of 10.67. It's comparison with some other methods are shown in Table 3 below.

Table 2. Comparison of text extraction methods

Algorithm	No of images	Result
Messalodi [9]	100 gray scale images of covers	54% precision, 91.2% recall
Otsu [10]	Gray level images of varied sizes	77.6% precision, 67.36% recall
Gllavata [11]	175 images of different types with and without text	84.94% precision 85.94% recall (with local threshold extension)
Kim [12]	50 true color images	124 text lines, 107 (86%) detected
Lee [13]	191 gray scale images	2096 characters, 1916 segmented correctly, 181 errors occurred
Color clustering [14]	83 text images	89.08% precision, 80.15% recall
HSV plane processing [20]	20 inscription and 24 manuscript images	89.6% precision, 78.2% recall

Table 3. Evaluation results based on measures used

Technique	F-measure (%)	PSNR
Cumulant based BSE	79.02	10.67
NGFICA method	63.36	9.95
Fast-ICA based method	57.99	8.21

- NGFICA Based Digitization of Historic Inscription Images [19]: The main problems that this paper helps solve in digitization of inscriptions is perspective distortion, lack of standardization in font and negligible distinction between foreground and background. The proposed method has improved the word recognition accuracy by 65.3% and character recognition accuracy by 54.3% of the OCR system [19].

4   Conclusion

Some of the text extraction and enhancement approaches for the ancient document images, manuscripts and inscription images are discussed in this paper. Proper pre-processing methods lead to good binarization which in turn helps in improving the segmentation process. It is being validated in [16] that no single binarization technique is suitable for all images. From this literature survey we found that the enhancement techniques applied for document images and palm leaf manuscripts cannot give good results for digitizing inscription images. ICA based techniques could be useful for text extraction especially in inscription images.

References

1. Cherala, S., Rege, P.P.: Palm leaf manuscript/color document image enhancement by using improved adaptive binarization method. In: Sixth Indian Conference on Computer Vision, Graphics and Image Processing. 978-0-7695-3476-3/08 $25.00 ©2008 IEEE doi:10.1109/ICVGIP.2008.64

2. Tan, C.L., Cao, R., Shen, P.: Restoration of archival documents using a wavelet technique. IEEE Trans. Pattern Anal. Mach. Intell. **24**(10) (2002)
3. Rao, A.V.S., Sunil, G., Rao, N.V., Prabhu, T.S.K., Reddy, L.P., Sastry, A.S.C.S.: Adaptive binarization of ancient documents. In: 2009 Second International Conference on Machine Vision. IEEE Computer society (2009)
4. Gangamma, B., Srikanta Murthy, K., Singh, A.V.: Restoration of degraded historical document image. J. Emerg. Trends Comput. Inf. Sci. **3**(5) (2012)
5. Chevalier, P., Albera, L., Comon, P., Ferreol, A.: Comparative performance analysis of eight blind source separation methods on radio communications signals. In: Proceedings of the International Joint Conference on Neural Networks, vol. 8, no. 2, pp. 251–276, July 2004
6. Babu, G.R.M., Srimayee, P., Srikrishna, A.: Text extraction from Heterogenous images using mathematical morphology. J. Theor. Appl. Inf. Technol. **15**(5), 795–825 (2008)
7. Garain, U., Jain, A., Maity, A., Chanda, B.: Machine reading of camera-held low quality text images an ICA based image enhancement approach for improving OCR accuracy. In: ICPR, pp. 1–4, June 2008
8. Nadernejad, E., Sharifzadeh, S., Hassanpour, H.: Edge detection techniques: evaluations and comparisons. Appl. Math. Sci. **2**(31), 1507–1520 (2008)
9. Hua, S., Yin, P., Zhang, H.J.: Efficient video text recognition using multiple frame integration. In: Proceedings of the International Conference on Image Processing, vol. 2, pp. 22–25, September 2004
10. Choi, S., Cichocki, A., Amari, S.: Flexible independent component analysis. J. VLSI Signal Process. **26**(2), 25–38 (2000)
11. Choi, S.: Independent component analysis. In: 12th WSEAS International Conference on Communications, pp. 159–162, July 2008
12. Tonazzini, A., Bedini, L., Salerno, E.: Independent component analysis for document restoration. Int. J. Doc. Anal. Recogn. (IJDAR) 7, 17–27 (2004). doi:10.1007/s10032-004-0121-8
13. Gupta, A., Kumar, S., Gupta, R., Chadhury, S., Joshi, S.D.: Enhancement of old manuscript images. In: Ninth International Conference on Document Analysis and Recognition, ICDAR 2007 (2007)
14. Gangamma, B., Murthy, S.K., Chandra, G.C.P., Kaushik, S., Kumar, S.: A combined approach for degraded historical documents denoising using curvelet and mathematical morphology. In: Computational Intelligence and Computing Research (ICCIC) (2010)
15. Pei, S.-C., Tzeng, M., Hsiao, Y.-Z.: Enhancement of uneven lighting text image using line-based empirical mode decomposition. In: ICASSP 2011. 978-1-4577-0539-7/11/$26.00 ©2011 IEEE
16. Shi, Z., Setlur, S., Govindaraju, V.: Digital enhancement of palm leaf manuscript images using normalization techniques. In: Center of Excellence for Document Analysis and Recognition (CEDAR), 5th International Conference On Knowledge Based Computer Systems, Hyderabad, India, 19–22 December 2004 (2004)
17. Chamchong, R., Fung, C.C.: Optimal Selection of Binarization Techniques for the Processing of Ancient Palm Leaf Manuscripts. 978-1-4244-6588-0/10/$25.00 ©2010 IEEE
18. Bouman, C.A.: Markov random fields and stochastic image models. Tutorial Presented at: 1995 IEEE International Conference on Image Processing, Washington, D.C., 23–26 October 1995. http://dynamo.ecn.purdue.edu/»bouman/
19. Sreedevi, I., Pandey, R., Jayanthi, N., Bhola, G., Chaudhury, S.: NGFICA based digitization of historic inscription images. ISRN Signal Process. **2013**, 7 p. Article ID 735857, Hindawi Publishing Corporation
20. Jayanthi, N., Indu, S., Tripathi, P., Gola, P.: Novel method for manuscript and inscription text extraction. In: IEEE SPIN (2016)

21. Jayanthi, N., Tomar, A., Raj, A., Indu, S., Chaudhary, S.: Digitization of historic inscription images using cumulants based simultaneous blind source extraction. In: ICVGIP 2014, 14–18 December 2014, Bangalore, India. Copyright 2014 ACM 978-1-4503-3061-9/14/ 12 …$15.00

22. Jayanthi, N., Gaur, A., Indu, S.: A Novel Approach for Text Extraction from Natural Scene Images

23. Schwarz, M.W., Cowan, W.B., Beatty, J.C.: An experimental comparison of RGB, YIQ, LAB, HSV, and opponent color models. ACM Trans. Graph. 6(2), 123–158 (1987). doi:10. 1145/31336.31338

24. H. R. Schantz, "The history of OCR", Recognition Technologies Users Association, 1972

25. Impedovo, S., Ottaviano, L., Occhinegro, S.: Optical Character Recognition: A Survey. Int. J. Patt. Recogn. Artif. Intell. 05, 1 (1991)

26. Nagy, G.: At the frontiers of OCR. Proc. IEEE 8(7) (1992)

27. Buzykanov, S.N.: Enhancement of poor resolution text images in the weighted sobolev space. In: 19th International Conference on Systems, Signals and Image Processing (IWSSIP), 2012. IEEE (2012)

Heart Disease Prediction System Using Random Forest

Yeshvendra K. Singh[1(✉)], Nikhil Sinha[2], and Sanjay K. Singh[3]

[1] Indian Institute of Technology (ISM), Dhanbad, Dhanbad, Jharkhand, India
yeshvendrasingh93@gmail.com
[2] Tech Mahindra, Pune, Maharashtra, India
nikhilsinha268@gmail.com
[3] Indian Institute of Technology (BHU), Varanasi, Varanasi, U.P., India
sks.cse@itbhu.ac.in

Abstract. The scope of Machine Learning algorithms are increasing in predicting various diseases. The nature of machine learning algorithm to think like a human being is making this concept so important and versatile. Here the challenge of increasing the accuracy of Heart disease prediction is taken upon. The non-linear tendency of the Cleveland heart disease dataset was exploited for applying Random Forest to get an accuracy of 85.81%. The method of predicting heart diseases using Random Forest with well-set attributes fetches us more accuracy. Random Forest was built by training 303 instances of data and authentication of accuracy was done using 10-fold cross validation. By the proposed algorithm for heart disease prediction, many lives could be saved in the future.

Keywords: Linear Regression · Logistic Regression · Support Vector Machine · Decision Tree · Random Forest · 10-fold cross validation

1 Introduction

Heart Disease or in other words cardiovascular disease is the common health problem in most of countries these days. The advancement of technology is making us lazy and prone to have heart diseases. People do less physical work, they have automation for everything, where they use their mental ability to work on these machines, build them, upgrade and maintain these automation system. Such a lifestyle causes a person to have big bellies, become smokers and alcoholic. Physical inactivity and malnutrition, overweight and obesity, tobacco and substance abuse are amongst the leading causes for cardiovascular disease as per University of Rochester's Medical centre. Alwan [9] presented a paper in WHO where he explained the prevention of cardiovascular disease focusing on low and middle income countries. They stated that cardiovascular disease is the leading non-communicable disease which accounts for one-third of the mortality rate and 10% of the global disease burden.

Heart disease causes sudden death without any premonition. 50% heart attacks will occur without warning. Some people suffer from severe chest pain and are brought to the hospital, where they get an ECG done so that the coronary syndrome could be detected, but the results could still be ambiguous. It may further require very costly and

© Springer Nature Singapore Pte Ltd. 2017
M. Singh et al. (Eds.): ICACDS 2016, CCIS 721, pp. 613–623, 2017.
DOI: 10.1007/978-981-10-5427-3_63

complicated, invasive and non-invasive tests to confirm heart disease. In many cases such attacks may be very severe and terminal, where life cannot be saved in spite of best treatment possible. So a better way of handling this would be to predict the heart disease before it occurs. In the past prediction of Heart Disease was challenging but due the advancement in Machine Learning algorithms it has become a common topic. Now the race is for increasing the accuracy so that the prediction system gets more precise and accurate.

The tests like ECG, MRA, Echo-cardiograph, Lipid profile, coronary angiography, etc., costs too much making it difficult for people or government in developing and under developed country to subsist. Heart Disease leads to maximum expenditure in exchequer. So predicting Heart Diseases early by data analysis of simple parameters like age, sex, blood pressure, etc. will be a boon to an individual, society or a country.

Many papers in the past stated that they were able to get a better accuracy by using either a linear classifier or an artificial neural network to solve this problem but due to lack of huge amount of data or nature of the dataset the accuracy couldn't be increased. The goal of this paper is to increase the accuracy by using more fitting algorithm based on the given dataset. The proposed solution for Heart Disease prediction is worth considering because of limited dataset and this solution works well in these kind of situations. Another advantage of this solution strategy is consideration of non-linear dependency of attribute in the dataset. An Algorithm like Random Forest for non-linear dependency of dataset needs a bit of adjustment in it to give better results, like it did in this case.

Structure of this paper is as follows: Sect. 2 will tell you about the background of heart disease prediction. Section 3 will briefly introduce you to the press-processing techniques and the machine learning algorithms used like Linear Regression, Logistic Regression, SVM, Decision Tree and Random Forest. Results and cross-validation technique will be discussed in Sect. 4. The paper is concluded in Sect. 5 by discussing the future.

2 Background

Many studies have already been done on prediction of heart disease. Every time we are getting one step closer than what we have achieved earlier. By the introduction of machine learning algorithms, huge amount of progress has been made in different fields, people are able to do things easily which they never thought anyone can do. By advancement of these machine learning algorithms, prediction of disease in a patient has become a common practice. One of the most common technique to predict heart disease is artificial neural network (ANN). Many scientists are using this technique for the better performance and accuracy but this also has some limitation like it requires a huge training set to give better results. Dilip et al. [2] used Multi-Layered Perceptron with BP learning to predict the neonatal disease. He also did a comparative analysis of MLP, Quick propagation method and Conjugate Gradient Descent where the highest achieved accuracy was 75%. Niti et al. [4] also used neural network to predict heart disease, blood pressure and diabetes. The training of this neural network was done using the back propagation method. Here ANN was used because ANN makes no assumptions about the distribution of the data hence gives a good result. Although the data size used in both the cases were small which could have been the reason for lesser accuracy.

Several other techniques were also used in the prediction of heart disease. Iqra et al. [5] stated that data mining has greater potential in understanding the unknown patterns in the dataset, hence helping us in disease prediction. They used Multi-nominal Logistic Regression as a classifier and 10-fold cross validation for validating the results. Milan et al. [3] did a comparative analysis of data mining classification techniques like RIPPER classifier, Decision Tree, ANN and Support Vector Machine. They were able to achieve an accuracy of 84.12% and stated that Support Vector Machine predicts cardiovascular disease with the least error rate. Micheal et al. [6] used cardiac score card system on the basis of lasso Logistic Regression to predict the heart wellness and heart failure, where lasso was used for feature extraction. Here the accuracy for Heart Disease prediction and Heart Failure Prediction came out to be 0.8403 AUC and 0.9412 AUC respectively. Heart disease prediction data could also have a non-linear dependency which was never tested by the above authors.

Few other authors tried solving this problem using ensemble methods, they were able to utilize the classification characteristics of every method they combined, if the combined classification characteristics didn't match the characteristics of the variable in the dataset, it won't be effective. Luyang et al. [8] modified 3 classical methods – Logistic Regression, Naïve Bayes and SVM and implemented them to predict cardiac arrhythmia. They found that by pairing Naïve Bayes and Support Vector Machine, the model gave better performance and feature selection can increase the accuracy of the model. Jabbar et al. [7] used PCA as a feature selection tool to reduce the dimensionality of the dataset and then applied ANN to get better results than the traditional classification techniques.

3 Methodology Used

Huge amount of work has been done in data analytics. We started with simple Linear Regression and now we deal with problems using deep learning or deep neural net. Here this power of Machine Learning algorithms is used in predicting heart disease. The procedure followed in doing same is shown in Fig. 1.

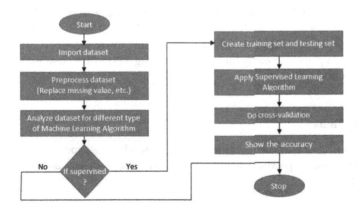

Fig. 1. Flow chart of procedure

3.1   Data Pre-processing

Cleveland Heart Disease [1] dataset have 74 attributes with 303 instances of each attribute, but only 14 of those attributes was ceased as it was observed that heart disease prediction was only dependent on 13 attributes. Some attributes among them were categorized in an undesirable way and few others had missing values. Like in the attribute Heart Disease Prediction, category 0 was given for having less than 50% blockage in the arteries and categories 1, 2, 3 and 4 stating different type of heart disease with blockage more than 50% in the arteries, however the requirement was only to predict that the patient had heart disease or not, so 1, 2, 3 and 4 were clubbed into a single category as all were the types of heart disease. A detailed description about the dataset is given in Table 1.

Table 1. Description of the Cleveland heart disease dataset

S. No.	Attribute	Characteristic
1.	Age	Integer
2.	Sex	Categorical
3.	Chest pain type	Categorical
4.	Resting blood pressure	Integer
5.	Serum cholesterol	Integer
6.	Fasting blood sugar	Categorical
7.	Maximum heart rate achieved	Integer
8.	Resting ECG results	Categorical
9.	Exercise induced angina	Categorical
10.	ST depression	Real
11.	Slope of the peak exercise ST segment	Categorical
12.	Fluoroscopy result	Categorical
13.	Thalassemia	Categorical
14.	Heart disease	Categorical

Further the dataset had some missing values in attribute 'number of major vessels colored by fluoroscopy', 'analysis of thalassemia', etc. Here the median of every attribute was taken in which the data was missing and this value was substituted at the missing value's place. By using this method missing values were removed from Heart Disease dataset.

3.2   Algorithms

There are two categories of machine learning algorithms: - supervised and unsupervised. In this paper supervised learning is used because our Cleveland dataset [1] is a labeled dataset.

The below mentioned linear classifiers and non-linear classifiers were developed using sklearn library of python. This library helps to learn the characteristics of the dataset which in turn could help in classification and building machine learning models.

3.2.1   Linear Regression

Linear Regression is a machine learning algorithm which determines the dependency of one attribute over the other so that it can be separated linearly. The equation (Eq. 1) to find the classification boundary is as follows (for k-dimensional data space):

$$Y = \alpha + \beta_1 X_1 + \beta_2 X_2 + \ldots + \beta_k X_k \tag{1}$$

Where Y is the dependent Variable, $\{X_1, X_2, \ldots, X_k\}$ are the independent variable, α is the error term and $\{\beta_1, \beta_2, \ldots, \beta_k\}$ are the regression coefficients. The wrongly categorized data set accounts for error in accuracy of the algorithm. All linearly separable data set can easily be categorized using Linear Regression.

By applying this algorithm an accuracy of 83.82% was achieved which can be improved further. To improve accuracy Logistic Regression is implemented which is a better form of Linear Regression.

3.2.2   Logistic Regression

Logistic Regression is probabilistic sense of Linear Regression, where the output of Linear Regression is mapped between 0 and 1. Logit function is used to map this output. If p is the probability of an event to occur, $\{X_1, X_2, \ldots, X_k\}$ are the independent variable, $\beta 0$ is the intercept from Linear Regression and $\{\beta_1, \beta_2, \ldots, \beta_k\}$ are the regression coefficient then the Logit function will be written as in Eq. 2.

$$Ln(p/1 - p) = \beta_0 + \beta_1 X_1 + \beta_2 X_2 + \ldots + \beta_k X_k \tag{2}$$

When this algorithm was applied on Heart Disease data set, surprisingly the accuracy decreased. The accuracy achieved was 83.16% which is less than the Linear Regression's accuracy that is 83.82% as depicted in the Fig. 2, which shows the comparison of accuracy of Linear Regression and Logistic Regression.

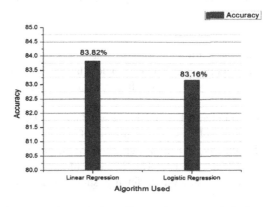

Fig. 2. Comparison of Linear Regression and Logistic Regression

3.2.3 Support Vector Machine

SVM is a machine learning algorithm just like Linear Regression but here the best possible line/hyper plane is found out that could separate the dataset into their respective categories.

The Heart Disease dataset's accuracy is checked against Linear Regression and Logistic Regression but the results were not satisfactory and could be improved further. Therefore Support Vector Machine is applied in order to get better results but that didn't happen. Instead the accuracy dropped down further to 82.83% which was lower than the accuracy of Linear Regression and Logistic Regression.

A comparative graph between all three algorithm's accuracy is given in Fig. 3, which shows the decrease in accuracy, as more perfect linear classification was applied.

By seeing this decreasing trend of accuracy we inferred that our dataset may not be completely linearly dependent on the heart disease. So we now had to find an algorithm that can work on non-linearly dependent dataset.

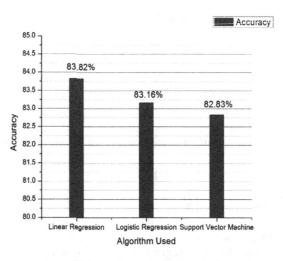

Fig. 3. Comparison of Linear Regression, Logistic Regression and SVM

3.2.4 Decision Tree

Decision Tree is a machine learning algorithm that works on non-linear tendency of data. It has a tree like structure with Boolean logic attached to it to split the data and reach to a conclusion or to classify a data. It can work well for both classification as well as regression.

This algorithm was implemented on the Heart dataset. Decision Tree can have different amount of splits as well as different amount of leave nodes which will fetch us different accuracies. So, the given Dataset is checked for the perfect tree that it can have and the highest accuracy it can achieve. The variation of number of splits and number of leaf nodes with different accuracy they fetch is shown in Fig. 4.

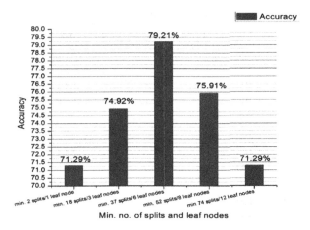

Fig. 4. Comparison of different accuracy with different parameters

In the above Fig. 4 it can be observed that with minimum number of splits 37 and minimum number of leaf nodes 6 the highest accuracy of 79.12% was achieved but this is the most basic algorithm for non-linearly dependent dataset. By using more sophisticated algorithm accuracy can be increased.

3.2.5 Random Forest (Our Proposed Method)

Random Forest is a machine learning algorithm which also works on non-linear tendency of data set but gives better results than Decision Tree algorithm. Random Forest is built up with hundreds of trees with randomized inputs and splits in it. The biggest drawback of a Decision Tree was over fitting, whereas this over fitting was dealt in Random Forest by averaging the output of every individual tree and then ranking them by comparing it with the original output.

Random Forest have a tendency to separate non-linearly dependent dataset, which helped implementing this algorithm on our Heart Disease dataset. Random Forest needs a proper adjustment to give better results, so by changing the parameters like randomness, number of trees, minimum number of splits and minimum number of leaf nodes the accuracy could be increased. First by keeping the randomness and minimum number of leave node to be 1 and checking the accuracy, the resultant Table 2 was generated which was not satisfactory. However, we were able to get better results by keeping randomness to 5 and minimum number of leaf nodes also to be 5.

Comparison of accuracy was done by keeping different parameters. By keeping minimum number of splits to be 10 accuracies achieved are shown in Fig. 5. Among them the highest accuracy achieved was 84.49%, which is better than any of the previous results.

Next we checked our accuracy by increasing the number of splits to be 15, but it was not as good as in the previous case. Here the highest accuracy achieved was 84.15%. By checked the accuracy with 20 splits, some trend of increasing or decreasing accuracy was expected but no trend was observed. However to our surprise the accuracy sore up to 85.81% which was quite good compared to earlier experiments.

Table 2. Results on changing number of tree and minimum number of splits

S. No.	Number of trees	Mini. no. of splits	Accuracy
1.	100	2	82.18%
3.	300	2	83.17%
5.	500	2	83.17%
6.	100	5	82.83%
8.	300	5	83.50%
10.	500	5	83.17%
11.	100	10	83.17%
13.	300	10	83.50%
15.	500	10	83.50%
16.	100	15	82.51%
18.	300	15	82.51%
20.	500	15	83.50%
21.	100	20	84.16%
23.	300	20	83.82%
25.	500	20	83.50%
26.	100	25	83.17%
28.	300	25	84.16%
30.	500	25	83.83%

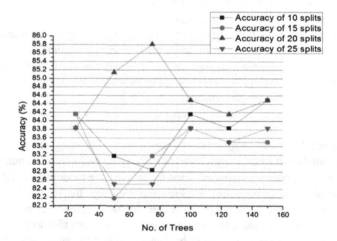

Fig. 5. Accuracy achieved with variable number of splits and trees

By seeing the increase in accuracy, the number of splits was increased by 5 and then the accuracy was calculated. But due to the randomness in the results the accuracy didn't exceed beyond 84%. The Fig. 5 shows us that with 25 number of splits the highest accuracy achieved was 83.83%. Different parameters were tried and accuracy corresponding to them were calculated but this was the best accuracy achieved.

By changing number of splits and number of trees the accuracy was changing but no trend was found in the accuracy. So, by seeing this it can be concluded that these features like randomness, number of leaf nodes, number of trees and number of splits depends on the nature of dataset and differs from one dataset to another. The perfect combination of these parameters can only be found by shear brute force.

Now let us compare the highest accuracy achieved in the above given variable splits and trees. Table 3 show that from all the mentioned data in the table highest accuracy is 85.81% for 20 number of splits and 75 number of trees.

Table 3. Comparison of accuracy by keeping different no. of splits and trees

Number of splits	Number of trees	Highest accuracy
10	150	84.49%
15	25	84.16%
20	75	85.81%
25	25/100/150	83.83%

4   Result

Heart Disease dataset had 303 instances which was quite less for training the model, so an optimal and effective 3-fold, 5-fold and 10-fold cross validation technique was used to compare the accuracy and it was observed that the robustness of the algorithm applied solely depends on the nature of dataset. However, only 10-fold cross validation technique was considered because it gives us a larger training set, giving us better results. After going through the validation technique it was observed that the proposed model achieved an accuracy of 85.81% using 10-fold cross validation which was better than the other models as shown in the Fig. 6.

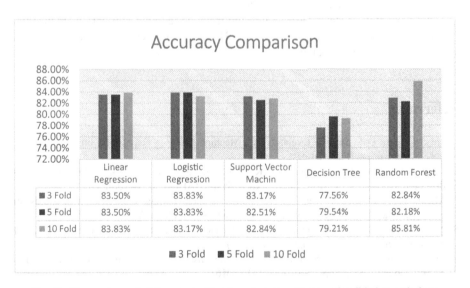

Fig. 6. Comparison of different machine learning algorithms and validation technique

Figure 6 shows us that in Linear Regression, Logistic Regression and Support Vector Machine there was not much change in the accuracy when validation function was changed but in case of Decision Tree and Random Forest there is marked difference in accuracy. Changing the validation technique changes the amount of training set and hence the nature of training set leading to change in the tree structure. But the highest accuracy remains the same i.e. 85.81% using 10-fold cross validation in Random Forest Algorithm.

No trend of accuracy was determined with variation of related parameters in Random Forest. This could be because the structure of Random Forest changes according to the nature of dataset. Although, few maxima around which the accuracy was relatively higher were found.

5 Conclusion and Future Work

Real world systems like Heart Disease dataset may have some linearly and some non-linearly dependent attributes. Hence, the proposed algorithm for detecting heart disease was much more effective than others. The characteristics of Random Forest was exploited, which yielded better results by a little adjustment in it. Predicting the Heart Disease by analysing the data will help saving lives of many patients.

The proposed algorithm can work very well on real world data and that's why it can be used very widely. We hope that this algorithm could be implemented in many different fields other than the Heart Disease dataset.

Although the accuracy was improved but still many more things can be done in future. More amount of data can be collected in order to increase the accuracy. The pre-processing of data can be reduced by collecting the original data and not synthesizing them. A user-friendly interactive environment can be made to deploy this method of predicting Heart Disease in hospitals.

This prediction of Heart Disease through machine learning will help us reduce the errors made by doctors in diagnosis of Heart Disease. However, the need of doctor will always be there for their patients.

References

1. Heart Disease Data Set of Cleveland, UCI Machine Learning Repository. http://archive.ics.uci.edu/ml/datasets/Heart+Disease
2. Dilip, R.C., Mridula, C., Samanta, R.K.: An artificial neural network model for neonatal disease diagnosis. Int. J. Artif. Intell. Expert Syst. (IJAE) 2(3), 96–106 (2011)
3. Milan, K., Sunila, G.: Comparative study of data mining classification methods in cardiovascular disease prediction. Int. J. Comput. Sci. Technol. 2(2), 304–308 (2011)
4. Niti, G., Anil, D., Navin, R.: Decision support system on heart disease diagnosis using neural network. Delhi Bus. Rev. 8(1), 99–101 (2007)
5. Iqra, B., Ali, R.A.: A framework for classifying unstructured data of cardiac patients. Int. J. Adv. Comput. Sci. Appl. 7(2), 133–141 (2016)

6. Michael, P.M., Biykem, B., Christie, M.B., Ximena, S., Nicolaos, C., Glennon, S., Vijay, N., Arunima, M., Craig, S.M., Jeffrey, L.E., Charles, C., John, T.M.: Cardiac ScoreCard: a diagnostic multivariate index assay system for predicting a spectrum of cardiovascular disease. Expert Syst. Appl. **54**, 136–147 (2016). Elsevier Ltd.
7. Jabbar, M.A., Deekshatulu, B.L., Chandra, P.: Classification of heart disease using artificial neural network and feature subset selection. Global J. Comput. Sci. Technol. **13**(3), 1–11 (2013). Ver. I
8. Luyang, C., Qi, C., Sihua, L., Xiao, J.: Predicting Heart Attacks. Stanford University, Stanford (2014)
9. Alwan, A.: Global Status Report on Non-communicable Diseases 2010. World Health Organization, Geneva (2011)

MapReduce Based Multilevel Association Rule Mining from Concept Hierarchical Sales Data

Dinesh J. Prajapati$^{(\boxtimes)}$ and Sanjay Garg

Computer Science and Engineering Department, Institute of Technology,
Nirma University, Ahmedabad, India
djprajapati.6054@gmail.com, gargsv@gmail.com

Abstract. Multilevel association rule mining is one of the important techniques of data mining to analyze the sales data. Multilevel association rules provide detailed information as compare to single level association rules. Today's era of e-commerce and e-business, various online marketing sites and social networking sites are generating tremendous amount of data in the form of sales, tweets, text mails, web usages and many more. The data generated from these sources is really too large so that it becomes tedious task to process and analyze using traditional approaches. This paper overcomes the drawback of single node computing by distributing the task to cluster of nodes. The performance of this system is analyzed using reduced minimum support threshold at different levels of concept hierarchy and by varying the database size. In this experiment, the transactional dataset is generated from big sales dataset then the distributed multilevel frequent pattern mining algorithm (DMFPM) is implemented to generate level-crossing frequent itemset using hadoop mapreduce framework. The multilevel association rules are generated from frequent itemset. The hierarchical redundant rule affects the efficiency of the system, so hierarchical redundancy is removed from it. Finally, the time efficiency of proposed algorithms is compared with existing Multilevel Frequent Pattern Mining Algorithm (MFPM).

Keywords: Distributed frequent pattern mining algorithm · Multilevel association rule · Mapreduce · Level crossing rules · Redundant rules

1 Introduction

The data mining is a technique to extract the useful knowledge and patterns from the data. One of the techniques used in data mining is called association rule mining. Association rule mining is used to discover the relationship among items. Association rule mining is used for market basket analysis where an organization is interested in identifying items that are frequently purchased together. The following terms are used in this paper.

Itemset: Let $I = \{I_1, I_2, \ldots, I_n\}$ be a set of distinct items. A set X which is subset of I is called itemset. An itemset X with k items is referred as k-itemset [1].

Support: The support is the percentage of transactions in the database D that contain both itemsets X and Y [2–4]. The equation for the support is given below.

M. Singh et al. (Eds.): ICACDS 2016, CCIS 721, pp. 624–636, 2017.
DOI: 10.1007/978-981-10-5427-3_64

$$Support = P(X \cup Y)$$

Confidence: The confidence is the percentage of transactions in the database D with itemset X also contains the itemset Y [2–4]. The equation for the confidence is given by the conditional probability is expressed in terms of itemset support.

$$Confidence = P(Y/X) = Support(X \cup Y) / Support(X)$$

Where, *Support* $(X \cup Y)$ is the number of transactions containing the itemsets X and Y both, and *Support(X)* is the number of transactions containing the itemset X.

Association Rule: Consider a transaction database D, where each transaction T_i is a set of items, and an association rule is the relationship between those items. An association rule is expressed in the form $X \rightarrow Y$, where X and Y are the itemsets. This rule exposes the relationship between the itemset X with the itemset Y. The interestingness of the rule $X \rightarrow Y$ is measured by the support and confidence [2–4].

An itemset is frequent, if its support is greater than or equal to the user defined minimum support threshold. Association rule mining process basically consists of two steps [3–5]: (i) first, all the itemsets that satisfies the minimum support thresholds are identified and referred as frequent itemset, (ii) then, Generate strong association rules from derived frequent itemsets that satisfies minimum confidence threshold. Big data is termed for a collection of large data sets which are complex and difficult to process using traditional data processing tools. For big data, the data reading is slower from physical storage than from the recent fast network. For example, to read 1 TB of data with 10 Mbps network speed, it takes about 28 h; however, if the dataset is divided into one hundred 10 GB datasets with 10 Mbps network speed each, it takes around 17 min only [6, 7]. The complex problem can be solved using divide and conquer strategy which consists of three phases [8]: (i) When the size of problem is small enough then solve the entire problem directly; otherwise, split the original problem into two or more sub-problems. (ii) Recursively, solve the sub-problems by again applying the divide-and-conquer strategy until the sub-problem is solvable. (iii) Finally, merge the solutions of the two sub-problems to get the solution of the original problem.

Multi-level Association Rule Mining: Association rules generated from mining data at multiple levels of concept hierarchy are called multilevel association rules [9, 10]. In multiple-level association rule mining, the items are categorized by level of concept hierarchy. This concept hierarchy is used to discover the association rules at multiple concept levels.

Each node in the concept-hierarchy tree represents single item available in the itemset. The AMUL dairy dataset contains four levels of the concept hierarchy tree. Any item at level i is child of item at level $i-1$ and so on. At level one, two items Fresh Products and Frozen Products are present. Further-more, Fresh Products has two children, Milk Products and Milk. Ice-cream and Snacks are the children of Frozen Products. This hierarchy continues accordingly. While mining multiple level association rule, the dataset is encoded in a concise numeric form to identify classification level as shown in Fig. 1. Encoding the taxonomy information as a sequence of digits makes multi-level association rule mining algorithm more efficient in terms of memory and processing. So, each node is assigned a number which represents the item id. This item id also provides encoding that gives taxonomy information about the hierarchy. The encoding is done from leftmost child, sibling and so on. For example, the item Skimmed Curd is encoded as 1122. The encoded code's first digit 1 represent Fresh Products at level 1 and second digit 1 represent Milk Products at level 2 and third digit 2 represent Curd at level 3.

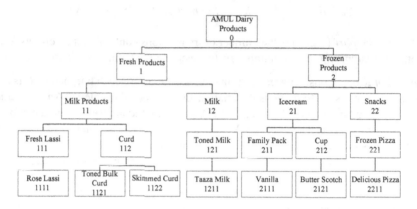

Fig. 1. Sample concept-hierarchy AMUL dairy products with taxonomy information

In brief, the contribution of this paper is summarized in three steps: (i) First of all, big sales hierarchical dataset is transformed into transactional dataset using hadoop mapreduce, (ii) The distributed multilevel frequent pattern mining algorithm is implemented to generate multilevel frequent itemsets including level crossing, (iii) Finally, Hierarchical redundant rules are eliminated to derive the interesting multilevel association rules. For the experimental purpose, multi-level frequent pattern mining algorithm and proposed algorithm are tested on sales dataset of AMUL dairy.

The remaining of this paper is organized as follows. Section 2 presents preliminaries for multilevel association rule mining from concept hierarchical sales big data in distributed environment. Related work is given in Sect. 3. Section 4 shows the proposed methodology. In Sect. 5, the performance of proposed method is evaluated on sales dataset of AMUL dairy. Finally, the conclusions and future scope is drawn in Sect. 6.

2   Preliminaries

This section covers the complete set of definitions, terminologies and assumptions used in this paper.

2.1   Data Pre-processing

Data pre-processing is the process of solving irrelevant or missing information and change the basic structure of data, collected from various sources [11]. In real world, the dataset may contain data in the format that cannot be used for further processing; such dataset can be converted into desired form using preprocessing.

2.2 Hadoop

Hadoop is an open source framework which implements the mapreduce programming model in the distributed environment [12]. In the hadoop framework, computer machine or node is classified as master node and slave nodes. The master node supervises data storage on machine and running parallel computations on that data. The slave nodes are the machines which perform the work of storing the data and running the computations.

2.2.1 Hadoop Distributed File System (HDFS)

The Hadoop runtime system is coupled with HDFS which provides parallelism and concurrency to achieve system reliability. HDFS is designed for storing huge files with streaming data access patterns, running on clusters of commodity hardware [12].

2.2.2 Mapreduce

Mapreduce is basically software introduced by Google to support distributed computing on big datasets using the cluster of nodes. The mapreduce framework consists of two functions [13]: Mapper and Reducer. The mapper and reducer function is basically written by the user. The data structure of map and reduce function is defined by *<key, value>* pairs. The mapper function takes an input as *<key, value>* pair and produces a set of intermediate result as *<key, value>* pairs. The reducer function receives an intermediate key generated and a set of values for that key. The reducer merges these values of the key to generate smaller set of values. The output of reducer is value zero or one typically.

2.3 Performance Analysis

The proposed approach can be evaluated on the basis of execution time of the algorithm, scalability & flexibility of data, and data heterogeneity to analyze the performance of the system [14].

2.3.1 Execution Time

The execution time is the time required to perform data mining or analysis task. The efficiency and time complexity of the algorithm is computed based on time required for getting the desired output quickly and efficiently.

2.3.2 Scalability and Flexibility

The performance of the system should not scale down even if data is scaled from thousands to billions of records. The system should be more flexible enough to handle heavy workload fast.

2.3.3 Data Heterogeneity

The data is coming from various sources due to the ease of internet and social media. The basic types of dataset may be of structured, semi structured and unstructured. Ideally, the system should accept heterogeneous data as an input then preprocess the data and finally, produce the desired output within stipulated time.

3 Related Work

Han and Fu [10] present various interestingness measures to find more interesting rules including level crossing rules. In this paper multiple level association rules discovers the interesting and strong rules from the large database. Authors also suggested modified methods for mining single level association rules to multiple level association rules which creates interesting issues for the further work. Thakur et al. [15] proposed a top-down approach for mining multilevel level-crossing association rules from the large transaction databases by using extension of existing approaches. In this paper, authors have used the concept of reducing support as well as filtered the transaction table, T for each levels of concept hierarchy. After generating a new filtered transaction tables at one concept level, similar process will be carried out for remaining level. This approach improves the processing time and generates less candidate itemsets. Wan et al. [16] proposed a novel approach to improve the efficiency, integrality and accuracy by analyzing multiple level association rules from primitive concept level of hierarchy. In this paper, the proposed method considers the dynamic concept hierarchies to generate multilevel association rules from customized point of view. The paper also mentioned various issues for the calculation of rule support and multilevel association rules at specific level.

The authors in [17, 18], proposed a method to remove the hierarchical redundancy using frequent closed itemsets. In this paper, hierarchical redundancy is removed to reduce the basic size of the association rules which improves the quality and usefulness of rule without losing any information. Author also suggests that this approach can be apply to the approximate basis rule to remove the redundancy. Hong et al. [19] proposed an incremental multilevel association rule mining algorithm based on the pre-large concept hierarchy with taxonomy information. The large frequent itemsets plays an important role to reduce database scan. Due to repeatedly scanning of the database, the efficiency of algorithm decreases. The author proposed algorithm to reduce the mining cost. Gautam and Pardasani [20] proposed boolean matrix based approach to discover frequent itemsets. The proposed approach scans the transaction database only one time and does not produce itemsets, but adopts the boolean vector relational calculus to discover frequent itemset. Boolean matrix based approach stores all transaction data in bits, so it needs less memory space. Ramana et al. [21] evaluated and compared traditional multilevel association rule mining algorithms like ML_T2L1, ML_T1LA, ML_TML1 and ML_T2LA. Algorithm ML_T2L1 finds multilevel large frequent itemsets from transactional database. ML_T1LA algorithm uses only single encoded transaction table. ML_TML1 algorithm generates multiple encoded transaction tables. ML_T2LA algorithm uses two encoded transaction tables and integrates the optimization techniques to find rules. Prakash et al. [22] proposed new approach to mine both the frequent and in-frequent interesting association rules without generating redundant rules. The proposed approach discovers the association rules that are complete according to propositional logic from a given dataset. The limitation of this approach is that if an unclassified dataset is used than classification must be performed before mining the rules.

Gautam and Pardasani [23] proposed partition and boolean based method to find frequent itemsets at each concept levels to reduce the number of database scans, I/O cost and CPU over-head. A top-down approach is used for efficient mining of multi-level rules. The algorithm proposed in this paper, uses boolean AND operator to reduce the time by removing unnecessary candidate itemset. The partitioning method is used to overcome the limitation of memory requirement. Gautam and Shukla [24] proposed a method for mining multilevel association rules using reduced minimum support threshold at each level. The authors have used the pincer search algorithm to mine multilevel frequent itemsets in a given transactional database. The algorithm presented in this paper, reduces both the number of database scan and candidates itemset; thus the time efficiency is improved. Karim et al. [25] proposed a distributed syatem for mining the transactional datasets using an improved mapreduce framework. In this paper, authors implemented "Associated-Correlated-Independent" algorithm to find the complete set of customer's purchase patterns along with the correlated, associated, associated-correlated, and independent purchase patterns. Butincu and Craus [26] present improved version of the frequent itemset mining algorithm as well as its generalized version. The authors introduced optimized formulas for generating valid candidates by reducing number of invalid candidates. By using the computations of previous steps by other processed nodes, it avoids generating redundant candidates. Authors also suggested to run the same algorithm in parallel or distributed system. Chandanan and Shukla [27] proposed an algorithm to remove hierarchical duplicate rules in multi-level using upper level closed frequent itemset and generator. The algorithm proposed in this paper, reduces the size of the rules to achieve good quality and improve the usefulness of rule without information loss. The basic goal behind this approach is to improve the time efficiency by removing the hierarchically redundant rules. Pumjun and Kreesuradej [28] proposed MLUpCS algorithm to mine multilevel association rules in dynamic databases under the different support threshold without rescanning of a whole dataset. This algorithm is extension the MLUp algorithm which mines multilevel association rules using the same minimum support threshold.

However, none of the above mentioned work deals with the problem of transforming sales data into transactional data and multilevel association rule mining including level crossing using mapreduce. Hence, mapreduce based data transformation is the initial part of this work then distributed multilevel frequent pattern mining algorithm is implemented to generate level-crossing frequent itemsets. Existing MFPM [15] algorithm generates large candidate set and its execution time is too high while dealing with big data. The proposed algorithm improves the drawback of existing multilevel frequent pattern mining algorithm and also improves the execution time of system by generating small candidate itemset.

4 Proposed Methodology

The overall architecture of the proposed methodology is shown in Fig. 2. Big hierarchical sales dataset of AMUL dairy is given as input to pre-processing unit to transform it into transactional dataset using hadoop mapreduce. These generated transactional dataset is given as input to the distributed frequent pattern mining algorithm for varying minimum support threshold which generates frequent k-itemset. Then, Multilevel association rules including level crossing rules are generated from it and finally hierarchical redundancy has to be removed to improve the performance of system. For this experiment, the hierarchical sales database of AMUL dairy having total size of 5 GB is used. The dataset contains more than 1500 different dairy products.

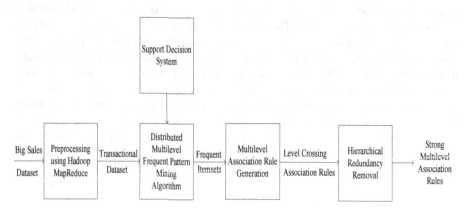

Fig. 2. Proposed methodology

4.1 Distributed Multilevel Frequent Pattern Mining (DMFPM) Algorithm

The existing multilevel frequent pattern mining algorithm generates large candidate itemset and execution time is also higher while dealing with big data. These drawbacks can be rectified by distributed multilevel frequent pattern mining algorithm proposed in this paper. Distributed multilevel frequent pattern mining algorithm is implemented to find frequent itemsets from the actual transactional dataset. Once the actual transactional dataset is stored in HDFS, the entire dataset is split into smaller segments. Each segment is transformed to the data nodes. The primary advantage of this approach is that, it exchanges the count values between each node rather than exchanging the data. The map function is executed on each data segment and it produces <*key, value*> pairs including level-crossing for each transaction of dataset. The mapreduce framework makes group of all <*key, value*> pairs having same items and executes the Reducer function by passing the list of values for candidate itemsets. The map function generates local candidate itemsets, and then the Reduce function gets global counts by adding individual local counts. For the overall computation, multiple iterations of mapreduce functions are necessary.

The distributed frequent pattern mining algorithm DMFPM shown in Fig. 3, uses notation $C[l, k]$ as a set of candidate k-itemset at level l and $L[l, k]$ as a set of frequent k-itemset at level l. The transactional data is given as an input to the mapper, line by line. Each line is split into itemset which is further split into items. Mapper generates the output *<key, value>* pair, where key is the item set and value is 1. Value here indicates the local frequency of the itemset. The reduce task combines the output of the mapper and generates frequent itemset at that level. For each level, the mapreduce function produces a frequent itemset including level-crossing at that specific level. The iteration continues until no further frequent itemsets are found for that level. Frequent itemsets are calculated based on different values of minimum support threshold at each level.

Input: Database in HDFS containing encoded concept hierarchy information (*D*),
         Maximum level of concept hierarchy (*Max_level*),
         Minimum Support Threshold for each level *l* (*Min_sup [l]*).
Output: *L [l]*, Level-crossing frequent itemsets for each level *l*.
Method:
For each level *l* in concept hierarchy do
        L[l,1] = find frequent1-itemsets from (*D*).
        For each frequent k-itemset in level *l* do
                C[l, k] = L[l, k-1] $\bowtie$ *L[l, k-1]*.
                If (*l* > 1) then
                        For *j*=1 to *l-1* do
                                C[l, k] + = *L[j, k-1]* $\bowtie$ *L[l, k-1]*.
                CT[l, k] = Apply Map function on *C[l, k]*.
                L[l, k] = Apply Reduce function on *CT[l, k]*.
        L [l] = *L [l]* U_k *L[l, k]*.

Map Function:
Input: Transaction *Tᵢ*
Output: *< candidate itemset, value>*
Method:
For each transaction *Tᵢ* ∈ *D* do
                For each itemset *Sᵢ* in Candidate Itemset do
                        For each item *Iᵢ* ∈ *Sᵢ* do
                                n = String_length (*Iᵢ*).
                                If (*Sub_string(Iᵢ, n)* ∉ *Tᵢ*) then
                                        Terminate the current itemset *Sᵢ*.
                        Generate the output *< Sᵢ, 1 >* as *< key, value >* pair.
Reduce Function:
Input: *< candidate itemset, list >*
Output: *< frequent itemset, support_count >*
Method:
count = 0.
For each number in *list* do
            count + = *number*.
If (*count* > = *Min_sup*) then
            Generate the output *< frequent itemset, count >* as *< key, value >* pair.

Fig. 3. The DMFPM algorithm

4.2 Multilevel Association Rule Generation

The output of distributed multilevel frequent mining algorithm is frequent itemsets at each level of concept hierarchy. These generated multilevel frequent itemset is given as input to the multilevel association rule generator module to generate meaningful multilevel association rules which satisfies minimum confidence threshold. Multilevel association rules can be generated as follows [3, 29].

- For each level of concept hierarchy,
  - For each level-crossing frequent k-itemset, f, generate all non-empty subsets of f.
  - For every non-empty subset s of f, generates the multilevel association rule as $s \rightarrow (f-s)$ such that $(Support\ (f)/Support\ (s)) \geq min\_conf$, where min_conf is the minimum confidence threshold at that level.

Since, the rules are generated from multilevel frequent itemsets; each rule automatically satisfies minimum support threshold.

4.3 Eliminating Hierarchical Redundant Rules

The hierarchical redundant rules are generated due to ancestor relationship among the items. The processing of such redundant rules degrades performance of the system. Hence, hierarchical redundant rules are eliminated to improve the quality and usefulness of the rules without loss of information. An association rule R_1 is an ancestor of another association rule R_2 if rule R_1 can be obtained by replacing the items in the rule R_2 by their ancestors in a concept hierarchy [3]. In such case, rule R_2 is not interesting since it does not provide new information and is less general than first rule R_1. Such rule is redundant and need to be eliminated.

5 Experimental Setup and Results

For the experimental purpose, a cluster of four desktop machines consisting of i5 processor with 4 GB DDR-3 RAM are used. Ubuntu 12.04 LTS operating system is installed in all the four nodes. Usually JVM is not a part of Ubuntu 12.04, so, JVM is also installed in all the nodes. Multi-node cluster is configured in three computers and single-node cluster is configured in a single computer using apache hadoop packages. The distributed multilevel frequent pattern mining algorithm is tested on both multi-node as well as single-node cluster and compared with existing algorithm.

5.1 Generation of Multilevel Frequent Pattern

After transforming transactional dataset into actual transactional dataset, actual transaction file is given as input to the proposed algorithm to find the frequent itemsets without level-crossing and including level-crossing.

5.1.1 Multilevel Frequent Pattern Mining Without Level Crossing

When a uniform minimum support threshold is used at each level of concept hierarchy, the search procedure is simplified but some of the interesting multilevel association rules may be missed. So, minimum support threshold is adjusted such that it reduces from higher level to lower level of the concept hierarchy. The MFPM and DMFPM algorithms are applied on 5 GB AMUL dataset using single node. For reducing minimum support threshold level–wise, the execution time for the MFPM and DMFPM algorithms is shown in Table 1. The level wise minimum support threshold 4-3-2-1 indicates *min_sup* of 4% for level 1, 3% for level 2, 2% for level 3 and 1% for level 4, respectively. It can be observed that the execution time of the proposed algorithms is significantly lower as compared to MFPM algorithm [15].

Table 1. Level-wise minimum support threshold vs execution time

Level-wise min. support threshold (%)	Execution time (in seconds)	
	The MFPM algorithm [15]	The DMFPM algorithm
4-3-2-1	36789	6800
5-4-3-2	31256	4800
6-5-4-3	24567	3900
7-6-5-4	16788	1987
8-7-6-5	13567	1178

5.1.2 Multilevel Frequent Pattern Mining Including Level Crossing

For finding multilevel frequent itemset including level-crossing, the minimum support threshold is considered similar for all the levels of concept hierarchy. The MFPM algorithm is applied on single node and DMFPM algorithm is applied on single, two as well as on three node cluster. The minimum support threshold is considered as 1%. The result of MFPM and DMFPM algorithms on AMUL datasets for the varying database size 256 MB, 512 MB, 1 GB, 2 GB and 5 GB is shown in Table 2. For a data set of size 5 GB that was distributed on single node, the execution time for the MFPM and DMFPM algorithms are 68000 s and 4800 s respectively. The experiment shows that the execution time of proposed algorithms is less as compared to the MFPM algorithm.

Table 2. Dataset size vs execution time

Dataset size (in MB)	Execution time (in seconds)			
	The MFPM algorithm [15]	The DMFPM algorithm (single node cluster)	The DMFPM algorithm (two node cluster)	The DMFPM algorithm (three node cluster)
256	3189	280	221	191
512	5000	490	380	258
1024	14980	896	696	405
2048	24000	1940	1640	1040
5120	68000	4800	4154	2300

The proposed algorithms provide much better performance as compared to MFPM when the size of the dataset is large. Furthermore, the efficiency of proposed algorithm is improved using cluster of nodes.

5.2 Hierarchical Interesting Association Rule Generation

Once the level-crossing association rules are generated for each level then, hierarchical redundant rules are eliminated from it to improve the efficiency. For this experiment, the number of hierarchical redundant association rules is calculated for minimum confidence threshold 40%, 50%, 60%, 70%, 80% and 90%, and minimum support threshold 1%, 2%, 3%, 4% and 5%, as shown in Fig. 4. It is observed from the experimental result that the number of hierarchically redundant rules generated is less when minimum confidence threshold and minimum support threshold are more than 70% and 3%, respectively.

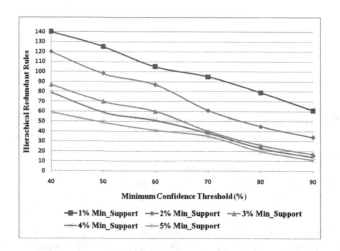

Fig. 4. Minimum confidence threshold vs hierarchical redundant rules

6 Conclusions and Future Scope

Traditional multilevel association rule mining algorithms have limitations of processing speed while analyzing the big data. HDFS and mapreduce play an important role in pre-processing, handling and analysis of such data. In this paper, hadoop based distributed approach is presented which process data by partitioning into cluster of nodes. The primary goal of this work is to reduce inter-node message passing in the cluster. In this paper, the proposed algorithm is used to mine multilevel association rules at same level and different levels of concept hierarchy. The proposed algorithm generates less number of candidate itemset and uses less message passing. Hence, the execution time of the proposed algorithms is comparatively less. The experimental results show that the distributed frequent pattern mining algorithm scale linearly with increasing database size. From the experimental results, it is observed that in order to reduce execution time, the number of node must increase accordingly. Furthermore, for the higher value of minimum confidence threshold and minimum support threshold, number of hierarchically redundant rules is less. The proposed algorithm is more flexible, scalable and efficient distributed multilevel frequent pattern mining algorithms for mining big data.

The time efficiency of the proposed algorithms can be yet improved by reducing the number of database scans for each level of concept hierarchy.

Acknowledgements. The authors take this opportunity to thank all the researchers from the domain of big data analysis for their immense knowledge and kind support throughout the work. Also would like to thank our institute for their resources and constant inspiration. Special thanks to the authority of AMUL dairy located at Anand, Gujarat, India for providing hierarchical big sales database. At last heartiest thanks to our family and friends for encouraging us to make this a success.

References

1. Srikumar, K., Bhasker, B.: Metamorphosis: mining maximal frequent sets in dense domains. Int. J. Artif. Intell. Tools **14**(3), 491–506 (2005)
2. Agrawal, R., Imielinski, T., Swami, A.: Mining association rules between sets of items in large databases. In: International Conference of ACM-SIGMOD on Management of Data, pp. 207–216 (1993)
3. Han, J., Kamber, M.: Data Mining Concepts & Techniques. Morgan Kaufmann Publishers, San Francisco (2004)
4. Olsan, D.L., Delen, D.: Advanced Data Mining Techniques. Springer, Heidelberg (2008)
5. Tseng, F.S.C., Chen, P.Y.: Parallel association rule mining by data de-clustering to support grid computing. Proc. PACIS **89**, 1071–1084 (2005)
6. Woo, J., Basopia, S., Kim, S.H.: Market basket analysis algorithm with NoSQL DB HBase and Hadoop. In: 3rd International Conference Emerging Databases (EDB2011), Korea, pp. 56–62 (2011)
7. Woo, J., Basopia, S., Kim, S.H.: Market basket analysis algorithm with map/reduce of cloud computing. In: Proceedings of the International Conference Parallel and Distributed Processing Techniques and Applications, USA (2011)
8. Tseng, F.S.C., Kuo, Y.H., Huang, Y.M.: Toward boosting distributed association rule mining by data de-clustering. Inf. Sci. **180**(22), 4263–4289 (2010). Elsevier
9. Angryk, R.A., Petry, F.E.: Mining multi-level associations with fuzzy hierarchies. In: The 14th IEEE International Conference on Fuzzy System, pp. 785–790 (2005)
10. Han, J., Fu, Y.: Mining multiple-level association rules in large databases. IEEE Trans. Knowl. Data Eng. **11**(5), 1–8 (1999)
11. Chang, F., Dean, J., Ghemawat, S., Hsieh, W.C., Wallach, D.A., Burrows, M., Gruber, R.E.: Bigtable: a distributed storage system for structured data. ACM Trans. Comput. Syst. (TOCS) **26**(2), 1–14 (2008)
12. Apache Hadoop. http://hadoop.apache.org/
13. Yeung, J.H.C., Tsang, C.C., Tsoi, K.H., Kwan, B., Cheung, C., Chan, A.P.C., Leong, P.H. W.: Map-reduce as a programming model for custom computing machines. In: 16th IEEE Symposium on Field-Programmable Custom Computing Machines FCCM 2008 (2008)

14. Jagdale, A.R., Sonawane, K.V., Khan, S.S.: Data mining and data pre-processing for big data. Int. J. Sci. Eng. Res. **5**(7), 1156–1161 (2014)
15. Thakur, R.S., Jain, R.C., Pardasani, K.R.: Mining level-crossing association rules from large databases. J. Comput. Sci. **2**(1), 76–81 (2006)
16. Wan, Y., Liang, Y., Ding, L.: Mining multilevel association rules with dynamic concept hierarchy. In: Proceedings of the 7th International Conference on Machine Learning and Cybernetics pp. 287–292. IEEE (2008)
17. Shaw, G., Xu, Y., Geva, S.: Eliminating redundant association rules in multilevel datasets. In: 4th International Conference on Data Mining, Las Vegas, USA, pp. 14–17 (2008)
18. Xu, Y., Shaw, G., Li, Y.: Concise representations for association rules in multilevel datasets. J. Syst. Sci. Syst. Eng. **18**, 53–70 (2009). Springer
19. Hong, T., Huang, T., Chang, C.: Mining multiple-level association rules based on pre-large concepts. In: Data Mining and Knowledge Discovery in Real Life Applications Austria, pp. 187–200 (2009)
20. Gautam, P., Pardasani, K.R.: A fast algorithm for mining multilevel association rule based on Boolean matrix. Int. J. Comput. Sci. Eng. **2**(3), 746–752 (2010)
21. Ramana, V.V., Rathnamma, M.V., Reddy, A.R.M.: Methods for mining cross level association rule in taxonomy data structures. Int. J. Comput. Appl. **7**(3), 28–35 (2010)
22. Prakash, S., Vijayakumar, M., Parvathi, R.M.S.: A novel method of mining association rule with multilevel concept hierarchy. Int. J. Comput. Appl. (IJCA), 26–29 (2011)
23. Gautam, P., Pardasani, K.R.: Efficient method for multiple-level association rules in large databases. J. Emerg. Trends Comput. Inf. Sci. **2**(12), 722–732 (2011)
24. Gautam, P., Shukla, R.: An efficient algorithm for mining multilevel association rule based on Pincer search. Int. J. Comput. Sci. Issues (IJCSI) **9**(4), 235–241 (2012)
25. Karim, M.R., Ahmed, C.F., Jeong, B., Choi, H.: An efficient distributed programming model for mining useful patterns in big datasets. IETE Tech. Rev. **30**(1), 53–63 (2013)
26. Butincu, C.N., Craus, M.: An improved version of the frequent itemset mining algorithm. In: Proceedings of the 14th IEEE International Conference Networking in Education and Research, Craiova, pp. 184–189 (2015)
27. Chandanan, A.K., Shukla, M.K.: Removal of duplicate rules for association rule mining from multilevel dataset. Procedia Comput. Sci. **45**, 143–149 (2015). Elsevier
28. Pumjun, N., Kreesuradej, W.: Maintenance of multi-level association rules discovery in dynamic database under a change of support threshold. In: 12th IEEE International Confernce on Fuzzy Systems and Knowledge Discovery (FSKD), pp. 618–623 (2015)
29. Ban, T., Eto, M., Guo, S., Inoue, D., Nakao, K., Huang, R.: A study on association rule mining of darknet big data. In: Proceedings of the IEEE International Joint Conference on Neural Network (IJCNN), pp. 1–7 (2015)

Author Index

Printed in the United States
By Bookmasters